ITALIAN AMERICANS
OF THE TWENTIETH CENTURY:
From the Same Vine

ITALIAN AMERICANS
OF THE TWENTIETH CENTURY:
From the Same Vine

GEORGE CARPETTO, Ph.D., *Editor*

DIANE M. EVANAC, Ed.D., *Associate Editor*

LOGGIA PRESS

Tampa, Florida

1999

STAFF

George Carpetto, Editor

Diane M. Evanac, Associate Editor

Leonard Salatino, Cover Design and Art Work

Special thanks to Dennis Piasio, Linda D'Andrea-Marino, and Mark Battiste
as major contributing authors.

ISBN 0-9673796-0-1

Library of Congress Catalog Number 99-73735

ITALIAN AMERICANS OF THE TWENTIETH CENTURY: *From the Same Vine.*

For information:
Loggia Press, 3315 Lemon Street, Tampa, Florida 33609

Printed in the United States of America
Loggia Press

CONTENTS

ITALIAN AMERICANS OF THE TWENTIETH CENTURY:
From the Same Vine

ADVISORY BOARD

PREFACE AND ACKNOWLEDGMENTS

Italian Americans of the Twentieth Century came about as an idea four years ago. The time had come to write a book that would highlight some of the many accomplishments of Italian Americans, and it would limit its scope to the Twentieth Century. The fact that the new millennium was imminent served as a major impetus. It seemed most fitting for Italian Americans to take stock of their achievements at this auspicious point in time.

In preparing this book, we opted for an abbreviated format in order to expand the number of persons included. Each biography would be presented in a uniform two-page format. This ensured that any given biography could be seen on two pages along with a list of sources. This format also made it possible to give equal prominence to each person selected as a biographical topic. Thus, social reformers, scientists, police, military, business people, administrators, educators, religious, political and government figures received the same visibility as some other groups who inherently enjoy the limelight more frequently such as movie stars and sports personalities.

We have also presented Italian Americans from all religious, political, socioeconomic, and sexual orientations. In particular, we emphasized the representation of women both in authoring these biographies and obviously in the subjects of the biographies. In addition, a democratic and inclusionary spirit prevailed from the outset so that even those people who did not have a professional writing background were invited to participate in the process. In response to the challenge, there were no less than sixty contributing authors.

Special thanks are very much in order for the State President of the Order Sons of Italy (OSIA) of Florida, Rose Marie Boniello. Without her vision and continued support, the project would not have come to fruition. Succinctly put by a theorist, the essence of leadership lies in successfully administering "future" situations from the present. It therefore involves looking at reality with the widest possible lens from the highest possible vantage point. In her years of tenure, President Boniello pioneered an entire set of bold initiatives to strengthen the Order Sons of Italy in the State of Florida. One of those areas touched by her foresight has been her sponsorship and continued belief in the realization of this enterprise.

The proposal to initiate the project was presented to the Grand Lodge of Florida, Order Sons of Italy, which convened in Tampa in 1995. This body of no less than sixty officers overwhelmingly supported the proposal. Subsequently, President Boniello (who is also the Chair Sons of Italy Florida Foundation, a nonprofit trust) with Salvatore D'Alessandro (President Sons of Italy Florida Foundation) and the trustees awarded a very substantial grant that made the first edition possible.

The reader may be interested in knowing that the monies derived from the sale of this book will be administered not only for statewide operational needs of OSIA in Florida—especially in the promotion and dissemination of Italian and Italian-American culture—but also for scholarships and for designated charitable organizations such as Cooley's Anemia, March of Dimes, and Alzheimer's.

Special thanks are in order for Dr. Diane Evanac for her untiring efforts in training sessions to statewide members to prepare them in tackling the challenges of writing biographies. Her skills in editing, formatting, and layout work have also been invaluable. The production of *Italian Americans of the Twentieth Century* also was strengthened by the presence of many people who are recognized authorities in their respective fields, such as Dr. Felix M. Berardo,

Professor of Sociology at the University of Florida. His suggestions and sociological insights helped to solidify the perspective of immigration phenomena, a major theme reflected throughout the biographies. He also made many suggestions of a practical nature that reflect his years of editorial direction on the staff of many scholarly journals.

There are others who gave of their time and talent and who have assisted in a variety of important roles. Frank Di Trolio, Humanities Bibliographer at the University of Florida, was invaluable in his knowledge of research tools and approaches. Greg Esposito, J.D., conducted the required legal searches for the logo documentation and other legal matters regarding this publication. Leonard Salatino, a Disney World graphic illustrator, was instrumental in doing the art work that includes the book jacket. Sheila Thomas, editorial consultant, shed much light on the publication process while offering her great sense of enthusiasm.

There were numerous others who assisted throughout the course of events. Among the most noteworthy is Dennis Piasio, State Second Vice President of the Grand Lodge of Florida, Order Sons of Italy. He was one of the prime movers in motivating people in the effort to get things started at the grass roots level. There are also Vincent and Irene Lamano who were responsible for videotaping and distributing Dr. Evanac's informative talks on writing biographies.

If there exists one regret this labor of love has generated, in particular for the editor, it regards the fact that many more biographies of Italian Americans might have been added, but a host of factors dealing with time and financial constraints limited us to two hundred. It is with this in mind that readers may rightfully expect a second volume in the near future to fulfill that expectation.

George Carpetto, Editor

INTRODUCTION

The great 17th-century philosopher-mathematician René Descartes openly disparaged the worth and usefulness of history because of its concomitant inaccuracies, its ample and deliberate distortions, and sometimes its downright lies. By extension, the same may be said of biographies, obviously a distinct form of history where admittedly the content of the narration may become woefully overselective and self-indulgent. And so, like Pontius Pilate of biblical repute, Descartes himself might aptly ask: "What is truth?"

While much may be said for Descartes' pessimistic position regarding the veracity of history and historical narratives, a rebuttal might aptly point out that essentially most writing—if not all writing—reflects a highly selective process, and for that very reason it surely represents an attempt at influencing the reader in some manner. If writing is an attempt to influence, then readers must inherently accept the challenge to be discerning in the quality and content of what they read.

Despite the futuristic speed at which some of our very sophisticated 20th-century scientific thought is moving, we are nonetheless getting closer to appreciating what Immanuel Kant taught and reiterated almost two hundred years ago: we can only approach the truth and cannot ever know it absolutely. Today's scientists, consciously or unintentionally, are corroborating this very wise Kantian perspective by their inescapable realization that each scientific discovery only seems to raise more intriguing questions. Inevitably it means going back to the drawing board. And so, we are in a dilemma of sorts. Again, we may ask: "What is truth?" And specifically, is there truth to be found in biographies?

Perhaps in an indirect way, Dr. Leo Buscaglia might have said it all stating that when we give our life serious thought and we begin to sort out the nonessential, the superfluous, the transient, and the incidental, what invariably do remain, front and center stage, are the human relationships that concomitantly surround us.

What necessarily becomes crucial within those relationships are our values, our philosophical position, and our spiritual beliefs. As far as the written word is concerned, biographies become one of the major ways we learn to appreciate and understand human existence. Or else, why read, why study, why do anything at all if it has no value or no meaning?

Biographies are a great source of inspiration for achievers who want to do more and also for those who with more effort and encouragement might achieve better outcomes and more rewarding lives. By reading biographies we also learn to distinguish the doers from the non-doers in the marketplace of human activity. We learn to appreciate exceptional qualities in thought and action from those that are mediocre. We learn what is useful to society's betterment and what is worthless. We learn—both in a personal and in a societal way—what is just and decent, what is essential and ennobling to society's proper functioning, existence, and ultimate survival: and what *isn't*.

What better time than now at the conclusion of one millennium and at the beginning of another to celebrate Italian Americans, their many accomplishments and contributions to America and to the world in the last one hundred years. There are so many people to celebrate and yet so little space afforded in the context of a book of this nature. It is for this reason that the reader should consider our selection of biographical topics as not exhaustive in any way.

Italians have constituted one of the key immigrant groups to have settled in the United States. Who are they? With the exception of a relatively small number of newly-arrived

Italians, most have become Italian Americans and are, therefore, second or multi-generational. In the majority of cases, they are able to trace their lineage with reasonable accuracy. With few exceptions, the Italian immigrants were very poor, mostly Roman Catholic, and strongly attached to family values and survival. Few were professionals and even fewer had enjoyed a twelve-year traditional education curriculum back in the "old country."

While a small number of Italians has come to the United States from some of Italy's northern towns and cities, most of them invariably came from the south and to a lesser degree from the central regions of Italy. Immigration usually took place in large waves. Rarely was immigration an even flow as is witnessed in more recent times where legal immigration is necessarily monitored. And since there was safety in numbers as is the case in so many societal situations, when immigrants arrived in America, they generally lived near one another, forming enclaves.

Today, precise figures on the number of Italian Americans (and other ethnic groups) present in the United States is difficult to calculate, due to a variety of factors such as intermarriage, census counting limitations, return migration (called *ritornati*), and so on. We do know that some Italians were present as early as the colonial days. For example, in 1656 more that a hundred Italian Protestants arrived in America under the sponsorship of the Dutch and resided in New York and Delaware.

However, the bulk of early Italian immigrants to this country arrived between 1880 and 1920. During that period, more than 4 million entered the United States, and that figure subsequently grew to 5 million. Today, it is estimated that the current generations that have flowed from those initial immigrants now number approximately 26 million Italian Americans—not an insignificant figure. It is an impressive 11 percent of that total population. Because they are by now essentially second generation or multi-generational, their efforts and struggles in the marketplace of opportunity have led them into virtually every field of endeavor. Our presentation of 200 Italian Americans recognizes what they have done to change life in America in some significant way.

While nearly all the subjects celebrated in this book are American citizens, citizenship status was not deemed by us as the critical criterion for inclusion. Therefore our criterion in deciding to include them lies in the fact that their best efforts took place while they were in the United States where they availed themselves of the opportunities that only America could offer them at that time. Guglielmo Marconi is perhaps the best case in point. While he discovered wireless communication in Italy, virtually all of the wireless developments and their applications took place in the United States.

In addition to our celebration of Italian Americans whose actions and thoughts we admire, we exhort the youth of America to emulate those creative personalities.

Finally, on a poetic note, like water to a parched mouth after a long and tiring journey, it is the good news that we bring.

George Carpetto, Editor

Alphabetic List of Biographies

Lombardi, John
Lombardi, Vince
Lombardo, Guy
Loren, Sophia
Lucci, Susan
Lupino, Ida
Luria, Salvador E.

M

Maglie, Salvatore "Sal"
Mancini, Henry
Mangione, Chuck
Mangione, Jerre
Manteo, Mike
Marciano, Rocky
Marconi, Guglielmo
Marino, Dan
Marshall, Penny
Martin, Dean
Menotti, Gian Carlo
Migliaccio, Eduardo
Millo, Aprile
Minnelli, Liza
Minnelli, Vincente
Modotti, Tina
Moffo, Anna
Montana, Joe
Mosconi, Willie
Muccio, John J.
Musmanno, Michael Angelo

O

Obici, Amedeo

P

Pacino, Al
Paglia, Camille
Panetta, Leon

Pascarelli, Emil F.
Pastore, John
Paterno, Joe
Patti, Adelina
Pavarotti, Luciano
Pei, Mario
Pellegrino, Edmund Daniel
Pesce, Michael
Petrillo, James Caesar
Petrone, Rocco
Petrosino, Giuseppe
Piccolo, Brian
Pinza, Ezio
Piston, Walter
Pitino, Rick
Politi, Leo
Ponselle, Rosa
Prestopino, Gregorio
Puzo, Mario

R

Riggio, Leonard
Rizzo, Frank
Rizzuto, Phil
Rodia, Sabato (Sam)
Rodino, Peter Wallace, Jr.
Rossi, Marie
Rozelle, Alvin Ray "Pete"

S

Sammartino, Peter
Sarandon, Susan
Scali, John Alfred
Scalia, Antonin
Scavullo, Francesco
Schirra, Walter M., Jr.
Scorsese, Martin
Secondari, John H.
Segale, Sister Blandina

Segrè, Emilio
Sergio, Lisa
Sinatra, Frank
Sirica, John J.
Siringo, Charles Angelo
Smeal, Eleanor Marie Cutri
Smith, Alfred Emanuel
Sofia, Sabatino
Soleri, Paolo
Stallone, Sylvester
Stella, Frank

T

Tagliabue, Paul
Talese, Gay
Tartaglione, Christine M.
Tesoro, Giuliana Cavaglieri
Torre, Joe
Toscanini, Arturo
Travolta, John
Turturro, John

V

Valenti, Jack
Valvano, Jim
Venturi, Robert Charles
Versace, Gianni
Villella, Edward
Viscardi, Henry, Jr.
Volpe, John Anthony

W

Warren, Harry

Z

Zamperini, Louis
Zappa, Frank

DANNY AIELLO (1933-   )

Danny Aiello, whose life has often been described as a rags-to-riches script worthy of Hollywood filming, was born in the depression era. He struggled as a youngster in elementary school and later became a high school dropout. His past, filled with many unorthodox behaviors–most of which he did to survive, he maintains–made him value his family highly and led him into acting, a profession he now enjoys as his life work. Without benefit of dramatic studies, he has earned more than fifty film, television, and stage credits in less than thirty years as a professional actor. For his Off-Broadway stage performance in *Gemini* (1977), he received an Obie Award; for his role in the film, *Do the Right Thing* (1989), he received Oscar and Golden Globe Award nominations as Best Supporting Actor. Along with these accomplishments, Aiello has also earned an Emmy for outstanding TV achievement in children's programming. He has appeared in a host of motion pictures many of which have become memorable movies and award-winning films, including Woody Allen's *The Purple Rose of Cairo* (1986), and Norman Jewison's *Moonstruck* (1987).

Danny Louis Aiello Jr., the sixth of seven children, was born on June 20, 1933 to Danny Louis Sr. and Frances (nee Pietrocova) Aiello. It appears that Danny's mother got married when she was only fifteen and had gotten herself into a troubled marriage. Danny was seven years old when the family moved from Manhattan's West Side to the South Bronx. It was about this point in time that his father, a truck driver with a long history of being derelict in his family duties and responsibilities, decided to abandon his family all together, causing great financial hardship to those he had left behind. Despite so many children, his mother Frances worked as a seamstress and tried hard to support her family single-handedly, but her family eventually went on public assistance.

As a six-year-old youngster, even before his father left the family, Danny had already been working shining shoes and selling newspapers at Grand Central Station. After attending elementary school in the Bronx, he went to James Monroe High School for a short-lived two-week stay after which he joined the National Guard by lying about his age. At that time, he also belonged to a Bronx gang called the Kingsmen who engaged in petty break-ins and stole from local grocery stores. During one such incident, Aiello remembers having gotten shot in the thigh by a zip gun. At sixteen, unhappy with this style of living, he again lied about his age, joined the U.S. Army and spent three years in (pre-unified) West Germany.

After an honorable discharge, he returned home, and in 1955 he married Sandy Cohen with whom he would have four children. Taking on odd jobs to earn income, which included hustling pool, he became a baggage clerk for the Greyhound Bus Company at its Manhattan terminal in 1957. By 1962 at age twenty-nine, he had worked so diligently that he earned the respect of his fellow workers and became elected president of Local 1202 of the Amalgamated Transit Union, the youngest person in Greyhound's history to have held such a title. Yet his efforts became all undone when a labor dispute arose, and the international union representatives sided with Greyhound and *not* with the union local. Aiello, who naturally sided with fellow workers of his union local, found himself removed as their local president and suddenly unemployed at Greyhound.

Without a job, Aiello referred to this disheartening episode as the lowest point in his adult life where his biggest fear had now become realized: not being able to support his home and honor his family duties. Yet crisis soon turned into opportunity. He had made many friends in those years working in New York City. His untimely burden was removed when a friend, Bud Friedman, the owner of the comedy nightclub Improvisation took him on as a bouncer. This position not only brought him a paycheck but also gave Friedman an opportunity to let Aiello act as master of ceremonies from time to time. This good fortune, in turn, also enabled Aiello to substitute for delinquent performers who either showed up late or had disappeared from town. Aiello soon discovered that he had talent singing, telling stories and jokes while thoroughly enjoying the limelight.

The turning point in his life occurred when he actively started looking for acting parts, auditioning, and answering casting calls for movies and plays. Aiello received his first opportunity to do professional acting in a film by screenwriter Louis LaRusso called *The Godmother* (1972). Though the film was never released, Aiello's fine acting led to other parts in movies that went on to become notable films like *Bang the Drum Slowly* (1973) and *The Godfather Part II* (1974).

In 1975 he had done so well that he went on to receive a Theater World Award as that season's outstanding new performer for his role as Biggie the Bartender in LaRusso's *Lamppost Reunion* (1975). A year later, he moved up to his first leading role on Broadway in another of LaRusso's plays called *Wheelbarrow Closers* (1976). In 1977 after only two years as a stage actor, he earned an Obie Award after appearing in Albert Innaurato's Off-Broadway comedy *Gemini*. When the play moved to Broadway, Aiello continued in the role for another year.

In all, by the end of the 1970s, Danny Aiello had clearly made his mark both in the theater and in film. Since then, he has averaged between two and three film appearances per year. He has also had the good fortune to have appeared in the works of some of the best directors in the film industry including Woody Allen's *Broadway Danny Rose* (1984), *The Purple Rose of Cairo* (1985), and *Radio Days (1987)*; Francis Coppola's *The Godfather Part II* (1974); and Sergio Leone's *Once Upon a Time in America* (1984).

Danny Aiello's life embodies a will to succeed–especially with his family that he calls "sacred." He is close to his children and to his wife with whom he has been married since 1955. While he has earned the respect of those close to him on the set, he has also earned respect from the film industry. He was nominated for both the Academy Award and the Golden Globe Award for Best Supporting Actor for his role in Spike Lee's *Do the Right Thing* (1989). For the theater, he also is widely respected for having won the 1977 Obie Award for Best Actor in Albert Innaurato's *Gemini* (1977). On the west coast, he also earned the Los Angeles Drama Critics Circle Award as the season's Best Actor in 1989 in Dave Rabe's long-running play *Hurlyburly*, which had had its debut four years prior in New York City in 1985.

General Sources:
1. *Contemporary Theatre, Film and Television*. Detroit, MI: Gale Research, 1989.
2. *Current Biography Yearbook*. New York: Wilson, 1992.
3. *International Motion Picture Almanac*. 1992 ed.
4. *New York Times* 10 Feb. 1991: 13+.
5. *New York Times Magazine* 21 Jan. 1990: 24.
6. Siegel, Scott, and Barbara Siegel. *The Encyclopedia of Hollywood*. New York: Facts on File, 1990.
7. *Who's Who in America*. 1999 ed.

–by ROCKY PESIRI

LICIA ALBANESE (1913-   )

The Italian-born American soprano began her career at the Teatro Lirico in Milan in 1934 when in a mid-program emergency (not as an official understudy but merely as a singer in training listening in the audience) she was "literally yanked from the audience" replacing the lead performer in *Madama Butterfly*, who had become ill. It has become an ironic fact of history that Licia Albanese's unscheduled characterization of Cio-Cio-San in the second half of that evening's program heralded what would become her signature role in Europe and later in the United States.

Licia Albanese was born in the Adriatic city of Bari, Italy on July 22, 1913, one of six children born to Michele and Maria (nee Ragusa) Albanese. As a youngster, she was depicted as a shy girl who studied in a convent school and who at age twelve decided to join her sister Stella in taking piano lessons. Her piano teacher recognized the good qualities of her voice and recommended she take singing lessons as well. Licia's father delighted in her singing an aria from *Tosca* as part of his birthday celebration–though her shyness forced her to sing the aria with her back turned to her listeners. He agreed with her piano teacher and soon located a voice teacher, a retired tenor Emanuel De Rosa, who lived close by, to give her lessons.

After three years of lessons, Licia accompanied her father to Naples where he consulted a physician for a serious ailment. In the interim, he had also arranged for Licia's audition with Mario Bellini, established conductor and operatic teacher. Mario Bellini was related to Vincenzo Bellini, the composer of the opera *Norma*. He advised her to remain in Naples and begin training in voice as soon as possible. She offered him, instead, instant disapproval as young Licia was more interested in returning home to aid her father whose doctor's report had not been very favorable. Yet a determined father eager to see his gifted daughter succeed, he made her promise she would eventually make singing her career. Three years later, just before dying, he reminded Licia of that commitment to him.

At age eighteen, she moved to Milan at her cousin's invitation. There she was able to meet and interview with Giuseppina Baldassare-Tedeschi, a voice teacher and soprano, noted for her singing role in *Madama Butterfly*. In 1932 Licia began her studies with the notable teacher. After two years, she made an unscheduled appearance one night at the Teatro Lirico when she substituted for the ailing lead singer. Despite her obvious success, she felt unready for the stage and returned to studying voice for another year.

A year later, she entered a government-sponsored contest. After winning locally, she was encouraged by teacher and friends alike to pursue the contest finals which would take place in Bologna. The ordeal consisted of four long arduous evenings with the competition including some three hundred singers from all parts of Italy. At its grueling conclusion, Licia was awarded not only the silver and gold medals but also first prize. This occasioned her formal debut as Cio-Cio-San on December 19, 1935 in the city of Parma at its Teatro Reale when she was only twenty-two years of age.

After a seasonal appearance at the Teatro San Carlo in Naples, Licia Albanese reached one of the epitomizing points in her early career in becoming a regular member of La Scala di Milano which did not preclude her making many guest appearances throughout Italy's principal cities; the Vatican's inauguration of its radio station in 1935: European cities such as Paris, London (Convent Garden), and Tunis in North Africa.

Licia Albanese had many accomplishments before leaving for America in 1940. She became one of the few women in history to perform at the Vatican (for Pope Pius XI), and she became the first woman to sing at the Vatican's radio station. She also performed for King Victor Emanuel in Rome in 1937 and as well for Sir Neville Chamberlain and Lord Halifax, also in Rome, in 1939. In that same year, when she had occasion to meet Beniamino Gigli in Italy, she joined him in making a recording of *La Bohème*. This mutually pleasant occasion to record together later prompted Gigli to recommend her to the New York Metropolitan Opera where she would eventually make her debut on February 9, 1940, singing the lead role in *Madama Butterfly*.

The debut marked the beginning of a twenty-six-year career in America much of which was spent with the Metropolitan Opera. Licia, who soon established a following of avid fans in America, was not without her detractors in the newspapers, especially in her early years. Her singing withstood the test of time, so much so that in 1946 (six years after her America debut) Toscanini selected Licia to sing the role of Mimi with the NBC Symphony Orchestra at the fiftieth anniversary celebration performance of *La Bohème*. A year earlier in April 1945, she had married Joseph A. Gimma, a stockbroker, also from Bari. They had never met until after their immigration to the United States. Eight months later in December, she applied for American citizenship.

In her entire career–some in Italy but mostly in America–she had made more than one-thousand appearances in some forty-eight different roles. While her specialty focused on Puccini's heroines, she was adept in Mozart operas and its female leads (Donna Anna, Serlina, Susanna), and similarly in French operas (Micaela, Manon, Marguerite). She became closely associated with the Metropolitan Opera where she would give her last performance on January 20, 1966 as Manon. Four months later in April, she also participated in singing a final farewell to the old Met as it was ready to close its doors before the opera company moved to its new Lincoln Center location.

After her official farewell to the Met, Licia Albanese taught opera and sang from time to time in concert. Besides the history of her many performances that have graced the Met, she is also remembered for her appearance on TV's memorable opera program, the *Voice of Firestone* series, where conductor Howard Barlow brought into the living rooms of viewing audiences many of the superstars of opera such as Licia Albanese. Presently, Licia Albanese devotes much of her time and energy directing the Licia Albanese-Puccini Foundation located in midtown Manhattan.

General Sources:

1. Bernheimer, Martin. "Licia Albanese." *The New Grove Dictionary of American Music*. New York: Grove's Dictionary of Music, 1992.

2. Bernheimer, Martin. "Licia Albanese." *The New Grove Dictionary of Music and Musicians*. New York: Grove's Dictionaries of Music, 1995.

3. *Current Biography*. New York: Wilson, 1946.

4. Ewen, David. *The New Encyclopedia of the Opera*. New York: Hill and Wang, 1971.

5. Hines, Jerome. *Great Singers on Great Singing*. Garden City, NY: Doubleday, 1982.

6. *The New Grove Dictionary of Opera*. Ed. Stanley Sadie. New York: Grove's Dictionaries of Music, 1992.

–by GEORGE CARPETTO, Ph.D.

ANNA MARIA ALBERGHETTI (1936-   )

Coming from a musical family in Pesaro, Italy and trained exclusively in voice by her father, Anna Maria started singing in the limelight from the age of six. She appeared in many European concert halls as a youngster, and she made her Carnegie Hall singing debut in 1950 at the age of thirteen, appearing also in the same year as a soloist with the New York Philharmonic. She then won the highly coveted Antoinette Perry (Tony) Award in 1961 as Best Actress in a musical for her role in *Carnival*. She was hailed by theater critics as having one of the purest voices in the music industry.

Anna Maria Alberghetti was born on May 15, 1936 in Pesaro, Italy, the eldest of three children of Daniele and Vittoria (nee Ricci) Alberghetti. Her parents were deeply committed musicians. Her father, Daniele, was a professional baritone and cellist. As a singer, he appeared with a number of Italian opera companies including the well-known La Scala di Milano, and he himself was concert master of the Rome Opera Company. Her mother Vittoria was a professional pianist and appeared regularly with the Scuola Reggia Musicale on the Island of Rhodes. Despite the dangers of World War II, Anna Maria performed in many European cities in 1942 after her family was led to safety, flying in a bomber, to the European mainland away from the beleaguered Island of Rhodes. Anna Maria was the singer, her mother the accompanist, and her father mentor and trainer.

Before traveling to the United States, Anna Maria first embarked upon a musical tour of Europe in the late 40s. After her debut at Carnegie Hall on April 28, 1950, the New York City critics unanimously raved over her performance as a thirteen-year-old coloratura. Two months later on June 29, appearing as the featured soloist with the New York Philharmonic at Lewisohn Stadium (New York City) she sang many challenging arias from such operas as *Lucia di Lammermoore* and *La Traviata* before a crowd of 13,000 people. After a standing ovation, she gave an encore of three Italian songs with her mother as accompanist at the piano.

In 1951 Anna Maria traveled back to Italy to appear in the Scalera Film Studios production of *The Medium*, the film version of Italian-American composer Gian Carlo Menotti's musical play of the same title, which had been first produced on Broadway in 1947. She played Monica, the medium's daughter, a role for which she received critically positive distinction both for her singing and her acting. She returned to Hollywood to appear in a Frank Capra production of *Here Comes the Groom* (1951), a film starring Bing Crosby and Jane Wyman. Alberghetti, who was featured in only one particularly important scene played the role of a blind war orphan who sang the "Caro Nome" aria from *Rigoletto*.

These two brief standout film performances in Fall 1951 received excellent reviews and prompted Paramount Studios to make a seven-year contract offer to Anna Maria, now only fourteen years of age. She appeared one year later in another Paramount movie, *The Stars are Singing*, which was not released until 1953. In this movie, which co-starred Rosemary Clooney and the well-known opera singer Lauritz Melchior, Anna Maria had a central role playing the part of a young Polish refugee who had entered the U.S. illegally. Unlike her two prior films, this film allowed her the opportunity to sing not only an aria from an opera (*La Traviata*) but also several lighter numbers.

Her film career expanded only moderately, appearing first in *Last Command* (1955) with Sterling Hayden and Ernest Borgnine, in *Duel at Apache Wells* (1956), in *Ten Thousand Bedrooms* (1957) where she co-starred with Dean Martin, and in her last movie *Cinderfella* (1960) which starred Jerry Lewis. It appears that the Alberghetti family had chosen a career route where Anna Maria could select from other options and not limit herself to film. Throughout the 50s she had consistently had the experience of performing in theater, television, nightclubs, and concert tours both in the United States and throughout Europe, Australia, and Latin America.

In Las Vegas Anna Maria appeared at the top nightclubs including the Sahara Hotel (1953-54), the Royal Nevada (1955), the Flamingo (1957), the Stardust (1960), and the Desert Inn (1958-62). In Miami she appeared at the Americana (1957), the Eden Roc (1959), and the Deauville Hotel (1960); in New York at the Waldorf-Astoria (1957) and the Latin Quarter (1958); in Philadelphia at Palumbo's (1960); in Chicago at the Palmer House (1960); and in Los Angeles at the Moulin Rouge (1958) and at the Cocoanut Grove (1960).

With the advent of TV in the 1950s, Anna Maria appeared often in that medium and became a well-known TV personality. She was no stranger to Ed Sullivan's *Toast of the Town* (1950) where she appeared as many as twelve times and to whom she attributed much of her TV success. She also appeared on more than thirty different programs, where she often did repeat appearances, including the *Eddie Fisher Show*, the *Red Skelton Show*, the *Colgate Hour*, the *Ford Theatre*, the *Jimmy Durante Show*, the *Loretta Young Show*, the *Steve Allen Show*, the *Bob Hope Show*, the *Perry Como Show*, the *Voice of Firestone*, *I've Got a Secret*, and the *Andy Williams Show*. She appeared in several summer theater productions such as *Rose Marie* (1957-60), *Fanny* (1958-59), *Firefly* (1959-63), and *West Side Story* (1963) throughout different parts of the United States.

Her most important role came in 1961 when she played the starring role of Lili in the Broadway hit musical *Carnival* for which she received the theater industry's most cherished honor, the Tony Award, for Best Actress in a musical. The portrayal of Lili became her signature role.

By the mid-60s, Anna Maria took leave from show business, a twenty-year departure, focusing on marriage and family. That hiatus from the limelight recently came to an end with her resumption of singing engagements in theater as in her nationwide tour in the role of Maria in the *Sound of Music*. She has also returned to the concert stage resuming her soloist role with major symphonic orchestras. A child-prodigy who had captured the hearts of Americans with her coloratura performances in the 1950s, she once more graces the American entertainment world.

General Sources:

1. *The Biographical Encyclopedia & Who's Who of the American Theatre.* New York: Heineman, 1966.
2. *Current Biography.* New York: Wilson, 1955.
3. Ganzl, Kurt. *The Encyclopedia of the Musical Theatre.* New York: Schirmer, 1994.
4. Katz, Ephraim. *The Film Encyclopedia.* New York: HarperCollins, 1998.
5. *Notable Women in the American Theatre: A Biographical Dictionary.* New York: Greenwood Press, 1989.
6. Null, Gary, and Carl Stone. *The Italian-Americans.* Harrisburg, PA: Stackpole Books, 1976.
7. *Who's Who of American Women: A Biographical Dictionary of Notable Living American Women.* Chicago: Marquis, 1963.

–by URSULA JACKSON

ALAN ALDA (1936-   )

Named Alfonso D'Abruzzo, Jr. at birth, Alan Alda would go on to win several Emmy Awards for acting, directing, and writing. In particular, for the 1973-74 season alone, he was named both Actor of the Year with the NBC Symphony Orchestra and Best Actor in a comedy series by the Academy of Television Arts and Sciences. Having the lead role as Captain Pierce, better known as "Hawkeye," in the hit-series *M*A*S*H*, he went on to write and direct many episodes of what was one of TV's most popular and long-running comedy series (1972-1983).

Alda was born on January 28, 1936, the only child of Robert and Joan D'Abruzzo. His first "stage appearances" were from a high chair in a Catskills, New York resort show performance. For the next few years, Alan would spend a great deal of time with his father backstage. After the family had moved to California, Alan contracted polio at age six. His mother devoted much of her time to him. For two years, he received daily treatments lasting an hour each, and during his recovery, he was tutored at home. It is reported that during this period of time the seeds of egalitarianism and feminism took root in his fertile mind. These attitudes were to influence a great deal of his life. At 16, he attended Fordham University as an English literature major. That year in Barnesville, Pennsylvania he ventured into summer stock with his father in the production of *Three Men on a Horse*.

In 1957, Alan married Arlene Weiss, three years his senior. His compulsive drive for family privacy stemmed, in part, from the turmoil of his parents' separation and divorce. Alan and Arlene had three daughters: Eve in 1958, Elizabeth in 1960, and Beatrice in 1961.

Arlene, a professional photographer, won many awards and published six books in photography.

Early in their marriage, before Alan's career took off, Arlene and Alan had agreed to have a normal life. The girls would be raised as other children from blue collar families. Their home in Leonia, New Jersey, would be as unpretentious as possible, and Alan would be just a plain "Joe." In his spare time, Alan started writing, acquiring quite a portfolio of articles. Eventually time would reveal that he was adept in many facets of entertainment.

Alan's adventures into television started with supporting roles in *Sergeant Bilko*, *The Nurses*, *Route 66*, and *The Trials of O'Brien*. During those early years, Alan tried to gain recognition by performing Off-Broadway, on Broadway, and summer stock in many states. He would do almost anything just to be working and be seen. He often referred to the on-stage appearance as an experience as effective as a shot of penicillin.

His work in *Second City* proved to be extremely beneficial in that it gave him greater confidence in his own abilities. In 1959, his official Broadway debut was in *Only in America*. This once Off-Broadway play dealt with interracial social relations. Although there is no evidence recorded about Alan's compassion or deep feelings about the injustices shown to southern blacks, he had the opportunity to gain new awareness while working in the play with black actors and minorities in general.

Purlie Victorious opened September 21, 1961 with Ruby Dee and Alan Alda. During the play, Alan's critical acting skills displayed tremendous ability to identify with minority rights issues. Alan, well liked by his fellow performers, also received excellent reviews for his role. It was reported at that time that he was a warm and sensitive person who could make a stranger feel like a member of his family. When Barbara Walters tried to paint Alan Alda as a sex symbol, Helen Martin, Alan's co-star in *Purlie Victorious*, defended him explaining that he was not a sex symbol, but just a family man who would go directly home to his wife and three daughters every night.

Purlie Victorious with its 261 performances was just that–victorious. Alan went on to repeat his success in the 1963 film version of *Gone with the Wind*. Throughout his career, Alan, sensitive to human values and respect for people of all kinds, became capable of launching devastating social statements in the guise of comic relief. He had proven himself quite a master of subtle innuendo and a gadfly for human sensitivity and respect.

In the mid-eighties, when his annual income, estimated in excess of $2 million, became known, Alan's typical humorous response was that he was worth every penny of it. While Alan was not yet critically accepted as a genius in his own right, and while no fans were lining up to see him, he was earning more money than ever before. Alan appeared in several soap operas such as *Love of Life*, *The Secret Storm*, and *Days of Our Lives*. He appeared numerous times on the TV panel show, *What's My Line*. In 1972, CBS Friday Night movies aired a feature-length film entitled *The Glass House*. This proved to be Alan's greatest moment on film thus far, and it furnished him with instant recognition all over the country.

During its filming, Alan's agent sent him a script that would soon radically change his life and career. It was at this juncture in his life, accepting the lead in the *M*A*S*H* series, that marked the beginning of a new Alan Alda where the character he played, Hawkeye, became a household word. From January 1973 to the end of the *M*A*S*H* series in February 1983, in everyone's mind he represented the main character whose excellent acting abilities influenced most of the pivotal and qualitative aspects of *M*A*S*H*. He had also written and directed many of the episodes of this series that would make TV history.

Extolled as actor-writer-director in the various media both during and subsequent to *M*A*S*H*, Alda acted in *California Suite* (1978) and in *Crimes and Misdemeanors* (1989); wrote and acted in *The Seduction of Joe Tynan* (1979); and wrote, directed and acted in *The Four Seasons* (1981), *Sweet Liberty* (1986), *A New Life* (1987), and *Betsy's Wedding* (1990).

In 1974 (just one year into *M*A*S*H*), Alan had come out in favor of the Equal Rights Amendment (ERA). He was made chairman of Men for the ERA. He testified before the Illinois Executive Committee when they were considering the fate of the ERA in that particular state. When the committee voted eleven to eight *not* to send the proposal to the Illinois Senate floor, it became a great personal loss for Alan, but that did not end his dedication to the cause of women's rights, human rights, and family values. The recipient of many prestigious professional awards (writing, directing and acting) and many civic awards (National Italian Foundation), Alda represents a model of Italian American achievements.

General Sources:
1.	Alda, Arlene. *The Last Days of MASH*. Verona, NJ: Unicorn, 1983.
2.	Katz, Ephraim. *The Film Encyclopedia*. New York: HarperCollins, 1998.
3.	Marchione, Margherita. *Americans of Italian Heritage*. Lanham, MD: University Press of America, 1995.
4.	Reiss, David. *M*A*S*H: The Exclusive, Inside Story of TV's Most Popular Show*. Indianapolis: Bobbs-Merrill, 1983.
5.	Strait, Raymond. *Alan Alda: A Biography*. New York: St. Martin's Press, 1983.

–by MARY JANE ADDONE

DON AMECHE (1908-1993)

One of the few actors in Hollywood history to have had three great and distinct successful periods in his career, Don Ameche was initially one of radio's superstars in the 1930s. After his radio fame, he became one of the most famous leading men in movies for almost forty years. Then, after a hiatus from acting in motion pictures, he returned to film in his seventies to enjoy a diverse and unusual series of acting roles, one of which earned him an Oscar for Best Supporting Actor in *Cocoon* (1985).

Dominic Felix Ameche, better known as Don Ameche, the second of eight children was born on May 31, 1908 to Felix and Barbara Etta (nee Hertle) Ameche in Kenosha, Wisconsin. His mother was of German and Scotch-Irish heritage, and his father was an emigrant from Ascoli Piceno, a city northeast of Rome, Italy. While he had done farming in Italy in the early part of his life, he now earned a living supporting his family by operating several saloons in Kenosha.

In 1926 after Don Ameche had graduated from the Columbia Academy, a Catholic prep school in Dubuque, Iowa, he attended its senior affiliate, Columbia College (later called Loras College). He had intentions of becoming a lawyer, and after leaving the college prior to completing the program, he continued to take courses at Marquette University in Milwaukee, Georgetown University in Washington, D.C., and the University of Wisconsin at Madison. In truth, he was drifting farther away from a once desired legal career and edging closer to a career in acting.

He had done some acting in his high school days, but he made his stage debut in his 20s while attending the University of Wisconsin (Law School) at Madison. He was performing at that time for a local stock company in Madison when he decided to go into acting professionally and give up law for good. Later in 1929 he had his first bit part as a butler in a Broadway play called *Jerry-For-Short* (1930); then, bit parts in *Illegal Practice* (1930) and in *Excess Baggage* (1930) after which he toured with a vaudeville show headed by Texas Guinan.

In the early 1930s, Ameche saw his career begin to move after he entered commercial radio. Later in his life, he would always be mindful of attributing his initial success to radio. The medium of radio was barely ten years old, and the 1930s was a period of time where, as a medium still in its early years, it freely allowed creative talent to thrive and presented new kinds of acting roles, personalities, and new programming ideas to a radio audience that was continually growing and captivated by the newness of the medium. Since radio, in effect, brought free entertainment into every home that could afford a radio set, vaudeville as an industry was losing much of its traditional vigor. Families could now huddle around the radio set and enjoy all kinds of programs for pennies of electricity per month.

Don Ameche and radio (as a medium) enjoyed a reciprocal relationship with each other. Radio helped make Don Ameche famous in his early days, and he in turn was one of the entertainers that helped shape radio's so-called Golden Age in the 1930s and 1940s. One of the most celebrated personalities for several years on the radio, he starred in well-known radio shows, such as *The First Nighter* and *Grand Hotel*. Yet his radio fame did not end in 1935 when he entered the movies. He was to return to radio to star in radio's *The Chase and Sanborn Hour* (1937-1939) and again in 1946 in the highly successful NBC *The Drene Show* where he together with Frances Langford teamed up in a series of humorous husband-and-wife sketches: "The Bickersons."

Because of his radio fame, 20th Century-Fox had quickly signed him up as an actor as early as 1935. Soon he became one of Hollywood's busiest actors who would in his lifetime play mostly leading roles in more than forty films between the mid-1930s to the mid-1940s, his heyday. Some of his most successful films included *Dante's Inferno* (1935), *Alexander's Ragtime Band* (1938), *The Story of Alexander Graham Bell* (1939), *Moon Over Miami* (1941), *Heaven Can Wait* (1943), and *Wing and a Prayer* (1944). Film historians have known that because of Ameche's good looks, charm, and mellow voice he became too easily typecast as a perennial mustachioed bon vivant and man-about-town, yet his acting abilities went beyond that, and his later years on the screen would vindicate that truth.

While he still appeared on the silver screen in the 1950s, 1960s, and 1970s, his film appearances became more intermittent especially in the 1970s during which he typically appeared more on stage and TV than on film. In 1975 he appeared with Alice Fay doing a national tour of the musical *Good News*. After a hiatus of about seven years, he made a big-screen comeback at age seventy-five in 1983 to the delight of his many admirers in the film *Trading Places* with another respected veteran actor, Ralph Bellamy. After playing the role of the greedy millionaire, Don Ameche, then in his mid-seventies, attracted much attention to his newly discovered potential on the screen.

As if starting a new career, he went to appear in ten or more films, including the role of one of many senior citizens in the cast of the dramatic film *Cocoon* (1985). The film, based on humanity's perennial search for the legendary fountain of youth, this time was created by extraterrestrials who had decided to place its location in Florida. For his dramatic acting, Ameche earned the Oscar for Best Supporting Actor in 1986. He continued acting in many other films, including *Cocoon: The Return* (1988) and *Things Change* (1988). For the latter film, he shared the award for Best Actor at the Venice Film Festival. He worked in the industry until he died in 1993 at age eighty-five. His last appearance was in the film *Corrina, Corrina*, released in 1994 after his death.

Though Oscar-award winner Don Ameche lived in Santa Monica, California and in New York City a good deal of his life, he died in Scottsdale, Arizona on December 6, 1993. He has left a legacy of fine acting and singing, spanning stage, screen, radio, and TV. In addition to his theater experience, he had not only witnessed three of these media grow (especially TV) from their infancy to the overwhelming proportions of influence they enjoy today but also participated in them as an intimate part of their growth. Because of his participation in them, especially in their early years, he will always have a permanent niche in their history.

General Sources:

1. Aylesworth, Thomas G. *The World Almanac Who's Who of Film*. New York: World Almanac, 1987.

2. *The Bickersons: Original Radio Comedy Classics from 1947-1948*. Sandy Hook, CT: Radiola, 1980.

3. *Current Biography Yearbook*. New York: Wilson, 1965; 1994.

4. Katz, Ephraim. *The Film Encyclopedia*. New York: HarperCollins, 1998.

5. "Obituary." *New York Times* 8 Dec. 1993: B8.

6. Siegel, Scott, and Barbara Siegel. *The Encyclopedia of Hollywood*. New York: Facts on File, 1990.

–by VINCENT LAMANO, Sr.

MARIO ANDRETTI (1940-   )

Many in the field have hailed Andretti as the greatest race car driver of all time. His impressively long series of successes began with his 1965 Indy Car championship as well as his finish as third in the Indy 500 in the same year. He concluded the 1965 season earning Rookie-of-the-Year honors as well as becoming the youngest driver ever to win the Indy Car season championship. In 1969, when he won the prestigious Indy 500, his fame and reputation were well on their way to creating the legendary figure that he has become today.

Mario Gabriel Andretti was born in the town of Montona near Trieste, Italy on February 28, 1940 to Alvise Louis and Rina (nee Giovanelli) Andretti. As one of three children, he has a twin brother Aldo, who has also engaged in car racing, and a sister Anna Maria. In 1948 the family decided to migrate to Lucca, Italy to keep their Italian citizenship as Montona (part of the Istrian peninsula) had become part of Yugoslavia shortly after World War II. Once living comfortably as a farm administrator and a property owner prior to the war, Mario's father, who had lost everything after the war, was now compelled to working in a toy factory. His family accordingly learned to live with less.

Mario's interests in car racing began when his uncle would take him and his brother Aldo to Florence to watch the car races which featured the then well-known Alberto Ascari (Mario's idol) and several other racers compete in the Mille Miglia, which was Italy's 1,000-mile cross-country road race. In their early teens, both Mario and his twin brother took to studying auto mechanics and passed much of their free time frequenting racing garages.

At thirteen, both brothers were already racing at the town of Ascona where races had been specifically developed for youthful drivers. Their father, opposed to car racing because many teen racers were injured and killed in accidents, never knew of his sons' involvement and active participation in the races. Mario contends that he secured the secrecy of their racing by shrewdly confessing this fact in the confessional to his priest uncle who was now bound by the oath of confession not to tell.

In 1955 when Mario and Aldo were fifteen years of age, the Andretti family decided to immigrate to the United States and specifically to Nazareth, Pennsylvania where they had relatives and where the father found work in a textile establishment. While attending high school, Mario had found work as a welder in a garage. In 1958, both Mario and Aldo had saved enough money to buy an old car, a Hudson Hornet, which they rebuilt and used for racing for the next three years. They shared its use on an alternating basis. In that three-year period, Mario himself had already won more than twenty stock car races. Mario, who dropped out of Nazareth High School before graduation, did eventually complete his secondary degree with the help of a correspondence course in 1959.

Because their father was still opposed to racing as a sport–much less as a career–the brothers had again managed to keep their racing a secret from the entire family. This surreptitious scenario came to an abrupt halt when in a race Aldo was seriously injured, requiring notification of the family. This event precipitated the father's absolute ban of auto racing. In an argument, Mario left home, and it was only at a later date that his father finally resigned himself to Mario's wishes for a career in racing, and the two eventually reconciled their differences.

In 1961 at age 21 Mario married Dee Ann Beverly Hoch, who had previously tutored him in English. It was from this point on that his racing career would accelerate. He and his wife had agreed to take a calculated risk which involved his quitting his job and devoting himself to racing full-time. He joined the United Racing Club (URC) and began doing sprint racing on the Eastern circuit. In 1963 he joined the American Race Drivers Club (ARDC) and began driving midgets, again on the Eastern circuit. On Labor Day of that year he won three races at two different locations which tallied up his wins to eleven for that ARDC season.

Having won the attention of a sponsor, Al Dean, through the efforts and initiatives of Clint Brawner, a chief mechanic and designer who had admired Andretti's aggressive and risk-taking driving, Mario Andretti had finally been offered the opportunity to drive in more prestigious races. With the strong backing of an established sponsor and the possibility of driving better equipment, he joined the United States Auto Club (USAC), and in his 1964 debut won the US Midget championship. This was succeeded by his 1965 Indy debut where he garnered the Indy Car championship together with finishing third place in the Indy 500, winning his biggest prize to date of $42,551, the Rookie-of-the-Year award, and the Hoosier Grand Prix competition.

After winning the Indy Car Championship between 1965 and 1968, he became determined to win it again in 1969 together with winning the Indy 500. Though he triumphantly went on to win both that year, he had encountered many serious challenges along the way. His newly purchased Lotus, which was supposed to be radically different in design, burned up in a qualifying race leaving him with severe burns on his face. His backup car, a Ford-Brawner Hawk, which qualified for the Indy 500 race, was plagued by untold minor problems both before and during the race.

Despite this difficult scenario, Andretti, known for perseverance, held up and together with his equipment set fifteen new records.

Since winning that eventful race of the 1969 Indy 500, which remained his one and only win for that race, he became instantly famous at home and abroad and began to drive in races in Europe, South America, and South Africa. Mario Andretti did remarkably well in a career that has lasted just less than 40 years, including 31 years in Indy Car competitions where in addition to winning several Indy Car championships (1965, 1966, 1967, 1968, 1969, 1984) and a total of 52 Indy Car victories, he won races all over the globe.

Among his many notable achievements, Mario remains one of three men to have won both the Formula One World Championship (1978) and Indy Car championships. Mario is also one of only two men to win Driver of the Year honors three times and the first to win that honor in three different decades. In 1992 he was named Driver of the Quarter Century. He has won every major car racing trophy imaginable except for the 24 Hour Le Mans. In all, Andretti's best accolade perhaps involves his frequently being referred to as "the greatest race car driver of all time" not only by his loyal fans but also by a large number of professionals in the industry worldwide.

General Sources:
1.   Andretti, Mario. *Andretti*. San Francisco: Collins, 1994.
2.   *Current Biography Yearbook*. New York: Wilson, 1968.
3.   Engel, Lyle Kenyon. *Mario Andretti, World Driving Champion*. New York: Arco, 1979.
4.   Murphy, Jim. *The Indy 500*. New York: Clarion Books, 1983.
5.   Prentzas, G.S. *Mario Andretti*. New York: Chelsea House, 1996.

–by ANNETTE RIZZO

EDDIE ARCARO (1916-1997)

As a world famous horse racer elected to the Hall of Fame (Saratoga Springs, NY in 1958), as a winner of the Kentucky Derby five times, and as top money-making jockey during his career, Eddie Arcaro's mounts won a total of more than $30 million in purses, and to date he remains the only jockey to have ridden two thoroughbreds to victory in the Triple Crown, once in 1941 with Whirlaway and, again, in 1948 with Citation. In his thirty-one years of horse racing, he had been in 24,921 races and finished first 4,779 times.

In 1949, along with Johnny Longden and Sam Resnick, he founded the Jockeys Guild and became its first president. When no one wanted to "front the money" to initiate the insurance coverage for the guild members, Arcaro gave his personal check to cover the first premium for the entire guild. He remained the principal force in getting his fellow jockeys health and injury protection insurance and in establishing safety measures and better working conditions. While Arcaro has been often called "the Master" for his many accomplishments on the track, fellow jockeys also admired him as an organizer and benefactor who showed concern for his peers in the work place. He worked as president of the Jockeys Guild until his retirement.

George Edward Arcaro, better known as Eddie Arcaro, was born on February 19, 1916, an only son to immigrant parents, Pasquale and Josephine (nee Giancola) Arcaro in Cincinnati, Ohio. Eddie weighed in at a mere three pounds when he came into the world; as a mature adult, he would eventually weigh 114 pounds at a height of five-foot three. A lover of sports as a youngster, he complained of not always getting picked when the players chose sides. Much of the time this was attributable to his less-than-

average height. He reported that this factor led to his going into racing where his height would be to his advantage.

Eddie left school at the age of fourteen, and he became a helper at the track as an exercise boy. A year later in 1931, he had his first race on May 18 at Bainbridge, Ohio where he finished sixth. He would go on to lose many more races–close to forty-five–before he would win his first race in 1932 at Agua Caliente in Mexico. By the mid-30s, Arcaro's reputation as a good racer had steadily grown while working at Calumet Farm. In 1933, however, Eddie had suffered a major setback. He had his first serious fall from a horse, and it had taken place at Chicago's Washington Park. His family who arrived soon after the mishap feared the worst and had taken him for dead. He remained unconscious for three days. He had suffered a fractured skull and a punctured lung, and it was three months before he was released from the hospital. Arcaro, who had experienced a prior mishap in the winter of 1928-29 in a sledding accident that could have left him crippled for life, had established the fact that he was a remarkably resilient person, and after his recuperation he resumed racing horses.

In his entire career as a racer, Arcaro concluded with twenty-one mounts in the Kentucky Derby alone, and he went on to win five of them. His first experience in the Kentucky Derby was in 1935 where he finished fourth riding Nellie Flag. His second attempt in 1938 proved more interesting as it became his first win when he rode Lawrin snatching the coveted prize by one length in the so-called Run for the Roses. His career, which had been improving steadily, finally arrived at a major benchmark with his winning the Kentucky Derby that year.

His win was a good omen of the Triple Crown that awaited him a few years down the road. The highest achievement in horse racing, the Triple Crown involves a driver and his horse winning in one year all three major races: the Kentucky Derby, the Preakness, and the Belmont Stakes. Arcaro, who still holds the record as the only racer to have captured the Triple Crown twice, won his first Triple Crown in 1941 with a horse named Whirlaway. It was a horse that Arcaro reportedly did not like very much at first but later described as "the most exciting horse I ever rode." This horse, described by Arcaro as a "little horse with steel springs," together with Arcaro's talents won the Kentucky Derby breaking the speed record by running just two minutes, one-and-two-fifths seconds. With Whirlaway, Arcaro then went on to win the Preakness and the Belmont Stakes that qualified him as the winner of the coveted Triple Crown.

After winning the Belmont Stakes in 1942 and the Kentucky Derby in 1945, he went on to win in 1948 his second Triple Crown with Citation described by Arcaro as "the most intelligent horse I ever rode." In all, he won the Belmont Stakes six times, the Preakness six times, the Kentucky Derby five times, the Suburban Handicap eight times, and the Jockey Club Gold Cup ten times. Arcaro also reached another milestone, becoming the third jockey in history to achieve 4,000 or more wins. He accomplished this in February 1958 at Santa Anita in Arcadia, California.

He retired from racing in 1961 at age forty-five. He was gratified at his sports achievements and his millionaire status, a station in life at which he had arrived by having wisely invested through the years in "oil, a chain of drive-in restaurants on the West Coast, and the wholesale saddlery business." He once stated that he would not like being away from racing. So, in retirement his interest in the world of horse racing did not come to a grinding halt as he shrewdly exchanged his riding crop for a microphone. Once more, he entered the spotlight–this time as a network television racing analyst.

Before dying from liver cancer on November 14, 1997 at age eighty-one, Eddie Arcaro had already been diagnosed with that disease a year earlier. He passed away at his home in Miami, Florida and his memorial services held at St. Martha's Catholic Church also in Miami were attended by many important people including sports celebrities like Joe DiMaggio. He leaves a legacy that includes not only the record of his personal triumphs on the track but also the example of his active involvement in the care and concern for his fellow jockeys when he helped establish the Jockeys Guild and was its president for twelve years. In a compilation of the One Hundred Greatest Athletes of All Time, Eddie Arcaro is listed as their fifty-sixth greatest. Perhaps another proof of his greatness is reflected by his many admirers who are racing professionals.

General Sources:
1. *Current Biography/Yearbook*. New York: Wilson, 1958; 1998.
2. "Fast Eddie." *People* 1 Dec. 1997: 87.
3. Nack, William. "The Headiest Horseman." *Sports Illustrated* 24 Nov. 1997: 21-22.
4. Ruby, Earl. *The Golden Goose: Story of the Jockey Who Won the Most Stunning Kentucky Derby and Then Became a Millionaire*. Verona, WI: Edco-Vis, 1974.
5. Stout, Nancy. *Great American Thoroughbred Racetracks*. New York: Rizzoli, 1991.
6. "Sunday Driver." *Wide Wide World*. Dir. Dick Schneider. NBC. 29 Apr. 1956.
7. Tilley, Chuck. *This is Horse Racing*. Miami, FL: Seemann, 1974.

–by GEORGE CARPETTO, Ph.D.

GERALD ARPINO (1925-   )

Dancer, choreographer, teacher, and director, Gerald Arpino was co-founder of the Joffrey Ballet and renowned creator of over forty choreographic numbers, expressing a most varied spectrum of dance possibilities on the modern stage. He enjoyed the best of times in the Joffrey Ballet's more than thirty-year worldwide celebrity status, which he and Robert Joffrey together had created. Arpino also endured several difficult years after Joffrey, his close partner, took ill and died in 1988. After Arpino had begun to devote himself exclusively to directing the Joffrey Ballet, there emerged the specter of unpaid bills and mounting expenses that forced the Ballet into bankruptcy in 1995. Overcoming the crisis, Arpino inaugurated a new ballet company, and in honor of his friend and colleague, called it the Joffrey Ballet of Chicago.

Gerald Peter Arpino was born on January 14, 1925 in the borough of Staten Island in New York City where his parents Luigi and Anna (nee Santana) who had emigrated from Sorrento, Italy had settled their family. Young Gerald went to school locally, and graduating with honors from Port Richmond High School, he entered Wagner College also located on Staten Island. A year later, he joined the United States Coast Guard during World War II. Stationed for a relatively long period of time in Seattle, Washington he had the opportunity to look up a family friend, Robert Joffrey, who together with Arpino would someday become famous, first as dancers and then as choreographers of international repute.

As a seventeen-year-old Coast Guardsman, Arpino had no prior exposure to dance. After visiting Joffrey, who had routinely attended dance classes at Ivan Novikoff's studio in Seattle, Arpino joined him and thereafter began dance training. Both of them then switched and studied for four years with Mary Ann Wells, described as a demanding teacher who had high expectations of Arpino. In an unusual move in his training, Arpino took not only her classes for aspiring professional dancers like most adults but also her classes for children as well.

In 1948 both Arpino and Joffrey returned to New York City. Arpino studied at the School of American Ballet of New York with Aleksandra Fedorova, Felia Doubrovska, Antonia Tumkovsky, and Muriel Stuart. Arpino continued his dance studies while he also performed with May O'Donnell and Gertrude Shurr (1949-1953). Well on his way to dancing professionally, he then toured with the Ballet Russe of Nana Gollner and Paul Petroff in South America in 1952. He subsequently appeared in Broadway musicals and in the relatively new medium of television in the early 50s.

When in 1953 Joffrey and Arpino founded their own school of ballet called the American Dance Center in New York City, Gerald Arpino focused on teaching. He became one of its faculty members and insisted on routinely offering children's lessons so as to supplement much needed income for their enterprise. Besides being co-founder of the Dance Center, Arpino was also its principal dancer and remained so until 1964 when he focused exclusively on choreography. Arpino had also been a principal dancer with the New York City Opera during Joffrey's tenure as the City Opera's resident choreographer between 1957 and 1962.

In 1961 Arpino began choreographing ballets, and becoming quite prolific, he created at least one original ballet per year and sometimes as many as three a year until the time he became director in 1989. Arpino staged his debut as a choreographer at the YM-YWHA on ninety-second street in Manhattan in 1961, and his first ballets were entitled *Partita for Four* and *Ropes*. The long-awaited creative momentum had begun, and in the following year he staged two more works, *Sea Shadow* and *Incubus*. By 1989 he would have created a total of forty-four ballets. A serious back injury and his increasing involvement in choreography phased him out of dancing completely. Becoming chief choreographer of the Joffrey Ballet in 1964, he assumed the title of associate director a year later.

Arpino, who became famous in part because he broke many of the rules of traditional dance and ballet, was innovative in many ways. He viewed ballet as a non-elitist medium. In modern times he remains one of the key players responsible for fostering the notion that dance as a form of expression is universal and not necessarily the domain of a privileged few. As a gifted choreographer, he is best known for his *Viva Vivaldi* (1964) and its boundless energy in motion; *The Clowns* (1968) became the first ballet in history to address the difficult theme of nuclear holocaust; *Trinity* (1970), a rock ballet, originally inspired by the Vietnam peace marches in Berkeley, California; *Light Rain* (1981) and its bold sensuality; and *Round of Angels* (1983), a romantic elegy. *Trinity* has now become the Joffrey Ballet's signature piece.

When Robert Joffrey incurred a severe illness in the mid-1980s and died in 1988, Arpino became artistic director of the Joffrey Ballet. As far as his own choreographic creativity was concerned, his last completed work remains *The Pantages and the Palace Present TWO-A-DAY* in 1989. In assuming the directorship of the Ballet and its responsibilities, he inherited its past financial liabilities. While Arpino devoted all his energies to operating the Ballet, the reality of accrued unpaid bills had suddenly surfaced and indeed created a major financial crisis.

It prompted the board of directors to discharge Arpino from his directorial control of the Ballet, and Arpino resigned and justifiably withdrew his ballets from the Ballet's repertoire. In a conciliatory stance, the board reinstated Arpino as artistic director. Despite many efforts to achieve financial viability in a time of mounting expenses, together with outstanding accruals payable, the Joffrey Ballet in 1995 was compelled to declare bankruptcy. In the same year, however, Arpino, intent on keeping the Joffrey Ballet alive, established the now financially viable Joffrey Ballet of Chicago.

Gerald Arpino, who has choreographed forty-four original ballets or choreographs, was in his earlier years in the 1960s nicknamed in a laudatory fashion "Arpinsky." This was to suggest that his *bravura* talents as a dancer had earned him the right to be associated with the long line of Russian dancers who had by tradition believed themselves as the best dancers in the world.

General Sources:
1. Anawalt, Sasha. "Gerald Arpino." *International Dictionary of Ballet*. Detroit, MI: St. James Press, 1993.
2. Cohen-Stratyner, Barbara Naomi. *Biographical Dictionary of Dance*. New York: Schirmer Books, 1982.
3. *Current Biography Yearbook*. New York: Wilson, 1970.
4. "The Joffrey Ballet of Chicago." 1 Jan. 1999. <http:www.joffrey.com/history.htm>.
5. Limarzi, Tullia. "Gerald Arpino." *International Encyclopedia of Dance*. New York: Oxford University Press, 1998.
6. *Who's Who in America*. 1999 ed.
7. Wulff, Helena. *Ballet Across Borders*. New York: Berg, 1998.

–by JUDY TERRANA

MAX ASCOLI (1898-1978)

Writer, publisher, political scientist, and university teacher, Max Ascoli remains one of the great literary heroes of the first half of twentieth-century political thought. As an astute student of law, politics, and philosophy, he was also a religious man who from the beginning saw through the facade and rhetorical pyrotechnics of Mussolini's speeches, his dangerously suppressive social programs, and his nationally vacuous imperialist agenda.

Born an Italian Jew, Dr. Ascoli was jailed and humiliated by state fascist police. When it was deemed legally possible, he fled to the freedom of the United States in 1931, a country which he devoutly admired and revered as one of humanity's few hopes for future world peace and redemption for world citizenry. His life, like that of many Jewish intellectuals in exile from their native countries in continental Europe, was most productive and inspiring to those who read and appreciated his political insights.

Max Ascoli was born on June 25, 1898, in Ferrara, Italy. He was the only child of Adriana (nee Finzi) and Enrico Ascoli, who was a successful coal and lumber merchant. From an early age, Max suffered from eye problems, a medical condition that would remain with him for the rest of his life. In 1920 he earned an LL.D. (Doctor of Laws) from the University of Ferrara, and in 1928 he was conferred another doctorate from the University of Rome.

He experienced the difficult art of expository writing early in his intellectual career. In 1921 at age twenty-three, he had his first book published. It was simply titled, *Georges Sorel* (1847-1922), an analysis of a French intellectual interested in revolutionary social philosophy whose ultimate vision included a *moral* climate where citizens based in a world society participated in lives full of creativity as "free producers." Sorel's ideas, however, far from being simplistic, were sociologically complicated because their content necessarily involved posing many challenging and uneasy questions as to the roles of many fundamental political, intellectual, and religious beliefs of Western culture.

In all, Sorel's thoughts were aimed directly at arousing the citizenry and encouraging them to strive for their well-being. Yet, history has repeatedly shown that philosophical writings, though inspirationally valid, are often subjected to exploitation for evil ends where, ironically, the outcome is the *reverse* of what was initially espoused. Clearly, by Sorel's standards, the people's good and their betterment were the principal thoughts as the goal and purpose of the state.

Dr. Ascoli, who had studied and understood Sorel's many intellectual matrices and complexities, would see Sorel's ideas and those of other thinkers (such as those of socialism and syndicalism of the late 1800s and early 1900s) as easy prey to the manipulation of power-seeking individuals whose ostensibly beneficent people-oriented platforms would yield different results in their programs unfolding in the middle and late 1920s. The unfolding involved the complete reversal of the ideal of a government *for the people*. Socialists such as Mussolini in Italy and Hitler in Germany knew how to utilize the appeal-to-the-masses approach as merely a dynamics of exploitation for systematically manipulating the people for the ends of totalitarianism. In Italy this negative process deteriorated into Fascism and in Germany, Nazism.

Not one to subscribe to Mussolini's rhetoric, Ascoli refused to join the Fascist party as early as 1922 and thereafter. When Mussolini became the dictator in 1925, Ascoli, through the means of a short-lived underground newspaper, began to speak out against the Fascists. However he stopped its publication when a man in Florence, mistakenly taken for Ascoli, was murdered. In the same year, his second book *Le Vie dalla Croce* was published, and a year later in 1926 he was employed by the Università Libera di Camerino to teach jurisprudence and political philosophy. In 1928 he earned another doctorate in philosophy from the University of Rome.

With Mussolini's power increasing, Ascoli again tried his hand at writing for an underground newspaper in Milan. Arrested and put in jail for three weeks, he feared that his identity as a writer for the underground antifascists might be uncovered; but he came to discover that the police had not yet made that connection and were merely harassing him because of his antifascist reputation. He was given two years house arrest which was later reduced to six months. Despite the sentence reduction, he was constantly followed by police. In effect, the arrest did much to ruin his university career as he was relieved of his university post and was later denied acceptance of a chair in philosophy at the University of Rome that he had legitimately acquired through Italy's system of competitive examinations, a common procedure for acquiring many university posts.

With no employment immediately available, he accepted a post at the University of Cagliari (Sardinia) in 1929. His refusal to join the education system's "society of university professors," a Fascist organization, eventually led to his dismissal in 1931. This event induced him to apply for and to receive that year an American grant, a Rockefeller Foundation fellowship. After complications in securing a passport and police confrontations at the port of departure (Naples), he arrived in America a week later.

After two years of study, he opted not to return to Italy, and remained in America in political exile. He found work as a teacher at the New School for Social Research in New York City in 1933. He became involved in writing, and in 1936 he wrote his first book in America, *Intelligence in Politics*. In 1939 he gladly received his American citizenship, and by 1941 he became Dean of the graduate faculty at the New School for Social Research. In 1940, as associate director of cultural relations in the government office of Inter-American Affairs in Washington, D.C., he did intelligence work in Latin America.

A prolific writer, his greatest achievement as a student of politics remains his initiation of and involvement in a biweekly magazine called the *Reporter* published from 1949 until 1968. It was known for its aggressive journalism and political analysis of such issues as McCarthyism, the Cold War, Communism, and the Vietnam War. A perceptive intellect of world politics and a victim of religious and political persecution in his earlier days abroad, Dr. Ascoli surely understood and disseminated as a lifetime mission the meaning of being an Italian American living in the freedom of the United States until the day he died in 1978.

General Sources:

1.	Ascoli, Max. *Intelligence in Politics*. New York: Norton, 1936.
2.	Ascoli, Max. *The Power of Freedom*. New York: Farrar-Straus, 1949.
3.	Ascoli, Max, ed. *The Reporter Reader*. Freeport, NY: Books for Libraries Press, 1969.
4.	Ascoli, Max, and Arthur Feiler. *Fascism for Whom?* New York: Norton, 1938.
5.	*Current Biography/Yearbook*. New York: Wilson, 1954; 1978.

–by DIANA VERICELLA

CHARLES ATLAS (1894-1972)

Angelo Siciliano, born in 1894 in the town of Acri, in Calabria, Italy would later assume a new name in the mid-1920s, calling himself Charles Atlas on his way to becoming the world-renowned bodybuilder and a "precursor of the modern bodybuilding movement." Angelo came to New York in 1904 at the age of ten. The product of a broken home, he came to America to live with his uncle. He lived on the waterfront area in one of Brooklyn's toughest neighborhoods. As a teenager, he was reportedly skinny and underweight, making easy prey for "bullies" in the area. At age fifteen, "he was attacked and severely beaten by a larger boy," an experience he would never forget.

Understandably, he brooded over that incident, and he started attending a gym at a Brooklyn YMCA. He did some weight-lifting to strengthen his body, but he remained unhappy with that kind of exercising which he saw as tiring. It appears that one day while visiting the zoo, he got the idea of exercising without the necessity of using weights. He learned this fact from observing a lion and noting how it stretched and flexed its muscles.

He had independently discovered this concept: that body muscles work not only in unison with each other but also in counterbalanced tension to each other. Movement takes place because of the body's highly dynamic rhythmic interplay of muscular contraction and relaxation. This notion, obviously known to doctors, became for Angelo a theoretical framework or starting point from which he developed a series of exercises which ultimately evolved into his famous bodybuilding program.

The key to understanding his program could be summed up in two words: dynamic tension. Angelo saw that by employing one muscle against the corresponding other, as a spring tightening and then releasing, he realized the answer to his problem of finding how to develop a well-built body without the strain of lifting weights. He created a series of exercises that he used for himself, and within a year he developed a highly sculptured body.

What made his program interesting was the fact that body muscles could naturally interact with each other with no need of special equipment or paraphernalia such as springs, pulleys, and weights. While employed as a janitor working in Brooklyn's Coney Island area in the 20s, he entered and won the 1922 contest titled The Most Perfectly Developed Man held at New York's Madison Square Garden. It was at that time that he decided to change his name to Charles Atlas. He won the same contest the following year, and his fame began to rise.

Angelo Siciliano had developed a strict regime which consisted of both physical exercises and nutritional practices. Upon awakening in the morning, he would drink a cup of warm water with lemon, then he would exercise for twenty-five minutes using the workout sequences he had developed from his dynamic tension theories. After a shower, he had a simple breakfast consisting of orange juice and bananas. His Spartan lunch included only figs and prunes. For dinner he would have a broiled steak and vegetables with fresh fruit. Then he would work out again for another twenty-five minutes. He had maintained this regimen for one year prior to the contest.

Sought after by artists for his magnificent physique, he became a model for artists earning $100 a week. This motivated him to want to bring his program to others. He developed the idea that everyone could develop a better physique by merely following the steps of the training program he had developed for himself. In 1924 Charles Atlas published his first book to meet the demands of his many fans.

Not only did the book succeed, but he had the good fortune to meet an advertising company owner, Charles Roman, who gave him a few ideas for promoting his program. In 1928, impressed with Roman's plans, he established a partnership with him, and Roman created ads of a cartoon which would soon become a media icon.

The cartoon was placed in many popular magazines, comic books, periodicals and Sunday newspaper supplements. The cartoon ad, one of the most successful and most recognizable ads in the history of advertising, depicted in a "before" scenario a skinny 97-pound weakling on the beach being kicked in the face with sand by a well-built lifeguard. To add to the weakling's slain ego, the bully takes off with the weakling's girlfriend.

Naturally, in the "after" scenario, the tables have turned. The once skinny weakling, now turned into a he-man with a very muscular physique (acquired only after having taken the Charles Atlas program, of course), punches the bully and in a single shot knocks him over and retrieves his attractive girlfriend. In response, the girlfriend says to her boyfriend what will become in the ensuing decades the proverbially sighed: "my hero."

By 1929, Angelo Siciliano and Charles Roman founded Charles Atlas Ltd., offering correspondence course programs. The mail-order book became so popular the world over that it was translated into at least seven languages, including Braille. Its success resulted in piles of correspondence as Charles Atlas received mail from as far away as Australia, the Orient, and Africa. What Charles Roman had done was develop a very successful marketing tool to promote Siciliano's excellent program.

They became millionaires within months, and when the stock market crashed in October 1929, they were unaffected. Charles Atlas had acquired celebrity status, and until the late 1960s, his image and his fitness program based on the concept of dynamic tension appeared regularly in newspapers and magazines around the globe. Angelo, still a stickler for his rigid schedule, continued to follow his strict course of bodily fitness living a Spartan life into his later years. In 1938, "weighing only 178 pounds, he (Atlas) pulled a 145,000-pound train 122 feet." With extensive nationwide coverage from the media, Atlas, at age 44, showed the world what his program could do for people.

Angelo Siciliano, once an emigrant from Calabria, now an American citizen named Charles Atlas, loved life and America. He believed that the body was more important than money. He had ensconced for posterity a respect for the importance of a physically fit and well-maintained body. Charles Atlas and his wife lived in a house furnished with his own hand-fashioned driftwood furniture on Point Lookout near Long Beach, Long Island, close to an unoccupied Coast Guard station. After his wife died in 1965, he continued to live there until his death in 1972 at the age of 78.

General Sources:
1.   *The Cambridge Dictionary of American Biography*. New York: Cambridge University Press, 1995.
2.   Gaines, Charles. *Yours in Perfect Manhood, Charles Atlas: The Most Effective Fitness Program Ever Devised*. New York: Simon & Schuster, 1982.
3.   Null, Gary, and Carl Stone. *The Italian-Americans*. Harrisburg, PA: Stackpole Books, 1976.
4.   "The World of Charles Atlas." 10 Oct. 1998. <http://fortress.am/users/rao/Atlas>.

–by PAUL N. CARLO

SALVATORE BACCALONI (1900-1969)

Salvatore Baccaloni, a most popular Italian-American opera singer, was a remarkable basso who set the standard for comic roles in the genre. At Arturo Toscanini's endorsement, he joined La Scala di Milano in 1925 and later went on to sing at the New York Metropolitan Opera Company where he remained from 1940 to 1962. Also appearing in several Hollywood movies, he graced the silver screen with his charm, warmth, and mellifluous voice.

He was born in Rome on April 14, 1900, the son of Joaquin and Ferminia (nee Desideri) Baccaloni. He began his musical training at the age of six when he was a boy soprano in the school of choristers which is affiliated with the Sistine Choir. With the group consisting of approximately 250 other boys, he received his musical training along with his education in other school subjects.

"As soon as he could read notes well, he was sent as a paid soloist to participate in the musical services of the various churches in Rome." Keeping half the fee for himself, the other half went toward his education at the chorister's school. When his voice began to change at age twelve, he left the Sistine Choir and was enrolled at the Academy of Fine Arts to study architecture. This he did to please his father, a building contractor, who wanted his son to develop "his gift for drawing and designing by becoming an architect." Baccaloni was indeed a bright, multi-talented, and hard-working student, and his father thought an architect's life would be a practical profession.

Like the lives of many others, Salvatore's studies were encroached upon by the necessity of military duty in World War I. In 1920 he graduated with a degree in architecture and was hired by an architectural firm as a draftsman in Rome. Yet in all his student years in studying architecture, he participated in many amateur operatic offerings, and he continued to do so even while working as a draftsman.

One night, at a private musical performance at the home of a prominent Roman hostess, his life changed significantly. Baccaloni had the good fortune to meet the well-known baritone and teacher, Giuseppe Kaschmann, a member of the first company which opened the New York Metropolitan Opera in 1883. After hearing Baccaloni sing that evening, he asked the young singer: "Why be an architect when you have such a beautiful voice?" Baccaloni had probably been looking for a sign, an omen of sorts, and he quickly responded to Kaschmann's suggestion by abandoning the draftsman's drawing board.

Within two years of study with Kaschmann, Baccaloni had mastered many operatic roles, and he made his debut at the Teatro Adriano in Rome in 1922 at the age of twenty-two appearing in the role of Bartolo in Rossini's *The Barber of Seville*. Soon after, he appeared in such roles as Dulcamara in Donizetti's *The Elixir of Love* and in Bellini's *Norma* in Rome's Teatro Augusteo. About three years later, Baccaloni's life was about to make another significant change.

At a performance in Bologna, Baccaloni sang the role of the tragic father in Charpentier's *Louise*. It was that night that Arturo Toscanini, who had been the principal conductor at La Scala di Milano at age thirty-one in 1898, recognized Baccaloni's powerful basso voice and his strong dramatic distinctness. Toscanini, who at the time of Baccaloni's performance was the director of the New York Philharmonic, used his influence in bringing him to the renowned Scala.

Baccaloni had already acquired a wide repertory which included both serious and comic operatic roles. Toscanini advised him to specialize in *buffo* parts, pointing out the many advantages of making lifetime work of comic roles in opera. Toscanini observed that the custom of fine voices in comic roles for some reason had not been maintained. Toscanini expounded that comic roles in opera were being relegated to older men many of whom were losing their voice. He saw in Baccaloni not only a full and youthful voice to play these roles but also a definite aptitude and spirit for comedy.

Baccaloni followed the maestro's advice which together with the maestro's influence, he was engaged as "La Scala's official *basso buffo*" after the death of La Scala's singer, Azzolini, in 1926. Thereafter, Baccaloni would sing regularly at La Scala until 1940. Two years later, in the late 20s, he traveled beyond Italy's borders and delighted audiences in England at Covent Garden (1928-29) and then several years later at the Glyndebourne Festival (1936-39).

In 1930 he sailed to the United States touring with the Chicago Opera Company making his North America debut in Chicago itself. Later, he traveled to Argentina to sing at the Teatro Colón in Buenos Aires beginning in 1931 and making many more subsequent appearances there until 1947. When he was on tour in 1938, San Francisco audiences particularly loved him, and his name would be maintained for many years to come on its Opera Association roster.

On December 21, 1940, making his first appearance at the Metropolitan Opera, Baccaloni captivated New York audiences with his antics on stage as the "lovesick, foolish old bachelor Don Pasquale" in Donizetti's opera bearing the same title, and later, as the "walrus-mustached Sergeant Sulpice" in Donizetti's *Daughter of the Regiment*. He would remain as a performer at the Metropolitan singing there until 1962. He gave 297 performances, most of which were in the Italian *buffo* repertory.

Baccaloni's instant success in New York soon won him a motion picture contract in 1941. Three of his several film appearances in the late 50s and early 60s include: *Full of Life* (1957), *Fanny* (1961), and *The Pigeon That Took Rome* (1962). Between engagements at the Metropolitan Opera, he devoted his talents to operatic concert tours throughout the United States. In his later years, the portly Baccaloni weighed in at 320 pounds. He was married to Elena (nee Svilarova), a Bulgarian, who was reputed to have been an excellent cook.

Good-natured and very approachable, he passed away on the last day of December in 1969, having earned the credit of a lifetime operatic repertoire that included 160 roles with critics agreeing that he set the standard of excellence for comic operatic roles.

General Sources:

1. Aylesworth, Thomas. *The World Almanac Who's Who in Film*. New York: World Almanac, 1987.

2. *Current Biography/Yearbook*. New York: Wilson, 1944; 1970.

3. *The Encyclopedia of Opera*. Ed. Leslie Orrey. New York: Scribner, 1976.

4. Ewen, David. *The New Encyclopedia of the Opera*. New York: Hill and Wang, 1971.

5. Katz, Ephraim. *The Film Encyclopedia*. New York: HarperCollins, 1998.

6. *The Metropolitan Opera Encyclopedia: A Comprehensive Guide to the World of Opera*. Ed. David Hamilton. New York: Simon and Schuster, 1987.

7. *The New Grove Dictionary of Opera*. Ed. Stanley Sadie. New York: Grove's Dictionaries of Music, 1992.

8. "Obituary." *New York Times* 1 Jan. 1970: 23.

–by ANTHONY TRIVELLI

ANGELA BAMBACE (1898-1975)

Angela Bambace, who would become a pioneer in American unionism, still remains today, relatively speaking, an unsung hero in the history of American labor. She dared to cross not only unionism's gender line in finally becoming elected the first woman vice-president of the ILGWU but also many ethnic and religious boundaries in the cause of justice in the labor force. She struggled valiantly for women and men alike for employee benefits, protection, and above all, for equity so that all workers received a day's pay for a day's work regardless of gender, color, or national origin.

She was born in Santos, Brazil on February 14, 1898 to an Italian couple, Antonio and Giuseppina (nee Calabrese) Bambace. Suffering from ill-health, Antonio had decided to move the family from Italy to Brazil and then later to New York City. The family settled in East Harlem, and it was a transition that would shape much of Angela's life. Like many immigrant women, Giuseppina took in sewing to help the family's income. Many women knew the needle trades because they had been trained as young girls in Italy when they prepared their dowries, which usually consisted of linens and cloth goods made by hand. These sewing skills had been transferred from mother to daughter for generations. Many of the women immigrants would form the backbone of the New York City garment industry.

The International Ladies Garment Workers Union (ILGWU) came into being in 1900 and the Women's Trade Union League would soon follow in 1903. Italian women, despite their expertise in needle trades, were initially slow in rallying to union causes and membership. Their upbringing had usually dictated that a woman's place was in the home and not in the workplace–and certainly not in strikes protesting for workers' rights.

However, that mind set would soon change because of the horrendous working conditions in sweatshops in urban areas. A protracted strike against shirtwaist makers of New York, which began in November 1909 and lasted until February 1910, remained a major benchmark for garment trade unionism. The historical event was still furthered by the indelible impression made by the Triangle Shirtwaist Company fire in 1911 that took the lives of 145 working women. This tragedy and the ensuing strikes secured a stronghold within the garment industry union.

These historical events had set the stage for Angela Bambace and her sister, Maria, when they entered the workforce as operators in a shirtwaist factory in 1917. Their mother, a staunch advocate of unionism, encouraged her two daughters to support unionism and attend its meetings. Reportedly, she herself would go to meetings with a rolling pin in hand to ward off any unsavory characters who typically intimidated workers especially if they had been strike supporters.

They learned from their mother's example, and it was not before long that in another sector of the garment industry that the Bambace sisters planned and organized a needle workers' strike in 1919. Soon after, Local #89, an Italian dressmakers' union, came into being as a direct result of their efforts. That same year, Angela married Romolo Camponeschi in an arranged marriage, and subsequently Angela gave birth to two sons, Oscar in 1920 and Philip in 1923. After withdrawing from union activities, she later returned to work and to her dedication to unionism in 1925.

In time, her fervent beliefs in the union cause would also exact its toll on her. Among other things, she was tossed down a flight of stairs, maligned, and even jailed. It also bore its toll on her marriage when she divorced, and her children were removed from her custody. Yet, throughout her life, Bambace's strategy remained a constant drive to foster long-range effectiveness rather than short-term gain. Every decade brought new work-related challenges to Angela, and her efforts were not limited to unionism. The 1920s and 1930s also witnessed her at one moment protesting for a reprieve in the Sacco and Vanzetti case and in the next moment striking in different parts of New Jersey and New York.

In Angela's struggle to expand unionism, she faced an even greater challenge, and it was from inside the union. ILGWU officials as well as other union officials were male dominated, and they considered Bambace an irritant. By the 1930s, tired of Bambace's complaints that no woman ever held executive status, they decided to offer her a project in Baltimore involving union organizing. Bambace got right to the task and organized Local #227, a union of women cloak makers. Angela became the one who had introduced the city of Baltimore to walkouts and sit-down strikes in dealing with non-union shops. Ahead of her time, she was instrumental in developing workers' educational programs for women in Maryland which served as a model elsewhere.

Having accomplished what she could in Baltimore, she was on the road again in 1940 heading for Pennsylvania. As was her trademark, union membership in this new area increased at a rapid rate. By 1942, she became union manager of the Maryland-Virginia district, and through her efforts, outpatient clinic services for union members were created. In 1956 a long-awaited ILGWU General Executive Board post came to Angela when she was finally elected vice-president of the ILGWU. Later in 1962 President Kennedy named her to his Commission on the Status of Women.

Angela who had cancer for a number of years, lost her final battle with it on April 3, 1975 in Baltimore, just three years after she retired from her union post. An Italian-American woman who fought battles on many fronts, including the war relief programs, the Histadrut (Zionist labor movement), and in local and state political affiliations, Angela Bambace and her intense passion for life and justice in times of adversity will always be remembered. In a field dominated by men, she set a great example of caring and commitment to just causes in labor. In remembrance of her devoted union work, the people of the city of Baltimore still refer to her as "Maryland's First Lady of the Labor Movement."

General Sources:
1. DiStasi, Lawrence. *The Big Book of Italian American Culture*. New York: HarperCollins, 1990.
2. Furio, Colomba M. "The Cultural Background of the Italian Immigrant Woman and Its Impact on Her Unionization in the New York City Garment Industry." In *Pane e Lavoro: The Italian American Working Class*. Ed. George E. Pozzetta. Staten Island, NY: The American Italian Historical Assn., 1978.
3. Mangione, Jerre, and Ben Morreale. *La Storia: Five Centuries of the Italian American Experience*. New York: HarperCollins, 1992.
4. Scarpaci, Jean A. "Angela Bambace and the International Ladies Garment Workers Union: the Search for an Elusive Activist." In *Pane e Lavoro: The Italian American Working Class*. Ed. George E. Pozzetta. Staten Island, NY: The American Italian Historical Assn., 1978.

–by LINDA D'ANDREA-MARINO

ANNE BANCROFT (1931-   )

A consummate actress who has graced both stage and screen, she was the recipient of two Tony Awards and the winner of an Oscar for best actress at the 1962 Academy Awards presentations. Her many years of training from her earliest age in New York City have served her well as she has consistently demonstrated superb skill and versatility as an actress. Beginning her professional career in the early 50s on TV, then on stage and in film, she has become known internationally and recognized as one of the world's finest actresses.

Born Anna Maria Louisa Italiano on September 17, 1931 in the Bronx, New York to Michael and Mildred (nee DiNapoli) Italiano, Anne Bancroft started training in dancing and acting at age four. One of three children (two sisters: Jo Anne and Phyllis), she was greatly influenced in her early years by her mother to aspire to join the entertainment world. Her mother had apparently decided that one of her three daughters would become an actress.

After attending Public School Number 35 and then graduating from Christopher Columbus High School (Bronx), she attended the American Academy of Dramatic Arts (AADA). Her mother supplied the financial support in the form of tuition. The AADA represented the "oldest actors' training school in the English-speaking world." Its curriculum required a two-year commitment. It had been established in 1884 in Manhattan, New York City, and its original name was the Lyceum Theater School for Acting. In addition to Anne Bancroft, it boasts such notable alumni as Cecil B. De Mille, Colleen Dewhurst, Ruth Gordon, Robert Redford, and Spencer Tracy, among many others.

In 1950, at age nineteen, she began her professional career on TV, and her first performance took place in the *Studio One* production of Turgenev's *The Torrents of Spring*. Using the stage name, Anne Marno, she also had a role in the TV series *The Goldbergs*. She appeared in many other TV programs, but it would be her reappearance on *Studio One* that would be decisive when Fred Coe, an influential Broadway producer, had taken notice of her. He would not forget her fine acting talents when she returned from her first excursion to Hollywood.

A successful screen test would win her an immediate 20th Century-Fox contract. From a stage name list supplied by Darryl F. Zanuck, the head of Fox Studios at that time, she chose the name Anne Bancroft. At 21, she made her motion picture debut in the 1952 movie, *Don't Bother to Knock*. Five years later, in 1957 at 26, she returned to New York having appeared in approximately fifteen movies of which she described herself as "not particularly proud" despite the experience.

After competing with several other more established actresses for the starring female role in *Two for the Seesaw*, she succeeded in impressing the play's producer Fred Coe and captured the lead female role opposite the veteran actor, Henry Fonda. *Two for the Seesaw* opened on Broadway on January 16, 1958, and it proved to be a huge success. It was a two-character play about an "affair between an Omaha lawyer on the brink of divorce and a generous Greenwich Village stray."

Anne Bancroft received immediate acknowledgment as a first-rate actress by theater critics. For that one role alone, she went on to receive many awards such as the Theater World, Variety, and the highly coveted

Antoinette Perry (Tony) Award. On February 13, 1958, a month after the play opened, her marriage of four years to Martin A. May culminated in divorce.

The next year Coe and his associates turned their attention to producing *The Miracle Worker*. There was no doubt that Bancroft would play the role of Annie Sullivan. She was the governess to Helen Keller who was "triply handicapped by blindness, muteness and deafness."

To prepare for this difficult role, she spent three weeks at the Institute of Physical Medicine and Rehabilitation in New York City where she worked with many of their disabled children so that she could learn and experience, first hand, what it would be like to have physical disabilities. In addition to those experiences, she would often close her eyelids with adhesive strips to sense and feel blindness.

The play opened on October 19, 1959 with Patty Duke playing the role of young Helen Keller. The drama was very much an instant success. Both actresses received immediate accolades from the theater critics, and Anne Bancroft's photograph would be seen on many magazine covers that year. Their roles, however, were to dispense to them, literally, many bumps and bruises due to the "nightly pommeling" they inflicted on each other during one of the scenes.

One critic of the *New York Times* (Dec. 20, 1959) reported that particular scene as best described as "never played exactly the same way twice . . . It is invariably followed by amazed applause . . . the scene may be played for laughs, tears, or tension . . . on occasion, it has been hilarious. Annie is a natural clown."

For her role as Annie Sullivan in *The Miracle Worker*, she received the Drama Critics Award as well as another Tony Award. Subsequently, she was invited to Hollywood to play the same role in the film version of that play. In 1962, she went on to receive an Oscar for Best Actress for that role. In addition, she subsequently received four nominations for Best Actress for the following films: *The Pumpkin Eater* (1964), *The Graduate* (1967), *The Turning Point* (1977), and *Agnes of God* (1985).

In 1979, she acted in, wrote, and directed *Fatso*, a movie about the trials and tribulations of an Italian American (role played by Dom DeLouise) in the battle of the "bulge." Combining humor and compassion for this character's plight, Anne Bancroft depicts this milieu with an incredible sense of scenic texture and warm detail, capturing on screen not only the specific theme of the culturally-driven "love affair" between Italians and good food but also the more universal theme of food as escape from reality and its associated psychological and interrelational scenarios.

Married to Mel Brooks, her marital and compatible creative partner for more than 30 years, Anne has appeared in a host of roles varying from lead role to cameo appearances. She represents a model of achievement for an Italian-American woman who earned her way and has made it to the top of the field. To date, she consistently earns the respect and acknowledgment of many moviegoers who see a movie simply because she is part of the cast.

General Sources:
1. *Contemporary Theatre, Film and Television*. Detroit, MI: Gale Research, 1989.
2. *Current Biography Yearbook*. New York: Wilson, 1960.
3. Holtzman, William. *Seesaw: A Dual Biography of Anne Bancroft & Mel Brooks*. Garden City, NY: Doubleday, 1979.
4. Katz, Ephraim. *The Film Encyclopedia*. New York: HarperCollins, 1998.
5. *Who's Who of American Women: A Biographical Dictionary of Notable Living American Women*. 1963 ed.

–by GEORGE CARPETTO, Ph.D.

BILLY BARTY (1924-   )

Billy Barty (nee William Bertanzetti) is probably one of Hollywood's best-known and best-loved "little people." He began performing for the movies as early as three years of age in the late 20s just when the silent movies were replaced by the "talkies." He also appeared on stage in the vaudeville era of the 30s with such people as Donald O'Connor. When TV came into being in the late 40s, he also became fairly active in that medium. Throughout his acting career he was engaged in the cause of defending and upholding the rights of people of small stature. He became responsible for eventually creating an organization called "The Little People of America in 1957 and the Billy Barty Foundation in 1975, offering psychological and financial assistance to little people in need."

He was born on October 25, 1924 in Millsboro, Pennsylvania. His film career, which spans more than seven decades, has offered him an opportunity to have a vast variety of roles ranging from that of a child to a Nazi spy. Standing 3 feet 9 inches tall and weighing about 80 pounds, he is presently an active and talented Hollywood personality.

Often described as an actor with the face of an innocent demon, it appears that it apparently was a quality that offered him a wide latitude of acting roles. He began performing as early as 1927 at three years of age appearing in a two-reeler called *Wedded Blisters*. Referring to his earliest roles as small children, he amusingly recalls: "I was four years old for eight years."

Then, playing in the *Mickey McGuire* series of comedy shorts between 1927 and 1934, he had the role of Mickey Rooney's kid brother. In feature films of that early era, he played a role in the *Gold Diggers of 1933* (1934) where he plays the child who offers Dick Powell a can opener to cut into Ruby Keeler's metal suit. He appeared in the 1934 production of *Alice in Wonderland* and also in the 1937 production of *A Midsummer Night's Dream*.

In the 1930s, vaudeville was still going strong when Billy was a youngster, and so before the advent of WWII he appeared on stage singing, dancing, and doing the patter, i.e., delivering rapidly amusing "gag" lines typical of that entertainment style. In the vaudeville theaters he also had the opportunity of playing together with Donald O'Connor who as an entertainer was also a youngster himself having been born in 1925: just a year after Barty.

In 1940 at age 16 Billy Barty left show business to complete his high school education. He later attended Los Angeles City College and then Los Angeles State College where he majored in journalism. Billy's dream was to be a sportswriter or announcer, and this seemed to go hand-in-hand with his desire to be a football or basketball coach. In his teenage years, sports were indeed a major part of his emotional life.

He had the opportunity to do broadcasting for some football games at L.A. City College, and in fact he did broadcast commentary on the first football game ever televised from the city of Los Angeles. His athletic abilities and desires were far from squelched because of his size. He coached little league, played baseball at L.A. City College, and for a brief period of time even played in semi-professional baseball where he batted .500, had 45 walks, and stole seven bases.

By 1947 he had returned to show business, and in 1949 he became the co-host of a children's TV show in New York City. At a time when TV was in its infancy and expanding so rapidly, he seemed to be at the right place at the right time as he became involved with a number of TV series in the 1950s. He was also a regular member of the Spike Jones' City Slickers, a musical group that did comedy and appeared in night clubs and regularly on TV.

At a time when Liberace's fame was growing nationwide, Billy Barty became an instant success, especially with TV audiences, when he did an unforgettable parody of Liberace playing piano. At one point during the piano presentation, the candelabra, Liberace's signature prop, unexpectedly exploded. To TV history buffs of that early, innocent TV era, this Billy Barty episode still ranks today as a comedy classic along with Ernie Kovacs' Nairobi trio. In the 1950s, Barty also appeared in a number of films such as *Pygmy Island* (1950), *The Clown* (1953), and *The Undead* (1957).

From 1963-1967 he moved up from co-hosting to having his own TV children's show, bearing his own name, *The Billy Barty Show*, that broadcast live from Los Angeles five days a week. During the 1960s, he appeared in a number of films such as *Jumbo* (1962), *Roustabout* (1964), and *Harum Scarum* (1965). In the 1970s, he became even more active in the movies, and he appeared in many films whose stars included celebrity status performers such as Joan Blondell, Elvis Presley, Ronald Reagan, Burt Lancaster, Kirk Douglas–to name a few.

At one point in his entertainment career, Barty decided to start a movement to raise the public awareness regarding "little people." This term represented the designation that he and many others with dwarfism preferred to the terms dwarf or midget. And so, as the motivating force in a group of twenty people who met in Reno, Nevada in 1957, he helped them initiate an organization called The Little People of America, Inc. whose purpose involved assisting little people and bringing them more into mainstream society.

Today, this supportive organization of little people represents the largest group in the world that focuses on people who are four feet ten inches tall or less. It helps its members to deal with their unique dilemmas and difficulties in a world where they constitute the minority in the context of height and its related social and psychological relationships.

Time is not passing him by as he remains energetic both mentally and physically in the kind of busy life that would wear out most people. He is currently working on his biography, and he remains very involved in the Little People of America and the Billy Barty Foundation, the latter of which he initiated to ensure the perpetuation of the movement's drive for small people's rights.

Still working on TV, he generally doesn't turn down a movie script if it is to his liking. He continues to offer encouragement and support to little people and their families through his own personal hot line. In a recent interview, when asked about his attitude in dealing with any life problem in a world of anomalies, his philosophy seemed best expressed when he replied, "...it may not work out–but my thinking is that as long as you try, you've done it." Just a few years ago, he was awarded an honorary doctorate from Los Angeles State College.

General Sources:
1.   Barty, Billy. *The Little People of America, Inc. Souvenir Book.* Studio City, CA: Billy Barty Foundation, 1982.
2.   *Contemporary Theatre, Film and Television.* Detroit, MI: Gale Research, 1989.
3.   Haliwell, Leslie. *The Filmgoer's Companion.* New York: Scribner's Sons, 1984.
4.   Katz, Ephraim. *The Film Encyclopedia.* New York: HarperCollins, 1998.
5.   Quinlan, David. *Quinlan's Illustrated Directory of Film Character Actors.* London: Batsford, 1995.

–by JANET B. TUCCI

CARMEN BASILIO (1927-   )

Hailing from Canastota, New York, this two-division champion was among the most popular boxing figures of his era. Honored by the Boxing Writers Association of America, he was voted Fighter of the Year for both 1955 and 1957. When he concluded his boxing career, he had a record of 79 bouts, 56 wins, 16 losses, and 7 draws. He won his first world-title bout as welterweight champ by defeating Tony DeMarco on June 10, 1955. Then, defeating Sugar Ray Robinson in one of boxing's most memorable championship bouts in the midst of a 38,000 person crowd at Yankee Stadium, Basilio became the new middleweight world champion in 1957.

Carmen's parents were born in Italy and came to the United States as youngsters. His mother Maria Lucia Basilio (nee Picciano) came from Campobasso when she was four years old. His father, Joseph, immigrated to Canastota from Rome, Italy in 1903 when he was 16 years of age. After Joseph married Maria Lucia in 1910, their union would bring forth a family of eleven children.

Joseph Basilio became a farmer growing mainly onions and other vegetables such as lettuce, carrots, and potatoes. He owned three plots of land amounting to 55 acres. One plot consisted of 9 acres and another of 14 acres, and both were located north of Canastota; the third plot of 32 acres was to be found in the Chittenango Station area of Madison County where, it appears, many of the local farmlands were worked mostly by southern Italians.

Carmen Basilio was born on April 2, 1927 into this relatively poor family. His father who was an avid boxing fan, encouraged his sons to embrace the boxing field. He bought boxing gloves for his three oldest sons Armando,

Carmen, and Paul not only for boxing practice but also for settling disputes with one another. It was fairly common for them to stay up together on Friday nights and listen to the boxing fights on the radio. In his youth Carmen had little interest in school, and he says he attended Canastota High School only because it featured boxing on its sports program. He fought regularly on its high school team, and he was often found getting into fights in the streets.

Carmen served in the United States Marine Corps in the final years of WWII. In the Marine Corps he also had done some boxing, and after his tour of duty, he was honorably discharged. He returned home and worked on the farm with his father and then decided to become a professional fighter. He trained hard and turned pro in 1948 with his first official match on November 24. In this pro bout, he knocked out his opponent (Jimmy Evans) in the third round. He won a whopping $50, and 33 percent of that amount went to his manager.

From the relative obscurity of fights tending to focus in and around locations in central and western New York State, things soon began to change during the next four years. His boxing activities began to capture the attention of lightweight and welterweight promoters especially after a draw and loss to Chuck Davey and to Billy Graham, who were far better known boxers. His fighting career really began to move when in a decision fight he beat the former lightweight champ Ike Williams in 1953. Then in a return match with Billy Graham, Basilio went on to defeat him in a title bout for the New York State welterweight crown.

Wanting to win the welterweight title (not limited to New York State), his forthcoming 11 bouts demonstrated a strong and determined 9-0-2 record. Ready as a crown contender on June 10, 1955, Basilio's first world title bout was an event that proved to be bloody for both fighters. After Basilio had dropped DeMarco twice in the 10th round, the referee decided to halt the bout in the 12th which made Basilio the new world welterweight champ. Temporarily losing his title in a subsequent bout in a 15-round decision to Johnny Saxton, Basilio quickly recaptured the title when in a rematch he beat Saxton in two rounds.

Perhaps the fight for which Basilio remains most famous was his 1957 title bout defeating the middleweight world champ Sugar Ray Robinson at Yankee Stadium. It took place at 10:30 p.m. on September 23. Rain showers that afternoon had prevented the event from becoming a sellout performance at the Stadium. In all, the otherwise 38,000 spectators were joined by thousands of others who watched the closed-circuit TV broadcast throughout the United States (in 174 theaters and arenas) including a sellout at the New York State Fair Coliseum.

No doubt, it was one of the most watched sports events of the decade where the interest levels were all the more sparked by the curious fact that (in those early days of television) both fighters had agreed to appear on Steve Allen's Sunday night television show about a week prior to the boxing match. The fighters fought intensely, and despite a badly cut left eye, Basilio went on to win the championship, which Robinson would retrieve a year later. After two more specific attempts at recapturing the title, he lost both times, once to Gene Fullmer who had supplanted Robinson, and another time in 1961 to Paul Pender who had supplanted Fullmer.

After his retirement from professional boxing in 1961, the townspeople in Canastota commissioned a statue to be built in his likeness and in his honor. He worked for a period of time at Le Moyne College athletic department in Syracuse, New York and also did some public relations work for Genesee Brewery, a New York-based enterprise. In his bid for the mayoralty election in his town of Chittenango in 1980, he lost by 66 votes. In 1986 he married for the second time. In 1990 he was inducted into the International Boxing Hall of Fame in Canastota. Now in his 70s, he and his wife, Josephine, live in Rochester, New York most of the year, and they winter in Florida.

In addition to having been a two-division champion who enjoyed a huge following of loyal fans, Basilio contends that in his professional career of 79 bouts he was never knocked down to the canvas despite the fact some people have erroneously claimed that Fullmer had once sent him to the canvas. Described as a very humble and approachable man with good listening skills, he has often expressed his happiness at the fact that he fulfilled his American dream. Coming from a small town and from a hard-working and respectable immigrant family, he trained diligently, determined to succeed; he fought hard and went on to win the middleweight championship of the world from a tough and formidable opponent at Yankee Stadium in 1957 while the whole boxing world was watching him make boxing history.

General Sources:
1.   Basilio, Carmen. Personal interview. 2 Sept. 1998.
2.   "Carmen Basilio." 11 Nov. 1998. <http://ww.ibhof.com.ibhfhome.htm>.
3.   "Carmen Basilio." 1 Dec. 1998. <http://www.ibhof.com/carmenb.htm>.
4.   Myler, Patrick. *A Century of Boxing Greats*. New York: Robson/Parkwest, 1998.
5.   *Sugar Ray Robinson vs. Carmen Basilio.* Buchanan Collection, Library of Congress. [Production company unknown], 1958.

–by MICHAEL T. GUARDINO, Sr.

JOHN BASILONE (1916-1945)

Tens of thousands of motorists every day race along the New Jersey Turnpike, one of the busiest highways in the United States. Most drivers focus on the pavement in front of them. Few notice that one of the service areas is named for John Basilone. The main purpose of those who stop is refreshment and relief, not reflection or remembrance. Few pause by the side of the main building to read an aging bronze plaque about Manila John, the only man in U.S. history to win the nation's two highest awards for valor in World War II: the Congressional Medal of Honor and the Navy Cross. An extraordinary United States Marine whose heroism has earned many monuments to his memory, John Basilone, who was nicknamed Manila John, fought valiantly and gave his life during World War II in the Pacific theater.

Few would have predicted from John Basilone's early life that he was heroic material. Born in Buffalo, New York on November 4, 1916, he spent his growing years in Raritan, New Jersey, a working class community about 35 miles southwest of New York City. His parents, Salvatore and Angelina Basilone, struggled to get by on their income from a small tailor shop, a task made more difficult by the fact that they had ten children crowded into a modest size home. John was a skinny kid who was often mischievous. He attended St. Bernard's parochial school before ending his education at age 15 to work, driving a laundry truck. He grew to be tall with black hair, a strong chin, a barrel chest, and movie-star looks.

The Great Depression was in full swing when he was a teenager. Jobs were scarce, and money was not easy to come by. At age 19, he joined the Army. Although the pay was low, military life at least offered him three square meals a day, clothing, lodging, and some adventure. John seemed to adapt quickly to peacetime soldiering. He won a Golden Gloves tournament as a lightweight boxer in the States before being sent to the Philippines, then an American possession. In Manila, the capital city, he acquired his nickname as well as large tattoos on both arms–a woman on the right and an unsheathed sword on the left with the legend "Death before Dishonor." During his stay in the Army, Basilone had developed such a fascination and facility with automatic weapons that before long he could break down a machine gun and reassemble it while blindfolded.

When his hitch was up in 1939, John returned to Raritan where his mother urged him to get married and raise a family. Economic conditions had improved, and he was able to find a job in a nearby chemical plant. But World War II had already begun in Europe, and although the United States was technically at peace, its armed forces were expanding rapidly. In 1940 Manila John reenlisted, this time in the United States Marines Corps. His specialty still remained machine guns, and because of prior military experience, he was quickly promoted from private first class to sergeant.

After the December 7, 1941 air attack on Pearl Harbor, the Japanese empire accelerated its military pace moving rapidly and acquiring land throughout much of the Pacific including the Philippines and stretching as far north as the Aleutian Islands off the coast of Alaska by early spring 1942. Yet by June of the same year, the tide would turn for Japan's massive offensive as American cryptoanalysts broke Japan's top-secret naval code. Admiral Nimitz now had access to the moves and intentions of Admiral Yamamato's fleet, which would result in Japan's losing four aircraft carriers in the span of a few days at the famous Battle of Midway.

At that time, Basilone, who was still in the States, was experiencing grueling amphibious Marine instruction in Maryland at a training site prophetically called Solomons. He was soon shipped off to the Pacific and headed to New Zealand by mid-June. Now with a major sea battle victory behind them, the American armed forces were on the offensive. Ironically, one of the first areas targeted by the Americans was the Solomon Islands. Located in the Southwest Pacific, it was a 900-mile long chain of volcanic islands. Guadalcanal, the largest island in this chain, became the scene of the U.S. first large-scale invasion.

Guadalcanal, described by many as a tropical hell consisting of infested jungle and swamp terrain, replete with crocodiles, leeches, scorpions, and malaria, was a key site that represented Japan's southernmost flank, a site the Americans knew they had to win. Unlike the sea-air battle at Midway which lasted only days, the struggle to secure Guadalcanal lasted five brutal months, where both sides ran out of supplies, took no prisoners, and had to resort to hand-to-hand combat. Sergeant Basilone was savvy in a machine-gun's fatal use and in doing repairs. He was vividly documented for his extraordinary heroic actions and single-handed bravery in the effort to secure Guadalcanal and its vitally important Henderson Airfield.

In light of his heroic actions, on January 19, 1943, John Basilone became the first U.S. Marine in World War II to earn the nation's highest award for bravery: the Congressional Medal of Honor. Lauded by President Roosevelt, Sergeant Basilone was brought back to the United States to receive a hero's welcome that included a New York City reception by Mayor La Guardia who offered him a key to the city. He soon became a public figure boosting wartime morale and appearing at social and political functions and as an emissary endorsing the purchase of U.S. Bonds for the war effort.

The wartime activity could have been over for Manila John if he had chosen to remain in the States, but he opted to re-enter the war seeking military action in the Pacific. He was assigned to the Fifth Marine Division, and it was his fervent desire to be present at the recapture of the Philippines, but that would never come to pass for him. On February 19, 1945, he was part of the first amphibious wave at Iwo Jima, a tiny island (about one-third the size of Manhattan), just 660 miles south of Tokyo, which would eventually become a critically strategic location for B-29 bombers.

Sergeant Basilone exercised great heroic efforts, and his valiant actions were vividly documented. Killed as he was by a mortar shell which landed right before him, Sergeant Basilone made the *New York Times* editorial column which acknowledged the loss of this great soldier. Posthumously, he was awarded the Navy Cross, the Marine Corps' second highest award for bravery after the Congressional Medal of Honor, and the Navy named a destroyer the USS Basilone in his honor. In 1949 the remains of his body were respectfully moved from Iwo Jima to Arlington National Cemetery in Virginia not far from the nation's capital in Washington, D.C.

General Sources:
1. Cutter, Phyllis (nee Basilone). Personal interview. 25 Sept. 1998.
2. Lepis, Louis. *Italian Heroes of American History*. New York: Americans of Italian Descent, Inc., 1976.
3. "Sergeant Basilone United States Marine Corps." 13 Oct. 1998. <http://www.direction.net/bcarr/basilone.htm>.
4. "Unico National, Inc." 20 Oct. 1998. <http://www.uniconat.com/>.
5. Ware, Susan, ed. *Forgotten Heroes*. New York: Free Press, 1998.

–by ANDREW VASCELLARO

GIUSEPPE BELLANCA (1886-1960)

Giuseppe Mario Bellanca was born on March 19, 1886, the son of a miller in the village of Sciacca, Sicily. He lived on the breezy slopes overlooking the Mediterranean Sea where he studied the flight of the sea gulls. He often dreamed of being able to fly one day. Known as "GM" to his friends, he attended the Technical Institute in Milan where he received a teaching certificate in mathematics. Then after attending the Politecnico, GM graduated in 1910 with a degree in engineering and mathematics. In school, GM continued to feed his fascination with flight. With the help of two classmates, he constructed an airplane which in 1909 became the first totally Italian-designed and Italian-built airplane.

In 1911, GM came to America with five brothers and a sister, settling in Brooklyn close to the airfields of Queens, Long Island. At age 25, he completed the construction of an airplane. He accomplished this feat in the back of his brother's grocery store, using family members as his assistants. GM first taught himself to fly, then opened a flying school in 1912 and started teaching others. Fiorello LaGuardia, a future Mayor of New York City, was one of his students.

GM formed the Bellanca Aeroplane Company and Flying School primarily to manufacture planes for their use in training pilots. Due to his successful designs through WWI and into the 1920s, GM had become known as the "professor." In fact, he was the only aeronautical engineer designing airplanes at that time.

GM's first cabin monoplane, completed in 1922, seated four passengers and an outside pilot, an outstanding feat for the time. Even now, some 70 years later with all the technical advances, his accomplishment at creating a five-seater plane still remains a remarkable achievement for its time since engineering skill was rare in those early decades of aviation. Quiet and shy by nature, GM avoided the limelight. He was always known to have a smile. Determined to make the best airplane possible, GM designed and built a sturdy high-wing monoplane called the Bellanca C.F. It first flew in June 1922. Unquestionably, it was the most efficient airplane in existence for its time. His airplane went on to break the endurance records for hours aloft without refueling, retaining that record for many years to come.

Despite his personal sense of achievement, hard times in 1925 forced GM to join forces with Wright Aero Corp. In New Jersey, he designed the Wright-Bellanca WB-1 and the WB-2 which would go on to win easily the efficiency and endurance records during the 1926 National Air Races. Wright's new power plant, the J5 Whirlwind, was a milestone in reliability, and aviators broke many records with this aircraft. The power plant, mated as it was with the overall Bellanca design, created aviation history. It was the first truly reliable engine and airframe combination.

Due to the demand for reliable engines, Wright decided to forgo manufacturing airframes and build only powerplants. Again, Bellanca was at a loss with his small company, receiving few offers to collaborate by such builders as Beech in Kansas and Ryan in California. Unfortunately, he elected to associate himself with a New York self-made millionaire, Charles Levine. This association turned out to be a setback as Bellanca assumed all men shared his honesty and forthrightness.

Bellanca and Levine joined forces, forming the Columbia Aircraft Corp. In early 1927, Wright Aero Corporation, in deference to Bellanca the designer, passed up orders for the WB-2, including a certified check for $25,000 from Charles Lingbergh who knew of the long range capabilities of the plane. The plane and all production rights were sold to Columbia Aircraft Corporation.

C. Chamberlin, a test pilot, joined GM. He with another renowned pilot, Bert Acosta, flew the airplane and stayed aloft for 51 hours and 11 minutes, breaking all previous endurance records. This flight covered a distance of 4,100 miles: 500 miles farther than the challenging distance of the forthcoming New York-to-Paris contest.

Levine, who wanted to bid on a lucrative government air mail contract, decided to make his own headlines and groom the WB-2, now renamed the Columbia, for the coveted New York-to-Paris contest. Levine, however, had failed to apply to enter the contest on time; thus, he decided to sell the airplane to Lindbergh for $25,000, allowing Lindbergh to win the $25,000 prize money.

Levine, however, had some demanding conditions. He wanted his own crew to fly the plane. This forced Lindbergh, who wanted to fly solo, to go with Ryan, the California-based company and use the modified Spirit of St. Louis with added fuel tanks. However, Lindbergh knew full well that the Columbia was the better of the two airplanes. He had even written to GM asking if a second or a duplicate airplane could be built for him for the contest.

Meanwhile, Lindbergh, on the cold, wet morning of May 20, 1927, took off for Paris to make history with the Ryan plane. The Columbia, fueled and ready, unfortunately remained grounded. Finally, on June 4 with legal problems resolved, the Columbia, with Chamberlin as pilot and Levine as passenger, took off, flew over Paris, and went farther into Germany landing outside of Berlin. This was a feat that far outweighed Lindbergh's solo accomplishment, proving that Bellanca's airplane could carry a greater load and remain aloft longer than any contemporary airplane.

GM soon parted with Levine. With a capital investment from the DuPont family, he formed the Bellanca Aircraft Corporation in Delaware. He went into production with his famous monoplane which would break many long distance records, including non-stop flights from New York to Istanbul and Japan to the United States. In 1931, a Bellanca plane actually remained aloft for 94 hours without refueling.

Bellanca had consistently made aviation history during his entire life, but he never fully received the recognition he assuredly deserved. Perhaps a more accurate rewriting of aviation history in the future will correct that. Bellanca died in 1960. An Italian-American visionary and innovator, Giuseppe Bellanca has profoundly influenced today's world of commercial aviation.

General Sources:

1. Magoun, Alexander, and Eric Hodgins. *A History of Aircraft*. New York: McGraw-Hill, 1931.
2. Matricardi, Paolo, and Eric Angelucci. *The Rand McNally Encyclopedia of Military Aircraft, 1914-1980*. Trans. S.M. Harris. Chicago: Rand McNally, 1981.
3. Morgan, Roger, ed. *Sunrise and Storm Clouds*. New York: Newsweek Books, 1975.
4. Simonson, Gene R., ed. *The History of the American Aircraft Industry: An Anthology*. Cambridge, MA: M.I.T. Press, 1968.
5. Spencer, Jay. *Bellanca C.F.: The Emergence of the Cabin Monoplane in the United States*. Washington, DC: Smithsonian Institution Press, 1982.

–by WALLY CRAWFORD

PIETRO BELLUSCHI (1899-1994)

Pietro Belluschi, born in Italy and licensed in 1928 as an architect in the United States, participated in the design and supervision of more than one thousand buildings. He was one of architecture's most influential twentieth century figures and one of the leading spokesmen for the modernist style in the United States northwestern region. In addition to his major influence especially in Oregon, he was also responsible for the design of many buildings elsewhere such as San Francisco's well-known Bank of America building. He also designed or codesigned many other structures such as the San Francisco St. Mary's Cathedral; the New York City Juilliard School of Music, Lincoln Center Alice Tully Hall, and the mid-town Manhattan Pan Am (now known as Met Life) Building with its pioneering heliport roof.

Pietro Belluschi was born in Ancona, Italy to Guido and Camilla (nee Dogliani) on August 18, 1899. He was the younger of two children. His sister, Margherita, four years older, would become an opera singer, a mezzo soprano of some repute. Pietro did not begin school until the family moved to Rome in 1905. The move was job-related with his father being transferred to Rome because of the nationalization of the railroads in Italy.

Pietro served in the Italian Army during World War I. He was discharged as a first lieutenant after having served three-and-a-half years in military service. Pietro whose education was interrupted by the war, continued his studies in Rome, earning his degree in 1922 as a doctor of architectural engineering at the University of Rome. After Pietro's father retired from his job, he started a small construction business. Pietro worked both for his father and for the state as a housing inspector. Unhappy with both jobs, he

viewed them as unchallenging.

In 1923, Pietro became an Italian exchange student at Cornell University in Ithaca, New York. After completing his civil engineering degree, he decided to remain in the States. He obtained his first job out west as an electrical engineer with an Idaho mining company. He then joined the architectural firm of A.E. Doyle and Associates in Portland, Oregon where he started as a draftsman in 1925, and two years later moved up to chief designer. In 1927, the organizational structure of the firm began to change. One of the principal partners resigned, and a year later the firm's head, Mr. Doyle, died. In 1928 Pietro passed the architecture examination and received his license.

He proceeded diligently at his profession, and in 1932 he became a partner in the firm. He was gradually becoming one of the foremost designers in the Pacific Northwest and a determined proponent of regional modernism. He viewed the mission of the architect as that of creating architectural form whose style and function were closely coordinated to geographic location. His designs conformed to landscape, climate, and availability (whenever possible) of local materials. He espoused what was called in architectural parlance as the "international style," a style that emphasizes simple, functional designs which serve the basic needs of the user. This outlook, European in origin from the 1920s and 1930s, which Belluschi adopted, would eventually affect his designs in the entire range of structures from the biggest to the smallest, from skyscrapers, factories, shopping centers, and public housing to private homes.

In 1943 he ultimately bought the firm where he had been a partner and changed the company's name to Pietro Belluschi, Architect. By the end of the 1940s and the early 1950s, he had already become one of the most highly respected architects in the entire country. Belluschi's career as a visionary architect in fact had begun in 1931 with the completion of his first major project, the realization of the Portland Art Museum where he employed his modernist style.

To the long list of the many secular structures he designed, there needs to be included a whole series of religious structures whose designs were also inspired by Belluschi's modernist style. That series began in 1938 with the completion of St. Thomas More Chapel in New Haven, Connecticut. Later that series included San Francisco's St. Mary's Cathedral whose overall shape parallels that of a bishop's miter, and the St. Louis Synagogue. His houses of worship with their creatively appealing designs that were cast in a modernist blend of simple and functional served as a model for many future religious structures across the country even in large urban areas.

Belluschi earned nationwide acclaim in 1948 when his design had come to fruition with the realization of a relatively small yet innovatively simple twelve-story glass-and-aluminum structure called the Equitable Savings and Loan Association Building (nowadays called the Commonwealth Building) in Portland, Oregon. It was the first postwar *curtain-wall* skyscraper, where its exterior wall had no weight-bearing function. The aluminum and glass were employed to seal and encapsulate the building: not support the structure. The design anticipated much of the inspiration behind such buildings as New York's United Nations and Lever Buildings. This had been preceded in 1942 by his design of a planned community in McLaughlin, Washington, where an integral part of the layout included the first modern shopping center in the United States.

As an Italian-born architect, Pietro Belluschi had the distinction of being the Dean of the School of Architecture and Planning at the prestigious Massachusetts Institute of Technology for fourteen years (1951-1965) and was one of the most prominent leaders in the development of an American-style architecture in the modernist tradition. The recipient of many commendations, awards, and honors including his appointment by President Truman to the National Commission of Fine Arts (1950), his election to the American Academy of Arts and Sciences (1952), his trusteeship of the American Federation of Arts (1954), his membership as a Fellow of the Royal Academy of Fine Arts (1954), and as a member of the National Institute of Arts and Letters (1955), Pietro Belluschi was more recently awarded the National Medal for the Arts in 1991 by President Bush in a White House ceremony. At age 94, Belluschi died February 14, 1994 in his home in Portland leaving an enormous architectural legacy to the United States.

General Sources:
1. Clausen, Meredith L. *Pietro Belluschi: Modern American Architect*. Cambridge, MA: MIT Press, 1994.
2. Clausen, Meredith L. *Spiritual Space: The Religious Architecture of Pietro Belluschi*. Seattle: University of Washington Press, 1992.
3. *Current Biography/Yearbook*. New York: Wilson, 1959; 1994.
4. Doumato, Lamia. *Pietro Belluschi*. Monticello, IL: Vance Bibliographies, 1980.
5. *Encyclopedia of American Architecture*. New York: McGraw-Hill, 1995.
6. Stubblebine, Jo, ed. *The Northwest Architecture of Pietro Belluschi*. New York: F.W. Dodge, 1953.
7. White, Anthony G. *Pietro Belluschi: A Selected Bibliography*. Monticello, IL: Vance Bibliographies, 1988.

–by MARIO GUECIA

MICHAEL BENNETT (1943-1987)

Remembered principally for his conception, choreography, and direction of *A Chorus Line*, one of the longest running musicals on Broadway (fifteen years) which won nine Tony Awards along with the 1976 Pulitzer Prize for drama, Michael Bennett was hailed by many as a Broadway genius. Involved in numerous musical shows, he became a leader in bridging the nuance of body movement on stage with its relation to revelation of character psychology. His work became synonymous with dance form and perfection of movement.

Michael DiFiglia, better know as Michael Bennett, was born April 8, 1943, in Buffalo, New York. He was the son of Joseph and Helen (nee Ternoff) DiFiglia. His parents had enrolled him at the age of three in a children's dancing school. Before reaching his teenage years, Michael had already taken lessons in ballet, tap, modern, and folk dance. He had performed in several variety shows produced by Mrs. John Dunn's Little Stars of Tomorrow. Because his parents were very supportive of his enthusiasm and love of dance, he was able to spend many summers in New York City where he studied at professional dance studios with such accomplished individuals as Aubrey Hitchins and Mat Maddox.

While attending Hutchison Central High School for Boys in Buffalo, he often appeared as a participant in community theater presentations, and he choreographed and directed many student productions. At age fifteen, he took the role of Baby John in a stock production of *West Side Story*. At age sixteen, just a few months away from his 1959 graduation, he dropped out of school to accept the role for the same part in Jerome Robbins' professional company which took that musical drama on a tour throughout Europe.

A year later, after he returned to New York City from abroad, he danced in Broadway musicals such as *Subways Are For Sleeping*, *Here's Love*, and *Bajour*. Having had the experience of being assistant to the choreographer for three Broadway productions, he was afforded the opportunity to choreograph his own show, *A Joyful Noise*. While the musical proved successful in summer stock, it lasted only twelve performances at Broadway's Mark Hellinger Theater in 1966. Bennett, who was now only twenty-three years of age, earned himself his first nomination for a Tony Award because most critics enjoyed his choreographic style, favorably described as "bouncy."

In the coming years between Broadway shows, Bennett was also acquiring TV choreographic experience, either performing or choreographing on such programs as the *Ed Sullivan Show*, the *Dean Martin Show*, and the *Hollywood Palace*. Then in 1967, much like his experience in *A Joyful Noise* a year prior, the musical, *The World of Henry Orient*, did not enjoy favorable reviews, yet the critics liked Bennett's choreography, citing the play's dances as the "most original aspect of the show." Another critic said it was as if Bennett was a "choreographer in search of a show." Bennett received a second Tony Award nomination for choreography after the closing of *Henry, Sweet Henry*, which ran for two months on Broadway in 1967.

Again, Bennett received his third consecutive Tony nomination for choreography in *Promises, Promises* in 1968, but unlike his prior nominations this one was for a musical that became a huge success, and it would run for two-and-one-half years to capacity crowds. As a Neil

Simon adaptation of Billy Wilder's 1960 smash hit movie (*The Apartment)*, the play contained the music and lyrics of Burt Bacharach and Hal David. Following the inception of the long run enjoyed by *Promises, Promises*, Bennett began staging the musical numbers for a new musical biography called *Coco*. It starred Katharine Hepburn, but despite the biggest box-office advance in history when it opened in 1969, the musical proved disappointing to most critics except, of course, for Bennett's consistently high-quality choreography, a strength that would allow him to move forward in other musicals.

Company, a play written by Stephen Sondheim, constituted a departure from traditional musicals as it was sparse in the use of large production numbers. Compensating for this situation, Bennett thought it best to choreograph into the play inventive dance numbers. The play went on to capture the majority of the 1971 Tony Awards, but despite his obvious efforts, Bennett himself was nominated but did not win the Tony that year.

Finally, after so many nominations, Bennett won two Tonys in 1972. One was for his choreography in Sondheim's *Follies*, a nostalgia play dealing with old Ziegfeld show girls who are awaiting the wrath of the wrecking ball that is about to destroy a building where they once performed. Bennett won a Tony for choreography and another for best direction of a musical. Soon afterwards, as was the nature of his personality, he rose to the occasion when, a mere six weeks before its opening date, he was asked to revamp the production of a musical, *Seesaw*, which was faltering. Again, his excellent work earned him a second Tony for choreography for this play.

At thirty years of age and after three Tonys, he decided to take a break from Broadway for a year. Reflecting upon his career with all its challenges, Bennett came up with the idea for *A Chorus Line*. He conceived, directed, choreographed, and co-produced this musical. Unlike any show before, Bennett creatively explored the lives and struggles of dancers and their dedication to the craft. In many ways, *A Chorus Line* also celebrates the struggle and the dedication of countless unsung dancers who have devoted their lives to the art of dancing. Poignant and psychologically well-grounded, the musical became an instant success in May 1975, and critics applauded it as the most exciting play since *West Side Story* from the early 60s.

In 1976, *A Chorus Line* brought in nine Tony Awards and a Pulitzer Prize for drama. Bennett and co-producer Joseph Papp sold the movie rights for $5.5 million. The musical, which concluded its Broadway performance in 1990, had made a record-setting fifteen-year run. Michael Bennett, however, who had died three years prior in Tucson, Arizona on July 2, 1987 due to an AIDS-related disease, was unable to enjoy the fruits of his hard labors and creative talents. A winner of eight Tony Awards in choreography and direction, he will be remembered as a hard working, innovative Italian American who set a standard for artistry and excelled in the love of his life: dancing.

General Sources:
1. *Contemporary Theatre, Film and Television.* Detroit, MI: Gale Research, 1986.
2. *Current Biography Yearbook.* New York: Wilson, 1981; 1987.
3. Flinn, Denny M. *What They Did for Love: The Untold Story Behind the Making of A Chorus Line.* New York: Bantam Books, 1989.
4. Kelly, Kevin. *One Singular Sensation: The Michael Bennett Story.* New York: Zebra Books, 1991.
5. Mandelbaum, Ken. *A Chorus Line and the Musicals of Michael Bennett.* New York: St. Martin's Press, 1989.
6. *Who's Who in America.* 1980-81 ed.
7. *Who's Who in the Theatre.* 1977 ed.

–by VINCENT J. LAMANO, Sr.

TONY BENNETT (1926-   )

Having been hailed as a "singer's singer," and reputedly Frank Sinatra's favorite crooner, Tony Bennett is currently enjoying the grandest of revivals in night club circuits while appealing to all age groups in concert, including MTV audiences. Starring in his own 1994 MTV special called *Tony Bennett Unplugged,* he went on to win two Grammy Awards: one for album of the year, and the other for best traditional vocal recording.

Anthony Dominick Benedetto was born in New York City on August 3, 1926. His parents John Benedetto a tailor, and Anna (Suraci) Benedetto were in many ways a typical New York City Italian family of modest means making it through the 1920s in Astoria, Queens.

When Tony was eight, his father died leaving young Tony, an older brother and sister, and his mother to carry on by themselves. For the next 17 years, Mrs. Benedetto worked at home as a seamstress for the garment industry. Putting in long hours of hard work for little pay during the time of the depression was no easy task; yet Tony remembers those days as very meaningful and happy. As a teenager, he worked for $30 a week at the Yukon Restaurant and Bar in New York as a singing waiter.

During World War II, he was drafted into the Army and served as an infantryman in Europe, including Germany. While in the Army, Tony Benedetto also sang with various military bands, and upon his honorable discharge, he enrolled in the American Theater Wings professional school, studying voice using the G.I. Bill of Rights. He worked as an elevator operator in the Park Sheraton Hotel.

In 1949, his big moment came when he won a spot on the Arthur Godfrey television show, *Talent Scouts,* finishing second behind Rosemary Clooney. After he and Rosemary Clooney appeared on the Jan Murray TV show, *Songs for Sale,* Pearl Bailey made Tony an offer to sing with her in the Greenwich Village Inn nightclub. Bob Hope, who had gone to hear Pearl Bailey's performance, became so impressed with Tony Bennett that he invited him to visit him the next day on-stage at the Paramount Theater. Bob Hope, who was appearing there, introduced Tony Benedetto to sing a few songs. Later, Bob Hope said that from now on he would be named "Tony Bennett," and so he was. Tony Bennett would accompany Hope on his forthcoming nationwide tour.

Soon after completion of the tour, Tony Bennett submitted a demonstration record, called "The Boulevard of Broken Dreams," to Mitch Miller, then the head of Columbia Records Artists and Repertoire Department. Miller then signed Tony Bennett to an exclusive recording contract. Although this demo record was a short-lived hit, it was soon followed by two others, "Because of You," and "Cold, Cold Heart." Both records sold more than one million copies each. Tony Bennett, the once unknown singer, had suddenly become a top male vocalist.

During October 1951, Tony Bennett became a major attraction at the Paramount Theater. He also appeared on the nightclub circuit as well as in the newly emerging medium called television. The trade magazine, *Cash Box,* had rated him as the top ranking male recording vocalist. Throughout the 1950s, Bennett's recordings became the rage of the bobby-soxers. His hits: "Rags to Riches" and "Stranger in Paradise" had remained number one on the charts for three consecutive weeks, each selling more than one million records. This brought Tony a most coveted Gold Record from

Columbia. Some other hit songs by Tony Bennett from that era include: "Lullaby of Broadway," "Always," "How About You," "Solitude," "April in Paris," "Blue Velvet," and "One For My Baby."

It was also during the late 1950s that a new craze, rock 'n' roll, would be fully emerging. Tony simply refused to get into this new style of music, and his once sweeping popularity started to wane as his records had lost their appeal to the younger generation. This lull lasted a few years until 1962 when things began to change for him.

The Fairmont Hotel in San Francisco had booked Tony Bennett. His piano accompanist, Ralph Sharon, was looking around for a song that would have an immediate local appeal for their performance. It happened, then, that what would become his signature song, "I Left My Heart in San Francisco"–an arrangement that had been collecting dust for the past seven years–suddenly launched Bennett into the limelight once more.

This became the most successful hit song of his career, and worldwide it became synonymous with the name Tony Bennett. A best-selling record for more than 100 weeks, there were over one-and-a-half million copies sold. In 1963, Tony Bennett was awarded two Grammy Awards that represented the record industry's highest honor. Presented by the National Academy of Recording Arts and Sciences, he was awarded the Grammies for Best Record of the Year and Best Solo Vocal Performance by a Male Singer. The award-winning song also earned him a gold record which he presented as a gift to the city of San Francisco.

With rock 'n' roll holding the lion's share of the marketplace throughout the 1960s and 1970s, Tony left Columbia Records and focused on live concerts and clubs "instead of having to worry about doing three albums a year." As a nightclub performer, Tony Bennett became one of the main attractions throughout the major night spots in the United States and abroad, especially England. In appraising Tony Bennett's singing success, spanning fifty years, one would have to acknowledge not only his unique voice but also his keen sense of pacing as he warms up to his listening audience. This becomes especially evident in smaller night clubs where he captivates his audiences to a point of mesmerization. A professional and personal friend of Frank Sinatra, Tony Bennett made an album in 1992, *Perfectly Frank*, featuring some of Frank's songs. This earned him his first Grammy in thirty years. In 1993, just a year later, he won another Grammy for the album, *Steppin' Out*, songs relatable to Fred Astaire. In 1994, he won a double Grammy for an album entitled *Tony Bennett Unplugged* based on an MTV program series.

As one of the most accomplished singers of our time, Tony Bennett has a demeanor just "short of shy" with a refreshing vulnerability not often found in the world of celebrities. A widely exhibited graphic artist, Tony Bennett's landscapes and cityscapes have earned him much admiration. In May 1995, Tony Bennett received the Lifetime Achievement Award at the World Music Awards ceremony. The dedication to his craft and the humanity reflected in his genuinely disarming warmth serves as an inspiration for people from all walks of life. A very successful Italian-American singer, he is admired by many the world over.

General Sources:
1. Balliett, Whitney. *Alec Wilder and His Friends*. New York: Da Capo Press, 1983.
2. *Current Biography Yearbook*. New York: Wilson, 1995.
3. *The New Grove Dictionary of American Music*. New York: Grove's Dictionaries of Music, 1986.
4. *Who's Who in America.* 1995 ed.

–by GOMY SMERALDI

CARDINAL JOSEPH L. BERNARDIN
(1928-1996)

Installed as a prince of the church in August 1982 in Chicago, Cardinal Joseph Bernardin became the leader of the largest and most prosperous archdiocese in the United States. Because of his affable personality and his deep concerns for implementing Vatican II's mandated plea for greater participation of the laity, he specifically requested his investiture have a "high degree of involvement by people who reflect the wide diversity of the archdiocese." His decision gave insight into what had been his life's work: caring for the people and reflecting a life of Catholic belief.

The older of two children of emigrant parents from northern Italy, Joseph Louis Bernardin was born in Columbia, South Carolina on April 2, 1928. His father, Joseph senior, a stonecutter with a granite company in Columbia, died succumbing to an early death from cancer when Joseph junior was only six. After the untimely death of their father, young Bernardin together with his sister, Elaine, persevered through their early years with their mother Maria (nee Simion) Bernardin, a seamstress.

After graduating from St. Peter's parochial school, young Bernardin attended public high school where he graduated at the remarkably young age of 16 despite the fact that he had held after-school odd jobs. He was reputed as being an avid reader and an eternal student while teens his age typically rushed off to high school football games and dated. His studying paid off when he earned a scholarship then earmarked for pre-med studies at the University of South Carolina. Yet it was while working at a Catholic hospital that he decided to relinquish the pursuit of a medical career in favor

of a religious vocation.

After one year at St. Mary's College in Kentucky (1945-46), he entered St. Mary's Seminary in Baltimore, and he graduated in 1948 with a B.A. in philosophy. Four years later, at Catholic University in Washington, D.C., he received both his master's degree in education and the sacrament of Holy Orders, being ordained a priest for the Diocese of Charleston, South Carolina. Even as early as his graduation day, he was already reputed by his peers as destined for higher church office and for greater responsibility as he seemed to possess in abundance a sense of personal warmth matched by a deep drive for hard work.

As predicted by many, Father Bernardin's career accelerated in the next 12 years. He was assistant pastor in Charleston for two years (1952-54), a typical entry level position. Yet, within the next ten years, he moved to diocesan vice-chancellor to chancellor (1956) to vicar general and to assistant to the bishop (1964). Two years later in 1966, Pope Paul VI appointed Bernardin as bishop. When consecrated Bishop of Atlanta, he became the youngest bishop in the U.S. At the same time, Bishop Bernardin was assigned as auxiliary to Archbishop Paul Hallinan of New Orleans who had recently returned from the ongoing Second Vatican Council in Rome, begun in 1962.

And so, right from the inception and implementation of Vatican II policies in their efforts to renew the Church from within, Bishop Bernardin remained at the cutting edge of change, fully aware of the challenges and difficulties it would entail. In 1968, Bishop Bernardin was named General Secretary of the

National Conference of Catholic Bishops (NCCB) in Washington. In 1972, Bernardin left Washington after Pope Paul VI appointed him the archbishop of Cincinnati's archdiocese of 2.6 million Catholics.

The power of his courage and convictions were demonstrated within his first two months of his Cincinnati post as archbishop when he called for an end to the American bombing in North Vietnam. Several weeks later, despite his opposition to official American policy in Vietnam, he participated in an ecumenical service in the White House on the occasion of President Richard Nixon's second inauguration. Bishop Bernardin, elected President of the National Conference of Catholic Bishops and member of the International Synod of Bishops, became Chairman of the Bishops Committee on War and Peace from 1974 until 1979.

During ten years of service to his flock in Cincinnati, he became known as assertive in local church matters. Yet he was reputed as a moderate ecclesiastic always seeking the counsel of rank-and-file clergy. He often spent holidays saying Mass in prisons; he regularly said Mass in Spanish for migrant workers, and he created emergency funds for them. In a pastoral letter on his 15th anniversary as bishop, he emphasized a bishop's ability to listen attentively to his flock. On July 10, 1982, Pope John Paul VI appointed Bernardin as Archbishop of Chicago to ameliorate the tarnished image left by Cardinal Cody who right before his death had been accused of fiscal improprieties.

It was reported that Bernardin's administrative talents brought renewed confidence to Catholics in his purview as he knew the needs of the Church and its new directives, but mostly, as most agree, he presented himself as a warm and compassionate man. In 1983, just a year later, Pope John Paul II carefully selected Archbishop Joseph Bernardin and elevated him to the lofty rank of cardinal. An enemy of pomp, Bernardin's legacy presents him as diligent, hard-working, and virtually accessible to everyone.

A false accusation of sexual misconduct (later recanted by the accuser, a former seminarian) sweeping through the media startled and devastated him. What's more, the dire diagnosis of pancreatic cancer and the return of liver cancer hampered his ordinarily dynamic and active personality. It is within the realm of these critical events that he decided to write his book, *The Gift of Peace*, a spiritual autobiography of the last three years of his life focusing on his courage and his strength in the search for spirituality and inner tranquillity.

On October 2, 1996 Cardinal Joseph Bernardin died. He was bestowed all the honors of a high prelate of the Roman Catholic Church. He will be remembered as a religious man, who with an eye on the times of worldwide social, moral, and political upheaval, exercised a calm and patient demeanor with his fellow humans. He remains in the hearts of many not only as an excellent mediator with those of the Jewish faith but also as a distinguished prelate *nulli secundus* both in the exercise of his temporal responsibilities and his spiritual life.

General Sources:

1.   Bernardin, Joseph. *Consistent Ethic of Life*. Kansas City, MO: Sheed & Ward, 1988.
2.   Bernardin, Joseph. *The Gift of Peace*. Chicago: Loyola Press, 1997.
3.   Bernardin, Joseph. *The Word of Cardinal Bernardin*. New York: Center for Migration Studies, 1996.
4.   *Current Biography Yearbook*. New York: Wilson, 1982; 1997.
5.   Kennedy, Eugene C. *Cardinal Bernardin: Easing Conflicts and Battling for the Soul of American Catholicism*. Chicago, IL: Bonus Books, 1989.
6.   *Who's Who in America*. 1995 ed.

–by MARGARET SCARFIA

LAWRENCE "YOGI" PETER BERRA (1925-)

Yogi Berra has become one of the most quoted baseball personalities in recent history but not so much for his baseball statistics as for his Berraisms or Yogi-isms, i.e. tautologies, or better, logical contradictions. For instance, he once said, "When you reach the fork in the road, take it;" "You can observe a lot by watching;" and "It was déjà vu all over again." He is a unique phenomenon that encapsulates a love of baseball together with an irrepressible penchant for humorously worded contradictions. A three-time winner of the American League MVP Award, and player on ten world championship teams, he was inducted into the Baseball Hall of Fame in 1972.

Lawrence Peter Berra was born to Pietro and Pauline (Longsoni) Berra of Milan, Italy on May 12, 1925. When Lawrence was seven years old, the Berras moved to the Italian "Hill" district of St. Louis, where Pietro Berra took a job in a shoe factory. Lawrence attended Wade Grammar School, where one of his boyhood friends named him "Yogi," after watching a film about India and its related practice of yoga. Ongoing deficiencies with reading and math led to Yogi's repeating the sixth grade. He became increasingly shy and self-conscious of the fact that he was older than his classmates. By the eighth grade, Berra found himself withdrawn, disinterested, and wishing he was doing what he did best–playing baseball.

At 15 Yogi quit school and went to work. Pietro Berra thought that baseball was a waste of time and that Yogi should be working to make a living. Yogi worked in a coal yard, as a soft-drink truck driver, and as a tack-puller in the shoe factory. Yet, in every spare moment, Yogi would play baseball.

Yogi and his friend, Joe Garagiola, played for the Stockham Post American Legion Baseball team. Yogi's lightning reflexes, strong arm, and powerful bat began to attract baseball scouts. However, it was Garagiola who was first signed to a major league contract because, unlike Berra, Garagiola didn't swing at "any pitch he could see." Rebuffed by the St. Louis Cardinals and Browns, the good fortune to sign Yogi Berra fell to the New York Yankees.

After one year (1943) in the minor leagues, Yogi joined the Navy, and participated in the invasion of Normandy, France in 1944. After the war, Yogi joined the Yankees top farm club, the Newark (N.J.) Bears, where he batted .314 and hit 15 home runs, in 1945. In 1947, his first full season with the New York Yankees, he batted .280, with 11 home-runs, and he hit the first pinch-hit home run in World Series history. Yogi Berra went on to establish a baseball career as one of the most outstanding catchers to ever play the game.

Yogi remained a notorious "bad ball hitter." Yet he hit with power finishing with 385 homers, and a career batting average of .285. Berra was named the American League Most Valuable Player in 1951, 1954, and 1955 (and finished second in the voting in 1953 and 1956). In addition, Berra was named to the All-Star team 15 times. Yogi led the mighty Yankees in runs batted in for six consecutive years, from 1950 through 1955.

Yogi Berra was a complete ballplayer as evidenced by his setting a fielding record for catchers where, from 1957 to 1959, he played 148 games without an error. His World Series records include: most games played (75) and most hits (71). Yogi, named manager of the New York Yankees in 1964, led them to the American League pennant. After losing to St. Louis in the World Series, Berra was released by the Yankees. The next chance to manage came in 1973 with the New York Mets, and again, Berra led his team to a pennant. Yogi coached with the Yankees and Houston from 1975 to 1989, when he decided to retire. The culmination of Yogi Berra's illustrious baseball career came in 1972 when he was named to the Baseball Hall of Fame.

Yogi married Corrine Short in 1949, and together they raised three sons: Lawrence, Timothy, and Dale (a former major league shortstop). During his early career, Yogi remained self-conscious about his lack of education and physical appearance (as he was once cruelly described as a cross between "a gorilla and bull penguin"). For years he kept the hurt inside until his accomplishments ended the harassment from teammates, opposing players, writers, and baseball management. Coinciding with his baseball achievements were Yogi's financial and business acumen. Yogi Berra was the only Yankee that the tyrannical, autocratic Yankee General Manager, George Weiss, could not intimidate into pay cuts or any raises.

Yogi's simple argument for Weiss would be to pay him what he wanted or trade him to a team that would pay! Berra went from someone who could not write a check to someone amassing considerable wealth as Vice President of the Yoo-Hoo soft drink company. Yogi had never taken a penny for his Yoo-Hoo endorsements; instead, he took stock. He eventually accumulated enough stock to leave him wealthy for life.

No biographical profile of Yogi Berra would serve its full purpose without some mention of his famous, or infamous, verbal *faux pas*, that came to be known as "Berraisms." Perhaps, his most noted malapropism was when he expressed his gratitude at a benefit dinner by commenting "I want to thank all those who made this evening necessary." Yogi once explained the difficulty in coping with the Yankee Stadium's left-field shadows by remarking that "it gets late early out there." Another trenchant observation held that no one goes to a particular restaurant anymore because it's always crowded. One Berraism has actually stood as a guiding philosophy and source of encouragement and fortitude in the face of seemingly insurmountable adversity, and that is: "it ain't over till it's over."

Today, Lawrence "Yogi" Berra, is a millionaire, but more importantly, he is a community-minded citizen, a dedicated family man, sportsman, and well-respected gentleman. He remains a tribute to Italian Americans as an example of having achieved so much success despite so many seemingly insurmountable obstacles.

Nobody laughs at Yogi anymore.

General Sources:
1. Berra, Yogi. *The Yogi Book*. New York: Workman Pub., 1998.
2. Borst, William A. "Berra, Lawrence Peter." *Biographical Dictionary of American Sports, Baseball*. Ed. David L. Porter. New York: Greenwood Press, 1987.
3. Braddock, Bill. "Berra, Yogi." *Encyclopedia Americana*. Danbury, CT: Grolier, 1997.
4. Golersbock, Peter. *Dynasty. The New York Yankees 1949-1964*. Englewood Cliffs, NJ: Prentice Hall, 1975.
5. Pepe, Phil. *The Wit and Wisdom of Yogi Berra*. Westport, CT: Meckler Books, 1988.
6. Windhausen, John D. "Yogi Berra." *Great Athletes, The Twentieth Century*. Englewood Cliffs, NJ: Salem Press, 1992.

–by CARMELO J. SIGONA

MARIO BIAGGI (1917-   )

One of the most popular congressmen in recent New York State history, he worked his way up from the ranks of one of the most decorated   New York City policemen to becoming a lawyer. Then, as a lawman turned lawyer, he focused his attention on politics where he could effect changes for the greatest number of people by introducing and supporting the enactment of better federal laws. A champion of the poor, the elderly, the handicapped, and those victimized by criminals, Mario Biaggi was also the friend of ethnic groups when injustices needed to be addressed and rectified.

Mario Biaggi was born on October 26, 1917 in a Harlem tenement in New York City. The oldest of three brothers, he came from a relatively poor family of emigrant parents, Salvatore and Mary (Campari) Biaggi, from northern Italy. As a youngster, he helped out his family financially by being a shoeshine boy and a laundry boy. As an adult, he worked his way up from the ranks of a highly decorated New York City policeman to that of a lawyer, becoming, eventually, a United States Congressman in 1969.

He attended Public School 171, and later studied automotive trades at Harren High School in mid-Manhattan. After graduating in 1934 in the middle of the depression, he worked in a factory for two years, then in the U.S. Post Office until 1942. He placed among the top one percent of the competing applicants, and he effectively joined the New York City Police Department.

The achievement of this exceedingly high test score was a harbinger of the many valiant and courageous acts he would perform in the line of duty. His distinguished police career both as an officer and a community liaison had exemplified 23 years of dedicated service and would earn him the Police Medal of Honor for Valor in 1960, the Police Department's highest award.

Similarly, for his many years of dedicated and heroic service, in 1961 he had the distinction of becoming the first N.Y.C. policeman to be inducted into the National Police Officers Hall of Fame. He earned a department record of 28 commendations for heroism, being wounded ten times in the line of duty.

A year prior, in 1960, Daniel Gutman, Dean of the New York Law School, became so impressed upon hearing Mario Biaggi as guest speaker at a dinner that he offered him a full scholarship to study law. Mario, who was a detective at that time, obtained a special dispensation from the American Bar Association waiving the college degree entrance requirement.

He completed law school in two-and-a-half years while on leave from the police department, and received his LL.B. degree in 1963. While studying law, he worked from 1961 to 1963 for the Republican Governor, Nelson A. Rockefeller, in community relations. In more actively addressing his future legal career, Mario then worked as assistant to the New York Secretary of State until 1965 thereupon formally retiring from the police department. Retiring with the rank of detective lieutenant, he was granted a disability pension for a leg injury incurred while attempting to stop a runaway horse.

After twice failing the qualifying examination for the bar, he finally succeeded in 1966. In the following year, he became partners in the law firm of Biaggi & Ehrlich. Despite his interest in private practice, the political arena had become near and dear to him. Running for office, he scored an easy victory in November 1968 in the race for the New York 24th Congressional District in the northeast Bronx. Right from the outset of his term, he introduced bills designed to curb narcotics peddling. He vehemently opposed President Nixon's 1969 crime package, as he personally found it insulting to Italian Americans because of the bill's wording and its unnecessary reference and use of the term Mafia.

He had quickly earned a reputation as New York's best congressman. A major factor contributing to Biaggi's reputation and political success included his genuine willingness to spend considerable time and effort attending to local constituent needs. For instance, he sponsored free "tax consultation" for senior citizens, and he created a "hot line" for senior citizens to be able to report easily narcotics related trade and crimes.

In 1973, Biaggi expended a great deal of his political efforts in a bruising battle to become mayor of New York City. After his campaign began, the *New York Times* published a report on Biaggi's secret testimony before a 1971 federal grand jury. This event seemed to raise serious questions as to his credibility since he had associated with other members of Congress who had allegedly collected fees for sponsoring private immigration bills. When Mario took the fifth amendment, this legal maneuver became a harsh blow to his credibility, triggering new investigations in other areas, and proving embarrassment to his "law and order" platform.

This, in turn, created a domino effect, arousing suspicions about everything he had achieved, causing the Bronx District Attorney's Office to reopen the inquiry into the 1959 shootout incident that had earned Biaggi his top-police heroism award. Even the IRS audited Biaggi's income history dating back to 1968.

Of course, the principal beneficiary of Biaggi's political collapse was former city controller Abraham Beame who won the Democratic Primary and then the election for mayor. Predictions that the disastrous mayoral campaign would finish Biaggi in politics once and for all proved untrue. None of the many investigations produced indictments against him, and the issues naturally disappeared from public scrutiny.

The enormous backlash created by his loyal Bronx constituents sent him back to Washington in 1974 once more as he went on to win reelection to Congress by an overwhelming margin. He supported much legislation, as his voting patterns indicated, consistent with preserving and expanding governmental assistance programs and with a strong stand on law and order issues.

Mario Biaggi and his wife, the former Marie Wassel whom he had married on April 20, 1941, still make their home in a South Bronx apartment where their children grew up. Their two sons, Richard and Mario II, became lawyers. Their daughter Jacqueline became a clinical psychologist, and another daughter Barbara, a nurse.

In 1980-81, Biaggi became an adjunct professor of political science at Lehman College in the Bronx. For his support of major labor, educational and welfare (aged and disabled) reforms, he received numerous honors and awards. He was also nominated for the 1982 Nobel Peace Prize for his assistance with the efforts to resolve civil strife in Northern Ireland. In gratitude for his start in law and politics, he endowed a lectureship at the New York Law School in honor of his sponsor, Dean Daniel Gutman.

General Sources:
1.   *Almanac of American Politics*. 1986 ed.
2.   *Congressional Directory*. 1985-86 ed.
3.   *Current Biography Yearbook*. New York: Wilson, 1986.
4.   *Who's Who in America*. 1984-1985 ed.

–by PAUL SPERA

BRIAN BOITANO (1963-   )

Brian Boitano, the 1988 figure-skating Olympic Gold Medal winner, was born on October 22, 1963 in Mount View, California. He grew up in Sunnyvale, a town west of San Jose, California, in an Italian-American family as the youngest of four children (one brother and two sisters) of Lew and Donna Boitano. He was eight years old when he began taking skating lessons, and it appears that he became inspired to do so after having attended with his parents a performance of the Ice Follies in San Francisco.

After his parents had agreed to his request for lessons, he began instructions at the Sunnyvale Ice Palace. He first started out in a group class, but soon after when his instructor Linda Leaver recognized his talents, she recommended him for private lessons. Amazingly, in his first lesson, young Brian achieved a minor miracle for a novice ice skater by doing five single-revolution jumps.

Within a brief period of time, Brian entered local contests, and while still eight years old, won first prize in the "pixie-derby boys" division, his first ice-skating competition. By the time he was ten, Linda Leaver reported that he was performing much like a twenty-year-old skater. Besides being his coach she soon became his personal manager. By the time Brian was twelve (1975), he had already won seventeen regional medals but was almost forced to give up figure skating due to a knee injury. By age fourteen (1978), he had captured the United States junior men's championship. In the following year, he moved up to the next division and placed eighth in the senior men's competition, and by 1983 and 1984 he had climbed to second place in that division.

At the 1982 U.S. Championship, in a particularly notable accomplishment, he became the first male skater to perform a triple axel (three and one-half revolutions) in competition. Yet in the 1983 World Championships he finished seventh despite the fact that he had successfully executed as many as six different types of triple axels and had become the first male to perform such a feat in international competition. Subsequent to this unique maneuver (and despite the judges' undervalued rating), he went on to achieve worldwide recognition as a daring and talented skater at age nineteen.

Still dissatisfied with the judges' evaluative prejudices from the 1983 competition, he nearly gave up the sport right before the 1984 Winter Olympics in Sarajevo. Finishing fifth in the Sarajevo events, he viewed that period of his career as the hardest phase of his life. After a series of disappointments, Boitano proceeded with his career taking comfort in having won the men's free-skating competition at the National Sports Festival in Baton Rouge, Louisiana, in July 1985.

In 1986, despite physical strain to his ankle tendons, he won his second consecutive United States title. A month later, in Geneva, Switzerland, he also went on to capture his first World title. A year later he won the United States title for the third consecutive time despite touching down and thus not fully completing a very difficult maneuver called the quadruple jump. His presentation also included his own now-famous "Tano triple lutz," a unique jump never before performed.

Boitano's career, which had taken off again with much vigor, met with disappointment once more when in 1987 at the world championship match in Cincinnati, Ohio he failed at fully executing a quadruple jump attempt when he fell. Boitano took second place to Canadian Brian Orser who was previously a runner-up on several other occasions. Boitano's loss did not come without its benefits. He decided to learn from the experience as he wanted to take no chances on losing in the coming 1988 Olympics.

To improve his style for the imminent challenges of the next Olympics, both he and his coach decided to hire the accomplished Canadian skate choreographer Sandra Bezic, herself a champ in pairs competition. She advised Boitano that at this point in his career he needed to emphasize less the technical aspects and focus more on feeling the emotion. With regard to emphasizing this factor in his skating routines, she changed his costuming and the music to which he would skate. Emphasizing music more along classical genres, she reasoned that Boitano could then better allow himself to act upon feeling the music as an integral part of skating.

In early 1988 when Boitano won his fourth consecutive men's single in Denver, Colorado, he became the third person (like his two predecessors Scott Hamilton and Charlie Tickner) to win four consecutive United States titles. Finally, in Calgary at the 1988 Winter Olympics, Boitano went on to offer a memorably outstanding display of his style performing almost flawlessly in all three phases of the competition. And despite a notably brilliant performance by his competitor, Brian Orser of Canada, Boitano won the gold medal. Many critics remained so impressed that they ranked Boitano's Calgary performance as among the best freestyle skating presentations in Olympic history.

A month later after the Olympics in Canada, Boitano took off for Budapest, Hungary for the World Figure-Skating Title, and he competed once more with Brian Orser, the prior year's champ. For Boitano, who went on to recapture the world title from Orser, this would represent his last event as an amateur. Boitano then traveled with the Tour of the World and Olympic Figure Skating Champions (sponsored by Campbell Soup) covering 76 cities throughout the world and concluding on July 14 at the San Jose Arena, not far from his native town of Sunnyvale. In December 1988 on ABC-TV Boitano made history with his own network special entitled *Brian Boitano: Canvas of Ice* that won at least two entertainment awards. In the same year, Boitano was honored with the Young Italian American of the Year Award from the Italian-American Foundation and the Victor Award for special contribution to sports. In 1989, along with other champion figure skaters (such as Brian Orser and Katarina Witt), Boitano toured the United States performing in 30 cities. Proceeds from the tour went toward amateur skating programs.

Later in 1990, he became involved in a made-for-TV full-length feature film (HBO), *Carmen on Ice*, for which both he and his starring partner (Katarina Witt) each won an Emmy. Boitano had also been enjoying a five-year winning streak in professional competitions until a loss in the 1992-1993 season. On several occasions in the 90s, Boitano directed and choreographed several programs with great success. Involved in several charitable efforts, including the Starlight Foundation dedicated to chronically and terminally ill children, all his colleagues agree Brian is affable and generous of his time and talent for others.

General Sources:
1. Boitano, Brian, and Suzanne Harper. *Boitano's Edge: Inside the Real World of Figure Skating*. New York: Simon & Schuster, 1997.
2. *Current Biography Yearbook*. New York: Wilson, 1989.
3. Marchione, Margherita. *Americans of Italian Heritage*. Lanham, MD: University Press of America, 1995.

–by LEE MATURO

CHARLES JOSEPH BONAPARTE
(1851-1921)

Worthy of greater recognition for his foresight, Charles Joseph Bonaparte was a hero in Italian-American history as the founder of the Federal Bureau of Investigation, Secretary of the United States Navy, and Attorney General of the United States.

Charles Joseph Bonaparte was born in Baltimore, Maryland on June 9, 1851, the son of Jerome Napoleon Bonaparte and Susan May Williams. Research has shown that he was one-fourth Italian as he was the grandson of Jerome Bonaparte, the King of Westphalia, and of Elizabeth Patterson of Baltimore, Maryland. Charles was named after his great-grandfather, Carlo Buonaparte who was Napoleon's father. The entire Buonaparte line emanated from the Italian island of Corsica and was therefore not French but Italian.

Charles attended Harvard where he received a Bachelor of Arts degree in 1871 and then a bachelor's degree in law in 1874. After being admitted to the Maryland bar, he practiced law in Baltimore for most of his life except for five years in public service at the federal government level. In 1905, the colorful and engaging President Theodore Roosevelt, who knew and was familiar with Bonaparte's "progressive" philosophies, chose him as Secretary of Navy. Bonaparte, who was now fifty-four years old, served in that office for one year. In 1906 Roosevelt then appointed him to the cabinet level post of Attorney General, a position he would keep until 1909.

In 1908, a year before Roosevelt's term as president would come to an end, Charles Bonaparte did something that would affect the way the federal government would investigate federal crimes in the future. He issued an executive order establishing a federal bureau replete with its own special agents to investigate offenses against the federal government, and these special agents would be serving specifically and exclusively as representatives of the United States Justice Department. In all, on July 26, 1908 he appointed ten former Secret Service agents and some special agents for the Department of Justice to become part of a new force of special agents who reported to their own chief within the Justice Department known as the Chief Examiner.

Bonaparte's action on that day constituted the beginning of what today is called the Federal Bureau of Investigation or the FBI. At its inception, it was a small unnamed force consisting of fewer than 20 special agents. Until that time, the Justice Department often had to resort to borrowing agents from the Treasury Department's Secret Service to handle and investigate violations of federal crimes. With Bonaparte's newly projected federal agency that likelihood would eventually disappear. In addition, on May 27, 1908, Congress passed legislation preventing the Justice Department from borrowing Secret Service agents. This made Bonaparte all the more motivated to realize his original strategy.

In the United States early history the so-called "secret service" was initially a branch of the federal government whose main function was to conduct secret investigations in matters of espionage. Later, the Treasury Department developed its own form of Secret Service (spelled in caps) whose concerns and duties involved protecting the President, Vice-

President, and their respective families. Their responsibilities also included the investigation and arrest of counterfeiters. Now, by establishing its own body of special agents, the Attorney General's office would no longer have to depend on other agencies.

In great part, Bonaparte's insightful vision had recognized that the conclusion of the 19th century and the beginning of the 20th century had brought many changes and that many more would be on the way. These new changes would necessarily include ways in which criminals would do business. What concerned Bonaparte was how criminals in particular might violate federal law or effect national security. In an industrialized society where government responsiveness to crime becomes crucial in assuring justice for its citizenry, Bonaparte strongly believed in the expansion of the Justice Department's investigative capabilities.

When Bonaparte completed his term of office, he strongly recommended along with President Roosevelt that the Department of Justice's recently acquired investigative force, which had grown to 34 agents, become a permanent part of the Justice Department. When Bonaparte's successor, Attorney General George Wickersham, of the incoming Taft administration took office, one of his first priorities was to follow Bonaparte's recommendation to continue the force and give it a name. He called that investigative body the Bureau of Investigation on March 16, 1909. It would take many more years–not until 1935–when after much experimentation with a variety of other names that the Bureau of Investigation was renamed to its now permanent Federal Bureau of Investigation.

Today the FBI has grown not only in number but also in quality of its hi-tech operations and services. It has become a nationwide center for research and database information for virtually all law enforcement agencies seeking assistance. In 1998 it celebrated its 90th anniversary. Since its early days at the turn of the century, it has acquired a worldwide reputation for its scientific methods and its hi-tech forensics research. The FBI today demands a $2.2 billion budget to support its bureau which has grown from its less-than-20-person original task force in 1908 to its present day 20,000-person work force which must deal not only with traditional crime but also with terrorism, cybercrimes, and the gruesome possibilities of biological or chemical crises affecting national security.

Charles Joseph Bonaparte died at seventy years of age at Bella Vista, his country home outside of Baltimore, Maryland on June 28, 1921. Highly respected both as a lawyer in private practice and as a civil servant, he also served as a trustee for the Catholic University of America and became the recipient of the Laetare Medal in 1903 from the University of Notre Dame. Charles Bonaparte has left an American legacy of legal, ethical, and administrative professionalism and innovation in government.

General Sources:
1. Bonaparte, Charles J. *Civil-Service Reform as a Moral Question*. New York: National Civil-Service Reform League, 1889.
2. Bonaparte, Charles J. *Papers: 1760-1921*. Washington, DC: Library of Congress Manuscript Division.
3. Bonaparte, Charles J. "The Spoils System in the Government of Dependencies." A Paper Read at the Nineteenth Annual Meeting of the National Civil Service Reform League. Indianapolis, 15 Dec. 1899." n.p., n.d.
4. "History of the Federal Bureau of Investigation." 1 Jan. 1999. <http://www.fbi.gov/history/hist.htm>.
5. Schiavo, Giovanni Ermenegildo. *Italian-American History*. New York: Vigo Press, 1947.

–by VINCENT TERRANA

JOHN JOSEPH BONICA (1917 -1994)

The year 1977 marked the 150th anniversary of obstetric anesthesia. In that light, Dr. John J. Bonica's labors of fifty years have been instrumental in defining and alleviating pain in the field of obstetrics, advocating regional anesthesia: caudal, epidural, and spinal. In addition to being responsible for many developments in these areas, Dr. Bonica's mandate that the endotracheal tube be a *sine qua non* in assisting parturient (birthing) women, who may have just eaten and who may possibly face the fatal danger involving the aspiration of regurgitated food during delivery.

Fifty or more years ago, a young father, flushed with emotions of joy and apprehension, was awaiting the delivery of his first child. His anticipation of fatherhood suddenly turned to fear and terror, when he, a physician, was asked to resuscitate his wife who had just aspirated (inhaled) part of her stomach contents while under open-drop ether anesthesia. This young doctor was unaware at the time that this mishap would prepare him to become one of the greatest champions of our century for the safety and care of parturient mothers and their babies. This physician, this father, who ultimately saved his wife and their child, was John J. Bonica, M.D.

Throughout history physicians have attempted to alleviate pain. As far as obstetrics was concerned, it wasn't until Queen Victoria who was administered chloroform by Dr. John Snow in Buckingham Palace on April 7, 1853 in the delivery of her eighth child that the course of modern obstetrics truly began. Her unequivocal approval literally meant that anesthesia would be "acceptable and respectable for women in labor."

Filicudi, a small island off Sicily, was the birthplace of John J. Bonica on February 16, 1917. His father, Antonino, and his mother, Angela (nee Zagame), immigrated to New York City in 1927, becoming naturalized citizens in 1928. On the death of his father in 1932, John shared in supporting his family by selling fruits and vegetables, shining shoes, and selling papers. It was from an early age that he dreamed of becoming a physician.

While attending high school, Bonica participated in amateur wrestling and won both city and state championships. He worked his way through college and received his Bachelor of Science degree from New York University in 1938. Still very engaged in wrestling, he eventually won the title of Light Heavyweight Champion of the world. Upon his graduation from Marquette University School of Medicine in Wisconsin in 1942, he married Emma Louise Baldetti after a six-year courtship.

After completing his internship and residency at St. Vincent's Hospital in New York City, Dr. Bonica joined the U.S. Army and was stationed at Fort Lewis in Washington State where, at age 27, he was appointed Chief of Anesthesiology at Madigan Hospital for the next three years. Becoming proficient in regional and block anesthesia, he pioneered and developed these forms of anesthesia for surgery and relief of pain for the more than 10,000 soldiers under his care who had been wounded in WWII action. His treatment of so many soldiers suffering severe pain inspired him to dedicate himself to a lifelong commitment to understand and alleviate pain.

Later, in 1947 as director of the Tacoma General Hospital Department of Anesthesiology, John Bonica instituted the first comprehensive obstetric anesthesiology service in the United States. This move was unprecedented in the 50s where before, a pregnant patient was usually down on the list of priorities. Among his innovations, there remains his introduction and general use of the endotracheal tube. Because of this innovation, the parturient patient no longer had to fear choking during delivery because of recently ingested food being aspirated into the lungs.

Dr. Bonica founded the Department of Anesthesiology at the University of Washington School of Medicine in Seattle in 1960. His studies, practices, and administrative policies not only set the professional agenda for the nationwide practice of modern day anesthesiology, but he founded the World Federation of the Societies of Anesthesiologists and the International Association for the Study of Pain. He became President of the American Society of Anesthesiologists (ASA) in 1966, and through his persistent programs and policies, obstetric anesthesia was no longer relegated to a subspecialty status. His residency program literally became a model and became renowned worldwide.

Bonica did research on acute and chronic pain, and he authored several books: *The Management of Pain* in 1953 (a second edition in 1990), and *The Practice of Obstetric Analgesia and Anesthesia* in 1967, considered "the Bible" of this discipline. Bonica also published in Italian and in Spanish his *Clinical Applications of Diagnostic and Therapeutic Block* (1959).

A worldwide lecturer and visiting professor of medicine, Bonica received international acclaim and awards: a Gold Medal from the University of Palermo in 1954; named Commendatore and received an Order of Merit from Italy in 1967; the Silver Medal from the Swedish Medical Society in 1969; the Gold Medal for Neuroscience from the German Neurophysiologic Society in 1972; and, appointed Fellow of the Royal College of Anesthesiologists from Great Britain. Bonica received the Distinguished Service Award from the American Society of Anesthesiologists and was a member of the American Medical Mission to China in 1973.

Women in the U.S.A. can be grateful for the safety, dignity, and painlessness of childbirth. Accolades can be bestowed upon Dr. John Bonica and other researchers because 20 years ago the mortality rate was 1 death in 10,000 during anesthesia, and now it has declined to 1 death in 250,000.

General Sources:
1. Bonica, John, ed. *Obstetric Analgesia and Anesthesia: A Manual for Medical Students, Physicians in Training, Midwives, Nurses, and Other Health Personnel.* Amsterdam: World Federation of Societies of Anaesthesiologists, 1980.
2. Bonica, John, ed. *Pain.* New York: Raven, 1980.
3. Bonica, John. *Principles and Practice of Obstetric Analgesia and Anaesthesia.* Philadelphia: F.A. Davis, 1967.
4. Bonica, John, et al. *The Management of Pain.* Philadelphia: Lea & Febiger, 1990.
5. Chapman, C.R. "A Tribute to the Founder of Interdisciplinary Pain Management: John Joseph Bonica, M.D. Dsc, FRCanes (1917-1994)." *Journal of Pharmaceutical Care in Pain and Symptom Control*, 3, (1995), 103-107.
6. Chapman, C.R., and John Bonica. *Chronic Pain.* Kalamazoo, MI: Upjohn, 1985.
7. McDonald, John S., M.D. "John J. Bonica Makes Obstetric Anesthesia an Academic Concern." *American Society of Anesthesiologist Newsletter*, 61(9), Sept. 1997, pp. 26-27.
8. *Who's Who in America.* 1990-91 ed.

–by PETER PAUL FRANCO, M.D.

SONNY BONO (1935-1998)

Sonny Bono, starting out as a pop music writer and later becoming a U.S. representative from California's 44th Congressional District, represents a remarkable person whose story invites praise and admiration. The son of Santo and Jean Bono, Sonny Bono's given name was Salvatore. Born in the Hawthorne section of Detroit, Michigan on February 16, 1935 to Sicilian immigrant parents, Sonny also had two older sisters: Betty and Fran. When Sonny was seven years old, his parents decided to move to Los Angeles, California where the family sought better economic opportunities and where Sonny grew up.

Years later, Sonny recalled that when his parents divorced, it was a traumatic event for him. In his earlier years in grammar school, he wrote skits, acted out sword fights, and continually told jokes. He did almost anything to get a reaction. Though gifted with imagination and creativity, he proved to be a poor student who seemed more intent on entertaining his fellow classmates.

Yet in his adolescent years, his family always emphasized the importance of getting a good education. Unfortunately, Sonny did poorly in school, and his underachievement became a common topic of discussion between family members. One day he retorted in anger blurting out, "Who cares about school, I'm going to be a movie star."

Eventually dropping out of high school, he worked as a delivery boy while learning about music and writing songs. In the early 50s, he picked up some bits of musical influence from his father, who had tried his hand at playing banjo and the accordion. In the early 50s, boys didn't sing; it was not the macho thing to do. If a young male wanted to be a singer, it meant taking a risk. And Sonny wanted to sing and write music.

After buying a homemade conga drum from a pawn shop for five dollars, he teamed up with a buddy, Corky, practicing as usual the ten most popular songs of the day. His dad was quite convinced that Sonny would become a failure, an attitude that caused Sonny much frustration. Sonny later recalled that he fought it, convinced to take any opportunity that came his way.

In February of 1954, at age 19, Sonny married a girl by the name of Donna Rankin, a pretty blond waitress. At his mother's insistence, the young couple had a big Catholic wedding. Though working at Douglas Aircraft, he thought of himself first as a songwriter, jumping at any chance to present his songs to those in positions of influence. That year Sonny wrote a song entitled "Ecstasy." The song failed to attract attention when Johnny Otis, a radio disc jockey, played the song on his show for several nights. But Sonny, who had written the song with Frankie Lane in mind, boldly decided to send him a demo which started Sonny on the road to becoming a hit songwriter.

Despite some recording success, the path was not always smooth. By July 1959 when their daughter Christine was born, their marriage had already begun falling apart. Soon after, both mother and daughter would move away from California and settle in Montana. Sonny had tried many different jobs related to the recording industry: first, with Specialty Records, and then finally with Philles Records where he learned the industry from top to bottom, from sound engineering to producing.

In 1963, he met Cher (Cherilyn Sarkisian LaPierre) when she was 16. A year later she would become his second wife when they married in Tijuana, Mexico. In their first singing act together, they were billed as Caesar and Cleo, and soon after they simply changed the billing to Sonny and Cher. They had some successful songs, but it was only after their 1965 hit "I Got You, Babe," which sold more than three million records in less than one month worldwide that they enjoyed celebrity status.

By the end of 1967, they had sold more than 40 million records around the world and had become rock's favorite couple. Some hits related to this period include: "Bang Bang," "What Now, My Love," "All I Really Want to Do," and "The Beat Goes On." The same year, they had also starred in a movie, *Good Times*, in which they played themselves as a pair of happily married stars singing their way through life. Two years later, in 1969 they produced their own film entitled *Chastity* which starred Cher.

As a dynamic and attractive entertainment duo in the nightclub and concert circuits, they had perfected what had been described as a supremely entertaining "song and chatter act." When they were asked to do their nightclub material for TV audiences, it worked so well for a six-week Sunday night TV series of one-hour shows in the summer of 1971 that *Sonny and Cher Comedy Hour* became a very successful and regularly scheduled TV program lasting three years until 1974.

In a classic format and formula for its time, Sonny engineered the dynamics of the program which included a mix of popular songs, old hits, and standard songs blended together with good-natured husband-and-wife repartee and good-old-fashioned gender ribbing. Often, Sonny became the brunt of Cher's sharp remarks critically teasing his "Italian" traits, his height of five feet six inches and his less-than-perfect singing abilities. It was a mixture of ingredients that Sonny himself had concocted, and it worked brilliantly to the delight of large TV audiences and to CBS' self-satisfaction at its TV rating.

Their unique image of a modern-day Camelot projected for so many years to their nightclub and TV audiences, came to an abrupt halt in 1975 when Sonny and Cher divorced. A successful restaurateur, Sonny married Mary Whitaker in 1986 and had two children. Sonny then pursued a career in politics and became mayor of Palm Springs, California for four years beginning in 1988 (the first year he ever voted in an election); then, in 1992 he ran for Congress and was defeated. Undaunted by his loss, two years later he ran again and was elected to the U.S. House of Representatives from California's 44th Congressional District earning 56 percent of the votes. While in Congress, he initiated several bills and served on the Congressional Bankers and Financial Services Committee and the Judiciary Committee.

The son of immigrant parents, Sonny was a man who started out as a delivery boy and became all he wanted to be: a songwriter with ten gold records to his name, an entertainer, a restaurateur and businessman, and a politician. The world mourned his death resulting from a skiing accident while on holiday with his family in Lake Tahoe, California on January 5, 1998. Sonny Bono was not the "bonehead" some people teasingly called him. Rather he was an Italian American who succeeded in all he pursued. He was delightful and sincere, and always stood for what he believed in–rare traits for someone who became a politician.

General Sources:
1. Bono, Sonny. *And the Beat Goes On*. New York: Simon & Schuster, 1991.
2. Braun, Thomas. *Sonny and Cher*. Mankato, MN: Creative Education, 1978.
3. *Current Biography Yearbook*. New York: Wilson, 1974; 1998.
4. "Obituary." *New York Times* 7 Jan. 1998: A16.

–by ROCKY PESIRI

LEO BUSCAGLIA (1924-1998)

Felice Leonardo Buscaglia, better known as Leo Buscaglia, was born on March 31, 1924 in Los Angeles, California. The son of Tullio and Rosa (nee Cagna) Buscaglia, Leo would become known to millions of his reading and viewing audiences as "Dr. Love," "The Love Merchant," or "Dr. Hug." This self-help author and celebrity lecturer became known as the unofficial ambassador of love. In 1983 he made publication history when he became the first author to have three different titles as bestsellers *simultaneously* on the *New York Times* bestsellers list.

Leo was one of ten siblings raised in an Italian immigrant family that emphasized cultural values. Discipline and personal responsibility were strong protocols in the home, and love and affection were given in abundance. The value of each child was recognized and respected by a family tradition whereby each person recounted at the dinner table his or her daily activities. Dinnertime, as Leo often explained, was not only a time to partake of food for the body but also a time to partake of food for the mind with the exchange of thoughts and feelings.

Shortly after Leo was born, his family moved back to Italy where he spent five years of early life in the Italian village of Aosta at the foot of the Italian Alps. He spoke only fluent Italian. When the family returned to Los Angeles, Leo was mistakenly assigned to a class for retarded children because he spoke no English. It took months before the problem was fully recognized and resolved, and he eventually was reassigned to a regular classroom setting.

After completing high school, Leo served in the U.S. Navy during World War II after which he began his academic pursuits. He earned his bachelor's degree in education in 1950, his master's degree in 1954 and finally his Ph.D. in languages and speech pathology in 1963. His career began as a school teacher in Pasadena, California but soon his curiosity coupled with a sense of adventure found him selling all his possessions including his house and car and taking off for Asia where he actively studied Eastern culture. He especially studied their religions and in particular Zen Buddhism and Hinduism which he correlated and compared to his Christian background. When he returned to the U.S., he remained in the Pasadena city school system for five more years as supervisor of special education.

Leo began his long association of more than 30 years with the University of Southern California (USC) as an assistant (1965), then associate, and finally full professor of education (1975-1998). It was at USC that Leo became the "guru" of a non-credit course entitled "Love 101." The course was existentially inspired and was a unique combination of psychology and sociology sprinkled with humor, storytelling, and appropriately given hugs. The entire course was initiated and designed by Dr. Leo himself. It appears that he was motivated to create this course when he became distraught after one of his most gifted students committed suicide. "Love 101" proved so popular on campus and drew so many students that Dr. Leo took the course on the lecture circuit.

It was on this circuit that Charles Slack, a New Jersey publisher, discovered Dr. Leo's ideas which focused on the importance and dignity of love. He persuaded Leo to publish his ideas. This discussion led to the publication of his first book dealing with the phenomenon of love: it was simply entitled *Love* (1972). Slack Incorporated went on to publish all of Dr. Leo's books. Five of them would eventually appear on the *New York Times* bestsellers list. It is estimated that Leo has had more than 18 million copies of his published works in circulation at the same time. Many titles were translated into 19 languages, and the core message of each book involved addressing the power and necessity of love in one's daily life.

Leo's very familiar and often stereotypical depictions of his Italian-American family life, including the kitchen and dining room table aromas of deliciously prepared foods and the strong emotional bonding of family members with one another, particularly during memorable occasions, formed the backdrop for his inspirational messages. In all, his universal focus on love was based on simple and elementary religious principles to which he rarely alluded and which he never touted as theological absolutes nor as emanating from any one particular religion.

Perhaps his appeal and his greatest strength involved simply reasserting the basic values of brotherly love as in the principle of loving "thy neighbor as thyself," yet he effectively shared his love messages without ever appearing preachy or even remotely supercilious. In effect, he lived out his philosophy, setting the example by modeling respectful behavior for fellow human beings. This was evident by his demonstration of candor, genuineness, and expressions of kindness in everyday activities. Based heavily on Maslow's concept of self-actualization, Buscaglia chose to focus less on Maslow's intellectual implications and more on striving for emotional well-being and wellness, and rarely dwelling on the negatives and psychological pathology.

Leo became acknowledged not only as an internationally known writer and lecturer but also as a prominent TV "philosopher" talking on the subject of love to the media, specifically on the education channels such as the PBS network. His numerous awards, tributes, honors, and personal popularity tended to make him

somewhat of a cult hero. In 1991 the University of Southern California recognized and affirmed the importance of his work by establishing the Leo Buscaglia Scholarship for Inner City Teachers Education. He himself also created the Felice Foundation, a nonprofit philanthropic organization to promote and encourage the dissemination of the ideals professed in his books and lectures.

Leo Buscaglia was not without his critics. Many had called into question his ideals of love vis-a-vis his life as a bachelor and not having a family of his own. Yet despite some negative voices in the background, when he passed away at age 74 on June 12, 1998 at his home in Lake Tahoe, Nevada he left behind a towering legacy of love, compassion, charity, and altruism for all to share. Surely an intellectual who was very much aware of the times and the related problems such as the high rate of teen suicide, divorce, drugs, alcoholism, and familial disintegration, he chose instead to appeal to his audiences at intuitive and emotional levels. He always focused on humanity's creative potential and resourcefulness in overcoming the existential problems of angst and individual feelings of isolation so that human beings might teach one another to get closer while respecting the other's personhood.

General Sources:
1. Buscaglia, Leo. *Because I am Human!* Thorofare, NJ: C.B. Slack, 1972.
2. Buscaglia, Leo. *Living, Loving, and Learning*. Thorofare, NJ: C.B. Slack, 1982.
3. Buscaglia, Leo. *Love*. Thorofare, NJ: C.B. Slack, 1972.
4. *Current Biography Yearbook*. New York: Wilson, 1983; 1998.
5. "Obituary." *New York Times* 13 June 1998: A10.
6. *Who's Who in America*. 1998 ed.

–by JOSEPH ANTONELLI

MOTHER F.X. CABRINI (1850-1917)

The first American citizen to be canonized, she came to the United States in 1889 knowing no English and bearing no material effects. In Italy in 1880 she had formed an order called the Missionary Sisters of the Sacred Heart. When she came to America with a small number of nuns from her order, they opened a mission in lower Manhattan. It was the first of scores of missions, hospitals, churches, and schools that would be realized through her fund-raising and charitable efforts both in the United States and in parts of Central and South America.

Maria Francesca Cabrini was the thirteenth child born to Stella and Augostino Cabrini on July 15, 1850 in the town of Lodigiano in Lombardy, Italy. Francesca was a beautiful child, but she was reportedly frail. It was recounted that as a young student she expressed a strong desire to travel to China to help the poor. Since she had heard that there were no sweets in China, she had decided early in life to give up eating candy.

As a child, Francesca would launch paper boats down a tiny stream near her home imagining that the violets she had placed on board were missionaries going to China. Intent on becoming a missionary, as a teenager she made application to two religious communities. Denied admission for reasons of ill health, Francesca was deemed unable to do the tedious work of religious. Unbeknown to her, the local pastor had opposed her admission for selfish reasons—he valued her contributions to the local parish. Having completed her schooling with the Daughters of the Sacred Heart, she resigned herself to becoming a teacher.

At age twenty-four she was asked by her pastor and bishop to serve for a few weeks at a poorly run orphanage. She agreed and was there for six years. Francesca persisted, and her desire to serve God grew stronger. Eventually the local bishop suggested that she initiate her own order of nuns. In 1880 she did so, starting a missionary order with seven women who were orphans themselves. They all took the vows of poverty, chastity, and obedience, and they called themselves the Missionary Sisters of the Sacred Heart. Before long, they acquired an abandoned Franciscan monastery and were ready to spread the "good news" of Christianity. Francesca took the name: Madre Francesca Saveria Cabrini.

In the next seven years, Mother Cabrini expanded her order in Italy, opened several community houses, and accepted new vocations. Churchmen marveled at her organizational abilities and her interpersonal rapport. Just as effective in haggling with a merchant as in beseeching a bishop to fund and support a new project, Mother Cabrini became a living paradox. She was quiet and humble but had a fierce determination.

Pope Leo XIII had heard about Mother Cabrini as an untiring nun from Lombardy who had always wanted to evangelize China. But since Italian immigrants were experiencing problems in America, he requested a meeting with her. Kneeling before him, Mother Cabrini was asked to make the United States, the new home for so many immigrants, her "China."

Mother Cabrini and six of her missionary sisters arrived in New York in 1889 to find a host of problems at the outset. They knew no English and had no living quarters. To make matters worse, the archbishop, who had invited the sisters to New York, met with them to inform them that his plans to assist them had fallen through. Mother Cabrini, who feared water because of a near-drowning childhood episode, had decided that she had crossed the ocean for a reason. She calmly informed the archbishop that she would remain in America.

She began her work by raising funds for orphans as she walked the streets of Little Italy. In short time, she opened a school and an orphanage. And, despite her fear of the ocean, she crisscrossed the Atlantic several times, sailing from America to Italy and to Central and South America. She had also traveled as far as Buenos Aires, making part of the trip by crossing the Andes seated atop a mule.

In 1899, the Sevite Fathers at Assumption Parish in Chicago invited her to establish an elementary school for Italian immigrants. When the school opened, 500 children quickly crowded into the available classrooms. Most of their parents were poor, first-generation immigrants. There was no tuition because the Missionary Sisters of the Sacred Heart worked for free. In addition to giving them an education, Mother Cabrini also set up food programs for the immigrant children.

Mother Cabrini continued her work venturing into the densely populated Italian neighborhoods hoping to ease their suffering and spread the love of God. In many areas, conditions were squalid and crime was rampant. Children often quit school at an early age to work side by side with their parents for low wages. Mother Cabrini's intense labors and dedication continued well into the twentieth century. During the course of her lifetime, this frail but determined woman had opened 67 hospitals, orphanages, and schools worldwide. Beginning with her arrival in New York in 1889, Mother Cabrini let no barriers get in her way. Her principal points of activity were New York, New Orleans, Chicago, Denver, Seattle, Philadelphia, and Los Angeles. Her work had expanded into the countries of Central and South America; also in France, Spain, and England. Mother Cabrini would often encourage her sisters by saying: "Work, let us

work. We have all eternity to rest."

At age 59, Mother Cabrini took her oath of citizenship in Seattle. She had crossed the ocean twenty-five times and returned to Chicago for the last time in April 1917. On December 22 of that year, she died of a cerebral hemorrhage at age 67—her age matching the number of institutions she had founded.

On November 21, 1938, twenty-one years after her death, Mother Cabrini was declared "blessed" by Pope Pius XI, and soon Catholics began campaigning for her canonization. On July 7, 1946, the Pope officially declared her a saint. Designated as the Patron Saint of Immigrants, she had become bigger than life, a living icon of charity. Canonized more than fifty years ago, people still refer to her today as *Mother* rather than *Saint* Cabrini. Her feast day is celebrated on November 13. In a world that is constantly redirecting its search for real heroes, Mother Cabrini surely fills that role.

General Sources:
1. Di Donato, Pietro. *Immigrant Saint: The Life of Mother Cabrini.* New York: McGraw-Hill, 1960.
2. Keyes, Frances Parkinson. *Mother Cabrini: Missionary to the World.* San Francisco: Ignatius Press, 1997.
3. Lorit, Sergio. *Frances Cabrini: A Saint for America.* New York: New City Press, 1988.
4. Maynard, Theodore. *Too Small a World: The Life of Francesca Cabrini.* Milwaukee: Bruce, 1945.
5. Null, Gary, and Carl Stone. *The Italian-Americans.* Harrisburg, PA: Stackpole, 1976.
6. Sullivan, Mary Louise. *Mother Cabrini: Italian Immigrant of the Century.* New York: Center for Migration Studies, 1992.

—by CAROLYN CIANCIOTTA

BIBA CAGGIANO (1936-   )

Biba Caggiano, a native of Bologna in the region of Tuscany, Italy is a cookbook author, chef, restaurateur, and TV celebrity with her own TV program. In 1960, she moved from Bologna to New York with her American-born husband. Ten years later, in 1970, she, her husband, and two daughters moved to Sacramento, California. At that time, she could not find any "real" Italian food in Sacramento, and she became inspired to fill that gap. In the ensuing years, she perfected the many cooking skills she had learned in Italy, and she would do much to change the dining scene in Sacramento. Additionally, she would teach many of her TV viewers the art of cooking.

She recalls that, as a child, the kitchen had always been the very soul of the house where her mother, an excellent cook, created simple, straightforward dishes whose aromas permeated the house. Biba learned to cook and would go a long way with the knowledge she had acquired growing up in Italy. Yet in the early days, before coming to America, one did not boast about being able to cook well since good cooking was taken for granted in Bologna.

When she eventually moved to Sacramento, she was asked to teach Italian cooking at a local school. Biba went on to teach for 12 years both in Sacramento and in many other western cities. She also began to do television shows on location in Italy. After collecting recipes in Italy and developing a program format, she regularly taught the art of cooking on NBC's Sacramento's affiliate KCRA.

When she and her doctor-husband had moved to Sacramento, she was delighted to have found a house with space that could easily be turned into a kitchen large enough to indulge her passion as well as serve as the hub of a house for a growing family. In what was once a small kitchen, breakfast area, and laundry room, she designed a new 18' x 16' kitchen.

She says that she was driven into the renovation mostly by the desire for a large gas cooktop stove with an efficient hood. Biba said the original electric stove had an oven on top that was so low she could barely stir pasta into a pot of boiling water. The chef stated that her needs were simple and that she had never wanted anything more than a conventional-size freezer and refrigerator.

She cooks everything fresh; freezes very little, except, of course, *gelato*. The kitchen has held up so well, in fact, that she is only now thinking about a second renovation. She said that the time has come for two ovens instead of one. When they first renovated the kitchen, she couldn't imagine needing two ovens. Ironically, for many years her family kitchen in Bologna had no oven. In fact, she said her mother owned only about four pots, and still she was a wonderful cook.

In 1986, she decided that she and the city of Sacramento were ready for an authentic Italian restaurant. She knew nothing about the business end of it, and so she hired experienced people to organize the kitchen and dining room areas and to keep track of the books. She learned fast. She said she has two wonderful young men as chefs: she was the coach, and together they were a team. So in 1986, she opened the restaurant, *Biba*, a stylish northern Italian eatery tucked away in the ground floor of a sprawling Bavarian-style building. With its mauve carpets, black marble bar, wraparound mirrors and abstract paintings, Biba's dining domain suggests an "understated neo-deco design"—the kind of place where you'd expect to find trendy items dominating the menu.

It, therefore, comes as a refreshing surprise to find that this very fashionable restaurant has succeeded precisely by avoiding culinary trendiness almost entirely. Biba has focused on good service, a superb wine list, consistent quality food, and good help. When her schedule allows, she spends as many as twelve hours a day, six days a week supervising the kitchen—and she's not about to relinquish that chore to anyone.

Her eating establishment has received glowing reviews from *Gourmet*, *Bon Appetit*, *Travel & Leisure*, and numerous other magazines. The restaurant, especially popular with many state legislators, has become very successful. Yet Biba still cannot understand people's confusion and misconceptions about Italian food. When people remark surprisingly that her food is so simple, she says that's precisely the point. The glory of Italian food is indeed its simplicity, but she believes it cannot be achieved unless one has fresh ingredients, which Sacramento's surrounding agricultural area so naturally provides. The right Italian ingredients such as good imported Italian olive oils and genuine Parmigiano-Reggiano cheese provide the finishing touch.

One thing had led to another in her life. From teaching engagements up and down the west coast, a weekly TV show, and then in 1986, *Biba* restaurant, and a series of best-selling cookbooks, Biba's schedule is most certainly full.

Biba is the host of her own internationally syndicated cooking show, *Biba's Italian Kitchen* on The Learning Channel. She demonstrates the preparation of classic Italian dishes. Many of the recipes she illustrates have appeared in her cookbooks. She is also the award-winning author of five best-selling cookbooks: *Northern Italian Cooking, Modern Italian Cooking, Leo Buscaglia's Love Cookbook with Biba Caggiano, Trattoria Cooking, From Biba's Italian Kitchen*, and the sixth book, *Italy al Dente*.

Regardless of the regional origins of the recipes, the food at *Biba*'s authoritatively and respectfully represents great Italian cooking. What's more, Biba tirelessly continues to explore still undiscovered dishes of her native Italy, and periodically introduces Sacramentans to even more delights of Italian cuisine.

Biba restaurant has consistently received glowing reviews from a variety of magazines such as *Gourmet Magazine*, *Bon Appetit*, and *Travel & Leisure*. The January 1995 issue of *Conde Nast Travelers* lists *Biba* restaurant among the best 200 restaurants in the country. In 1996, Biba was chosen as one of the six recipients in the prestigious Robert Mondavi Culinary Award of Excellence. Biba Caggiano is a member of The International Association of Cooking Professionals and of Women Chefs and Restaurateurs. As a regular TV host and personality on The Learning Channel, she has become internationally known as one of the great Italian-American chefs and restaurateurs of our time.

General Sources:

1. Bates, Carolyn. *Gourmet Magazine* May 1989: 24.
2. Caggiano, Biba. *From Biba's Italian Kitchen*. New York: Hearst Press, 1995.
3. Caggiano, Biba. *Italy Al Dente*. New York: William Morrow, 1998.
4. Caggiano, Biba. *Modern Italian Cooking*. New York: Simon & Schuster, 1987.
5. Caggiano, Biba. *Trattoria Cooking*. New York: Macmillan, 1992.
6. *HOME* Oct. 1997.
7. Houston-Duff, Marlena. "Dining Out." *Sacramento Magazine* Dec.1992: 73.
8. Roth, David M. *Travel & Leisure* Dec. 1990: E16.
9. *Vinotizie* Aug./Sept. 1994.

—by GLORIA SCALZITTI WALKER

FRANK A. CALDERONE (1901-1987)

A physician and public health official whose specialties lay in preventive medicine, Frank Calderone was deputy health commissioner for New York City from 1943 to 1946. His notable achievement to humanity consisted of his contribution of time and expertise in organizing the United Nations World Health Organization in 1948, becoming the medical director of its headquarters, directing the drafting of its constitution, and directing the United Nations Secretariat health services from 1951 to 1954.

Frank Anthony Calderone was born on the Lower East Side of Manhattan on March 10, 1901. He was one of three children born to Salvatore and Rosaria (nee Spoleti) Calderone. His father, Salvatore, who had immigrated to the United States from Sicily in 1895, got involved in newspaper work. Despite some linguistic barriers usually inherent in most immigrant experiences, he was responsible for having built and then operated a chain of vaudeville and motion picture theaters in Nassau County (Long Island). It was a burgeoning business at the time, and it represented a timely investment that grew into a relatively large corporation with many real estate holdings for his family.

Young Calderone attended a local grammar school in the Lower East Side and then graduated from Stuyvesant High School in 1916. Calderone first attended Columbia University in upper Manhattan to complete his premedical program and then graduated from New York University (NYU) in 1924 with a medical degree. From 1931 to 1936 he served on the NYU Medical School staff as a teacher of pharmacology and researcher in pharmacology and anesthesia.

Dr. Calderone was also a student of public health issues, and in 1937 he received a Master of Public Health degree from Johns Hopkins University at their School of Public Health, a pioneer institution in the area of public health administration. Calderone was now in the enviable position of having an M.D. and a masters in public health, a relatively new degree combination for its day. New York University quickly promoted him, and Dr. Calderone focused most of his class curriculum on preventive medicine and on matters of public health concerns, statistical analysis of populations, epidemiological studies, and general public health issues and administration. He remained on the NYU teaching staff until 1940.

Dr. Calderone was also associated with the New York State Department of Health, and during 1937 he bore the title of "epidemiologist-in-training," in preparation for his becoming a state district health officer the following year. In his new capacity as district officer, he became instrumental in promoting the Lower East Side Health and Teaching Center in Manhattan in 1939. He and some colleagues also established in the same vicinity the Mother's Health Organization which specifically fostered the aim of educating the public in the area of understanding nutritional problems, needs, and solutions. This highly innovative community-based program seemed to have attracted nationwide attention, and Calderone acquired instant recognition as a leader in the community health area.

Dr. Calderone was appointed acting secretary of the New York City Department of Health in 1942, and ten months later, he was appointed deputy commissioner by Dr. Ernest Stebbins. With this wide array of administrative experience, Dr. Calderone resigned from this post on January 23, 1946. He soon accepted the position of director of the Interim Commission of the World Health Organization (WHO) headquarters office in New York City.

As the first director of this interim arm of the United Nations organization, whose International Health Conference met for the first time in the summer of 1946 in New York, he directed the drafting of WHO's new constitution. Among the founding principles, there emerged the distinct idea that the realization of worldwide health was essential to achieving peace. "The health of all peoples is fundamental to the attainment of peace and security and is dependent upon the fullest cooperation of individuals and states."

This interim commission headed by Dr. Calderone awaited ratification by at least 26 U.N. member nations. In the meantime, it carried out preparatory work for the ratification of the permanent WHO, which was eventually ratified in 1948. During this preparatory interval of almost two years under Dr. Calderone's direction, WHO began to define itself and set its guidelines. In its specifics, the World Health Organization was to become a clearinghouse for medical and scientific information, set standards for drugs and vaccines, administer international sanitary regulations governing land, sea, and air traffic, and upon a state's request help fight disease in any way possible.

The broad principles set up by the International Health Conference in 1946 and the more operationally comprehensive guidelines hammered out over the ensuing two-year period (both of which were conducted under Dr. Calderone's leadership) went beyond the former League of Nations Health Organization and the Office International d'Hygiene Publique whose services were more limited in scope. The newly envisioned World Health Organization represented a unique achievement in humanity's history in asserting the dignity of the individual and the right for medical care and assistance.

The Interim Commission of the World Health Organization got off to a good start in 1947, setting a good example of its work when it swiftly shipped out enough anticholera vaccine to inoculate three million people in Egypt. This decisive action had the effect of thwarting a major epidemic in the Mediterranean region, limiting the outbreak of cholera to Egypt and resolving that problem within two months. Dr. Calderone remarked that this was the first time in medical history that a potentially devastating epidemic was checked in such little time.

The world nations ratified WHO in 1948. At the end of the following year, Dr. Calderone withdrew from the directorship of WHO but continued on as consultant and advisor. In 1951, he returned to the United Nations as medical director of Health Services at its Secretariat, which at the time involved more than 3,000 staff members. He remained in that position until 1954.

As a unique personality whose special talents involved medical and administrative expertise shortly after the devastation of World War II, Calderone led the operational development of a worldwide health network that was new to the world and is still with us today. Dr. Calderone died on February 10, 1987 in New York City having left a legacy of medical and administrative savvy that has spanned the globe. He has served humanity with a deep sense of compassion.

General Sources:
1. *Current Biography/Yearbook*. New York: Wilson, 1952; 1987.
2. "Obituary." *New York Times* 24 Feb. 1987: A25.
3. Tulin, Miriam. *The Calderone Theatres on Long Island*. Hempstead, NY: Long Island Studies Institute, Hofstra University, 1991.
4. *Who's Who in the United Nations*. 1975 ed.

—by FRANK V. CASTELLANO

JOSEPH A. CALIFANO, JR. (1931-   )

One of the unsung heroes of the troubled Johnson era, Joseph Califano, as special assistant to the President, did much of the work and bore much of the burden of President Johnson's well-intentioned but faltering Great Society program. As Johnson's increasing role and energies became inextricably involved in the Vietnam conflict, Califano was in charge of coordinating federally funded programs for the poor. Later, in the Carter administration, Califano was appointed Secretary of Health, Education, and Welfare. He had the monumental task of reforming federal programs and downsizing the administrative sprawl that had been generated since the inception of the socioeconomic programs that went as far back as the Kennedy/Johnson administration. A doer, an executive, and an administrator in every sense of the word, Califano was probably best described by consumer advocate Ralph Nader as "a corporate lawyer with a conscience," who, while being tough on wasting federal dollars in medicare and in welfare programs, always remained sensitive to the poor.

Joseph Califano, Jr. was born on May 15, 1931 in Brooklyn, New York. His father, Califano senior, was a middle level administrative assistant at IBM before his retirement. His mother Katherine (nee Gill) Califano, of Irish descent, was a public school teacher. Joseph Jr.'s early education was in Catholic school settings which included Brooklyn Preparatory High School. After attending Holy Cross College in Worcester, Massachusetts and receiving his B.A. in 1952, he went on to Harvard Law School where he became one of the editors of the *Harvard Law Review* and earned his LL.B. degree *magna cum laude* in 1955.

Upon graduation Califano entered the U.S. Navy for three years and served as a legal officer in the Office of the Judge Advocate General. After he was discharged in 1958 with the rank of lieutenant, he became employed with the Wall Street firm of Dewey, Ballantine, Bushby, Palmer, and Wood where he handled tax cases and corporate law. Apparently, it was through his wife's initiative that he became interested in public service during the time of the 1960 elections, the Kennedy era. It all began with his involvement in New York City's reform democratic movement during that election.

Bored with "splitting stocks" and the like, he then decided to actively seek a position in the Kennedy administration. In 1961 Califano wrote a letter describing his experience to Cyrus R. Vance, who was the newly-appointed general counsel for the Department of Defense. Vance soon hired Califano as special assistant, and when at a later date Vance was promoted to Secretary of the Army, he took Califano along, still with the title of special assistant. In 1963 Califano was appointed general counsel of the Department of the Army. One of his major responsibilities involved supervision of the Army Corps of Engineers and its enormous civil works program. Califano, as a major government lawyer, also handled Army-related international hearings in the investigation of the 1964 Panama Canal Zone riots.

In spring 1964, Secretary of Defense Robert McNamara appointed Califano special assistant, and in effect Califano became McNamara's right-hand man, troubleshooting in many areas including the development of the supersonic transport, various cost-reductions programs, and the supervision of federal troops in Selma, Alabama's period of social unrest during the civil rights demonstrations. President Johnson, who was highly impressed with Califano's work whenever he would visit the White House on a liaison assignment for McNamara, was unable to wrest Califano from McNamara until a year later in July 1965 when Johnson acquired Califano's services and appointed him as special assistant in charge of legislative coordination and troubleshooting.

Bill Moyers withdrew from the Johnson administration in early 1967, at the time when Johnson was in the throes of the Vietnam War. Califano was entrusted with the monumental task of overseeing the Great Society program that Johnson had previously outlined in his political platform. Califano became involved in enforcing civil rights, generating consumer protection and anti-pollution legislation, creating the Department of Transportation, the Office of Economic Opportunity, and the Model Cities programs. Domestically those were, indeed, unusually difficult years, and Califano as special assistant to the President in the capacity of Chief Domestic Advisor bore the brunt of having to deal with burgeoning political unrest and its concomitant socioeconomic problems including the complexities of welfarism, the problems of implementing the poverty programs, and the Watts riots in Los Angeles.

In 1968 Johnson decided not to run for reelection, and in January of 1969 Califano's White House job as special assistant came to a conclusion. During the administration of the Nixon years (1969-1974) and Ford years (1974-1977), Califano remained in the public sector in the Washington, D.C. area at the firm of Arnold & Porter and then became a partner in Williams, Connolly & Califano. During the presidential campaign, he served as a personal aide to Carter. After Carter became President, Califano was nominated Secretary of Health, Education, and Welfare. With one dissenter, Califano was approved for that position which he held from 1977 to 1979. During that time he worked hard to implement Carter's pledge to overhaul HEW which accounted for one-third the federal budget.

A man devoted to public service, Califano has written several books. As a prolific and insightful writer, he has presented and discussed from first-hand experience working in the White House America's domestically troubled years during the Vietnam era; the student revolts of the 60s in America and its globalized effects; the Herculean demands placed upon the office of the American presidency; and, the needed health care reform for the 90s. Diligent in the cause of good government and compassionate for those less privileged, he is still active today lecturing in the hope of building more bridges between community action and government so that in the end justice will prevail in our complex society.

General Sources:
1. Califano, Joseph A. *America's Health Care Revolution: Who Lives? Who Dies? Who Pays?* New York: Random House, 1986.
2. Califano, Joseph A. *Governing America: An Insider's Report from the White House and the Cabinet.* New York: Simon & Schuster, 1981.
3. Califano, Joseph A. *A Presidential Nation.* New York: Norton, 1975.
4. Califano, Joseph A. *Radical Surgery: What Next for America's Health Care.* New York: Times Books, 1994.
5. Califano, Joseph A. *The Student Revolution: A Global Confrontation.* New York: Norton, 1969.
6. Califano, Joseph A. *The Triumph and Tragedy of Lyndon Johnson: The White House Years.* New York: Simon & Schuster, 1991.
7. *Current Biography Yearbook.* New York: Wilson, 1977.
8. *Who's Who in America.* 1976-77 ed.

—by DENNIS PIASIO

ROY CAMPANELLA (1921-1993)

Voted three times Most Valuable Player in the National League, Roy Campanella started his baseball career at the age of fifteen. Born November 19, 1921 in the town of Homestead, Pennsylvania his father, John Campanella, was Italian American, and his mother, Ida Mercer, was African-American. John Campanella's parents had emigrated from Sicily.

Roy was a child when his family moved to North Philadelphia. He had one brother, Lawrence, and two sisters, Gladys and Doris. During the depression, his father, who was a fruit and vegetable vendor, labored long hours. Even Roy, at age twelve, would be up in the early morning hours helping his brother with his milk delivery route, going house-to-house on a horse-driven cart.

In his early years, Roy had been subjected to racial slurs, being called a half-breed by those of different races in his neighborhood. Though not very scholastic, his athletic abilities were outstanding, and he was "lettered" in several different sports. It was at fifteen, while still at Simon Gratz High School, that his career in baseball was launched.

He began playing weekend baseball with the Bacharach Giants, a popular Negro semi-pro team in Philadelphia, a notable accomplishment for his age. Almost incredibly, before the season was over, Roy was signed up and played for the Baltimore Elites, among the best-known Negro teams. In the beginning of the 1937-38 school year, Roy decided not to return to high school because, in a sense, Roy's dreams of playing baseball had been fulfilled at the young age of fifteen.

Playing professional ball with the Baltimore Elite Giants was a challenge. They traveled in their own bus and slept in it between cities. Often they played a doubleheader during the afternoon and went on to play another doubleheader that same evening in a different city. On occasion, Roy would play all four games. As a catcher, he was known to have a "rifle" arm and was considered to be the best. He had a talent for handling a pitcher with his calm attitude and motivational pep talks.

In the Negro Leagues, he played with and against some great ball players: Satchel Paige, Josh Gibson, Don Newcombe, Biz Mackey, Bill Boyd, Coop Papa Bell, and Jackie Robinson, among others. During this era, ball players in the Negro Leagues played in Cuba, Mexico, Puerto Rico, Venezuela, and Santo Domingo. Roy worked year-round, catching 220 games, and resting for only two weeks before going to the Latin America games. In 1949, he was instrumental in getting the Elites to win the Negro League championship by making five hits in his five times at bat in the playoff game.

In 1948, Jackie Robinson became the first Negro player in what was once an all-white baseball establishment. Roy Campanella and Don Newcombe would soon follow. Unlike Robinson, who was more outspoken regarding racial issues, Roy Campanella was more reticent. "Campy," as he was often called, preached patience, not militancy. Roy was quoted as saying "I'm a ball player, not a pioneer." He understood the slow progress of civil rights changes, reasoning that the blacks were at least headed on the right path.

In 1948, Roy Campanella was hired by the Brooklyn Dodgers, but he did not play at Ebbets Field until mid-season. By summer of 1949, he was batting .400 and by mid-season played behind the plate more often than the regular catcher. That year he appeared in the All-Star Game for the National League. Roy also became one of the key players who helped the Dodgers win the 1949 pennant. In 1951, he won the New York Baseball Writers' Award as Most Valuable Player in the National League. He won that award two more times during his baseball career. In his nine-year career, he had hit 242 home runs and batted in 856 runs.

Roy Campanella's future with the Dodgers was expected to have extended beyond his catcher-playing days. In the early 50s, Dodger President Walter O'Malley had laid plans for Roy to become baseball's first Negro manager in major league baseball. When this was made known to Roy, it came as a welcome relief. He felt his future in baseball would be secure.

Generally, the 50s were good years for him. Roy opened a liquor store in Harlem as an investment. Wanting to provide a future for all of them, he hired some friends who formerly played with him in the Negro Leagues. His career was doing well, and like Jackie Robinson, he had become a celebrity. He and his wife, Ruthe Willis, married in 1939, were the parents of five children and lived comfortably in St. Albans, Queens, NY.

Everything seemed perfect until early morning on January 28, 1958. Roy was driving his car when it skidded over an icy spot on the road, and he lost control of it. That tragic auto accident nearly cost him his life. He crashed into a telephone pole and had seriously injured his neck leaving him permanently paralyzed. His baseball career came to an abrupt halt.

These were difficult times for Roy Campanella. One of his doctors understood Roy's feelings of the lack of acceptance by others and helped him to understand that he first had to accept himself. It was then that he began his physical therapy in earnest, participating in his daily exercise program to regain movement where he formerly had not been able. He became a role model for other quadriplegics by helping them learn to accept their affliction and live meaningful lives.

In 1959, one year after his devastating accident, Campy wrote his well-known autobiography, *It's Good to Be Alive*. That same year, the Yankees and Dodgers honored him by playing an exhibition game at Los Angeles. With over 93,000 in attendance, that number still remains a record in the history of baseball. In 1969, Campy was voted into the National Baseball Hall of Fame on the first round.

Roy's compassion is evidenced by the fact that he often related a poignant episode about a young boy who had asked him to autograph a baseball. He explained to the boy that his hands were paralyzed and that he wasn't able to sign it but that he would let him have an official league baseball. The young boy responded that would be fine because he couldn't see. Roy was informed later that the blind boy was the son of oil tycoon, J. Paul Getty.

Roy Campanella died on June 26, 1993. He will long be remembered as a champion baseball player and a fine human being who exhibited love, compassion, and determination until his final days.

General Sources:
1. *African-American Sports Greats: A Biographical Dictionary*. Westport, CT: Greenwood Press, 1995.
2. Campanella, Roy. *It's Good To Be Alive*. Boston: Little Brown, 1959.
3. Green, Carol. *Roy Campanella, Major League Champion*. Chicago: Childrens Press, 1994.
4. Macht, Norman. *Roy Campanella: Baseball Star*. New York: Chelsea House, 1996.
5. May, Julian. *Roy Campanella: Brave Man of Baseball*. Mankato, MN: Crestwood House, 1974.

—by DENNIS PIASIO

FRANK CAPRA (1897-1991)

Frank Capra's early life seems like a roller-coaster ride of events full of endless struggle. As a chemical engineer finding a meager market place for the knowledge he possessed, he drifted for years knocking on many doors and finding nothing. For a while, he even played poker for a living. Because of his scientific background he managed to get the opportunity to direct a film short, *Fultah Fischer's Boarding House* in 1922. He realized how little he knew about the craft of making movies, and so he learned as much as possible in the coming years. Despite competition within the industry itself, he finally directed several films in the late 20s but only achieved fame for his 30s' films.

Francesco Capra, better known as Frank Capra, was born at 18A Via Santo Cono on the 18th of May 1897, in the small Sicilian village of Bisaquino outside Palermo, the regional capital of Sicily. He was the sixth surviving child of Salvatore and Rosaria Capra.

At fifteen years of age, his oldest brother, Benedetto, persuaded his parents to pay for passage to America. Benedetto would be the first of his family to be part of the turn-of-the-century Italian migration to the United States. He settled in Los Angeles. In May of 1903, his parents and his siblings joined him there. Frank was only six at the time, and in later years he described the place where they had settled as a "ghetto" area. It was a terrible feeling he would not forget as he was highly motivated to transcend this part of his immigrant past.

Frank attended the local schools. He took jobs selling papers and playing his banjo in honky-tonks to help increase the family income and secure his higher education. In due time, he enrolled at Throop College of Technology, later to be known as Cal-Tech. While Frank was in his sophomore year, his father was killed in a tragic accident. Frank thought this would mean quitting school and taking care of his mother and sister. But the school student loan fund solved that problem, and he completed his final two-and-a-half years.

The records show that his grades had suffered in the aftermath of his father's death. A very weak showing in the first two-thirds of his junior year and a series of dismal rebounds in the terms to follow prevented him from earning a degree in chemical engineering. Yet he eventually received a Bachelor of Science degree. Just before his graduation, the United States had declared war on Germany. In a burst of patriotism, Frank went to enlist in the Army. He was told to continue his scientific training, and after being sworn in, he was sent back to Throop College as a private where he also received his military training in ROTC.

He was discharged after the war but was unable to find work. Then finally, an unlikely opportunity came his way that started him off in his future career in the movies. In early 1919, he was hired by the Christie Film Company which was one of the leading producers of slapstick comedies. His position as janitor at first seemed irrelevant, but he was eager to learn film, and he made himself useful to others in whatever way he could. Being on the movie lots kept fueling his desire to pursue a career in filmmaking.

As early as 1920, Capra and a down-on-his-luck Shakespearean actor named Walter Montague came together with a scheme to make film equivalents of famous poems. Montague raised the funding from a local investor and hired a theatrical promoter to organize the filming and keep it within budget. Capra was to direct and help with the set design, and he decided to hire only actors who had never appeared in films so they would not realize how little *he* knew.

The film-short was entitled *Fultah Fisher's Boarding House*. After its filming, he edited it, and a nationwide distributor purchased it for $3,500, which more than doubled the initial investment. It opened on April 2, 1922 to receive rave revues. Shortly afterwards, Montague and Capra had a series of disagreements and Capra resigned from the partnership. In the next several years, he did much apprentice work, learning the hands-on knowledge that would serve him so well in the coming years.

Eventually in 1928, Columbia Pictures hired him as a director. The films he made there from 1928 to 1939 helped Columbia Pictures rise from what was called a "quickie" studio to a major one. As a director he had acquired the reputation for being efficient and reliable. The major turning point in his career came when he teamed up with Robert Riskin, a screenwriter. They collaborated on seven projects which all turned out to be highly profitable. In 1934, they released *It Happened One Night*, and to their surprise it swept the Academy Awards winning five major Oscars.

This made Frank Capra the first Italian American to win an Oscar for film directing. With this award, he found a new level of respect and prestige, and he began to produce as well as direct all his future projects. In 1936 and 1938, he won two more Oscars: *Mr. Deeds Goes to Town* and *You Can't Take It With You*. Capra returned to military service during World War II, and General George C. Marshall asked Capra to prepare a series of films that he hoped would educate the troops about why they were fighting. The general hoped to motivate them to make the sacrifices he knew would have to be made. The series was simply called *Why We Fight*. The first film of that series, *Prelude to War,* went on to win the Best Documentary Oscar in 1942. Capra was discharged with the rank of colonel, and on June 14, 1945 he received the Distinguished Service Medal that General Marshall had awarded him for his special film efforts for the military.

With WWII concluded, he decided to form his own production company which he called Liberty Films. His first film, *It's A Wonderful Life*, was not as successful as he had hoped. Times had changed after the war, and the simple premise of good triumphing over evil no longer captivated post-WWII audiences. Ironically, that movie remains today the one for which Capra is best remembered. His first marriage ended in divorce, and in 1932 he married the former Lucille Warner Reyburn with whom he would have four children, one of whom went on to become a producer.

Frank Capra, the noted director, producer, and screenwriter, died at the age of ninety-four on September 3, 1991 in La Quinta, California. He has left a legacy of innovative ideas that film students continue to study today, and he remains an example of an Italian American who came to Hollywood with nothing, ventured into a relatively new medium of expression, employed innovative ideas, and made it to the top of his field. He indeed helped to shape the way movies were made, and his influence in American cinema is still with us today.

General Sources:
1. Capra, Frank. *The Name Above the Title.* New York: Vintage, 1985.
2. Carney, Raymond. *American Vision: The Films of Frank Capra.* New York: Cambridge University Press, 1986.
3. McBride, Joseph. *Frank Capra: The Catastrophe of Success.* New York: Simon & Schuster, 1992.
4. Schickel, Richard. *The Men Who Made the Movies.* New York: Atheneum, 1975.

—by LORRAINE LANZELOTTI

LEWIS JOHN CARLINO (1932-   )

A novelist, playwright, screenwriter, and film director, Lewis John Carlino whose trademark involves the creative exploration of interpersonal relationships has developed and amplified many Pirandellian motifs and notions of the difficulties of human communication and has placed them in the more contemporary arena of late twentieth-century life. Carlino won immediate recognition in the early 60s when he received the tenth Drama Desk-Vernon Award for outstanding contribution to Off-Broadway theater. His themes deal with the difficult crucible of human feelings or, rather, the frustrations caused by the impenetrability of certain feelings when they become roadblocks to growth and understanding between people. He is probably best remembered for his writing and directing the screenplay for the film, *The Great Santini* (1979), based on Pat Conroy's award-winning novel.

The youngest of three children, Carlino was born in New York City on New Year's Day, 1932. When he was 12 years old, he and his family moved to California. After high school, he attended El Camino College, a junior college in Lawndale, until his enlistment in the United States Air Force in about 1951. After four years of military service, he enrolled under the G.I Bill at the University of Southern California where he majored in film studies. To earn money, he worked summers as a camp counselor and as a hospital surgical technician. When he earned his B.A. in 1959, he had graduated *magna cum laude* with Phi Beta Kappa status. He pursued his education and earned a master's degree in one year.

In his undergraduate days at the University of Southern California, Carlino gratified his creative urges and interests in theater by writing a series of one-act plays which included *The Brick and the Rose*, *A Collage for Voices*, *Used Car for Sale*, and *Junk Yard*. *The Brick and the Rose*, a study of narcotics addiction, was first produced by the Los Angeles chapter of the American National Theater and Academy in 1957. Then in 1960 it was also presented on the *CBS Television Workshop*. From these early works, Carlino went on to earn the 1960 British Drama League Prize in International Playwriting.

After his master's degree, Carlino did some extensive traveling around the world. On his return to the United States, he settled in New York City where he obtained a job teaching at Columbia University. He pursued writing one-act plays such as *Objective Case*, *Mr. Flannery's Ocean*, and *The Beach*, which were performed by local theatrical groups. He experienced his Off-Broadway debut with the production of *Cages*, a double-bill title of two-character, one-act plays: *Snowangel* and *Epiphany*. Starring Shelley Winters and Jack Warden, two veteran performers of stage and screen, *Cages* enjoyed a run of 176 performances at the York Playhouse.

Both one-act plays involved the intriguing and critical use of the reversal of personal identities. *Snowangel* dealt with the thematic examination of one's youth. In this particular case, the recollection takes place through the eyes of a "good-hearted prostitute" and her dreams of long-lost love: *not* so much through the eyes of her client. In *Epiphany* a husband attempts to regain his sense of identity and authority over his own life countering a domineering wife. The conflict is exacerbated by the husband's fears dealing with his latent homosexuality.

Carlino earned immediate and—mostly favorable—critical attention. His success inspired a return to examining some of his earlier works. In November 1963, *Telemachus Clay: A Collage for Voices* opened on Off-Broadway at The Writers' Stage Theater. In the tradition of George Bernard Shaw's *Man and Superman*, Carlino's *Telemachus Clay* involved the use of actors seated on stools facing the audience dramatically reading their lines directly to the viewers. It consisted of 11 actors undertaking about 90 roles in a "Joycean odyssey" of a young artist in search of self and meaning in life.

In May 1964, *Doubletalk* had its premiere performance at the Off-Broadway Theater de Lys. Like the play *Cages,* it was a double-bill performance consisting of *Sarah and the Sax* and *The Dirty Old Man.* Both were two-character, one-act plays where the dramatic conflict in each play unfolded around the meeting of strangers from diverse backgrounds and different age groups. In the former, it was the encounter of an elderly Jewish widow and young black musician, and in the latter it was the encounter of an enamored teen-age girl and a lonely but sensitive elderly man.

Doubletalk became ultimately responsible for allowing Hollywood producers to enter Carlino's creative life. While he would continue his work in theater, he would also begin to write screenplays and occasionally to direct a film. Beginning with his first film, *Seconds* (1966), he was involved in either writing or directing (or both) well over ten Hollywood films including *The Brotherhood* (1968), *The Mechanic* (1972), *Crazy Joe* (1974), *I Never Promised You a Rose Garden* (1977). *The Great Santini* (1979) has remained the most memorable film that he wrote and directed. It remains, perhaps, his signature film as he artistically brings out the contradictory feelings of characters in their existential conflict and personal crisis.

Carlino's artistic odyssey essentially focuses on humanity's unique position in the known universe. A human being's feelings about personal existence, about intuitive interpretations of the world at large, and about the cosmos in general can and do come into conflict with other fellow human beings. Within the realm of human interactive behavior where people indeed do differ, those personal meanings can often represent deceptively limiting, self-restrictive, and self-destructive forces. The conflictive meeting points constitute social and familial matrices that can become opportunities for change and growth, or, simply may be reduced to the redundant reality of throwbacks to freeze-framed human predicaments where change is hopeless.

In many ways reminiscent of Pirandello's thematic outlines dealing with the problems of human communication, Carlino (also of Sicilian heritage like Pirandello) has added new and fresh context to the traditional unities of time, place, and action to dramatically and artistically portraying human conflict throughout his works. He is the recipient of many awards and honors, and he surely exemplifies success in his chosen field of drama and film.

General Sources:

1. *Contemporary Authors.* Farmington Hills, MI: Gale Research, 1998.

2. *Contemporary Dramatists.* Detroit, MI: St. James Press, 1993.

3. *Current Biography Yearbook.* New York: Wilson, 1983.

4. D'Acierno, Pellegrino, ed. *The Italian American Heritage: A Companion to Literature and Arts.* New York: Garland Publ., 1999.

5. Rigdon, W., ed. *Notable Names in the American Theatre.* Clifton, NJ: White, 1976.

6. Siegel, Scott, and Barbara Siegel. *The Encyclopedia of Hollywood.* New York: Facts on File, 1990.

—by CHARLES HARRINGTON

FRANK CARLUCCI (1930-   )

A veteran of four presidential administrations whose career began in 1971 in the Office of Economic Opportunity, then in the Office of Management and Budget, HEW, an Ambassadorship to Portugal, the Deputy Directorship of the Central Intelligence Agency, the office of Secretary of Defense in the Reagan administration, Frank Carlucci was noted for his nonpartisan approaches to international affairs. As former president of Sears World Trade, Frank Carlucci has also earned the respect of Americans for his business acumen.

The grandson of an Italian immigrant stonecutter, Frank Charles Carlucci, III was born on October 18, 1930 in Scranton, Pennsylvania to Frank Charles Carlucci Jr. and to Roxanne (nee Bacon) Carlucci. He attended Wyoming Seminary College, a prep school in Kingston, Pennsylvania. After earning his A.B. from Princeton University in 1952, he completed two years in the U.S. Navy, and he then concluded one year of a two-year curriculum at Harvard Graduate School of Business Administration.

After a dissatisfying stint in sales and management, Carlucci decided to join the U.S. Foreign Service in July 1956. A year later, he was stationed in Johannesburg, South Africa as vice-consul and economic officer at the American Embassy until 1959. Later in March 1960 he was assigned a post in the American Embassy in the city of Leopoldville, Belgian Congo (today called Zaire). Highly unstable as a newly emerging state, the Congo remained for a long time a dangerously volatile country to all those assigned to work there.

Among the many perilous situations in that area during Carlucci's assignment, there was reported one particular incident where Carlucci's physical prowess and agility played a vital role in his being able to rescue a carload of Americans from mob violence when a traffic accident caused the death of a Congolese. Carlucci in helping the Americans get to safety narrowly escaped with his life as he was stabbed in the nape of his neck. His assignment in the Congo proved to be his most precarious job as his life was always in danger whenever leaving the Embassy on monthly fact-finding trips for the American government.

After a two-year assignment in the State Department at the Congo desk in 1962, he was assigned the post as consul general in Zanzibar. Due to political unrest, he was expelled a year later by that volatile African government. After returning to the U.S., he was assigned to South America, holding several consecutive posts at the American Embassy in Rio de Janeiro from 1965-1969, his longest stay abroad. Quite by chance, at a Washington reunion, Carlucci met with his former wrestling teammate from Princeton University, Donald Rumsfeld, who had been recently selected to be director of the Office of Economic Opportunity (OEO). Instead of pursuing a one-year study at Massachusetts Institute of Technology, Carlucci was persuaded by Rumsfeld to become deputy director at the OEO.

Once Rumsfeld was appointed adviser to the Nixon staff in the fall of 1970, Carlucci, whose work at the OEO was flawless in the anti-poverty program, became nominated as its new director, but he was not confirmed until several months later in March 1971 only after some partisan issues were overcome. Carlucci consistently sought to defuse potentially dangerous partisan bombshells by creating mutually agreeable compromise positions. There existed at that time the perceived notion that

Nixon wanted to undo many federal programs by decentralizing them. Many legislative leaders in retaliation sought instead stronger federal controls to insure delivery of these anti-poverty programs to the less privileged areas. Carlucci saw the political situation clearly, and he resolved the problem by his hands-on approach at both the federal and local levels.

Carlucci was acquiring an excellent track record from his quality work and receiving a growing trust in Congress. The number of different positions he would hold began to accelerate rapidly. Within months of his previous post at OEO, Carlucci was appointed by Nixon to be associate director of the Office of Management and Budget, then its deputy director in 1972, and undersecretary of Health, Education, and Welfare (HEW) for 1972-1974. In December 1974 in a curious change in Carlucci's career, President Ford assigned Carlucci as ambassador to Portugal.

At that time, Portugal was in danger of becoming Communist, and Henry Kissinger, then Secretary of State, became particularly concerned at the implications of a growing Communist threat at the most western tip of Europe. After arriving in Portugal in January 1975, Carlucci soon worked with its government to restore many democratic measures to its political process with the hope of averting a Communist takeover. In the April 1975 elections, after the Communists failed to achieve any significant power base as had been feared by the U.S., political observers gave much of the credit to Carlucci's dedicated and savvy efforts.

During the Carter administration, Carlucci was nominated and approved in January 1978 to become the second in command at the CIA as its Deputy Director. According to many observers, his style of administering the CIA did much to restore its badly tarnished image from the mid-1970s when its excess of power had come to light. Outspoken on such matters of CIA personnel security and CIA information-gathering abilities, in April 1979 he severely criticized the Freedom of Information Act (1974) for endangering the well-being of domestic and foreign sources, and he advocated severe penalties for unauthorized disclosure of intelligence personnel.

When President Reagan was elected in 1981, Carlucci became Deputy Secretary of Defense for one year (1981-1982), second in command to Casper Weinberger. After a departure from government, he was president and later CEO of Sears World Trade between 1983 and 1986. He returned in 1986 to continue serving in the Reagan administration, first, as Assistant to the President on National Security for 1986-1987 and, then, becoming Secretary of Defense for 1987-1989.

Carlucci received many awards including honorary doctorates from Wilkes College (1973), Kings College (1973), and an honorary LL.D. from the University of Scranton (1989). He was awarded the State Department's highest foreign service citation, the Superior Service Award for his courageous work in the Congo (1960). Before leaving office, he also received other government awards. Many were from the various departments where he had served, including the Woodrow Wilson Award (1988) and the George C. Marshall Award (1989).

General Sources:
1. *Current Biography Yearbook*. New York: Wilson, 1981.
2. International Roundtable Conference (1988: Washington, D.C.). *The Atlantic Alliance and Western Security as NATO Turns Forty*. Cambridge, MA: The Institute, 1989.
3. Leech, John. *Halt! Who Goes Where? The Future of NATO in the New Europe.* New York: Macmillan, 1991.
4. *Who's Who in America*. 1989 ed.
5. *Who's Who in American Politics*. 1989 ed.

—by PEGGY M. BOMPADRE

UGO CARUSI (1902-1994)

The first Italian American to have been appointed to the position of Commissioner of Immigration and Naturalization, Ugo Carusi made history in 1945 when his responsibilities involved the awesome task of facilitating the processing of the paperwork and organizing the application procedures for the mounting number of displaced persons (DPs) who were the victims of the devastating effects of World War II and the concentration camps. Despite limited allocation of resources, he established in little time the process and procedures for approximately 400,000 displaced persons who were ready for entry into the U.S. But he would have to wait until Congress enacted the necessary laws for them in 1948.

His legal acumen and administrative savvy did not end with the DPs of post-WWII Europe. Under Truman's administration, he also headed the Washington branch of the U.N. High Commissioner for Refugees. Still embracing the same responsibilities under Eisenhower's new administration in 1953, he also worked in the Hungarian Refugee Relief efforts that followed the Hungarian Revolution of 1956. Tireless in his humanitarian efforts, even after his retirement (1963), he joined the efforts of American voluntary relief organizations in 1967 to assist in studying and fine-tuning the relocation of homeless South Vietnamese children.

Ugo Carusi was born on March 17, 1902 in Carrara, Italy. The son of Eugenio Abramo and Eva (nee Bertoli) Carusi, he was born while his parents were visiting relatives in Italy. His parents, who had indeed been immigrants to the United States in 1893, had since become naturalized American citizens. While they were on their first return trip to Italy since their immigration to America, Ugo was born.

Several months after his birth, the family returned to the United States, and they made their home in Barre, Vermont. After Ugo attended the public school system and finished his secondary school at sixteen, he found work in a Vermont law office where he remained for four years. In 1922 at age twenty, Ugo became secretary to the state of Vermont's attorney general, a position he would keep for three years. In 1925, when President Coolidge's Attorney General, John G. Sargent, made Carusi's acquaintance and offered him a job as his private secretary and special assistant, Carusi gave up his Vermont post and moved to Washington, D.C.

Now finding himself at the heart of the nation's political center, Carusi wasted no time in getting started towards a law degree even if it meant going to school part-time. While working at the Department of Justice, Carusi attended the Law School at National University (now known as George Washington University). In 1930, when Attorney General Sargent's job came to an end, Carusi was appointed executive assistant to the incoming Attorney General William D. Mitchell. Carusi, in fact, would go on to serve in that capacity for each successive Attorney General until 1944.

Meanwhile, he earned his LL.B. degree in 1931 and graduated as class valedictorian. In the same year he was admitted to the District of Columbia's bar; and one year later in 1932, he earned his LL.M. degree. By 1936 he had become a faculty member of the law school where he had studied, and between 1936 and 1944 he lectured on constitutional and administrative law. Carusi's job as executive assistant involved varied and often disparate responsibilities such as simply greeting callers to the Justice Department or as representing the U.S. abroad. In October 1938, President Roosevelt appointed Carusi as the U.S. delegate to the First International Congress on Criminology which was held in Rome.

In January 1945, only months before President Roosevelt's untimely death, Ugo Carusi was appointed the commissioner of Immigration and Naturalization. Within months of this noteworthy event as the first Italian American to such a post, Carusi announced to the world his great satisfaction at having given the authorization for the naturalization of over 100,000 armed services personnel. He also announced the immediate deportation of over 7,000 illegal aliens. Most of them had been found guilty of illegal entry through the Mexican and Canadian borders.

On the other end of the spectrum, one of the more pressing concerns involved the high number of refugees flowing out of Central Europe who were seeking a home in the U.S. In 1946, with limited personnel and funding, Carusi took off for Germany to establish the offices and organization for processing the paperwork of nearly 400,000 refugees (displaced persons). In this humanitarian effort, Carusi was most effective in being responsible for the supervision of almost one million DPs, who mainly came from Poland, the Baltic states, and the Balkan countries. About half of this large displaced population was located in so-called safe American zones and the other half in camps maintained by the U.S.

In effect, this situation amounted to Carusi having to maintain a holding pattern overseas while trying hard to accommodate refugees with the serious needs of resettlement while U.S. legislators decided when to enact legislation that would permit the legal entry of DPs into the United States. In the interim, in 1947 President Truman appointed Carusi as special assistant to the Attorney General and as chairman of the U.S. Displaced Persons Commission, in essence, a temporary commission in charge of studying how the DPs might be settled once they arrived in the U.S. Truman's planning and timing were excellent as the enactment of legislation took place in 1948.

Ugo Carusi had exercised an untiring humanitarian spirit during an uninspiring three-year legislative limbo. With a steadfast dedication to the belief that those displaced persons who awaited entry would someday be among the best future citizens of the United States, he worked hard to expedite matters so that once Congress approved the needed legislation the refugees would have a minimum of legal entanglements and would find a settlement program in the U.S.

When Carusi died on July 21, 1994, it was clear that his role as public servant, which had begun early in his legal career and became especially crucial in the post-WWII era, represented humanitarianism in one of its finest hours where government service and compassion become one through the person of Ugo Carusi vis-a-vis WWII displaced persons. Reported by his peers and colleagues as a social and gregarious individual, he was a member of many civic and professional organizations including the Order Sons of Italy in America.

General Sources:

1. *Concise Dictionary of American Biography*. New York: Scribner, 1964.
2. *Current Biography/Yearbook*. New York: Wilson, 1948; 1994.
3. *New York Post Magazine* 2 Dec. 1948: 43.
4. *New York Times* 16 Aug. 1944: 11.
5. Saxon, Wolfgang. "Ugo Carusi, 92, Immigrants' Son Who Helped Wartime Refugees." *New York Times* 30 July 1994: 27.
6. *Who's Who in America*. 1958-59 ed.
7. *World Biography*. New York: Institute for Research in Biography, 1948.

—by DENNIS PIASIO

ENRICO CARUSO (1873-1921)

Considered by many critics as the greatest tenor of all time in the annals of opera, Caruso made his New York debut at the Metropolitan Opera in 1903 as the duke in *Rigoletto*. He would enthrall his American audiences at the Met for the next eighteen consecutive seasons. He became an operatic idol for many opera lovers, and his name was a metaphor for the beautiful, artistic, and meaningful in opera.

Enrico Caruso was born on February 25, 1873 in Naples, Italy. His parents, Marcellino and Anna, had moved to Naples from the village of Piedimonte D'Alife, just north of Naples. His mother, who taught him to read in his early years, wanted Enrico to become an educated person, but his father specifically wanted him to become an engineer.

At school, one of Enrico's teachers, Allessandro Fasanro, discovered Enrico's rich contralto voice. Enrico, who loved to sing, soon became the principal soloist of the school choir. His extraordinary voice came to the attention of many others. At ten, Enrico was taken under the tutelage of pianist Ernesto Schirari and maestro Raffaele de Luto for opera lessons.

Though Enrico appeared to have a natural musical talent, his father, at a certain point, insisted that he give up his schooling and singing all together and simply work full-time. Yielding partly to his father's wishes, he discontinued school, but he continued singing at social and church functions. When Enrico was fifteen, his mother became seriously ill and died. Enrico, who had been closely attached to his mother, became devastated by her premature death.

The responsibility of caring for his younger brother Giovanni and sister Assunta,

prevented him from continuing his voice studies. But that situation was short-lived because his father, Marcellino, remarried five months after his wife's death. His stepmother, Maria Castaldi, managed the household and cared for Enrico's siblings. Caruso returned to a training schedule and to singing at local establishments.

At eighteen, Enrico frequented many cafes, often participating in their local singing groups. Both the entertainers and cafe patrons urged Enrico to seek voice lessons. One evening, after singing, Enrico was approached by Eduardo Missiano, a young baritone who was the son of a well-to-do Neapolitan family. He offered Enrico the services of Guglielmo Vergine, a distinguished voice teacher. In 1891, Enrico began his new training which would lead him to his great career. In 1894, Vergine after properly training Caruso agreed that his student, then twenty-one, was ready to start his career.

In that year, at the Teatro Nuovo in Naples, he made his debut singing in Morelli's *L'Amico Francesco*. Though not always singing with great success in the small theaters of southern Italy, he did achieve notable success in 1897 singing in *La Gioconda* in the city of Palermo. This appearance plus subsequent performances in Milan led him to more performances in northern and central Italy that marked the definite beginning of his fame and, eventually, of his international stardom.

By 1899, Caruso emerged as the most sought after opera singer, appearing in Russia, Egypt, and (Buenos Aires) Argentina. Also singing in his native Italy, he won over audiences in Rome, Bologna, and particularly in Milan at La Scala. In 1902, he made his famous debut in Covent Garden, England, and a year later, he made his American debut singing the role of the

Duke of Mantua in Verdi's *Rigoletto*. In 1904, Caruso made his second appearance before an American audience at the Metropolitan Opera House in New York City where he would perform most frequently between 1904 and 1920. Hailed as the world's best tenor, he began recording for Victor and touring the United States from coast to coast.

Following his engagement in America in 1904, Caruso began a tour of Europe during 1905 and early 1906. One brilliant performance seemed to follow another whenever he would sing in London, Vienna, Berlin, and Hamburg. On his return to America, he sang in Pittsburgh, Chicago, St. Louis, Baltimore, Washington, D.C., and San Francisco. While in Washington, President Theodore Roosevelt invited him to sing at the White House.

When Caruso appeared in San Francisco with his touring company, he seemed to show signs of fatigue for the first time in his career. In a period of twenty-five days, he had sung six different operas in thirteen performances. On April 18, while still in San Francisco, Caruso experienced firsthand the effects of the great earthquake of 1906 that devastated the city. Over the next decade, Caruso continued singing in America, which had now become his new home. After traveling to Italy for short intervals of time, he returned to sing for American audiences who apparently could not get enough of this great tenor.

Caruso enjoyed an extraordinary career in America, but by the year 1920 it seemed that illness was catching up to him. He managed to open the season at the Metropolitan Opera on November 15, but his schedule had caused him to become exhausted both physically and emotionally. In fact, he had become ill apparently with a cold and severe chest pains several months prior to the November opening. On December 8, while singing his most noted aria, "Vesti la giubba," his voice broke and he tripped and stumbled off the stage. Caruso insisted on continuing the opera session and did so after a short period of rest.

On December 21, Caruso again became ill after a performance. He insisted on continuing his vigorous schedule despite a continual deterioration in his health. Three days later, on December 24, on the date of his 607th performance at the Metropolitan Opera House, he sang what would be his last performance. Caruso, described as weak and faltering, completed the performance exhausted and in deep pain. Throughout the following months, Caruso's condition worsened. He had lost over fifty pounds and had become gravely ill.

He decided to return to Italy, and on May 28, 1921, he sailed for Naples, arriving on June 9. Upon arrival in the port of Naples, his fellow Neapolitans gave him a hero's welcome. He spent the following months in Sorrento, but his condition still grew worse. He was taken to Rome on July 31 for a kidney operation which would never take place as he died on August 2. The great tenor, dying at a mere 48 years of age, was given by his native Neapolitans a funeral befitting a highly respected and beloved monarch. The world bid farewell to the man who gave so much joy to all those who had heard his incomparable voice.

General Sources:
1. Caruso, Dorothy. *Enrico Caruso, His Life and Death*. Wesport, CT: Greenwood Press, 1987.
2. Caruso, Enrico, Jr., and Andrew Farkas. *Enrico Caruso: My Father and My Family*. Portland, OR: Amadeus Press, 1997.
3. Greenfeld, Howard. *Caruso*. New York: Putnam, 1983.
4. Sadie, Stanley, ed. *The New Grove Dictionary of Opera*. New York: Grove's Dictionaries of Music, 1992.
5. Schiavo, Giovanni. *Italian-American History*. New York: Vigo Press, 1947.

—by EDWARD MOTTOLA, Jr.

OLEG CASSINI (1913-   )

One of the world's leading fashion designers and manufacturers of clothing, fashion-related accessories, and perfumes, Oleg Cassini devoted most of his career to designing clothes for women, and that group included many well-known personalities like Jacqueline Kennedy, Brigitte Bardot, and Grace Kelly. He began designing clothes as early as eleven years of age, and at the age of twenty-one he won the top five prizes at La Mostra della Moda (fashion show) in Turin (1934).

Coming from an expatriated family that was once a well-to-do diplomat Russian-Italian family, Oleg worked his way up from little or no money to a point where today his businesses and personal worth have brought him well into billionaire status. Oleg Cassini was born in Paris on April 11, 1913 to a Russian diplomat, Alexander Loiewski, and an Italian Countess, Marguerite Cassini. At the inception of the marriage, their last name started out as the hyphenated Loiewski-Cassini but later became simply abbreviated to Cassini. As a child, Oleg became fluent in many languages including Russian, Italian, Danish, and English, but French was his earliest language and his family's most commonly spoken tongue. Oleg also had a brother, Igor, who was born in 1915. Oleg's Italian courtly lineage comes from his maternal grandfather's side, Count Arturo Cassini, the last in a line of Italians (from the city of Trieste) who had served Czar Nicholas as ambassador to the United States during the eras of Presidents William McKinley (1897-1901) and Theodore Roosevelt (1901-1909).

Oleg's father, Alexander Loiewski, for many years had been a Russian diplomat in Czarist Russia. However, when the Communist-inspired revolution took place in 1917 and overthrew the Czarist family, the Cassinis who were at the time in Copenhagen, Denmark suddenly found themselves isolated and permanently cut off from Russia. Oleg was only four years old at the time. The Cassini family, which was associated with the recently defunct Czarist Russian family, was now considered finished, and it quickly became part of the displaced European "nobility." The Cassinis sold what they had and decided to relocate themselves to Florence, Italy their new haven.

Oleg's father, who for years had enjoyed a reputation as a diplomat and a dandy, lost not only his post and international standing but also his family fortune back in Russia. The once well-to-do family now suddenly found itself poor, but it had made its way from Copenhagen to Florence where they had found friendship and support to start anew. Oleg's mother, a survivor at heart, quickly took to business and opened a dress shop which, among other things, attempted to cater to personalities in high society and in diplomatic circles, something with which the Cassinis were familiar.

By the age of eleven, Oleg was familiar with the operation of his mother's boutique and had already demonstrated both an unusually deep interest and talent as a designer. From the books he had read, he had designed cowboy and Indian costumes for himself and his brother Igor. At age thirteen, he had the good fortune to visit the city of Paris, his birthplace, with Madame Cardenas (the daughter of the Dictator of Venezuela) who had befriended Countess Cassini. Cardenas traveled to Paris with her three daughters, and she had generously asked Oleg to come along. On his return to Florence, to the delight of his mother, Oleg presented her with sketches he had made while observing fashion wear in Paris. Entrusted by his mother to realize those sketches, he designed and created three gowns for his mother's boutique collection. The gowns immediately became popular locally that year, and it meant good business for his mother and the Cassini family.

During his teenage years he attended the best of schools in Florence including the English Catholic School and the Accademia delle Belle Arti where he graduated in 1934. Raised as an aristocrat at the insistence of his mother, he was exposed to all the arts, sports, and all things befitting a "gentleman." After studying art in Rome and also doing some designing there, Oleg decided in 1936 to travel with his brother to the United States. Of course, this was the era of the great depression and jobs were scarce. It was a struggle at first when Oleg and his brother had no money living in a mid-Manhattan rooming house. Designer jobs were scarce, and despite finding work in New York City, Oleg found the competition difficult. Clothes executives also found his designs too European for the times.

By 1940, Oleg decided to move to Hollywood, California where he found work in the costume department of Paramount Pictures and later at 20th Century-Fox. In 1942 he became an American citizen and joined the U.S. Army. After attending officers' candidate school, he went overseas during the war, and in 1946 he was discharged with the rank of first lieutenant. He returned to work in Hollywood after the war, but afterwards in 1950 he successfully opened up in New York City's garment district his own business of ready-to-wear clothing for women.

While establishing his own business, he also began designing costumes for Broadway shows and for programs on the new medium of TV. In addition, Oleg not only appeared as a guest on TV shows but also had acquired his own program. Incredibly, within a decade's time from the conclusion of WWII, Oleg had become not only an established manufacturer and designer of women's name-brand fashions but also a TV personality. Physically appealing and always the fashion-plate himself, he made it easy for consumers to be able to associate the Cassini label with the charming and well-spoken person on the TV screen. In short, he had became a phenomenal success and was quickly joining the ranks of the rich and famous clothes designers.

Although Oleg Cassini's family had lost everything during the Russian Revolution, his mother prepared him from his earliest years to think and act as a gentleman and an aristocrat. Having received an excellent cultural education in Europe, it is no wonder that Oleg would make it his business to hobnob with America's cultural and financial "aristocrats." Oleg, who designed clothes for the Kennedy family, was responsible for the "Jackie" look, a simple-yet-chic sense of "luxurious simplicity," an American standard that the whole world noticed.

General Sources:
1.   Behbehani, Mandy. "Cassini Revives Designs Jackie Made Famous." *San Francisco Examiner* 7 Sept. 1995: G1+.
2.   Cassini, Marguerite. *Never a Dull Moment*. New York: Harper, 1956.
3.   Cassini, Oleg. *In My Own Fashion: An Autobiography*. New York: Simon & Schuster, 1987.
4.   Cassini, Oleg. *A Thousand Days of Magic: Dressing Jacqueline Kennedy for the White House*. New York: Rizzoli, 1995.
5.   *Current Biography Yearbook*. New York: Wilson, 1961.
6.   Fitzpatrick, Catherine. "Cassini Royale." *Milwaukee Journal Sentinel* 18 May 1997: F5+.
7.   Hoobler, Dorothy. *Vanity Rules: A History of American Fashion and Beauty*. Brookfield, CT: Millbrook Press, 1999.
8.   *Who's Who in America*. 1992-93 ed.

—by IRENE LAMANO

LUIGI LUCA CAVALLI-SFORZA (1922-   )

Geneticist, researcher, writer, and teacher who, in blending the relatively newborn field of molecular genetics with models from statistical evolutionary studies, Cavalli-Sforza has been able to create a new science called genography. It is the molecular study of genes based on a breakthrough whereby the analysis of certain markers in genetic structures indicate the migration patterns in humanity's early evolution, well before the terms European or African came into existence. The "genetic atlas" that has been produced by his work and by that of his colleagues is one more major scientific component in understanding the geographic patterns of early *homo sapiens* and subsequent human populations.

In addition to these pioneering efforts in genography, Cavalli-Sforza has espoused many ideas that run counter to some of the prevailing views that subscribe to racial superiority. Simply stated, Cavalli-Sforza's latest research on human genetic structures has shown that there is no scientific evidence—at least from a genetic perspective—that one race is *inherently* superior to another. His studies have consistently shown that the "genetic variation among *individuals* is greater than the variation among *groups*." In other words, given appropriate and conducive conditions in the environment, some individuals will excel more than others from the norm in any given group, but since all human groups are genetically built the same, according to Cavalli-Sforza, those two realities in essence destroy the notion of an inherent racial superiority of any one group.

Luigi Luca Cavalli-Sforza was born on January 25, 1922 in Genoa, Italy. He received his M.D. in 1944 at twenty-two years age at the University of Pavia (Italy). He studied blood groups and immunology while he worked as an assistant researcher at the Istituto Sieroterapico, a serum institute in Milan. Venturing on to England, he did further research from 1948 to 1950 at Cambridge University where he studied with Sir Ronald Fisher, a British statistician and geneticist whose work, *The Genetical Theory of Natural Selection* (Oxford, 1930) bridged both fields of genetics and statistics that enabled him to postulate many scientific truths that have come to be regarded as cornerstones of modern population and evolutionary genetics.

Inspired by Fisher's work, Cavalli-Sforza wondered if through molecular genetics a time line factor in human genes could reveal information leading to migration patterns tens of thousands of years ago. It was Fisher who had first promoted the use of blood-group analysis as an essential vehicle in studies dealing with human evolution problems. Cavalli-Sforza, a pioneer in the field, first started mapping out humanity's migratory changes by considering what information could be derived from the most basic kinds of blood testing in the ABO blood-group system, which in turn is made of four basic blood groups A, B, O and AB.

In addition to the ABO blood-group system, he also availed himself of another system. It was based on a 1940 discovery of a substance found in the blood that was either Rh negative or Rh positive. Now with Fisher's theories behind him, Cavalli-Sforza reasoned that with the proper use of blood sampling on a worldwide basis and through the analysis of these two blood systems, variations in the distribution of blood testing factors among different populations could be used to show "distance" among different groups, thus establishing a more accurate picture historically of humanity's migratory benchmarks.

By 1960, three newly discovered blood systems also began to be employed. This raised the number of blood-based methods for identifying markers up to five. These newly discovered blood systems have been curiously named MN, Diego, and Duffy. Now armed with five markers, or identifiers, Cavalli-Sforza and his colleague could improve upon the accuracy of their ongoing studies and derive from them more reliable scientific results regarding human migration patterns. In effect, their new techniques now rendered obsolete much of the data-gathering practices and older methods employed by anthropometry, which had relied on external data and measurements such as cranial structure and skin color.

Cavalli-Sforza had held several research and teaching jobs in Italy, but in the early 1970s he accepted a position in the United States at Stanford University School of Medicine in California where he has since remained. Towards the end of the 1970s, Cavalli-Sforza and two of his colleagues, Paolo Menozzi and Albert Piazza, started an ambitious 16-year project which would involve investigating the blood samples of more than 100,000 people from 2,000 communities and tribes around the globe. To insure greater accuracy of their data, they selected areas that were known to have been unaffected by any post-1492 European colonization efforts. With risk of life and limb, this project involved journeying to remote and dangerous areas where often taking blood samples particularly from children was perceived by tribesmen as hostile and "magically" malevolent.

The results of this unprecedented kind of endeavor produced many interesting outcomes. By having consolidated and confirmed many prior studies dating back to 1960s that Cavalli-Sforza and some colleagues had done, it validated a new scientific area of learning called genography. Much to Cavalli-Sforza's credit, the latest undertaking produced a human family tree that was quite similar to the one he had constructed in the 1960s where he had been limited by having had access to only as much as one-fifteenth of the data. The historic collaborative tome, *The History and Geography of Human Genes*, appeared in 1994.

In 1991 while completing the previously mentioned study, Cavalli-Sforza and four colleagues had published a paper on genomics (the study of genetic material), thus announcing the advent of another project called by the acronym HGDP, the Human Genome Diversity Project to do DNA sampling from blood, sputum, hair roots, and more—again, from a worldwide range of human populations to learn more about early human behavior. An acknowledged pioneer in genetics, medical researcher, and creator of genography, he has earned a long list of academic honors, honorary doctorates, and awards from Italy, England, Japan, and the Unites States to have made him one of the most recognized scientists in the world today.

General Sources:
1. Cavalli-Sforza, L.L. *Elements of Human Genetics*. Menlo Park, CA: W.A. Benjamin, 1977.
2. Cavalli-Sforza, L.L., and Francesco Cavalli-Sforza. *The Great Human Diasporas: The History of Diversity and Evolution*. Trans. Sarah Thorne. Reading, MA: Addison-Wesley, 1995.
3. Cavalli-Sforza, L.L., P. Menozzi, A. Piazza. *The History and Geography of Human Genes*. Princeton: Princeton University Press, 1994.
4. *Current Biography Yearbook*. New York: Wilson, 1997.
5. *New York Times* 27 July 1993: C1.
6. *Scientist* 14 Oct. 1996: 1.
7. *Time* 16 Jan. 1995: 54-55.
8. *Who's Who in America*. 1996 ed.

—by GEORGE CARPETTO, Ph.D.

ANTHONY J. CELEBREZZE, Sr.
(1910-   )

As the well-honored and respected mayor of Cleveland, whose years of mayoral service spanned almost a decade (1953-62), Anthony Joseph Celebrezze went on to become U.S. Secretary of Health, Education, and Welfare under both the Kennedy and Johnson administrations. As a key player in designing much of the 60s legislation regarding clean air and water, civil rights, medicare, and educational programs, he left the HEW office having done much honor and dignity to the integrity of federal government programs, their personnel, and their operations.

He was born on September 4, 1910 in Anzi, a small village in Potenza in southern Italy. Anthony was the ninth of thirteen children. When his family immigrated to America, settling in Cleveland, Ohio he was only two years old. Hard-working from the start, as early as age six he started helping his brother sell papers at a newsstand in Cleveland's downtown area.

He played halfback in high school, but in addition to that he did some non-school-related boxing in local sports programs to make extra money. After graduation, he attended John Carroll University for one year, then switched to Ohio Northern University where he completed his LL.B. in 1936. To support himself through his college years during the depression of the 30s, he loaded freight cars for the New York Central Railroad.

After graduating with a law degree and being admitted to the Ohio bar, Celebrezze worked for three years at the Ohio Bureau of Unemployment Compensation. In 1938, he married his high school sweetheart, Anne Marco, a graduate of Western Reserve University who taught in the public school system. In the ensuing years, they had three children: Anthony, Jr., Jeanne Anne, and Susan Maria. Subsequent to his legal experience at the Compensation Bureau, he opened his own law practice. Both his private practice and his marriage were interrupted by WWII where he served in the Navy.

On his return to Ohio from military service, he continued his law practice, but he kept a steady eye on running for public office at the state level for the Democratic Party. He campaigned and was elected to the Ohio Senate in 1950 and was reelected in 1952. Voted twice as one of the top senators in Ohio, he distinguished himself in the areas of taxation and veterans affairs. In 1953, he vied for the mayor's office on the independent Democratic ticket. He became Cleveland's newly elected mayor and remained in that position for five consecutive terms until 1962, relinquishing his final year's term as mayor because of his confirmation to the Presidential cabinet.

He had won his last term's election with an unprecedented 73.8% of the votes, carrying all of Cleveland's 33 wards. As mayor of Cleveland, he became well known throughout the United States as a committed, hard-working leader. Engaged relentlessly in his five mayoral terms, he was a dedicated peacemaker keeping harmony among Cleveland's various ethnic communities, and especially in his efforts to eradicate slum areas. He helped develop the Erieview Project and the St. Lawrence Seaway in an effort to raise Cleveland Port's status to an international level.

He enjoyed the distinction of being the

only Cleveland mayor to have been elected for five consecutive terms in office by the voters. Also deemed an innovative administrator and an energetic leader by his associates and colleagues, in 1958 he was elected president of the American Municipal Association and in 1962 President of the U.S. Conference of Mayors. Because of his excellent nationwide reputation in mayoral leadership, President Eisenhower appointed him in 1959 to the Advisory Committee on Intergovernmental Relations. In early 1962, President Kennedy re-appointed him to the same post and also to the Red Cross Board of Governors.

While serving in the second year of his fifth term as mayor, Celebrezze was nominated in July of 1962 by President Kennedy to the post of Secretary of Health, Education, and Welfare (HEW). Unanimously approved by Congress, he became, in effect, the first Italian-born American in the history of the United States to achieve cabinet-level status. Because of his administrative savvy, long experience, and responsiveness to minority issues, Celebrezze was entrusted with many other duties directly related to his status in HEW. These included appointments to the President's Committee on Equal Opportunity and to the President's Commission on the Status of Women.

In an era of federally enacted legislation in the form of monies for the burgeoning medical, housing, welfare, and educational assistance programs under the Kennedy and Johnson administrations, Celebrezze worked harder than ever before to meet the huge challenges created in expediting the mandates involved in the fair and equitable distribution of federally apportioned funds while accounting for the needs of the recipients at various community levels.

In August 1965, Celebrezze resigned his post of Secretary of HEW to become a United States 6th Circuit Court Judge. Acutely aware of problems besetting all minorities, immigrants, unemployed, elderly, and disabled people,

Celebrezze was lauded by many individuals throughout the nation, including Lyndon Johnson and his cabinet, for his humanitarian spirit and his worthy accomplishments in his three years as HEW Secretary.

His excellent record both as mayor of Cleveland and as Secretary of HEW did not go unnoticed even by organizations that had not necessarily benefitted directly from his efforts, and thus, he was the recipient of many awards, citations, and honorary degrees, too numerous to mention. From his Italian admirers across the sea he was awarded The Order of Merit of the Republic of Italy (1955) and the Gold Medallion of Rome (1963). In the United States he received from Italian Americans The National Fiorello La Guardia Award (1961).

Celebrezze was a humanitarian, and since he touched the lives of many ethnic groups in the United States, he was accordingly acknowledged by most of them, including a citation in 1956 from the United Negro College Fund, the B'nai Brith Award for Promoting Harmony and Brotherhood, and the Salvation Army Centennial Citation. He was a tireless and dedicated public servant whether at the local or at the national level. He died on October 29, 1998 leaving a legacy of a life of activity, integrity, and humanitarian concern for all the citizens he served.

General Sources:

1. *Chamber's Biographical Dictionary*. Ed. J.O. Thorne. New York: St. Martin's Press, 1962.

2. *Current Biography Yearbook*. New York: Wilson, 1963; 1999.

3. Marchione, Margherita. *Americans of Italian Heritage*. Lanham, MD: University Press of America, 1995.

4. "Obituary." *New York Times* 31 Oct. 1998: C16.

5. *Who's Who in America*. 1962-63 ed.

—by ANTHONY CIANCIOTTA

LUIGI PALMA di CESNOLA (1832-1904)

Many Italian Americans have led exciting and colorful lives, but few have exceeded that of Luigi Palma di Cesnola. Just one year after leaving Italy and entering the United States in 1860, he was commissioned a lieutenant colonel in the Union Army and fought in the American Civil War. After leading three successful battles, he was captured and imprisoned by the Confederacy. As part of a prison exchange negotiation, he was returned to the Union forces. He resumed fighting along with General Sheridan's troops. He was decorated several times after the war, but he felt most honored when many years after the Civil War he received his most cherished decoration, the Congressional Medal of Honor.

Cesnola had a meeting with President Lincoln who appointed him United States Consul to Cyprus. There, in addition to his role as administrator and diplomat, he took up archeology as a hobby and came across exceedingly large amounts of archeological treasures worth in the millions of dollars in as many as sixty-five of the island's necropolises obscured by centuries of time. Unintentionally, he began a whole new career for himself recovering and preserving ancient works of art and artifacts. In 1880, Cesnola began his directorship of the now world-renowned New York Metropolitan Museum of Art, a position he would hold for twenty-five years until his death in 1904. On its opening day ceremonies, he had the privilege of giving a private tour to U.S. President Rutherford B. Hayes.

Luigi Palma di Cesnola was born into a military family on June 28, 1832 in a town just outside the city of Turin. His father, a Piedmontese count and an experienced soldier, had served under Napoleon; and Luigi, too, a product of military schools, had fought against Austria and was the youngest officer in King Charles Albert's Royal Army of Piedmont. Barely seventeen years of age, he fought in the Battle of Novara in 1849.

In 1860 he decided to travel to the United States. He arrived in New York City, and having little money he supported himself by giving French and Italian lessons. Subsequently, he met Mary Reid, a 30-year-old woman of New York society who became a student of his. Despite pleas from her family and friends against a hasty marriage to Cesnola, she wedded Luigi in 1861 after a brief courtship, and their marriage remained unwavering despite his interesting and tumultuous life.

In the same year, he joined the Union Army to fight against the Confederacy, and because of his military training and experience as a cavalryman, he was commissioned a lieutenant colonel. This created difficulties in protocol with many of his superiors who often had less experience than he. He proved to be a valiant and capable officer despite the fact that he had been arrested twice by angry superiors whom he had defied on occasion.

He was granted a new commission after his arrests. Leading his men into fierce battle at Aldie Gap in Virginia, he would earn for himself thirty-four years later in 1897 the famous Congressional Medal of Honor. Re-entering the war as he did and fighting in many battles, he was subsequently captured and incarcerated by the Confederacy and was placed in Richmond's infamous Libby Prison. As soon as Cesnola was exchanged for a Confederate colonel in 1864, he resumed his fighting along with General Sheridan's Union troops. By September of the same year, Cesnola and his entire unit were honorably discharged from the military because their tour of military duty had ended.

Cesnola then made an appointment to meet with President Lincoln. The meeting took place just two days before the President would be assassinated. Reportedly, Cesnola had negotiated with the President both an advancement in military rank (despite his then non-military status) and a government post. The latter was realized by his subsequent appointment as American Consul to Cyprus, which took place after Lincoln's death. Yet because Lincoln had never put to paper his apparent agreement to make Cesnola a brigadier general, Cesnola called himself "general" nonetheless for the rest of his life having avowed repeatedly the veracity of this verbal agreement under sworn testimony.

The island of Cyprus, which occupied a strategic location in the Mediterranean area, had oscillated for varying periods of time between Turkish and Greek rule. At that time it was a Turkish protectorate. The early part of his tour of duty in Cyprus proved to be initially difficult for him and his wife because of the unexpected primitive surroundings and the lack of urban amenities. In time, he had acquired a taste for doing archeological digs, which at first were those of a neophyte. After searching the remains of over sixty-five cemetery areas and over twenty other sites on the island on his own, he had learned much about archeology and its treasures.

Many of the sites proved to be unusually rich in yielding buried treasures from antiquity, long abandoned well over 2,000 years before. One of his most important finds was the Golgoi Temple which contained a well-preserved mosaic pavement, many burial vaults, a huge cache of gold and silver jewelry, gems, and various artifacts such as vases, lamps, and sculptures. Since from time to time his diplomatic position on the island also involved his representing Russia and Greece vis-a-vis the Turks who ruled the island, he had developed many strategies to circumvent the Turkish authorities in order to transport the ancient treasures off the island and send them safely to the United States where he negotiated a personal agreement with the trustees of the soon-to-be-opened Metropolitan Museum of Art in New York City.

As an extraordinary man who fought as a soldier in his native Italy and also in the American Civil War, he also served well in his newly adopted country as a versatile diplomat and archeologist. He would go on to become a great administrator of the renowned New York City Metropolitan Museum of Art for twenty-five years and a famous author of a most popular book in its day, *Cyprus: Its Ancient Cities, Tombs, and Temples*. Few people have come close to his bravery, resourcefulness, and versatility. When he died on November 20, 1904 at the age of seventy-two, his funeral at St. Patrick's Cathedral was attended by many of New York City's most influential people who had come to pay their respects to this Italian American who had accomplished so much in one lifetime and would influence future generations through his work at the New York Metropolitan Museum of Art.

General Sources:
1. Cesnola, Luigi Palma di. *Cyprus: Its Ancient Cities, Tombs, and Temples*. Nicosia, Cyprus: Star Graphics, 1991.
2. Marinacci, Barbara. *They Came from Italy: The Stories of Famous Italian Americans*. New York: Dodd Mead, 1967.
3. Null, Gary, and Carl Stone. *The Italian-Americans*. Harrisburg, PA: Stackpole Books, 1976.
4. Tomkins, Calvin. *Merchants and Masterpieces: The Story of the Metropolitan Museum of Art*. New York: Dutton, 1970.

—by ANDREW VASCELLARO

ALFRED CHECCHI (1948-   )

In 1989 at age 41, Alfred Checchi became co-chairman of Northwest Airlines, the fourth largest American airline. He has been aptly described as a highly charismatic person along the lines of the late John Kennedy. Through his labors as an administrator and businessman, he has become a centimillionaire in a relatively short period of time. In addition to his business goals, it appears that his future aspirations also include an eye on California's gubernatorial seat, and ultimately, perhaps, the White House. An aggressive and dynamic Harvard M.B.A. graduate, he earned his millions by authoring deals either for or with large American corporations such as Disney, Marriot, Bass Brothers and Northwest Airlines. His relatively brief yet very accomplished business career represents quite an achievement in light of the fact that just two generations ago his paternal grandparents had emigrated from the island of Elba and the city of Parma. Bearing all the problems of most immigrants with the additional problem of not speaking English, his paternal grandparents adapted to this country and raised their children encouraging them to become educated. Arthur Checchi, Alfred's father, went to college and eventually obtained a high-ranking position in the Food and Drug Administration where he worked from 1946-1960. Similarly, Alfred's mother Josephine (nee Soldati) Checchi received business college training.

Alfred Checchi, born on June 6, 1948, attended Good Counsel High School in Wheaton, Maryland where he was elected student council president and the student most likely to succeed. Attending a top-rated college and a prestigious university, he earned a B.A. and an M.A. at Amherst College followed by an M.B.A. at Harvard University's Graduate School of Business. Upon graduation Alfred went to Washington, D.C., and started his own economic consulting firm and afterwards joined the Marriott Corp.

While at Marriott from 1975-1982, he used his savvy to achieve a spectacular vertical climb in the corporation network as he engineered many astute financing packages for Marriott's expansion programs both at home and abroad. Aside Marriott's notable growth since his arrival, he has been credited for having made Marriott the number one hotel for customer preference by the time he left that corporation.

Seeking entrepreneurial goals beyond his administrative challenges he left Marriott, then a highly prospering business, and joined the Bass Brothers of Fort Worth, Texas for the period 1982 to 1986. Again, using his business acumen, he has been credited with catalyzing several lucrative financial packages dealing with Texaco, Arvida, and Disney. For the Disney agreement alone, he was responsible for the Bass Brothers securing a 25% holding in the then distressed Disney empire. Reportedly, Checchi earned for himself $50 million in that business deal alone. In addition, serving as consultant to Disney's Michael Eisner, he strategized both Disney's financial restructuring, its general expansion, and in particular, its planning of acquisition of real estate and its development.

In 1986, he launched his own consulting firm in Los Angeles which dealt with investment portfolios and acquisitions programs. In 1989, while still maintaining his own company, he teamed up with a former colleague from Marriott, Gary L. Wilson. Together they spearheaded a new enterprise that involved the creation of an investment group that successfully executed a $3.65 billion leveraged buyout of Northwest Airlines whose corporate headquarters are still located in St. Paul, Minnesota. With approximately $12 million of his own money invested in the Northwest buyout, he and his partner Wilson became co-chairmen of Northwest's board of directors.

Critics have since pointed out that he had nearly brought Northwest to the brink of bankruptcy from the debt incurred by the highly leveraged buyout. Yet Checchi feels vindicated by his financial maneuvers and obviously by his successful outcome. He rebuts his critics by pointing out that he prevented Northwest from going down the abysmal path of Eastern Airlines, and he precluded Northwest from being torn apart by asset strippers. In a very penetrating interview, he defended his position by saying that, "we took one of the worst airlines in America and made it one of the most profitable." Most of Checchi's present fortune is attributable to the 11.4 million shares he owns in Northwest.

Again Checchi was criticized for extracting $800 million in union concessions and an additional $837 million in state and local bonds and tax credits. He rebutted by stating that Northwest's survival, ultimate growth, and its personnel were his top priorities, and that is why Northwest knowingly absorbed losses while its personnel enjoyed full employment during the Gulf War when most airlines were admittedly laying off many of their workers because of the crisis. Touting his track record of good relationships not only with his customers but also with his employees, he claims that one of his principal goals has always been to provide for his employees the best possible place in which to work. He is fond of reminding people that Northwest used to be called North*worst* prior to his management. With Checchi at the helm, it was rated first in on-time performance.

Proof of his arguments was realized when in recognition of his care and concern for his personnel, he was given the Boss of the Year award in May 1990, an award offered by the National Association of Working Women. In 1996 Checchi also accepted the Businessman of the Year Award at the National Italian-American Foundation in Washington, D.C. where he had an opportunity to speak of the contributions of his ethnic heritage and the importance of family in his life. Of his family background, he paid particular attention to the respect and admiration he had for his paternal grandmother for her fortitude and courage when she and her family experienced many struggles.

His wife Kathryn, an attorney, and their three children, Adam, Kristin, and Kate live in a Beverly Hills estate once owned by Sidney Poitier. Both he and his wife are actively involved in promoting educational values. He is Chairman of Partners for Excellence Campaign for the Minnesota Academic Excellence Foundation. He and his wife have contributed monies to further scholastic achievement in Minnesota's primary and secondary school system. Checchi's young age, his dynamic personality, leadership, and financial savvy make one wonder what other surprising accomplishments, perhaps in politics, may lie ahead.

General Sources:
1.   Booth, Cathy. "Can't Buy Me Love." *Time* 1 Dec. 1997: 50-51.
2.   Green, Laura Speciale. "OSIA News." *Italian America* June 1996: 14-16.
3.   Grover, Ronald. "Al Checchi Wants To Make California Fly Right." *Business Week* 3 Feb. 1997: 44.
4.   Marchione, Margherita. *Americans of Italian Heritage*. Lanham, MD: University Press of America, 1995.
5.   *Who's Who in Business*. 1989 ed.
6.   Will, George. "A Splash in California." *Washington Post* 19 Oct. 1997: C9.

—by GEORGE CARPETTO, Ph.D.

JOHN CIARDI (1916-1986)

Public radio introduced John Ciardi to many people who would have otherwise not known him and his writings. With his deep, mellifluent voice he was the wordsmith who explained the meaning of words in this quirky, plastic language that we call English. His presentations were amusing, often irreverent, but always highly educational; and that helps explain why so many radio listeners eagerly awaited his program called *A Word in Your Ear*.

Though English was the context of his work as a poet and critic, a radio listener could not help but intuit and feel Ciardi's deep sense of culture. To a considerable degree there was a certain sense of Italianicity in his poems, and this would often find itself expressed in the colorations of his metaphors especially with regard to family relationships.

John Ciardi was born on June 24, 1916 in Boston, Massachusetts. He was the only child of Carminantonio and Concetta (nee Di Benedictis) Ciardi who had separately emigrated from the town of Avellino, Italy, met in the U.S., and later married in 1906. John Ciardi's Italian-Catholic experience and his Italian American biculturalism created sharp contrasts for him in his growing years where the values of his parents' "Old World" heritage and the pressing "New World" realities came to clash. It was no surprise that those very dichotomies eventually provided him with much of the rich subject matter and dialectic for his poetic cosmos.

Ciardi's early poetry indicated his preference for short poems, often compressing into a few verses a history of familial experiences and his personal adventures in America, a land offering so many new perspectives, especially to immigrants. Although John was too young to have had many personal memories of his father

who had died an early death, his father's historical presence was kept alive by his mother's most frequent and vivid recollections. Ciardi addressed this interesting dilemma when he wrote of his father's funeral in the poem: "It Took Four Flowerboats to Convoy My Father's Black."

...I mean, God,
it was a regatta, I tell you, she told me,
half of which I remember, and half of
which
I remember being told after I had
forgotten it once.

Recognition for his poetic talent came early to him. Already a scholarship student at the University of Michigan, he won first prize in the Avery Hopwood Awards along with a stipend of $1,200—a fair sum of money in 1938! For twenty years he would dedicate himself to the teaching profession; first, at the University of Kansas City in 1940; then, after serving in World War II at Harvard University from 1948-1953; and, finally, at Rutgers University from 1954-1961.

During this twenty-year span, many events occurred in his life. He married, became the father of three children, served as poetry editor for a publishing house, edited a book on mid-century American poets, became elected a Fellow of both the American Academy of Arts and Sciences and the National Institute of Arts and Letters, won the Prix de Rome, published several books of his poetry, published his first book of children's poems, won many other awards and, generally speaking was quite prosperous and prolific.

Even after formally leaving academics,

Ciardi returned to lecturing. He was a natural teacher, feeling a deep sense of responsibility to teach his generation, both the tender young and many adults of the so-called literate public with its unrecognized sensibilities and self-imposed poetic limitations. The vehemence with which he carried out this crusade often became controversial, and his critical essays had brought him national literary prominence.

Ciardi had also begun a long association with Norman Cousins, the editor of the *Saturday Review*, who eventually would encourage Ciardi to leave the academic life for the challenges of the publishing world. Several of Ciardi's poems had already been published in the *Saturday Review*; and, in 1956, he became its poetry editor. One of his first tasks was to set a poetry policy for the magazine which immediately caused trouble and controversy. His policy effectively screened out 213 poems that had already been accepted for publication! After threatening to resign, he was reluctantly given permission by Cousins to send back over 200 of these poems with a letter explaining his position. Within two weeks he had a carton full of letters written with rage and anguish.

Soon Ciardi began writing a regular column under the title "Manner of Speaking" which was mostly about poetry and his views and experiences as editor, critic and lecturer, but it was also about those things that excited or infuriated him. His negative review of Anne Morrow Lindbergh's *The Unicorn* caused a major controversy among his readers who responded with verbal attacks upon him. Cousins tried to soothe the public but, in so doing, riled Ciardi to the point that he quit. Cousins and Ciardi did patch up their differences, but it was with the understanding that Ciardi's criticism would be confined to his column where it was unequivocally seen as personal. Although his critiques would cause more confrontation with the editor, Ciardi and Cousins worked together until the *Saturday Review* filed for bankruptcy in 1977.

This poet, teacher, and literary critic was also a translator. Ciardi had long been interested in the works of Dante, often finding there inspiration for his own poetry. In 1954, his classic translation of Dante's *Inferno* was published; it was followed by *Purgatorio* in 1961, and by *Paradiso* in 1970. These three translations have since become standard texts for English-speaking people studying Dante's literary triptych called *The Divine Comedy*.

John Ciardi died of a heart attack at the end of March 1986. He left a poetic legacy of precious words available for each of us to take and use, such as in his poem: "Poetry."

Whether or not you like it is not my
business/whether or not you can take
it is, finally, yours/whether or not
it makes any difference to you it does
make its own, whether or not you see it.

John Ciardi's life has, indeed, exemplified the literary success of a second generation Italian American achieving academic and artistic acclaim while graciously integrating much of his Italian heritage in virtually everything he did.

General Sources:
1.   Alighieri, Dante. *Inferno*. Trans. John Ciardi. New Brunswick, NJ: Rutgers University Press, 1954.
2.   Ciardi, John. *The Birds of Pompeii: Poems*. Fayetteville, AR: University of Arkansas Press, 1985.
3.   Ciardi, John. *Selected Poems*. Fayetteville, AR: University of Arkansas Press, 1984.
4.   Ciardi, John. *This Strangest Everything*. New Brunswick, NJ: Rutgers University Press, 1966.
5.   Krickel, Edward. *John Ciardi*. Boston: Twayne, 1980.
6.   *Who's Who in America*. 1984-85 ed.

—by CONI GESUALDI

MICHAEL CIMINO (1943-   )

Director, screenwriter, and producer, he entered the film industry with a broad academic background and great cultural savvy. Initially aspiring to become an architect, he attended the best of schools and immersed himself in the arts, including ballet, graphic arts, painting, and writing. After earning a degree in graphic arts at Michigan State University, he continued on to completing a Masters in Fine Arts (MFA) at Yale University. He became involved in dramatics and ballet, and by the end of the 60s he had done editing for documentary productions, eventually doing directing work in TV commercials. When he moved to Hollywood in 1971, he started in the industry by first co-writing two films and then began directing as early as 1974.

The Deer Hunter (1978) was a three-hour highly charged Vietnam saga whose huge box-office appeal made critics take notice of Cimino's film craft and his treatment of violence. Not without his detractors, Cimino was hailed by many critics as having created the most significant anti-war statement since *The Grand Illusion* (1937). Because of the film's overwhelmingly intense visual experience and script, *The Deer Hunter* generated nine Academy Award nominations and went on to secure five Oscars, including Best Picture and Best Director. Over twenty years have passed since its first showing, and it seems that the test of time has so far conferred upon *The Deer Hunter* a permanent place among Hollywood's more recent classic films.

According to the best available information, Michael Cimino was born in 1943 (or possibly two or three years earlier). He has a younger brother, and his father was a well-to-do music publisher. The Cimino family lived rather comfortably in Old Westbury, Long Island, New York. While growing up he attended the best of private schools in the area; and as counterpoint to his own economically satisfying existence, one of his fascinations had involved his constant observation of people who occupied the other extreme of his privileged socioeconomic position. He became captivated by the toughness, passion, and intensity of the underprivileged.

At Michigan State University, he studied graphic arts and edited the university's satirical journal. He worked out physically, often competing in weightlifting matches. After obtaining a degree from his undergraduate college, he attended graduate school at Yale University working towards a fine arts degree where he had the opportunity to study a wide range of subjects including art history, painting, and architecture. While attending Yale, he joined the Army Reserve in 1962, spending six months training time in Fort Dix, New Jersey and several weeks in Houston, Texas for basic medical instruction.

After receiving his masters (MFA) in 1963, he moved to New York City to fulfill his need to study acting and ballet. To earn a living, he worked for a relatively small company that made documentary films for commercial and industrial purposes. He was an editing apprentice, and this work experience afforded him the opportunity to learn to use the Movieola, a trademark name for a projection device for editing motion picture film and sound. It was at this crucial point in his life that he decided that he wanted to become a filmmaker. His interest in making films was also retrospectively reinforced by the prior influence of his grandfather who often took young Cimino to the movies—sometimes as often as three times a week.

By the end of the 60s, Cimino's creative efforts had made him become well known in New York City circles as a TV director of commercials. In 1971 Cimino made off for Hollywood where he soon began co-writing screenplays. His first Hollywood work involved co-writing *Silent Running* (1971), a nuclear disaster film replete with impressive futuristic pyrotechnics in a doomsday scenario where the few remaining people struggle with the vestiges of earthly vegetation. Later, critics viewed Cimino's second experience at co-writing in the film *Magnum Force* (1973) as much more favorable. Many seemed to agree that Cimino's probable input into this second installment in the *Dirty Harry* series did much to enhance the dramatic credibility and intensity of the roles by realistically complicating plot and motivation of the characters around the San Francisco police inspector and his involvements with violent scenarios.

A Clint Eastwood production film, *Thunderbolt and Lightfoot* (1974), was Cimino's first experience involving a full-length movie that he wrote and directed. It was a most successful movie with many talented actors such as Clint Eastwood, Jeff Bridges, and George Kennedy. It dealt with a Vietnam vet's fervent dream to pull off a big heist and then simply retire for life. A countercultural twist on thematics of the "American dream," the movie, picaresque in quality, contained many hilarious episodes that captured the essence of male camaraderie and especially modern male subculture.

The Deer Hunter (1978), Cimino's most important and popular film, and winner of five Oscars, remained highly controversial for some segments of the movie critics and viewing audiences. It seems that they had erroneously interpreted Cimino's perspective that the Vietcong were murderers. In an interview, Cimino explained that from his point of view the focus of the film was always on the ordinary, everyday people who fought the war, how the war affected them, and how it often destroyed them. Cimino generally described the film's focus as depicting the violation of three very ordinary American people—in this case steelworkers from Pennsylvania—who were summoned to war to suffer *extraordinary* pain and exercise *extraordinary* courage. He professed to having had no politically inspired ideological or intellectual agenda as to whether this particular war should or should have not been fought.

Though Cimino had been involved in about nine films, some of which were so demanding and ambitious that they fell into cost overruns, he is typically a risk-taker whose art attempts to accurately depict characters and scenes with a great deal of visual intensity. His films include *Silent Running* (1971), *Magnum Force* (1973), *Thunderbolt and Lightfoot* (1974), *The Deer Hunter* (1978), *Heaven's Gate* (1980), *Year of the Dragon* (1985), *The Sicilian* (1987), *Desperate Hours* (1990), and *The Sunchaser* (1996). Perhaps, the best tribute ever paid by some critics to Michael Cimino involved associating him with Jean Renoir (1894-1979), the internationally renowned French director, whose film *The Grand Illusion* (1937) has been a traditional touchstone for film excellence.

General Sources:

1. Bliss, Michael. *Martin Scorsese and Michael Cimino*. Metuchen, NJ: Scarecrow Press, 1985.

2. *Current Biography Yearbook*. New York: Wilson, 1981.

3. Katz, Ephraim. *The Film Encyclopedia*. New York: HarperCollins, 1998.

4. Monaco, James. *The Encyclopedia of Film*. New York: Perigee Books, 1991.

5. Monaco, James. *Who's Who in American Film Now*. New York: New York Zoetrope, 1987.

—by CHARLES HARRINGTON

BENJAMIN CIVILETTI (1935-   )

Nominated by President Jimmy Carter to be Assistant Attorney General, Benjamin Civiletti, an esteemed and highly professional attorney, often called "a lawyer's lawyer," left a prestigious private law firm in Baltimore, Maryland to accept this cabinet position during the Carter administration in 1977. About a year later in 1978, again nominated by the President and approved by the Senate to become Deputy Attorney General, he held the second most powerful position in that sphere of the cabinet where he was responsible for the operational network involving a budget that was close to $2 billion for the FBI, the Drug Enforcement Administration, and the U.S. Marshals Service.

In 1979, after Attorney General Griffin Bell had announced his resignation, Benjamin Civiletti was nominated to replace him, and, once more, was approved by the Senate to become President Carter's new Attorney General. Inheriting a host of problems, he proved to be a highly gifted tactician who faced each challenge with a professionalism and composure that was second to none. In those days when President Carter strove hard to mend the many wounds the country had endured since the 60s, Civiletti more than filled expectations in assisting Carter to those ideological and spiritual ends, adhering to the letter and the spirit of the law in all the legal matters in his purview.

Benjamin Richard Civiletti, born in Peekskill, New York on July 17, 1935, was of Italian heritage. He attended Johns Hopkins University in Baltimore, Maryland where he received his B.A. degree in 1957 and later attended the University of Maryland, also in Baltimore, where he received his LL.B. in 1961. After passing the Maryland bar exam, he began his fast-moving career track by first working for Judge William Calvin Chestnut as a clerk in the United States district court system. About a year later in September 1962 he became assistant United States attorney in Baltimore where he spent most of his time prosecuting fraud cases. After a two-year experience in this area, he returned to private practice.

In October 1964 Civiletti joined the prestigious firm of Venable, Baetjer & Howard, located in Baltimore. Starting as an associate, he became a partner in the firm five years later in 1969. By 1971, while heading its litigation department, which dealt with all kinds of criminal and civil lawsuits, he also became active on many commissions and task forces spanning the gamut from the mayoral level in Baltimore up to state legislative matters. He was quietly building a reputation as a dedicated and squeaky clean private attorney/administrator and a most willing ex-officio public servant.

Among the many political and legal personalities he came across in his years, Civiletti had made the acquaintance of Charles Kirbo, who in the early 1970s was an adviser to Jimmy Carter—then the Governor of Georgia. Kirbo had admired Civiletti's work in handling a Maryland action in a federal antitrust case which, similarly, Kirbo's firm in Atlanta, Georgia also had to handle. In 1977, Kirbo recommended Civiletti both to President Carter and to Attorney General Bell as successor to Richard Thornburgh in the capacity of Assistant Attorney General whose main responsibility involved heading the criminal division of the Justice Department.

As the third ranking administrator in the Attorney General's office, Benjamin Civiletti was systematically the recipient of many negative feelings that Congress—in a strong and sustained bipartisanship—still harbored anger over the Watergate scandals and the issues of obstruction of justice which had ultimately implicated Nixon's Attorney General's office. This widespread feeling of mistrust for the Attorney General's office persisted despite President Ford's neutralizing efforts during the 1974-1977 intervening years.

When Bert Lance, President Carter's friend, resigned as Director of the Office of Management and Budget in September 1977 after Senate hearings on banking, it came as no surprise that Civiletti and the office he represented were also being closely examined for the fulfillment of their due diligence of their duties in this investigation. Similarly, there was the same scenario of mistrust and ruthless scrutiny of the Justice area during the congressional investigation of South Korea and its alleged attempts at buying influence with members of Congress and other Washingtonians. In all, Civiletti, true to form and to his fine reputation, working with a staff of 350 lawyers, performed the necessary duties to bring that matter to a conclusion.

Despite questions raised by some members of Congress, Carter's nomination of Civiletti to Deputy Attorney General was approved by the Senate on May 9, 1978. This position which typically included supervision of federal enforcement agencies such as the FBI also involved Civiletti's responsibility for the management of the agency's $2 billion budget. One of the major achievements during his tenure involved his efforts on cracking down on white-collar crime perpetrated at the federal level.

In 1979, when Attorney General Bell resigned from his position, it took the Senate only three days to approve Carter's nomination of Civiletti as the new Attorney General. The vote, reflecting a fervent respect that Civiletti had earned from Congress in his prior two years of service in the justice area, was a resounding 94 to 1. Having worked arduously to leave the Attorney General's office untarnished by his efforts, Civiletti succeeded in helping to restore much of the vitality, credibility and effectiveness of federal enforcement agencies. Respected by his peers in government and admired by young aspiring lawyers, he returned to private practice after ending his work with the Carter administration in 1981.

Benjamin Civiletti was honored both during and after his tenure in government office on many occasions. In just recognition of his outstanding public service, his practice of upholding the highest standards of the legal profession, and his administrative acumen in justice matters, he received honorary doctorates in law from many notable schools of higher learning including the University of Baltimore (1978), New York Law School (1979), Tulane University (1979), St. John's University (1979), University of Notre Dame (1981), and University of Maryland (1983). In addition, he most appropriately received the Herbert H. Lehman Ethics Award. He leaves a legacy of integrity, respect, and competency. Presently, he is chairman of Venable, Baetjer & Howard in its Baltimore office, and he is a fellow of the American College of Trial Lawyers.

General Sources:
1.   *Current Biography Yearbook*. New York: Wilson, 1980.
2.   "MBNA America Bank. N.A.: Directors and Officers." 4 Jan. 1999. <http://www.mbnainternational.com/stocks/q297/page 8. htm>.
3.   United States. Congress. Senate. Committee on the Judiciary. *Confirmation Hearings on Benjamin R. Civiletti, Nominee, Attorney General...July 25, 26, and 27, 1979.* Washington: U.S. Government Printing Office, 1980.
4.   *Who's Who in America*. 1986-87 ed.
5.   *Who's Who in American Law*. 1978 ed.

—by SAM PITTARO

PERRY COMO (1913-   )

Perry Como, the Italian-American crooner with the baritone voice, was noted for his authentically relaxed and mellow style. He was a radio and recording star in the 40s who had also appeared in films such as *Doll Face* (1945) and *Words and Music* (1948). In addition to his success in radio, night clubs, and film, he achieved the acme of his career with the advent of television as the star of his own long-running and popular programs. Affectionately referred to as "Mr. C" by his nationwide audiences in the 50s and 60s, he was one of TV's most established singing performers. His telegenic personality, charm, and soft charisma, all ensconced within his uniquely mellow voice, soothed the hearts and minds of those who watched his show.

Perry Como was born in Canonsburg, Pennsylvania on May 18, 1913. His parents, Pietro and Lucia Como, had both emigrated from Italy in the early 1900s. Perry, baptized Pierino, was one of thirteen children. To help ease his parents' financial burden, he began working after school in a barber shop at age 11. Although within a few years he was making installments on his own barber shop, his father compelled him to finish school first.

At 21, he owned his shop, and he ran his business for six years. He became adept at barbershop singing. His friends encouraged him to audition in Cleveland for Freddy Carlone's Orchestra, and he was hired. He and his bride, the former Roselle Belline, toured the Midwest with Carlone's band for three years.

In 1937, the popular orchestra leader, Ted Weems, signed him on to work in his show. Six years later, when Weems joined the Army, the orchestra dispersed and Como returned to Canonsburg, fully intending to reopen his barber shop. However, before resuming his business, CBS offered him a spot on a radio program. Como accepted only after being assured that he would be permitted to live in New York for the duration of the program.

Shortly thereafter, he signed for a two-week trial at the highly popular New York City nightclub, the Copacabana. Though he faced daunting competition from Frank Sinatra, Como measured up very well in the eyes of the public and the critics. Harriet Van Horne, radio critic for the *New York World Telegram*, considered him refreshing because he was "handsome, pleasantly wholesome and mercifully unaffected. His voice is a clear, full-throated baritone and, when he sings, he appears to be suffering no pain at all—not even that private, exquisite pain that is peculiar to nightclub crooners."

Two years after his nightclub debut, Como was paid $10,000 for two out-of-New York shows: the highest ever for one-night stands. In the summer of 1943, RCA Victor launched Como on a successful recording career. His rich, vibrant voice, which he himself has described as "somewhere between a tenor and a light baritone," soon emanated from juke boxes all over the country, disc-jockey booths and music stores catering to different ages. By the fall of 1946, he had become the first popular singer to achieve the two-million mark in two of his recordings released at the same time. The entertainment industry's *Variety* magazine applauded Como for being "Victor's star salesman" and for reviving two old songs: "If You Were the Only Girl in the World" and "Prisoner of Love" after other singers had failed.

His popularity in nightclubs, on radio, and on disc-jockey lists attracted Hollywood interest at 20th Century-Fox amounting to a seven-year contract. The four pictures he had made were not memorable, but the write-ups were. They welcomed him as "a pleasant addition to the Hollywood crooners." Despite his success in Hollywood, Como sought an early release from his film contract in order to concentrate on other facets of his career such as his new radio program, *The Supper Club*. It seemed that "Mr C" became the idol of the post-World War II "bobby-soxers" and then a leading recording and television star of the Big Ballad era of the 50s.

After years as a band vocalist, he became an even bigger star on television, making many appearances on TV specials as guest host. But he was particularly known for hosting his own weekly variety show, *The Kraft Music Hall* program, from 1955 until 1963. One of the highlights of the show was the request segment where Como sang favorites while perched on a stool next to the ever-present music stand where there was ensconced a beautiful rose. Sporting his familiar cardigan, Como would speak relaxed with informality and warmth creating an instant union with his audience even before he sang. Then his smooth, virile baritone had the effect of romancing both young and old.

Como continued to make records of songs which had been best received on the radio. Many became bestsellers, some gold discs. Most notably between 1944 and 1958, Como had forty-two top hits on the billboard charts. "Prisoner of Love," "Because," "Catch a Falling Star," "Papa Loves Mambo," "Wanted," "Hot Diggity" "Delaware," and "More" are just a few examples of gold disc and multi-million-selling records. *It's Impossible* in 1970 and *And I Love You So* in 1973 were also multimillion-selling albums. Occasionally doing specials, guest spots or commercials on television, he remained rather consistently on the pop-music charts through 1973. He received a Grammy Award for the Best Vocal Performance in his rendering of "Catch a Falling Star."

After that era there were only sporadic appearances, notably in television such as in the presentation, *Cole Porter in Paris*. On many occasions, he also broke attendance records and was enthusiastically received by fans and critics alike. Close to 70 years of age when he began making world tours in the 1980s, his performances sold out in advance. Perry Como who has been one of the most commercially successful of all the pop recording artists and vocalists of his generation, still found time to play a role in ethnic and charitable events and to become one of the founders of the Hospitalized Veterans' National Radio Foundation.

Perhaps among the most remarkable and heralded achievements of this talented Italian-American singer was not only his rise from rags to riches and his transition from small-town barber to superstar, but also his obvious commitment to his family, integrity, and privacy. During his active years in show business and in his early semi-retirement, Perry Como succeeded in enjoying his family, his privacy, and his own chosen way of life. After celebrating 65 years of marriage in early August 1998, Perry Como suffered the loss of his wife Roselle just two weeks later.

General Sources:
1. *Contemporary Theatre, Film and Television*. Detroit, MI: Gale Research, 1999.
2. *Current Biography*. New York: Wilson, 1947.
3. Kinkle, Roger. *The Complete Encyclopedia of Popular Music and Jazz, 1900-1950*. New Rochelle, NY: Arlington House, 1974.
4. Larkin, Colin. *The Encyclopedia of Popular Music*. London, UK: MUZE UK Ltd, 1997.
5. *The New Grove Dictionary of American Music*. New York: Grove's Dictionaries of Music, 1986.

—by GLORIA SCALZITTI WALKER

BILL CONTI (1942-   )

A most popular and highly prolific composer of over one hundred film scores, TV movies, music specials, mini-series, episodic and melodrama series, he has become one of the most renowned music composers in show business. He was Grammy-nominated and Oscar-nominated for best score or best song on several occasions including the film *Rocky* (1976); he earned an Oscar for Best Original Film Score for *The Right Stuff* (1983) and an Emmy Award in 1992 for outstanding achievement in TV music direction. Holding two degrees from Juilliard School of Music and a Ph.D. from Louisiana State University, he brings the richness of academic credentials as a background to his refreshingly original talents whose protean nature adapts incredibly to a kaleidoscope of music scores ranging the entire spectrum of possible movie themes.

Once the film industry had recognized his talents in his film scores from the late 1960s and early 1970s, it took little time for him to become part of mainstream Hollywood. Since then Bill Conti has been enjoying a well-deserved and solidly-based popularity that recognizes his versatility and talent. Having worked actively for thirty years in the film industry, he is known and respected for his work worldwide, especially in Europe. In the late 1970s, his great talents easily crossed over into television where he started composing scores for TV movies and TV series. Recently his name has just about become synonymous with the music direction of the Academy Award presentations and its entertainment portions of the program.

Bill Conti was born on April 13, 1942 in Providence, Rhode Island to William and Lucetta Conti. He formally began studying music in 1949 at age seven and quickly became a piano prodigy. It came as no surprise when he later formed his own band at fifteen years of age. After graduating from high school, he attended Louisiana State University and received his B.A. in 1964. But he was not yet finished with education as he had higher aspirations. He went on to the Juilliard School of Music in New York City to earn another bachelor's degree which was followed by a masters degree in music (1967). Then, returning later to Louisiana State University to complete the requirements for his doctorate, he eventually earned his Ph.D. in 1985.

Bill Conti received his initial success in composing film scores from European-made movies. While touring with a jazz band in Italy in the 1960s, he was asked to write a film score for a British-backed movie called *Juliette De Sade* (1969). This was soon followed by his music scores for three other Italian-made films: *Candidate for a Killing* (1969), *The Garden of the Finzi-Continis* (1970), and *Liquid Subway* (1972). The third of these four films was particularly well received by American critics as well as by international audiences. The film's difficult and delicate subject matter—based on a popular Italian novel by Giorgio Bassani—dealt with the discriminatory treatment that Italian Jews received under Mussolini's regime preceding and especially during World War II.

Once Conti had established himself with these four film scores, his career moved rather rapidly. For starters, Conti wrote the score for *Blume in Love* (1973), a popular film whose story dealt with a divorce lawyer and the problems facing him when his wife decided to leave their marriage. This film was followed by Conti's musical score to the award-winning film *Harry and Tonto* (1974). It starred Art Carney, and for his performance in this film he went on to win an Oscar for Best Actor. It dealt with the touching story of an aging widower and his endearing cat, Tonto. With the friendship of his feline companion, Harry leaves his city home in an attempt to find a better life living with each of his children. He discovers that it was much more fun getting there rather than staying with them.

Among the 30 or so film scores he wrote in the 1970s alone, Bill Conti will probably be best remembered by and forever associated with the film *Rocky* (1976) that won the Oscar for Best Picture. Despite the stirring and haunting refrains of the theme music from *Rocky*, his most famous and popular movie score, the nomination for best score category did not earn him an Oscar, and Bill Conti would have to wait until another year when another of his film nominees, *The Right Stuff* (1983), would capture an Oscar for Best Original Score. *Rocky*, of course, went on to have four sequels (*Rocky II, III, IV,* and *V*) respectively in 1979, 1982, 1985 and 1990, and Bill Conti was responsible for all of those scores.

The 1980s represented Bill Conti's most voluminous period of productivity where he composed over sixty music scores covering both Hollywood movies and TV series and mini-series. As for his mainstream movies, it was during that decade that he worked to complete the music for *Rocky III* (1982) and *Rocky IV* (1985). It was also the decade where he won his Oscar for Best Original Score for the film, *The Right Stuff* (1983). In addition to Bill Conti's Oscar, *The Right Stuff* also won three other Oscars. The script was based on the historical story of seven overconfident American pilots and their involvement with the Mercury program which launched the U.S. spaceflights in response to the U.S.S.R.'s April 1961 pioneering launch of Yuri Gagarin, the first human in spaceflight.

In addition to writing scores for many mainstream Hollywood movies such as *The Formula* (1980), *The Karate Kid* (1984), and *Lean On Me* (1989), Bill Conti also did an enormous amount of work for television, another major area of productivity for him in the 1980s. He wrote the scores for the following TV series or mini-series: *Dynasty* (1981), *Falcon Crest* (1981), *North and South* (1985), *North and South: Book II* (1986); and for the following, he wrote the theme music: *Cagney and Lacey* (1983), *Emerald Point N.A.S.* (1983), *Lifestyles of The Rich and Famous* (1984), *The Master* (1984), *The Colbys* (1986), *Mariah* (1987), *Napoleon & Josephine: A Love Story* (1987). Beginning in the 1980s Bill Conti became music director for the Academy Awards TV broadcast program, and he has been doing that for twelve consecutive years.

Bill Conti's consistently excellent performance as a music director and conductor and, of course, as a highly creative composer for over thirty years in mainstream film and in TV's multi-faceted area of movies, melodramatic series, and specials, have attested to his great talents. They recall his obviously persistent nature from his childhood piano-prodigy days. Respected and admired particularly by those in the film and television industries, he is viewed as one of Hollywood's living music legends.

General Sources:
1. *Baker's Biographical Dictionary of Musicians.* New York: Schirmer, 1991.
2. "Bill Conti Filmography and Discography." 20 Jan. 1999. <http://www.ruhr.de/home/eckhardw/bconti.html>.
3. *Contemporary Theater, Film and Television.* Detroit: Gale Research, 1994.
4. Katz, Ephraim. *The Film Encyclopedia.* New York: HarperCollins, 1998.
5. *The New Grove Dictionary of American Music.* New York: Grove's Dictionaries of Music, 1989.
6. *Who's Who in America.* 1999 ed.

—by GEORGE CARPETTO, Ph.D.

FRANCIS FORD COPPOLA (1939-)

Director, producer, and screenwriter, most known for his direction of *The Godfather* (1972) and the ensuing *The Godfather Part II* (1974) and *The Godfather Part III* (1990), the winner of five Academy Awards from ten nominations, and winner of two Palme D'Or awards at the Cannes Film Festival, Francis Ford Coppola holds a long list of film credits that clearly indicates a most daring and gifted artist whose works will be discussed by future historians. Like many Hollywood luminaries, he has also had his share of negative moments in the industry.

Francis Ford Coppola was born on April 7, 1939 in Detroit, Michigan. The second of three children, Francis has an older brother and a sister, Talia Shire (Coppola). His parents were both talented people. His father, Carmine Coppola (1910-1991), was a Neapolitan flutist and composer who played not only for the Detroit Symphony Orchestra but also for the NBC Symphony Orchestra when the latter was under the direction of Arturo Toscanini. His mother, the former Italia Pennino, had appeared as an actress in several Italian films.

Though born in Detroit, young Francis grew up in Queens, New York City. He nurtured an avid interest in filmmaking from an early age, and after surviving a one-year encounter with polio, he decided at age ten to make his first amateur film with an 8 mm camera. Francis was also a talented musician and tuba player, and in view of those strengths, he accepted a scholarship at the New York Military Academy at Cornwall-On-The-Hudson. After 18 months there, he lost interest, and not wanting to face his parents, he fled to Los Angeles spending the summer with his brother. After returning to New York, he completed his high school studies, and at the young age of 16 he won a partial scholarship and began studying drama at Hofstra College on Long Island where he was involved in school musicals and plays.

After completing his degree at Hofstra in 1960, Francis, who was now in his early 20s, moved to California and attended UCLA for several years focusing his attention on filmmaking. While attending UCLA he directed and produced an inauspicious soft-core "nudie" film, *Tonight for Sure* (1961). The presence of this ill-fated movie was later aptly balanced by his award-winning screenplay, *Pilma, Pilma*, which (though never released) earned him the Samuel Goldwyn Award in 1962.

Francis Coppola, who—in many different capacities—had assisted Roger Corman's avid filmmaking enterprises, was given his first major break when Corman assigned him to direct *Dementia 13* (1963), a low-budget horror movie produced by Corman. Filmed in Ireland, Coppola met and married that year Eleanor Neil, the movie set decorator. On his return to Hollywood, Coppola worked on a number of film projects, and he completed his course work at UCLA and concluded his next film, *You're a Big Boy Now* (1967) that he presented as his M.F.A. thesis. A light-hearted comedy, it was successfully distributed by Warner Brothers.

The film's relative success brought Coppola recognition, and he moved up to directing more expensive studio films including *Finian's Rainbow* (1968) and *The Rain People* (1969). Both films failed to achieve any distinction, but he persevered in the craft in different capacities such as co-writer and unit director in many films throughout the 60s such as *The Young Racers* (1963), *The Terror* (1963), *This Property is Condemned* (1966), *Is Paris Burning?* (1966), and *The Wild Racers* (1968).

In a sense, these efforts served as a preparation for his success in co-writing the script for what became a major box-office hit, the film *Patton* (1970), a nearly three-hour long biographical study of one of America's legendary and controversial war heros from WWII. *Patton* swept away eight Oscars that year, including Coppola and co-writer Edmund North winning Oscars for Best Screenplay. Two years later, the intensity of Coppola's career reached new heights when he directed *The Godfather* (1972) for Paramount Studios.

The Godfather became not only one of the all-time money makers in Hollywood history but also an instant American movie classic of epic proportions where myth and reality met on the silver screen and where, thematically, mythic family ties experienced an uneasy relationship with the harshness of underworld business. Both Coppola and Mario Puzo (author of the best-selling novel of the same name) won Oscars for Best Screenplay Adaptation. The film earned a nomination for Best Director; it earned an Oscar for Best Picture; and Marlon Brando garnered an Oscar for Best Actor.

In 1973 Coppola produced *American Graffiti* which under George Lucas' direction was nominated for five Oscars. The year 1974, however, reached one of the highest points in Coppola's entire career. Collectively that year, Coppola outdid all of his prior work including *The Godfather* (1972). After writing the screenplay for the popular *The Great Gatsby* (1974), Coppola also produced, directed and wrote the script for *The Conversation* (1974), a film dealing with a hi-tech surveillance expert and his unexpected discovery of tragedy through his eavesdropping. It received two Academy Award nominations and won the Palme d'Or.

This was also the same year in which Coppola directed and co-wrote with Mario Puzo *The Godfather Part II* (1974) which went on to win six Academy Awards, including three Oscars for Coppola for Best Picture, Best Director and Best Screenplay; and three Oscars for Best Score, Best Supporting Actor, and Best Art Direction/Set Direction. This film was creatively shaped by two major film sequences in which one served as a prelude to *The Godfather* story and the other one functioned as its sequel. In its entirety, the film reached dramatically epic proportions that surpassed the original film.

Apocalypse Now (1979) produced and directed by Coppola has become a classic in its own right. It remains as one of the most compelling war films ever made, a penetrating odyssey within the era of the Vietnam War where in a mythic setting a CIA operative goes out in search of Colonel Kurtz, a renegade American military heavy who took refuge in Cambodia to establish his own bizarre jungle empire. Nominated for eight Academy Awards, it won three.

Since then Coppola has made a number of films including *The Cotton Club* (1984), *Captain Eo* (1986), *Peggy Sue Got Married* (1986), *Gardens of Stone* (1987), *Tucker: The Man and His Dream* (1988), *The Godfather Part III* (1990), *Bram Stoker's Dracula* (1992), *Jack* (1996), and *The Rainmaker* (1997). He remains as one of the most creative minds Hollywood has ever experienced. Relatively young, Coppola is sure to create many more great films for the silver screen.

General Sources:
1. Ayelsworth, Thomas, G. *The World Almanac Who's Who of Film.* New York: World Almanac, 1987.
2. Johnson, Robert K. *Francis Ford Coppola.* Boston: Twayne, 1977.
3. Katz, Ephraim. *The Film Encyclopedia.* New York: HarperCollins, 1998.
4. *Who's Who in Entertainment.* 1998-1999 ed.
5. Zuker, Joel S. *Francis Ford Coppola: A Guide to References and Resources.* Boston: G.K. Hall, 1984.

—by MICHAEL T. GUARDINO, Sr.

CHICK COREA (1941-   )

Pianist, crossover keyboardist, composer, recording artist, bandleader, and arranger of jazz, Chick Corea has received scores of awards and honors, including eight Grammy Awards from his thirty-three nominations to date. A perpetual student of music since age four, he was trained in the basics of music from his earliest years by his musician father. Vaulting over much of the phenomenon of the rock'n'roll era during his teens and young adult years, Chick Corea was virtually unaffected by the broad impact that rock'n'roll had made on others of his age as he devoted his efforts to learning and composing jazz music. He became an artistic innovator, one of the earliest composers to incorporate synthesizers into his compositions. His musical form has been described as a broad orchestrated blend of Latin, classical, bop, and jazz-rock fusion.

Anthony Armando Corea, better known today as Chick Corea, is a third-generation Italian American, born in Chelsea, Massachusetts on June 12, 1941 to Armando John and Anna (nee Zaccone) Corea. His father, a professional musician, trumpet player, and bandleader, was Chick's first teacher, inspiring Chick at the age of four to study piano at home. Later in his childhood, Chick studied classical piano under the tutelage of a local teacher, Salvatore Sullo.

As a pre-adolescent and adolescent, he listened regularly to the works of jazz greats such as Dizzy Gillespie, Charlie Parker, Miles Davis, Art Tatum, and Bud Powell. He often transcribed some of their works and committed them to memory. In particular, he studied and transcribed the entire works of the pianist, Horace Silver; and Corea went on to improvise solos based on Silver's style. In all, by the time he was a young adult, he composed music, basing most of his style on jazz and classical artists, and occasionally borrowing elements from rock'n'roll, which at the time was the dominant voice in popular music. What elements he did adopt from rock'n'roll usually related to its use of "guitars, electronics, and backbeat rhythms and high energy."

In his teenage years, he first played music at high school functions; then, away from home in the Boston area, and finally in Cape Cod's supper club circuit. After graduating from Chelsea High School in 1959, he moved to New York City. Intending to get a college education, he lasted only one month at Columbia University's undergraduate school of liberal arts, and only two months of classes at the Juilliard School of Music. In order to support himself, Corea played at local dances, a job he obtained through a bandleader relative living in Brooklyn.

His more decisive professional work began in 1962-63 when he performed as pianist for the Latin band of Mongo Santamaria and that of Willie Bobo. From these Latin-based musical experiences he derived what would become an ongoing infatuation for fusing Latin rhythms with his prior knowledge of jazz protocols and patterns. His next significant move involved joining Blue Mitchell, a jazz trumpeter. While working between 1964-1966 as a pianist for Mitchell, he dedicated himself to composing; and he managed to record for the first time some of his compositions in Mitchell's recording sessions for Blue Note records. He recorded his first album as a leader in his *Tones for Joan's Bones* (1966) and eventually his *Now He Sings, Now He Sobs* (1968).

Between 1966 and 1968 Corea worked with different jazz greats for varying periods of time. These included Stan Getz, Sarah

Vaughan, Herbie Mann, and Elvin Jones. Afterwards, he joined Miles Davis in 1969 as Herbie Hancock's gradual replacement. Davis introduced Corea to the electric piano and persuaded him to pursue that instrument for the band. In effect, as the new electric piano player, Corea became a member in many of Miles Davis' much acclaimed classic numbers such as *In a Silent Way, Filles de Kilimanjaro,* and *Bitches Brew.* When Corea joined Davis, the latter had already been experimenting as of the late 1960s with a form of electronic jazz-rock which would become responsible for introducing the "fusion" movement of the 1970s.

Corea, who was in search of his own style of free jazz, did not agree entirely with Davis' electric approach. Thus in 1970, Corea and the double bass player, Dave Holland, left Davis' group, and along with two other jazz musicians, created a new group called Circle which ended up disbanding within a year. It was at this time in his life that Corea avowed that he made the second biggest discovery of his life after that of discovering music; the discovery involved L. Ron Hubbard's scientology. After studying Hubbard's teachings, Corea claimed that he finally began to reshape his life after having already fruitlessly "searched through rebellion, drugs, diets, mysticism, religions, intellectualism." Corea professed to have found inner peace with the simple truths espoused by Hubbard that, in brief, contain a fundamental dualism. In order to avoid the vicious cycle of negativism, an individual must first learn to deal with one's own self-defeating mechanisms and then learn ways to communicate better.

Since his conversion, Corea's career grew as it had never grown before. It was during this period that he recorded many of his most popular albums, and he began touring with his band around the globe with much success. In 1972 he founded a new group called Return to Forever that attracted a larger audience by focusing on a jazz style that employed what some critics have aptly described as "infectious Latin rhythms." This group went on to record eight popular albums, including some of his most popular pieces such as "La Fiesta" and "Crystal Silence."

In 1986 Corea founded another group, the Elektric Band that professionally has constituted the highest point in his career as he seemed to have found a working combination between acoustic and keyboard instruments. The Elektric Band went on to record well over 100 records and over fifty albums. In all, Corea has kept busy playing his own style of jazz and composing hundreds of works. Chick Corea has been the recipient of scores of awards, including eight Grammys, nineteen *Downbeat* awards (Best Electric Pianist, 1987, Best Electric Group, 1988, Best Electric Piano, 1988), 17 *Keyboard Magazine* readers' polls, and many more. In 1992 Corea achieved a lifetime goal when he established his own record label called Stretch Records with its commitment to focus more on creativity than established musical patterns and styles.

General Sources:
1. *Baker's Biographical Dictionary of Musicians.* Ed. Nicholas Slonimsky. New York: Schirmer, 1991.
2. *Current Biography Yearbook.* New York: Wilson, 1988.
3. Feather, Leonard G. *The Biographical Encyclopedia of Jazz.* New York: Oxford University Press, 1999.
4. Feather, Leonard G. *The Pleasures of Jazz.* New York: Horizon Press, 1976.
5. Hitchcock, Wiley, and Stanley Sadie. *The New Grove Dictionary of American Music.* New York: Grove's Dictionaries of Music, 1989.
6. Lyons, Len. *The Great Jazz Pianists.* New York: Morrow, 1983.
7. *Rolling Stone* 15 July 1976: 24.
8. *Who's Who in America.* 1988-89 ed.

—by SAM PITTARO

JOHN PAUL CORIGLIANO (1938-   )

A world renowned composer of orchestral and chamber music, opera, and film scores, and winner of innumerable national and international music awards, including two Grammy Awards, John Corigliano (to be distinguished from his father who was an accomplished violinist) represents an unusually gifted musical phenomenon of our generation. As a composer he is unique in our contemporary times because he has written an abundant treasure of music that may be appreciated by traditional lovers of classical music as well as by music specialists trained in the difficulties of modern atonal music.

He has accomplished this feat by creatively employing the conventional repertoire of melodic and harmonic relationships together with a well-balanced combination of the not-too-easily-understood intricacies of modern, esoteric atonal music, that is, music whose melodic and harmonic patterns do not make reference to traditional music's system of patterns and scales. He has indeed spent much of his creative life honing in on a style that is, at once, respectful of both traditional tonal music and modern atonal music. This remarkable accomplishment may very well be one of his major achievements.

John Corigliano was born on February 16, 1938 in New York City to John Sr. and Rose (nee Buzen) Corigliano. His parents lived intermittently as a couple. His father maintained an apartment in Manhattan, and his mother had a place in Brooklyn. Young John spent much of his early years commuting between both locations experiencing a sadness "torn between loyalties" and sensing a confusion brought about by distanced parents.

Both parents were artistically talented. Working for the New York Philharmonic from 1943 to 1966, his father was its concertmaster, i.e., the principal violinist, who usually serves as assistant to the conductor. His mother was a well-known piano teacher as well as an accomplished pianist. After young John's first piano lesson—with his mother as teacher—which ended in an argument, he refused any further instruction in piano. But he tinkered by himself, and by age six he had developed the uncanny ability to improvise fluently on the piano so that he could imitate a composer's style.

As a teenager he started studying clarinet with Stanley Drucker of the New York Philharmonic, but curiously, when his instrument was stolen, he decided to drop clarinet lessons. Meanwhile, at Midwood High School in Brooklyn (NY), he tried his hand at every available school band instrument, and in a short time became adept at all of them. He seemed to drop his interest in classical music for a while and devoted his musical pursuits to popular music. It was a period of searching, trying to discern for himself a proper trajectory he could follow into the future. After a talk with his father about Walton's *Violin Concerto*, his interest in classical music was suddenly revived.

He learned from that conversation that he needed to focus his attention on the uniqueness of certain musical sounds and how they functioned in an orchestral piece. For instance, he started listening to recordings such as Aaron Copland's popular classical score, *Billy the Kid*. From a technical perspective, he began liking and appreciating Copland's use of "7/4 time, the irregular rhythms, the flattened fifths in the harmony, the spacey sounds." A new world of music suddenly opened up to him, and he discovered the intimations of the kind of style he would eventually nurture and develop.

In 1955, Corigliano began his college studies at Columbia University. Ironically, his father vowed not to support him if he majored in music. This was rendered even more difficult when Corigliano admitted that he wanted to be involved in music not as a performer but quite possibly as a composer. The father openly discouraged him from entering a classical music career since he feared that his son would have to endure the uphill battle, the mistreatment, and the toils that most contemporary composers face. His father's feelings were so adamant that even on the day John graduated *cum laude* in 1959, he remained saddened to see his son venture into a risky music world not known nor understood by most of the general public.

After graduation he steadfastly kept writing his musical compositions while he held many jobs. From 1959 to 1964 he was program director of WQXR-FM and later WBAI-FM; assistant to Leonard Bernstein's innovative and well-received music series on CBS-TV called *Young People's Concerts*; producer for Columbia Masterworks classical recordings; and, an orchestrator for many "pop" classical albums. Simultaneous to these jobs, he completed as early as 1961 "Fern Hill," the first part of a musical trilogy of Dylan Thomas' poems that he had performed at New York City's Carnegie Hall. He would go on to complete this choral symphony, *A Dylan Thomas Trilogy*, in 1976.

"Fern Hill" was followed by his 1964 *Violin and Piano Sonata* that won first prize at the Spoleto Chamber Music Competition (Italy). His father, to whom this musical work was dedicated and who refused to acknowledge it at first, became its featured violinist when it was performed at Carnegie Hall in 1966. Later, Corigliano's *Concert for Piano and Orchestra* (commissioned by the San Antonio Symphony), written for the 1968 World's Fair at San Antonio, Texas was later recorded for Mercury Records in 1971, and he received the Ester Award for Best Contemporary Recording.

John Corigliano's career has since skyrocketed, expressing a dynamic eclecticism, moving freely in rich forms of musical expression, uniting in a continuous marriage of old nineteenth-century romantic musical articulation and twentieth-century atonality, thus creating fresh musical works. In all, Corigliano has been responsible thus far for having written well over 60 musical works whose wide range in content and style has only added to his creative genius. His more recent works such as *Symphony No. 1* (1991) and *The Ghosts of Versailles* (1991) have earned him many awards.

After being elected in 1991 to the American Academy of Arts and Letters, which consists of 250 of America's most creative minds in art, sculpture, music, architecture, and writing, he was also named by *Musical America* as Composer of the Year in 1992. He was nominated for Academy and Grammy Awards on several occasions, and he went on to win two Grammy Awards. His broad appeal has steadily grown not only because of his obvious success as a composer of film scores such as for the movies *Altered States*, *The Revolution*, and *The Red Violin*, but also because of his refreshingly unique, eclectic, modern style.

General Sources:
1.   Cockrell, Dale. "John Corigliano." *The New Grove Dictionary of American Music*. New York: Macmillan, 1986.
2.   *Current Biography Yearbook*. New York: Wilson, 1989.
3.   Holland, Bernard. "Highbrow Music to Hum." *New York Times Magazine* 31 Jan. 1982: 24+.
4.   Kozinn, A. "The 'Unfashionably Romantic' Music of John Corigliano." *New York Times* 27 April 1980: 19+.
5.   Slonimsky, Nicolas. *Baker's Biographical Dictionary of Twentieth-Century Classical Musicians*. New York: Schirmer Books, 1997.

—by THERESA BRANCIFORTE

LOU COSTELLO (1906-1959)

Louis Francis Cristello, better known as Lou Costello of the comedy team of Abbott and Costello, had worked as a laborer and as a stunt man for MGM and Warner Brothers in the late 20s. When nothing came of it, he joined the world of vaudeville and burlesque. In 1931 he met Bud Abbott, and they went on to become a most successful comedy team. Later, they would become an even bigger hit in the movies of the 40s and early 50s.

Lou Costello was born on March 6, 1906 in Paterson, New Jersey. Sebastian, his father, was born in Caserta, Italy a town just north of Rome. In 1898 Sebastian came to America and in 1902 married an Irish girl, Helen (nee Rege). From his early youth, Lou reportedly wanted to be in show business. At age four, he play acted both alone and with friends in front of a mirror. He grew up idolizing Charlie Chaplin, and it was Chaplin, indirectly, who later on would influence Lou to change from dramatic acting to comedy. After grammar school, Lou entered Paterson's Central High School, and it seems that he excelled at baseball and basketball. It was sports that had apparently kept Lou in school. Later he became a prizefighter, but his boxing career came to an abrupt end after about 11 fights when his Dad learned about Lou's boxing matches.

After graduating from high school, he worked in several local stores in the Paterson area until 1927 when he asked his dad for permission to go to Hollywood. Finally, Lou's father, who was against Lou's attempting a Hollywood career gave in, and Lou was off to Los Angeles. Upon his arrival, he took up jobs such as laborer on the MGM and Warner movie sets awaiting, naturally, his "big break." It never came, and in 1928 he decided to return home for

schooling. En route, Lou picked up a part-time job as a comic in St. Joseph, a town in Missouri. After a year's experience, Lou left the Midwest and resumed his journey back home.

Upon arrival, Lou officially changed his last name to Costello. Still having to resort to taking on many odd jobs, Lou finally got his first break when a producer named Mat Fields hired him to be a rue comic in a show called *Take a Chance* at the Orpheum Theater in New York. The show ran for over a year, and Lou continued his quest for stardom by picking up bit roles wherever possible in the New York area.

Lou, who had continued to bounce around the vaudeville and burlesque circuits, worked on 42nd Street (Manhattan) and in Brooklyn. In 1931, he first became acquainted with Bud Abbott quite coincidentally. It appeared that Costello, who was working shows in Brooklyn, lost his partner to illness that day. Abbott, who was looking to get into show business and had repeatedly had unsuccessful attempts, got his big break when working as a cashier at a Brooklyn theater, was asked to substitute as Costello's straight-man partner. Abbott and Costello worked so well together that they teamed up permanently.

It was during this early part of their career that on one of his many side jobs Lou met and fell in love with Anne Battler who hailed from Providence, Rhode Island. She too was a bit player, and they married on January 30, 1934. On September 28, 1936, Lou and Anne became the proud parents of Patricia Ann. In the years that followed, Lou and Anne had a second child, Carol Lou, born on December 23, 1939, and a third child, Lou Costello, Jr., born on November 6, 1942.

Meanwhile, the Abbott and Costello

team grew, and a brilliant career was about to ensue. Before long, Abbott and Costello had audiences rolling in the aisles with their famous "mudder" routine and their legendary baseball routine "Who's on First" that have remained comic classics until this day. With tall and lean Abbott playing the straight-man and the short and pudgy Costello playing the funnyman, they worked their way up to becoming stars in vaudeville, burlesque, and night clubs. In 1938 they broke into radio becoming a huge success, and a year later they starred in a Broadway revue entitled *Streets of Paris*.

They had become big names in radio, vaudeville, burlesque theaters, night clubs, and now Broadway and were now ready to break into the film industry. Their first film *One Night in the Tropics* (1940) got little attention despite the team's popularity elsewhere in the media. Yet, just a year later, their second film *Buck Privates* (1941) grossed a whopping $10 million that had the effect of making them headliners on the silver screen in addition to their great success in radio.

The comedy team's career skyrocketed, especially during the late 40s and in the early 50s. By 1956, when they made their last movie together *Dance With Me Henry*, Lou and Bud had made more than 30 slapstick films in addition to their more recent TV show success series, which would go into reruns. The team had achieved top box-office attraction in films, well-known status in radio and then TV. In short, they had become household words akin to the fame of Laurel and Hardy.

They had done well as a team, and plenty of money had come into their respective lives as it had never come before. Yet Lou's life was not without its sad moments. In the middle of his blossoming film career, tragedy struck Lou when his son, Lou, Jr., two days shy of his first birthday, drowned in the family pool. Lou was devastated, and many remarked that he never really recovered from his son's death.

Once more tragedy struck on May 9,

1947 when Lou's Dad suffered a heart attack and died. Although Lou continued working his comic routines with Abbott after his son's death, Lou reportedly fell apart after the death of his father. A light came back into his life on August 15, 1947 when he became the father of another daughter, Chris, who would later write her father's popular biography: *Lou's on First*.

Lou continued his partnership with Bud Abbott for more than another decade, and they played their last engagement as a team in December 1956. Lou continued his career until February 1959 when suddenly he became ill. It was just before his fatal heart attack that Lou had appeared in a film entitled *The 30-Foot Bride of Candy Rock* (1959). He died on March 3, 1959, at the early age of 53. From humble beginnings, Costello was determined to perform and make people laugh, and he surely accomplished that. His humor was always wholesome, and the quality of his humor also seemed to reflect a certain innocence and clearly the efforts of a caring, gentle, and loving person.

General Sources:
1. Anobile, Richard J. *Who's on First?* New York: Darien House, 1973.
2. *Contemporary Theatre, Film and Television*. Detroit, MI: Gale Research, 1997.
3. Costello, Chris, and Raymond Strait. *Lou's on First: A Biography*. New York: St. Martin's Press, 1981.
4. Cox, Stephen, and John Lofflin. *The Official Abbott and Costello Scrapbook*. Chicago: Contemporary Books, 1990.
5. *Current Biography*. New York: Wilson, 1941.
6. Katz, Ephraim. *The Film Encyclopedia*. New York: Putnam, 1979.
7. Thomas, Bob. *Bud and Lou: The Abbott & Costello Story*. Philadelphia: Lippincott, 1977.

—by EDWARD MOTTOLA, Jr.

MARIO MATTHEW CUOMO (1932-)

When Democrat Lieutenant-Governor Mario Cuomo defeated Republican Lewis E. Lehrman on election day in 1982, he became in effect the fifty-second governor of New York State and the first Italian-American to have been elected to the highest office in the Empire State. He went on to serve twelve years as governor and has since become one of the most respected people in national politics. In the hearts and minds of many Americans, Cuomo has been and still remains the most desirable and viable candidate for the United States presidency.

Mario Cuomo was born on June 15, 1932, in Queens, New York. His father, Andrea, who had been born in Brooklyn, New York in 1901, returned to his parents' native Italy in 1904. Andrea met and then married Immaculata Giordano in Salerno (Italy), and he returned to the United States in 1926 with his wife where they raised four children. Mario's father dug ditches and was a pushcart vendor before the family finally opened a grocery store in 1931 in the height of the depression.

Mario was the third child and second of two sons. He and his siblings were raised in South Jamaica (Queens), which at that time was a melting pot of Polish, Italian, and Jewish immigrants, and blacks. Mario attended the local elementary and junior high schools and then St. John's Prep School. During his early years, Mario helped out in his parents' grocery store, but, whenever he could, he played baseball, his favorite sport.

It was while attending St. John's Prep that Mario was offered a minor league contract with the Pittsburgh Pirates. Mario's father objected to this move, seeing this as impacting negatively on Mario's brilliant scholastic records. Finally, it was only after Mario agreed to continue schooling while playing baseball that his father agreed to allow Mario to sign the contract. He received a $2,000 bonus for signing the agreement and was assigned to a Salisbury team in North Carolina in 1951.

The following year in 1952, Mario was assigned as a center fielder to the Brunswick team in Georgia. After receiving high marks for his batting and fielding, he was classified by the Pirate organization as a potential major league ball player. However, it was during the 1952 season that things started to go awry for Mario when he ran into an outfield wall severely injuring his wrists and later receiving a serious head injury from a wild pitch. Hospitalized for a month, he decided to leave baseball.

Mario continued his education attending St. John's University. He earned a B.A. in Latin American Studies and graduated *summa cum laude* in 1953. Mario married his sweetheart, Matilda Raffa, in June 1954 at St. John the Baptist Church in Brooklyn, New York. They had five children: Margaret, Andrew, Christopher, Madeline, and Maria. His wife, a school teacher, contributed significantly to their finances while Mario attended St. John's Law School. He graduated and tied for top class honors in 1956, and in the same year he was admitted to the New York State bar.

For two years he was confidential legal assistant to the Honorable Adrian P. Burke of the N.Y. State Court of Appeals. In 1958, Mario became affiliated with the private law firm of Corner, Weisbrod, Froeb & Charles in Brooklyn where he eventually became a partner in 1963 and he remained until 1975. At the same time, Mario also taught as an adjunct law professor at St. John's Law School from 1963 through 1973.

In the 1960s, Mario Cuomo had legally represented many community groups from Willett's Point and Corona, Queens. From one such predicament involving the proposal to build low-cost housing, Cuomo's commissioned report to Mayor John Lindsay regarding the problem eventually became a book, *Forest Hills Diary: The Crisis of Low-Income Housing in 1974.* The success of this book along with his active involvement in community issues eventually brought him much acknowledgment from the public.

With his growing interests in public service, in 1974 he announced his candidacy for the position of lieutenant-governor of New York State. While he was unsuccessful in the primaries, Governor Carey offered Cuomo the post of secretary of state in 1975. Cuomo accepted it; he resigned from his professorship and his legal partnership. Unlike many secretaries of state for whom that post was essentially a job entailing honorific duties, Cuomo actively pursued troubleshooting assignments statewide. He proved to be a fair but stern negotiator in land disputes, rent-strike movements, and most instrumental in bringing about sorely needed legal reforms in nursing home operations, lobbying protocols, real estate brokering, and blockbusting.

When Governor Carey asked Mario to become Chairman of the New York State Democratic Party in 1976, Mario turned down the offer because he was planning to run in the Democratic primary for mayor of New York City a year later that ended in defeat. In 1978, when Governor Carey, who was running poorly in public opinion polls, requested Mario to run as lieutenant-governor on his ticket, Cuomo accepted and was elected along with Governor Carey to a four-year term from 1979-82. In 1980, Cuomo pledged his leadership in running President Carter's election campaign in New York State, and in effect Cuomo became a delegate at the Democratic National Convention.

In January 1982 when Governor Carey announced he would not seek reelection, a bitter Democratic Party primary battle for the governor's office pitted Mario Cuomo against New York City Mayor Ed Koch. In a close match, Mario Cuomo became the Democratic candidate with 52% of the vote. Cuomo then defeated his Republican opponent, Lewis Lehrman, and on election day in 1982 he became New York's fifty-second governor. After he began his term in 1983, he remained governor for 12 years until 1995.

In 1984, perhaps Cuomo's finest hour, he was the keynote speaker at the 1984 Democratic National Convention where his steadily growing appeal as a nationwide figure grew even more. Considered by many as future presidential timber, he continued as governor and did not actively pursue a nomination at presidential primaries. After serving 12 years as governor, he lost his bid for a fourth term in 1995. Many citizens still feel his leadership role in politics has not ended. As a writer of many books and articles and as a recipient of many awards from both professional and civic groups, Cuomo has indeed achieved respect and admiration from all sectors of society, most notably for his inspiring leadership, his actively engaged and committed posture, his trustworthy personality, and his genuine concern for citizenry and community life.

General Sources:
1. Cuomo, Mario M. *Diaries of Mario M. Cuomo: The Campaign for Governor.* New York: Random House, 1984.
2. Cuomo, Mario M. *Forest Hills Diary: The Crisis of Low-Income Housing.* New York: Vintage Books, 1975.
3 *Current Biography Yearbook.* New York: Wilson, 1983.
4. McElvaine, Robert S. *Mario Cuomo, A Biography.* New York: Scribner's, 1988.
5. *Who's Who in America.* 1995 ed.

—by EDWARD MOTTOLA, Jr.

ALFONSE MARCELLO D'AMATO
(1937-   )

Having risen remarkably fast from the predominance of local politics to the level of national government and having overcome a strong opposition from the liberal Republican camp in the 1980 New York primary, Alfonse D'Amato became living proof as the newly-elected U.S. senator from the state of New York that the incipient 80s were indicating a decidedly clear shift to the right. As a Republican and an ultraconservative, originally emerging from a small suburban constituency, he established his reputation rapidly on many Senate committees as a hard-nosed pragmatist dedicated to hard work and detail, quite adept at the art of legislative maneuvering in Congress.

Born in Brooklyn, New York on August 1, 1937, Alfonse Marcello D'Amato was the oldest of three children of Armand Michael and Antoinette (nee Cioffari) D'Amato. In the mid-1940s his family moved to Island Park, a suburban community in Nassau County not far from Kennedy Airport. After attending a local elementary school, he attended Chaminade, a Roman Catholic high school in the town of Mineola (Nassau County) from which he graduated in 1955. He attended Syracuse University's College of Business Administration where he graduated in 1959. Remaining at the same institution, he went on to earn his J.D. degree in 1961 and was admitted to the New York State bar a year later.

He later reported having experienced ethnic discrimination first-hand when he had begun his initial search for employment at several New York City law firms. Assisted by a longtime family friend, Joseph Carlino, who happened to be a state assemblyman, D'Amato started practicing law and became active in Republican politics in the early 1960s. In retrospect, it now seems clear that he began his political career in 1964 when he was chosen a Republican Party committeeman for Island Park's representation.

D'Amato served as Nassau County public administrator from 1965 to 1968, the receiver of taxes for the town of Hempstead in 1969; Hempstead town supervisor from 1971 to 1977; and finally, from 1978 to 1981, presiding supervisor. His chief priorities as presiding supervisor included holding the line on expenses so that an already overtaxed town and county could look forward to no additional taxes. He accomplished this by a series of cost-cutting maneuvers including the attrition of four hundred positions, by downsizing the number of town commissions, and by decreasing fuel usage in town-related buildings.

As a harbinger of future nationwide change that would become more typically associated with the late 90s, D'Amato created—twenty years sooner—his own welfare reduction program in the late 70s which completely bypassed Nassau County's CETA program (Comprehensive Education and Training Act). His unique brand of training program proved to be far more effective since in a relatively short period of time the town of Hempstead was able to boast that it had taken 1,000 people off their welfare roles, trained them for jobs, and went on to place the former welfare recipients in meaningful positions.

D'Amato was more politically ambitious than he had let on to those around him. Most people thought he was simply interested in becoming the political leader of Nassau County. Yet even before D'Amato announced his decision to run in the 1980 Republican primary against Senator Jacob Javits, the four-term Republican incumbent from New York State, there were some politically astute observers who had viewed D'Amato as having political savvy and as having a good handle on timing. D'Amato had aptly seized upon his opportunity in sensing that the trend of the times was changing. Newly invigorated conservative attitudes were emerging in the Republican party. Javits, an avowed liberal, would now have to face great risk and become more vulnerable at the primary because of his liberal stance.

Despite the fact that D'Amato was a virtual unknown outside of the Long Island and New York City areas, the media and the campaign process became major players in generating the publicity that D'Amato sorely needed. It was a difficult primary where both contenders touched upon sensitive areas. Despite their vast ideological differences, the primary seemed to focus less on national issues and more on their personal backgrounds and personality. Javits focused on D'Amato's inexperience and ill-suited temperament while D'Amato concentrated on Javits' potentially severe health problems. In a sense, time proved D'Amato correct as he took 56.1 percent of the total vote and, perhaps, even more significantly, winning in every sector of New York State.

In the general election, D'Amato now faced his Democratic opponent Elizabeth Holtzman, a four-term veteran of the state House of Representatives. Unfortunately, this campaign proved more caustic than his primary with Javits. Holtzman capitalized on D'Amato's inexperience, his opposition to the E.R.A. and to abortion. D'Amato, by contrast, stressed Holtzman's ineffectual "Cadillac" welfarism, her multi-faceted neglect of middle class workers and small business people. The *Village Voice* published allegations of D'Amato's involvement in Nassau County's kickback schemes. Later cleared of all charges, the apparently negative publicity worked to his advantage in the form of a sympathy vote.

D'Amato won the election by a slim margin of 80,000 votes out of approximately six million votes cast. The nationwide general election in 1980 corroborated D'Amato's sense of change as Republicans took control of the Senate for the first time in twenty-five years. This political factor together with D'Amato's new friendship with Senator Howard Baker, Senate Majority Leader, offered D'Amato golden opportunities. He served on some key Senate committees including those on Banking, Housing and Urban Affairs, and Appropriations.

Sole author of the *Report on Earthquake Reconstruction in Italy* (1981), he co-authored two other major book-length reports published by Congress through the Government Printing Office: *Report on U.S. Presence in the Persian Gulf* (1988) and *U.S. Chemical and Biological Warfare-Related Dual Use of Exports to Iraq and Their Possible Impact on the Health Consequences of the Persian Gulf War* (1994). Having served dutifully as senator from New York State between 1981 and 1999 and known for his eighteen-hour workdays, he left office leaving behind a legacy of eighteen years of hard work and dedicated service for his constituents and his country.

General Sources:
1. *Congressional Directory*. 1998 ed.
2. *Current Biography Yearbook*. New York: Wilson, 1983.
3. D'Amato, Alfonse. *Power, Pasta & Politics: The World According to Senator Al D'Amato*. New York: Hyperion, 1995.
4. Tonev, Gavril. *Alfonse D'Amato— Senator Without a Toga*. Durham, NH: Sofia Press, 1985.
5. *Who's Who in America*. 1982-83 ed.

—by MARY JANE ADDONE

BOBBY DARIN (1936-1973)

Singer, songwriter, motion picture actor, nightclub and TV entertainer, he rose from the depths of poverty earning, first, the rock 'n' roll status of teenage idol, later the admiration of adult audiences, and finally two Grammys and an Oscar nomination for his supporting role in *Captain Newman, M.D.* (1963).

Walden Robert Cassotto, better known as Bobby Darin, was born, according to the most recently corrected and updated accounts, in the Bronx on May 14, 1936. Countering prior narratives of his life, the actual circumstances surrounding his birth appear to be somewhat unusual. Bobby's mother, Nina, was seventeen years old when she gave birth to him. He was born out of wedlock, and he never knew his natural father (Saverio Cassotto) whom Darin assumed as deceased. He was brought up thinking Nina (his seventeen year-old mother) was his older sister, and he grew up believing that his grandmother was his mother. Her name was Vivian Fern Walden Cassotto, and she coincidentally had been an entertainer in vaudeville prior to these events.

In May 1937, young Nina, now eighteen, met and fell in love with Charles Maffia, the second man in her life. He subsequently moved in with Nina, Vivian, and young Bobby. This union of the two lovers later resulted in the birth of Vivienne Carla Maffia, nicknamed Vee Vee; and so, Bobby, at a young age, was told he had become an uncle. In the same year, Bobby began his schooling at P.S. 43 in the Bronx. School officials wanted to place him in kindergarten, but Vivian, who had spent many days teaching him at home, demanded he be placed at least in first grade. Bobby was bright, and he proved Vivian's claims by correctly reading excerpts from a book. As school progressed, he exceeded the school's expectation by the end of the semester, and he was transferred from the first to the third grade.

Bobby enjoyed school and took a deep interest in school plays. He was chosen to play Santa Claus in the school Christmas pageant, but, strangely, he became ill on the day of the performance. He complained of pains in his joints and was running a high fever. He was diagnosed as having a serious case of rheumatic fever. Later the family doctor, Dr. Spindell, examined him and brought the family the tragic news that Bobby could only live possibly to 16 and at the very best until 21. It appeared that the only hope would be the advent of new drugs. Bobby suffered many more similar attacks between his eighth and twelfth birthdays. He took sulfa drugs on a daily basis and was always aware that death could come at any moment.

Through it all, Bobby entered the highly competitive Bronx High School of Science in 1948, and it was there where he became friends with four other fledgling musicians who decided to form a band. Bobby taught himself to play piano and the drums. The band played at many of the high school dances, and they wound up at a Catskills (New York) resort called the Sunnylands Hotel. Bobby started doing more and more singing, and this experience seemed pivotal in his deciding upon singing as a career.

In June 1952, Bobby graduated high school at 16 years of age. He enrolled as a theater arts major at Hunter College and later appeared in several of its college plays. He discovered that he liked acting in addition to singing. Yet, unhappy with the college scene, Bobby left college in 1953 and wanted to make it into show business on his own. After many small jobs, his life seemed to be going nowhere.

His success would not really begin until 1958 with his hit number, "Splish, Splash." It was during this relative lull in his now slow-moving career that he met Connie Francis, another young promising star, with whom he fell in love. Reportedly because of her father's strong objections, their marriage plans were scrapped and, so too, their relationship.

During one of his employment lulls, he decided to change his surname, and from a phone book, he simply selected "Darin." Then working closely with a new friend, Don Kirshner, he started writing and singing radio commercials. With money from this new-found opportunity, he invested in cutting two demos for Decca Records in 1956 which earned him a one-year contract. Despite the resulting exposure he received, such as singing with the Tommy Dorsey Orchestra on TV, his Decca Records proved unsuccessful and his contract with them expired.

In 1957, Atco Records, a subsidiary of Atlantic Records, offered him a one-year contract and eventually released in 1958 what would become his well-known "Splish Splash" that marked the beginning of his rise to stardom. Suddenly, Bobby's career went into high gear playing at the top clubs in New York and Hollywood, Atlantic City, and Las Vegas. He also became involved in film-acting, and while filming in Italy, he met his future wife, Sandra Dee whom he married on December 1, 1960. Making their home in Bel Air, California, they had a rocky two-career marriage exacerbated by Sandra's sense of loneliness. They had one child, named Dodd, and they later divorced in 1967.

After his 1957 success of "Splish Splash," Bobby had decided to finance the making of an album of old favorites entitled *That's All*. It became a highly successful album that had captured the attention of the adult population, his new target audience. Darin had cleverly accomplished this by writing his own unique arrangements. One such arrangement included a totally new version of Kurt Weill's "Mack the Knife" that later became his signature piece. Later in 1959, selling as a single, it sold over 2 million records, and it earned Bobby a Grammy for Best Single of the Year and another Grammy for Best New Performer.

Bobby's clever renditions of new and old songs became high in demand in nightclubs throughout the United States. He also continued appearing in Hollywood films in the 1960s and writing songs for some of those movies. In 1971 both his movie acting (appearing in over ten films) and singing engagements started to progressively diminish in frequency when the doctors discovered he had developed an irregular heart beat. In July 1973, he married Andrea Yeager who remained constantly at his side until his death several months later, on December 20 of the same year. An innovator in composing new renditions of older songs and no less an electrifying entertainer, Bobby Darin accomplished so much in so little time. One can only imagine what else he might have created.

General Sources:
1. Bleilel, Jeff. *That's All: Bobby Darin on Record, Stage & Screen.* Ann Arbor, MI: Popular Culture, 1993.
2. *Current Biography Yearbook.* New York: Wilson, 1963; 1974.
3. Darin, Dodd. *Dream Lovers: The Magnificent Shattered Lives of Bobby Darin and Sandra Dee.* New York: Warner Books, 1994.
4. Di Orio, Al. *Borrowed Time: The 37 Years of Bobby Darin.* Philadelphia: Running Press, 1998.
5. Katz, Ephraim. *The Film Encyclopedia.* New York: HarperCollins, 1998.
6. Larkin, Colin. *The Encyclopedia of Popular Music.* London, UK: MUZE UK Ltd, 1998.
7. *The New Grove Dictionary of American Music.* London: Macmillan, 1989.

—by EDWARD MOTTOLA, JR.

DENNIS DECONCINI (1937-   )

Despite the fact that he comes from the ultraconservative and Republican state of Arizona, Senator Dennis DeConcini has distinguished himself as a three-term Democrat who often found himself in conflict with the leadership principals of his own party. Essentially a conservative himself, he managed to thrive as a Democrat despite the existence and persistence of that indistinguishable area of anomalies between the political parties where textbook definitions usually serve little use. Being his own person, independent in his thinking, he typically bucked the common tendency of many senators to vote strictly by party lines.

Dennis Webster DeConcini was born on May 8, 1937 in Tucson, Arizona the son of Evo and Ora (nee Webster) DeConcini. He is one of four children. His father was a justice on the Arizona Supreme Court, and he also served as Arizona's state attorney general. His mother, also involved in politics, was a Democratic National Committeewoman from 1972 to 1980. His brother, Dino, also active in politics, was an aide to Arizona's Governor Raul H. Castro in the mid-1970s, and he himself ran for the Democratic gubernatorial nomination. His oldest brother, David, administers the family holdings in real estate.

Dennis DeConcini attended the public schools in Arizona, and after graduating from Tucson Senior High School in 1955, he attended the University of Arizona where received his B.A. in 1959 majoring in political science. He then joined the United States Army and became a second lieutenant. Discharged a year later in 1960, he would serve seven remaining years in the army reserves. While he worked in his father's law office, he studied towards his law

degree. After receiving his LL.B. in 1963, he was subsequently admitted to the state bar the same year. He continued as a researcher in his father's law office in Tucson.

In 1964 DeConcini served for two years as vice-chairman of the Arizona Democratic Committee from 1970 to 1972. He also became chief of staff for Arizona's Governor Samuel P. Goddard from 1965 to 1967. In 1975 he was named Arizona's Attorney of the Year after he had successfully prosecuted many high-profile criminals beginning in 1973. As a lawyer, his law-and-order approach, his tough stand on illicit drugs, and his decisively pro-consumer orientation gained him some national prominence.

In 1976 he entered the senatorial race as a Democrat hoping to take the seat of retiring Republican Senator Paul Fannin in Arizona, a staunchly conservative and Republican state, the land and abode of the late Barry Goldwater. In the Democratic primary he faced Carolyn Warner, and he went on to win by a wide margin. In the Republican primary, the principal members of the leadership feuded bitterly in choosing between the candidates in a troubling scenario. Sam Steiger, who is Jewish, eventually won the nomination beating John Conlan, an Evangelical Christian, who was viewed by many as having employed religious innuendo in the campaign.

In short, the acrimony caused within the Republican ranks did nothing to help its candidate as DeConcini went on to win the senatorial seat with a relatively strong 55-45 percent outcome. In 1972 DeConcini ran for a second term earning 59 percent of the vote and defeating Pete Dunn. Again in 1988, running for a third term, he defeated Keith DeGreen by capturing 57 percent of the vote. In all, DeConcini seemed to act as a positive and stabilizing force among the Democrats in Arizona's senatorial races as opposed to many of his Republican opponents, who often, lingering in the throes of intra-party confrontations and mutual accusations, emitted a negative message to the voting public.

Perhaps one of DeConcini's finest moments occurred in his first term in office in regard to the Panama Canal treaties. Dissatisfied with one of the major conditions in a treaty that involved relinquishing the Panama Canal by the year 2000 and at the same time deeming the canal to be a neutral area politically, DeConcini, whose senatorial vote President Jimmy Carter needed, insisted both in the Senate and with the President that changes be made to the language of the treaty.

This change in wording included the fact that the United States could intervene with military force—if necessary—whenever the operation and security of the canal were threatened. Despite some reluctance, President Carter eventually agreed to the wording demanded by DeConcini, and the entire treaty was approved on March 1978 by a vote of 68-32, only one vote more than the two-thirds majority required for the ratification of a treaty.

DeConcini was a member and, in some instances, chairman of many senatorial subcommittees including the Appropriations, Judiciary, Treasury, Defense, Constitution, Veterans Affairs, Indian Affairs, Intelligence; Energy and Water Development; Anti-trust, Monopolies, & Business Rights; and Patents, Copyrights & Trademarks. Again, as a senator who is difficult to categorize, especially since he crossed party lines on numerous occasions, he often held what has been called the "swing vote" in many situations in committee. Uniquely, he was one of the few Democrats who voted consistently for an amendment to the constitution in support of a balanced budget.

DeConcini, who had been against gun control legislation for years, sponsored a Senate bill which suspended for three years the manufacture and sale of semiautomatic assault rifles in 1990. Serving on the Senate Select Committee on Indian Affairs and after concluding its findings in a seventeen-month inquiry, DeConcini was one of the most vocal members in pointing out not only the federal government's negligence in monitoring Indian programs but also the abuses within Indian tribes themselves such as tribal leaders' corruption and the presence of organized crime in Indian gambling concessions, and a host of other criminal offenses.

As a senator who typically voted his conscience, he had such a remarkably squeaky-clean conservative record and reflected such total support of Reagan's anti-crime legislation that President Reagan considered appointing him as FBI director in 1987, which he declined. Despite some Congressional committee efforts at discrediting his track record after years of flawless public service, he endured accusations of malfeasance and survived unscathed in a 1989 investigation that involved a bank failure in California. DeConcini who had been a senator for eighteen years from 1977 to 1995 and who has since become a consultant, rightfully possesses in the eyes of most the image of an exceedingly independent thinker and incorruptible person.

General Sources:
1. *Almanac of American Politics*. 1990 ed.
2. *Congressional Directory*. 1995 ed.
3. *Current Biography Yearbook*. New York: Wilson, 1992.
4. *New York Times* 13 Apr. 1978: A10.
5. Radcliffe, Donnie. *Washington Post* 14 Apr. 1978: B1.
6. *Who's Who in America*. 1999 ed.
7. *Who's Who in American Politics*. 1997-1998 ed.

—by DENNIS PIASIO

JERRY DELLA FEMINA (1936-   )

During the height of the 1960s advertising revolution on Madison Avenue, Jerry Della Femina, who had previously started in the 1950s as an advertising messenger for the *New York Times*, became one of the legendary leaders in nationwide advertising. Convinced that he could do advertising copywriting by the insight and experience he had acquired as a messenger visiting department store copywriters, he worked at a series of jobs, and at the age of thirty-one in 1967 as the CEO of Della Femina, Travisano & Partners, his agency had billings totaling one-tenth of a billion dollars. In 1978 he was hailed as being among the top three advertising copywriters in the industry at the American Association of Advertising Agencies at it annual meeting.

Jerry Della Femina was born on July 22, 1936 in Brooklyn, New York to Michael and Concetta (nee Cossaro) Della Femina. It appears that from 1909 to 1939 the core members of the Della Femina family left their native village near the city of Naples, Italy and settled in the Gravesend section of Brooklyn, a forty-square-block area which at that time was predominantly immigrant Italian. Jerry's grandparents lived with his family in the same house where the adults spoke their native Neapolitan dialect as a matter of course. Consequently, Jerry spoke little or no English at home. At age six when he began elementary school, his English might be best described as that of a young immigrant having recently arrived from Italy.

He graduated from Lafayette High School in 1954, and although he hadn't selected a career for himself, his lackluster academic performance was more than compensated for by an adamant and relentless drive to succeed. His first job was that of an advertising messenger for the *New York Times* where his father, coincidentally, had been employed as a paper cutter for many years. His inspiration to focus on something where he could succeed occurred repeatedly whenever he would visit the offices of department store ad copywriters who did their work "sitting around with their feet propped up on desks." Animated by the kind of job where thinking creatively at a desk about advertisements could bring handsome rewards, he quickly enrolled at Brooklyn College to take one year of advertising courses.

Despite his stint at the *New York Times* and the experience of his college courses in advertising, he had a rather difficult six-year period of odd jobs (even an interval of unemployment) which, overall, lasted from 1955 to 1961. It was during this time frame that he also married his first wife, Barbara Rizzi with whom he had three children, Donna, Michael, and Jodi. Despite this series of dead-end jobs, he was very determined to obtain a position as an advertising copywriter. After being unemployed for some months, he chose the firm of Daniel & Charles as a likely taker for some ads he had developed. He sent these sample ads unsolicitedly and merely signed them J.D.F. His plan worked, and Jerry was overjoyed to get his first full-time job as an advertising copywriter. Out of work and eager to join the industry, this event became the major pivotal point in his entire career. "After that it was the easiest thing in the world," Jerry later related.

His first ads at Daniel & Charles were for Kayser-Roth, a well-known apparel company. In just a short time, Jerry had developed a reputation not only for his talents but also for his eccentricity, two qualities that actually go well together in a field that is focused on soliciting sales by capturing buyer attention. Two years later in 1963, he joined the firm of Fuller & Smith & Ross. Six months later he was made copy chief at Ashe & Anglemore and refused its vice presidency.

Finally, in 1964 he became creative director of the firm Delehanty, Kurnit and Geller (DKG). It was during his two and a half years at DKG that Della Femina performed the kind of quality work that earned awards, namely, his ads for Pretty Feet and Talon Zippers. He went on to win two Gold Key awards presented by Advertising Writers Association and two ANDYs from the Advertising Club of New York, each award reportedly worth $5,000 to $10,000. His many awards received while working at DKG and his many disputes with upper management where his ad outcomes often proved him correct in being on the money for his clients made him realize that he should open up his own agency.

Yet before realizing that desire he decided he still needed to understand how bigger agencies functioned, and so he decided to join Ted Bates Agency in 1966, a larger but more conservative firm. Earning $50,000 a year as a creative supervisor for Bates, he had proven himself to be from the start too provocative and outspoken. Upper management established new protocols that in effect were to control Della Femina from making remarks perceived as detrimental to the firm. In all, despite these facts, he was given the credit for turning around the faltering Panasonic account at Bates.

But in September 1967 Jerry took the risk to create his own firm along with Ron Travisano and two members from Bates. The firm Della Femina, Travisano & Partners finally became a reality. The growing pains as a new ad agency proved to be almost devastating at first. Yet Della Femina and his uncanny ways of attracting high visibility for his firm's creative talents not only survived the era of the 1960s with its proliferation of short-lived "hot shop"

agencies but also went on to become by 1970 a $100 million agency with offices in New York and Los Angeles.

The publication of his book, *From Those Wonderful Folks Who Gave You Pearl Harbor* (1970), remained controversial within the industry because of its insider revelations, but it brought in many new clients amounting to as much as $8 million in new revenue. In 1986 Jerry sold his agency and officially left it in June 1992. In the next six months, he opened two successful restaurants in the Hamptons (Long Island, New York) but quickly returned to the industry in December 1992 starting a new ad company simply called Jerry, Inc. In 1994 it merged with Ketchum Advertising, forming Jerry & Ketchum.

Jerry is now married to Judy Licht, a television news reporter, and they have two children, Jessie and James. Jerry has been involved on the boards of WNYC-TV, The Children's Aid Society, Citymeals-on-Wheels, and an ad industry initiative called Ads Against AIDS, and he has been cited by *The Wall Street Journal* as a "Creative Leader" since 1980.

General Sources:
1. *Current Biography Yearbook*. New York: Wilson, 1979.
2. Della Femina, Jerry. *An Italian Tree Grows in Brooklyn*. Boston: Little Brown, 1978.
3. Della Femina, Jerry. *From Those Wonderful Folks Who Gave You Pearl Harbor: Front-line Dispatches from the Advertising War*. New York: Simon & Schuster, 1970.
4. Fox, Stephen. *The Mirror Makers: A History of American Advertising*. New York: William Morrow, 1984.
5. Rothenberg, Randall. *Where the Suckers Moon*. New York: Vintage Books, 1994.
6. *Who's Who in America*. 1978-79 ed.

—by THERESA BRANCIFORTE

NORMAN DELLO JOIO (1913-   )

Pulitzer Prize-winning music composer, educator, and professor emeritus at Boston University, Norman Dello Joio has been for almost a half century one of the most recognized American figures in classical music composition. Having received his formal training at the Institute of Musical Art, the Juilliard School of Music, the Berkshire Music Center, and Yale University School of Music with Paul Hindemith, he excelled both as composer and teacher, winning many music awards from the different media. While working at Mannes College (1956-1972), he conceived and spearheaded a project whose program was funded by the Ford Foundation which encouraged aspiring musicians in high schools to compose classical music for school ensembles. When he became professor and dean of the School of Fine and Applied Arts at Boston University, he served as a nationwide model of music creativity and leadership.

Norman Dello Joio was born in New York City on January 24, 1913, the only child of Casimir (a turn-of-the-century immigrant) and Antoinette (nee Garramore) Dello Joio. A descendent of three generations of Italian organists, young Norman grew up with music all around him. His father Casimir was organist at New York City's Our Lady of Mount Carmel Church; and his godfather Pietro Yon was organist at St. Patrick's Cathedral. Norman began playing piano at an early age; then, after learning the organ, he had become so proficient by age fourteen that he was appointed organist and choir director at Star of the Sea Church on City Island.

He obtained his education attending All Hallows Institute (1926-1930) and then City College of New York (1932-1934). In his teens he enjoyed jazz sounds, and after belonging to several jazz bands, he had one of his own by age twenty. He began his formal full-time training in music at the Institute of Musical Art in 1936, and went on to earn an Elizabeth Sprague Coolidge Award for his *Piano Trio* (1937). Then on a fellowship he attended the Juilliard Graduate School of Music (1939-1941) where he studied composition.

He received another fellowship to attend the Berkshire Music Center in Tanglewood, Massachusetts where he studied composition under the guidance of Paul Hindemith who at the time was its resident composer. In 1942 Dello Joio received a Town Hall Composition Award for his orchestral work, *Magnificat*. Dello Joio then attended the Yale School of Music where Hindemith had relocated. After he received two Guggenheim fellowships in 1943 and 1944 and a grant from the American Academy of Arts and Letters in 1945, he pursued composition more actively.

Critics agree that despite the relatively brief training time that Dello Joio experienced with the renowned Hindemith, the latter's influence was to have a lifetime effect on the former. In addition to offering training to Dello Joio, Hindemith urged his student to develop his own "voice" and to write "naturally," eschewing established models if, in effect, they have little relevance to the temperament and experience of a composer. He suggested this as a key relationship to which he should adhere.

Dello Joio's likes consisted of a delightful combination including Catholic church music, 19th-century Italian opera, the popular music, and New York jazz sounds that prevailed during the 1920s and 1930s. In a sense, Dello Joio was already on his way to developing his own style with his 1942 *Magnificat*. As a musical genre, which has been ultimately based on literary precedents, the *Magnificat* was usually shaped as a kind of *crescendo* which thematically "magnified" the image of the Virgin Mary according to the readings in St. Luke's gospel.

After his studies with Hindemith and while continuing his composition of musical works in the latter part of the 1940s, Dello Joio also embarked on a new career, teaching college. He began as early as 1945 teaching music composition at Sarah Lawrence College near Bronxville, New York. His teaching presence, like that of his growing number of compositions, would blossom through the years.

In 1959, for instance, while teaching at Mannes College (1956-1972), he began a fourteen-year association with the Contemporary Music Project for Creativity in Music Education. There he established a nationwide program through the Ford Foundation's backing to encourage high school students to compose classical music. In 1972 he became professor of music and dean at Boston University where he directed its School of Fine and Applied Arts until 1978.

In regard to Dello Joio's creativity in music, his greatest initial efforts took off in the late 1940s. His *Variations, Chaccone and Finale*, first performed by the New York Philharmonic Orchestra under the direction of Bruno Walter, earned him a New York Music Critics Circle Award for Best Orchestral Work in 1948. Then in 1957, Dello Joio earned the prestigious Pulitzer Prize in music based on his *Meditations on Ecclesiastes* (1956) for string orchestra. Here, perhaps, the listener can best appreciate Dello Joio's unique synthesis of traditional Gregorian chant melodic elements and modern approaches. Fourteen years after he had received his first New York Music Critics Circle Award, he obtained a second one in 1962 for his opera, *The Triumph of St. Joan*.

Dello Joio who did not limit himself to the concert stage, also wrote extensively for television. Enjoying and exercising his delight in popular and jazz motifs in his orchestral works, he wrote one of the best known television musical scores for a program called *Air Power*, a twenty-two week series for CBS (1956-1957). Included in his works for television, his score for a program entitled *The Louvre* earned him an Emmy Award in 1965.

Norman Dello Joio has led an enormously creative life. A list of his works with requisite brief descriptions of them would take several pages to fill. While his works contain a richness of expression, he as a composer possesses a great versatility that is reflected in a variety of musical forms including stage orchestral, television scores, modern opera, chamber and instrumental, choral, and solo vocal. Aside Dello Joio's varied interests in traditionally-based religious musical motifs and their fusion with popular and jazz motifs, many critics have aptly described his style as a refreshingly unique blend of well-crafted and colorful music that is meaningful to the modern ear.

General Sources:
1. Bumgardner, Thomas A. *Norman Dello Joio*. Boston: Twayne, 1986.
2. *Current Biography Yearbook*. New York: Wilson, 1957.
3. Giordano, Joseph, ed. *The Italian-American Catalog*. Garden City, NY: Doubleday, 1986.
4. Jackson, Richard. "Norman Dello Joio." *The New Grove Dictionary of American Music*. Eds. H. Wiley Hitchcock and Stanley Sadie. New York: Macmillan, 1986.
5. Sadie, Stanley, ed. *The New Grove Dictionary of Music and Musicians*. Washington, DC: Grove's Dictionaries of Music, 1980.
6. *Who's Who in America*. 1998 ed.

—by FRANK SUSCA

DAVID DEL TREDICI (1937-   )

An unusually gifted contemporary classical composer, he has been hailed by many authorities in the field as a genius. Unlike many contemporary composers who have become heavily involved in atonal music (music which has little reference to traditional scales and melodies), Del Tredici has continued in the trajectory of the classical traditions (tonal music) producing many valuable creations in light of those traditions. Despite enjoying great success as a musical performer in his early days and winning many awards, he chose music composition as a career. After winning in 1959 the prestigious Woodrow Wilson Fellowship at Princeton University, he went on to earn a Pulitzer Prize in music composition in 1980.

David Del Tredici was born on March 16, 1937 in Cloverdale, California to Walter and Helen (nee Wegele) Del Tredici. Of Italian-German descent, he has often depicted himself kiddingly as "a freak in an unmusical family." He himself did not know of his own talents until he was 12 years old when he began taking piano lessons. He was so talented even for a beginner that he surpassed rather quickly the talents of his teachers at the Sisters of Holy Name.

At age seventeen, he went on to study piano with Bernhard Abramowitsch in 1954, and the music lessons with this maestro in Berkeley, California lasted until 1960. Del Tredici's interests focused on the romantic era and particularly on the works of Robert Schumann (1810-1856). Despite his rather late start in music, it seems that to whatever he was introduced he learned quickly and well. During that period of time where he studied with Abramowitsch, he precociously started giving recitals in various cities including San Francisco with its symphony orchestra. He gave his recital debut at age seventeen, the very same year in which he started studying with Abramowitsch. Subsequently appearing with many other symphonic orchestras nationwide and three more appearances with the San Francisco Symphony, he won in 1955 the Kimber Award, one of the most prestigious awards given to pianists at that time.

Graduating as a Phi Beta Kappa student, he earned his B.A. from the University of California at Berkeley in 1959. Later he pursued graduate work as a Woodrow Wilson Fellow at Princeton University where he eventually received his M.F.A. in music composition in 1964. Unhappy with Princeton's music faculty who were very much invested in modern atonal music, Del Tredici took a release from the program to study piano with Robert Helps in New York City. Returning to Princeton in 1963, he completed his work to earn a M.F.A. degree in music one year later.

In his years at Princeton University and in the subsequent years following that academic experience, he was—more than anything else— a composer in search of his own unique style. It was a period of discovery for him, and while he naturally preferred allying his efforts to composing tonal music, he did experiment limitedly in the composition of atonal music. Most of that experience had been made mandatory by virtue of the kind of music composition being taught by the Princeton faculty.

In retrospect, according to many music critics, when Del Tredici's early compositions are examined closely, they clearly belie any real attempt at atonality and, if anything, reflect his aversion to it. In fact, Del Tredici himself euphemistically used to refer to those early student works as "impressionistic." And it was during that period of transition and experimentation, overlapping his studies at Princeton University, that Del Tredici became attracted to the literary figure of James Joyce. Del Tredici seemed to identify with Joyce's inner journey and, among other things, the common predicament of being a "troubled, lapsed" introspective Catholic. Many Joycean poems during that six-year phase became the starting point for Del Tredici's musical compositions such as "I Hear an Army" (1964) based on Joyce's poem of the same title.

After tiring of the Joycean themes in 1967, Del Tredici began experimenting some more, but this time with a soprano and rock group music. He wrote a composition entitled *The Last Gospel*, based on St. John's gospel. Here he made an attempt at basing what affects the sounds and rhythms of the words might directly have on the musical composition. This experience led him to explore a newly-found intrigue with the "energy" which words could possess for a music composer, and this brought him to his second major phase involving his attraction to literature and how its words might become a starting point for the music composer.

This time it was Lewis Carroll (1832-1898) and, indeed, his *Alice's Adventures in Wonderland* (1865) and *Through the Looking-Glass and What Alice Found There* (1872), both of which constituted a creative mingling of fantasy and satirical observations. This world of fantasy and satire, which he had known as a child, now offered him the context and opportunity to fully return to the classical romantic notions of music and helped him develop his own neo-romantic style utilizing all those things he had learned when he had studied atonal music.

The thematics of this Alicean world would keep him composing music for the next 30 years, and in that light, he received numerous commissions along the way. He wrote most of his best works in this area, including *An Alice Symphony* (1969), *Final Alice* (1976), and *Child Alice* (1977-81).

Del Tredici has received many awards and honors in his lifetime. In addition to having earned a prestigious Pulitzer Prize (1980) for his composition "In Memory of a Summer Day," he also possesses to his credit a Woodrow Wilson Fellowship (1959), a Hertz Award (1962), a Guggenheim Fellowship (1966), election to membership in the American Academy of Arts and Letters (1968), the Naumbergh Recording Award (1972), a Creative Arts Award from Brandeis University (1973), and a Friedheim Award (1982).

He has taught music and music composition at many universities such as Harvard and Boston Universities, and is presently titled Distinguished Professor of Music at the City College of New York and a faculty member of the Juillard School of Music. His most recent composition *The Spider and the Fly*, a 30-minute work for voice (soprano, baritone) and orchestra, representing a kind of thematic conclusion to his many works inspired by *Alice in Wonderland*, was commissioned by the New York Philharmonic and enjoyed a successful premiere in May 1998.

General Sources:
1. *Current Biography Yearbook*. New York: Wilson, 1983.
2. Del Tredici, David. *David Del Tredici, the "Alice in Wonderland" Series (1968-1981)*. New York: Bossey & Hawkes, 1982.
3. Sadie, Stanley, ed. *The New Grove Dictionary of Music and Musicians*. Washington, DC: Grove's Dictionaries of Music, 1980.
4. Slonimsky, Nicolas. *Baker's Biographical Dictionary of Musicians*. 8th ed. New York: Macmillan, 1992.
5. *Who's Who in America*. 1995 ed.

—by MARY JANE ADDONE

ROBERT DE NIRO (1943-   )

Recipient of two Oscars, one for Best Supporting Actor in 1974 for *The Godfather, Part II* and another for Best Actor in 1980 for *Raging Bull*, and co-recipient of the Best Actor Award at the Venice Film Festival in 1981 for *True Confessions*, Robert De Niro may be most appropriately called the man of a thousand faces, transforming himself into each persona that he so credibly portrays. In his latest film, *Analyze This*, this long-time actor's hilarious comedic performance as a mobster plagued by panic (anxiety) attacks, which lead him, at first reluctantly, to demand therapy from an uncooperative psychiatrist reminds us once again of the incredible range of characters he has successfully depicted.

He is recognized particularly for the uncanny ability of acting any type of person from different eras and genres: a saxophone player in *New York, New York*, an enigmatic and heroic Green Beret returning from the Vietnam War in *The Deer Hunter*, a professional boxer (based on the life of Jake La Motta) in *Raging Bull*, an ambitious priest in *True Confessions*, a frustrated comedian in the *King of Comedy*, a reflective gangster in *Once Upon A Time In America*, a future plumber in *Brazil*, a former violent Christian follower in *The Mission*, Al Capone in *The Untouchables*, an obsessed but kind-hearted bounty hunter in *Midnight Run*, a small time mobster in *Good Fellows*, a psychotic patient in *Awakenings*, a fire detective in *Backdraft*, a bad tempered husband in *This Boy's Life*, an insecure cop in *Mad Dog and Glory*, a local bus driver and father in *Bronx Tale*, a gambling casino owner in *Casino*, a psychopathic ex-con in *Cape Fear*, a fanatical baseball lover in *The Fan*, and a perfect thief in *Heat*.

These are just a few of the roles that well illustrate his versatile talents that have led many in and outside of the movie industry to characterize him as the leading actor of his generation. In more than fifty films to date, De Niro has clearly demonstrated that he is equally adept at playing unambiguously evil characters as he is at portraying passive figures. As one biographer notes: "He totally inhabits each character he assumes, and as a result, he is impenetrable to the media and even to his costars." He is a consummate artist, an actor's actor.

Robert De Niro, Jr., was born on August 17, 1943 into a family of artists. His father Robert De Niro, Sr., was a Greenwich Village abstract expressionist painter as well as a sculptor and poet. His mother, Virginia Admiral, also a painter, has been quoted as attributing her son's secret to success to simply a "force of will." In 1946 his parents separated, apparently amicably, with their only child Robert remaining with his mother. To make a living she started a typing and proofreading service. Despite the separation, the son and father maintained regular contact with one another throughout Robert's growing years, and they often attended movies together.

While growing up in his Little Italy neighborhood he was known by the nickname "Bobby Milk," due to his scrawniness and skin pallor. As a youngster he was shy and taciturn, and he eventually overcame this timidity when he began to hang out on the streets as a member of a small-time gang. Fortunately, the acting bug took hold early on so that at age ten he had his first acting role—the cowardly lion in *The Wizard of Oz* staged at Public School 41. This was followed by his first paid acting job at age sixteen (the year he dropped out of school) with a touring company in Chekhov's *The Bear*.

For the next fifteen years he sharpened his skills through performances in dinner theater and in Off-Broadway productions. Along the way, he studied drama with Stella Adler at the Dramatic Workshop and with Lee Strasberg at the Actors Studio, where many aspiring stars learned the famous Method acting. When asked what attracted him to acting, he is reported to have said it gave one the opportunity "to totally submerge into another character...to do things you would never dare to do yourself."

De Niro's movie career was launched in the early 1960s with a series of films directed by Brian De Palma—*The Wedding* (1967), *Greetings* (1968), and *Hi Mom!* (1970). These went relatively unnoticed, but in 1973, his portrayal of a dying baseball player in *Bang the Drum Slowly* brought him the New York Critics Award for Best Actor, and his star began to shine. In the same year, De Niro appeared as a psychotic gangster in Martin Scorsese's *Mean Streets*, and that was the beginning of a longtime collaboration that thus far has produced eight films. They discovered to their delight that they had grown up in the same neighborhood.

It is generally acknowledged that De Niro achieved superstar status with his superb performance as the young Vito Corleone in Francis Ford Coppola's *The Godfather Part II* (1974). His understated portrayal of the early adult years of the Godfather "was a masterpiece of nuanced gestures, glances, and speech patterns that captured the pride and inner reserve of Brando's mature 'Godfather.'" In preparing for this role he spent much time mastering the Sicilian dialect while he visited Sicily. That portrayal brought him an Oscar for Best Supporting Actor and, in the eyes of many, nailed down his reputation as the next Marlon Brando.

Before embarking upon a film, De Niro usually studies the characterization of the persona, real or fictional. In the case of *Raging Bull*, after gaining sixty pounds to play the role of aging boxer Jake La Motta, De Niro also spent an entire year "training and boxing with him, studying him and film footage of his bouts, and recording conversations with him." Throughout his career De Niro carefully tried to avoid being typecast as an ethnic, and he has obviously succeeded since both movie viewers and critical reviewers consistently marvel at his capacity to "climb into the skin of assorted unsavories better than anyone," and on the other hand his "equal facility at playing kinder, gentler characters."

As we head toward the millennium, Robert De Niro will accompany us into a new century as one of the most gifted actors of our times. There are still many more exciting movies and characters to look forward to as this well-known Italian American continues to entertain and enlighten us on the big screen.

General Sources:

1. Agan, Patrick. *Robert De Niro: The Man, the Myth, and the Movies*. London: R. Hale, 1996.

2. Brode, Douglas. *The Films of Robert De Niro*. Secaucus, NJ: Carol Pub. Group, 1996.

3. *Current Biography Yearbook*. New York: Wilson, 1993.

4. Dougan, Andy. *Untouchable: A Biography of Robert De Niro*. New York: Thunder's Mouth Press, 1996.

5. McKay, Keith. *Robert De Niro, the Hero Behind the Masks*. New York: St. Martin's Press, 1986.

6. Powell, Elfreda. *Robert De Niro*. Philadelphia: Chelsea House, 1997.

7. Ragan, David. *Who's Who in Hollywood: The Largest Cast of International Film Personalities Ever Assembled*. New York: Facts on File, 1992.

—by FELIX M. BERARDO, Ph.D.

BRIAN DE PALMA (1940-   )

Universally accepted nowadays as the movie director most closely following the footsteps of Alfred Hitchcock, Brian De Palma has explored—with pioneering efforts—a greater technical usage of the movie camera, special effects, and his own brand of film editing. Very much a man who marches to the beat of his own drum, he had gone beyond Hitchcock and is presently considered by many film critics the master of the psychological thriller and has been dubbed a genius especially in a particular area of filmmaking referred to by technical critics as "rhythmic editing." He is especially noted for his terrifying film openings that compel instant and sustained viewer attention.

Psychological thrillers represent a growing segment of the movie continuum, and De Palma has surely become the master of his craft not only as director but also as screenwriter. His career of over 30 years and of almost 25 films, which include such movies as *Mission Impossible* (1996), *Carrie* (1976), and *Sisters* (1973), attest both to his knowledge of the growing complexities and demands of the subject matter and to his technical expertise in the almost obligatory maximization of visual effects inextricably involved in the realm of making movie thrillers.

Brian Russell De Palma was born in Newark, New Jersey on September 11, 1940 but was raised in Philadelphia. He was the youngest of three sons of Dr. Anthony Frederick De Palma and Vivienne (nee Muti) De Palma. His father, an orthopedic surgeon, was in part responsible for availing Brian opportunities to learn about surgery and to have access to the scientific aspects of the human body. Brian apparently did develop an interest in body workings and its structures—not to mention a fascination with its possible pulsating gore.

Although both parents came from Italian Roman Catholic backgrounds, he was raised in the Presbyterian faith; yet, for his movies, he admits to regularly relying upon Catholicism's visually rich repertoire of images and iconography that he found mysterious and sometimes terrifying. Gifted in the sciences, he built his own computer and competed in nationwide science contests during his high school years. During summer vacations he often worked part-time in a hospital particularly in settings that allowed him to frequently observe surgical procedures and operations.

After graduation, he enrolled at Columbia University intending to major in physics, his forte, but while attending there, he joined the Columbia players because of his growing interest in drama. It was during this time frame that he concedes to having become obsessed by movies, particularly by those Hitchcock and Polanski thrillers and by Godard's films which exuded experimental and non-traditional camera techniques such as using a hand-held camera for moving shots and innovative restructuring of film sequences done essentially for visual effect with spontaneous and often impulsive rhythms.

With a hand-held 16 mm Bolex camera he started making film shorts: first, *Icarus* (1960); then *660124: The Story of an IBM Card* (1961); and finally, *Wotan's Wake* (1962). He graduated from Columbia with a major in fine arts and a minor in physics. Based primarily on his third film short, he won several awards including an MCA writing fellowship to Sarah Lawrence College which allowed him to obtain an M.A. degree in 1964.

After graduation he earned a living doing

documentary and promotional films for organizations such as the NAACP, the Museum of Modern Art, and other business and cultural institutions. On a shoestring, De Palma had been working all along on making his first full-length film, *The Wedding Party* (1966) with the help of Sarah Lawrence faculty and student assistants. While produced in 1966, it was not released until 1969.

Similarly, on a shoestring, he made his second feature film *Murder à la Mode* (1967) where he successfully experimented in depicting a murder event viewed from three rather different points of view, each one supported by a correspondingly different cinematographic technique. Although it was his second full-length film, it became his first to be released. His third full-length, low-budget film, *Greetings* (1968), an anarchic and often satirical look at 60s social phenomena, went on to win the Silver Bear Prize in the 1969 Berlin Film Festival. De Palma became, in part, responsible for introducing Robert De Niro to the silver screen in this film. De Niro had only had a bit part in a 1965 French movie, *Trois Chambres à Manhattan*.

After doing some other films such as *Dionysus in '69* (1969), *Hi Mom!* (1970), and *Get to Know Your Rabbit* (1972), De Palma completed the first major phase of his development whose themes of satire and off-beat comedy bore the marks of many different influences. With the making of *Sisters* (1973), however, he initiated a recognizably Hitchcockian phase where, while borrowing openly from Hitchcock's thematic structures and techniques, he went well beyond the ostensibly didactic foundations to create a style of his own.

While *Sisters* (1973), *Phantom of the Paradise* (1974), and *Obsession* (1976) were only modest commercial successes, *Carrie* (1976) based on Stephen King's best-selling horror novel, featuring Sissy Spacek in the title movie role, became a top money maker. Based on a low-budget ($1.6 million) investment, the movie became a box-office smash hit, which fully established De Palma as a leading director whose experiments with film shorts begun in the early 1960s paid off.

While enjoying the vigorous pace of making almost a movie a year, De Palma took time off to teach an undergraduate filmmaking course gratis at Sarah Lawrence in gratitude for the opportunity and fellowship he had received at that school. His more recent movies include: *The Fury* (1978), *Home Movies* (1979), *Dressed to Kill* (1980), *Blow Out* (1981), *Scarface* (1983), *Body Double* (1984), *Wise Guys* (1986), *The Untouchables* (1987), *Casualties of War* (1989), *The Bonfire of the Vanities* (1990), *Raising Cain* (1992), *Carlito's Way* (1993), *Mission Impossible* (1996), *Snake Eyes* (1998).

As a director and writer who takes risks, De Palma has earned his way to the top of his field as the leader of the psychological thriller. On occasion, De Palma has been enviously referred to as a "movie brat," that is, someone who has learned the craft of filmmaking on one's own essentially outside of the mainstream of the film industry. That may explain, in part, some of the reasons why he has become one of the industry's dominant directors, ready to experiment and try out new ideas and avail himself of his scientific and technical background.

General Sources:
1.   Andrew, Geoff. *The Film Handbook.* Boston: G.H. Hall, 1989.
2.   Bliss, Michael. *Brian De Palma.* Metuchen, NJ: Scarecrow Press, 1983.
3.   *Current Biography Yearbook.* New York: Wilson, 1982.
4.   Gandini, Leonardo. *Brian De Palma.* Roma: Gremese, 1996.
5.   Katz, Ephraim. *The Film Encyclopedia.* New York: HarperCollins, 1998.
6.   *Who's Who in America.* 1998 ed.

—by THERESA BRANCIFORTE

BERNARD DE VOTO (1897-1955)

A noted columnist for *Harper's Magazine,* a popular professor at Northwestern and Harvard Universities, and famed trilogist on the theme of the American West, he won the 1948 Pulitzer Prize for nonfiction: *Across the Wide Missouri*, published in 1947. As a World War I army lieutenant, history scholar, literary critic, editor, journalist, novelist, educator, and conservationist, De Voto's life story represents an engaging amalgam of interests and experiences—not to mention his unusual family background that included having an apostate Catholic father of Italian origin and an apostate Mormon mother whose family members had been pioneers in the Mormon faith movement.

Bernard De Voto was born on January 11, 1897 in Ogden, Utah. His father, Florian Bernard De Voto, had come to Utah where he taught mathematics, ostensibly working for the Catholic church. He met and married Rhoda Dye, the daughter of a Mormon pioneer family. From young Bernard's genealogy, it appears that his paternal grandfather had been a Piedmontese cavalry officer; and reportedly, it seems that after he had married a Roman aristocratic woman, he decided that his marriage would be best served by simply moving to America.

Young Bernard's education began at a convent school, Sacred Heart Academy. Then, switching to the public school system, he eventually graduated from Ogden High School in 1914. He had quickly taken to writing in his teens as he did reporting for the *Ogden Evening Standard* registering events for the community calendar. In his teenage years, he had also taken an avid interest in exploring the foothills and canyons, scaling the peaks of the surrounding mountainous regions. He and his friends often did primitive camping without the benefit of tents and other basic amenities.

He attended the University of Utah for one year and then switched schools enrolling at Harvard University which would prove to be a different setting for him not only geographically but also socially and intellectually. At the University of Utah he had been an active student, organizing a collegiate chapter of the Socialist Society. However, after the University of Utah had dissolved his socialist chapter and had dismissed four faculty members for having similar "socialist" notions, De Voto decided that he would leave Utah and attend Harvard.

Despite his pacifist ideals toward the "Great War" proceeding in Europe, he did enlist in the Army and was commissioned a lieutenant in the infantry where he remained for two years as an Army instructor in the United States for the duration of the war. Resuming his college education at the war's conclusion, he graduated from Harvard University in 1920 as a Phi Beta Kappa student. The degree itself was "pre-dated 1918" to reflect the interruption of the war.

In an apparent contradiction to the ugly remembrance of the "socialist" episode back at the University of Utah, he decided to move back west. But motivated as he was to write a challenging trilogy tracking the historical developments of Northern Utah, he took two years to do research in specific geographic areas of the west during which time he also worked as a history teacher in Ogden Junior High School for one year.

In 1922 he again left Utah and accepted an instructorship to teach English and creative writing at Northwestern University in Evanston, Illinois where he would teach until 1927. There he met his future wife, Helen Avis MacVicar, one of his first-year students. Within the span of four years, he published three novels: *The Crooked Mile* (1924), *The Chariot of Fire* (1926), and *The House of Sun-Goes-Down* (1928). In addition to these novels, he also sold many of his articles to established magazines such as *Harper's*, *Saturday Evening Post*, and *American Mercury*.

Despite receiving an assistant professorship at Northwestern in 1927, he returned once more to the New England area in Cambridge, Massachusetts where he had easy access to the Harvard Library. His goal was to continue doing research for his writings without the pressures of teaching. Without a teaching job, he earned a living writing light fiction for magazines. In 1929, Harvard University, his *alma mater*, hired him to teach, and he would remain in that capacity until 1936.

Influenced by the writings of the Italian sociologist Vilfredo Pareto (1848-1923), De Voto sought to find tangible connections between environment and literary creativity. Taking this social historian perspective as applied to literature, De Voto produced *Mark Twain's America* (1932) to correct errors and badly framed generalizations about the American frontier and its people in Van Wyck Brooks' book *The Ordeal of Mark Twain* (1920). De Voto was the first in the U.S. to employ the methods of social history to resolve literary problems. Then, in 1934 De Voto published what became a highly discussed novel, *We Accept with Pleasure*. It treated the theme involving young Midwesterners who with high expectations for positive change take off for post-WWI Boston and become severely disappointed with the New England area.

While serving briefly as editor for the *Saturday Review of Literature* from 1936-1938, it was his 1935 acceptance of the position of editor of the "Easy Chair" column in *Harper's* magazine for which De Voto would best be remembered. It was a position he kept for the rest of his life, and it served him as an influential conduit for introducing fresh ideas to its wide and highly educated reading audience.

De Voto went on to fulfill his youthful dream to complete his historical trilogy dealing with Western expansion and growth: *The Year of Decision: 1846* (1942); *Across the Wide Missouri* (1947), which earned him both the Pulitzer Prize for nonfiction and the Bancroft Prize; and *The Course of the Empire* (1952), which earned him the National Book Award. He also topped his many literary achievements by editing *The Journals of Lewis and Clark* (1953). Typical of his style, his interest in literature became intimately involved with the importance that he attributed to understanding history, and that remains as one of his trademarks. It may very well be that his concern for social improvement and his curiosity in understanding people as social beings became thematic qualities that permeated all his works.

General Sources:
1. "Bernard De Voto." *Dictionary of Literary Biography*. Ed. James J. Martine. Detroit, MI: Gale Research, 1981.
2. *Current Biography/Yearbook*. New York: Wilson, 1943; 1956.
3. De Voto, Bernard. *Mark Twain's America*. Boston: Little Brown, 1932.
4. De Voto, Bernard, ed. *The Journals of Lewis and Clark*. Boston: Houghton Mifflin, 1953.
5. "Obituary." *New York Times* 14 Nov. 1955: 1.
6. Sawey, Orlan. *Bernard De Voto*. New York: Twayne, 1969.
7. Stegner, Wallace, ed. *The Letters of Bernard De Voto*. Garden City, NY: Doubleday, 1975.
8. Stegner, Wallace. *The Uneasy Chair: A Biography of Bernard De Voto*. Garden City, NY: Doubleday, 1974.
9. *Who's Who in America*. 1954-1955 ed.

—by SAM PITTARO

PIETRO DI DONATO (1911-1992)

With the publication of his highly autobiographical novel, *Christ in Concrete,* in 1939, Pietro Di Donato produced the first undisputed literary masterpiece inspired by the Italian American experience, and in a sense he became the "grandfather of Italian American letters." Paulie, Pietro Di Donato's persona and principal character of the novel, is a twelve-year-old son of a bricklayer who must shoulder the responsibility of supporting his mother and seven younger brothers and sisters after his father is killed by the collapse of a building at a construction site. Despite the intensity of the immigrant context, the novel has been viewed by critics as a most original and universal work well within the American experimental literary traditions.

Pietro Di Donato, the eldest of eight children, was born on April 13, 1911 in the tenement district of West Hoboken, New Jersey. His parents, Domenic and Annunziata (nee Cinquina) Di Donato, were emigrants from the same town in Abruzzi. Like many of his townsmen who had immigrated to America, Domenic worked as a bricklayer and eventually became a master mason. On Good Friday 1923, the thirty-six-year-old mason met with a fatal accident. The scaffolding at his construction site collapsed, and he plummeted to his death into a pool of stone and mortar. It would become Pietro's lifetime belief that his father's death occurred because of faulty materials used by the builders to save money.

Annunziata was pregnant with her eighth child when her husband died, and twelve-year-old Pietro had to help support a family of nine by becoming a part-time bricklayer himself through the intervention of his father's friends. After spending only a few days in the ninth grade, he quit daytime high school and continued his studies at night. Nine years later, when his mother died of cancer in 1932, he, as head of household, moved his brothers and sisters to Northport, Long Island. It was at this point in his life that his writing career began.

The premature death of both his parents together with the ongoing struggle to manage a large family were traumatic to young Di Donato. To a considerable degree, the struggles must have triggered his creative energies and shaped many of his political, social, and religious views. Di Donato, who was a voracious reader and frequented the Northport library, studied Zola, Melville, and the Russian masters of the nineteenth century. When a friend showed him a play by Clifford Odets, Di Donato thought he (Di Donato) could write a lot better if he were to put on paper his father's love for life who "only wanted to live and work for his family, and was deprived of that."

The short story that evolved from his impromptu reaction and challenge to himself was published in *Esquire* in March 1937. It met with such success that various publishers each scrambled in an effort to recruit Di Donato into turning it into a novel, which is what Di Donato ultimately did for Bobbs-Merrill in 1939. His novel, *Christ in Concrete,* turned out to be a success and was chosen by the Book-of-the-Month Club as the main selection over Steinbeck's *Grapes of Wrath.* *Christ in Concrete* soon became a quasi "sacred text" for Italian-American letters. It was noted for having vividly chronicled the life of first and second generation Italian Americans during the first two decades of the twentieth century. Through his fictional protagonist, Di Donato offers a realistic and unflinching portrait of his growing up in such a unique and challenging era for Italian immigrants.

At the same time, he portrays in poignant terms the values that his characters placed on family life and on the generosity of neighboring families as together they struggled to survive in what was perceived as a foreign land. On another level, his narrative may also be viewed as social protest in an indictment of the turn-of-the-century American capitalist experience where workers' lives were expendable and working conditions neglectful and often dangerous. As a person who lived his life with intensity and feeling and acted upon his beliefs, Di Donato had joined the Communist Party as protest in his emotional reaction to the American court system's unjust execution of Sacco and Vanzetti in August of 1927. In all, the great popularity of his 1939 novel set the conditions for its being made into a 1949 movie, *Give Us This Day*, directed by Edward Dmytryk.

Di Donato, who went on to write many articles of a literary and political nature, wrote two more novels and two biographies of religious personages. His second novel, *This Woman* (1959), is a narrative that deals with the world of sexual obsession and the struggle between earthly seduction and ideals. Filled with realistic sexual detail, it becomes an allegorical account, suggestive of political, social, and economic dialectics. Di Donato's third novel, *Three Circles of Light* (1960), is a return to the turn-of-the-century immigrant world of Italians. While the narrative deals with the overt dialectic between the loyal wife and the adulterous husband, its themes run into questions of traditional organized religion and the depths of "folk religion" whose perennial substratum of values transcend the present. Di Donato also did two biographical studies: *Immigrant Saint: The Life of Mother Cabrini* (1960), and *The Penitent* (1962), the life of Saint Maria Goretti.

In order to raise money to help out a publisher friend of his, Di Donato published an anthology of short stories and other writings under the title *Naked Author* (1970). This constituted his last narrative work, but he continued to write articles for a number of magazines. One such article for was for *Penthouse* (October 1977) where he wrote about Aldo Moro, Italy's President, who had been recently kidnapped and would be murdered by Italian terrorists. The article entitled "Christ in Plastic" won the Overseas Press Club Award in 1978.

Predeceased by his wife in a marriage of more than forty years, Pietro Di Donato died in Long Island, New York on January 19, 1992 at the age of eighty. Autodidactic in many respects, he was a novelist, playwright, biographer, and critic whose life experience spanned just about an entire century. He leaves a proud legacy in his writing *Christ in Concrete*, a brilliant depiction of an essential immigrant experience in a narrative medium for all peoples to enjoy and appreciate.

General Sources:
1. D'Acierno, Pellegrino, ed. *The Italian American Heritage: A Companion to Literature and Arts*. New York: Garland Publ., 1999.
2. Diomede, Matthew. *Pietro Di Donato, the Master Builder*. Lewisburg, PA: Bucknell University Press, 1995.
3. Gardaphé, Fred. *Italian Signs, American Streets: The Evolution of Italian American Narrative*. Durham, NC: Duke U.P., 1996.
4. Green, Rose Basile. "Pietro Di Donato." *Dictionary of Literary Biography*. Detroit, MI: Gale Research, 1981.
5. Locher, Frances C., ed. *Contemporary Authors*. Detroit, MI: Gale Research, 1981.
6. Napolitano, Louise. *An American Story: Pietro Di Donato's Christ in Concrete*. New York: Peter Lang, 1995.

—by FRANK DI TROLIO

JOE DIMAGGIO (1914-1999)

Joseph Paul DiMaggio, born on November 25, 1914 in Martinez, California would become one of the biggest baseball legends. His name would appear both in song and in writing as a touchstone for greatness in sports. Known as "The Yankee Clipper," he also answered to the name "Joltin' Joe DiMaggio." His friends and fellow baseball players universally acclaimed him not only great at his game but also loyal, humble, and a loving human being in his personal life.

Born of modest means, Joe was the eighth of nine children. His father, Giuseppe, a fisherman, and his mother, Rosalie (nee Mercurio), were of Sicilian heritage. As a youngster, Joe sold newspapers to help out his family. They lived in the North Beach section of San Francisco. Two of Joe's brothers, Vince and Dom, also played in major league baseball. Joe, who was interested in baseball, looked up to Vince who played for the San Francisco Seals.

Just about the time when Joe finished his high school freshman year, Vince, knowing Joe's interests in baseball, let him practice on the field with the team. Joe's opportunity to play baseball came when a player left the team, and Joe filled in as a shortstop and quickly became known for his excellent batting abilities. At a later date, when his brother Vince could no longer play due to a shoulder injury, Joe substituted for him also in the outfield. His reputation was steadily growing, and he became acknowledged as the greatest player of the Coast League.

At a mere 18 years of age, Joe had already achieved celebrity status, breaking records held by Jack Ness and many other notables of the time. The bidding for him to play in the majors started in 1934, and by 1935 he found himself on the New York Yankees team.

Unfortunately, at the beginning of his first year, he hurt his knee and instep, and so he missed many games, but his dedication to the game kept him going. He did play 138 games and finished the season with a .323 average.

Friends have acknowledged that Joe was modest by nature and had a great sense of moral and family responsibility, attributable in great part to his Sicilian-American upbringing. He had dark eyes and hair, a prominent nose, large mouth, and a slow but friendly smile. Lanky in build, he was more than six feet tall and weighed 195 pounds. He and Babe Ruth, also an outfielder, never seemed to be in a hurry, except for the speed needed going around the bases. His ability to judge fielding a ball has been described by many as artistic.

Nurturing a deep sense of loyalty, Joe always saw himself as part of a team. In his early years in the Big League, he seemed to have built up an aloof, casual front that some took as brashness. Many were unkind to him for that. Most sports writers, however, saw Joe for his achievements, and in 1939 voted him Best for All-Star, Best Outfielder, and Most Valuable Player. Having an average of .347 and having hit 46 home runs, he won the Home Run Championship award and was considered a phenomenon of his time. He was acclaimed the only person to have played in four pennants, winning in the first four years in the majors.

Joe was just short of 25 when he married a lovely actress, Dorothy Arnold, who was 21. On their wedding day, over 30,000 admirers attended in and around the well-known San Francisco landmark, the Church of Saints Peter and Paul. As their place of residence, they lived in New York City in a West End Avenue penthouse. They soon had a baby son, "Little

Joe," but their marriage did not last very long.

In 1941, playing centerfield for the Yankees, he hit safely in 56 consecutive games. His streak was stopped by great playing by other teams, only to pick up a new streak for the next 16 days. Then he went on to hit safely in 72 of 73 games. Indeed, he had become an American sports hero.

In 1942, Joe was called to military duty, and in 1943 he joined the Army Air Force serving until 1945. Despite the loss of three years, he returned to baseball to resume a brilliant career. He managed to have a .325 lifetime batting average, connected for 2,214 base hits and hit 361 home runs. He was elected to participate in 11 All-Star teams and played in 10 World Series. He was elected to the National Baseball Hall of Fame and Museum at Cooperstown, New York in 1955. It was clear to all that Joe DiMaggio represented the American Dream: the son of immigrant parents who had made it to the top.

After his retirement from baseball, Joe married the famous movie star, Marilyn Monroe. It was 1954, and Joe was 40 years old. Although it was a relatively brief marriage, lasting only nine months, their divorce became one of Joe's saddest points in his life. When Marilyn died in 1962, just eight years later, he handled all the funeral arrangements. He never remarried, and it was reported that he regularly brought flowers to her grave site for the rest of his life.

One memorable event in Joe's life was the "Old-Timers Game." The clubhouse was packed with newspaper reporters and old team mates like Mantle and Ford. Then it was time for the old-timers to leave the clubhouse and appear on the field where 50,000 people looked on awaiting this once-in-a-lifetime event. As each name was called, the individual moved out to the field. Casey Stengel, then age 84, was among the notables at this event. There was also the voice of broadcaster Frank Misser. Everyone was waiting in anticipation of Joe DiMaggio. Joe jogged next to the long line of players already introduced to the fans. He waved his cap, acknowledging the ovation. He then kissed Mrs. Gehrig and Mrs. Ruth and shook hands with all the celebrities.

This event was a ritual. Each old-timer would walk up to the plate, swing his bat against the ball, hoping the crowd would lose itself in reverie. When it was Joe's turn at bat, he hit the ball really hard. The sound of it shook everyone. Mel Allen, the announcer of the Yankee games, described the hit as a high drive out to left field—going, going, and stopping just short of the wall! The crowd went wild.

Joe DiMaggio died on March 8, 1999 in Hollywood, Florida after a long bout with lung cancer. Both he and Babe Ruth remain today the two players most associated with the nation's favorite pastime, baseball. He leaves a legacy of a modest, clean-living athlete. He was for many years the idol of aspiring young sports players, and his name has since been immortalized by history books, movies, and song as a metaphor for sports greatness.

General Sources:
1. *Current Biography/Yearbook*. New York: Wilson, 1941; 1999.
2. Durso, Joseph. *DiMaggio: The Last American Knight.* Boston: Little Brown, 1995.
3. Lehmann-Haupt, Christo. *Me and DiMaggio*. New York: Simon & Schuster, 1986.
4. Moore, Jack B. *Joe DiMaggio: A Bio-Bibliography.* New York: Greenwood Press, 1986.
5. Schoor, Gene. *Joe DiMaggio: A Biography*. Garden City, NY: Doubleday, 1980.
6. Seidel, Michael. *Streak: Joe DiMaggio and the Summer of '41*. New York: McGraw-Hill, 1988.

—by ANTHONY MINAFRA

PETE DOMENICI (1932-   )

Pietro Vichi Domenici, better known as Pete Domenici, has been one of the most dynamic and forthright senators this country has ever known. The youngest of six children, he was born on May 7, 1932, the only son in the family. Born of Northern Italian emigrants, young Pietro was reared in the traditional customs of his heritage. His parents, Cherubino ("Choppo") and Alda (Vichi) Domenici had come to America to create a better life for themselves and their children.

Their dreams of fulfillment were realized through good business practices, strong family values, and love and respect for each other. Choppo Domenici, at age 14, had begun by working in his uncle's grocery store in Albuquerque, New Mexico. He developed this "mom and pop" grocery store into a major wholesale distributor outlet that ranged up to a 100-mile radius. Young Pete worked in the family business, driving trucks, laboring in the warehouse, selling and putting orders together.

Taking care of a growing business kept senior Domenici at work much of the time, but his love of family was always steadfast, and his concerns that his children receive an education were paramount in his thinking. This explains in part why he negotiated a deal with his son Pete. He promised to pay for his son's college education provided that young Pete understood he would have to repay it in the event that he quit school. Pete Domenici persevered and met the task head on earning his bachelor's degree and later his LL.B. degree in 1958. Within a year he was admitted to the New Mexico bar.

In a short time he set up a private law firm, Domenici and Bonham, together with a colleague. Pete had always complained about the problems in government, and so his friends encouraged him to run for a seat on the city commission of Albuquerque. Upon his election to the commission, he was also chosen to act as their chairman or *ex officio* mayor in October 1967. As chairman, Pete Domenici brought about many positive changes: providing for more jobs, extending government services to the heavily populated Hispanic communities, and bringing in private companies to renew the city's neglected downtown area.

The year 1969 saw Domenici on the National League of Cities Revenue and Finance Steering Committee, the Resolutions Committee for the 1969 Annual Conference of Mayors, and the State Republican Finance Committee. He was also appointed to the Governor's Policy Board for Law Enforcement, and the Middle Rio Grande Conference of Governments.

In 1970, Pete Domenici ran and lost his bid for the governor's position by just two percentage points. But two years later, he won the Senate Congressional seat when he competed with Jack Daniels, a wealthy business executive. Domenici's platform was a major factor in his victory, earning him 54% of the popular vote. This was the first time since 1936 that New Mexico voted a Republican to the Senate.

On the Senate floor, Pete Domenici became known as a staunch, although flexible, conservative. Under President Nixon he was always in favor of maintaining a strong military position in foreign countries, balancing the budget, and increasing defense spending. He generally took a firm stand regarding Communist countries, and it was after the Vietnam war that Pete Domenici stood firm in his conviction to not assist the Vietnamese postwar government with economic assistance until the Americans classified as missing in action (MIA's) were accounted for and sent back home.

He pursued the same stance in trying to reduce financial aid to the United Nations until they would investigate the fate of those missing Americans. He was also opposed to many of the conditions in President Carter's negotiations process concerning the Strategic Arms Limitations Treaty as well as the Panama Canal Treaty which might jeopardize North American security. Pete Domenici was the most outspoken Republican on the Senate's Energy and Natural Resources Committee. He proposed funds be authorized in research of synthetic fuels and alternative energy sources. Typically voting his own conscience, he would also cross party lines siding with Democrats on other issues.

Pete always kept in mind his home state of New Mexico, and so he was instrumental in bringing about the federal government's directive to remove the toxic waste materials from plant sites. He also brought about a clean water project to be administered by his own state officials. While duly concerned as a responsible representative of his state, he disliked self-serving senators who competed for continuance of "pork barrel" projects costing the federal taxpayers millions of unnecessary dollars annually. This steadfastness was evident in his collaboration, often crossing party lines, and working jointly on projects with such senators as Daniel Patrick Moynahan, a Democrat.

A high point in Domenici's political career came about in 1980 when the Republicans captured the majority both in the United States House and Senate during the Reagan years. Domenici became the chairman of the Budget Committee, and after chairing the committee, it was reported that he was responsible for having saved the American taxpayers $36.4 billion through cutbacks in federal spending. He was influential in much of the success of Reagan's economic policies, including the lowering of interest rates for business and the American home buyer.

Pete Domenici remains today an ardent, dedicated voice of the people, committed to the principles of good government and high standards of traditional *old country* family values. Senator Domenici has been married since 1958 to the former Nancy Burk, and they have eight children. Pete Domenici has consistently affirmed strong family values and high moral and political leadership. It began when he was elected to local office in his home state in 1967, and it has persisted after many years in office at the national level. Despite the alluring power and prestige of senatorial office, Pete Domenici has maintained high standards of personal conduct and civic responsibility in serving both his constituents who elected him and America as a political unity.

General Sources:

1. *Congressional Directory*. 1999 ed.
2. *Current Biography Yearbook*. New York: Wilson, 1982.
3. Domenici, Pete, et al. *Balanced Budget Reconciliation Act of 1997*. Washington, DC: U.S. G.P.O., 1997.
4. Domenici, Pete, et al. *A Changing America: Conservatives View the '80s from the United States Senate*. South Bend, IN: Regnery/Gateway, 1980.
5. Domenici, Pete, et al. *Disposing of Weapons—Grade Plutonium*. Washington, DC: Center for Strategic and International Studies, 1998.
6. Fenno, Richard F. *The Emergence of a Senate Leader: Pete Domenici and the Reagan Budget*. Washington, DC: Congressional Quarterly Press, 1991.
7. Nunn, Sam, and Pete Domenici. *Principles for Health Care Reform*. Washington, DC: Center for Strategic and International Studies, 1994.
8. *Who's Who in American Politics*. 1982.
9. *Who's Who in America*. 1999 ed.

—by DENNIS PIASIO

RENATO DULBECCO (1914-   )

One of the pioneering virologists of the twentieth century, Renato Dulbecco began his efforts in the study of viruses after he immigrated to the United States in 1947. As a physician embarking upon a research career, he soon produced the "plaque assay technique" that has since become a standardized procedure in the lab for facilitating the measurements of viral units in any given laboratory culture. With his career off to a good start, he would devote his entire life to studies in virology. In doing extensive work in the area of carcinogenics, he went on to earn the Nobel Prize in medicine or physiology in 1975, sharing the prize with David Baltimore, a microbiologist, and Howard Temin, an oncologist.

Renato Dulbecco was born on February 22, 1914 to Leonardo and Maria (nee Virdia) Dulbecco in the city of Catanzaro, an old Byzantine city dating back over 1,000 years and located in the southernmost part of the Italian peninsula. His father, an engineer, was called into military service during World War I, and upon his departure, his mother quickly went to northern Italy with the children where she lived in the cities of Turin and Cuneo. After World War I, the family moved to the Ligurian area in the town of Imperia where young Renato started elementary school and in 1930 at sixteen graduated from high school.

At first persuaded by his mother to study medicine, he entered the University of Turin and discovered by the end of the year that he preferred biological research more than traditional medicine. Within a year he was working in Professor Giuseppe Levi's laboratory, a specialist in nerve tissue. Unwittingly, Dulbecco found himself quite by coincidence in the company of two fellow students, Rita Levi-Montalcini and Salvador Edward Luria who someday would all win a Nobel Prize after separately having relocated themselves to the United States.

After Dulbecco earned his degree in medicine in 1936 at the University of Turin's Medical School, he was summoned by the Italian government into military service; and after army basic training, he became a medical officer. This was the time of Mussolini and his deepening alliance with Hitler and the unfortunate prelude to World War II. After Dulbecco had finished two years of service, he was discharged and resumed his research studies in pathology. However, with the onset of the wartime conflict, he was called back into military service in 1939. He was first sent to the French front; then, when he was shifted to the Russian front in 1942, he suffered a severe injury during a major offensive that resulted in his hospitalization and his being sent back to Italy.

After Mussolini's government finally toppled, Dulbecco became a partisan, and hiding with the local resistance groups, he was their physician in the fight against the Nazi military who had by now occupied most of Italy. At the end of World War II, he was deemed a hero and elected to Turin's City Council, but he soon gave up political life to resume his research in the lab. He harbored a dream that involved finding radiation as a means of effecting the genetics of simple organisms. Returning to the University of Turin where he had previously done work, he did research, collaborating with Levi-Montalcini who had similar interests in the use of radiation as a research tool.

Eventually, it was through Salvador Luria's timely efforts that Dulbecco was invited to the United States to participate in Luria's research group in Bloomington at the University of Indiana. Dulbecco accepted and his first major accomplishment at Indiana involved an observation that dealt with bacteriophage, i.e., viruses that kill bacteria (literally: eat up). His immediate discovery involved the fact that through a process called photoreactivation—in this case the use of short wavelength white light— he could reactivate bacteriophage that was previously made inactive by ultraviolet light.

This fact captured the attention of the well-known German-born microbiologist Max Delbrück in Pasadena at the California Institute of Technology (Caltech) who in 1949 then offered Dulbecco a position as a research fellow. Dulbecco moved to California and remained at Caltech until 1963. By the early 1950s, Dulbecco took to work, and at Caltech he developed the plaque assay technique used in the measurement of viral units whose application later became instrumental in the development of the Sabin's polio vaccine (made from living virus) which supplanted the Salk Vaccine (made from dead virus).

By the late 1950s Dulbecco devoted his energies to the study of animal viruses and their relationship to cancer. The major purpose of his studies investigated the exact manner in which particular viruses effected changes in host cells. Upon invasion by a virus, the host cell was either destroyed or reproduced indefinitely, i.e., became cancerous. After working with a known virus that caused cancer in chickens, he then focused on the polyoma virus which was known to cause cancer in mice.

He and his staff of researchers discovered that the invading virus' DNA (deoxyribonucleic acid), the main component of the cell's chromosome, insidiously combined with the host cell's DNA. This invasive combination now makes the invading virus achieve a new fatal status called a provirus. In the next stage, a process called cell transformation, the provirus goes on to control the genetic mechanism of the cell, allowing the cell to multiply by producing cancer-like cells.

In 1972 Dulbecco worked in the laboratories of the Imperial Cancer Research Fund in London where he became assistant director and where he headed much of the research pertaining specifically to cancer and its relationship to human cancers, and in particular, breast cancer. It was during his stay in England that he together with David Baltimore and Howard Temin were jointly awarded the Nobel Prize for their work on tumor virology. On his return to America in 1977, Dulbecco first became a Distinguished Research Professor at the Salk Institute and then its President in 1982, holding that position until his retirement in 1993 when he became its Emeritus President and Distinguished Professor. In addition to receiving the Nobel Prize in 1975, Renato Dulbecco received in his lifetime well over fifteen major awards in Europe and in the U.S. including the Lasker Award for Medical Research (1964) and the Louisa Gross Horwitz Prize (1967).

General Sources:
1. *American Men & Women of Science.* New Providence, NJ: R.R. Bowker, 1998-99.
2. Dulbecco, Renato. *The Design of Life.* New Haven: Yale Univ. Press, 1987.
3. Dulbecco, Renato. *Induction of Host Systems, Integration and Excision.* Cambridge, MA: Cambridge Univ. Press, 1975.
4. Dulbecco, Renato, ed. *Encyclopedia of Human Biology.* San Diego: Academic Press, 1991.
5. Dulbecco, Renato, and Harold S. Ginsberg. *Virology.* Philadelphia: Lippincott, 1988.
6. *Notable Twentieth-Century Scientists.* Detroit, MI: Gale Research, 1995.
7. Wasson, Tyler, ed. *Nobel Prize Winners.* New York: Wilson, 1987.

—by MARK BATTISTE

JIMMY DURANTE (1893-1980)

Jimmy Francis Durante, better known as "The Schnozzola" or "The Schnoz," whose entertainment career spanned more than six decades, is remembered as one of the greatest and most beloved comedians of twentieth-century America. Besides being a comedian, songwriter, and entertainer, he also became famous for his bulbous nose, penguin strut, and gravelly voice. Jimmy routinely created some of the oddest expressions and funniest malapropisms in the English-speaking world. With his easy saloon-style piano playing and singing, he skillfully projected a soft, warm, and pleasant showmanship for all age groups.

"The Schnoz" was born on February 10, 1893 in New York City in Manhattan's Lower East Side on Catherine Street. The youngest of four children, he had two brothers and a sister. His parents, Bartolomeo and Rosa, who had emigrated from Salerno, Italy to the United States first settled in Brooklyn where they had their first three children: Michael, Albert and Lillian. Bartolomeo, who was also part French and a barber by profession, moved his family to Manhattan where the family lived in an apartment behind his barbershop where he often shaved many Tammany Hall politicians.

Jimmy began going to public school at six years of age. He did well at first, but the endless taunting he received from his fellow school mates through those early and tender years proved to be very disconcerting to him. By the seventh grade, he had had enough, soon missing classes and finally quitting school altogether. Beginning at 13 years of age, he took on a series of mostly part-time jobs. He assisted his father in the barber shop, and he also did some work in a funeral parlor and drove a coal wagon. As a teenage boxer, he experienced his one and only professional bout where he was knocked out in the first round.

While these somewhat inconsequential experiences were going on, Jimmy had been taking piano lessons. It seemed that his father, who reportedly was also a part-time barker at sideshows, had managed to obtain a piano from one of Jimmy's cousins. This familial agreement apparently included in exchange for the piano free lifetime haircuts for the donor family. Jimmy began piano lessons under the guidance of a local music teacher, Angelo Fiori, at the cost of 50 cents a lesson. He took to music and spent much of his time sneaking in and out of a local saloon to hear and memorize the ragtime music of the local piano player "Eight-Fingers Rogers." Jimmy used to run home and try to play exactly what he had just heard, and this is how his love for the ragtime beat began.

In 1909 at age 16, he began his show business career by playing ragtime piano in the Bowery nightclubs (lower Manhattan). Then, a year later, one of Jimmy's neighbors, who worked as a bartender in Diamond Tony's Saloon, a beer hall in Coney Island, Brooklyn, told Jimmy about an opening there. Against the wishes of his parents who believed he might get mixed up with gangsters, he took the job anyway. Towards the end of 1911 Jimmy tried a new job playing piano at the Chatham Club in New York City's Chinatown section, noted for its gangster element. After a period of time, Jimmy decided he wanted to return to the relative safety of the Coney Island area.

By the summer of 1912 he was again working there playing ragtime piano at Carey Walsh's, a cabaret not far from Diamond Tony's. Jimmy befriended a singing waiter, Eddie Cantor, and soon they paired up as a piano and singing team. They became close friends, and it was Cantor who encouraged Jimmy to become a comedian since most piano jobs in those days usually became dead-end situations.

In 1915 Eddie Jackson, who would also become one of Jimmy's closest friends, entered his life. They would remain close for the next 65 years. By now, Jimmy was working at the Alamo Club in the Bronx. Besides playing piano, Jimmy was also in charge of hiring the entertainers. Jackson was hired as a singing waiter and soon became part of Jimmy's team. In 1918 Jimmy met a female singer, Jeanne Olson. They feel in love and married on June 19, 1921.

On November 18, 1923 Jimmy opened his own nightclub called the Club Durant in New York City, located on 58th Street. Because the name Durante had been clipped to appear Anglo-Saxon, he used to kiddingly claim that he couldn't afford the "e" on the marquee. There he formed a partnership with his friends Eddie Jackson, Lou Clayton, and Frank Nolan. Although the club was quite successful, it was forced to shut down in October 1925 because it was a speakeasy.

Shortly after that, Jimmy, Jackson, and Clayton created a new act called "The Three Sawdust Bums." They became successful in the vaudeville and nightclub circuits, especially at the Dover Club (for over two and one-half years). Then, after appearing at the New York Palace Theater in 1928, they became a smash hit, and it seemed nothing could hold them back. As a team, they appeared on Broadway featured in Ziegfeld's *Show Girl* (1929), *The New Yorkers* and also in a film, *Roadhouse Nights* (1929).

Ushered off to Hollywood, Jimmy started a new career in film that skyrocketed him. In his lifetime he appeared in more than 35 movies. In 1943 tragedy struck when his wife, Jeanne, of 22 years died of a heart attack. He continued with his work making movies, doing nightclub appearances, and radio shows. With the advent of the late 40s medium of television, he enjoyed an even bigger success starring in many programs as he had the perfect personality that matched TV's fledgling wholesomeness.

In 1960, at age 67 he married 39-year-old Margaret Little, a showgirl he had met more than 15 years earlier, and they adopted two daughters. When Jimmy suffered a series of strokes in the 1960s, his work gradually tapered off, and eventually he became unable to be an entertainer. After 20 years in a second marriage, he died on January 29, 1980 at the age of 87. He was buried in Holy Cross Cemetery outside Culver City, California.

This gentle and kind entertainer from New York City was loved and mourned by everyone from the White House to the everyday person. His signature enigmatic closing line, "Goodnight, Mrs. Calabash, wherever you are," which has become proverbial, still brings a smile to the faces of Durante fans. His tender sense of humor peppered with funny malapropisms and his squeaky-clean showmanship attracted attention from people of all ages. A paragon of wholesome entertainment, this Italian American offered love and kindness to virtually everyone who entered his life.

General Sources:
1. Adler, Irene. *I Remember Jimmy*. Westport, CT: Arlington House, 1980.
2. Bakish, David. *Jimmy Durante: His Show Business Career*. Jefferson, NC: McFarland, 1995.
3. *Current Biography/Yearbook*. New York: Wilson, 1946; 1980.
4. Fowler, Gene. *Schnozzola, the Story of Jimmy Durante*. New York: Viking Press, 1951.
5. Katz, Ephraim. *The Film Encyclopedia*. New York: HarperCollins, 1998.
6. Robbins, Jhan. *Inka Dinka Doo: The Life of Jimmy Durante*. New York: Paragon House, 1991.

—by EDWARD MOTTOLA, Jr.

LOU DUVA (1922-   )

People in the world of boxing have often said: "Boxing is Lou Duva" and "Lou Duva is boxing." Today he is dubbed as having the most recognizable physical profile in boxing as that of Alfred Hitchcock for the film industry. From boxer, trainer, manager to manager/promoter, he has made it to the top of his field financially and professionally.

Born on May 28, 1922 in a section of Manhattan, New York called Hell's Kitchen, Lou was the second of seven children. His parents, Salvatore and Saveria (nee Damiano) Duva, both born and raised in Foggia, Italy came to America in the early 1900s. First settling in Hell's Kitchen, his parents later moved to Paterson, New Jersey where Lou's education began in Public School 4. He started attending Central High School, but after three months Lou was asked to leave school because he apparently was always sleeping in class.

At that time in his life, it so happened that Lou not only delivered newspapers in the early morning hours before school and also sold papers on street corners late at night, but he also worked the bowling alleys as pin boy at McNeers Bowling Alley sometimes as late as four in the morning. This was during the depression era, and essentially all his earnings went to his family.

Then his older brother Carl had introduced Lou, who was ten years of age, to boxing. He immediately took to the sport, and by the age of fifteen, he began boxing in "bar-room" smokers, which were boxing matches that took place behind bars and restaurants. Lou usually received between three and five dollars per evening bout.

In 1938, Lou joined the federal government's Civilian Conservation Corps (CCC). He worked as a truck driver in Boise, Idaho; Walla Walla, Washington; and in Nyssin, Oregon. During this period, he earned thirty dollars a week, and he sent twenty-five of it to his mother. It was in CCC that Lou became a boxing instructor in addition to being a fighter himself. Despite what others might have said about his having been dismissed from high school, he believed in education, and to further it he began taking correspondence courses.

When WWII began, he returned home and enlisted in the Army, and he would continue to box while serving his two-and-one-half years in the service. He went off to do his three-month basic training in Jackson, Mississippi, but on his first weekend furlough Lou got his earliest lesson in discrimination. While riding to town on a city bus, Lou gave up his seat to accommodate an elderly black woman. He was frowned upon by the bus driver and some white men. Because of his convictions, Lou had refused to let this lady stand, and then a fight ensued. Lou and three of his buddies ended up in the stockade that day.

When he returned home, Lou pursued his professional boxing career as a welterweight fighter establishing a modest 15-7 record. His losses were in part attributable to his limited training time. Thinking he would not make it as a boxer, he started his own trucking firm. In 1947, he also met his future wife and became married in 1949 at age twenty-seven. Lou married Enes Rizio, and together they raised five children: two sons, Daniel and Dino; and, three daughters, Donna, Deanna, and Denise.

While his trucking business grew from three trucks to a fleet of thirty-two, he would often spend much of his time in Stillman's Gym on Eighth Avenue in Manhattan. There he had the opportunity to meet top contenders and the celebrities who came to visit. Encouraged by his wife, Lou opened his own gym, the Garden Gym, in Totowa, New Jersey. Later, investing funds from his trucking business profits, he ventured into a new area establishing himself as a promoter.

He persevered and did well as a promoter. In 1963, Joey Giardello, a protege of Lou Duva, defeated Dick Tiger to win the middleweight prize. This constituted the first of thirteen world championships that would be garnered by trainees under the direction of Lou Duva and his staff. Rocky Marciano, the world heavyweight champ, was a close friend and business associate of Lou Duva. Together they had promoted many fights until the untimely death of Rocky in 1969.

After Lou Duva's children graduated from college, they all participated in shaping and running the Duva family enterprise—a successful promotional company called *Main Events, Inc.* The firm first began by promoting monthly fights in Ice World in Totowa, NJ. Then in 1979, when the new sports network (ESPN) was planning its yearly schedule, *Main Events* was contracted to broadcast one boxing show a month from Ice World. That successful year was a bittersweet time for Lou because he also suffered a heart attack. After surviving the ordeal, Lou cut down on his work, resigned as president of Teamster Local 286, and focused only on boxing.

Under the direction of his son Dan, *Main Events* went on to grow to even bigger heights in TV syndication, and it is reputed today as having become the largest boxing videotape company in the country. Their overall company growth and tape acquisitions have made it the major source of regularly shown boxing programs on HBO television. Lou Duva and his family, while blessed with many successes, also had their tragic losses. In 1986, Lou lost his wife, Enes, of thirty-seven years to multiple sclerosis. Ten years later, he went on to lose his son, Dan, to brain cancer; he had been a business lawyer and president of *Main Events*.

Besides being a savvy promoter and businessman, Lou Duva has also taken interest in his fighters both in and out of the ring. He actively encouraged his fighters to get an education, achieve personal goals, and economic stability. Duva also established scholarship programs for amateur fighters. In all, at a personal level, he has offered to boxers a winning combination: a boxer's discipline in the ring that is matched with getting an education outside the ring.

Lou has personally trained fighters from all over the world including men from Australia and New Zealand. World champions who have worked under the auspices of Lou Duva include: Joey Giardello, Mark Breland, Evander Holyfield, Rocky Lockridge, John-John Molina, Vinny Pazienza, Darren Van Horn, Livingston Bramble, Johnny Bumphus, Ed Hopson, Mike McCallum, Michael Moorer, Meldrick Taylor, and Pernell Whitaker. His favorite fighters still remain Rocky Marciano, Sugar Ray Robinson, and Muhammad Ali. Because of his many achievements in boxing, on June 14, 1998, Lou Duva was inducted into the International Boxing Hall of Fame in Canastota, NY. He remains a living tribute to his fellow Italian Americans.

General Sources:
1. Duva, Lou. Personal interview. 11 Nov. 1997.
2. "Main Events-Biography of Lou Duva." 7 Aug.1998. <http://mainevents.com/duva/duva_bio.htm>.
3. Myler, Patrick. *A Century of Boxing Greats: Inside the Ring with the Hundred Best Boxers*. New York: Robson/Parkwest, 1998.
4. Odd, Gilbert. *Encyclopedia of Boxing*. New York: Crescent Books, 1983.

—by DENNIS PIASIO

RALPH FASANELLA (1914-1997)

An anomaly of our times, Ralph Fasanella, at barely twenty-two years of age, joined the Abraham Lincoln Brigade to fight with Loyalists against Gen. Francisco Franco in the Spanish Civil War (1936-1939). Upon returning home, he joined the U.S. Navy only to receive a medical discharge at a later date. After being a union organizer for the CIO between 1940-45, he ran for office as a Labor Party candidate for New York City councilman. He was soon blacklisted and peculiarly unable to find a union job. He resigned himself to being a service station attendant pumping gas by day and painting pictures by night. His artistic cosmos usually centered on working people, especially the immigrants in urban milieus such as New York City and the Massachusetts New Bedford area. He became a fresh and colorful voice on canvas depicting workers' struggles.

For more than thirty years, his art works were barely known except for perfunctory acknowledgment by local some New York City galleries and newspapers. It was not until October 30, 1972 when a cover story in *New York* magazine together with a penetrating book entitled *Fasanella's City* in 1973 by Patrick Watson brought him to the attention of art critics and the general public. Suddenly, the recognition of his artistry propelled his work into exhibitions across the country as far as San Francisco. Today, one of his most well-known paintings, *Family Supper* (1972), hangs at the Ellis Island Museum of Immigration.

Ralph Fasanella, who would become the quintessential painter of struggling immigrant workers, was prophetically born on Labor Day, September 2, 1914 to Giuseppe and Ginevra (nee Spagnoletti) Fasanella in New York City's Greenwich Village area. Both Italian born, his parents met and married in the United States. Ralph was the third of their six children. His mother came from Bari, a major city on Italy's southeast Adriatic coast, and his father came from Andria, a nearby seaport town.

Both parents had a decidedly clear influence on Ralph's emotional and philosophic view of the world in affirming the values of hard work and compassion. His father was a dedicated family man who performed back-breaking work as an iceman, one who delivered heavy blocks of ice to individual homes and businesses for refrigeration purposes. To help out the family finances, his mother was a buttonhole maker in a coat factory. In addition to her family and work life, she also found the time to be a Socialist activist and antifascist.

As a family of eight, Ralph, his parents, and his five siblings lived in a three-room walk-up apartment on Sullivan Street. His father, who arose at 4 a.m. to deliver ice with his horse-drawn wagon, often expressed that he felt no better than a draft animal. Ralph was regularly compelled to help out his father on the job, and he did this as early as age nine. As a result of having to carry ice blocks up many floors in Manhattan tenement dwellings at an early age, he learned about hard work, large families living in tight quarters, and the metaphorical importance of the kitchen and eating together as a family. A multitude of themes dealing with these experiences first-hand as a youngster would unwittingly become for him the magma of his painting repertoire when, as an adult artist, he would look back and give meaning, form, and expression to those experiences.

Ralph's early years were also troubled times for him. He had run away from home at age nine. Later, on three other occasions his family placed him in a Catholic reform school for considerable periods of time. After his last release from reform school, he witnessed his tired, frustrated father leave the family. Now in his mid-teens, Ralph pitched in to help support them. The economic depression of the 30s was in full swing, and his mother, an activist, spoke of Socialist reform. Quite literate, she was involved in producing antifascist newsletters written in Italian. Ralph joined her at many Socialist rallies and demonstrations; and at her urging, he went to Europe to fight for two years against Franco in Spain's civil war.

Upon his return home, he enlisted in the U.S. Navy but was soon given a medical discharge. After serving as a union organizer from 1940 to 1945, he became disillusioned with the CIO's bureaucracy and inertia. It was during these years that Fasanella taught himself to paint. After some major disappointments with the CIO, he became highly engrossed in art and in painting, devoting his energies to visiting museums and learning whatever he could on his own so he could improve his painting skills. He began his career by sketching and painting on cardboard with 10-cent paint tubes.

While he had had some paintings on display in the 60s and early 70s, he received his major recognition as an artist in a cover article in *New York* magazine, constituting the "discovery" of this new artist. He was extolled as the greatest *primitive* painter since Grandma Moses (1860-1961). Because of that initial 1972 article and a 1973 book devoted entirely to Fasanella's art (*Fasanella's City*), his arts works, consisting of urban scenes and panoramas, were exhibited throughout the United States and Europe.

While *primitive painting* may mean the kind of art work that is reflective of an artist who is presumably unschooled, unpolished, or even naive, it can also mean an art where the artist prefers to be very much in touch with deep, rudimentary feelings regarding survival, a sense of societal belonging, and where spatial relationships reflect movement and the radiation of activity. Fasanella's scenes do precisely the latter. This is beautifully illustrated, for instance, in his depictions of scenes from Coney Island, Greenwich Village, the San Gennaro Festival, Yankee Stadium, and New York City subway rush hour.

Ralph Fasanella, an autodidactic marvel of our times, died at age 83 on December 9, 1997 in New York. He left the world a legacy of a uniquely expressive art that arouses in the viewer a deep compassion for workers and their struggles in industrialized settings. With depth of feeling, he depicts working-class neighborhoods, their factories, sports stadiums, and street culture. In a nutshell, it is the working-class people in its moments of joy and also in its struggle for subsistence and survival. In recognition of Ralph Fasanella's concern for human rights and workers equity, the United Nations Postal Administration announced in 1991 that one of Fasanella's paintings would commemorate a United Nations Article of the Universal Declaration of Human Rights.

General Sources:
1. Beaird, Joe. "Ralph Fasanella, Champion of Labor, Dies." *The Standard-Times* 18 Dec. 1997.
2. *Current Biography Yearbook*. New York: Wilson, 1975; 1998.
3. D'Acierno, Pellegrino, ed. *The Italian American Heritage: A Companion to Literature and Arts*. New York: Garland Publ., 1999.
4. Hemphill, Herbert W., and Julia Weissman. *Twentieth-Century American Folk Art and Artists*. New York: Dutton, 1974.
5. *Ralph Fasanella: A Song of the City*. (no dir.). Hudson, NY: Bowling Green Films, 1979.
6. Watson, Patrick. *Fasanella's City*. New York: Knopf, 1973.

—by GEORGE CARPETTO, Ph.D.

ANTHONY STEPHEN FAUCI (1940-   )

Anthony Stephen Fauci has become an internationally celebrated scientist. One of the most articulate leaders of the federal government's efforts in AIDS research today, he has been the director of the National Institute of Allergy and Infectious Diseases (NIAID) since 1984 and coordinator of all AIDS research programs since 1985.

Born in Brooklyn, New York on December 24, 1940, Dr. Fauci was one of two children born to Stephen and Eugenia Fauci, both of whom were graduates of Columbia University. His father became a pharmacist and his mother worked as a homemaker. Fauci describes his mother as a "self-starter and a perfectionist" and he readily admits, "I probably got a lot of drive from my mother."

He graduated from Regis, a Jesuit high school in Manhattan, noted for its vigorous scholastic standards. Excelling academically, he still found time to become one of its star basketball players. After he attended Holy Cross College in Worcester, Massachusetts and received a baccalaureate in 1962, he enrolled at Cornell University Medical Center in Ithaca, New York, and in 1966 he received his M.D. degree. He completed his residency at Cornell University Medical Center in NYC in 1968.

He joined the Laboratory of Clinical Investigation at the National Institutes of Allergy and Infectious Diseases (NIAID), a division of the National Institutes of Health (NIH). He also spent one year (1971-1972) as chief resident in the Department of Medicine at Cornell Medical Center in New York City, thus completing his residency in internal medicine.

In 1984, Fauci was appointed director of NIAID and chief of the NIAID's Laboratory of Immunoregulation in 1985. He has also held positions as clinical professor at Georgetown University College of Medicine and George Washington School of Medicine. Fauci has devoted his life's work to researching infectious diseases and their effects on the immune system. He was a pioneer in immunoregulation long before the identification of the Acquired Immune Deficiency Syndrome or AIDS in 1981.

Early in his research career, Fauci pioneered work on an uncommon, but fatal disease: Wegener's granulomatosis. This disease starts with lesions in the upper and lower respiratory tract that eventually causes inflammation of all bodily organs, kidney failure, and then death. In 1971, Fauci and two other physicians found that an immunosuppressive agent called cyclophosphamide acted most favorably on the immune response to Wegener's granulomatosis. The therapy plan which was developed through his research saves 95% of those afflicted with it.

Fauci was also instrumental in developing a cure for two other fatal diseases, namely, polyarteritis nodosa and lymphomatoid granulomatosis. According to the American Rheumatism Association, a 1985 survey by the Stanford University Arthritis Center claims that Fauci's work on treating those two diseases ranked "as one of the most important advances in patient management and rheumatology over the past 20 years." A 1995 study by the Institute of Science Information acknowledged that Fauci was the fifth most cited scientist among more than one million researchers published from 1981 through 1994.

A 15-hour workday is typical for Fauci during which he evaluates laboratory scientific data and prepares articles for publication in the world's many and varied scientific journals.

Throughout his career, Fauci has written and edited more than 600 papers. He is the Associate Editor of *Current Therapy in Internal Medicine*, and the editor of the text, *Harrison's Principles of Internal Medicine*.

His professional activities include membership in many medical and scientific organizations, including the National Academy of Sciences (NAS). He has addressed a multitude of audiences at home and abroad on pertinent topics concerning infectious diseases and their respective therapies as well as research for newer and better vaccines, hopefully one of which may put an end to the scourge of the late twentieth century—AIDS.

The Human Immunodeficiency Virus (HIV) is a virus of the retrovirus family and is the agent that causes Acquired Immune Deficiency Syndrome, otherwise known as AIDS. A person infected with AIDS loses immune function and becomes vulnerable to opportunistic diseases such as tuberculosis, various pneumoniae, Kaposi's sarcoma, cancers, and a myriad of other diseases.

What makes HIV unique is that the body's formidable, early, immune response, the greatly expanded-in-number cytotoxic T lymphocytes (CTLs), known as Killer T-cells, annihilate and reduce the virus to very low levels in the bloodstream. Yet Dr. Fauci and researchers found that this greatly enlarged population of Killer T-cells, effective initially in killing the virus, then disappears completely from the bloodstream leaving the HIV in the lymph nodes to replicate and disseminate throughout the body. This is the dilemma confronting researchers today in establishing a therapeutic cure for AIDS.

Fauci and his research colleagues have pioneered the most important advances in therapeutics for the HIV disease. The first drug found to be effective in prolonging life in AIDS patients was AZT (Zidovudine). Dr. Fauci believes that the development of "a vaccine is the only surefire way to put an end to the HIV epidemic." The NIAID in consort with pharmaceutical companies is presently engaged in extensive research for the eventual development of a vaccine for HIV.

Dr. Anthony Fauci's many contributions in medicine and scientific research have blossomed in the form of improvements in health for humanity. He believes that the public needs to become more aware of the newly emerging diseases, many of which are becoming resistant to antibiotics. The public also needs to give its support to efforts to detect these new microbes. Once more, educating the public in these areas is extremely important, and proper funding for research by U.S. Congress is crucial.

Dr. Fauci lives in Washington, D.C., with his wife and daughter not far from his NIAID office in Bethesda, Maryland. Fauci is the recipient of numerous awards and at least eighteen honorary doctorate degrees both at home and abroad.

General Sources:

1. *American Men and Women of Science.* New Providence, NJ: R.R. Bowker, 1998-1999.

2. *Current Biography Yearbook.* New York: Wilson, 1988.

3. Fauci, Anthony. "Host Factors in Pathogenesis of HIV Disease." Third Conference on Retroviruses and Opportunistic Infections. Washington, DC, 28 Jan. 1996.

4. Fauci, Anthony, and G. Pantaleo, eds. *Immunopathogenesis of HIV Infection.* New York: Springer, 1997.

5. Fauci, Anthony, et al., eds. *Harrison's Principles of Internal Medicine: Companion Handbook.* New York: McGraw-Hill, 1998.

6. *Notable Twentieth-Century Scientists.* Detroit, MI: Gale Research, 1995.

7. *Who's Who in America.* 1999 ed.

—by PETER PAUL FRANCO, M.D.

LAWRENCE FERLINGHETTI (1919-   )

A writer of no less than ten books of poetry, two novels, and many plays; a publisher, a book entrepreneur, and a major spokesman for American Beat Literature, Lawrence Ferlinghetti was—and still is today—an important literary figure whose influence began in the 50s. His writings are quintessentially embedded in the social and political issues of our times, and his value system is clearly countercultural and champions liberal causes.

Based on much of the anguish he weathered in his childhood years as an orphan shuttling between households and based on his wartime experiences, which included his witnessing the shattered remains of Nagasaki, Japan after "the bomb," he became a pacifist and a dedicated liberal. His close collaboration and spiritual kinship with Allen Ginsburg in organizing a conference of poets named the Pan American Cultural Conference, held at the Universidad de Concepción, Chile in 1960, helped to establish the term "beat generation," its poets, and their poetry as standard entities in the parlance of modern literary critics.

Lawrence Ferlinghetti was born in Yonkers, New York on March 24, 1919 to Clemence Monsanto and Charles Furling. As many immigrants had done, Furling anglicized his last name from the Italian, Ferlinghetti, which his yet-to-be-born-son, would reassume at a later date. Charles Furling came from Northern Italy where he had worked as an auctioneer. In America he used those skills—plus his ability to speak several European languages—to appeal to many immigrants. He created a successful retail business on forty-second street in Manhattan.

Furling, who at first lived in Brooklyn's Bath Beach area, met his future wife, Clemence Mendes-Monsanto in the 1890s at Coney Island, Brooklyn, at that time a fashionable and popular beach resort area and amusement center. They married and had five boys of whom Lawrence was the last. Furling died suddenly from a heart attack or stroke a few months before Lawrence's birth, and this event would precipitate untold hardships for the surviving family. Clemence, pregnant with Lawrence, had four boys who were 17, 14, 10 and 6 years of age.

After moving several times to smaller quarters and unable to endure the stress of family responsibilities and dwindling assets, Lawrence's mother became emotionally disturbed and was hospitalized in a state institution in Poughkeepsie, NY. Lawrence, now a one-year old, was adopted by his mother's uncle Ludwig Monsanto and his wife Emily, while his older brothers were placed in a boarding school in Ossining, NY. Not long afterwards, Ludwig and Emily encountered marital difficulties and eight months later were divorced. Emily together with young Ferlinghetti retreated to her French-German speaking hometown in Strasbourg, France.

Emily had remained in Europe almost four years, and it seems that Ludwig's persistent letter writing persuaded her to return to America and remarry him. She and Lawrence returned to New York. Soon after remarrying, Ludwig and Emily faced financial troubles, and again they went their separate ways. Emily and Lawrence returned to Strasbourg and, again, came back to the United States. She joined Ludwig to be a couple again with Lawrence as their child, only to leave each other for the last time. Emily finally decided to place Lawrence, now six years of age, in an orphanage located not far from where his mother was hospitalized. Lawrence's subsequent growing years were spent in two other adoptive households, the Bislands and the Wilsons, until placed in a missionary school where he finished his high school education.

Ferlinghetti then attended the University of North Carolina at Chapel Hill where he was circulation manager for the college newspaper and where he continued to write poetry, something he had begun when he was sixteen. Upon graduation he joined the United States Navy and served during World War II. After his war experiences, he attended Columbia College in New York City where he received a master's degree and shortly thereafter began his studies at the Sorbonne in Paris, France, where he earned his doctorate in 1950. His doctoral dissertation, a literary thematic study, was entitled "The City as Symbol in Modern Poetry."

From Paris he moved to San Francisco. There in 1953, he and Peter Martin launched a magazine publication called *City Lights* which overtly addressed the cultural needs of the San Francisco Bay area, but, realistically reflected a newly fermenting countercultural dissension. It came in the form of what seemed to be a vaguely defined yet deeply-seated fear, precipitated in great part by a new sensibility reacting against the apparent peace of a post-war new world order. This "order" was in truth based more on an escalating cold war, an arms race, a space race, and a series of nuclear confrontational threats, which for the first time in humanity's history raised the distinct specter of human extinction.

Viewed in this light, then, the shock-value encapsulated in much of the brashness, lewdness, and stark insolence in some of the "beat generation" authors, vis-a-vis the dominant and seemingly all-too-complacent American culture of the 50s, acquires new meaning. Beneath the bold and brash veneer of the "beat generation" there lies the intuition of a gnawing and all-too-real insight that humanity could be on the brink of extinction. We can say this now with the advantage of hindsight that the so-called beatniks, who evolved as followers of the "beat generation" writers together with their incidental trappings of "free love" and their drug culture, were really reflective and symbolic of a much more essential reality characterized by a primal fear of extinction.

It is no wonder that below their second floor magazine offices, Martin and Ferlinghetti decided to open up a bookstore, aptly called the City Lights Bookstore that could, at low prices, disseminate poems, plays, novels, and protest literature to raise the consciousness of this uneasy world scenario that was being ignored by the average person. The retail store went on to become one of the most famous bookstores in the world. It became a focal point, a symbolic beacon for the growing number of countercultural movements of the 50s and 60s. At their most elevated level, the writers who were promoted by *City Lights* magazine and the City Lights Bookstore preached nuclear sanity, peace, and brotherhood. In 1997, Ferlinghetti received the 67th Annual California Book Award for his *A Far Rockaway of the Heart*.

General Sources:
1. Cherkovski, Neeli. *Ferlinghetti, A Biography*. Garden City, NY: Doubleday, 1979.
2. Felver, Christopher. *Ferlinghetti Portrait*. Salt Lake City: Gibbs Smith, 1998.
3. Ferlinghetti, Lawrence. *A Coney Island of the Mind*. New York: New Directions, 1958.
4. Ferlinghetti, Lawrence. *Endless Life: Selected Poems*. New York: New Directions, 1981.
5. Ferlinghetti, Lawrence. *A Far Rockaway of the Heart*. New York: New Directions, 1997.
6. Silesky, Barry. *Ferlinghetti, the Artist in His Time*. New York: Warner Books, 1990.

—by KATHY FREEPERSON

ENRICO FERMI (1901-1954)

Born in Rome, Italy on September 29, 1901, Enrico Fermi was the youngest of three children born to Ida de Gattis, a teacher, and Alberto Fermi, a railroad official. A self-starter, Enrico advanced his knowledge of mathematics and physics as a young lad. In 1918, he won a fellowship to the Scuola Normale Superiore at the University of Pisa. At the age of twenty-one, Enrico Fermi was awarded a doctorate in physics, graduating *magna cum laude*.

Enrico Fermi continued his study of physics in Germany and then became lecturer of mechanics and mathematical physics at the University of Florence, Italy. Having earned an international reputation early in life, he was given a newly created chair in theoretical physics in 1927. In 1929, one year after his marriage to Laura Capon, Benito Mussolini appointed Fermi honorary member to the Royal Academy of Italy.

From his research in nuclear physics in 1933, Fermi described a new phenomenon which involved *beta* decay (neutrons decaying into electrons and protons) with resulting *beta* emissions, and he coined these particles with the term "neutrinos." In 1934, when Fermi learned of the creation of artificial radioactivity by Jolet and Jolet-Curie, this inspired him to push beyond Jolet and Jolet-Curie's work, creating hundreds of new radioactive isotopes. In 1935, Fermi and his associates also discovered a sub-atomic process called *moderation* that showed neutrons as more effective in causing reactions when they are slowed down.

With the rise of Mussolini and his attack on Ethiopia in 1935, atomic research in Italy now assumed more complicated dimensions. To make matters worse, in 1936 Mussolini allied himself with Hitler. With the enactment of anti-Semitic civil service laws in 1938, Fermi and his wife, a Jew from a prominent Roman family, quickly immigrated to the United States. After accepting an offer to become professor of physics at Columbia University, Fermi informed the Fascist government that he was making a six-month visit. In November of that year, he learned that he had been awarded the Nobel Prize in physics for the discoveries resulting from neutron bombardment. After the awards ceremony in Sweden, he quickly left Stockholm and returned to New York to apply for immigration status as a prelude to American citizenship.

The pace of events began to accelerate in the Western world, especially in world politics and in atomic research. Neils Bohr came from Copenhagen to teach at Princeton University. He revealed that prominent scientists had already performed Fermi's neutron bombardment experiment with uranium, and they witnessed the splitting of the uranium atom into smaller units. This very isolated and controlled nuclear fission produced energy and more neutrons as by-products. It was speculated that if this process of neutron bombardment of uranium were continued into a full sequenced chain reaction, it could produce unbelievable amounts of explosive energy unlike anything ever produced before.

This phenomenon generated much discussion in the scientific community. In 1939, Fermi discussed creating a weapon utilizing such a chain reaction to the Department of the Navy. He received federal funds for further research, which ultimately pointed toward the use of plutonium, a hypothetical element of atomic mass 239 for use in a chain reaction device, referred to as an atomic bomb. He and his colleague (and former student), Emilio Segrè, argued that such an element would certainly be fissionable and could be readily produced.

In 1942, the United States government created the "Manhattan Project" at Columbia University. Fermi, at first, had reason to believe that he would not be included in the group because of his alien status. Nonetheless, he was given responsibility for the project's research into chain reactions and the use of plutonium. Late in that year, the operation moved to the University of Chicago campus. Fermi, Chairman of the Theoretical Aspects Subsection of the Uranium Committee, directed the construction of the world's first nuclear reactor located on a squash court beneath the University's Stagg Stadium. Referred to as "the pile" because of the blocks of graphite piled up to slow down neutrons, it contained uranium oxide, the neutron source; and uranium, the target. The reaction would be controlled by the manipulation of cadmium rods.

On December 2, 1942 these rods were withdrawn, resulting in humanity's first self-sustaining atomic chain reaction. Fermi had ushered in the atomic age! He was named head of the advanced physics department, and a new atomic laboratory was built in Los Alamos, New Mexico where an atomic bomb would be built and tested. After having become American citizens a month earlier, he and his wife moved to the secret lab site in August 1944 where almost a year later on July 16, 1945, the world's first atomic bomb was detonated.

Returning to the University of Chicago after the war, Fermi joined that school's newly created Institute for Nuclear Studies where he held the Swift Distinguished Service Chair in Physics. He became involved in the construction of a cyclotron, that is, a sub-atomic particle accelerator. He soon began running experiments dealing with the interactions of neutrons and some recently discovered particles, "pi-mesons."

When Fermi traveled to Italy in 1954, he suddenly became seriously ill. On his return to Chicago in October, he had exploratory surgery and learned of an inoperable tumor in his stomach. Fermi began to talk pessimistically regarding the Earth's future and the role of humans in the use of atomic power. Atomic weapons in the wrong hands could make world destruction a possibility. He began writing down his lectures on nuclear physics.

Close to death, Fermi revealed to his former student, Emilio Segrè, that he had been blessed by a Catholic priest, a Protestant pastor, and a rabbi. He had granted permission to all three since "it pleased them and it did not harm me." Fermi died during the early morning hours of November 30, 1954, a few months after his fifty-third birthday. His wife wrote a biography of him, and Segrè wrote one as well. The Atomic Energy Commission established a Fermi Prize in his honor and awarded him with the first one in 1954.

General Sources:
1. *American Men and Women of Science.* New Providence, NJ: R.R. Bowker, 1998-99.

2. Fermi, Laura. *Atoms in the Family: My Life with Enrico Fermi.* Albuquerque: Univ. of New Mexico Press, 1988.

3. Gottfried, Ted. *Enrico Fermi, Pioneer of the Atomic Age.* New York: Facts on File, 1992.

4. International School of Physics Enrico Fermi. *History of Twentieth-Century Physics.* New York: Academic Press, 1977.

5. Lichello, Robert. *Enrico Fermi, Father of the Atomic Bomb.* Charlottevile, NY: SamHar Press, 1971.

6. *Notable Twentieth-Century Scientists.* Detroit, MI: Gale Research, 1995.

7. Segrè, Emilio. *Enrico Fermi Physicist.* Chicago: University of Chicago Press, 1970.

—by MARK BATTISTE

GERALDINE A. FERRARO (1935-   )

Geraldine Anne Ferraro is a woman of firsts! First Italian American to be nominated for Vice President of the United States in a major party. First female candidate for Vice President of the United States of a major political party. First woman named chair of the National Platform Committee of the Democratic party. First female elected to represent the 9th Congressional District in New York.

Born August 26, 1935 in Newburgh, New York, Geraldine was the fourth child of Dominick and Antonetta (nee Corrieri) Ferraro. Her birth was preceded by twin brothers, one of whom died at birth, and another brother, Gerard, who died in an automobile accident at three years of age while sleeping on his mother's lap. Geraldine, named for her deceased brother, breathed new life into her parents.

Arriving in New York from Italy, her father Dominick developed a thriving restaurant and a five and dime store in Newburgh, NY. Dominick would sometimes leave work early to spend time with Geraldine, and he showered her with affection and toys. When her father suddenly died of a heart attack in May 1943, Geraldine was so traumatized she became anemic and stayed out of school for a year.

Antonetta, left alone with two young children, had to provide for her family. Forced to leave their home in Newburgh, they found a small apartment in the Bronx and then later on in Queens. Antonetta worked sewing beads and sequins on dresses and gowns—a skill she had learned when she was twelve years of age. This allowed her to send Geraldine to an all-girls Catholic school, Marymount, in Tarrytown. She believed Geraldine could be whatever she decided to be, and she scrimped and saved to make that happen. Ms. Ferraro's college career at the elite Marymount College in NYC was financed by scholarships. Although Geraldine wanted to be a doctor, she chose to major in English because women just didn't become doctors in the 1950s. In 1956, Geraldine became a second-grade teacher in the NYC public school system. She entered Fordham Law School night classes that same year and was granted her J.D. in 1960. Shortly after graduation, Ms. Ferraro married John Zaccaro, a real estate developer. Rather than take John's last name, Geraldine kept her maiden name to honor her mother for all the love and support she had given her.

Because Wall Street law firms were not "female friendly" at the time, Geraldine worked as a civil lawyer part-time for her husband's real estate business. She always provided her mother with a portion of her legal fees. Ms. Ferraro continued in John's business for the next fourteen years as she raised her three children, Donna, John, and Laura. Wanting to maintain contact with the legal profession, she became active in her local Democratic club and got involved in community politics.

In 1974 Nicholas Ferraro, cousin to Ms. Ferraro and successful district attorney in Queens, hired Geraldine as an assistant district attorney in the Investigations Division. She handled child abuse, domestic violence, rape, and other cases. In 1978, Geraldine had her eye on the Congressional seat for the 9th District which was occupied by James Delaney. When he retired, to get her name on the ballot, she stood on street corners and got passers-by to sign a petition. Told that she would have trouble with Italian males in her district, they became her biggest supporters. With her strong stand on law and order, senior citizens, and the community, she became the first woman elected to the House of Representatives from the 9th Congressional District. She won two more successive terms in 1980 and 1982. Geraldine was known to be a team player who represented her constituents well. A strong advocate of women's rights, her pro-abortion stand caused some of her fellow Roman Catholics to be at odds with her. Her personal belief against abortion did not hinder her from standing up for what she considered a woman's right. Ms. Ferraro is a person of principle who follows her conscience and her heart.

House Speaker Tip O'Neill took a strong liking to Ms. Ferraro and made her a member of the Democratic Steering and Policy Committee, secretary to the House Democratic Caucus, and in 1983 a member of the Budget Committee, a powerful position. In 1984, Ferraro was appointed chair of the Democratic Platform Committee, another first for a woman. This position had the effect of catapulting her to party prominence and nationwide recognition.

Shortly afterwards at the age of forty-eight, Geraldine Ferraro became the first woman and the first Italian American to run for Vice President for a major political party. Although she concedes that Walter Mondale probably chose her for her gender, she believes that her selection was based on her qualifications.

Though she was scrutinized and tortured by the press, quizzed at news conferences, and debated over in peoples' homes, Geraldine's mother reminded her that her name means "iron" and that she was strong enough to handle whatever came her way. Excepting a movie star, she received more coverage than any other woman up to that time. Because of the unprecedented factor that a woman was on the ballot, not even the sophisticated pre-election polls could predict the outcome of the election.

Although the Mondale-Ferraro ticket was unsuccessful, Geraldine Ferraro's nomination forever changed the role of women in politics. There was no job a woman could not do. Women became equal members of society.

After the election, Ferraro taught at Harvard, served as the founding president of the International Institute for Women's Political Leadership, and started the Political Action Committee to increase the number of Democratic women in Congress and a Democratic majority in the U.S. Senate.

In 1992 Ms. Ferraro ran for the Senate and lost the primary by a small margin. She became a co-host on CNN's *Crossfire* and was ambassador to the U.N. Commission on Human Rights. She believes in basic human obligations to *every* person, a health care system that works, education, civil rights, domestic partner legislation, environmental responsibility, ethical medical decisions, and volunteerism. Proud to be an Italian American, Ms. Ferraro beckons her fellow Italian Americans to join her in speaking up against bigotry.

In 1998, Geraldine sought the Democratic nomination for Senate in her desire to eventually take over the seat from Republican Al D'Amato. When Charles Schumer won the nomination, Geraldine vowed to support him all the way. One thing is for certain, the name Geraldine Ferraro and politics will be forever bound. In *Changing History*, a book she authored, she stated: "Once you've been involved in the inner workings of government, in the legislative bodies that set policy, in the debates that involve the future of this country, you don't just walk away."

General Sources:
1. Church, George J., and Ed Magnuson. "A Break with Tradition." *Time* 23 July 1984: 12-16.
2. *Current Biography Yearbook*. New York: Wilson, 1984.
3. Ferraro, Geraldine A. *Changing History: Women, Power, and Politics*. Wakefield, RI: Moyer Bell, 1993.

—by DIANE M. EVANAC, Ed.D.

JAMES JOSEPH FLORIO (1937-   )

A former eight-term Democratic congressman (1975-1990) and former governor of New Jersey (1990-1994), Jim Florio is presently a senior partner in Florio & Perrucci in its Piscataway, New Jersey office and a Rutgers University professor of public policy and administration. Recognized by many as having been a dedicated civil servant and authority in such areas as international trade, energy, health care, environmental and transportation issues, he is perhaps best remembered for and associated with his leadership and design of the 1980 Superfund law that dealt with handling the dangers of nationwide toxic waste found at industrial sites in particular. A tireless, no-nonsense legislator, he worked out the details of the planning and enactment of crucially essential legislation that—while difficult enough to discuss among politicians—often remained obscure in the minds of average citizens who did not always fully perceive or understand the inherent dangers of deferring environmental problems.

James Joseph Florio, better known as Jim Florio, was born on August 29, 1937 in the Red Hook section of New York City's borough of Brooklyn. He was the son of Vincenzo Florio, a Brooklyn Navy Yard painter, and Lillian (Hazel) Florio who was of Irish heritage. His paternal grandfather was an immigrant whose jobs included that of delivering coal and ice. Though born in Red Hook, Jim did most of his growing up in the Flatbush area of Brooklyn. When his father lost his job at the Navy Yard because of the post-WWII downsizing of military bases and installations, young Jim worked hard to help out the family. Later, at age seventeen, he dropped out of Erasmus Hall High School and joined the United States Navy where he served as a weather technician in Alaska and Florida for four years. Discharged from the Navy's full-time service with the rank of ensign in 1958, he served in the reserves for sixteen more years and would then retire as a lieutenant commander.

Upon receiving his high school equivalency diploma, he enrolled at Trenton State College (NJ) where he studied diligently and was elected president of the student body and graduated *magna cum laude* in 1962. After earning a Woodrow Wilson Fellowship, he did a year's additional studies in government at Columbia University and then pursued a law degree at Rutgers University Law School while he worked as a night watchman at the Camden County Courthouse. He joined the New Jersey bar in 1967 and set up practice in Camden County where he had already shown interest in political office. While serving and learning the business of politics in a number of state positions in the state assembly from 1967 to 1968—together with the assistance of local Democratic machinery—he eventually was elected to the state assembly in 1969 and, reelected for two more consecutive terms, focused his efforts on tax, environmental, and transportation issues.

In 1972 he challenged Republican incumbent, John E. Hunt. As a newcomer and not winning that first competition at the federal level, he earned a commendable 47% of the vote. Two years later, profiting from the negative publicity that Hunt had acquired for his sustained alliance with President Nixon and then from the president's subsequent August 9, 1974 resignation, Florio was quickly elected in November 1974 and then reelected biennially seven more times, serving in the House of Representatives until 1990. As chairman of the

Energy and Commerce Subcommittee on Commerce, Transportation and Tourism, Florio pursued as one of his major objectives resolving toxic waste problems. Ultimately he was responsible for overseeing the drafting of the Comprehensive Environmental Response, Compensation and Liability Act of 1980, more commonly referred to as the Superfund law. It amounted to a five-year program involving over one-half billion dollars in clean-up funds that were to be equally matched by whatever chemical companies the Environmental Protection Agency found responsible for polluting the environment.

In 1985 when the Superfund was up for renewal and Florio faced heavy opposition from many legislators who balked at the cleanup costs, he fought relentlessly for increased funding to insure the program's long-range effectiveness. A renewal package was realized even though it fell short of his desired $10 billion. Florio was also involved in drafting laws that started the nationwide inspection and elimination of asbestos insulation in our country's schools. In his long tenure as a congressman, he also voted for legislation that favored the nation's war veterans, the elderly, the deregulation of the railroad system, the increase in product disclosure data for consumer protection, the support for the legality of abortion but denial of its funding, and finally the support for more gun-control legislation.

Florio's journey to becoming governor of New Jersey began as far back as 1977. Contending with a relatively popular Republican incumbent in office, Florio finally had his day in the sun in 1990 when he was elected by 62% of the vote, sweeping seventeen of the twenty-one counties. In his January 16, 1990 inaugural address, Florio's resounding theme of "new ideas to preserve old ideals" reiterated the goal of striving for an economically viable New Jersey as a unified people working hand-in-hand with industry and business: *not* a state reflecting a disparately dichotomized people, one in well-to-do cities and towns and, in sharp contrast, the other in decaying, polluted and often abandoned areas. In his office as governor, he continued the many federal programs he had supported as a congressman. He dealt with industry and working people to improve their relationships; he introduced programs to improve schools, the quality of the environment, and consumer protection such as in the area of insurance assessments.

As a public servant who tirelessly performed his duties of elected office, he represented the electorate from 1975 to 1994. While Jim Florio had also had his moments with the press, he proved himself to be an engaging legislator and a determined leader in the purview of both state and federal programs and in effect received the John F. Kennedy Profile in Courage Award in 1993. In all, as a recognized statesman respecting the rights of people's health and economic well-being, he also emulated some of the best traditions of Ralph Nader's consumer rights movement and philosophy. As a consummate environmentalist, he leaves a legacy of almost twenty years of public service dedicated to the belief that modern health care necessarily begins with a clean environment. He leaves a legacy of unswerving dedication, hard work, and duty to the common good of the electorate both in their present and future needs.

General Sources:
1. *Congressional Directory*. 1989 ed.
2. *Current Biography Yearbook*. New York: Wilson, 1990.
3. Florio, Jim. Personal interview. 12 Dec. 1998.
4. *Taylor's Encyclopedia of Government Officials: Federal and State*. Dallas, TX: Political Research, 1989.
5. *Who's Who in America*. 1998 ed.
6. *Who's Who in American Politics*. 1989-1990 ed.

—by FILIBERTO P. BORDI

THOMAS FOGLIETTA (1928-   )

Thomas Michael Foglietta, after forty years of dedicated service as a United States congressman representing the people from the state of Pennsylvania, was nominated by President Clinton on September 5, 1997 and later confirmed by the Senate on Oct. 21 of the same year as the American Ambassador to Italy, his ancestral homeland. Thomas, the son of Michael and Rose Foglietta, was born in Philadelphia on December 3, 1928. As a young Italian-American man maturing in the 1940s, Thomas was afforded the opportunity to obtain a good education graduating from St. Joseph's College with a B.A. degree and then from Temple University with a law degree. He began his practice in south Philadelphia's well-known Italian district.

He became politically involved early in his legal career, and he would continue in politics for the ensuing 40 years. He began as a Republican city councilman opposing the entrenched Democratic machine. Yet in 1980, when he was elected to the House of Representatives, he did so as an independent; soon after, he switched to the Democratic Party. For about ten years the majority of his constituency had been overwhelmingly White; and Blacks and Hispanics constituted the minority.

When redistricting started in 1992, Tom Foglietta found himself as the only white representing what had become a black majority House district. In 1994, a reelection year, he faced a very determined black challenger, but he maintained his seat campaigning on the record of his efforts in having preserved jobs in the Philadelphia area and on the value of a projected extension of his seat on the House Appropriations Committee which he had gotten

at the start of the 103rd Congress. He had also sat on the Transportation Sub-Committee and on the Military Construction Sub-Committee.

His reputation had grown, and he became well known as a catalyst in keeping the Philadelphia Naval Shipyards active even after an independent commission was set up to review the needs of the Pentagon's facilities. Through his energetic efforts, he pursued lobbying efforts that kept the shipyard off the list of bases to be terminated. At one point, he even traveled to Russia in hopes of negotiating a deal whereby the Philadelphia Shipyard would dismantle contaminated Russian naval vessels.

Another instance of Foglietta's aggressive strategy in maintaining a strong work-force policy for his constituency involved his disagreement with Florida Democrat, Earl Hutto. The latter attempted to have the Navy remove a ship that was located in Philadelphia to be brought to Pensacola and then be decommissioned in Hutto's state. Foglietta, who had thwarted Hutto's efforts, then lobbied for funding to refit the aircraft carrier U.S.S. Kennedy in Philadelphia. Time and again, Tom Foglietta would fight to preserve employment for his constituents. Proving to be an excellent tactician, he had developed quite a following among his electorate.

Foglietta had earned his very positive congressional reputation in many ways by first being a "people person" and by typically fighting for minority causes. Without a doubt, one could safely say that party affiliation was very much a secondary consideration in his style. His interests lay first and foremost with the people's needs: For instance, in his early career as a Republican in Philadelphia, he successfully aligned himself with forces to fight the dominant

Democratic machinery. Then when he ran successfully as an independent in 1980 and won, he had again effectively aligned himself with forces that opposed both major parties.

It came as no surprise that when he eventually became a Democrat, he still served his constituents with the same zeal and drive. Party almost didn't seem to matter as far as his style and personality were concerned. Being a Caucasian politician in a predominantly Black and Hispanic House District and facing a strong black contender in this 52% minority district, the veteran incumbent, Tom Foglietta, was reelected to office nonetheless. Ironically, in all his electoral scenarios, he was the minority candidate. His track record in preserving jobs in his city together with his dynamic personality made the difference.

It was during the 103rd Congress that the pressure was mounting in the Republican-controlled Congress to bring closure to the crime prevention legislation contained in a crime bill backed by the Clinton administration. This was when Congressman Foglietta took a stand to defend the inclusion of programs aimed at helping adolescents get off the streets by keeping them in facilities. This prompted innovative ideas such as midnight basketball.

He also was only one of three House Democrats voting in 1994 against the revision of the Hatch Act whose changes would have expanded opportunities for federal employees to take part in the political decision-making processes. Foglietta's concerns involved the fact that if federal officials and agents in bureaus like the IRS, the FBI, or Immigration would be given these concessions, those newly acquired revised rights would then enable them to exert pressure in skewing voting trends.

It would mean that in their day-to-day contact with the public or through mass media, they could influence and possibly intimidate voters. Concerning this matter, Foglietta made this insightful and forceful statement commenting from the House floor: "Imagine the pressure an IRS or an Immigration agent could exert in a close-knit urban neighborhood? We cannot allow even a hint of this potential abuse to taint the electoral process."

Tom Foglietta was also involved in bringing about the restoration of a democratically elected government in Haiti. He was part of a Congressional delegation investigating the human rights abuses there. For his many hard-working years in Congress (1981-97) as a U.S. House Representative, Foglietta has left a legacy of dedication and genuine concern for the people he so respectfully represented. A wise and independent thinker, he continues to set a model of excellence in political life.

Nominated as Ambassador to Italy by President Clinton on September 5, 1997, Foglietta was confirmed by the Senate on October 21. He was sworn in on Nov. 12. 1997 after relinquishing his Congressional seat that he had held for many decades. At age 69, his energy is still abounding. His commitment and his political experience will serve him well in the land of his ancestors. As a man with a reputation for getting the job done, he was no doubt the right person appointed to this especially prestigious post in downtown Rome.

General Sources:
1. "Ambassador Thomas M. Foglietta's Biography." 21 Apr. 1999. <http://www.usis.it/mission/bios/ambioen.htm>.
2. *Facts on File*. 1997 ed.
3. "Foglietta." *New York Times* 7 Sept. 1997, I: 37.
4. *Taylor's Encyclopedia of Government Officials: Federal and State*. Dallas, TX: Political Research, 1999.
5. *Who's Who in America*. 1999 ed.
6. *Who's Who in American Politics*. 1997-1998.

—by DENNIS PIASIO

HENRY FONDA (1905-1982)

Oscar-award winning actor and 6th recipient of the Life Achievement Award from the American Film Institute, Henry Fonda has become one of the great American legends in world cinema. Born May 16, 1905 in Grand Island, Nebraska, Henry Jaynes Fonda descended from a titled Italian family that had fled from Genoa, Italy to the Netherlands to escape political persecution.

When Henry was six months old, the family moved to Omaha where his father ran a printing shop. In 1923, Henry graduated Omaha Central High School, and aspiring to become a newspaperman, he went to the University of Minnesota to study journalism. While in college, he worked for Northwestern Bell and then in a settlement house directing sports. In his second year, he dropped out of college and returned to Omaha to work as a file clerk.

But things began to change when in 1925, Dorothy "Do" Brando (mother of the then one-year-old Marlon Brando), a talent recruiter, part-time actress, member of the Board of Directors with the Omaha Community Playhouse, and a friend of the Fonda family, encouraged Henry to audition for a play in the Phil Barry Production of *You and I*. Despite the lack of faith in his ability to act, Henry managed to be persuaded to do so. He trudged downtown to read the part for director Greg Foley and officially won the role. His first season with the play lasted eight months. He became totally involved in theater, including building and painting scenery, hanging lights, and much more.

The theater helped him overcome his extremely shy, self-conscious personality. Rather than support Henry's pursuit of an acting career, his father felt he should get a "real" job.

When director Greg Foley offered him the lead role in *Merton of the Monies*, Henry's father became appalled that Henry would take on another play. Heated arguments between them led to their not speaking to each other. Despite their differences, the entire family attended opening night. When they returned home that evening, Henry's sister criticized his acting. Henry's father slammed down his newspaper and affirmed that Henry's performance was just perfect. Henry soon left his old clerk job and went with the small amateur playhouse. Though the salary was minimal, he remained working with them for three years.

In 1928 while playing summer stock in New England, he befriended a group of young aspiring theater people including Joshua Logan, Jimmy Stewart, Mildred Natwick, and Myron McCormick. He played some occasional bit parts on Broadway that seemed to be leading nowhere and decided to move to Cape Cod near the University Playhouse where he again met up with Joshua Logan. Henry joined the acting troop and met his first wife, Margaret Sullivan, a Virginia belle. At noon on Christmas Day 1931, Henry and Margaret married with the acting company serving as their witnesses. Margaret's career was soaring while Henry's was still in its infancy. Their marriage ended without bitterness in 1933.

Henry returned to Manhattan where he shared an apartment with Jimmy Stewart, Joshua Logan, and Myron McCormick. In 1934, Henry obtained his first major role in Leonard Sillman's Broadway play, *New Faces*. The same year, he secured the lead role in *A Farmer Takes a Wife*. His acting career was beginning to reach new heights when Leland Hayward, a theatrical agent, signed Fonda to a contract. Hayward paid for Fonda's move to California, a move that would change Henry's life significantly. Walter Wanger, a producer, signed him on to do two pictures a year at a salary of $1,000 per week.

While in England in the summer of 1936, Henry met Frances Seymour Brokaw. He married her in New York on September 16 that same year. They had two children: Jane Seymour born December 21, 1937, and Peter Henry, born February 23, 1939. The family had settled in Bel-Air, California when, in August 1942, Henry joined the war effort by enlisting in the Navy. Discharged as lieutenant senior grade in 1945, he was the recipient of a bronze star and a presidential citation. Henry returned to acting in the postwar years, both on stage and in the movies. In 1948, he achieved one of his biggest successes. He landed the starring role in the Broadway play *Mister Roberts* with which he is most identified by his fans.

After the war years, while Henry's theatrical career soared, his family life was besieged by problems. His wife Frances, who had experienced several bouts of severe depression, suffered a mental collapse and committed suicide in April 1950. Nine months later, Henry married his third wife, Susan Blanchard. While on their honeymoon, they received word that Henry's son Peter was seriously wounded by a .22 caliber pistol, and they rushed home to attend to him.

After five years of marriage and after having adopted a daughter, Henry lost both his third wife and his adopted daughter to divorce. In 1961, Fonda's fourth marriage also ended in divorce. Four years later at age 60, Henry married his fifth wife, Shirlie Mae Adams, 33, a former airline stewardess and model.

The most notable plays in which Henry Fonda starred include *A Farmer Takes a Wife* (1934), *Mister Roberts* (1948), *The Caine Mutiny Court Martial* (1953), *Clarence Darrow* (1974), and *Two for the Seesaw* (1958). He also appeared in more than 100 movies, including *Young Mr. Lincoln* (1939), *The Grapes of*

Wrath (1940), *The Male Animal* (1942), *Mister Roberts* (1955), *Twelve Angry Men* (1957), *The Best Man* (1964), and *On Golden Pond* (1981). His last film, *On Golden Pond* (1981), in which he appeared with Katharine Hepburn, earned him the Academy Award as Best Actor. Three years prior, in 1978, Fonda had also received the American Film Institute's sixth Life Achievement Award.

In Los Angeles, Henry Fonda's life came to an end on August 12, 1982. His legend endures with theater goers as they fondly recall his dramatic stage presence; and, seasoned movie buffs still marvel at his superb acting in his movie roles, such as young Mr. Lincoln or Tom Joad (*The Grapes of Wrath*). In truth, many critics have come to realize that in the better part of his acting career, Henry Fonda tackled the most difficult acting roles, portraying with great clarity and credibility quintessential, down-to-earth men characterized by deep moral principles and a sense of decency.

General Sources:
1. Collier, Peter. *The Fondas: A Hollywood Dynasty*. New York: Putnam, 1991.
2. *Current Biography Yearbook*. New York: Wilson, 1974; 1982.
3. Fonda, Henry. *Fonda, My Life, As Told to Howard Teichmann*. New York: New American Library, 1982.
4. Katz, Ephraim. *The Film Encyclopedia*. New York: HarperCollins, 1998.
5. Roberts, Allen, and Max Goldstein. *Henry Fonda: A Biography*. Jefferson, NC: McFarland, 1984.
6. Sweeney, Kevin. *Henry Fonda: A Bio-Bibliography*. New York: Greenwood Press, 1992.
7. Thomas, Tony. *The Films of Henry Fonda*. Secaucus, NJ: Citadel Press, 1983.
8. *Who's Who in America*. 1982 ed.

—by MARY JANE ADDONE

CONNIE FRANCIS (1938-   )

Concetta Rosa Maria Franconero, better known as Connie Francis, born on December 12, 1938 in Newark, New Jersey, was the daughter of George and Ida (nee Ferrara) Franconero. Both sets of her grandparents had come to America as immigrants, coincidentally, in the same year, 1905. Her maternal grandparents came from the town Mondo Virginina near Naples and her paternal grandparents from Reggio, Calabria. They all settled in Newark, New Jersey.

At the tender age of three, Connie attended Miss Masciola's Music School in Newark, taking lessons on the miniature accordion. By age four, she made her first performance at a music recital playing "Anchors Aweigh." Connie Francis went to the Bergen Street School and the Arts High School in Newark, and later, Belleville High School from which she graduated in June 1955.

During her high school career, she displayed an unbelievable amount of energy and involvement in numerous curricular and extra-curricular activities. She was a member of the National Honor Society, editor of the school newspaper, and a member of the glee, dramatic, debating, and international relations clubs. She organized student groups and wrote and produced musical comedies. At 15 she won the New Jersey State typing championship.

Connie's parents arranged for her to play benefits, private parties, church socials, and other community gatherings. Her father was instrumental in having Connie audition for many radio shows with her accordion. Though initially not successful, her first victory would come not from radio but ironically from TV on the *Arthur Godfrey Talent Scout Show* where she won first prize. At Godfrey's suggestion, her stage name became Connie Francis.

At 13 after a successful audition for George Scheck's *Startime*, a television show geared to youngsters, Connie appeared weekly and would do so for the next four years. Still in her early teens, she had the experience of touring the "borscht belt" in the New York Catskills during the summer months. She left few stones unturned, becoming involved in many aspects of show business: working backstage, doing the lighting, makeup, camera work, contributing production ideas, and typing scripts.

When the *Startime* show closed, George Scheck became Connie Francis' personal manager. When she was 17, she began singing in small night clubs and cocktail lounges around the country. From June 1955 to September 1957, she was under contract with MGM Records and agreed to record ten records for them. Her first nine recordings did not become hits. Yet her voice had already been heard on the soundtrack of movies such as *Jamboree* and *Rock, Rock, Rock*.

Connie then auditioned for nearly 200 large night clubs, radio, and television shows. With only three tryout successes, she became discouraged and decided to leave the performance end of the entertainment field. She received a scholarship to New York University and began classes in radio and television production. Her commitment with MGM involved having to make one more record which she would do in late 1957. Despite her reluctance, she was persuaded by her father to record an old favorite of his from 1923 entitled "Who's Sorry Now." It was given a rock 'n' roll beat, and she recorded it to fulfill her contractual agreement with MGM.

In 1957 a most popular TV show called

American Bandstand had become a way of life for many teenagers viewing late afternoon TV. Hosted by disc jockey Dick Clark, the show launched many singing careers because it regularly introduced new recordings as part of its format. Once presented on the air, these new recordings were rated on the spot by the show's teenage dance participants. It was Connie's good fortune that her new song, "Who's Sorry Now," made its debut on *American Bandstand*, and within three months it would sell over a million records. Her new-found success had put to an end her five-month study stint at New York University.

At age 20 Connie Francis began to enjoy her first string of hits. Many were reworkings of oldies such as "Mama" and "Among My Souvenirs"—and some were new—such as "Lipstick On Your Collar" and "Where The Boys Are," and "Everybody's Somebody's Fool." After 1958, she would become celebrated four times as the Best Female Singer of the Year by *American Bandstand* viewers; as the Most Programmed Vocalist of the Year by *Billboard*; Best Female Singer of the Year by *Cash Box*; and Best Female Vocalist of the Year by *Photoplay Magazine*. She appeared on several major television shows including *Perry Como, Jack Benny, Ed Sullivan, Jimmy Rodgers, What's My Line, This is Your Life*, and *Person to Person*.

After her early TV successes, Connie Francis began touring throughout the United States, Australia, New Zealand, Europe, South America and the Far East. Much to her credit, she recorded songs in Italian, Spanish, French, German, Portuguese, and Hebrew. Many of these songs became hits in the countries where those languages were spoken. She was later awarded Radio Luxembourg's Golden Lion Award for being the most programmed singing artist in Europe.

At age 36 Connie was besieged by several traumatic experiences. Beginning in November 1974, while on tour in Westbury, Long Island, she was raped in a hotel by an intruder. The trauma caused her to become a recluse, putting an end to her performing for a seven-year period. Abandoned by her third husband soon after the rape, their marriage ended in divorce. Connie plummeted into a deep depression.

Plagued by nasal problems, she underwent several corrective surgeries. Then in 1981, her brother George, who was cooperating with federal officials in the investigation of a kickback scheme, was gunned down gangland style right in front of his home. All these tragic events took their toll on Connie's personal and professional life. Diagnosed manic depressive, she spent much recuperative time in several institutions. On one occasion, she took an overdose of pills, but she was fortunately revived. Having overcome many setbacks in her personal and family life, Connie Francis has since returned to the stage where her concerts continue to be sold out. Her talents, unique style, youthful exuberance, and charitable works for national organizations and worldwide causes such as UNICEF, and for entertaining U.S. troops in Vietnam will always be remembered.

General Sources:
1. *Current Biography Yearbook*. New York: Wilson, 1962.
2. *The Encyclopedia of Popular Music*. Ed. Colin Larkin. London, UK: MUZE UK Ltd, 1997.
3. Francis, Connie. *Who's Sorry Now?* New York: St. Martin's Press, 1984.
4. Katz, Ephraim. *The Film Encyclopedia*. New York: HarperCollins, 1998.
5. *The New Grove Dictionary of American Music*. New York: Grove's Dictionaries of Music, 1986.
6. Shaw, Arnold. *Dictionary of American Pop/Rock*. New York: Schirmer Books, 1982.

—by JAMES L. MORSE

LOUIS J. FREEH (1950-   )

The second of three brothers, Louis J. Freeh was born on January 6, 1950 in Jersey City, New Jersey to William Freeh, a real-estate broker of German-Irish descent, and to Bernice Freeh, nee Chinchiolo, a former bookkeeper of Italian descent who had been raised in the Bronx (NY) by immigrant parents.

Louis grew up in North Bergen, NJ where he attended St. Joseph of the Palisades Elementary School. As a youth, he exhibited exemplary character serving as an altar boy for his local Catholic church and as an Eagle Scout. It is reported that at the tender age of nine he already knew that he wanted to become an FBI agent. He attended St. Joseph's Boys High School in West New York, New Jersey. While there, he became leader of the Christian Youth Group. During his junior and senior years, along with some other students, he went to Appalachia to do volunteer work for the poor in Lancaster, Kentucky. This experience reportedly had a profound influence on his decision to marshal his interests towards public service.

Freeh grew up in a working class family and neighborhood. In his early years, they lived in small quarters; and they were able to own their own house by renting out their second floor apartment. Louis has said that he was fortunate in having had loving parents who taught him a sense of fairness, morality, and family values. That is the kind of background, he reiterated, that stays around for the rest of one's life.

As a young man, Louis had gotten a taste of discrimination and social injustice when his mother related to him a story about when she, at age eighteen, had applied for a job with a large brokerage firm on Wall Street. Highly qualified for the position, she was rejected, she relates, not because of lack of qualifications but for their openly-stated preference for someone from non-Italian heritage. This scenario became a particularly incisive example of discrimination that Louis would never forget.

He attended Rutgers University at the New Brunswick campus where he graduated in 1971 as a Phi Beta Kappa student with a B.A. degree in American Studies. He continued his education attending night classes at Rutgers Law School in Newark, New Jersey; and in 1974 after three years of study, he was awarded a law degree. He practiced law for about a year when at age 25 he entered the FBI Academy in Quantico, Virginia; and upon completing his 6-week training course in 1976, he became an FBI agent.

His first assignment took him to the FBI's New York City office where he spent his first five years of investigative focus on organized crime, particularly on the city's waterfront activities. As an undercover agent employing hi-tech equipment, he was able to expose criminal activity, and he gathered sufficient incriminating evidence to bring to court many union leaders and as many as "125 others for extortion, racketeering, and tax evasion, among other charges." After the successful prosecution of these crime figures, Freeh was promoted to the position of supervisor of the organized crime division at FBI Headquarters in Washington, D.C. It was here that he met his wife to be, Marilyn Coyle, who also worked for the FBI as a paralegal. They would marry and have four sons.

A mere ten months later after his transfer to Washington when a host of bureaucratic frustrations reached high levels, he left the FBI to become an assistant attorney in the United States Attorney's Office for the Southern

District of New York. He became involved as one of the leading prosecutors in what was later to be called the "Pizza Connection" case. The trial, which began in 1985 and indicted and convicted 18 defendants, brought to a conclusion a five-year FBI investigation that dealt with a billion-dollar heroin and money-laundering operation.

It was one of the lengthiest and most costly trials dealing with organized crime figures. It was dubbed the "Pizza Connection" because pizza parlors throughout the U.S. were often used as focal points for drug distribution and money laundering. As the most outstanding of the prosecuting attorneys in this famous case lasting 17 months, Freeh had successfully litigated against organized crime. "Promoted to the rank of deputy and associate United States attorney in 1989, Freeh was named interim second-in-command when Rudolph Giuliani, then the United States attorney in the Southern District of New York, left office."

In 1990 he was asked to oversee the investigation of letter-bombings which were taking place in the southern United States. Among other things, those criminal acts had resulted in the death of a federal judge, Robert Vance, and a civil rights attorney, Robert Robinson. For his role in the successful prosecution and conviction of the letter-bomber, Freeh received the Attorney General's Award for Distinguished Service. In 1991, President Bush appointed Freeh to a lifetime federal judgeship in the Southern District of New York.

On July 16, 1993, Freeh was summoned to the White House where President Clinton and Attorney General Janet Reno offered him the post of FBI Director. Reportedly, this was an offer he had already twice rejected because of his concerns about the impact it would have on his family and his family life. Before accepting, he reportedly asked for assurances that regarded his independence as director and quality-time allowances for his family life. Clinton, who had called Freeh "a law enforcement legend," agreed to the requests, and Freeh became the new director on July 20, 1993.

As director, Freeh has been noted for his work in getting prosecutions in organized crime, drugs, racketeering, fraud, and terrorism. In 1987 and 1991, he had been the recipient of the Attorney General's Award for Distinguished Service, the second highest honor awarded by the Department of Justice annually. He has also received the John Marshall Award for Preparation of Litigation and the Federal Law Enforcement Officers Association Award.

The FBI now has a $2.2 billion budget and a 20,000 person bureaucracy that engenders a host of administrative challenges. In addition to the traditional responsibilities in his post, Freeh also faces many new challenges such as the threat of Asian organized crime, Islamic terrorism, domestic terrorism, and the resurgence of urban street gangs. Because of the respect and credibility that Freeh has earned, many citizens view him as the right man at the right time for the FBI director job. As a dedicated person who is never seeking self-aggrandizement, Freeh is a true leader, a role model of honesty, diligence, and respectability for his lofty position.

General Sources:
1. *Current Biography Yearbook*. New York: Wilson, 1996.
2. Freeh, Louis. "Remarks." John Carroll Society's Annual Dinner. Washington, DC, 23 Apr. 1994.
3. Kessler, Ronald, and Paul McCarthy. *The FBI: Inside the World's Most Powerful Law Enforcement Agency*. New York: Pocket Books, 1994.
4. "A Short History of the FBI." <http://www.fbi.gov/history/hist.htm>.
5. "What Can Be Done About Terrorism?" *USA Today* 6 Jan. 1996: 24-26.
6. *Who's Who in America*. 1999 ed.

—by LEO V. ZANATTA

ANNETTE FUNICELLO (1942-   )

Actress, singer, dancer, entrepreneur, recording artist, and one of the original and most popular of the Mouseketeers, Annette Funicello was one of the key players in Walt Disney's early family of stars. After her tenure with the Mouseketeers, she remained under contract with Disney. She moved up to senior status and appeared in a host of TV programs always linked to the Disney family name and, of course, appearing as a leading lady in as many as ten Disney movies particularly in the 1960s. A few years after returning to the silver screen with Frankie Avalon in 1987 to make a Paramount Pictures film entitled *Back to the Beach*, they made a successful yearlong nostalgia concert tour (1989-90), focusing on the teenage beach songs of the 60s.

Annette then made front-page headlines in 1992 when she announced to the world that she was in the throes of battling multiple sclerosis (MS). Today, she represents a symbol of hope and courage to all those afflicted with chronic and terminal diseases of the central nervous system. As America's sweetheart since her appearance on the *The Mickey Mouse Club* in 1955, she was simply referred to as "Annette" by millions of TV viewers fifty years ago. Now she is a highly determined entrepreneur, running two very successful businesses, using their profits to fund her foundation for MS research.

Annette Funicello was born in Utica, New York on October 22, 1942 to Joseph and Virginia Funicello and grew up in a middle class Italian-American family. Her grandparents were the emigrant generation from Italy. Her father, a master mechanic, worked hard to provide for his family, but having had enough of the cold weather he relocated the family to sunny California when Annette was four years old. No one in the family ever imagined the future she would find in the Walt Disney enterprises and in the Hollywood film industry.

They settled in the Los Angeles San Fernando Valley. After their arrival, young Annette began taking lessons in music and dance. With her mother's encouragement, Annette steadily improved her singing and dancing abilities, and in 1954 at age twelve she had an opportunity to appear as the lead in the ballet *Swan Lake* at the Starlight Bowl in Burbank. Walt Disney who was in attendance that evening was impressed with her abilities. Annette was called in for an audition for what would become a pathway for a career into show business, and it all began with a newly emerging television show called *The Mickey Mouse Club*.

The original series of *The Mickey Mouse Club* started in 1955 and concluded in 1959 after a successful four-year run. The one-hour show aired five days a week for the first two seasons, and it was reduced to one-half hour for the remaining two seasons. Unlike most children's programs of the time, it did not use a studio audience but depended upon its Mouseketeers for that. Its format was usually based on a theme that was developed through the use of film-shorts, newsreel footage, documentaries, a sketch, an episode from a serial program, and a Disney cartoon. The show's themes were held together by the engaging participation of the Mouseketeers who did the singing and the dancing. They also starred in the serialized episodes and served as an interactive audience with guests who were invited to the show.

Annette Funicello, among the most congenial and active participants, was one of the ten Mouseketeers to return in each of the four TV seasons. The program's syndication took place in 1962 and again in 1975. This program proved to be highly popular and innovative since, among other Disney firsts, it was the first program to offer made-for-TV serials designed specifically for children. Annette Funicello is well remembered for her role in one of these series, the *New Adventures of Spin and Marty*. In the fall of 1976, a revised version of the original show took place, and it was renamed *The New Mickey Mouse Club*; and, of course, it later switched to Disney's own TV channel in April 1989.

While Disney's original *The Mickey Mouse Club* underwent syndication in the 60s, Annette, who was now in her late teens and early twenties, started making as many as ten full-length feature films for Disney including *Babes in Toyland* (1961), *Beach Party* (1963), and *Pajama Party* (1964). Annette had also appeared in many TV programs and TV movies, as early as the 50s after *The Mickey Mouse Club* began, in a sense being an ambassador for the family-oriented Disney image. In addition to her film and TV work, Annette had her share of music hit records. Later in her career, she also did a yearlong concert tour (1989-90) with Frankie Avalon evoking memories of the teenage beach songs of the 60s.

After Annette Funicello had discovered she had MS, she also revealed some of her deepest feelings regarding the illness. In the opposing alternatives in attitude she might have adopted in reacting to the illness, she speaks of becoming determined to fight the disease and not ever yielding. As proof of her efforts, she started two businesses, and both businesses have become sources for subsidizing the Annette Funicello Research Fund for Neurological Diseases, a private foundation established by Annette to assist in the effort to study their possible cure. The first business she launched was the Annette Funicello Teddy Bear Company which markets a line of collectible bears. Then, in conjunction with Baywood International Inc., she launched her second business, promoting her own perfume fragrance named *Cello, by Annette*. In light of the aims of Annette's private foundation, the Walt Disney Company began in 1993 to support and distribute the latter product, and a percentage of the proceeds has gone to Annette's foundation enterprise.

In October 1992 the Walt Disney Company presented Annette with its Disney Legends Award. The award is intended to recognize those individuals whose work for the Disney family has made a significant impact on the Walt Disney legacy. Her autobiography published in 1994 was also made into a CBS-TV movie in 1995 bearing the same title: *A Dream is a Wish Your Heart Makes*. In 1997 Annette became the recipient of the Bella Rackoff Humanitarian Award for her charitable work with people afflicted with neuromuscular diseases. She remains steadfast to an ideal that cherishes life in its fullest familial and humanitarian sense of the word and, therefore, remains for many people a source of strength, courage, and charity.

General Sources:
1. Cerio, G. "A Sweetheart in Autumn." *People Weekly* 5 Oct. 1995: 111-12+.
2. D'Acierno, Pellegrino, ed. *The Italian American Heritage: A Companion to Literature and Arts*. New York: Garland Publ., 1999.
3. Funicello, Annette. *A Dream is a Wish Your Heart Makes*. New York: Hyperion, 1994.
4. Matsumoto, Nancy. "Hope in Her Heart." *People Weekly* 17 Aug. 1992: 74-78+.
5. McNeil, Alex. *Total Television*. New York: Penguin Books, 1992.
6. "Walt Disney Records: Biography of Annette Funicello." 1 Jan. 1999. <http://www.cowtown.net/users/annette/Anniebio.htm>.

—by KATHLEEN ZAPPIA

PAUL GALLICO (1897-1976)

A journalist for the *New York Daily News*, a war correspondent in both World Wars, a fiction writer, movie critic, screenplay writer, sports columnist, fable and ghost-story writer, and the author of forty-one books including *The Snow Goose*, *Confessions of a Story Writer*, and *The Poseidon Adventure*, Paul Gallico was a prolific creator who led a colorful and interesting life.

Paul William Gallico was born on July 26, 1897 in a New York City boarding house to immigrant parents Paolo and Hortense (nee Ehrlich) Gallico. His mother was from Vienna; and his father, who was from Trieste, had once traveled to the United States to make his first appearance as a concert pianist at age fourteen in New York City. He returned ten years later as soloist appearing with many symphonic orchestras and then decided to settle in New York City and become a music teacher.

The Gallicos' travels to and from Europe meant that young Paul had the unusual opportunity as a child to experience, firsthand, turn-of-the-century lifestyles especially those of musicians like his father and other artistic performers. He also had the chance to sense the opulence and luxury of ocean liner voyages, different cultures, languages, and the arts in general. His exposure as a youngster to culture and the arts influenced by the European ethos of the time would constitute a significant influence in many of his writings as an adult.

In addition to having knowledgeable parents from whom to learn, Paul attended the New York City school system to get his grade school and high school education. He then attended Columbia College of Columbia University by working in a variety of job capacities from those that were back-breaking to those that were cultural. Being muscular and heavily built, he helped load and unload ships at the New York City docks, was a munitions plant worker, did ushering at the Metropolitan Opera House, wrote free-lance fiction for magazines, and tutored students in German. He was active on the Columbia crew team, and eventually he completed his college degree in 1921 after having served in the United States Navy as a seaman gunner in WWI and also having done some war correspondence for the media.

In 1921 he not only obtained his first professional full-time position as review secretary for the National Board of Motion Picture Review but also married a newspaper woman, Alva Taylor, the daughter of Bert Leston Taylor, noted *Chicago Tribune* columnist. With the help of her father's ties to the newspaper industry, he started working for the *New York Daily News* as a motion picture reviewer in 1922; then, he transferred to its sports area as a writer and finally became a sports editor and columnist. Remaining in that position for the next twelve years and becoming popularly read, he was responsible for creating and promoting in 1927 through the *Daily News* in conjunction with the *Chicago Tribune* what then became known as the annual Golden Gloves amateur boxing tournament.

Gallico's career style contained some unusually daring practices. For his newspaper columns, he not only interviewed sports figures from all fields but also interacted with them in their sports milieu. For instance, he once boxed with Jack Dempsey, then the heavyweight champion, and went one round with him in the ring. Similarly, he competed in a swimming match with Johnny Weissmuller. He repeated these kinds of maneuvers in almost thirty or more sports, thus becoming lifetime friends with many of those people about whom he wrote.

He later explained that he was attempting literally to immerse himself into those sports, especially if he had never tried them before; and, his main purpose, of course, was just to understand "how it feels" to compete so that his columns could better reflect the qualities and challenges unique to the sports discussed. He tried a series of sports that were entirely new to him including flying single-engine planes, racing cars and boats, and skiing.

By 1936 Gallico's reputation and salary had grown, and he had already penned fourteen short stories that appeared in the *Saturday Evening Post* for which he was handsomely paid. After taking on his last assignment to cover the Olympic games in Berlin, which in fact became the last Olympic games to be played before Europe descended into the horrors of WWII, he decided to leave both the *Daily News* and the traditional full-time job in order to write more of the things in which he was interested. This usually involved writing fiction and covering special assignments.

Gallico now entered a new phase in his life where he was mostly occupied with free-lancing for special newspaper coverage, doing feature magazine articles, and writing fiction and screenplays. Though best known at the time for his many short stories, he excelled in full-length fiction and screenplays. In 1942 he received an Oscar nomination for his original MGM screenplay *Pride of the Yankees*, the biography of the legendary baseball hero, Lou Gehrig, who had been stricken with Amyotrophic Lateral Sclerosis (ALS) disease.

Immediately after the success of this film, Gallico went off once more to fight in Europe with the U.S. Expeditionary Forces. Gallico, who had already been decorated after WWI with the Victory Medal (1918), returned home after WWII and was again decorated with the Ribbon with Battle Star (1945). Right after his return to the States, he wrote another successful MGM screenplay, *The Clock* (1945), which starred Judy Garland and Robert Walker.

The Poseidon Adventure, a work of fiction published in 1969, would became his best remembered book, and it was popularized by an all-time great disaster film in 1972 based on that book and bearing the same name. A luxury liner, caught in a storm and in the path of an enormous tidal wave, capsizes turning over 180 degrees. In order to escape, the few survivors stuck inside the vessel must struggle to reach the bottom (now the top) of the ship. For its day in 1972, the film caused quite a stir commercially especially with its star-studded cast of Gene Hackman, Shelley Winters, old-time TV favorite Red Buttons, and Jack Albertson.

A popular and multi-talented writer who understood his film audiences and his reading public, he was and still is considered by many literary critics one of the best of America's entertaining and successful columnists and feature writers. As a masterful author of forty-one books, numerous short stories, several screenplays, and after enjoying an enviably interesting and productive career, he died at the age of seventy-nine in Monaco on July 15, 1976.

General Sources:

1.	*Current Biography/Yearbook*. New York: Wilson, 1946; 1976.
2.	Gallico, Paul. *Lou Gehrig, Pride of the Yankees*. New York: Grosset & Dunlap, 1942.
3.	Gallico, Paul. *Miracle in the Wilderness: A Christmas Story of Colonial America*. New York: Delacorte Press, 1975.
4.	Gallico, Paul. *The Poseidon Adventure*. London: Heinemann, 1969.
5.	Gallico, Paul. *The Snow Goose*. New York: Knopf, 1941.
6.	"Obituary." *New York Times* 17 July 1976: 26.
7.	*Who's Who in America*. 1946-47 ed.

—by MARIAN LILES

ERNEST GALLO (1909-   ) & JULIO GALLO (1910-1993)

The Gallo Winery in Modesto, California reputed the world's largest wine empire, produces more wine than the combined production of their three largest competitors. As they had once succinctly put it, their family-owned business philosophy encapsulated the notion: "To do whatever was to be long-range benefits of our company regardless of its effects on current profits." This idea, of course, runs contrary to the ideas of most publicly-owned companies whose primary interests are wedded to the idea of more immediate favorable earnings. The idea of deferring short-term bottom line profits for greater future profits remains, more often, a more realistic option for privately-run enterprises. The Gallo message contains the unremitting desire for commitment, hard work, striving for perfection, and the occasional good fortune that is concomitant with those attributes.

Their parents, Giuseppe and Susie Gallo, were immigrants who started with virtually nothing. In 1909, Ernest was born in Jackson and a year later Julio was born in Oakland, both cities in California. The San Joaquin Valley became home to the Gallo family where his father had a small grape-growing business. Ernest remembered drinking wine for the first time when he was five years old. It all happened very much by accident. After his father had crushed the grapes, and they lay fermenting for several days, Ernest managed to drink some wine drippings, but they amounted to as many as two cupfuls. The next thing he remembered was walking up to his grandmother's bed and feeling ill while his head was spinning. He experienced what was his first and reportedly last hangover.

Prohibition, described as a philosophy for enacting legal methods of controlling the manufacture, distribution, and sale of alcoholic beverages, went back as far as 1869 with the formation of a minor yet militant party called, appropriately, the Prohibition Party. Because of this party's efforts, national prohibition became law right after World War I through the enactment of the Eighteenth Amendment to the United States Constitution. Prohibition lasted for little over a decade because it was repealed in 1933 by the Twenty-first Amendment.

When Prohibition had come with its many restrictions, it put many wineries out of business. But homeowners could make as many as 200 gallons of wine for their own use. As a result, home winemaking had become an annual event for many Italian immigrant families who, coming to America to make a better life for themselves, did not want to give up an Italian tradition that included wine as part of their cultural heritage. And so, during the 1920s, the Gallo family like many Italian emigrant families that had access to farmlands, did what they could to grow their own grapes and to make wine from them. As teenagers growing up during Prohibition, Ernest and Julio naturally helped out their father by working the fields, and also learning the process of winemaking.

The 1930s proved to be a decade of happiness and extreme pain for the Gallos. For one thing, in August 1931 Ernest married Amelia Franzia, daughter of Italian homemade winemaker; and similarly, in May 1933 Julio married Aileen Lowe, who was of German-Austrian descent. However, in the same year it was also a very disturbing time when the Gallo brothers' parents were found shot to death. The police reported the tragic event as an apparent murder/suicide where Joe senior shot his wife and then himself.

In 1933 when Prohibition ended, it allowed the Gallos to embark upon their wine business. But because it was the middle of the Depression era, it was a difficult time for most fledgling businesses to succeed. The brothers worked hard to create E. & J. Winery. While they had only the experience of making homemade wine during Prohibition and possessed no marketing experience, they started with $900.23 in savings and a $5,000 loan.

In their first year (1934), they produced 177,847 gallons of red wine for a profit of $30,000. In the second year, 230,000 gallons; and in the third year, 941,000 gallons. During that period, the Gallo wine industry had grown, and by 1936 they had the storage capacity for one million gallons. Along with their successes, they also experienced health problems. Ernest had contracted tuberculosis and spent six months in a TB ward and was later operated for a ruptured appendix. In 1941 Julio experienced a nervous breakdown with a relapse a year later.

During WWII the Gallo wineries also assisted in the war effort. They converted their existing equipment to make tartrate (an industrial chemical) and alcohol for use in the making of synthetic rubber tires for military vehicles. Ironically, after WWII had ended, many wine companies emerged from the military war years only to create their own price wars with each other. The Gallo wineries indeed survived, and they started creating more wine varieties by combining different kinds of grapes. They expanded their operations by acquiring more properties, updating old equipment, using more stainless steel holding tanks, and investing vertically in the wine industry by doing such things as building their own glass plant and storage facilities.

With the advent of TV, wine became advertised nationwide in the 1950s; it would forever change the dining and beverage habits of Americans, and so drinking wine, which was once thought of as European, had now become an American phenomenon. Ernest Gallo had always said that he wanted the Gallo Winery to be the "Campbell Soup company of the wine industry." In the year 1960, the Gallo Winery became the leading wine producer in the U.S. by selling 30 million gallons of wine, and it was supplying wine to as many as 31 of the states.

Noticing that there was not much of a domestic champagne business in the U.S., the Gallos introduced successfully a whole new line of sparkling wine products. By 1971, Andre Cold Duck topped 2 million cases. Similarly, they created a revolution by introducing wine coolers, Boone's Farm apple wine. An overnight success in 1971, it went on to sell 56 million cases of wine coolers in 1987. No longer a winery that sells to Americans alone, nowadays Gallo wines supply about 43% of the world's wine market. Both brothers believed in dedication and in the perfection of combining scientific methods and vinicultural craft. As such, they represent an excellent tribute to all hard working Italian Americans and their desire to succeed. Julio died on May 2, 1993 in a jeep accident on his farm, and Ernest still continues monitoring his family-owned business daily, often spending long hours in nurturing the fruits and labors of his American dream.

General Sources:

1.   Gallo, Ernest, & Julio Gallo. *Ernest & Julio: Our Story*. New York: Random House, 1994.
2.   Hawkes, Ellen. *Blood and Wine*. New York: Simon & Schuster, 1993.
3.   Sullivan, Charles L. *A Companion to California Wine: An Encyclopedia of Wine and Winemaking From the Mission Period to the Present*. Berkeley: University of California Press, 1998.

—by JOSEPH PIGNATIELLO

ROBERT CHARLES GALLO (1937-   )

Robert Charles Gallo, born in Waterbury, Connecticut on March 23, 1937, was the son of Mary (Cianciulli) Gallo and Francis Anton Gallo. When Robert was a teenager, his younger sister, Judy, contracted leukemia. Dr. Marcus Cox, a pathologist at St. Mary's Hospital in Waterbury, diagnosed and treated Judy's disease. Despite efforts of an early chemotherapy treatment program and an ensuing remission, she relapsed and died. His sister's youthful demise together with Dr. Cox's care and influence would inevitably shape much of Robert's future career choice in the field of medical research.

In 1959, about ten years later, he graduated with a B.A. degree from Providence College in Rhode Island. He went on to Thomas Jefferson Medical College in Philadelphia. For periods of time between 1962-63, he also worked at Yale University Medical School as a clinical clerk. After medical school, he did his internship and residency at the University of Chicago (1963-1965).

As a medical student, he performed many experiments dealing with the growth of red blood cells. Much of his research was published, and upon completing his internship, he had already captured the attention of officials at the National Cancer Institute in Bethesda, Maryland. He was soon hired, becoming a clinical associate in 1965, and then promoted in 1968 to senior investigator in the laboratory of human tumor cell biology.

At the Institute, he focused on the growth properties of white blood cells (leukocytes). His interest in this was fostered not only by this area's potential for sustained research funding into the future but also by the memory of his sister's death caused by leukemia, a white blood cell disease. Much had been written since 1908 indicting viral causes for certain forms of cancers in animals, yet until the 1960s it had seemed virtually impossible to establish an analogous link in humans.

New technologies in biochemistry and in electronics had now made it possible to analyze viruses and their structures, functions, and their reproductive and parasitic operations. It inherently meant being able to study a virus' genetic composition called DNA and RNA. This new, virtually unexplored frontier of biochemistry raised the obligatory question as to how a virus enters a host cell and eventually incapacitates it.

In 1970 Dr. Gallo and fellow researchers were to demonstrate the existence of viral activity in leukocytes taken from leukemia patients. After growing these incapacitating viruses in an appropriate laboratory medium, they were able to limitedly observe the viruses through the use of the electron microscope. They began identifying different types of viruses. One such type categorized as Type C RNA, was associated with tumor developments in animals. Optimism grew as it would be just a matter of time before definite linkages could be established between viruses and its causation in certain human cancers.

Unfortunately, in January 1975, Gallo had prematurely announced that his group had isolated the human leukemia virus. Since follow-up experiments were not able to replicate the original experiments, Gallo and his colleagues moved in another direction, studying malignant human T-cells. By 1978, it seems that Gallo and his research staff had isolated and matched an unknown virus from the blood of a leukemia patient with that of T-cells developed in the laboratory. Because of cautionary attitudes, this phenomenon was not published until 1981 in the October issue of *Science*.

He named this virus the human T-cell leukemia virus and its two variants: HTLV-I and HTLV-II. After obtaining an ample collection of malignant samples from around the world, he discovered that the HTLV-related leukemia was "more common in Africa, the Caribbean, and Japan," and was transmittable "by intimate contact, such as breast-feeding or sexual intercourse, or through blood transfusions." Replications of his studies concluded that the HTLV virus was carcinogenic and it became classified as a "retrovirus."

Gallo's research attempted to understand the mechanisms of the retrovirus and how cancers grew from normal cells. He discovered that when the virus enters the invaded cell, the virus's RNA (genetic material) imposes its own instructions on the cell's operations by changing the cell's nucleus where the DNA (the command center of the cell) is located. In effect, the changes in the cell's DNA (now dictated by the virus' agenda) causes the cell to function differently, growing abnormally and, regrettably, undetected by the body's immune system.

In 1981, when a growing number of people were dying from an inexplicably fatal disease related to problems with their immune system, it immediately raised many challenges that seemed relatable to the research that Gallo and his staff had done on the leukemia virus. Naturally, Gallo sought to find and identify a comparable virus that was involved in the explanation of this newly emerging fatal disease, later to be designated as the AIDS virus.

His research encountered many roadblocks. He tried in vain to grow this new virus in the laboratory. After many unsuccessful months, Gallo came to the conclusion that this virus was acting radically different from prior viruses he had studied. Unlike the previous leukemia viruses which made the host cell grow abnormally by creating more cells which were cancerous, the newer virus simply killed its host cell and "wiped out its own tracks" by first invading the cell and then killing it.

Gallo and his staff were compelled to use alternative methods to study this newer virus. Eventually, they were able to determine their theories as true in discovering the AIDS virus, publishing their findings in a series of four scientific papers in the May 1984 issue of *Science*. They named the AIDS virus with the acronym HTLV-III, representing "Human T-Cell Lymphotropic Virus Type III."

Dr. Robert Gallo married Mary Jane Hayes in 1961 and they have two children, Robert and Marcus. As a virologist, he went on to receive many awards for research, including two prestigious and highly coveted Lasker Awards, once in 1982 and again in 1986. Serving as chief of the National Cancer Institute, his research goes on unabated, attempting to find a resolution to the AIDS epidemic.

General Sources:
1. *American Men and Women of Science*. New Providence, NJ: R.R. Bowker, 1998-99.
2. Carey, J. "Bob Gallo's New Weapon Against AIDS." *Business Week* 15 Jan. 1996: 87-88.
3. *Current Biography Yearbook*. New York: Wilson, 1986.
4. Gallo, Robert C. *Virus Hunting: AIDS, Cancer, and the Human Retrovirus: A Story of Scientific Discovery*. New York: Basic Books, 1991.
5. Gallo, Robert C., and Flossie Wong-Staal, eds. *Retrovirus Biology and Human Disease*. New York: Dekker, 1990.
6. Gallo, Robert C., and Gilbert Jay, eds. *The Human Retroviruses*. San Diego: Academic Press, 1991.
7. *Notable Twentieth-Century Scientists*. Detroit, MI: Gale Research, 1995.

—by ANTHONY SOLDANO

GIULIO GATTI-CASAZZA (1869-1940)

The most charismatic of the New York Metropolitan Opera's impresarios, Giulio Gatti-Casazza nurtured its growth and directed its development for twenty-seven years from 1908 to his retirement in 1935. A frequent traveler to Europe to observe firsthand potentially great opera stars and musicians, he was ultimately responsible for much of its worldwide reputation and for the powerful image that the words "Metropolitan Opera" or simply the "Met" would evoke in people's minds as the showcase of the best opera and opera singers in the world. Among the many personalities that he either discovered or mentored, Enrico Caruso and Arturo Toscanini top the lofty list.

Giulio Gatti-Casazza was born in Udine, Italy on February 3, 1869. Udine, located in the Friuli-Venezia region, just northeast of Venice and close to the Yugoslavian border, is a city replete with gothic, renaissance, and baroque art works and structures. It has claimed to have had Palladio (1508-1580), one of Italy's notable architects, design some of its architecture. Giulio, proud of his city's northeast Italian culture, intended to become an engineer, but in 1893 at age twenty-four he succeeded his father as director of the Municipal Theater in Ferrara, a city just south of Venice.

Despite his relatively young age, Giulio apparently excelled in directing the operations of this municipal theater so well that five years later in 1898 he was offered the highest managerial position imaginable in the world of Italian culture at that time, the direction of La Scala di Milano. He accepted the challenge and for an entire decade the reputation of La Scala blossomed. He had many excellent administrative qualities, and one of his strongest included his ability to intuit the wishes of his audiences whereupon he would simply provide their realization. He had developed and employed from an early age an effective win/win strategy.

It was close to the turn of the century when he had accepted that job, and in Europe there was hope for a new dawn looming on the horizon. German opera, particularly that of Wagner (1813-1883), was imbued with a strong desire for historical change. Infused with German mythology and Nietzschean philosophy suggesting philosophical changes to challenge the era, Wagner's works became for many opera aficionados the ideal vehicle for reflecting those needs.

Gatti-Casazza, who apparently was keenly aware of this Zeitgeist, did much during his tenure at La Scala to counter conventional opera wisdom and joined in popularizing Wagnerian opera in Italy in addition to having La Scala perform the usual regime of Italian operas. Yet, careful to maintain a happy balance, he also introduced new operas from France. In all, he kept La Scala at its traditionally high level of achievement as he was inventive, highly intuitive, and managerially on target with his audiences' desires so that the box office was always busy.

Gatti-Casazza's reputation as an astute and resourceful manager at La Scala became known quickly even among opera executives and administrators in the United States. This helps explain why when the New York Metropolitan Opera became steeped in financial problems, Gatti-Casazza was asked to assume its direction. It seems that the prior director of the Metropolitan, Heinrich Conried, who had held the reigns from 1903 to 1908, was actually quite effective in many ways, appropriately featuring many German operas, offering old favorites as well as American premieres such as *Parsifal* and *Salome*, and improving the overall quality of productions. He also was responsible for the introduction of partial nudity on the stage in the opera *Salome* (January 1907) and, again, in the opera *Faust* (November 1907) in the characterization of Mephistopheles.

The latter events created a furor in the media and caused an editorial backlash for Conried's daring use of nudity, but this was all incidental. While he did resign in 1908 claiming illness, historians have pointed out that it was no secret that competition from the newly founded Manhattan Opera Company had already been adversely effecting the Metropolitan's ability to meet its financial obligations. In 1908 the board of directors at the Metropolitan Opera, intent on redesigning the entire operation, placed Gatti-Casazza at the helm, making him the director as well as its general manager. In effect, he would be held responsible for maintaining both the Met's liquidity and its high artistic standards.

With competition a short distance away, it was no small order, but in his twenty-seven-year tenure, Gatti-Casazza more than fulfilled that directive. He began systematically setting standards of efficiency and high performance. He insisted that all operas be sung in the language of original composition (and not English translations). He sought and hired the best operatic conductors of the time such as Gustav Mahler (1908-1910), Arturo Toscanini (1908-1915) who made his American debut in November 1908 with a performance of *Aida*, Alfred Hertz (1902-1915), Arthur Bodansky (1915-1939), and Tullio Serfin (1924-1934).

In a 24-week season, he often would have to his credit as many as 48 different works so there was variety in addition to high quality. He was also responsible for the debut of American operas, such as Frederick Converse's *The Pipe of Desire* (1910), Horatio Parker's *Mona* (1912), and the world premieres of Giacomo Puccini's *La Fanciulla del West* and

Engelbert Humperdinck's *Königskinder*. A purist in many respects, he had Wagner's operas performed without cuts; and, taking full advantage of the new medium of radio in the 1920s, he had the Met's performances aired on a weekly basis. Spearheading an administration to make the Met survive especially during the challenging days of the depression era, he then retired in 1935 after 27 years of tireless, impeccable leadership.

During his fifth year of retirement in Italy, Giulio Gatti-Casazza died in the city of Ferrara on September 2, 1940 just a few months after the death of his wife of ten years, Rosina Galli, who had been a prima ballerina and later the ballet mistress at the Met. Just before his death, he had completed his autobiography entitled *Memories of the Opera*. He left a legacy of dedication to the high standards as the leading opera impresario of his time. An astute and daring manager of money and people, he made the New York Metropolitan Opera survive the 1929 stock market crash and the resulting economic depression. He maintained the highest standards for over a quarter of a century, and it is no wonder that today his name is still the one most associated with the Metropolitan Opera's greatness.

General Sources:
1. *Current Biography*. New York: Wilson, 1940.
2. Ewen, David. *The New Encyclopedia of the Opera*. New York: Hill and Wang, 1971.
3. Gatti-Casazza, Giulio. *Memories of the Opera*. New York: Vienna House, 1973.
4. Hamilton, David, et al. *The Metropolitan Opera Encyclopedia: A Comprehensive Guide to the World of Opera*. New York: Simon & Schuster, 1987.
5. Sadie, Stanley, ed. *History of Opera*. New York: Norton, 1990.

—by GEORGE CARPETTO, Ph.D.

BEN GAZZARA (1930-   )

Actor of stage, screen and television, occasional director and narrator, Emmy Award recipient, and winner of several theater awards, Ben Gazzara has had a long and engaging career both as an actor in the United States and in Italy, often having played roles opposite such notables as Anna Magnani and Totò in *The Passionate Thief* (1960). A method actor by training at Irwin Piscator's workshop at the New School in the Village (NYC) and at the Actors Studio with mentor Lee Strasberg, Gazzara has proven himself to be a versatile actor on stage with three Tony nominations. In television he had three Emmy nominations for his three-year hit-series in the 60s *Run for Your Life,* and he was a recipient of an Emmy for a 1986 miniseries.

Biaggio Anthony Gazzara, better known as Ben Gazzara, was called Ben or Bennie from his earliest years. He was born on August 28, 1930 in Manhattan (New York City) in a heavily populated Italian area on 29th Street and Second Avenue. One of two boys, Ben's brother Anthony was five years older. They both spoke the Sicilian dialect as their first childhood language. His parents, Antonio and Angela (nee Cusumano) Gazzara were immigrants. His father, a carpenter and roofer by trade, died early in life during the Depression years while his boys were still young.

Raised with a Catholic education, Ben was an altar boy and attended Our Lady of the Scapular of Mount Carmel Elementary School run by the Carmelite nuns. Before graduating from elementary school, he was already appearing in amateur productions at the Madison Square Boys Club, where reportedly he had been described as serious and immersed in his roles even during rehearsals when most other "kids would start horsing around..." He then attended Stuyvesant High School, which he disliked; and in his third year, he took to truancy for about eight weeks. His time away from school was usually spent in movie houses where he watched his favorite screen stars including James Cagney, Clark Gable, John Garfield, Edward G. Robinson, and Spencer Tracy.

After his school impropriety was disclosed to his mother, he negotiated a switch to a coed Catholic high school in the Bronx, St. Simon Stock School from which he would eventually graduate in 1947 when he was seventeen. Though he sorely wanted to become an actor, he thought it more practical to study engineering. In the fall of that year, he enrolled in the night program at City College of New York, and during the day he worked at a job on Canal Street, but this would be short-lived.

A year later in 1948, his desire for acting was rekindled when he saw a production of Jean-Paul Sartre's *The Flies* by the Dramatic Workshop at the New School for Social Research. Responsible for the supervision of that workshop was a man called Erwin Max Piscator (1893-1966). Hired by the New School, he was a German radical theater and movie director who in the 1920s had become the chief exponent of avant-garde leftist drama, which was often viewed as a form of "epic theater" in that it was theatrically designed to involve the audience with multi-media effects through the use of slides or film. A Communist in political orientation, Piscator's theatrical style (not his political objectives) had thoroughly fascinated Gazzara so much so that he quit his engineering studies and auditioned for and won scholarship money to Piscator's workshop.

At the New School in the Village, Gazzara studied under Raiken Ben-Ari, who years prior had studied in Moscow under Stanislavski and Vakhtangov, two noted theorists in acting. Gazzara learned a great deal at their workshop, and two years later he was admitted to the famous Actors Studio headed by Lee Strasberg who also taught in the tradition of Stanislavski's principle of intuitive realism, more commonly referred to as the Method or method acting. Gazzara, who as a youngster had exercised his natural inclination towards acting, found renewed vitality after the experience of these two major courses of study. He now felt he had in his possession the theory and the practice in method acting and was ready for his profession.

Gazzara began his professional career in acting in 1952 at the Cape May Playhouse (NJ) as Micah in *Jezebel's Husband*, then as Jocko de Paris in *End as a Man*, which began on Off-Broadway and then successfully moved to Broadway in two different theaters for the following two years (1953-54). When he played the lead role of a psychopathic sadist in a southern military academy, it turned out to be one of the finest moments of his stage career with his winning in 1953 the Drama Critics Award and the World Theatre Award.

In 1955 it was his good fortune to have a part in what would become a very successful Broadway play, *Cat on a Hot Tin Roof*, a drama by the renowned Tennessee Williams who went on to win the Pulitzer Prize and the New York Drama Critics Award. Gazzara played the part of Brick, an alcoholic and distanced husband in a southern family drama. Seven months later in 1955, however, Gazzara left the William's drama to take the lead role in Michael Gazzo's *A Hatful of Rain* where he played the role of Johnny Pope, a drug addict. The critics praised Gazzara extensively for having demonstrated his broad acting ranges from roles depicting power and control to those of depression and suffering.

After doing the movie version of *End as a Man* retitled for film as *The Strange One* (1957), Gazzara continued in theater in another of Gazzo's plays, *The Night Circus* (1958). While he would go on to do ten or more major theater appearances as recent as *Chinese Coffee* in 1994, Gazzara spent most of his time doing movies and working in television. Among his many excellent film roles, he was particularly successful in *Anatomy of a Murder* (1959) and *Husbands* (1970). While Gazzara had appeared in television throughout the 50s, it wasn't until the 60s that his name became well known in two very successful TV series. In *Arrest and Trial* (1963-64) he played a detective and co-starred with Chuck Connors; and in *Run for Your Life* (1965-68) Gazzara plays the role of a man stricken with a fatal disease who is trying to pack into life as much as he can in the time remaining.

Having acted in over sixty movies inclusive of foreign films, and having appeared in four TV series/miniseries in addition to over forty TV appearances, Ben Gazzara has rightfully earned his niche as an esteemed actor in modern film, theater, and television. In 1986 he earned an Emmy for a TV miniseries *An Early Frost* (1985). From his long list of film credits, including his recent appearance in Joel Coen's *The Big Lebowski* (1998), Ben Gazzara will probably be best remembered for his starring role in the mid-60s hit-series, *Run for Your Life*, that for three years had captivated TV viewing audiences.

General Sources:

1. *Contemporary Theatre, Film and Television*. Detroit, MI: Gale Research, 1998.

2. *Current Biography Yearbook*. New York: Wilson, 1967.

3. Katz, Ephraim. *The Film Encyclopedia*. New York: HarperCollins, 1998.

4. Ragan, David. *Who's Who in Hollywood*. New York: Facts on File, 1992.

—by GEORGE CARPETTO, Ph.D.

PETER GENNARO (1919-   )

A dancer, producer, director and choreographer most associated with modern jazz dancing in theater, Peter Gennaro has also achieved many memorable and notable moments in film, ballet, and in the medium of television. A WWII entertainer, a Broadway and Radio City Musical Hall choreographer, in addition to having been a Hollywood and TV dancer and choreographer, he has been in all the facets of entertainment that have involved dancing.

Peter Gennaro, whose date of birth is uncertain, was most likely born on November 23, 1919 in Metairie, Louisiana to Italian emigrant parents, Charles and Concetta (nee Sabella) Gennaro. The youngest of three children, he contracted as a child an ear infection which managed to effect his hearing causing a chronic hearing problem for the rest of his life. Ever since then, he has had to actively compensate for that hearing deficit all the more because of the dancing lessons he pursued from a young age through his adolescent years and into his future career as a dancer and a choreographer.

When stationed in the military in India doing routine work in the Army Air Corps, he came across quite by accident an opportunity to dance. Melvyn Douglas, a Broadway actor and director by profession and also a Hollywood screen star, was touring India with his military entertainment group. He needed dancers in his shows being staged for the American military. Peter managed to join his military troupe and worked with them for eight months. When he returned to Louisiana after the war and worked in his father's tavern and restaurant called Gennaro's Inn, Peter discovered that the sharp contrast in activities precipitated his thinking through what he wanted to do with his life.

After six months, he took off for New York City to study dance with his specific destination being the American Theatre Wing. Empowered by his military entertainment days and the G.I. Bill's educational benefits, he began studying modern dance under Katherine Dunham, José Limón, and Archie Savage in 1946. He obtained his first professional job in September 1947 in the ballet chorus of the San Carlo Opera, an itinerant company whose home town was Chicago. There he met and married Jean Kinsella who also danced for the San Carlo Opera. They married in January 1948. In the same year, they began dancing in musical comedies that were basically road shows. As his experience and exposure grew, he obtained parts in Broadway shows such as *Subway Circuit* (1949), *Kiss Me Kate* (1950), and *Guys and Dolls* (1950).

It was in May 1954 that he secured his first important role at the St. James Theater in a Broadway musical called *Pajama Game*. This appearance was significant because his dancing to the music of "Steam Heat" with Carol Haney brought him to the attention of Broadway critics for the first time. Gennaro had also been teaching dance, especially modern jazz movements, to Broadway, TV, and Hollywood stars. One of his pupils was the famed movie actress Grace Kelly. When she mentioned that the producers of a play, *Seventh Heaven*, were looking for a choreographer, he inquired and obtained the position; and this became the first time he choreographed a Broadway show. The musical opened at the ANTA Theater in May 1955 lasting only 44 performances. While the critics had generally panned the musical itself, they lauded Gennaro's efforts in the choreographic numbers.

Based on the strength of his growing experience, he obtained a leading dance role in the November 1956 Broadway production of *Bells Are Ringing*. Later, Gennaro worked as co-choreographer with the well-established Jerome Robbins on one of the all time Broadway musical greats *West Side Story*, which opened in September 1957 at the Winter Garden Theater. It was an instant success in the eyes of the critics as well as in the hearts and pocketbooks of Broadway musical aficionados. This 1957-58 show ran for 284 performances, and due to its great popularity it was revived in 1960.

Critically important in Gennaro's work and involvement as a choreographer in *West Side Story* remained his expert introduction of "jazz" movements into the dance numbers, especially in the classic "America." Henceforth, Gennaro's popularity grew, and he was able to work in an even wider range of dance expressions demonstrating his expertise in modern jazz sequences and its complexities that eventually became recognizable by critics and audiences alike. *Fiorello*, a Broadway musical opening in November 1959, instantly captured favorable reviews particularly for its Gennaro dance numbers. The musical and choreographic success of *Fiorello*, dealing with the life of Fiorello La Guardia, was immediately followed by his November 1960 choreography of *The Unsinkable Molly Brown*, set in turn-of-the-century Denver, Colorado which, despite lukewarm responses from critics, went on to run for a lengthy 532 performances. Moved by its popularity, MGM made it into a movie in 1964 choreographed by Gennaro.

Though Gennaro would become a name frequently synonymous with 60s and 70s Broadway musicals, confirmed by three nominations for a Tony Award (*Bajour* in 1964, *Irene* in 1973, *Little Me* in 1982) and winning a Tony and a Drama Desk Award for the musical *Annie* in 1977, he spent the greater part of his time directing choreography for shows at the Radio City Music Hall (1971-78) and for the burgeoning TV media with its apparently insatiable appetite for variety shows, musicals, specials, and family-oriented comedy hours. Gennaro achieved the status of being the most visible and prominent TV choreographer. He worked on many popular TV programs that starred personalities such as Arthur Murray, Red Skelton, Perry Como, Ed Sullivan, Sid Caesar, Bing Crosby, Fred Astaire, and Andy Williams.

Perhaps one must attribute to Gennaro a marvelous sixth sense of timing in adapting and blending the medium of dance to present times and to the popular needs of the theater-going public. This unique and cherished adaptability was made possible in great part by his professionalism in a wide range of styles from traditional ballet to the complexities of the not-so-apparently-easy freestyle movements or improvisation that are often synonymous with jazz dance. Gennaro still remains active in the industry while his son, Michael, is managing director of the Steppenwolf Acting Company of Chicago, and his daughter, Liza, is a choreographer.

General Sources:
1. *Contemporary Theatre, Film and Television.* Detroit: Gale Research, 1987.
2. *Current Biography Yearbook.* New York: Wilson, 1964.
3. Feuer, Jane. *The Hollywood Musical.* Bloomington, IN: Indiana University Press, 1993.
4. Kislan, Richard. *Hoofing on Broadway: A History of Show Dancing.* New York: Prentice Hall, 1987.
5. Kislan, Richard. *The Musical: A Look at the American Musical Theater.* New York: Applause, 1995.
6. Marcus, Alford. *Jazz Danceology.* n.p.: Dance Press, 1991.

—by SAM PITTARO

RICCARDO GIACCONI (1931-   )

Known as the founder of X-ray astronomy from which he was able to generate many astronomical discoveries, recipient of many honors and awards, heading the team in the design of the Hubble Space Telescope, director of the European Southern Observatory (ESO) in Chile, world-renowned lecturer in the relatively new field of astronomy known as high-energy astrophysics, Riccardo Giacconi has become one of the most sought-after lecturers in the world addressing both physicists and laymen alike about the complicated hi-tech field of astronomy and its role in the 21st century.

Riccardo Giacconi was born on October 6, 1931 in Milan, Italy to Antonio and Elsa (nee Canni) Giacconi. He attended the University of Milan and earned his doctorate in 1954 under the guidance of his mentor, the distinguished physicist Giuseppe Occhialini. Riccardo wrote his dissertation on elementary particles, and while teaching at the university he applied for and won a two-year Fulbright grant to study abroad in 1956 at Occhialini's suggestion. While at the University of Indiana as a Fulbright fellow, he studied cosmic rays activity. During that time he met and married Mirella Manaira in 1957, and they would have a family of three children.

In 1958 after completing his Fulbright, he became a research associate at Princeton University. Unfortunately, while doing research there, he came to the sobering conclusion that his methods were growing into obsolescence. It appears that as magnetic particle accelerators were becoming available towards the end of the 50s, they had all but pre-empted the older methods of doing research including those of Giacconi who had usually collected cosmic rays as a means of studying fundamental atomic particles. He suddenly was faced with the problem of learning newer methods and finding the commensurate equipment to continue his research, so he had to change direction.

The apparent dilemma became resolved in 1959 when he met Bruno Rossi, a reputed pioneer in cosmic-ray physics, who invited him to look into working at a private Massachusetts firm (located not far from MIT) called American Science and Engineering (AS&E), which did work for the federal government. AS&E was interested in the commercial and defense-related uses of X-ray physics. There he met Martin Annis and George Clark, both students of Bruno Rossi. Giacconi soon started to work at AS&E, and his career began to move rapidly.

Clark exhorted Giacconi to pursue astronomy research by starting with the study of the properties of charged particles in the Van Allen radiation belts. The Van Allen belts are the names given to two belts of radiation which are found outside the earth's atmosphere extending between 400 and 40,000 miles above the Earth. Their ethereal layers are not uniform in density, and this irregularity would act to further complicate a scenario that included America's plans for satellite navigation and communication. The radioactivity of the belts could also pose many dangers to personnel and equipment in future space launches.

Sputnik 1 (10/4/57) and *Sputnik 2* (11/3/57) had already been launched by the Soviet Union, and the American space program was trailing with its *Explorer 1* (1/31/58) by several months. While the race for outer space had indeed begun, more data was sorely needed to assess the potential lethality of cosmic rays activity. While Giacconi undertook this space program project, he also searched for ways to improve the detection of X-rays and gamma rays emanating from nuclear testing, a cold war reality of the 1950s where both the United States and the Soviet Union were testing nuclear weapons. Giacconi and his team were afforded the opportunity with their latest equipment to observe X-ray and gamma ray activity within the Earth's atmosphere.

In September 1959 at Rossi's prompting, Giacconi also began exploring what possibilities X-ray astronomy, a totally new field at the time, might produce by designing the world's first X-ray telescope. In all, the mass of data collected by Giacconi's program was instrumental in the AS&E designing and building twenty-four rocket payloads and six satellite payloads in a subsequent eight-month period. Giacconi's program to explore and monitor X-ray activity in outer space, initially inspired by Rossi and then instituted by the AS&E test facilities, were ultimately responsible for a 95 percent success rate in monitoring outer space activity.

The methods of gathering that information had proven to be so successful that it had the effect of creating a new data-gathering protocol extending beyond the solar system in the search for more X-ray sources. On June 18, 1962, a rocket launch containing data-gathering equipment sent back totally new information indicating the Scorpius constellation as a definite source of cosmic X-rays. By 1967 Giacconi's team had discovered more than thirty X-ray sources beyond that of the solar system.

After NASA's launch of its HEAO-1 (High Energy Astronomy Observatory) satellite in 1977 which involved Giacconi's design of its instrumentation (X-ray telescope observatory), Giacconi and his team quickly went on to improve the design of the telescope designated for the HEAO-2, a satellite called *Einstein*. Launched from the Kennedy Space Center in November 1978, it remained operational until April 1981, and its success revolutionized celestial mapmaking. In 1981 Giaccioni was named head of the Space Telescope Science Institute where he led the team that carried out the design for the launching of the unprecedented Hubble Space Telescope. Perched above the Earth's atmosphere, it would be able to see farther into the universe than any other telescope to date.

Starting from his early university days, Giacconi has been a recipient of close to twenty important honors, awards, and prizes including a Fulbright (1956), the Dannie Heineman Prize for Astrophysics (1981), the Cressy Morrison Award from the New York Academy of Sciences (1982), and the Wolfe Prize (1987). In 1993 he left the Space Telescope Science Institute to become the director of the European Southern Observatory. From the structure's very inception, he became responsible for overseeing the construction of this $200 million observatory in Northern Chile (South America) which is purported to be the most up-to-date facility of its kind on Earth. It is called a VLT (acronym for Very Large Telescope), an architectural monument with which we may associate Giacconi's scientific accomplishments.

General Sources:
1.   Giacconi, Riccardo. "The Einstein X-Ray Observatory." *Scientific American* Feb. 1980.
2.   Giacconi, Riccardo, and Giancarlo Setti, eds. *X-Ray Astronomy*. Proceedings of the NATO Advanced Study Institute held at Erice, Sicily, 1-14 July 1979. Boston: D. Reidel Pub., 1980.
3.   Maffei, Paolo. *Monsters in the Sky*. Trans. Mirella and Riccardo Giacconi. Cambridge, MA: MIT Press, 1980.
4   *Notable Twentieth-Century Scientists*. Detroit, MI: Gale Research, 1995.
5.   O'Meara, Stephen. *Sky & Telescope* Jan. 1991: 18.
6.   Tucker, Wallace, and Riccardo Giacconi. *The X-Ray Universe*. Cambridge, MA: Harvard University Press, 1985.

—by MARK BATTISTE

173

ANGELO BARTLETT GIAMATTI
(1938-1989)

Beginning as a distinguished teacher, a scholar in English and in comparative literature at Princeton University, and then president of Yale University, he went on to become president of baseball's National League and eventually the commissioner of baseball. He achieved all of these things in the brief span of fifty-one years.

Angelo Barlett Giamatti was born on April 4, 1938 in Boston, Massachusetts. He grew up in South Hadley, Massachusetts where he enjoyed the privileges of being raised in an educationally-oriented family. His father Valentine Giamatti, a Yale graduate himself, taught Italian at Mount Holyoke College, a prestigious college for women. His mother, Mary (nee Claybaugh Walton) Giamatti, was herself a graduate of Smith College for women, another time-honored Massachusetts college.

Angelo Bartlett Giamatti, often called "Bart," enjoyed a fine education from his earliest years. Demonstrating a propensity for languages and literature, he was encouraged to pursue that area. As a pre-schooler, Bart had already learned Italian at home; and in the ensuing years while he attended school, reading, appreciating and discussing good literature had become the daily fare at family gatherings. In addition to experiencing a substantial educational foundation in his home environment, he also enjoyed a series of excellent educational experiences in fine schools.

After spending some time in South Hadley High School, Bart spent a year abroad at the International School of Rome where he had the opportunity to explore his Italian heritage firsthand. Returning from Europe, he completed his high school education at Phillips Academy in Andover, Massachusetts. He entered Yale University, majoring in English and being active in many student associations. It came as no surprise when in 1960 he graduated *magna cum laude*. In the same year, before starting graduate school, he married Toni Smith, a graduate of Columbia University. They would have three children, Marcus Barlett, Elena Walton, and Paul Edward Valentine, born in 1961, 1964, and 1967, respectively.

Bolstered by being a recipient of a coveted Woodrow Wilson Fellowship, Bart went on to receive his Ph.D. in comparative literature in 1964. Shortly after he had graduated that year, Bart obtained his first full-time position as instructor in Italian and comparative literature at Princeton University. His doctoral dissertation, *The Earthly Paradise in the Renaissance Epic*, was revised and published just two years later in 1966 by Princeton University Press. At the relatively young age of twenty-eight, he had established himself as a scholar teaching at Princeton and published by its prestigious press.

He had been quickly promoted to assistant professor in 1965. After teaching at New York University's summer program in 1966, he began his second full-time position as assistant professor of English by returning to his alma mater, Yale University. There he became a full professor by 1971, but more importantly, his experiential trajectories as teacher, scholar, and administrator were moving rapidly.

He was intensely involved in many aspects of teaching and was reputed as a teacher who made the class materials come alive. His classes were heavily attended, yet he was not known as an easy marker. Unlike many scholars who are great in scholarship but not as brilliant in their teaching, Giamatti was most successful in easily bridging that gap so that among his undergraduate students he was particularly known for his excellent teaching. On many occasions, he also had the opportunity to teach in summer programs and abroad.

As a scholar, he continued his work especially in English and Italian literatures. With the critical eye of the scholar, he edited and/or coedited several works especially in the area of Renaissance poetry, such as *The Songs of Bernart de Ventadorn* (1965), *A Variorum Commentary on the Poems of John Milton* (1970), and Stewart Baker's edition of Ariosto's *Orlando Furioso* (1970). Being on the editorial board for Princeton University Press, he had occasion to become general editor of a three-volume anthology entitled *Western Literature* in 1971. He also went on to publish in 1975 his second major book, *The Play of Double Senses: Spencer's "Faerie Queene,"* which functioned as an undergraduate guide to understanding Spencer's work.

As an administrator, Giamatti had many responsibilities in different areas. He was director ("Master") in Erza Stiles College, one of Yale's twelve residential colleges. He was also director of the Yale Visiting Faculty Program and associate director of the Yale National Humanities Institute. Giamatti's most notable administrative role took place when he served as its president from July 1, 1978 to 1986.

Yale had been experiencing a host of deteriorating financial problems in the late 1960s, which included a deficit of $2.6 million by its fiscal year 1970-71. At this time, its $563 million endowment had lost much of its purchasing power; and the expected rate of contribution was declining. Despite numerous cost-cutting efforts, by 1977 there was an accumulated deficit of $16 million.

A fund-rasing effort begun in 1974 had brought in $250 million by mid-1978, and it soon appeared clear that Yale's downward spiral was not just a money issue but also an image issue—and many alumni were disenchanted with Yale's tarnished image. Many arduous months were spent in search of a new president who could revive Yale's reputation after President Brewster had resigned in 1976. When the search narrowed to two candidates—Giamatti and the dean of the arts and sciences—the dean declined making Giamatti Yale's 19th and youngest president. He also represented the first of a partly non-WASP heritage to hold that position of authority.

In his lifetime, Giamatti had the good fortune to have distinguished himself in distinct areas. Before his untimely death, Giamatti had experienced three successful careers: a highly respected Renaissance scholar, an administratively innovative president at Yale University, both the president of the National League (1986-89) and, then, commissioner of baseball (1989). Loving baseball almost as much as he loved his books, Giamatti was probably the most educated commissioner of baseball in its history. His life pays tribute to his fellow Italian Americans in his having accomplished so much in such a short time.

General Sources:

1. *Current Biography Yearbook*. New York: Wilson, 1978.
2. Giamatti, Bartlett. *The Earthly Paradise and the Renaissance Epic*. New York: Norton, 1966.
3. Giamatti, Bartlett. *A Free and Ordered Space: The Real World of the University*. New York: Norton, 1988.
4. Giamatti, Bartlett. *A Great and Glorious Game: Baseball Writings of A. Bartlett Giamatti*. Chapel Hill, NC: Algonquin Books, 1998.
5. Marchione, Margherita. *Americans of Italian Heritage*. Lanham, MD: University Press of America, 1995.

—by WILLIAM WALKER

AMADEO PETER GIANNINI (1870-1949)

As the originator of branch banking in the United States and as the founder and developer of the Bank of Italy, which today is called the Bank of America National Trust and Savings Association (the largest bank in the United States and the largest privately held bank in the world), Giannini represents a legend in American history, banking, philanthropy, and biographic exuberance.

Amadeo Giannini was born in San Jose, California, on May 6, 1870, the son of Italian emigrants from Genoa, Luigi and Virginia (nee Demartini) Giannini. When Amadeo was seven years of age, his father died. A year later, his mother remarried, and her second husband, Lorenzo Scatena, moved the family to San Francisco where he would own and operate a wholesale fruit and vegetable business. This type of business, which normally began its work schedule at midnight, thoroughly fascinated young Amadeo who would often slip away late in the evening after his mother fell asleep, and he would join his stepfather at the produce wharves.

After Amadeo graduated from Washington Grammar School, he attended a five-month business program. At age 13, he went to work at his stepfather's prospering wholesale business. By age 15, he became a wagon driver in the San Joaquin and Sacramento Valleys, competing with veteran buyers and vying for the produce from the farmers. Tireless in his efforts to succeed and seemingly a born trader, he often carried bread and cheese in his pocket so he would not have to stop for lunch.

Over the years, he had creatively engineered cost-effective techniques in the business operations, eventually earning for himself a partnership in his stepfather's enterprise

in 1889 at age 19. Continuing his efforts to succeed while taking on more of the decision-making activities, he went on to make it the largest wholesale produce business on the Pacific coast in ten years, and by the time he was 25 years of age in 1895, Amadeo had already become a millionaire.

In 1901, at the age of 31, after he had worked for eighteen years (1883-1901) in this business, he announced his retirement. Yet his 1901 retirement became short-lived when his wealthy father-in-law, Joseph Cuneo, died in 1902, leaving Giannini in charge of the Cuneo estate and his chair on the board of directors at Columbus Savings Bank. By 1904, Giannini had become disenchanted with that bank's business policies, and with the help of five partners he opened up his own bank, the Bank of Italy in San Francisco.

At that time, Giannini was considered by other bankers as financially radical because he not only made loans to small businessmen and farmers but also solicited customers actively. In fact, in the beginning of his enterprise, he would walk around town explaining the purpose of his bank to everyday people in the streets. When his bank first opened on October 17, 1904, he personally greeted each person at the door and offered them a glass of wine. By early 1906, the Bank of Italy had acquired $2 million in gold and securities on deposit.

On the morning of April 18, 1906, however, an earthquake and an ensuing fire ravaged and engulfed most of what was then San Francisco. Giannini, who lived 25 miles away, rushed into the city before the flames could burn down his bank. He rescued its gold and currency by hiding them in a wagon, covered with produce, and headed home. Later when the city began rebuilding, his losses had been so minimal that he was the only banker who was able to resume business as usual.

The soundness of his advanced banking policies also enabled him to survive the Panic of 1907 (stock market crash) that he had perceptively anticipated and for which he had shrewdly prepared. The financial crash caused many banks to dissolve, but Giannini's Bank of Italy continued with its growth unabated, issuing currency and paying gold on demand, surviving the crash while other banks faltered and failed.

Giannini continued to make loans available to both large and small enterprises, including the newly emerging motion picture industry. He also continued his policy of providing assistance in the form of farming loans and farm mortgages. He was in great part responsible for the phenomenal growth of agriculture in central and northern California.

In 1909, he began aggressively buying up other banks throughout the state of California. In effect he converted them into branches of the Bank of Italy, thus establishing the first statewide branch banking system in the history of the United States. Twenty years later, in 1927, he began acquiring a second network of branch banks, and in 1929 he unified this latter group under the name: Bank of America of California.

Finally, after having created a holding company in 1928 for his banking interests under the name Transamerica Corporation, he set the stage for the 1930 merger of his two banking networks which resulted in the establishment of the Bank of America National Trust and Savings Association, becoming by the 1940s the largest bank in the United States, and today the largest privately-owned bank in the world.

In 1930, his second attempt at retirement was also short-lived. It seems that a year later when his successor inaugurated conservative policies in face the of the growing depression, Giannini waged a proxy fight, ousted his rivals, and resumed the chairmanship of Transamerica and the Bank of America. In 1934, he once again relinquished the chairmanship of the Bank of America but continued as board chairman of Transamerica until his death on June 3, 1949, in San Mateo, California.

By that time, Bank of America had more than 500 branch banks with more than $6 billion in deposits. Yet it came as no surprise when President Roosevelt, who would predecease Giannini by several years, paid tribute to Giannini's historical importance. The President professed his belief that Giannini's personal efforts through his innovative banking policies had done more to build California than any other Californian of his day.

A philanthropist of the highest order, he gave much of his monies to foundations and research institutes that are extant today. Beginning as early as 1927, he donated $1.5 million to the University of California thereby establishing the Giannini Foundation of Agricultural Economics for its statewide university system. Most of his money was left for posterity in another foundation: the Bank of America-Giannini Foundation devoted to medical research and distribution of educational scholarships. No other businessman has helped the working man and the small businessman as much as this great Italian-American banker.

General Sources:

1. Bonadio, Felice A. *A.P. Giannini: Banker of America.* Berkeley: University of California Press, 1994.
2. *Current Biography.* New York: Wilson, 1947; 1949.
3. James, Marquis. *Biography of a Bank*: *The Story of Bank of America N.T. & S.A.* Westport, CT: Greenwood Press, 1971.
4. Nash, Gerald D. *A.P. Giannini and the Bank of America.* Norman, OK: University of Oklahoma Press, 1992.

—by ANDREW VASCELLARO

RUDOLPH WILLIAM GIULIANI (1944-   )

Rudolph Giuliani was born on May 28, 1944, the son of Harold and Helen Giuliani, small store owners in Brooklyn, New York. As Giuliani had learned of his grandfather's turn-of-the-century struggle against the protection racket of the Mafia, he acquired early in his life the family's animosity toward organized crime and how that organization tarnished the image of all Italians and provided an excuse for anti-Italian sentiments. After receiving his law degree, he worked for the U.S. Justice Department, and by 1981 he became Associate Attorney General, the third highest position in the Justice Department. Twelve years later, on election day (1993), he went on to become New York City's 107th mayor, and he is now serving his second term.

Giuliani attended a Roman Catholic elementary school and then Bishop Loughlin High School in Brooklyn. He continued at Manhattan College where he became president of his fraternity and many other college groups. He acquired a lasting passion for political philosophy and debating. Unsettled as to whether to enter medicine or the priesthood, he decided in his junior year to become a lawyer. In 1968 after graduating *magna cum laude* from New York University's law school, he began his first job in the field as a law clerk for Lloyd MacMahon, a federal district judge.

Then, while serving as assistant United States attorney for the Southern District of New York between the years 1970-1975, he established himself as an intelligent prosecutor and an expert practitioner in the art of cross-examination. In his first year, he tried as many as nineteen cases. In 1972, one of his first triumphs occurred with his assignment to investigate corruption involving the use of drugs and drug money in the New York City Police Department (NYPD). Acting on information given him by a policeman that recorded incriminating conversations with his peers, Giuliani was so persistent in his questioning of the policeman that the latter confessed to being part of the NYPD's corruption.

In 1974 Giuliani enhanced his reputation as an expert prosecutor during a bribery trial in which he cross-examined Bertram T. Podell, a Democratic congressman from Brooklyn. His volley of questions was delivered with such intense precision that it made Podell so nervous he broke his eyeglasses, asked for a recess and then, later, pleaded guilty. In 1975 during the Ford administration, Giuliani went to Washington, D.C. and served as assistant to Judge Harold Tyler, the Deputy Attorney General of the Justice Department. In 1977, he returned to New York and became a partner in the firm of Patterson, Belknap, Webb & Tyler.

Later, in 1981, Rudolph Giuliani became the Associate Attorney General. In effect, he assumed the number-three position in the Justice Department. During the next two years, he would emphasize the department's determined efforts to fight narcotics by widening the FBI's drug enforcement capabilities in the establishment of twelve specific task forces.

Later, reflecting on his career, he realized that he had spent five of the most interesting years in New York. He developed a longing to return to the United States attorney job. In 1983, he did just that by leaving the Justice Department and returning to the U.S. attorney position where one of his first actions involved taking some lawyers from his 133-lawyer office and adding them as mobilizing forces to the New York City Police Department in its crackdown on dope peddling in Manhattan's Lower East Side. By the end of 1984, the number of indictments for the Southern District had risen to 1,038 as compared to 843 in 1983.

Giuliani had formed his battle plans on four fronts: "narcotics, white-collar crime, organized crime, and public corruption." In 1985, when Giuliani's office secured a guilty plea from Edward A. Markowitz, Giuliani suddenly became known as the avenging angel in the world of white-collar crime. Markowitz's crime was reputed as "the biggest tax fraud scheme in government history." Giuliani then availed himself of the use of the newly created RICO Act to secure a conviction against not only Carmine Persico but also eight other members of the Colombo family in 1986.

Giuliani then orchestrated a second major case against organized crime, which later became dubbed in the media as the "Pizza Connection." In many ways, this was the realization of efforts to legally link organized crime and drugs by charging the New York Bonanno crime family with conspiring with the Sicilian Mafia to distribute drugs from coast to coast through pizza parlors. The RICO Act allowed not only for the prosecution of specific crimes of members of a crime family but also for the prosecution of the family itself that was breaking the law by its very existence. The inspiration behind Giuliani's use of the RICO Act "secured seventeen convictions out of twenty-one defendants." It was estimated that the "Pizza Connection" had involved over $1.6 billion in drug traffic monies.

Giuliani used hundreds of FBI informers and wire taps in his arsenal of weapons. His assistants perused government transcripts and amassed evidence that in effect secured the indictment of the bosses who directed Mafia activities throughout the United States. He later emerged as one of the most effective figures in law enforcement in securing convictions of organized crime leaders.

In 1986, he again invoked the RICO Act against municipal corruption by indicting Bronx Democratic leader, Stanley Friedman, charging him with orchestrating a bribery ring in the New York City Parking Violations Bureau. In the same year, Giuliani turned his attention to inside trading in the stock market community. When he indicted Dennis Levine, shock waves hit Wall Street. That arrest so frightened Ivan Boesky that he went to Giuliani's office and confessed to inside trading violations. The legal investigation and the SEC efforts resulted in the eventual indictment of Boesky who pleaded guilty to tax evasion and criminal conspiracy.

Giuliani's hard work, dedication, and organizational savvy have uncovered many major crimes and scandals. His track-record resulted in having established him with a reputation as a tough and persistent fighter with high ethical standards. Giuliani's name had been proposed as a Republican candidate for the U.S. Senate as well as for the governor's position. To the good fortune of New York City, he was elected its mayor in 1993 and then re-elected in 1997 for another term to continue his great work. He wields a strong and determined personality for the common good of the people.

General Sources:

1.   Burby, Liza N. *A Day in the Life of a Mayor: Featuring New York City Mayor Rudy Giuliani*. New York: Powerkids Press, 1999.

2.   *Current Biography Yearbook*. New York: Wilson, 1988.

3.   Giuliani, Rudolph W. "How New York is Becoming the Safest Big City in America." *USA Today* Jan. 1997: 28-31.

4.   Jacobson, M. "Rudy's Oval Office Dream." *New York* 10 Nov. 1997: 46-53.

5.   Marks, J. "New York, New York." *U.S. News and World Report* 29 Sept. 1997: 44-49+.

—by SAM PITTARO

ELLA TAMBUSSI GRASSO (1919-1981)

Ella (nee Tambussi) Grasso, who was born on May 10, 1919 in Windsor Locks, Connecticut, would become on election day in November 1974 the first woman duly elected to the office of governor who had not been the wife of a previous incumbent. This was a record-breaking achievement for women in the United States especially since Governor Grasso became noted for her sense of fiscal and ethical responsibility to the people she represented. Winner of numerous civic awards, including the Marconi Award from the Sons of Italy, she set a standard that has not gone by unnoticed.

She attended parochial school and won scholarships to the Chaffee School (Windsor) and to Mount Holyoke College in the state of Massachusetts where in 1940 she graduated with a B.A. *magna cum laude*. In the same year, 1942, she received a masters degree in sociology and economics, and she married Dr. Thomas Grasso, a high school principal with whom she had two children: James and Susanne.

From 1943 to 1946, she served as Assistant State Director of Research for the Federal War Manpower Commission for the state of Connecticut. She developed an interest in politics, and she became a political speech writer and campaign supporter. Her political interests intensified in the forthcoming years, and she herself would run for office. Elected to the Connecticut House of Representatives, she would serve from 1952 to 1957. She also would serve as Secretary of State for Connecticut from 1958 to 1970.

During that time she had served on numerous state committees which included: the Connecticut Board of Mental Health, Long Lane Farm Study Commission (1953-55), Highway Financing Study Commission (1953-55), Suffield

League of Women Voters, and state chairperson of the Cystic Fibrosis Campaign (1960). Her work ethic would make her the recipient of many awards granted by business professional groups and by political associations. President Kennedy appointed her to the Board of Foreign Scholarships, and later President Johnson would reappoint her to the same position. She also became a member of the National Platform Committee in 1960 and co-chairperson of the Resolutions Committee of the Democratic National Conventions in 1964 and in 1968.

Elected to the United States Congress in 1970 and, then re-elected in 1972, Grasso served in the House of Representatives from 1971 to 1975. During that time she also became involved in the Democratic National Committee, actively opposing the American policy in Vietnam. She served as vice chair of the Executive Committee on Human Rights and Opportunities and also as chair for the Planning Committee for the Governor's Commission on the Status of Women. Connecticut Democrats supported her progressive ideas for streamlining state governmental departments. She was respected by both business people and political colleagues alike because of her self-confident, non-threatening, humane manner in presenting her arguments, proposals, and ideals.

In 1974, the state Democratic Party nominated her for the governorship of Connecticut. She won the election in a landslide victory. She made history in becoming the first woman to be elected governor without having followed her husband into office. *Time Magazine* named her one of twelve Women of the Year in 1975, and *Ladies Home Journal* designated her Woman of the Year in 1976. Her sustained concern both for business development and for many of Connecticut's struggling, underprivileged families earned her respect and success as governor. To reduce the huge state debt, she proposed a one-percent hike in the sales tax. Concomitantly, she also tightened government spending. She returned her "earned" raise in salary to the Connecticut state treasury in the form of a gift. In 1978, she was reelected governor.

She promised an open government and, accordingly, she asked the legislature for a "right to know" statute which would open government records and meetings to the public. She also made proposals to solve the problems dealing with the ever-climbing public utility rates and the complaints of utility executives who deplored the lack of money for capital improvements. Grasso asked the legislature to enact laws which allowed state-borrowed monies for the construction programs for those companies.

She was most admired in her home state not only for her work as governor but also for her long track record of dedicated work in a long list of diverse committees and charitable organizations whose efforts effected the lives of many people. Her love and loyalty to her Italian roots, her particular devotion to her immigrant parents, Giacomo and Maria, and her love for her immediate family endeared the Connecticut population. She spoke fluent Italian and enjoyed cultural events. Most importantly, she possessed a deep understanding for all ethnic minorities and, particularly, for immigrants.

She consistently supported expanded opportunities for women, but rarely made reference to herself or to the feminist movement. In a 1975 speech on women in politics, she stated that there was a great need for more women to participate in public service even though she readily admitted that: "it has been my good fortune not to experience any discernible discrimination even from the earliest days of my public career. The 93rd Congress had 12 women members, the 94th Congress 16, plus scores of women holding key elected positions in state and local governments...In the future, an effective Congress will include many more women members—and the day will come when the nation's First Lady will be the nation's first woman President."

Her history includes her having received many awards: in 1959, the Amita Award as outstanding woman of Italian parentage; in 1963, Italian-American Gold Medal from the Connecticut Lodge Order Sons of Italy in America; in 1968, the Marconi Award from the Order Sons of Italy at the national level, and many other awards too numerous to mention. In 1968, she also became a Knight in the Order of Merit of the Italian Republic.

Tragedy struck her and her family, and her many political admirers when in the middle of her second term in office in 1980, she was diagnosed with cancer. Incredibly, she went on to run the state government from her hospital room. She died in 1981 after a distinguished career in politics. She remains in the minds of many a paragon of political honesty, dedication and determination.

General Sources:
1. *Biographical Directory of the Governors of the United States 1789-1978*. Westport, CT: Meckler Books, 1987.
2. *Current Biography Yearbook*. New York: Wilson, 1975; 1981.
3. Nelson, Barbara J. *American Women and Politics*. New York: Garland Pub., 1984.
4. Uglow, Jennifer S. *The Continuum Dictionary of Women's Biography*. New York: Continuum, 1989.
5. Weis, Ina J. *Women in Politics: A Bibliography*. Monticello, IL: Vance Bibliographies, 1979.
6. *Who's Who of American Women*. 1981-1982 ed.

—by MIKE DINA

RICHARD A. GRASSO (1946-   )

On June 1, 1995, Richard A. Grasso became chairman and chief executive officer of the New York Stock Exchange (NYSE), the most prestigious and powerful equities market in the world. Because he had held other positions within the Exchange's organization, such as president and chief operating officer since 1988, in effect he made stock market history in that he became the first member of the Exchange's own staff in its more than 200 year history to have been elected to any of those positions—much less to have occupied all three positions at the same time. Like many successful executives, he rose from the lower administrative ranks which, in his case, was from a corporate listings representative.

Richard Grasso was born on July 26, 1946 in Elmhurst, Queens, New York where he lived in a lower-middle class neighborhood. When he was 13 years of age, he purchased his first stocks. Naturally, because of his youthful status, his mother had to transact the purchase of the stocks for him. Richard held a part-time job in a pharmacy, and he decided to invest $1,000 from the money he had prudently saved up. He was intrigued by stocks, and he attempted to learn as much as possible about them from the pharmacist at whose place of business he worked. Reportedly, he often sat with the pharmacist when the latter placed stock orders in a brokerage firm which was conveniently located next to the pharmacy.

He attended Pace University and received a B.S. in accounting. After serving in the United States Army during the period between 1966-68, he joined the Exchange's staff in April 1968 in the listing department. In 1973 he was assigned the directorship of listing and marketing, commissioned with adding qualified companies to the NYSE list of participating companies. In December 1977, he was promoted to vice president of corporate services; and almost a year later, in November 1981, he was promoted to senior vice president of corporate services with the added responsibility for acting as liaison among participating NYSE companies.

In the coming decade these promotions were followed by two major upward moves which led to his becoming president of the Exchange. He first became executive vice president for marketing in 1983 and then vice president for capital markets in 1986, which also included responsibilities for all of the NYSE's financial products and its market data. During this engaging period he received certification in advanced management in a postgraduate program from Harvard University in 1985. Eventually, in 1988 he was elected president and chief operating officer of the NYSE. While maintaining these positions, he later became Executive Vice Chairman of the Exchange on January 1, 1991. While he held these positions with their responsibilities, he became chairman and chief executive officer of the New York Stock Exchange. In effect, he became the first person to have secured any of those positions working his way internally through the ranks.

Throughout his years of service, Grasso had always upheld the importance of integrity and professionalism in maintaining the NYSE as the leader in the global equities market. His broad-based experience and knowledge have since continually enhanced the NYSE's trading, regulatory, and administrative operations through the sustained use of cutting-edge technology. In all, as a highly focused leader, he has stressed, on the one hand, respecting fiscal integrity and a customer-comes-first attitude while, on the other hand, undertaking the NYSE's serious globalization strategies.

In an effort to globalize the NYSE and launch its operations into the twenty-first century, he has encouraged, implemented, and utilized the latest hi-tech equipment for monitoring the Big Board and for in-house wireless communication. For instance, on the trading floor, the use of a hand-held "personal digital assistant" has become one of the major component aspects of the NYSE's more recent wireless network enhancement revolution.

It has had the effect not only of increasing the efficiency of market professionals and the NYSE's first-rate market system but also of supporting the operational and regulatory staff in their pursuit of precision, speed, and possible investigative evaluations. In 1996 under Grasso's direction, the NYSE had already initiated the use of televising real-time stock prices on CNBC and CNN*fn* with great success in an effort to provide the TV viewer with instantly displayed market activity. Despite his responsibilities as head of the most renowned and influential equities market in the world, Grasso has always made time for his participation in community and professionally related activities. He is on the board of directors of the NYSE-listed Computer Associates International, the International Capital Markets Advisory Committee for the Federal Reserve Bank of New York, the advisory board for the Yale School of Management, and the National Italian American Foundation.

As for community, Mr. Grasso is a member of the YMCA of Greater New York, the Centurion Foundation, and the New York City Police Foundation. In 1992, which marked 500 years after Columbus' discovery of America, Grasso was named chairman of the New York City Columbus Quincentennial Commission. Since 1992 he has also served as honorary chairman of the Friends of the Statue of Liberty National Monument-Ellis Island Foundation.

In 1996 he chaired the Metro New York Region of the U.S. Olympic Committee for the 1996 Olympics. More recently in 1997, Mayor Rudolph Giuliani appointed Grasso to two key programs involving public education.

Today, he, his wife, son, and three daughters reside in Locust Valley, New York. Grasso has been the recipient of numerous awards, honors, and commendations, including two honorary doctorates: a Doctor of Law degree from Fordham University and a Doctor of Commercial Science from Pace University. A person unusually active in community-based affairs, he has received the Special Award in Business from the National Italian American Foundation, several awards from the Boy Scouts of America, the Brotherhood Award from the National Conference of Christians and Jews, and Man of the Year Award by Catholic Big Brothers. From abroad, he was honored with the title of Cavaliere di Gran Croce by the President of Italy. His life activities and his work ethic consistently through the years have clearly embodied the model of dedication, professionalism, community spirit, and leadership in the many roles he has held.

General Sources:
1. Angrist, Stanley. "Bring on the Business." *Forbes* 11 July 1988: 137.
2. Grasso, Richard. "The Best is Yet to Come." *Vital Speeches of the Day* 15 Jan. 1997: 215-219.
3. *Hoover's Handbook of American Business.* Austin, TX: Hoover's Business Press, 1999.
4. Kansas, Dave. "Richard Grasso Assumes Posts of Chairman, CEO of Big Board." *The Wall Street Journal* 1 June 1995: B8+.
5. *Who's Who in America.* 1999 ed.
6. Woolley, S. "The Booming Big Board." *Business Week* 4 Aug. 1997: 58-64.

—by GEORGE CARPETTO, Ph.D.

ROCKY GRAZIANO (1922-1990)

When Paul Newman starred in *Somebody Up There Likes Me* (1956), portraying Rocky Graziano, a film based on Rocky's autobiography published just a year earlier, Rocky suddenly achieved national celebrity status that went well beyond that of his fans and boxing audiences. This silver screen phenomenon in turn caused Rocky to embark on a new career. And so, besides having become an overnight success as a best-selling autobiographical writer, he suddenly acquired an unexpected career status in show business, and in the next twenty-five years would appear as a regular on TV variety programs, game shows, and as an endorser of commercials products.

Yet Rocky Graziano's beginnings were quite different. He was born Thomas Rocco Barbella on the Lower East Side of Manhattan (New York City) on January 1, 1922. His formative teenage years took place during the Great Depression era. He spent much of his time around the boxing gym learning about boxing after dropping out of school in the seventh grade. His home also presented many problems. His father, Joseph Barbella, an ex-boxer, was an alcoholic and a spouse abuser.

Being rough and tough had become a way of life, a survival mechanism, especially for a youngster caught in these difficult circumstances. One of the consequences of his quest for survival often involved street fighting. In the 1930s, Rocky had become a juvenile delinquent who often found himself in and out of jail. Fighting came easily to Rocky, and in order to earn some quick cash, he turned to boxing. In 1942 he turned to professional boxing to use all the skills he had learned in those prior years. It was at this time that he was also drafted into military service.

Rocky had a difficult time adjusting to military discipline and taking orders. It seems that one day when he felt he had had enough, he punched an officer, and to avoid punishment, he went AWOL. Ironically, Rocky decided to make this poorly calculated move the beginning of his boxing career, and he attempted to do so by changing his name to Graziano in hopes of remaining undetected by the Military Police. His ill-founded freedom was short-lived since soon afterwards he was arrested, court-martialed, sent to military prison for nine months, and then dishonorably discharged from the service.

Now out of the Army, Rocky felt free once more to start his boxing career full-time. In 1943, he chalked up an impressive sixteen wins and two losses. Yet Rocky was still amidst the element he had known all too well, and again he became involved in criminal activities including narcotics and alcohol. Luckily, it was at this time that he made a decision to rely on a higher power to help him, and so he turned to God. He decided he would use boxing to climb out of poverty while leaving behind an old lifestyle he no longer wanted.

In order for Rocky to improve as a professional boxer, he knew he had to learn more and train harder. It simply wasn't enough to be a tough fighter if he wanted to become a champ. Beginning in the welterweight division, Rocky began to draw attention when he defeated Billy Arnold and Al Davis in 1945. By 1946 Rocky had managed to get some impressive knockouts to his credit and these included such names as Freddie Cochrane, Marty Servo, and Harold Green who were among the most prominent welterweights at that time.

By now Rocky had so impressed the boxing community that he became matched with middleweight champion Tony Zale at Madison Square Garden in the fall of 1946. That night the audience witnessed one of the most brutal and savage championship fights of all times. Rocky almost won, but in the 6th round Zale rallied and managed to knock out Rocky.

Rocky's great performance that night prompted the fight promoters to immediately set up a rematch for the middleweight crown on July 16, 1947. Typical of his style, Rocky appeared tireless in his unending attack on his opponent, and he possessed a remarkable resiliency in being able to take a punch. In many ways, the rematch turned out to be a duplicate of the powerfully aggressive prior match, and both men fought hard. There was a difference, however, when in the sixth round Rocky knocked out Tony Zale. Suddenly, Rocky became the Middleweight Champion of the World, and he had finally achieved his dream.

In January 1948, he was rematched with Tony Zale for a second time. Rocky's reign didn't endure because he only lasted three rounds thereby returning the championship to Zale. Yet during the next three years, Rocky continued to box scoring an impressive nineteen knockouts out of twenty-one fights. Once again the boxing community was so impressed that promoters matched Rocky with the then middleweight champ Sugar Ray Robinson on April 16, 1952. The bout lasted three rounds when Sugar Ray knocked out Rocky. Rocky's career was not yet over. In the same year, Rocky fought the then-champion Chuck Davey who went on to win, but it was only by decision, not by a knockout. This was to be Rocky's last fight because he would soon announce his decision to retire from the boxing world.

In retirement, Rocky wrote (together with Rowland Barber) his now famous autobiography which made him a best-selling author practically overnight and offered him celebrity status when his autobiography became the subject of a Hollywood feature movie starring Paul Newman. Among his business enterprises, Rocky decided to open his own restaurant in New York that became a mecca for celebrities especially from the field of boxing.

In 1971 Rocky was inducted into the International Boxing Hall of Fame and Museum. From a total of 83 professional bouts, he had won 67, lost 10, and drew on 6. He had 52 knockouts to his name. In 1985 at age sixty-three, Rocky decided to give up all his business ventures and enterprises. About five years later on May 23, 1990, at age 68 he died in his New York City home.

Given the bleak and dire circumstances of his early ghetto background during the depression of the 30s, he realized his dream to climb out of a life of poverty and achieve success. Although Rocky was appreciated and admired during his boxing days, most notably he remained not only popular as a celebrity but also well liked as a kind and generous person until the last days of his life.

General Sources:
1. Graziano, Rocky, and Howard Liss. *Rocky's Boxing Book*. New York: Sayre Pub., 1978.
2. Graziano, Rocky, and Ralph Corsel. *Somebody Down There Likes Me, Too*. New York: Stein & Day, 1981.
3. Graziano, Rocky, and Rowland Barber. *The Rocky Road to Physical Fitness*. Englewood Cliffs, NJ: Prentice Hall, 1968.
4. Graziano, Rocco, and Rowland Barber. *Somebody Up There Likes Me*. New York: Simon & Schuster, 1955.
5. "IBHOF / Rocky Graziano." Nov. 1 1998. <http://www.ibhof.com/graziano.htm>.
6. Myler, Patrick. *A Century of Boxing Greats: Inside the Ring with the Hundred Best Boxers*. New York: Robson/Parkwest, 1998.

—by ANTHONY ZAPPIA

ROSE BASILE GREEN (1914-   )

A teacher, writer, scholar, poet, and administrator, Dr. Rose Basile Green whose area of expertise involved American and English literatures also nurtured eclectic interests throughout her life especially in those related to concerns in the Italian-American immigrant experience. With a great eagerness and discerning focus, her volumes of poetry and prose have thematically treated the deep existential concerns of Italian immigrant's biculturalism and the process of change which crosses the lives of all those immersed in the everyday aspects of living in a new country.

Rose Basile was born on December 19, 1914 to Salvatore and Carolina (nee Galgano) Basile in the town of New Rochelle (north of New York City). Her parents did well in business for many years in the New Rochelle area until illness struck Salvatore, and they were compelled to move. They purchased a large farm in the small town of Harwinton in the northwest area of Connecticut where young Rose attended a one-room schoolhouse to get her education.

Rose eventually returned to the New Rochelle area in order to attend the College of New Rochelle where she earned her B.A. *cum laude* in 1935. She began her career working for one year (1935-1936) as a writer and researcher for the federally sponsored Work Progress Administration (WPA) in its Writers' Project in the town of Torrington, a small city not far from her parents' town of Harwinton. Immediately after that experience, she worked for Torrington High School where she taught English and Italian for the next six years from 1936-1942.

She earned her M.A. at Columbia University in 1941, and she went on to marry Raymond S. Green on June 20, 1942. After working for one year as an Associate Professor of English and Registrar at the University of Tampa (1942-1943), Rose Basile Green became a freelance writer of radio scripts for the Cavalcade of America on the National Broadcasting Company (NBC) from 1943 to 1953. It was during this interval of time that the Greens had two children, Carol Rae and Raymond Ferguson.

In 1953, Rose began her years in university teaching with a position as special instructor in English at Temple University (Philadelphia) where she taught for four years until 1957. In the interim, she became involved in the formation of a new college, Cabrini College, in Radnor, Pennsylvania in 1957 and became one of its founders. There she taught in the English Department and became its first chairperson. During her administrative and teaching responsibilities at Cabrini College, she received her Ph.D. from the University of Pennsylvania in 1962. Dr. Basile Green worked at Cabrini College until her retirement in 1970. It was during this time that she published her *Cabrinian Philosophy of Education* in 1967.

It seems that retirement came not so much as a conclusion but as a new beginning. Dr. Basile Green's literary output increased, and she became more active in Italian-American cultural and educational organizations. In one of her more noted books, *The Italian-American Novel, a Document of the Interaction of Two Cultures* (1973), she evaluated 70 writers of Italian descent and discussed their contributions to American culture and literature from the perspective of the writers' initial bicultural foundations and their evolving formations.

A champion of immigrants needing to

receive their due recognition for overcoming the hardships incurred in their cultural transition from Italian to Italian-American, Dr. Basile Green has also emphasized the necessity of recognizing specifically the role of Italian women in this powerful transitional process. It therefore comes as no small surprise that she found it important to translate and edit the biography of Mother Cabrini from Italian into English which was then published in 1984.

Mother Cabrini, the first American citizen to be elevated to the status of sainthood, had indeed epitomized the Christian values of giving especially to immigrant populations. The reader gets to appreciate the irony in Mother Cabrini's life in that she, a poor immigrant herself who initially spoke no English, devoted her entire life to helping Italian emigrants and emigrants from all other European countries who had come to North and South Americas.

In much of her writings, Dr. Basile Green worked thematically in the recognition of the worth and value of women immigrants: not only the religious (like Mother Cabrini and her missionary sisters whose shelters, schools and hospitals spanned two continents) but also women immigrants in general who had come across the ocean to begin a new life. To this important theme, Dr. Basile Green has devoted much of her poetry and many of her books including: *Woman, the Second Coming* (1982) and *The Distaff Side: Great Women of American History* (1995). Also, in writing the "foreword" to a book entitled *Immigrant Woman in North America*, (by Francesco Cordasco), she reiterated the importance of the women's role in the immigrant experience.

Dr. Green was also involved in many organizations that promoted educational values and brotherhood. They include being vice president of the National Italian Foundation, chairperson of the National Advisory Council of Ethnic Heritage Studies (U.S. Dept. of Education), member of the Academy of American Poets, member of the American Academy of Political and Social Science, member of the American-Italian Historical Association, and the Academy of Vocal Arts of the Opera Company of Philadelphia.

Dr. Rose Basile Green maintains the strong belief that "pressure must be exerted nationally" through "the printed and visual media, to affirm the accomplishments of Americans of Italian ancestry," and to this belief she has dedicated much of her intellectual and emotional being, especially as poet and prose writer. She has been the recipient of many awards that reflect her stamina and great intellectual prowess. Many of these awards have been both academic and civic, and they include those from Columbia University, the College of New Rochelle, the City of Philadelphia, the Daughters of the American Revolution, and a Doctorate of Humane Letters (honorary LHD) from Gwynedd-Mercy College. In 1975 she was named Woman of the Year by the Pennsylvania Order Sons of Italy, and in 1976 she was the recipient of the National Amita Award for literature. She has also been decorated by the state of Italy as Cavaliere della Repubblica.

General Sources:
1. Green, Rose Basile. *The Distaff Side: Great Women of American History.* New York: Cornwall Books, 1995.
2. Green, Rose Basile. *Five Hundred Years of America, 1492-1992.* New York: Cornwall Books, 1992.
3. Green, Rose Basile. *The Italian-American Novel, a Document of the Interaction of Two Cultures.* Rutherford, NJ: Fairleigh Dickinson University, 1974.
4. Marchione, Margherita. *Americans of Italian Heritage.* Lanham, MD: University Press of America, 1995.
5. *Who's Who of American Women.* 1997-1998.

—by THERESA BRANCIFORTE

FELIX GRUCCI, SR. (1905-1993)

Felix Grucci, Sr. along with his dedicated family members were responsible for raising the ranks of their fireworks company from a relatively small domestic operation to one of international stature when it won the coveted Gold Medal at the Monte Carlo International Fireworks competition in 1979. Presently producing about 300 fireworks displays a year, it also enjoys the honor of having produced fireworks displays not only for the Brooklyn Bridge's Centennial (1983) and the Statue of Liberty Centennial (1986) and other major historical events in New York State but also for the last five presidential inaugurations in Washington, D.C.

The Grucci story goes back to 1850 when Angelo Lanzetta started a fireworks business in Bari, Italy. Deciding to immigrate to the United States, Angelo moved to Long Island, New York in 1870 where he continued working with fireworks. He had two children Anthony and Maria. They both had knowledge of the trade, but it was Anthony who would run the business after his father's death. At a certain point, he then enlisted the help of his nephew Felix (Maria's son) to be his assistant in an apprenticeship arrangement. In the first few decades of the 20th century, the family ran the business exclusively from their Long Island base, and with their fireworks displays they graced the New York City skyline and dazzled spectators on such holidays as the Fourth of July and Catholic feast days, especially saints' holidays.

Felix's mother Maria (nee Lanzetta) Grucci was married to James Grucci, and they had Felix in 1905 in Bellport (Long Island), New York. Felix's mother who previously had lived in Italy knew about fireworks quite well since as a youngster before coming to America she had won a prize bestowed to her by the King of Italy for a fireworks display she designed, which involved fireworks being raised to the sky by a balloon. Her son Felix learned all he could from his uncle Anthony. For several years the Lanzettas and the Gruccis moved to Miami with the hope of making their business grow, but by 1929 they returned to Bellport, Long Island.

Felix continued working for his uncle in fireworks, but he still worked nights as a musician (drummer) with a local band. When his uncle Angelo died in 1938, Felix took over the leadership of the business. It was around this time that he met Concetta DiDio, and they married on February 4, 1940 becoming lifelong partners both in marriage and in business. They had three children, James, Donna, and Felix, Jr. who in time would all become part of the family fireworks legacy. The company went through several name changes over the course of time such as "Suffolk Novelty Fireworks Company" and "New York Pyrotechnics Products," before settling on "Fireworks by Grucci."

By the 1970s Felix Grucci together with his family took their fireworks business to new heights. Felix invented a stringless shell which eliminated the problem of burning fallout. He then developed an "atomic" simulator for troop-training purposes for the U.S. Department of Defense. Also, for the first time in their career they ventured out of New York and produced the fireworks display on the Charles River in Boston, Massachusetts for Arthur Fiedler's Boston Pops Orchestra at the memorable U.S. Bicentennial Celebration in 1976.

On October 22, 1977 near Titusville, Florida the Gruccis detonated the largest fireworks in history and was recorded in the *Guinness Book of World Records*. It was named the Fat Man II (alluding to the Fat Man—the first atomic bomb built in Nevada in 1945), and it weighed in at 720 lbs with a shell enclosure that was 40-1/2 inches in diameter. During Felix's lifetime there were two other major changes introduced by his fireworks family. First, it involved the introduction and use of electronic firing which insured greater accuracy, timing, and safety; second, the introduction and use of musically choreographed displays.

Their defining year took place in 1979 when the Gruccis took the Gold Medal at the Monte Carlo International Fireworks Competition whose contestants came by invitation only, which made their award even more prestigious. This was the first time in history that an American company won this honor. Before the medal was awarded, Felix received accolades from the crowds that moved him to tears. Horns honked for nearly ten minutes in appreciation of the awarding-winning fireworks display presented that night. This honor and achievement earned Felix and his family members from the New York press the title of America's First Family of Fireworks.

Unfortunately, not without tragedy in the course of its history, the Grucci family witnessed on two occasions their entire business operation destroyed by explosions, and more painfully, they experienced the catastrophic loss of two family members to the same hazard despite their safety precautions. Their facilities are monitored and equipped with safeguards to minimize risk factors. For instance, copper plates must be touched when one enters a facility to eliminate static electricity. And for the same reason, no one is permitted to wear silk garments or undergarments, and no one is allowed hair-combing. Precautions naturally become an even bigger concern when they are on the road where external factors may unexpectedly occur and cause dangerous situations.

To date the best work written on the Grucci family is to be found in Plimpton's book titled *Fireworks* (1984) where he discusses the Grucci's Gold Medal achievement in Monte Carlo (1979) and their fireworks performance at the Lake Placid Winter Olympics (1981). The Gruccis have also given memorable fireworks performances at the most recent U.S. presidential inaugurations. The Grucci family did the fireworks display at the last five inaugurations in 1981, 1985, 1989, 1993, and 1997: twice for Reagan, once for Bush, and twice for Clinton. In addition, the Gruccis also did a performance for the Smithsonian Institute's 150th anniversary in Washington, D.C.

Felix Grucci, Sr., who died on January 9, 1993, knew full well that the company he had worked so hard to build was enjoying legendary status worldwide and had already acquired bookings for the year 2000 that read like a *Who's Who of American Cities*. Today his wife and children and their respective spouses carry on the business, proud of their very uplifting and edifying work. How fitting it must be for the Grucci family to recall that their biggest performance to date still remains their display at the Statue of Liberty's Centennial in 1986 where they required a minimum of 33 firing stations in order to shower the New York City harbor and skyline for necessary brilliance to celebrate the glory of America's Statue of Liberty.

General Sources:
1.   "CCN*fn*-Grucci Family Lights up the Sky." 4 July 1996. <http://www.cnnfn.com/news/9607/04/interview_grucci>.
2.   "Felix Grucci, Sr." *New York Times* 18 Jan. 1981: 1.
3.   "Felix Grucci, Sr." *New York Times* 29 June 1980, VI: 25.
4.   "Felix Grucci, Sr." *New York Times* 23 May 1983, II: 7.
5.   Plimpton, George. *Fireworks: A History and Celebration*. Garden City, NY: Doubleday, 1984.

—by LINDA D'ANDREA-MARINO

FRANCO HARRIS (1950-   )

Franco Harris, who was the third of nine children and was born in Fort Dix, New Jersey on March 7, 1950, would go on one day in 1990 to become enshrined in the Pro Football Hall of Fame. A running back for the Pittsburgh Steelers from 1972 to 1983, he provided the necessary power to help bring his team into eight Pro Bowls. Upon his retirement from football, he began enriching his life and that of his family with many successful business ventures.

"Cad" Cadillac Harris, his father, an African-American, who served as a medic for twenty years in the U.S. Army, and Gina (nee Parenti) Harris, his mother, a native Italian, met in the town of Piero Sanca outside of Lucca, Italy during WWII.

In discussing her interracial marriage for the *New York Post* in 1975, Franco's mother recalls that, during the War, the "people where I lived liked the black people. They liked the American soldiers. So many of us were helped by Americans. They gave us food. They helped us to live." When the Harris family left Italy, they moved to Mount Holly, New Jersey not far from Fort Dix.

Franco worked hard as a youngster, shining shoes, hustling for those extra nickels and dimes. Later, he worked in local supermarkets bagging and stocking shelves, but he always made time for sports. He was selected high school All-American in football. Also starring in baseball and basketball at Rancocas Valley Regional High School in Mount Holly, New Jersey, he was eventually recruited by Pennsylvania State University where he earned a B.S. degree in hotel and food services.

At Penn State, Harris "played football, at that time, in the shadow of Lydell Mitchell" who as "a swift break-away runner" had already set many college records. Harris together with Lydell Mitchell gained 2,002 yards in 380 carries and helped Penn State to victories over the University of Missouri in the 1970 Orange Bowl and over the University of Texas in the 1972 Cotton Bowl. These became very important factors in the eventual draft selections for the National Football League.

At 6 foot 3 inches and 235 pounds, Harris had a big enough size to bowl over would-be tacklers. His balance, quickness, and explosive acceleration made him hard to catch, and other teams could soon attest to that. He became an integral part of the driving force of the Steelers from 1972 to 1984. Yet having been the first draft pick, Harris' abilities were at first in doubt by many fans who thought Lydell Mitchell should have been drafted by the Pittsburgh Steelers. In 1974, Franco Harris began to silence all his critics. He passed the 1,000 yard mark in rushing and led the Steelers into Super Bowl IX against the Minnesota Vikings and their "Purple People Eaters" defense. Harris carried the ball 34 times and gained a Super Bowl record, 158 yards to help the Steelers win: 16-6.

Franco Harris will always be remembered for his "Immaculate Reception." This refers to the much needed miracle the Steelers were looking for in order to win. The scenario went as follows: score, Oakland Raiders 7, Pittsburgh Steelers 6. There were only 22 seconds left on the clock; 4th down and 10 yards to go. The game was being played on frozen turf in Three Rivers Stadium, Pittsburgh. Terry Bradshaw, quarterback for the Steelers, was scrambling around the back field dodging the on-rushing tough Oakland defense. He spotted Frenchy

Fuqua, running back for the Steelers, and let go with a long pass. The ball was deflected by Jack Tatum, Raiders' defensive back; it went slightly upwards and continued its descent.

Franco Harris had been running up field to help out with blocking. Suddenly, there was the ball, not more than six inches from the ground, when Harris reached way down, held on to it, and, simultaneously, kept running for the touchdown. The final score: Pittsburgh 13, Raiders 6. This signaled the first divisional playoff game ever. Pandemonium took over in the stadium, and it was the beginning of a great player and a great team with a bright future. NFL Coach George Allen was quoted as saying "Franco Harris has been a great pass catcher, a great blocker, and a great runner, and he has the knack of making the big play."

The following year the Steelers won Super Bowl X, defeating the Dallas Cowboys, 21-7. After barely falling short in 1977 and 1978, the same team led by Coach Chuck Hall returned to win Super Bowl XIII over the Cowboys and Super Bowl XIV over the Los Angeles Rams. Harris, Bradshaw, wide receiver Lynn Swann, and John Stallworth, and the "Steel Curtain" defense, including linemen Joe Greene and L. C. Greenwood, linebackers Jack Ham and Jack Lambert, won four Super Bowls in six years for an unprecedented achievement.

The durable, determined Harris helped lead the way, missing only 9 games due to injuries in his first 12 NFL seasons. During his career, Franco gained the most rushing yardage in 13 of his 19 post-season games. Altogether he gained 12,120 yards (4th all time) on 2,949 carries, (2nd all time), scored 100 touchdowns, and caught 307 passes for 2,287 yards; played in winning Super Bowls 1975, 1976, 1979, 1980; selected for the nine Pro Bowls every year from 1972 to 1980.

After spending the 1984 season with the Seattle Seahawks, Harris retired and returned to Pittsburgh. In 1990, Franco Harris was inducted in the Professional Football Hall of Fame.

Harris pursued his business challenges with the same spirit and determination with which he had played football despite the fact that in the latter the training was more mental than physical. Franco was quoted as saying: "I can't learn enough now. I wish I had known reading and gathering information was so much fun." His enterprises include The Super Bakery, which he started not only with profits in mind but also with customer needs. With an interest in health-consciousness, he developed a new product: a low-fat super donut. He tried it out on his son, Dok. It met not only Dok's taste requirements but also the requirements of the U.S. Department of Agriculture's standards for the child nutrition programs.

Harris also partly owns trading-card and comic book companies and a professional cycling team. "They say if you love what you do, you never have to work a day in your life." Franco has also stated: "Today my passion is business." Accustomed to running downfield to help and blocking against the defense, he is now on his way to helping those in need.

General Sources:
1. *African-American Sports Greats: A Biographical Dictionary*. Westport, CT: Greenwood Press, 1995.
2. *Current Biography Yearbook*. New York: Wilson, 1976.
3. Kowet, Don. *Franco Harris*. New York: Coward, McCann & Geoghegan, 1977.
4. Neft, David S., et al. *The Football Encyclopedia: The Complete History of Professional Football from 1892 to the Present*. New York: St. Martin's Press, 1994.
5. Reiss, Bob, and Gary Wohl. *Franco Harris*. New York: Tempo Books, 1977.
6. Treat, Roger. *The Encyclopedia of Football*. South Brunswick: Barnes, 1979.

—by DENNIS PIASIO

LEE IACOCCA (1924-   )

As a student excelling in his course of study, Lee Iacocca earned his masters degree in mechanical engineering in record time. In 1966 he created the legendary Mustang for the Ford Motor Company and became its president. Later, after becoming chairman and CEO of the ailing Chrysler Corporation, he not only rescued this large corporation from bankruptcy but also brought it to new innovative heights by making and marketing smaller and more efficient cars.

Lee Iacocca was born on October 15, 1924 in Allentown, Pennsylvania. His parents, Nicola and Antoinette (nee Perrotto) Iacocca, were both natives of San Marco, a town outside Naples, Italy. Lee grew up in Allentown with his older sister Delma. His father, an astute and innovative businessman, was involved in many enterprises, including one of the first car rental agencies in the 1920s. In 1929, however, the Great Depression came, and like most of the nation, the Iacoccas suffered financially. They had lost everything except their home.

As a teenager, Lee was bright but shy. One of his school teachers, Miss Raber, was credited for awakening his talent for writing and public speaking. In his sophomore year, Lee contracted rheumatic fever. He was bedridden for six months, and during that time he read avidly and did much thinking to motivate himself. He became more involved in school activities, focused on studying and preparing for a career. He joined extracurricular activities, the drama club and the debate team. He became a member of the National Honor Society, and he graduated twelfth in a high school class of nine hundred in 1942.

At the time of his high school graduation, World War II had already been underway. Although Lee wanted to join the military service,

he was classified as 4F (medical deferment) because of his history of rheumatic fever. He went to college, and by 1945 Lee had earned a B.S. degree in industrial engineering at Lehigh University in Bethlehem, Pennsylvania.

After graduating in three years, Iacocca was hired by the Ford Motor Company and was sent for training in Dearborn, Michigan. Before completing the program, he was granted a leave of absence to accept a Wallace Memorial Fellowship for a masters in mechanical engineering at Princeton University. Incredibly, he had earned both degrees in just four years. He returned to Ford completing the training program in half the time normally required.

By 1949, Lee would become zone manager in the Wilkes-Barre Pennsylvania area. In 1953, he then became the assistant sales manager of the Philadelphia area. In 1956, he initiated a sales campaign with the slogan: "56 for 56," meaning: buy a 1956 Ford for only $56 a month for three years. His district quickly became number one in Ford national sales. Ford imitated Lee's sales approach nationwide, and its sales also rose substantially. Also in 1956, Lee married Mary McCleary, a receptionist at the Ford sales office in Chester, Pennsylvania. Their marriage took place in Chester at St. Robert's Church, and they would go on to have two children, daughters Kathryn and Lia.

Lee was part of the marketing group at Ford, which offered safety devices in its 1956 models. With the help of the engineers at Ford, Lee developed a device called "interlock" whereby a car's ignition wouldn't operate unless the seat belts were in use. In 1956, Ford offered seat belts for the first time, but only 2% of its customers ordered them. The public was opposed to the use of the "interlock" system, and Ford simply replaced it with an eight-second buzzer. By 1964, seat belts would become standard equipment in all passenger cars.

Safety always was Lee's primary concern. He believed that seat belts, and not airbags, were key to reducing traffic fatalities. He argued that air bags posed dangers related to delayed or inadvertent inflation. In Lee's eyes it seemed that the use of seat belts needed to be made mandatory. In 1966, Lee made automotive history with the introduction of the Ford Mustang whose unique sporty style was to affect the whole industry. On December 10, 1970, Iacocca became president of the Ford Motor Company. In 1978, however, after thirty-two years of service and money-making innovations for Ford, he was asked to resign over personal differences with Henry Ford II.

Only a little over a year after, on January 1, 1980, Iacocca became chairman and CEO of the Chrysler Corporation. Chrysler had been indeed on the verge of bankruptcy, and Iacocca had accepted the challenge to turn things around. He began by being actively involved in Chrysler's advertising. He created the "K-car" series and a top-selling minivan series. He actively competed with the imported cars market and simultaneously expanded Chrysler's own markets overseas. He developed and intensely advertised Chrysler's fuel-efficient vehicles at a time when American car-makers were still far behind in responding effectively with the emergence and success of the phenomenon of smaller foreign cars that were flooding the American marketplace.

Iacocca's achievements included not only saving the Chrysler Corporation from bankruptcy but also setting the standard for American-produced vehicles that were smaller and more efficient. On August 15, 1983, Iacocca repaid, in advance by seven years, the loan the Federal Government had made to Chrysler. By the time Iacocca retired from Chrysler in 1992, the international business community considered him as an industrial and market innovator.

Iacocca received many awards and honors in his lifetime. One such honor involved President Reagan appointing Iacocca in 1986 chairman of the Statue of Liberty/Ellis Island Centennial Commission. But sadness struck the Iacocca family when Lee's wife, at age fifty-seven, died from complications resulting from diabetes. Lee then assigned all royalties from his best-selling autobiography to benefit the Mary Iacocca Joslin Diabetes Center in Boston, Massachusetts. He also established the Iacocca Foundation that has since supported diabetes research and offered scholarships to the children of Chrysler employees.

Lee presently enjoys an oceanfront condominium in Boca Raton, Florida and an estate in Tuscany, Italy named Villa Nicola, that produces table wine and olive oil. His daughters operate this family-run business venture called Villa Nicola Ltd. Lee Iacocca, an erudite businessman and philanthropist, has made his indelible mark on contemporary America's business mores.

General Sources:
1. Collins, David. *Lee Iacocca: Chrysler's Good Fortune*. Ada, OK: Garrett Educational Corp., 1992.
2. *Current Biography Yearbook*. New York: Wilson, 1988.
3. Gordon, Maynard M. *The Iacocca Management Technique*. New York: Dodd, Mead, 1985.
4. Iacocca, Lee. *I Gotta Tell You: Speeches of Iacocca*. Detroit, MI: Wayne State University Press, 1994.
5. Iacocca, Lee, and William Novak. *Iacocca: An Autobiography*. Boston, MA: G.K. Hall, 1984.
6. Levin, Doron. *Behind the Wheel at Chrysler: The Iacocca Legacy*. New York: Harcourt Brace, 1995.

—by ELEANOR FEE

ALBERT INNAURATO (1947-   )

Winner of two Obie Awards in the 1970s for *Gemini* (running over four years on Broadway) and for *The Transfiguration of Benno Blimpie*, Albert Innaurato also went on to receive an Emmy for *Verna the USO Girl* in 1980. A recipient of many grants including a Guggenheim (1976), a Rockefeller (1977), and a National Endowment for the Arts (1986), he has displayed a wide range of interests and concerns regarding contemporary American culture. As a playwright he has become known for his own unique blend of present-day themes unified by a farcical style, much hyperbole, and touches of morbidity. Also talented as an opera critic, he has demonstrated this expertise as a regular contributing author to many magazines including the *New York Times*, *Opera News*, and *Vanity Fair*.

Albert Innaurato was born on June 2, 1947 in Philadelphia to Albert, Sr., and Mary (nee Walker) Innaurato. His mother was a nurse; and, his father, while a printer by trade, was autodidactic in world literature and also enjoyed the reputation as a storyteller. These highly literate skills have reportedly served as a strong source of energy and motivation for his playwright son. Young Albert, who was an opera aficionado from an early age, has attributed a good deal of his use of theatrical gestures and effects to his exposure to opera.

Before the age of ten, young Albert had already become aware of the divergence of his thoughts and actions from those of his age group. For one thing, he had written an opera libretto, and by age twelve he had already begun reading European literary heavies like Freud and Nietzsche. Transferring out of a parochial school setting into a public high school designated for gifted students, he eventually adjusted to the new and often frightening freedom before him. Eternally curious about people deemed as outcasts by society or who simply do not fall within the parameters of so-called normalcy, he began writing as a teenager depicting through the craft of drama what it might be like to experience their world from an emotional and intuitive perspective.

After graduation from high school, he at first attended Temple University and then transferred to California Institute of the Arts where he realized how badly he wanted to be a playwright. After earning his bachelor's degree in fine arts in 1972, he returned to the east coast attending Yale University's School of Drama where he received his master's degree in 1975 also in fine arts. Before he completed his studies, he had written and produced *Urlicht* (1971), a play that involved an irreverent and comic treatment of his religious past. With fellow student collaborator, Christopher Durang, he wrote three other plays: *I Don't Generally Like Poetry, But Have You Read "Trees"* (1972), *The Life of Mitzi Gaynor, or Gyp* (1973), and *The Idiots Karamazov* (1974).

Before graduating from Yale, he also wrote another play, *Earthworms*, which was produced at the Eugene O'Neill Memorial Theatre in Waterford, Connecticut in 1974. Its outrageously bizarre and improbable story line involves the relationship of a homosexual and a young hillbilly woman that is complicated by the intrusion of a strange assortment of hustlers and transvestites. Despite the improbability of the mix of characters and their relationships, the overall impact of the play succeeds quite well in alluding to the dangerously persistent amalgam of sex, sadism, and violence in contemporary American society. The play probably served also as a catharsis for the writer's misgivings with the severities of Catholic schools of the 50s.

The 70s were very creative years for Innaurato as his next play, *The Transfiguration of Benno Blimpie*, which many critics have considered his darkest of comedies, would earn him an Obie Award in 1977. Innaurato started writing the play in 1972; then completing it two years later, the brief play had its premiere performance in New Haven, Connecticut in 1974. It opened in New York City in 1977 where the talented James Coco played the title role. It deals with an obese male character who in a series of monologues relates his life sufferings, and he speaks with equal and almost magical fluidity regarding past and present events, blending them into a coherent whole. Despite the character's use of many scatological terms and grotesque depictions, many critics did not find those elements to be ever gratuitous but as an integral part of the painful and difficult dramatic themes of obesity, sex, and family ties.

In the same year, Innaurato received another Obie Award for *Gemini*, a two-act play, dealing with growing up sexually in the contemporary urban world, complicated by ethnic factors, bodily self-image, gender-identity and its uncertainties. Containing more humor than his previous plays, this long-running comedy, first on Off-Off Broadway, then Off-Broadway, and finally on Broadway, ran for over four years. It was made into a TV movie and re-titled *Happy Birthday, Gemini* (1980).

Again, as in his previous play, the author cautions that the homosexual aspect (homophobia) may be easily misconstrued as the central conflict; instead, the play's fundamental drama deals with sexual identity in general, especially when the factors of ethnicity and family come into play. One might aptly add to the author's observations that there persist the overpowering influence of the media, the world of advertising, and their overt and, also, their not-so-overt subliminal messages suggesting sex for sale in the marketplace of goods. Innaurato's

baby boomer birth date (1947) clearly identifies the 60s as the period of his teenage years. It was the era of educational reform where students were redefined by the government. It was also the era of sexual liberation, the burgeoning use of illicit drugs (hallucinogenics), the Woodstock Festival, the Vietnam War, the assassinations of President Kennedy, Bobby Kennedy and the Rev. Martin Luther King, and the Cuban Missile Crisis that almost brought the world to nuclear confrontation.

When Innaurato's works are examined in this broad context, it becomes clear that homophobia and homosexuality are thematically not the essential concerns even though they are surely important issues. They are indeed topical but merely remain coincidental to the broader and more pressing issues of sexuality and violence, gender-identity, and the problems of personal identity in a technocratic, dehumanizing society. This expansive scenario explains in part Innaurato's use of scatological and grotesque elements as reactive components that delineate the turmoil and anger generated when the individual as a societal being and the inner self become assaulted and overwhelmed. When these issues are fully recognized in Innaurato's dramas, they almost necessarily call into question—with some reasonable discomfort to the viewer—one's own moral value system.

General Sources:
1. *Contemporary Theatre, Film and Television*. Detroit, MI: Gale Research, 1987.
2. *Current Biography Yearbook*. New York: Wilson, 1988.
3. D'Acierno, Pellegrino, ed. *The Italian American Heritage: A Companion to Literature and Arts*. New York: Garland Publ., 1999.
4. Katz, Ephraim. *The Film Encyclopedia*. New York: HarperCollins, 1998.

—by GEORGE CARPETTO, Ph.D.

GREGORY LA CAVA (1892-1952)

Born in Towanda, Pennsylvania on March 10, 1892, the son of Pascal Nicholas and Eva (nee Wolz) La Cava, Gregory would someday become a film director legend. In his time, La Cava was as well known as Hollywood film heavy Frank Capra. As a movie director, La Cava would be recognized for his single-mindedness, his nonconformity, and his own brand of rugged individualism fitting into no one's slot but his own. His need to work independently was so great that he was reputed to having had the lengthiest and most detailed legal contracts in Hollywood's early film history, sometimes as long as sixty pages.

His native town of Towanda was essentially Irish, and Gregory's family apparently constituted the only Italian people living there. After attending elementary school, Gregory moved with his family to Rochester, New York where in addition to attending high school he worked for more than a year as a young reporter for the *Rochester Evening Times*. Having demonstrated many talents both in writing and in art, he decided to attend the Chicago Art Institute and later the National Academy of Design in New York City. He then became a newspaper cartoonist managing to earn a living at that trade working for the American Press Association in the *Evening World* and in the *Sunday Herald*.

After a few years as a magazine and newspaper cartoonist, he became increasingly fascinated by the growing possibilities that animated cartoons held for the future. An ardent cartoonist, he studied the early phases of the development of cartoons as applied to animation on the silver screen whose successful origins had begun around 1908. This desire led him to become employed by the Walter Lantz studios, and there during WWI he had the opportunity to work with early cartoon animation. He became involved in comic strip characterizations such as the well-known "Mutt and Jeff" and the "Katzenjammer Kids."

In many ways, Gregory had become one of the pioneers in cartoon production, and later while working for the William Randolph Hearst Enterprises, he organized and developed their animated cartoon department becoming the editor in chief of its International Comic Films division. While film animation was still in its infancy, Gregory had done more than four years' work of animated cartoon production and experimentation by the year 1921.

Gregory, who was a contemporary of Walt Disney, in actuality had more experience in that medium by the beginning of the 1920s than Disney. Yet both of these strong, determined personalities took very different paths. While Disney in the late twenties began to take animation to new heights, Gregory had already left the developmental area of cartoon animation in the early twenties and began writing and directing in the burgeoning realm of silent motion pictures in New York City.

In the early 1920s, he first started writing stories and directing comedy shorts for the screen. He then switched to directing feature films. In 1922, Gregory directed both Johnny Hines (a star comedian of the silent movies) and the then unknown Clara Bow in her screen debut, *Beyond the Rainbow* (1922). With the broad success of this La Cava film, Paramount shrewdly began grooming Clara Bow as a new symbol of the flapper age of the Roaring Twenties.

After successfully working for Paramount in New York City for several years as a writer and director, Gregory moved to Hollywood in 1927 along with Paramount when it decided to relocate its major operations to sunny California. It was at this moment in history that film production operations were beginning to change very rapidly, and the silent movies would soon be replaced. Not all the actors, actresses, and directors of the silent era would continue to be successful.

The inception of the sound era (when the movie audiences heard the actors voices) that traditionally is said to have begun in part with Warner Brothers' motion picture, *The Jazz Singer*, was released in October 1927. Not quite perfected, sound was tried again in an all-talking movie in the 1928 Warner Brother's *Lights of New York*. Representing a major benchmark in movie history, within months it caused all movie studios to switch to "talkies" making silent movies become virtually a thing of the past.

By 1929, Gregory switched his place of employment from Paramount to First National, a smaller and more aggressive production and distribution company (later assimilated by Warner Bros). There he directed Corinne Griffith in a film entitled *Saturday's Children* (1929). She was nicknamed the "Orchid Lady" and reputed the world's most beautiful woman. Unlike Clara Bow, Corinne Griffith had already established herself as a sex symbol of the silent movies era dating as far back as 1916. It was Gregory's good fortune that when he directed her in this 1929 "talkie" film, it was a huge success.

With "talkies" in full swing and the path clearly obvious as to its potential as a newer and fuller medium of expression, Gregory began focusing all his efforts on directing and put aside any interests in writing, film animation, or drawing. His decision proved to be a fruitful one, and despite the overbearing presence of the forthcoming depression era, both he and Frank Capra became among the highest paid and most well-known directors in Hollywood at that time. When he concluded his film career in 1948, he had directed close to forty feature films spanning the era of the late 20s to the late 40s.

Gregory La Cava was a director who had witnessed and experienced, firsthand, the art of filmmaking in all of its major production transitions from its infancy in the silent era into the more modern film era as it blossomed into the second half of the 20th century. Though he himself often used some techniques that were throwbacks to the silent movie era, he was also modern in many ways in that he kept himself psychologically interactive with his actors. He believed that because "the script" is never completed until the movie is shot in its entirety, he allowed his actors full freedom to suggest changes. In all, he went on to evolve his craft setting a standard in the industry as he created hit movies with such periodic consistency that he made both audiences and producers happy.

In the history of moviemaking, Gregory La Cava represents a uniquely powerful personality with whom critics and students of film must reckon. His undeniably rich and varied experience, his seasoned background in early cartoon animation, in silent movies, and in sound-era films together with his rugged individualism had struck for his time a most successful balance between artistic and commercial ends. A veteran filmmaker and a pioneer in the medium of film, this Italian American who died in 1952 stands as a tribute to all Americans for his contribution to the arts.

General Sources:
1. *Current Biography.* New York: Wilson, 1941; 1952.
2. *The Encyclopedia of Hollywood.* New York: Facts on File, 1990.
3. Katz, Ephraim. *The Film Encyclopedia.* New York: HarperCollins, 1998.
4. *World Encyclopedia of Film.* Ed. John Smith and Tim Cawkwell. New York: Galahad Books, 1974.

—by GEORGE CARPETTO, Ph.D.

FIORELLO LA GUARDIA (1882-1947)

Achille La Guardia (a young musician from Foggia, Italy) and his wife, Irene (a young Austrian Jew from Trieste), arrived in New York City in late 1880 and settled in Manhattan's Greenwich Village area. They had a daughter Gemma; and on December 11, 1882, they had a son Fiorello who prophetically was born less than a mile away from City Hall. Achille, unable to earn a living as a full-time musician, enlisted in the U.S. Army and became a bandmaster with the 11th infantry regiment. Later that year, the regiment and the La Guardia family were transferred west to a territory that would not become the state of North Dakota until 1889. As a result of their travels, Fiorello grew up among Indians, cowboys, and soldiers rather than New York City street urchins.

After serving at several other posts, the regiment was moved to the city of Prescott in the Arizona Territory. Here, Fiorello completed grammar school and had barely started a two-year high school. He soon became an involuntary dropout when the USS Maine blew up in Havana harbor, and the regiment was sent to Tampa, Florida to then be shipped out to the war in Cuba. Achille and his family, however, were left behind. His health had been damaged permanently after having eaten diseased meat, which had been sold to the Army. With a meager pension of $8.00 a month, he was discharged. A short while later, he would lose that pension because Army officials had decided that his illness was not the result of combat duty.

By the end of 1889, unable to support his family, Achille and his family returned to Trieste. In 1900, Fiorello became a clerk at the American Consulate in Budapest and later in Fiume where he worked with immigrants. He became enraged at the poor treatment they typically received by dishonest officials. His father, at age 55, died in 1904 leaving Fiorello head of the household at age 18.

While working at the consulate, Fiorello learned to speak Italian (which was never spoken at home), German, Spanish, Hungarian, and from his mother, Yiddish. Later, in political life, his knowledge of these languages would enable him to go into ethnic neighborhoods in New York and speak to the voters in their own language. In 1906, Fiorello finally returned to his native New York, and in 1907 he became an interpreter on Ellis Island. He recognized that the treatment of the immigrants was not much better there either.

He had already experienced bigotry as expressed against the native Americans when he lived out West as a child, and now he saw it again in the poor treatment of immigrants perpetrated by corrupt public officials. This kind of scenario was instrumental in shaping his character. He would become the man that Harry S. Truman, President of the United States, would later describe as "incorruptible as the sun." In 1910, Fiorello earned a law degree from New York University and later that year he was admitted to the New York bar. He immediately terminated his job with civil service, and with barely $6 in his pocket, opened his own law office, specializing in immigration law.

Fiorello joined the Republican Party in 1914 because he "could not stomach the Tammany Hall mob." In 1917, he became the first Republican since the Civil War to become a congressman from the 14th District and the first Italian American to serve in the House of Representatives. Fiorello's first Congressional term was stormy and short-lived. When the United States joined the Allies in WWI, a long and bitter debate on selective service ensued, and he voted yes for its acceptance. He wondered aloud how many congressmen would join in the war effort. La Guardia stood up and was the first to volunteer. Four others joined him later. In July 1917, he enlisted in the Aviation Section of the Signal Corps and was sent to Europe to fly planes. Discharged as a major at the end of the war, he returned to Congress to receive a hero's welcome.

In 1919, he married the girl he had left behind, Thea Almerigotti. Sadly, in 1921, he would lose both his daughter Fiorella and his wife to tuberculosis. He served in Congress from 1917 to 1921 and again from 1923 to 1932. His conflicts with the "establishment" in Congress kept him from being assigned to any meaningful committees, and so most of his proposals were defeated. After he left the House, in a twist of irony each of his important proposals that earlier had been defeated would eventually become law. Minimum wages, old-age pensions, child-labor laws, workmen's compensation, social security, and government regulation of utilities and the stock market became part of American life.

On February 28, 1929, Fiorello married Marie Fisher who had been his secretary for fifteen years. He began to think of running for the job of mayor of NYC. He knew his chances were next to none. The big landowners, whom he had accused of not paying their fair share of taxes, chose to ignore him. His early campaign picked up some steam only when he began to attack Tammany Hall, though apparently not enough to defeat Jimmy Walker. One week before the election on Tuesday, October 29, 1929 the stock market crashed and the Great Depression would begin.

Later in 1932 when Jimmy Walker could not explain his personal finances to an investigative committee, he resigned as mayor. LaGuardia, who had led the fight against Tammany Hall and Jimmy Walker, was now favored by the people. On January 1, 1934, Fiorello became the 99th mayor of the city, a job he held for 12 years. He had caught the fancy of New Yorkers and the media, and the general public loved him. Over the years he became simply known as the "Little Flower."

He was undersized: a roughneck, wearing a brown suit to his own inauguration. As he took office, he faced the awesome task of a city hurt by the Depression, mismanaged, and on the brink of bankruptcy. The banks and the federal government had refused the city's applications for loans. Yet one hundred days after he took office, New York City sold a $7.65 million bond issue at 4 percent interest. The budget became balanced and the city received a $100 million loan from the federal government, restoring New York City's credit.

Even his detractors admitted that he was incorruptible. To many New Yorkers, he was the best mayor the city had ever had. When the "Little Flower" died at his home on September 20, 1947, he was mourned by friend and foe alike. He was an Italian American in whom all Americans could take pride.

General Sources:
1. *Current Biography*. New York: Wilson, 1940; 1947.
2. Elliott, Lawrence. *The Little Flower: The Life and Times of Fiorello La Guardia*. New York: Morrow, 1983.
3. Kessner, Thomas. *Fiorello H. La Guardia and the Making of Modern New York*. New York: Penguin Books, 1991.
4. La Guardia, Fiorello H. *The Making of an Insurgent: An Autobiography, 1882-1919*. Philadelphia, PA: Lippincott, 1948.
5. "Obituary." *New York Times* 21 Sept. 1947: 1+.
6. Zinn, Howard. *La Guardia in Congress*. Westport, CT: Greenwood Press, 1972.

—by AUGUST BERARDINELLI

FRANKIE LAINE (1913-   )

A popular singer of the 40s and 50s, and a Hollywood actor in movies of that era, he captured the hearts and minds of many music lovers. As ten of his recordings had sold more than one million copies by 1956, he eventually garnered a grand total of sixteen recordings that qualified as gold records. As a talented entertainer and a contemporary to Tony Bennett, Perry Como, Frank Sinatra and to their collective popularity in the music industry of the post World War II decades, Frankie Laine was considered without a doubt among the foremost of America's vocalists of that era.

In addition to his popularity in the United States on radio and in nightclub circuits during that period, he also was among the very first vocalists to have his own fifteen-minute TV show by the fall of 1955 on CBS-TV. It was a singer-focused TV format that would soon become standard programming in the ensuing TV decades. Having a pleasant and relaxed personality, Frankie Laine filled in for Arthur Godfrey on the latter's CBS-TV show during the summers of 1955 and 1956. He also outsold all other American vocalists in Europe during the 50s era when Europeans considered American songs fashionable.

Francis Paul LoVecchio, better known as Frankie Laine, was born on March 30, 1913, in Chicago, Illinois the oldest of eight children. Both of his parents were native to Monreale, Palermo (Sicily). His parents, who later met by coincidence in Chicago, did not know each other when they had made their way to America. His father Giovanni immigrated to the United States in the year 1906, and he came over from Sicily in steerage. Similarly, in the same year, his mother Anna (nee Salerno) and six other siblings were luckier in that they traveled in third class when they immigrated to America.

Frankie Laine's parents, who were immediately attracted to each other when they met, had their share of initial family problems getting together as a couple since her hand had been promised in marriage to someone else. However, once that problem was overcome, they married. When his father first had come to America, he started employment for the Chicago Railroad as a water boy and worked his way up to laying rails. When he found that job grueling, he enrolled in a trade school intent on becoming a barber. Though Frankie was born in a primarily Italian area on Townsend Street where his parents had their first apartment, the family soon moved not too far to another apartment across the street from the Church of the Immaculate Conception, a church that served the needs of many different immigrant groups.

The church had a parochial school where Frankie started attending at the second grade level. Frankie vividly recalls that there were two major influences in his life that made him appreciate music and want to pursue it as a career. First, there was his grade school teacher, Sister Norbert, generally described by him as wonderful, who was also like "a tyrant" driving the fundamentals of music into his head. Secondly, years later in high school he skipped class one day to see and hear Al Jolson in a "talkie" movie, *The Singing Fool* (1928). When he saw Jolson sink to his knees and captivate the audience while singing "Sonny Boy," Frankie knew he wanted to be a singer and move people the same way Jolson did.

Naturally, Frankie had done his first singing in the church choir, and while attending Lane Technical High School, he sang on an occasional basis in local cabarets and night clubs, literally singing for his supper and often being the bouncer too. He did all kinds of things to earn money including dance marathons. By 1931 at age eighteen, Frankie had won two dance marathons, and he won $500 in prize money when he set an all-time dance marathon record of 3,051 hours in 145 days in 1932 in Atlantic City, New Jersey, a feat that was recorded in the *Guinness Book of World Records*.

But it wasn't until he went to New York City during the years of the Great Depression that he auditioned for a five-dollar-a-week singing job on radio station WINS. The show featured other vocalists as well, but he began to learn the trade. He developed his own style focusing on the use of jazz-like rhythmic phrasing that worked around musical tones rather than singing them directly, done by emphasizing their downbeat aspects, using his voice, as he once said, "like a horn." Though now possessing a style of his own, nothing happened to propel him into fame.

After moving to Los Angeles, he worked at a defense plant by day and sang by night. When WWII ended in May 1945, Frankie lost his defense job, and he would struggle financially until 1946 when he would receive his first break. One night when Frankie was singing without pay at Billy Berg's Vine Street Club, Hoagy Carmichael, the renowned composer of "Stardust," liked Laine's voice, and before he left the premises he made sure Billy Berg put Laine on salary. Frankie soon began earning $75 per week. Several nights later, when he introduced his version of an old song, "That's My Desire," the audience became so enthusiastic that before the evening was over, he had sung it five times.

Within months Mercury Records signed him up, and his first recording of that song alone in 1947 would go on to sell more than one million records. Heard by millions of people on the radio, Laine saw his career skyrocket as he was invited to perform in top nightclubs where he often received as much as $5,000 for a one-time guest appearance. By this time, Frankie Laine fan clubs had mushroomed around the globe as far as Australia and South Africa.

He also appeared in as many as nine Hollywood movies including *Make-Believe Ballroom* (1949), *When You're Smiling* (1950), *Sunny Side of the Street* (1951), *Rainbow 'Round My Shoulder* (1952), and *Meet Me in Las Vegas* (1956). He often provided the voice for Hollywood film backgrounds or for TV series theme songs as in Clint Eastwood's classic Western TV series, *Rawhide* (1960s).

Frankie Laine, who has been through the ordeal of quadruple bypass surgery, continues to perform in his eighties. He has had a long history of having done considerable charity work, especially for underprivileged children and for needy young vocalists looking for a start.

He claims fervently that nothing worthwhile in his life came about without a price or a struggle. A warm and talented personality, he will always be remembered for his legacy of 40s and 50s popular music where he had scores of hit songs many of which have since become classics such as *That's My Desire* (1947), *Mule Train* (1949), *Jezebel* (1950), *On the Sunny Side of the Street* (1951), *I Believe* (1953), the last of which alone sold more than 11 million records.

General Sources:
1. *Current Biography*. New York: Wilson, 1956.
2. *The Encyclopedia of Popular Music*. Ed. Colin Larkin. London, UK: MUZE UK Ltd, 1998.
3. Katz, Ephraim. *The Film Encyclopedia*. New York: HarperCollins, 1998.
4. Laine, Frankie. *That Lucky Old Son: The Autobiography of Frankie Laine*. Venture, CA: Pathfinder, 1993.
5. *The New Grove Dictionary of American Music*. New York: Grove's Dictionaries of Music, 1986.

—by ANGELA HARRINGTON

MARIO LANZA (1921-1959)

An Italian-American tenor, whose career skyrocketed and ended in such a brief lifetime of thirty-eight years, became the first singer in recording history to have sold two-and-a-half million albums, the only classical music artist to have sold one million copies of a single record in a year, and the recipient of the world's greatest royalty check as of 1951 for a ten-month period amounting to $746,000. Popular in the concert hall as well as on the film stage, Lanza preferred singing and acting in the film medium. Appealing to people of all ages from bobby-soxers to senior citizens, he garnered one of the largest followings of fans a film star could have ever imagined in Hollywood history.

Alfred Arnold Cocozza, better known as Mario Lanza, who adapted his stage name almost entirely from his mother's maiden name Maria Lanza, was born in South Philadelphia on January 31, 1921. His father Antonio Cocozza was a decorated World War I combat veteran who lived on a total disability pension. His mother, a seamstress, worked hard for many years so that the family was financially stable. Mario was unusual as a youngster as he took to operatic music as early as seven years of age, listening avidly to opera records on the family Victrola (an early phonograph trade name), singing along, learning the lyrics, and studying the operatic plots.

Later in life, Lanza admitted that as an only child he was pampered by his parents to the point that he became reckless in his habits and attitudes. In high school, teachers disliked the deliberate use of his weight (230 lbs.) and his loud voice to taunt and intimidate fellow students. One day when he got out of hand by socking one of his teachers, Lanza was expelled. It was just two months prior to graduation at Southern High School. Never finishing his secondary education, his pampered life continued unabated. His permissive parents, who had spoiled him all those years, allowed him to do little or no work.

His parents had only come to seriously recognize his music talents when he was in his late teens after his high school failure. This all came about when Lanza tried to learn to play the piano and had no success, so his parents suggested his taking singing lessons. Luckily, his parents found a former opera singer, Irene Williams, who agreed to teach him. They settled upon a lesson every other day, and this schedule lasted for almost two years. Reportedly, his mother gladly worked extra hours to pay for his lessons to see him succeed.

After two years of training, it was Lanza's good fortune—now twenty-one years of age and having had such a conscientious music teacher—that Irene Williams arranged through some of her friends (Dr. John Noble and concert manager William Huff) at the Philadelphia Academy of Music to have him audition, however minimally, for its busy guest conductor Serge Koussevitzky right before the evening's scheduled performance. Koussevitzky, upon hearing Mario sing an aria that afternoon, offered him on the spot a summer scholarship at the Berkshire Music Festival at Tanglewood. The music center, located on the Tanglewood Estate in the beautiful Berkshire Hills in west Massachusetts that the maestro had founded in 1934, offered up-and-coming artists the unique possibility to sharpen their skills and the opportunity to perform during Tanglewood's summer music programs.

After Lanza appeared in concert on August 7, 1942, his life suddenly changed. The

New York Times columnist Noel Straus offered Mario excellent reviews, and not before long he was put under contract by Columbia Concerts to do singing tours around the country. This serendipitous moment in his life was cut short when he was drafted into the armed forces. Subsequent to basic training, the U.S. Army designated him as a military policeman. He was sent first to Florida and then to Texas for a limited period of time, which must have appeared to him an eternity. He despaired for months over his severed musical career, but he finally received a reprieve when he was offered to sing and entertain members of the U.S. Army.

Now being able to leave the MPs and become part of Special Services (entertainment) through the efforts of Johnny Silver, Lanza toured with him in GI shows and sang regularly on military radio programs for the duration of World War II. After being discharged from the service, Lanza acquired a New York manager, Sam Weiler, who made him take music lessons under the tutelage of Enrico Rosati. From mid-1947 to mid-1948, he made a series of singing appearances including one at the Hollywood Bowl that earned him the attention of MGM.

Initially, MGM's Louis B. Mayer showed some reluctance but was convinced by movie producer Joe Pasternak to sign him up. Lanza was taken on at MGM, and he performed his first film role in *That Midnight Kiss* (1949). Despite the fact that Lanza surprisingly suffered from stage fright and had canceled fifteen out of twenty-seven promotional appearances for the movie, the film was very successful, and Lanza gained immediate nationwide recognition. He went on to make seven other films including *The Toast of New Orleans* (1950) where he sang what would become his signature song "Be my Love." Then, with *The Great Caruso* (1951), his greatest singing achievement where he portrayed the legendary Caruso, he broke all house records at Radio City Music Hall to sellout crowds for a ten-week period that earned the music hall a record $1.5 million.

Lanza's other films included *Because You're Mine* (1952), *The Student Prince* (1953), *Serenade* (1956), *The Seven Hills of Rome* (1957), and *For the First Time* (1959). In all, his meteoric rise seemed to have all the predictably necessary conditions for more success. Yet Lanza's personal problems would dictate otherwise. He had always had a penchant for overeating and excessive drinking, and by the time the *Student Prince* was completed in 1953, his drinking was increasing at an alarming rate, and it exacerbated his heavy use of barbiturates. Lanza's untimely death surely came as a shock to his admirers and followers who knew little of his problems. His death has been attributed to many different causes including his drinking, his ongoing obesity problem, his long history of binge eating and alternating starvation diets, and drug use. Sadly, he died of a heart attack at a young age in a Rome clinic on October 7, 1959. He left a musical legacy both in recorded music and in film that in many respects—both in quantity and in quality—was second to none.

General Sources:

1. Bessette, Roland L. *Mario Lanza: Tenor in Exile*. Portland, OR: Amadeus Press, 1999.
2. Hitchcock, Wiley, and Stanley Sadie, eds. *The New Grove Dictionary of American Music*. New York: Grove's Dictionaries of Music, 1986.
3. Katz, Ephraim. *The Film Encyclopedia*. New York: HarperCollins, 1998.
4. "Million-Dollar Voice." *Time* 6 Aug. 1951: 60-61+.
5. Null, Gary, and Carl Stone. *The Italian-Americans*. Harrisburg, PA: Stackpole Books, 1976.
6. Strait, Raymond, and Terry Robinson. *Lanza: His Tragic Life*. Englewood Cliffs, NJ: Prentice Hall, 1980.

—by GEORGE CARPETTO, Ph.D.

TOMMY LASORDA (1927-   )

As a twenty-year manager of the L.A. Dodgers and as an almost fifty-year veteran of the Dodger organization, Lasorda brought many years of prominence and prosperity to the L.A. Dodgers and its nationwide organization. After being inducted into the National Baseball Hall of Fame in Cooperstown, New York on March 5, 1997, he became baseball's 14th manager to be so honored, and, in effect, he also became the 15th hall of famer as a Dodger. After having led the Dodgers to two World Championships, four National League pennants and seven Western Division titles in his twenty years as manager, he has earned the deep respect of his profession and has received many honors.

Thomas Charles Lasorda, better known as Tommy Lasorda, was born on September 22, 1927 in Norristown, Pennsylvania. He was the second of five boys born to Italian immigrant parents Sabatino and Carmela (nee Covatto) Lasorda. Sabatino, who had come from the Abruzzi area of Italy, worked as a truck driver for Bethlehem Steel. He has been depicted as a jovial person who considered himself both grateful and privileged to be in America and able to work and raise a family here. In his off-hours, he was typically portrayed as singing, playing the concertina, and telling old stories to family and friends. In all, Tommy's father set a fine example of camaraderie to his children and all those around him, and he often expressed his gratitude for his new found home in America.

Tommy Lasorda would take a different route from that of his four brothers who entered the restaurant business. Tommy wanted to get into baseball. Since his early days, he had admittedly depicted himself as a "third-string" pitcher when he played for his high school team. Despite the lackluster record of these teenage wannabee years, he managed to obtain a minor-league contract with the Phillies. Overtaken by this relatively minor feat during the war years, he quit school in his senior year (1944-45). His pitching win-loss record for the 1945-1948 period (which subsumed two years away in military service) was an unimpressive 12-24. Modest in playing talent, he possessed, instead, his signature trademark: a great will to succeed in baseball as he was about to discover his forte.

Soon after, he joined the Dodger farm team system, and by 1949 he was pitching with an improved 7-7 record, playing as a member of the Greenville Spinners in South Carolina. He was later sent up north to Montreal, Canada to its AAA farm club. Encouraged by the shift, Lasorda became even more determined to succeed and, in fact, decided he would stick with the Dodger organization as far as he could go. He dreamed of making it to the Dodgers' major league team, which at that time was located in Brooklyn, New York until its move to Los Angeles in 1958.

After spending nine years with the Montreal farm club, his pitching record was a much improved 107-57. He had been offered some experience at participating in major leagues games, but his general performance proved fruitless, and he returned to Canada. Finally, in 1960 after a dismal pitching record of 2-5 in Montreal, the Dodger organization decided to make him a scout. In essence, this ironically became the turning point in his career as his strengths lay in the management areas of baseball, and his first assignment was in Pocatello, Idaho.

By the year 1965, the team he managed placed second in its league. Later, as manager of the Ogden (Utah) Dodgers, his team went on to win the pennant for three consecutive years (1966-68) in the Pioneer League. The crowning achievement in this part of his life arrived when he became a Triple-A manager (1969-1972), and two of his teams, Spokane in 1970 and Albuquerque in 1972, each won a pennant. In 1970, getting the recognition that he deserved for his persistent efforts in management, he was voted Minor League Manager of the Year. As a manager in the Dodger farm system, he had a record that showed 478 wins and 367 losses. In addition to his notable pennant wins, he had also acquired a reputation for developing and sending good players up to the majors of whom there amassed an impressive group numbering 57.

This did not go unnoticed, and in 1973 he was promoted from the minor to the major league becoming the third-base coach for the Los Angeles Dodgers. Dedicated to the Dodger organization as he had consistently avowed, he turned down managerial offers from several other major league baseball teams. Walter Alston, who had been manager of the Dodgers since 1954 when the Dodgers were still based in Brooklyn, had been in charge of the team and had led the Dodgers to seven pennants and four world championships. After two consecutive years (1975 and 1976) during which the Dodgers (under his aegis) finished a "distant second" in the National League West, Alston sought retirement in September 1976.

Peter O'Malley, president of the Dodger organization, then named Lasorda to succeed Alston as manager. Suddenly reports coming out of Vero Beach, Florida during the 1977 spring training discussed Lasorda's very different style of management described as loud yet complimentary, garrulous yet precise in directions. When the season opened at Dodger Stadium, Frank Sinatra, a close friend of Lasorda, inaugurated the occasion by singing the national anthem to the cheers of many Dodger fans.

That summer the Dodgers went on to win hands down the National League West title by defeating the Cincinnati Reds and then winning the National League Championship by defeating the Phillies. In the following year, Lasorda led his team to win the pennant; and he became the second baseball manager in history to win the pennant in his first two years as manager.

Lasorda has a long list of achievements. Under his 20-year leadership as manager, the Dodgers won a total of four National League pennants (1977, 1978, 1981, 1988), and they also won two World Championships (1981, 1988). Lasorda also managed six All-Star teams, leading the National League teams to triumph in 1978, 1979, 1982, and 1984. In 1988 he became the first recipient of the Milton Richman Memorial Award by the Association of Professional Baseball Players of America. As a fitting tribute to his dedication to baseball, to his many contributions, and to his successes in the field, he was inducted into the Baseball Hall of Fame in 1997. Even after he had given up his baseball uniform, Lasorda remained an integral part of the Dodgers as he became a vice president of the Dodgers organization.

General Sources:
1.   Bjarkman, Peter C., ed. *Encyclopedia of Major League Baseball Team Histories: National League.* Westport, CT: Meckler, 1991.

2.   *Current Biography Yearbook.* New York: Wilson, 1989.

3.   Lasorda, Tommy. *The Artful Dodger.* New York: Arbor House, 1985.

4.   "Tommy Lasorda Tribute." 10 Dec. 1998.<http://www.dodgers.com/tommy/tommy.htm>.

5.   Whittingham, Richard. *The Los Angeles Dodgers: An Illustrated History.* New York: Harper & Row, 1982.

6.   *Who's Who in America.* 1997 ed.

—by SAM PITTARO

RITA LEVI-MONTALCINI (1909-   )

In October 1986 Dr. Rita Levi-Montalcini became the recipient of the Nobel Prize. In effect, she became the fourth woman to be awarded the Nobel Prize in the area of physiology/medicine. She had made some groundbreaking discoveries in the early 1950s in regard to what later became called nerve growth factor, or, N.G.F. It is a protein that is instrumental in the growth and the differentiation of cells in the nervous system whose knowledge has since been vitally important in the study of cancer, birth defects, Alzheimer's, and virtually all diseases related to the neurological systems.

She received this award jointly with her colleague, biochemist Stanley Cohen, who worked with her at Washington University in St. Louis, Missouri in the early 1950s. More recently, with the advent of more sophisticated scientific instrumentation in the area of genetic engineering, their innovative work from the 1950s acquired newer significance as researchers explored how the nerve growth factor could better help them understand diseases such as cancer, Alzheimer's, and AIDS.

Rita and her twin sister, Paola, were born in Turin, Italy, on April 22, 1909. Born to Adamo Levi, an engineer and plant manager, and Adele Montalcini, the twin sisters had two siblings: a brother, Gino, seven years older than they, and a sister, Anna, five years older. The family might best be described as upper middle class Jewish Italian. The family environment was reportedly "brimming" with affection and hardly troubled by disagreement between the parents.

Yet her parents were a study in contrasts. While it appeared that her mother was a woman of serenity, Rita had characterized her father as a dynamic yet hot-tempered man who was the undisputed master of the house despite the fact that his work sometimes took him away from home. Rita saw him often for lunch and dinner, and even when he was away for his job, it was he who controlled her life to the smallest detail. Adamo Levi's authoritarian ways and his Victorian-era views had often inspired awe and fear in his young daughter Rita.

Rita, in turn, had many inner strengths to counterbalance some of her father's notions that included the idea that women were not suited for the professions and that they were to receive only a limited education, marry, and have children. Rita, indeed, had other ideas. When she had reached twenty years of age, she told him that she wanted neither married life nor babies, and she wished to return to her studies. Her father, expressing strong doubts, reluctantly approved her plans to study.

After passing qualifying examinations and then appearing at the top of the list of candidates, she entered Turin's School of Medicine in the fall of 1930. One of her second-year teachers was Dr. Giuseppe Levi, a renowned professor of human anatomy and histology, the study of cellular structures of both plant and animal tissue. Until his death in 1965, Dr. Levi would remain Rita's friend, mentor, and second father. Studying under Dr. Levi's guidance, Rita did her very first work with nervous-system cells that would become her lifelong area of expertise.

When she graduated in 1936, she had specialized in neurology and worked as Dr. Levi's assistant. However, Fascist-motivated governmental decrees barred Jews from all university positions and forbade them to practice medicine. In March 1939, Dr. Rita Levi-Montalcini left Italy and traveled to Belgium, undertaking neurological research at the Neurological Institute of Brussels. When she returned to Turin in December 1939, she practiced medicine clandestinely as a doctor among the city's poor. She eventually gave up her efforts a few months later since pharmacists would not fill her patients' prescriptions.

Being compelled to give up the practice of medicine, she again turned to research. She set up a primitive laboratory in her bedroom. Under a microscope, she operated on chicken embryos from eggs. She analyzed the way in which the removal of peripheral limb tissues (which still lacked nerves) effected the differentiation and development of motor cells in the spinal cord and sensory cells in the ganglia at the rear of the spinal cord.

In July 1943, Mussolini resigned. The Fascist nightmare was over only to be replaced by Nazi troops occupying key cities in Italy, including Turin. Armed with counterfeit ID cards, Dr. Levi-Montalcini and her family fled to Florence. Seeking shelter there, they tried to assure a landlady that they were not Jewish. The landlady saw through their ruse and gave them refuge anyway. Dr. Levi-Montalcini and her sister then began "manufacturing" false ID cards for friends to flee to Florence. She remained in Florence until September of 1944 when the British troops liberated the city.

In the summer of 1946, Dr. Levi-Montalcini's article where she had summarized her wartime neuroembryology studies in her makeshift lab at home came to the attention of Dr. Viktor Hamburger, chairman of zoology at Washington University in St. Louis, Missouri. He invited her there for a semester to conduct further research. This "invitation" went on to last no less than thirty years. She worked in research from 1947 to 1951, became associate professor from 1951 to 1958, then full professor from 1958 to 1977. In 1956 she became an American citizen and in effect acquired dual citizenship status.

In 1968 she was elected to the prestigious National Academy of Sciences, the tenth woman to be elected to the academy since it was founded in 1863. Eighteen years later in September 1986, Dr. Levi-Montalcini and five other researchers became recipients of the highly coveted Lasker Medical Research Award, a harbinger of many Nobel Prize recipients. In fact, one month later, Dr. Rita Levi-Montalcini and Dr. Stanley Cohen became joint recipients of the 1986 Nobel Prize in physiology or medicine.

A year later in 1987, along with two dozen prominent scientists honored at the White House in a special ceremony in the Rose Garden, Dr. Rita Levi-Montalcini became the recipient of the National Medal of Science, the highest American scientific award. She remains a proud example of her Jewish heritage in its traditional thirst for knowledge and a model of the Italian-American experience that allowed her to soar to the heights of her field. She is a paragon for women in future generations to emulate.

General Sources:
1. *American Men and Women of Science.* New Providence, NJ: R.R. Bowker, 1998-1999.
2. *Current Biography Yearbook.* New York: Wilson, 1989.
3. Dash, Joan. *The Triumph of Discovery: Women Scientists Who Won the Nobel Prize.* Englewood Cliffs, NJ: Messner, 1991.
4. *International Who's Who.* 1989-90 ed.
5. Levi-Montalcini, Rita. *In Praise of Imperfection: My Life and Work.* New York: Basic Books, 1988.
6. Levi-Montalcini, Rita. *The Saga of the Nerve Growth Factor: Preliminary Studies, Discovery, Further Development.* River Edge, NJ: World Scientific, 1997.
7. *Notable Twentieth-Century Scientists.* Detroit, MI: Gale Research, 1995.

—by VICTOR PASSARELLA

LIBERACE (1919-1987)

Wladziu Valentino Liberace, better known as Liberace, was a talented and famous pianist. Excelling in showmanship, he became a TV icon and a major concert performer known for breaking many box office records both for attendance and income, especially at the Radio City Music Hall in the 1980s. As a performer with a dazzling draw, he was in great part responsible for helping to make Las Vegas an entertainment mecca in the 70s and 80s.

He was born on May 16, 1919 in West Allis, a suburb of Milwaukee, Wisconsin to an Italian-born father, Salvatore Liberace, and a Polish-born mother, Frances (nee Zuchowski) Liberace. Walter, as he was called, was one of four children: an older brother, George, who later became his manager and orchestra leader, and an older sister, Angelina, and the youngest brother, Rudy. All four were given piano lessons at an early age, and all four had the benefit of having both parents come from musical families back in Italy and in Poland, respectively.

Walter was able to play piano "by ear" before the age of four, and his talent won him a scholarship to the Wisconsin College of Music at the age of seven for a more formal course of study. He continued there, tuition-free, well into his young adulthood. Later, the famous Polish pianist, Paderewski, who listened to the young Liberace play the piano, further inspired his parents to groom him for a musical career.

After the stock market crash of 1929, the Liberace family moved to Milwaukee. In elementary school, young Walter proved to be a sickly child, often missing school with frequent bouts of pneumonia. His preference to remain indoors to practice the piano unfortunately earned him the title "sissy." Yet this all changed when at eleven he played piano in the local theaters at the end of the silent movies era. Suddenly he became popular with people of all ages, including those who had taunted him.

Walter had consistently trained himself to accommodate all kinds of musical requests. His growing confidence helped him to develop his own trademark style of playing "down home" (and often schmaltzy) songs and cleverly alternating those tunes with abbreviated renditions of classical and semi-classical numbers, which he referred to as "my *Reader's Digest* versions" that his fans loved so much. Yet his brilliant arrangements condensing lengthy and complicated works into more easily appreciated music were criticized by the purists.

Enjoying the challenge of being versatile both in classical and popular music, he built his reputation in high school with his five-piece teenage band, the Mixers, playing at school dances regularly. Yet in 1936, still in high school, he appeared as soloist with the Chicago Symphony and later performed with the Milwaukee Symphony. Despite his school absenteeism due to his frequent illnesses, he did well scholastically graduating 21st in a class of 76 students in 1937.

While playing pop music in local clubs with his band under the stage name Walter Busterkeys, he also performed classical recitals. At one such performance at La Crosse, Wisconsin in 1939, Liberace recalled that after the audience had requested an encore and he amusingly played a new pop novelty song, "Three Little Fishies," the audience seemed to become disturbed and much criticism ensued. Yet for him this served as a liberating event. He changed his stage name becoming simply Liberace and his style was no longer subservient to audiences' narrow expectations.

In 1940, he ventured off to New York City and got booked as an intermission pianist at the Plaza Hotel Persian Room. New York City proved to be a mixed blessing. On the one hand, it was a city bustling with creativity; yet, on the other, it also had a wealthy "café society" that perpetuated indiscretions by heckling him despite his many talents simply because he was a "nonentity" financially. This kind of treatment epitomized a low point in his life.

Exempted from the military draft of WWII due to a spinal injury, Liberace retreated to Wisconsin to further his career for the remainder of the war years. Upon his return to New York to play once again at the Plaza a few years later, he brought props with him such as an oversized grand piano adorned with elaborate candelabra that became his signature prop. The demand for his appearance increased, and finally there was no stopping his success.

He starting playing regularly in major cities from New York to Los Angeles. In 1952 he moved to California, and after some TV appearances on NBC, he obtained a five-year contract involving syndication. By this time he had become a notable solo performer playing to sell out audiences at Carnegie Hall and Madison Square Garden in New York and setting box-office records at the Hollywood Bowl in California. By 1954 he had made numerous record albums, and he soon garnered two Emmys and six gold albums.

Liberace had already been working regularly in Las Vegas for several months each year for many years until 1980 when he began touring. This was the high point of his career where in 1984 and 1985 he broke all house records at Radio City Music Hall. First, in 1984, after a 30-year hiatus away from New York, he set a new house record, having in 14 performances a total attendance of 82,000. In 1985, on a return engagement, Liberace "gave an unprecedented 21 standing-room-only performances, selling 103,000 tickets and grossing $2.4 million, a house record."

Despite his extravagance in dress and showmanship and despite his many lavishly furnished homes and his huge collections of art works, antique automobiles and pianos, his many interviewers had consistently remarked as to the paradox that Liberace remained "a charming man, gentle, unaffected, polite, and almost shy, with a childlike sincerity and joyfulness in his own flamboyance." The child from within seemed ever present and ever ready to explore the artistic and the human with sensitivity.

Due to an opportunistic disease caused by acquired immune deficiency syndrome, he died on February 4, 1987 at his vacation home in Palm Springs, California. He will long be remembered for his performance of classical, semi-classical, popular and even "old parlor favorites" done with florid and romantic touches exclusively in his own inimitable style. Both to his sell-out concert audiences and to his huge number of TV fans, he brought many fine hours of musical joy and showmanship. In his own unique way, with his ever present gaze into the eye of the TV camera, he always radiated an uncommonly genuine sense of warmth and sensitivity while displaying a most unusual adroitness at the piano keys.

General Sources:

1. *Current Biography/Yearbook.* New York: Wilson, 1954; 1987.

2. Faris, Jocelyn. *Liberace: A Bio-Bibliography.* Westport, CT: Greenwood Press, 1995.

3. Liberace. *Liberace.* New York: Putnam, 1973.

4. Mungo, Raymond. *Liberace.* New York: Chelsea House, 1995.

5. "Obituary." *New York Times* 5 Feb. 1987: B6.

6. Thomas, Bob. *Liberace: The True Story.* New York: St. Martin's Press, 1987.

—by RICKY ETHELBAH

JOHN LOMBARDI (1942-   )

At a time when many university presidents sense burnout after about five years, John Lombardi remains as vigorous as when he first arrived in 1990. During this period he has moved the University of Florida into greater national prominence. But he is not standing on his many past accomplishments. As he prepares to lead his institution into the 21st century and toward becoming a world-class site of higher learning, he carries with him a full agenda of ideas and innovations. That has been the hallmark of the man and his presidency.

Students at the University of Florida have rapidly come to love the unique president of their campus—John Lombardi. He exhibits a youthful exuberance with which they can easily identify. For example, he typically slaps "high fives" at graduations and other events, and is often seen tooling around the campus in his rusted 1985 red pickup truck that has registered more than 185,000 miles.

A writer for the *Orlando Sentinel* reports: "Students know the truck, love the Prez. When he parks on campus, his windshield accumulates more notes than a dormitory bulletin board: complaints, hellos, suggestions to invest in some Bondo and paint." For nearly two years, his enthusiasm for automobiles led him and a colleague to operate an auto repair shop. "Lombardi may be the only university president in the country that does his own brakes and engine work."

His energy seems boundless, and his ability to present idea-packed extemporaneous speeches—sometimes with breakneck rhetoric— is envied by many, and his articulation skills have earned him the accolade, among many, as a "master communicator." Sid Martin, a former state legislator once remarked: "He has more common sense than anybody I know. He can talk to a bunch of plumbers, and before you know it, they're cheering, and they all think he's a plumber, too." This highly visible and innovative Italian American truly relishes the daily challenge of leading one of the nation's largest and better-known public institutions of higher learning.

An article in *The Gainesville Sun* (1995), the local *New York Times*-owned newspaper, noted that in a short five years at the helm, Lombardi has emerged to be "what many believe the most powerful and articulate voice for UF and higher education in the history of Florida." In that same article, the dean of the College of Arts and Sciences states that "to deans around the country," the Lombardi administration is "legendary." His official biography reveals that Lombardi comes from a family with a passion for education. He was born in Los Angeles in 1942. His mother was a college librarian. His father was the president of Los Angeles City College and a well-known pioneer administrator in California's junior college system.

Lombardi earned his bachelor's degree from Pomona College and his M.A. and Ph.D. in history from Columbia University in New York City. His specialization has always been Latin American history with a particular emphasis on Venezuelan history. As he began to climb the typical academic career ladder, he held positions in Mexico and at Purdue University. He came to the University of Florida from Johns Hopkins University where he was provost and vice-president of academic affairs.

Lombardi is an unusual academician. He speaks several languages, reviews software for a computer magazine—he has written numerous product reviews, and every week leaves his office to teach a history course. He discovered early on that for him, "teaching is as natural as falling off a log." A specialist in Latin American history, he is the author of seven books focused mostly on Venezuela. His wife Cathryn Lee co-authored one of those books and illustrated two others. Anyone can "speak" to him via e-mail. He also plays the clarinet with the UF alumni band. He attends and enjoys many of the ongoing sports activities on campus, especially the football and baseball games. He is one of the most visible university presidents in the U.S.

During his tenure as president, the University of Florida was selected to be a member of the elite group of American public universities. Lombardi has introduced many innovative programs designed to enhance the lives of faculty and students alike. For instance, the Florida Quality Evaluation Project, begun in 1992, initiated programs for greater accountability in the state and the university system. Focusing on quality and productivity of the university programs, it evaluates them and compares them to comparable institutions. The Teaching Improvement Program (TIP), put into effect in 1993, provides performance-based, state monetary rewards for teaching excellence.

Similarly, the Professional Excellence Program (PEP), also state-funded, provides performance-based state monetary rewards based on faculty members' sustained quality achievements since their promotion to the rank of professor. Lombardi also has instituted a model tracking program to guarantee students the ability to graduate in four years, thereby providing for the earlier admission of the freshman applicants.

President Lombardi, tested from the day he arrived, would prove to be highly adept at administering crises even during his very first year. The crises included scandals associated with some sports programs, simmering campus racial tensions, the horrendous murder of several campus students, and the ongoing reduction in state educational funding. In each instance, he exhibited a calm but compassionate form of leadership.

The Lombardi family is close knit. His wife Cathryn Lee provides an interesting contrast to her energy-driven husband. An author in her own right, Cathryn Lee has written a text on Latin American history. They met in junior college in California, married, and now have two grown children. John Lee received his master's degree from the University of Florida, and Mary Anne completed her bachelor's at the University of Michigan.

The Lombardi family has turned the university president's home into one of the most visited places by students and faculty alike. On average, they host about eight events a week. Cathryn Lee has restored the residence to its earlier charm, and she is presently writing a history of that home. Guests and visitors are quickly welcomed into its genuinely cordial atmosphere. What better way to describe this Italian-American university president.

General Sources:
1. Lombardi, Cathryn L. *Latin American History: A Teaching Atlas*. Madison, WI: Univ. of Wisconsin Press, 1983.
2. Lombardi, John V. *Computer Literacy: The Basic Concepts and Language*. Bloomington, IN: Indiana University Press, 1983.
3. Lombardi, John V. *People and Places in Colonial Venezuela*. Bloomington, IN: Indiana University Press, 1976.
4. Lombardi, John V. *Venezuela: The Search for Order, The Dream of Progress*. New York: Oxford University Press, 1982.
5. McLeod, Michael. "Roaring Gator." *The Orlando Sentinel* 28 Jan. 1996.
6. Washington, Ray. "Lombardi Proves to Be a True Leader." *The Gainesville Sun* 5 March 1995.

—by FELIX M. BERARDO, Ph.D.

VINCE LOMBARDI (1913-1970)

Vince Lombardi's name has become synonymous with football. When he took the Green Bay Packers from the status of a poorly playing team into a leading team in the Western Conference of the NFL within two years' time, he created a huge stir. Then he created genuine excitement for football fans when he led them to five championships and then on to win the first two Super Bowl games. He accomplished this unusual feat in the span of only nine seasons.

Vince's father Enrico Lombardi was born in the town of Salerno, Italy on November 28, 1890. His family immigrated to America in 1892 settling in New York City in Manhattan's Mulberry Street section known as Little Italy. He was one among many Italian emigrants who had left their villages in Italy and moved to this particular area of New York, looking forward to the wonderful opportunities America had to offer. But especially in the begining, they often found the living conditions to be poor and jobs low-paying and full of strife.   For most immigrants, their major consolations consisted of friendship and the dream of a brighter tomorrow for themselves and their children.

Enrico worked hard and eventually acquired skills as a butcher. He later opened his own wholesale meat business that prospered. In fact, at the early age of 22 and as a success in business, he met, courted, and in the customary Italian manner, soon married his bride, Matilda lzzo.   Their first child, Vincent Thomas Lombardi, who someday would become a legendary football coach, was the first of four children born on July 11, 1913.

As the oldest, Vincent was often given the responsibility of looking after the children while his parents worked to better their status. Through this early experience it is reported that he developed self-reliance, responsibility, and leadership qualities which would stay with him throughout his lifetime, both in his personal life as well as in his professional life.

After completing his academic studies at St. Cecilia's High School, Vincent continued his education attending Fordham College located in the Bronx.   Despite a demanding academic program, he found time to play football. As a college athlete, he soon became known as one of the "seven blocks of granite" for his prowess in the football team's offensive and defensive lines. His determination and abilities as a lineman made him quickly earn the respect and admiration of his fellow opponents.

Upon graduating from Fordham College, he was unsure of his future plans, vacillating between becoming a religious and going to law school. During this period of uncertainty, he was contacted by his former *alma mater*, St. Cecilia's High School, offering him a position as head coach of the football team. With no hesitation he made his choice to accept. This was a pivotal decision in his life as football would become his new found profession.

His career at St. Cecilia's was so successful that he was invited to Fordham College to take on the position of assistant coach. His position at Fordham College would be brief, lasting just about one year between 1947-1948. His fine reputation had apparently captured the attention of West Point Academy officials who courted him until they convinced him to become assistant head coach of their prestigious football team.

The years he spent at West Point would become the most formidable years of his career. Under the watchful leadership of head coach Earl "Red" Blaike, Vince Lombardi would become one of the most sought after coaches in the history of football. Vince was tough, he was demanding, he was feared, but he was respected by his peers and his team. He remained at West Point from 1949-1953. Lombardi's talents as a leader and coach preceded him, and he was sought after by the N.Y. Giants organization. Hired as offensive coach along with Tom Landry as defensive coach and under the guidance of head coach Jim Lee Howell, the Giants would become the leaders in their league.

After several extremely successful years with the Giants, Vince's dream of being a head coach was about to become a reality. He was notified to appear at the office of the Green Bay Packers to discuss a lucrative coaching contract. It was signed on January 28, 1969. As head coach, Vince had now inherited a team with a record of one win, ten losses, one game tied. It was a terrible time when the Green Bay Packers had hit bottom and were in complete disarray.

The team was owned by the people of Green Bay, Wisconsin. The Board of Directors, made up of business people with very little knowledge of football, knew that the team and the franchise were in deep financial trouble. Lombardi, knowing the severity of the problem, accepted the position, but only on his own terms. He made it very clear to the Board of Directors as well as to the fans that he was to be in complete control. His method of coaching, his disciplinary actions, his motivational skills and his knowledge of the game brought about many changes. Some liked the changes, and some did not. But his determination did not let public opinion deter him from making judgments he thought were vital and necessary.

During his first year at Green Bay, his Packers won seven games and lost five. He was awarded the honor of Coach of the Year by a landslide selection, and it was the best year the Green Bay Packers had since 1944. Incredibly, in only nine seasons (1959-1968), Lombardi's Packers won 103 regular season games, lost only 20, and tied 3. During those memorable years, the Green Bay Packers won five championships in the National Football League. The team was the first to play in the newly created Super Bowl in 1967, and they went on the win football's first two Super Bowls in 1967 and in 1968.

In 1969, Vince Lombardi joined the Washington Redskins as head coach and executive vice-president. In his first year as coach, he brought the team to a 7 win, 5 loss, 2 tie record, the first time the Redskins had been over .500 in fourteen years. In 1970, Vince Lombardi was to learn that he had colon cancer. Despite all his successes, this was one game he would not win, but he fought the battle to the very end. On September 3, 1970, Vince Lombardi, "the legend," succumbed to this dreadful disease, but the memory of his achievements would live on in the minds of everyone for years to come. The son of an Italian emigrant, he left such a mark in the world of sports that people only vaguely familiar with sports recognize his name. His self-discipline and his motivational style may be best likened to his phrase, "winners never quit and quitters never win," the way he lived his life.

General Sources:

1. Lombardi, Vince. *Baby Steps to Success.* Lancaster, PA: Starburst Publ., 1997.
2. Lombardi, Vince. *Coaching for Teamwork: Winning Concepts for Business in the Twenty-First Century.* Bellevue, WA: Reinforcement Press, 1996.
3. Lombardi, Vince. *Strive to Excel: The Wit and Wisdom of Vince Lombardi.* Comp. Jennifer Briggs. Nashville, TN: Rutledge Hill Press, 1997.
4. Lombardi, Vince. *Winning is a Habit.* New York: HarperCollins, 1997.
5. Wells, Robert. *Vince Lombardi: His Life and Times.* Madison, WI: Prairie Oak Press, 1997.

—by DENNIS PIASIO

GUY LOMBARDO (1902-1977)

Probably the person most associated with New Year's Eve celebrations with his inaugural "Auld Lang Syne" musically defined by a predominantly velvety saxophone style—the signature sound of his Royal Canadians orchestra—Guy Lombardo has remained on record as having had the longest career as an American bandleader delineated by more than fifty years of continuous popularity spanning from the early 1920s until into the 1970s when he died.

Consistently an entrepreneur as well as an excellent musician, he was also a reputed daredevil who since 1939 pushed the throttle on many a speedboat, another of his interests for which he won the Gold Cup in 1946 and Silver Cup in 1952. As a risk-taker in speedboat racing, his whole life has been a reflection of someone who came from relative obscurity and creatively used his musical and organizational talents to become a legendary bandleader.

Guy Lombardo was born on June 19, 1902, in London (Ontario), Canada. His parents Gaetano and Angelina (nee Paladino) met and married in London (Ontario) and raised a family. Guy's father Gaetano had emigrated from the Lipari Islands of Italy in 1887 to Canada where he operated a successful tailor shop. Guy was the oldest of seven children; he had four brothers, Carmen, Victor, Liebert and Joseph; and two sisters, Elaine and Rose Marie. Guy and his siblings all attended St. Peter's, a Roman Catholic parochial (elementary and high) school where Guy studied the violin and his brother Carmen played the flute. Guy completed high school in 1920, but in addition to studying music at school, Guy and most of his siblings also took music lessons.

Often they would practice their instruments in their father's tailor shop. Eventually during high school, Guy and Carmen formed a small band playing at local events and at neighborhood festivities. In 1919 Guy obtained a job for his band where he could steadily earn $45 per week. He saw the earning potential in music, and so he decided not to continue on to college. He channeled his energy into his desired career as a musician, and he and his brother formed the nucleus of the band around which they kept adding more musicians.

In 1924, Guy and his brother decided to seek their future in the United States. When Guy and his band entered the United States, they decided to call themselves Guy Lombardo and Company. They began their work in the Cleveland area, playing at the Claremont Café, which was a roadhouse, that is, a nightclub beyond city limits. It was here that Guy's desire to create a unique style of music was realized into what would become his signature style, recognizable not only to his fans but also to the public at large.

Coincidentally, it was at this time in the 1920s that radio began its commercial history. It became the newest medium of mass communication providing a relatively accessible and inexpensive form of entertainment for the public. Guy shrewdly negotiated a one-hour radio slot at WTAM in Akron, Ohio that would broadcast his performances from the Claremont Café. The station offered no remuneration and no work benefits, but that didn't matter to Guy as he was more interested in getting exposure to the American radio-listening public. It was in September 1926 that Guy met and married his lifelong partner Lilliebell Glen, who had been one of his earliest fans from Cleveland.

Having created a distinct style of music

marked by a heavy but mellow saxophone prominence, Guy obtained bookings elsewhere. In 1927, before he began playing at the Granada Café in Chicago, Lombardo decided to dub his band "Guy Lombardo and His Royal Canadians," a title that would remain as an integral part of their image. At that time, Guy's unique style of music was competing with jazz groups that dominated the band styles of the "roaring twenties." Guy was soon able to win a double victory by convincing club owner Al Quodbach, whose business income needed improvement, to allow the band's performance from the club to be on radio broadcast. Guy met his jazz competition head on—this time, through radio station WBBM Chicago. Many listeners of his newly created audience found his sound very attractive. Guy offered not only an alternative to listening to instrumentally heavy Dixieland-style improvisational music but also a kind of music that was more melodic and easy to dance to.

Because of the Granada Café radio broadcast experience, Lombardo's fame grew, and he soon began playing at top Chicago showplaces such as the Palace Theater. Finally, in October 1929, Guy Lombardo made his first appearance in New York City. It was a radio-broadcast performance at the lavish Roosevelt Hotel which was packed with avid Lombardo fans. He became such a hit that despite the infamous October 29 stock market crash, better known as "Black Tuesday," people still poured in to hear Guy and his orchestra play. Throughout the years of the Depression, his popularity actually increased making him the number one bandleader of the era. Guy, who became a conduit for introducing new songs, was reputed as having introduced some 300 hit songs to the public in those early years.

In 1929, he also began what would become a tradition in twentieth-century America—people observing his New Year's Eve gala party through the media, which at first was heard on radio and later in the 1950s televised; always, of course, punctuated with his unique rendition of the Robert Burns classic "Auld Lang Syne," Guy's signature piece. Although most of Lombardo's hit songs were in the 30s and 40s, he put his entrepreneurial talents to work well into the 1970s maintaining his popularity by producing Broadway-style shows at the Jones Beach Amphitheater during the summers as early as 1954, creating lavish productions of hit musical classics such as *Showboat*, and *The Sound of Music*.

Although Guy Lombardo passed away on November 5, 1977, his orchestra still continues to perform today in the same style he had created in the 1920s. In retrospect, Guy Lombardo was a pioneer in being among the first to employ the medium of radio for broadcasting band or orchestral music. His style and his orchestral renditions became an institution in establishing what has been called the "sweetest music this side of heaven." By 1975, his orchestra had recorded and sold more records than any other recording artist or group in the world. Guy Lombardo has bestowed upon the United States a legacy of a special kind of American music that has become timeless.

General Sources:
1. *Current Biography Yearbook*. New York: Wilson, 1975; 1978.
2. Fox, Hugh. *The Face of Guy Lombardo: Poems*. Fremont, CA: Fault Press, 1976.
3. Kressley, Dave, and Charles Garrod. *Guy Lombardo and His Royal Canadians*. Zephyrhills, FL: Joyce Record Club Publications, 1995.
4. Lombardo, Guy, and Jack Altshul. *Auld Acquaintance*. Garden City, NY: Doubleday, 1975.
5. *The New Grove Dictionary of American Music*. New York: Grove's Dictionaries of Music, 1986.
6. "Obituary." *New York Times* 7 Nov. 19 1977: 38.

—by JOSEPHINE NARDONE CLUM

SOPHIA LOREN (1934-   )

Like many children whose childhood years were right before and during World War II, Sophia experienced firsthand the pain of hunger and ravages of war. Particularly towards the end of WWII, Naples and its environs where she lived were bombed for months on a daily basis by Allied aircraft. Yet, in some ways, her life reads like a fairy tale where the main character goes from a reputed "ugly duckling" status in her childhood—earning the nickname "stecchetto" ("skinny stick")—from a poor and struggling single-parent household, living in an industrial town adjacent to the port of Naples—to becoming a film extra, a model, an impressive lead in a documentary movie, a film celebrity, and then achieving worldwide stardom status and eventual wealth.

Sophia Loren was born on September 20, 1934, in Rome, Italy in a ward for unwed mothers in the Clinica Regina Margherita. Her unmarried parents (who would never marry) were Riccardo Scicolone and Romilda Villani. Sophia's mother Romilda, who hailed from Pozzuoli (a suburb of Naples), had come to Rome in search of a film career. It appears that Romilda, who was attractive and had won a Greta Garbo look-alike contest, left Pozzuoli despite attempts by her parents to dissuade her from seeking a movie career. There she met Riccardo, Sophia's natural father, reputedly a charmer who was an engineering student and did not want a marital commitment.

Shortly after Sophia's birth, her mother left Rome with Sophia, returning to Pozzuoli, a relatively industrialized seaport town, where Sophia's maternal grandparents lived. After the birth of Sophia's younger sister, Maria, both sisters were granted the right to take their father's surname. Sophia's name became Sofia

Villani Scicolone. Her first name, spelled "Sofia," reflected the traditional Italian spelling. Her entire name would eventually change to Sophia Loren some time after the start of her film career.

In 1949, at age fifteen, at her mother's prodding, she entered the first of several beauty contests in Naples. When Sophia won second place in one contest and did as well in the other beauty contests, these successes not only rekindled her mother's desire to become a movie star herself but also ignited in Sophia a serious interest in wanting to do the same. And so, mother and daughter soon returned to Rome to try their luck at Cinecittà, Italy's film capital located in the outskirts of Rome.

In search of movie careers, they both began by working as movie extras in the film, *Quo Vadis*, filmed in 1949 but not released until 1951. In 1949 Sophia also entered the Miss Italy beauty contest and won not only a consolation prize but also received the opportunity to do some special modeling work, posing for photographs to be used as stills in comic books and illustrated pulp fiction "soaps." Appearing in yet another contest, the Miss Rome beauty contest, Sophia received her first significant break when, while competing, she came to the attention of Carlo Ponti. He was an established Milanese lawyer and movie producer, who that day was one of the judges and would be her future husband.

Ponti had her take a screen test and requested that she study acting and perfect her Italian. She was groomed for a film career and given bit parts in low-budget films. By 1953, in the span of two-and-one-half years, Sophia had already accumulated appearances in almost 18 films. She usually maintained the name Sofia

Scicolone, but on many occasions she used the name Sofia Lazzaro in Ponti films.

In 1953, she landed her first substantial part appearing in a Carlo Ponti film named *Africa Sotto I Mari* (*Africa Under the Sea*), a semi-documentary underwater movie. Her name also changed. Sofia was anglicized to Sophia; Lazzaro was dropped. Loren, its replacement, was supposedly based on a modification of Marta *Toren*, a Swedish actress. More importantly, the truncated ending in the name Loren (not common to the Italian ear) may have also suggested something French and titillating at a time when anything French was still considered chic and fashionable.

Carlo Ponti's reputation as a film producer, which dated back to the early 40s, afforded Sophia powerful exposure to the viewing public and to other producers and directors as well. Her career soon began to skyrocket. Before the year was out, she had already been asked to perform as the female lead in a movie version of the opera *Aida* (a lead role which was turned down by Gina Lollobrigida) where Sophia acted and did the lip-synching to the operatic lyrics sung by Renata Tebaldi.

After making many American movies (shot in Italy) such as *The Pride and the Passion*, which co-starred Cary Grant and Frank Sinatra, she ventured to Hollywood in 1958, preceded by much publicity, to do seven films for Paramount Studios. Among those movies, *Houseboat* (1958) with Cary Grant and *Desire Under the Elms* (1958) were well received by the public, and she went on to win the Venice Festival Award for her role in *The Black Orchid* (1959).

On her return to Italy she starred in a De Sica film, *La Ciociara/Two Women* (1961), that many critics believe is her most memorable acting performance. She earned an Oscar and the Cannes Festival Award for Best Actress for that riveting portrayal of a mother and her young daughter who were raped together by a band of foreign soldiers in war-ravaged Italy during WWII. Under the direction of De Sica, Sophia also went on to give many more memorable performances in the 1960s including such timeless masterpieces as *Yesterday, Today and Tomorrow* (1963) and *Marriage Italian Style* (1964), both international hits.

Sophia Loren, whose career now spans almost 50 years and has been in no less than 80 films, has received many honors and awards both in her native Italy and internationally for her incredibly rich acting talents. In 1991 she received perhaps the most impressive award to date when the Academy of Motion Picture Art and Sciences awarded her a special Oscar for Lifetime Achievement. On a lesser note, she achieved a first that same year she was chosen as the first female grand marshal of New York City's Columbus Day Parade. Equally notable has been the United Nations decision to place her image on its commemorative coin to depict Ceres, the Roman goddess of grain and harvests.

General Sources:
1. *Current Biography Yearbook*. New York: Wilson, 1959.
2. Harris, Warren G. *Sophia Loren: A Biography*. New York: Simon & Schuster, 1998.
3. Katz, Ephraim. *The Film Encyclopedia*. New York: HarperCollins, 1998.
4. Levy, Alan. *Forever, Sophia: An Intimate Portrait*. New York: St. Martin's Press, 1986.
5. Loren, Sophia. *Sophia Loren's Recipes and Memories*. New York: GT Publishers, 1998.
6. Loren, Sophia. *Women & Beauty*. New York: Morrow, 1984.
7. Loren, Sophia, and A.E. Hotchner. *Sophia: Living and Loving*. New York: Liberty Pub. House, 1991.
8. Shaw, Sam. *Sophia Loren in the Camera Eye*. London: Hamlyn, 1980.

—by MARY JANE ADDONE

SUSAN LUCCI (1948-   )

Portraying Erica Kane in the TV melodrama, *All My Children,* from its premiere in 1970, Susan Lucci has become the most famous soap opera actress in daytime TV history. While she has won many awards and recognition for her fine acting, she also remained known for *not* having won the prestigious daytime Emmy Award for Best Actress despite eighteen prior nominations. On the evening of May 21, 1999, however, that all changed when she succeeded in being selected the winner for Best Actress in portraying Erica Kane on *All My Children.* Talented and equally beautiful, her list of credits includes appearances in Hollywood films, over twelve roles in prime-time made-for-TV movies, roles in scores of TV specials, TV miniseries, and a host of episodic programs. Acknowledged by many critics as having defied the stereotype of the "lowly soap actress," she has indeed created for herself an unprecedented popularity and charisma for her daytime TV role in one of America's most watched programs.

Susan Lucci was born on December 23, most likely in 1946 (but some say, 1948) in Scarsdale, a residential community in Westchester County just north of New York City. Her family then moved to Garden City, Long Island where she spent most of her growing years. Susan and her older brother Jim were raised in a comfortable upper-middle-class environment. Their father, who was of Italian heritage, earned his living as a building contractor, and their mother, who was of Swedish background, worked as a nurse.

As is often the case with many in the acting profession, Susan professed having felt incredibly shy as a child. Then at age eleven, she seemed to have acquired a sense of freedom from her shyness when she appeared in a local Girl Scout production of a play during which she experienced the feeling of being at ease in the presence of other people. This freedom served as a gateway to her taking lessons in a variety of areas including painting, piano, skating, horseback riding, and more.

After attending a local Roman Catholic grammar school, she enrolled in Garden City High School where she graduated with honors. During her high school years, she was a hospital volunteer, a cheerleader, a member of the newspaper staff, and often played the lead role in many of the student productions such as her appearance in *The King and I.* Her sense of freedom had blossomed to such a point that she ventured to Norway as an exchange student. A student deeply committed to her studies and talents, she employed her communication skills so well in her senior year that she placed second in a statewide contest for "oral interpretation."

After graduating from high school, she revealed to her parents her desire to forgo college and to move to New York City to pursue an acting career. It did not sit well with them, and it became a highly debated family issue. A compromise was reached, and the terms of the agreement involved her going to Marymount College, a Roman Catholic college for women, which had an excellent theater department. It was located in Tarrytown, just north of New York City where she studied theater and acted in many of the college-based plays and also in some of the local productions.

At the end of her senior year, she became a beauty queen achieving semifinalist status in the New York State Miss Universe Beauty Pageant. After there arose a conflict between completing her course work and meeting the demands of the final phases of the beauty contest, Susan opted to finish school. She graduated with a B.A. from Marymount in 1968, but much to the disappointment of her parents who thought she would go on to *teach* drama, she proclaimed that she had not taken any education courses and wanted to become a professional actress.

Despite many acting skills and techniques she had developed at Marymount College and despite her exposure to the difficulties of experimental theater, her first job entailed doing non-acting work at the Ed Sullivan Theater. She worked as a "color girl" sitting daily in front of TV cameras so that the technicians could fine-tune the lighting systems for the demands of color TV programs. While employed in that capacity, she also auditioned for serious acting jobs but had little significant success. She had landed only bit parts in several soap operas and in two Hollywood films: *Goodbye Columbus* (1969) and *Me, Natalie* (1969). Finally, in late 1969, Susan Lucci auditioned for a new soap opera developed by soap opera impresario Agnes Nixon whose many credits included *Guiding Light*, one of Lucci's favorite programs when she was a young TV viewer.

The new TV melodrama, *All My Children*, was to have its story line develop around the lives of a high school foursome: Phil, Chuck, Tara, and Erica. Lucci had already passed a preliminary audition for the role of Tara, but many in the studio agreed that Lucci would be better cast in the role of Erica who, as a character and personality, was more powerful, self-engrossed, tantalizing, and complicated. Lucci's 30-year experience in that role as a consistently dynamic actress remains today a key landmark in TV's history of serialized programs.

The actions and interactions of this foursome would become the raw materials of their personal lives, struggling in a new world replete with drug phenomena, the sexual revolution, and the changing political, social, and economic structures of the times. In a sense, *All My Children* and the issues upon which it focused maintained a certain topical flavor and matched the changes in society with dramatic scenarios employing a language that reflected and depicted those societal changes.

Given this ongoing and complicated milieu, Lucci's continuous role as Erica throughout the years presented its acting challenges as the character's basic emotional and cognitive ranges spanned the gamut from a most calculating and often villainous person to a very vulnerable one. This complex character matrix together with Lucci's consistently excellent acting, no doubt, has helped explain in great part the paradoxical spell and love/hate relationship that Erica has exercised over so many TV viewers and daytime soap aficionados.

Susan Lucci, who is no doubt overjoyed at finally receiving the Emmy on her nineteenth nomination in 1999, had also earned many other quality awards. She had received Harvard University's Award for Best Actress of the Year as far back as 1980; the *Soap Opera Digest* Editor's Award for Outstanding Contribution to Daytime TV (1988); the Canadian *TV Guide* People's Choice Award for Best Soap Actress (1989); and New York City's Golden Apple Award in 1994.

General Sources:
1. Allen, Robert Clyde. *Speaking of Soap Operas*. Chapel Hill, NC: University of North Carolina Press, 1985.
2. *Contemporary Theatre, Film and Television*. Detroit, MI: Gale Research, 1996.
3. *Current Biography Yearbook*. New York: Wilson, 1989.
4. "Lucci Ends Drought with Daytime Emmy." *The Gainesville Sun* 22 May 1999: 3A.
5. Siegel, Barbara, and Scott Siegel. *Susan Lucci: The Woman Behind Erica Kane*. New York: St. Martin's Press, 1986.

—by DOLORES PESIRI

IDA LUPINO (1918-1995)

Ida Lupino, star of stage, screen, and television, was born in London, England on February 14, 1918 to comedian Stanley Lupino and actress Connie Emerald. The Lupino home, a stomping ground for movie and theater people of their day, offered young Ida a front-and-center seat encountering actors and actresses all around her. This made for a host of indelible impressions that she would remember for the rest of her life.

For her schooling, her parents sent her to Hove (England) where she attended the Clarence House School until age eleven. She became proficient in French, dance, and music, but it seemed that her calling would be acting. At the mere age of seven, she wrote and directed a play called *Mademoiselle* for her classmates.

At age thirteen, Ida entered the Royal Academy of Dramatic Arts. By the time she reached fifteen, the pace of her career would suddenly move very quickly. In 1932, she would perform in a total of five British films. Incredibly, when Ida's mother could not fill the role of a "Lolita" type, Ida who had accompanied her mother for the audition was offered that part, and she had her first dramatic part as the lead female in a movie entitled *Her First Affair*, produced by an American, Allen Dwan. Appearing much older than fifteen, Ida became billed as "the English Jean Harlow." And later that year, she would gain even greater notoriety by appearing in a film called *Money for Speed* where she played a dual role: that of a gold digger and that of an innocent girl.

The second of the five movies especially caught Hollywood's attention, and at sixteen years of age, she received a contract from Paramount to appear as Alice in the movie version of *Alice in Wonderland*. Both she and

her mother left England and made off for sunny Hollywood. After she had screen-tested, she surprisingly became viewed, instead, as "a potential Clara Bow." Rather than featuring Ida as Alice, the film studio gave her a role in *Search for Beauty* (1933), which was followed by a succession of other movies: first, as "a stage-struck" girl in *Ready for Love* (1934), then a young woman contemplating suicide in *Paris in the Spring* (1935); *Peter Ibbetson* (1935), *Anything Goes* (1936), *Yours for the Asking* (1936), *One Rainy Afternoon* (1936), *The Gay Desperado* (1936), *Artists and Models* (1937), and *Let's Get Married* (1937). Before reaching the age of twenty, she had already appeared in fourteen films.

Ida Lupino would have three marriages. In 1938, she married Louis Hayward, a leading man and a Hollywood star in his own right, and she would remain married to him until 1945. Then she would marry Collier Young, a Columbia executive (1948-50). Together they attempted to work as a team creating a business of filmmaking. She would marry her third husband, Howard Duff, an actor, who had acted with her in many films and in a 50s TV series.

Despite appearing in a relatively large number of films at such a young age in the 1930s, Lupino began resenting most of the roles she played. She felt typecast appearing as "the sweet young thing" or the classic "ingenue." Tired of being just another pretty face on the screen, she retreated from the spotlight for one year at age twenty, in 1938, awaiting more serious dramatic roles. Eventually, in 1939 she received the kind of role that would relaunch her career in the direction that she had desired. It was the role of a cockney prostitute, Bessie Broke, in a film entitled *The Light That Failed*.

In this dramatic role she played a loathsome character, ironically gaining for herself the once unlikely, yet now welcomed, epithet as "the girl you love to hate."

After her 1940 film entitled *They Drive by Night*, it seemed that success would become all the more certain. Lupino portrayed the life of a woman, Lana Carlsen, who, unrequited in her love for a long-haul truck driver on the west coast, committed murder and then drives herself to insanity. The often-mentioned courtroom scene where Ida portrayed unscripted emotional states in the character of a stark-raving woman got the instant attention of the producer and that of Jack Warner who immediately signed her up for a long-term contract after they had seen the rushes. They were convinced now more than ever that they had just witnessed the work of an actress comparable to that of Bette Davis.

Warner Brothers would now do their best to match her newly "discovered" talents with highly appropriate dramatic roles. In 1941 alone, she would star in four very successful films. She starred as a loyal gun moll in *High Sierra*, an escaped convict in *The Sea Wolf*, and a murderous housekeeper in *Ladies in Retirement*. In this film, Ida returned to play the role of a psychopath: a housekeeper who murders her employer so that she might acquire the victim's home as a place for her two insane sisters. In *Out of the Fog*, which was a film adaptation of Irwin Shaw's play, *The Gentle People*, Lupino would receive many accolades from movie critics.

In 1942, she returned to the sentimental drama in *Life Begins at Eight-Thirty* playing the role of a crippled daughter of a selfish Hollywood has-been. Then, in 1943, after a small role in *Forever and a Day*, Ida returned to a lead role in *The Hard Way* as a ruthless and murderous woman. As an ambitiously crazed business manager for her sister's Hollywood career, she wrecks the lives of all those who stand in her way. For this role, she would receive in 1943 the highly coveted New York Film Critics Award.

In 1946, she appeared in *Devotion*, a study of Emily Brontë; in 1948, she starred as a tavern singer in a melodrama entitled *Road House*. She appeared as a vicious warden in *Women's Prison* in 1955. In addition to having amassed as an actress more than fifty screen credits, she was a producer, director, and co-writer both for many Hollywood films and for many dramatic episodes in the newly emerging TV media. In the 1950s, Lupino directed and co-authored many episodes for TV series such as: *Have Gun, Will Travel*; *The Untouchables*, and *Alfred Hitchcock Presents*.

In addition to appearing in dramatic roles quite regularly on TV's *Four Star Playhouse*, she also produced and co-starred with her husband Howard Duff in a situation comedy called *Mr. Adams and Eve*. Ida Lupino died on August 3, 1995 in Burbank, California. As an actress, writer, and producer, she is rightly credited for being ahead of her time in the way she broached very difficult and painful topics such as rape, homicide, criminal and pathological behavior with directness and sensitivity when TV was in its early formative years.

General Sources:
1. *Current Biography/Yearbook*. New York: Wilson, 1943; 1995.
2. Donati, William. *Ida Lupino: A Biography*. Lexington, KY: University Press of Kentucky, 1996.
3. Katz, Ephraim. *The Film Encyclopedia*. New York: HarperCollins, 1998.
4. *Queen of the "B's:" Ida Lupino Behind the Camera*. Ed. Annette Kuhn. Westport, CT: Greenwood Press, 1995.
5. Ragan, David. *Who's Who in Hollywood*. New York: Facts on File, 1992.
6. Vermilye, Jerry. *Ida Lupino*. New York: Pyramid Publications, 1977.

—by MICHAEL T. GUARDINO, SR.

SALVADOR E. LURIA (1912-1991)

Graduating as a medical doctor *summa cum laude* in 1935 from the University of Turin, Italy, he subsequently studied at the Institute of Radium in Paris examining medical physics and bacteriophage (viruses that attack bacteria). A Guggenheim fellow at Princeton and Vanderbilt Universities, and professor of bacteriology and microbiology at several American universities, he became in 1964 a Sedgwick Professor of Biology at the Massachusetts Institute of Technology (MIT) and went on to win the Nobel Prize for physiology or medicine in 1969, a prize he shared with two colleagues, Max Delbrück and Al Hershey.

Salvador Luria was born on August 13, 1912 in Turin to David Luria and Ester Sacerdote. He received his primary and secondary education from the Italian public school system. Graduated in 1929 from one of the best prep high schools in Italy, the Liceo D'Azeglio, Luria entered medical school at the University of Turin. He soon developed an interest in research, some of which he performed under the mentoring of Dr. Giuseppe Levi, professor of histology (the study of tissue).

In 1935, after graduating with the highest of honors next to his medical degree, he served as an officer in the Italian Army Medical Corps. Those two years of service convinced him that a life of scientific research based on medical physics would be preferable. To those ends, he decided to do postgraduate work, and he went off to the University of Rome to study radiation biology and to study physics and their possible applications to biology. Ugo Fano, an old friend from his high school days, became instrumental in convincing Enrico Fermi, director of the Physics Institute to accept Luria as a postgraduate student.

Once accepted, Luria was introduced to a novel idea by one of his professors, Franco Rasetti. He presented Luria with a series of articles published by a German scientist Max Delbrück whose articles proposed the concept of the *gene as a molecule*. Luria became impressed by this concept, and metaphorically he saw this novel idea as a modern day "Holy Grail" that could potentially open up the entire world of biophysics. By 1938, both the increasing systematic pressure wielded upon Italian Jews by Mussolini's regime and the looming Nazi domination of Italy alarmed many Jews like Luria who now felt compelled to emigrate. He left Italy and quickly moved to France.

A recommendation from Fermi allowed him to attend the Curie Institute in Paris where he studied medical physics and where he witnessed firsthand how radiation produced mutations in viruses called bacteriophages that typically attack bacteria. Two years later when it appeared imminent that Hitler's forces would be taking over France, Luria again fled—this time to the United States on September 12, 1940 to start a new life and pursue his research in biophysics.

In the immigration process, he discovered that he had the right to change his name. Not wanting to change his last name, he reshaped his first. His name at birth was Salvatore, the way it is typically written in Italian. He now took the final "e," and made that the initial to a fictitious middle name Eduardo (Edward); he then changed the remainder of his first name from Italian into a Spanish-sounding Salvador.

He found his first place of employment in New York City at Columbia University where he became a research assistant at its College of

Physicians and Surgeons. Before the year 1940 came to a close, Luria had already met Max Delbrück whose work he had read and admired. Delbrück, also Jewish, had fled Nazi oppression, and he was now at Vanderbilt University (Tennessee) doing research. After Luria became a recipient of a Guggenheim fellowship, he joined Delbrück at Vanderbilt to do research.

Delbrück offered an invitation to Alfred Hershey to join them in discussing what all three apparently had in common: their interest regarding bacteriophage, a little-studied virus. They joined forces so as not to duplicate their efforts, forming what is now called the "phage group." While they worked independently, they also met with regularity to experiment and share information at Carnegie's Department of Genetics at Cold Spring Harbor (New York) in the 1940s. Collectively, their goal was to identify the physical nature of the gene (biophysics). In order to do this, they used bacteriophages which were in effect the simplest "creatures" they could find that had genes.

From 1943 to 1959, Luria taught and did research at the University of Indiana. Among many other achievements, it was during this period that Luria worked on proving that bacteria typically undergo spontaneous mutation and are not necessarily triggered by adaptive responses. This new knowledge contradicted the conventional wisdom of the time, and, in turn, it shed new light, adding a new twist to all the biostatistical information that to date had been amassed especially in the area of oncology.

In 1959, he was appointed professor and chairman of the Department of Microbiology at MIT where he researched the noxious qualities of colicins, a deadly protein that disrupts normal cell functions. Ten years later in 1969, Luria, together with his colleagues of the 40s "phage group," Delbrück and Hershey, went on to receive the Nobel Prize for physiology or medicine. A man of many talents and interests, he was an avid reader of world literature, did painting and sculpting, and was politically active.

Salvador Luria passed on at age 78 on February 6, 1991 in his home in Lexington, Massachusetts. He has left a legacy of innovative research in a revolutionary area of human endeavor: the study of the genetic structure of viruses, their reproduction and mutation processes. An editor and board member of several scholarly journals in biology-related fields, he earned many awards, prizes, and commendations, including a Guggenheim Fellowship (1942-1943), the Lenghi Prize from Italy's Accademia dei Lincei (1965), the Louisa Gross Horwitz Prize in 1969 from Columbia University, and, of course, the Nobel Prize for physiology or medicine in 1969 for his pioneering work on viruses.

In 1974, Luria won a National Book Award for his popularly received text which was precisely aimed for the general reader, *Life: The Unfinished Experiment* (1973). While at MIT he was responsible for founding its Cancer Research Center (1972), which he directed from its inception until he retired in 1985.

General Sources:
1. *American Men and Women of Science.* New Providence, NJ: R.R. Bowker, 1998-1999.
2. *Current Biography Yearbook.* New York: Wilson, 1970; 1991.
3. Luria, Salvador. *Life: The Unfinished Experiment.* New York: Scribner, 1973.
4. Luria, Salvador. *A Slot Machine, A Broken Test Tube: An Autobiography.* New York: Harper & Row, 1984.
5. Luria, Salvador, et al. *A View of Life.* Menlo Park, CA: Benjamin/Cummings, 1981.
6. McMurray, Emily J., ed. *Notable Twentieth-Century Scientists.* Detroit, MI: Gale Research, 1995.
7. "Obituary." *The Boston Globe* 7 Feb. 1991.

—by MARK BATTISTE

SALVATORE (SAL) MAGLIE (1917-1992)

Sal Maglie, who someday would be a famous pitcher for the New York Giants, was born April 26, 1917 in Niagara Falls, New York. While attending grade school and playing traditional outdoor sports, Salvatore Anthony Maglie, the son of an Italian emigrant, did not show any particularly great aptitude for sports. Yet while attending Niagara Falls High School, he made it onto its baseball team, and he did so well on the team that he was pitching two and three times a week for semi-professional clubs. Sal was even more popular in high school basketball, and when he was awarded a Niagara University scholarship for basketball, he rejected it inexplicably and went to work for his father who owned and operated a grocery store.

In 1937 while working for an industrial firm, Sal tried out for the Rochester baseball club of the International League. In the summer of 1938, he landed a $275 a month contract with Steve O'Neill, manager of the Buffalo Bisons in the International League. In August of 1938, Sal made his first professional minor league appearance as a relief pitcher against Newark. Apparently very nervous in his first game, Maglie hit two batters; and, after he walked a couple of batters and the opposing team got some homers, O'Neill pulled him out of the game. In a lackluster first season, Maglie appeared in 5 games, pitching 12 innings with an earned run average (ERA) of 3.75. His record got worse the following two seasons.

As a consequence, he requested to step down to a lower league, the Jamestown New York Club of the Pony League where he brought his ERA up to a much improved 2.73. In 1941 Maglie played for the Elmira New York Club of the Eastern League where he was given steady work, pitching 270 innings, winning 20 games, losing 15 games, and having an ERA of 2.67.

In 1942 Sal was brought up to the Jersey City Giants and became a relief pitcher. He won 9 games, lost 6, and his ERA was 2.78. He then decided to help out in the war effort by leaving baseball and becoming a pipe fitter. His only remaining contact with baseball was as manager/pitcher for amateur Canadian teams. During 1945 Maglie returned to "Triple A" baseball pitching 118 innings, mainly in relief, winning 6 and losing 7. He felt stronger, but he wasn't happy because he wasn't getting the hitters out at the right time. Late in the season, Mel Ott, then manager of the New York Giants, called up Maglie to join the Giants.

As a New York Giant, Sal got to do relief work and also became a starter. He hadn't been a starter since 1941 with Elmira, and he remained grateful for Mel Ott's confidence in him. He had started out 10 or 11 times, and 3 of his first 6 games became shutouts. He was in fact far better that his "5 wins and 4 losses" record showed because he had only walked 22 batters in 84 innings and his ERA was 2.36, the best of his entire career.

In February 1946 Maglie changed his whole career as a major league baseball player by signing with the brothers Bernardo and Jorge Pasquel in the Mexican League. He played on the Puebla team where his salary almost doubled. As a starting pitcher in this newly formed Mexican League, Sal Maglie's debut was disastrous and the ensuing games he pitched were equally bad. It was through the intervention of his manager Adolfo Lugue that Sal suddenly became an avid student of pitching. He was quick to learn that his curve ball wasn't working so well, due in part to the high altitude where he was pitching.

Lugue then taught Maglie to become a control pitcher: He told Sal never to throw the same pitch twice and to only pitch to spots, keeping the batter off stride. This sage advice led Sal to win 20 games in 1946 and another 20 in 1947. In 1948 when the Pasquel brothers decided to cut salaries, they lost most of their players. However, former American and National League players who had gone to the Mexican League were suspended from playing organized baseball in the U.S. for 5 years by baseball Commissioner A.B. (Happy) Chandler. The commissioner only reinstated them when in 1949 lawsuits started piling up on his desk.

Sal Maglie then rejoined the Giants in 1950, but he was used mainly in the bullpen by manager Leo Durocher. As a relief pitcher, he gave up only 5 runs in 33 innings. After he got his first start on June 25, and gave up 9 runs, including 3 homers, he was placed back in the bullpen. He wasn't called on to start another game until July 24 after the Giants were on a nine-game losing streak, and Durocher took another chance with Sal.

Maglie pitched against the St. Louis Cardinals and won the game 5-4. Starting again, he went on to win the next 11 consecutive games with the last 4 as shut-outs, compiling an 18-4 record that year. He fell short by just 4 "outs" of topping Carl Hubbell's 1933 record of 43-1/3 scoreless innings. Maglie had stated his formula for pitching success: "pitch 'em high inside and low outside...Pitch him tight inside and he can't get set on you." The "high inside" pitch forces the batter to back away from the plate, or to duck to avoid being hit.

This strategy resulted in his being nicknamed "The Barber," that is, one who gives close shaves. He was reputed by most critics as being the best in the business because of his legendary curve ball. A late bloomer, Sal Maglie achieved in the year 1951 a 23-6 record, the highest in the National League; he had only lost 6 games while pitching 298 exceptional innings. He had also enjoyed another winning streak of 10 straight games until defeated by the St. Louis Cardinals in June. "The Barber" also became the winning pitcher for the National League All-Star Game on July 10 of that year.

On September 29 against the Boston Braves, his final victory of the season by 3-0 represented a major factor in the Giants winning their first pennant since 1937. In the 1952 season Maglie won 18 games, lost 8, and pitched 216 innings for a 2.91 average. Again in 1954, he helped the Giants get the National League pennant once more. As of the mid-50s, Sal Maglie had achieved the highest lifetime winning average for any pitcher currently active in both leagues with 64 victories and 22 losses.

In 1956 Sal Maglie was traded to the Brooklyn Dodgers, his former immediate rivals. Both the Giants and the Dodgers were part of the National League and both shared the same city of New York. As a Dodger, Sal's pitching savvy was a major factor in helping them win the pennant in 1956. A year later, Maglie was sent to the New York Yankees where he finished his final pitching season. He had compiled a career record of 119 victories, 62 losses, a 3.15 ERA with 25 shut-outs. Sal "the Barber" Maglie died December 28, 1992 in his hometown of Niagara Falls. He was a great pitcher who will long be remembered especially by those who were fortunate enough to watch him play baseball.

General Sources:
1. Bjarkman, Peter C., ed. *Encyclopedia of Major League Baseball Team Histories: National League*. Westport, CT: Meckler, 1991.
2. *Current Biography/Yearbook*. New York: Wilson, 1953; 1993.
3. "Obituary." *New York Times* 29 Dec. 1992: A12.
4. *Saturday Evening Post* 5 May 1951.
5. Shapiro, Milton J. *The Sal Maglie Story*. New York: Messner, 1957.

—by DENNIS PIASIO

HENRY MANCINI (1924-1994)

An exceptionally prolific composer, talented arranger, and skillful conductor, Henry Mancini left a musical legacy that still remains second to none in the industry. He displayed a versatility for creating hauntingly memorable songs, scores, and theme music both for movies and television programs. His musical artistry indeed revealed a composer who was equally at ease in composing for drama, comedy, romance, or mystery. As a craftsman in his art, he was able to write the softest and most romantic kinds of music such as "Moon River," but he was equally talented in composing bold and captivating theme music such as that of the *Peter Gunn* TV series using jazz-like improvisational motifs.

In addition to having recorded over 50 successful albums and published over 500 works of music, he was honored by many awards including two Emmys and 20 Grammys from 70 nominations. For the motion picture industry, he composed the music for about 250 films and won a total of four Academy Awards from 18 nominations. He earned an Academy Award for the Best Score in *Breakfast at Tiffany's* (1961), for the Best Song "Moon River" also from the same movie; for the Best Title Song in *Days of Wine and Roses* (1962), and for the Best Score in *Victor/Victoria* (1982).

Enrico Nicola Mancini, better known as Henry Mancini, was born April 16, 1924, in Cleveland, Ohio to Quinto and Anna (nee Pece) Mancini. When he was five years old, his family moved to the industrial town of Aliquippa, Pennsylvania where his father labored as a steelworker. His father, a native of Abruzzi, Italy possessed and exhibited his love for music not only by encouraging his son to study music but also by playing the flute and piccolo in the local Sons of Italy band. He taught young Henry to play the piccolo by the time he was eight. Henry then switched to the flute, and, remarkably, taught himself to play the piano by age 12 imitating his neighbor's player piano and later picking up on several other instruments.

Like many youngsters he was torn between music and playing sports, especially football. One day this conflict came to a halt when he discovered jazz. The excitement led him to join the school band, and his talents eventually steered him to becoming first flutist in the Pennsylvania All-State High School Band. Mancini was barely 14 when he became a member of the local Ambridge Community and the Sons of Italy Bands. He was also soon playing—usually piano—with many orchestras and bands that were not local. Before enrolling to study music at the Carnegie Institute of Technology in Philadelphia and later at the Juilliard School of Music in New York City, he had also begun studying music with Max Adkins who was the leader of the pit band at the Stanley Theater in Pittsburgh.

There Mancini began his formal training in orchestration and musical arranging. Later, his studies at Juilliard were cut short by the military draft. Trained as an infantryman in World War II, Mancini joined the Army Air Force Band upon bandleader Glenn Miller's recommendation. After World War II and Glenn Miller's untimely death, Mancini then joined the reorganized Miller Orchestra (led by Tex Beneke) as pianist and arranger. He married Virginia (Ginny) O'Connor, who at that time was a vocalist with the Mellolarks. In 1947, they decided to move closer to the movie industry and set up home in Burbank, California where they began raising a family, one son and twin daughters.

It was at this point in his career where Mancini began learning to do scoring for radio shows while teaching himself the craft of scoring music particularly for dramatic shows. His wife's recording stint with the Jimmy Dorsey Orchestra in 1952 finally led Henry to the attention of Universal International Film Studios where he was asked to do a two-week assignment on an Abbott and Costello movie. This brief assignment become a six-year job as a staff composer and arranger. Given the opportunity to demonstrate his talents, he went on to do the musical arrangement both for *The Glenn Miller Story* (1954) for which he received his first of many Academy Award nominations, and later for *The Benny Goodman Story* (1956).

After receiving public attention for his musical score of Orson Welles' film, *Touch of Evil* (1958), he went on to achieve creative distinction with his pulsating and haunting theme music to Blake Edwards' popular TV private-detective series *Peter Gunn* (1959) for which Mancini won his first two Grammy Awards: one for Album of the Year and one for Best Arrangement of the Year. Mancini saw this particular score as being a major turning point in his career, and he attributed this to his creative use of the "jazz idiom." Encouraged by the enormous success of this series, Blake Edwards together with Mancini pursued the creation of another successful TV private detective series, *Mr. Lucky* (1959). Mancini also received two more Grammys for Best Arrangement and Best Performance for this series.

With two TV hit shows and several Grammys to his credit, Mancini returned to the Hollywood movie studios as a freelance composer-arranger working for Columbia, Metro-Goldwyn-Mayer, Paramount, 20th Century-Fox, and Universal Studios. He went on to compose some of his most memorable film scores including *Breakfast at Tiffany's* (1961) with its haunting song "Moon River," *The Days of Wine and Roses* (1962), *Charade* (1963), *The Pink Panther* (1964) with its five sequels (1975, 1976, 1978, 1982, and 1983), *Victor/Victoria* (1982), and other popular films.

Henry Mancini passed away on June 14, 1994 at 70 years of age in Los Angeles. In all, as a composer-arranger involved in about 250 films, as a winner of four Oscars and twenty Grammys, two Emmys, and as a recipient of many magazine awards and honorary degrees in his lifetime, he was a very private person who maintained high moral values and a deep sense of modesty despite so many achievements.

As a family man who was married for 47 years to his spouse Ginny since 1947, he believed in the importance of family, good teachers and good schools, dedication to one's work, and discipline in one's life. In order to honor his lasting memory, the American Society of Composers, Authors and Publishers (ASCAP) established in 1995 (a year after his death) the ASCAP/Henry Mancini Award for its annual awards ceremonies. The award has been tailored for those creative individuals who excel in achieving outstanding contributions to film music.

General Sources:

1. *Current Biography Yearbook*. New York: Wilson, 1964; 1994.

2. *The Encyclopedia of Popular Music*. London, UK: MUZE UK Ltd, 1998.

3. Katz, Ephraim. *The Film Encyclopedia*. New York: HarperCollins, 1998.

4. Mancini, Henry. *Did They Mention The Music?* Chicago: Contemporary Books, 1989.

5. Mancini, Henry. *Sounds and Scores: A Practical Guide to Professional Orchestration*. n.p.: Northridge Music Corporation, 1973.

6. *New Grove Dictionary of American Music*. New York: Grove's Dictionaries of Music, 1986.

—by CHARLES CAGNO

CHUCK MANGIONE (1940-   )

Charles Frank Mangione, better known as Chuck Mangione, came into this world on November 29, 1940. Recognized today as a multi-talented master musician and composer bearing his own uniquely identifiable style of modern jazz often characterized by Afro-Cuban rhythms, he comes from a most interesting and rich Italian family background.

He was born in Rochester, New York to Frank and Nancy (nee Bellavia) Mangione, who were first generation Italian-American parents of Sicilian ancestry. His father, who had been a grocer for many years, had a strong feel for music but was never quite afforded the opportunity to develop in that area. The Mangiones had two other children besides Chuck, an older son Gaspar, and the youngest of the three, a daughter Josephine.

All three children received music lessons, and Chuck began to study the piano at eight years of age. Two years later, inspired by a movie depicting the life of the famous jazz cornetist Bix Beiderbecke (*Young Man with a Horn*, c. 1950), he picked up the trumpet, and music—from that point on—became his lifelong love. It was this film biography that had influenced and literally changed his life. Thereafter, in his early teens, he actively played at Italian and Jewish weddings and bar mitzvahs. Perhaps, more importantly, he together with his father and brother would frequent many different local musical events.

Interestingly, it appears that what Chuck's father had apparently lacked in musical ability he had a hundredfold in determination and drive in promoting his children's musical future. For instance, often after having attended a concert with his two sons, he would introduce himself to the performers as if he knew them,

introduce his sons, and then invite the performers over his house for a Sunday Italian meal, including, of course, the obligatory pasta and wine combination. Operating in this inviting fashion, it had become quite common for the Mangione household to have as their guests such notables as Dizzy Gillespie, Jimmy Cobb, Ron Carter, or Sam Jones.

Naturally, given the time, place, and inclination, like most jazz musicians, they would create their own jam session right in the middle of the Mangione living room with Chuck and Gaspar joining this uniquely private home-based performance. It was a special kind of experience that a young musician like Chuck was able to have with much consistency in his early years.

Chuck was influenced by many musicians in those fledgling years, but he regarded Dizzy Gillespie, most importantly, as his "musical godfather." From so much of Gillespie's musical repertoire, Chuck seemed to be especially attracted to Afro-Cuban rhythms. Chuck also admired the work of two other jazz greats: Miles Davis and Stan Getz. Interestingly, in addition to the influence of these superstars of the jazz world, he pleasantly recalls his utter fascination as a youngster with listening to the theme music of the *Cisco Kid* TV series.

As a teenager Chuck first studied trumpet and music theory at the preparatory school at Eastman School of Music, and then after graduating, he entered its undergraduate program in 1958. The Mangione brothers together with a friend, Sal Nistico, then created a musical combo called the Jazz Brothers. In the next five years, they cut three albums on the Riverside label: *The Jazz Brothers*, *Hey Baby!*, and *Spring Fever*. During this time, they also had the opportunity to perform at the Randall's

Island Jazz Festival and at lower Manhattan's Half Note nightclub.

Another major benchmark in Chuck's musical history occurred when the Eastman program needed a replacement on the flügelhorn. Chuck volunteered and he immediately fell in love with that instrument, particularly with its more mellow sound and feel. The instrument, which has remained his trademark, is a three-valve brass wind, usually pitched in B flat, and in many ways is similar to a saxhorn. Before he completed his bachelor's degree (1963), he composed his first jazz work for orchestra, *Feel of a Vision*, which was performed at his graduation recital. One year earlier, under his name he had already cut his first album, *Recuerdo* (1962).

After graduating and then teaching music for one year at the Hochstein School of Music in Rochester, he freelanced as a jazz musician in New York City. In 1965 Chuck played in the trumpet section for both the Woody Herman and Maynard Ferguson bands, eventually remaining with the Art Blakey group for two-and-a-half years. In 1968 he returned to his native Rochester where for the next four years he was director of a newly established jazz ensemble at the Eastman School of Music. He also had formed a group that played six nights a week at the Shakespeare Club where performers like Chick Corea and Ron Carter often sat in to play.

After only a mixed reaction to *Kaleidoscope*, his orchestral composition, he conducted the Rochester Philharmonic in a performance of another orchestral work he had written, *Friends and Love,* in 1970. The performance was a huge success, and it marked the beginning of Chuck's nationwide popularity. Most critics agree that much of Mangione's popular success, which took off in the 1970s and has since endured for three decades, is in great part attributable to his unique style.

It is a style which has managed to blend the more palatable qualities of jazz's complexities and intricacies into a form of music that audiences who are nonspecialists in jazz might better appreciate and enjoy. And the same may be said for the majority of musicians who, not being specialists in jazz, can also perform his works with some reasonable comfort and ease. In a sense, Mangione has proven to be not only an excellent composer and successful musician but also a very good teacher in the broadest sense of the word aiming for the largest possible audience understanding and enjoyment.

Since the 70s, Mangione has performed at the finest of recital halls throughout the United States, Canada, and Europe. Both individually and as part of musical groups, Mangione was nominated on several occasions for a Grammy. Finally in 1976, his second album for A&M Records, *Bellavia*, which he dedicated to his mother, earned him a Grammy. In 1978, a single, "Feels So Good," perhaps his signature piece, reached the pop top-ten, and its album version remained only second to *Saturday Night Fever*. Additionally in 1978, the musical score he had written for the film, *Children of Sanchez,* earned him his second Grammy for the Best Pop Instrumental Performance. Teacher, composer, and musician, Mangione remains a tribute to his Italian-American heritage.

General Sources:
1. Clarke, Donald, ed. *The Penguin Encyclopedia of Popular Music.* New York: Viking Penguin, 1989.
2. *Current Biography Yearbook.* New York: Wilson, 1980.
3. Feather, Leonard G. *The Biographical Encyclopedia of Jazz.* New York: Oxford Press, 1999.
4. Feather, Leonard, and Ira Gitler. *The Encyclopedia of Jazz in the Seventies.* New York: Horizon Press, 1976.
5. Kernfeld, Barry, ed. *New Grove Dictionary of Jazz.* New York: Macmillan, 1988.

—by MARY JANE ADDONE

JERRE MANGIONE (1909-1998)

Author, editor, critic, novelist, historian, and professor emeritus at the University of Pennsylvania, his works reflect one of the strongest voices echoing with special emphasis the struggles and values characteristic of the second generation of the Italian-American immigrant experience. As a writer who was deliberately creating a non-fictional account of his experiences growing up in Rochester, New York in a book named *Mount Allegro* (1943), he was asked to modify it at the publisher's request to read more like fiction, and that work has since become an acknowledged classic in ethnic literature read both by Italian Americans and the general public alike.

Gifted with a sense of history and based on a thorough documentation of facts, Mangione together with Ben Morreale recently completed in 1992 a rather comprehensive book entitled *La Storia: Five Centuries of the Italian American Experience*. It begins with the depiction of Italians as being present among the early American colonizers, and the historical narrative continues in the delineation of subsequent immigration patterns, especially the major waves of Italian immigrants in the late nineteenth and early twentieth centuries.

Gerlando Mangione, better known as Jerre Mangione, was born on March 20, 1909 in Rochester, New York the first of four children to Gaspare and Giuseppina (nee Polizzi) Mangione, both Sicilian emigrants, who met and married in the United States but had never known each other although they had lived only a few miles apart in Sicily. His father, a pastry chef and paper-hanger, and his mother, a homemaker and part-time seamstress, both expected their children to maintain their Sicilian language that was spoken at home all the time.

When young Mangione started East High School, his writing talents soon emerged, and he worked his way up to becoming the editor of the *Clarion*, the school weekly. After graduation he went on to Syracuse University where his interests in writing blossomed as he founded the *Chap Book*, a literary magazine. His parents, who had hoped that Jerre would major in something prestigious and practical, balked when he announced he wanted to be a newspaperman. When he graduated from the college in 1931 with a B.A. in English, he found his first job in New York City with *Time* magazine. In 1934 Mangione then switched to working on the editorial staff of McBride, a publishing firm.

In 1936 he decided to visit Sicily in what turned out to be a frightening and disappointing recognition of Sicily's poverty under Mussolini's Fascist regime. On his return to America, he wrote about his reactions to those experiences for the *New Republic* and several other magazines. Mangione became among the first to become very vocal about antifascism, and he expressed his hatred of Fascist control of people's everyday lives and particularly its denigration of Italians and their spirit. From his journey to Italy, Mangione had also acquired what would become a lifelong love affair with Sicily, its people, its cultural strengths, and its unique sense of dignity under even the most difficult political and economic conditions.

While working for the publishing firm, Mangione had also served as a book reviewer on many top-quality newspapers of the time such as the *New York Post*, the *New York Herald Tribune*, and the *New York Sun*. He also was a freelance writer of articles and short stories for name magazines such as *Harper's Bazaar*. Then after moving to Washington, D.C. in 1937, Mangione held a series of jobs in the federal government including national coordinating editor of the Federal Writers' Project until 1939, public relations specialist for the Department of Commerce at the Census Bureau (1939), information specialist in the Department of Justice (1940), public relations specialist also in the Department of Justice (1941-42), and special assistant to the commissioner in the Immigration and Naturalization Service (1942-48), serving first in Washington, D.C. and later in Philadelphia as editor in chief of its *Monthly Review* (1945-47).

From 1948 to 1961, he worked as a writer in a variety of positions in industry including the Columbia Broadcasting System. In 1961 at age fifty-two, he started an academic career at the University of Pennsylvania as director of freshman composition, and by the end of the 60s he ultimately became full-professor of English and director of its writing program. Even before the inception of his academic position, Mangione had consistently received creative writing funds (such as Yaddo and MacDowell Colony Fellowships) which allowed him the time to write; and, indeed, Mangione wrote a huge body of works.

Many of Mangione's numerous critical writings are found in his abundant submissions of analytical articles and book reviews to literary journals, magazines and newspapers. His historical narratives and various memoirs include: *A Passion for Sicilians: The World Around Danilo Dolci* (1968); *The Dream and the Deal: The Federal Writers' Project, 1935-1943* (1972); and *An Ethnic at Large: A Memoir of America in the Thirties and Forties* (1978). In addition to his short stories and his book of fables, *Life Sentences for Everyone* (1966), there are also his novels, such as *The Ship and the Flame* (1948), and *To Walk the Night* (1967).

Jerre Mangione died on August 16, 1998 at his home in Haverford, Pennsylvania. In his lifetime, he was the recipient of well over thirty awards and honors, including a Guggenheim Fellowship (1945), a Fulbright Fellowship (1965), and a Rockefeller Grant (1968). He received both an honorary M.A. (1971) and a doctorate in literature (1980) from the University of Pennsylvania where he established a Center for Italian Studies and became its first director in 1978. From the Italian Republic, Mangione was awarded the decoration of Commendatore in 1971 for his lifetime work; and, also from Italy, he also won Il Premio Nazionale Empedocle in 1984 for his literary work *Mount Allegro*.

So talented to have met and surpassed the challenges of industry, government, and academia, Jerre Mangione's biography together with his literary works have left a legacy reflecting an undeniably deep, aesthetic, and historical sensitivity to the Italian-American immigrant experience, including the struggles and the victories of a people so eager to engage their energies and improve their condition in this land of freedom and opportunity.

General Sources:
1. *Current Biography/Yearbook*. New York: Wilson, 1943; 1998.
2. LaGumina, Salvatore. *The Italian American Experience: An Encyclopedia*. New York: Garland Publ., 1999.
3. Mangione, Jerre. *America is Also Italian*. New York: Putnam, 1969.
4. Mangione, Jerre. *Mount Allegro: A Memoir of Italian American Life*. New York: Columbia University Press, 1981.
5. Mangione, Jerre, and Ben Morreale. *La Storia: Five Centuries of the Italian American Experience*. New York: HarperPerennial, 1993.
6. Trotsky, Susan M., ed. *Contemporary Authors*. Detroit, MI: Gale Research, 1994.
7. *Who's Who in America*. 1995 ed.

—by GEORGE CARPETTO, Ph.D.

MIKE MANTEO (1909-1989)

Entertainment where the performers are puppets and where vignettes or stories are related to an open air crowd or inside a small theater has been called the puppet show or puppet play. It has been a tradition that in Europe went as far back as the Medieval Ages. Among the many themes portrayed, the most common have been the adventures of Charlemagne, King Arthur and the Knights of the Round Table, and the stories of Orlando Furioso, a legendary Italian knight based on Ariosto's Renaissance book of the same name. Before the advent of modern media, puppet shows and its counterpart, public storytellers, along with church morality plays and pageantry stood side-by-side with the conventional theater as forms of public entertainment.

Sicily, in particular, had one of the longest love affairs with puppetry. Today many elderly Italian-American immigrants—particularly Sicilians—can still remember in great detail their witnessing in Italy the phenomenon of the roving puppeteers going from town to town putting on their shows for children. Generally, in Italian the puppeteer has been called *il marionettista* and in Sicily *il pupista*. Such was the heritage and the tradition of the twentieth-century Manteo family and its long line of *pupisti* from the city of Catania.

Mike Manteo who would someday carry on the family tradition of Sicilian puppetry was born on September 2, 1909 to Agrippino and Caterina Manteo in Mendoza, Argentina where the family had immigrated. There in Mendoza, Agrippino, who now possessed the collection of marionettes he had inherited from his father, was determined to carry on the family tradition. He started having his own marionette show when he opened up a makeshift theater for the public behind his bakery shop.

In 1919, when Mike was ten years old, the family decided to immigrate to the United States. They made their home in New York City; and at 109 Mulberry Street in lower Manhattan, Agrippino's dream to continue having his own little puppet theater and to appeal to a larger audience became a reality. His theater became known as Papa Manteo's Life-Size Marionettes or *Opera dei Pupi*. In those days, there were also other marionette theaters in New York City, and immigrants naturally constituted the mainstay of the audiences that attended those marionette programs.

However, with the passing of time, the advent of silent movies, public radio in the 20s, and then the "talkies," many immigrants simply did not patronize the shows sufficiently as they had in the past, and so many puppet theaters began to close down. Agrippino refused to let his dream die. He purchased marionettes from closing theaters and taught Mike and his other sons and daughters everything he knew about puppetry. The Manteo family's electrical business helped in subsidizing the marionette shows. Mike Manteo, who had experienced puppet shows from his earliest days, had made it his business to learn everything else he needed to know from his father to carry on the dream, including the process of learning how to create and craft the life-size marionettes from scratch.

Marionettes had to be hand-crafted. The heads were usually carved out of hard wood, usually cherry wood. Iron rods ran throughout the body interior to establish the frame. A key rod controlled the puppet's right hand, used for brandishing the knight's sword. Mike's sister, Aida, learned to adorn the puppets' frames with garments that she fashioned from satin and velvet material. The large marionettes sometimes could weigh as much as 100 pounds and were suspended from an overhead platform.

In 1929, the Manteo family was the main subject of *Theater Arts*, a monthly magazine, which described the Manteo family's two-hundred marionettes. At that time, the family went all out giving performances almost nightly. Reportedly, a theatergoer wishing to experience all the episodes of *Orlando Furioso* would have to attend 394 consecutive performances. This was the kind of effort that the Manteo family had put into puppetry. In 1932, to honor the Manteo family's work, a film was made called *Knock on Wood*.

Agrippino, who had dedicated a good deal of his life to keeping this family tradition, built his last puppet in 1937. A year later, he closed down his marionette theater and gave the marionettes to his son Mike. Agrippino died shortly thereafter, leaving Mike to become the next "Papa Manteo." Empowered as he was, Mike now became in charge of the family tradition bearing all the responsibilities regarding the continuance of the family marionettes and preservation of the hundreds of improvisational scripts that had survived decades of use.

Mike Manteo fulfilled his father's dying wish, spending the rest of his life disseminating the experience of this age-old cultural phenomenon. The family members remained close with one another in order to perform whenever there was an opportunity. The family moved and thought as one body, and with Mike at the helm, the family did much charity work, performing for school children, religious, and other public organizations both locally and at nationwide events.

In June 1983, Mike Manteo received a National Heritage Fellowship Award from the N.Y.S. Council for the Arts for his outstanding contribution to American culture. During that same time, at the National Museum of American History, a marionette called Agricane di Tana was displayed along with a backdrop which had been painted by Mike's father in 1923. The Manteo family also gave several performances in January 1984 in New York City at the Symphony Space Theater in upper Manhattan. When an international puppetry convention took place in the nation's capital, the Manteo family and its marionettes were among the most active participants, proudly doing their demonstrations.

In 1989, Mike Manteo, who died at age eighty, had indeed devoted many years to the transmission of this unique cultural phenomenon that dated back to Medieval times. Before dying he passed the title of "Papa Manteo" to his son Agrippino, also known as Pino. Pino hopes that this family tradition will somehow continue into the future, perhaps in a new and different way. In a recent interview, Pino stated that there remain about 150 marionettes in his possession, but it would take six to eight months to train and prepare family members to put on marionette shows. Recently, the cable station CUNY made a documentary of the Manteo family and its marionettes; and more recently in June 1998 the Italian television network RAI interviewed the Manteo family as to its history and its many accomplishments. The new "Papa Manteo," Pino, is confident that somehow his family's historically important puppets will continue for posterity, perhaps through institutional or governmental assistance and cooperation.

General Sources:
1. Gold, Donna Lauren. "Far From Sicily." *Smithsonian Magazine* Aug. 1983: 68-73.
2. Manteo, Agrippino (Pino). Personal Interview. 29 May 1998.
3. Schoenberg, Harold C. "Marionette Mix of Fun and Tradition." *New York Times* 20 Jan. 1984: C3.
4. Singer, Mark. "Manteo Marionettes-Opera Dei Pupi." *New Yorker Magazine* 17 Sept. 1979: 154-164.

—by LINDA D'ANDREA-MARINO

ROCKY MARCIANO (1923-1969)

Rocco Francis Marchegiano, the world famous heavyweight fighter and champion, professionally known as Rocky Marciano, was born on September 1, 1923 in Brockton, Massachusetts. Rocky was the oldest of three sons of Pierino and Pasqualina (nee Piccento) Marchegiano, who also had three daughters.

Pierino, who had immigrated to the U.S., fought with the American Expeditionary Force in World War I. When he returned home from fighting the Germans, he was seriously wounded from having endured shrapnel, especially to his face. He also had endured the rigors of poisonous gas trench warfare. Because of these grueling wartime afflictions, he would experience ill-health for the rest of his life, being able to work only intermittently in the Brockton shoe factories. He and Pasqualina were married in 1921.

More illness struck the family in 1925 when Rocky, only 19 months of age, lay critically ill with pneumonia. With very little hope for recovery, his mother Pasqualina and many local *paesane* gathered around the crib to pray for Rocky's healing. A friend Fiorena Foscaldi even performed an old Neapolitan ritualistic exercise stirring water and oil to chase away the *malocchio,* the evil eye. Later, it seemed that a ninety-year-old aunt Paolina Mangifesti reportedly took a dish of warm water and with a little spoon let the water trickle into Rocky's mouth. To everyone's amazement, Rocky blinked his eyes and began to move his lips. That week, the fever subsided, and Rocky was on his way to recovery.

From Rocky's earliest youth, Brockton was always a great sports city. In the cool shadow of the trees at James Edgar playground, Rocky dreamed of becoming a star athlete who could command respect and wealth. Baseball was his first love. He idolized power hitters like Babe Ruth, Joe DiMaggio and Ted Williams. At that time, he never imagined that he would become a prize fighter.

From the time he was 13 until he quit school at 16 to go to work, Rocky's reputation as an athlete grew. Rocky was a catcher on St. Patrick's Church baseball team and a first string linebacker on the high school football team. He was never a serious student and did just enough to get by in most subjects. When Rocky said he'd be leaving school, his mother was opposed to it, but he assured her he would get a job and help support the family. This was during the difficulties of the Depression, and the Marchegiano family with Pasqualina's careful money management survived.

It was his uncle who got Rocky interested in boxing. During the early period of his training, Marciano focused on learning "to hit with both hands." He also began to develop what he would later call the "Susie-Que," the potent punch of an overhand right swing. Yet, his interest in boxing really took place only after he had been drafted into the Army at the age of twenty in March 1943. It was at the induction center where he learned that "the winning of a recreation-period bout would get him a three-day pass." Before returning to civilian life in 1947, he had gained much boxing experience both overseas in Wales and later in the States.

Still intent on making baseball his career, he returned disappointed from Fayetteville, North Carolina where his three-week tryout for the Chicago Cubs proved negative. Allie Colombo, a friend, told Rocky to not waste time and that he should concentrate on boxing. Gene Caggiano, a local boxing promoter, then began working with Rocky and asked him to enter the Golden Gloves in Lowell, Massachusetts. In January 1948, Rocky surprisingly started with three straight knockouts. Observers described him as superbly conditioned, punching, clawing, and mauling his opponents to the canvas.

Charlie Mortimer, a top 19 year-old amateur, had 12 amateur fights and won them all. When they met, Mortimer was boxing well and won the first two rounds. With 20 seconds left in the third round, Rocky hit Mortimer with a tremendous right uppercut and knocked him out, and after that, Mortimer never fought again. Rocky now qualified to go to New York as the New England representative to the Golden Gloves All-East Championship Tournament.

When Rocky officially qualified to enter professional boxing, his first bout took place in Providence, R.I. He fought and won his first fight by knocking out Harry Balzerian in the first round. After winning several other fights in the New England area, he then appeared in New York's Madison Square Garden knocking out Pat Richards in December 1949 and, a month later, Carmine Vingo.

In 1951, he most notably defeated ex-champion Joe Louis in a non-title bout. A year later on September 23, 1952, he won the heavyweight championship title from Jersey Joe Walcott. Rocky Marciano, the son of Italian immigrants, was the only heavyweight champion ever to complete a professional career without a loss. With a record of 49-0 with 43 knockouts, he was the greatest slugger in boxing history having knocked out 88% of his opponents. Rocky then went on to retire undefeated on April 27, 1956. As a tribute to his boxing history where he set a world record winning all forty-nine of his professional bouts since 1947, he was elected to Madison Square Garden's Hall of Fame in 1967.

It was now thirteen years after his retirement. The date was August 31, 1969. It was at 5:30 p.m. at Midway Airport in Chicago when Glenn Beiz readied his plane for the flight to Des Moines. It was a Sunday, the day before his 46th birthday when tragedy would occur. A weather briefing included stormy skies, fog, clouds, and low ceiling in the Iowa area. The warning was ignored as Rocky was looking forward to returning to Ft. Lauderdale to celebrate his birthday with his wife and two children. At nine o'clock that evening, the plane crashed into a lone oak tree in the middle of a cornfield two miles short of the runway killing all three passengers.

In Rocky's honor and memory, the Marciano brothers, Sonny and Peter, established the Marciano Foundation, an organization dedicated to helping underprivileged youths develop their potential in sports. As a fitting remembrance of his life, many of Rocky's friends have aptly stated, "The Rock was the greatest, and there'll never be another like him."

General Sources:
1. Bunce, Steve. *Boxing Greats: An Illustrated History of the Legends of the Ring*. Philadelphia: Courage Books, 1998.
2. *Current Biography/Yearbook*. New York: Wilson, 1952; 1969.
3. Cutter, Robert. *The Rocky Marciano Story*. New York: Allen Publ., 1954.
4. Libby, Bill. *Rocky: The Story of a Champion*. New York: Messner, 1971.
5. McCallum, John Dennis. *The Encyclopedia of World Boxing Since 1882*. Radnor, PA: Chilton, 1975.
6. Myler, Patrick. *A Century of Boxing Greats: Inside the Ring with the Hundred Best Boxers*. New York: Robson/Parkwest, 1998.
7. "Obituary." *New York Times* 1 Sept. 1969: 1; 2 Sept. 1969: 44.
8. Skehan, Everett. M. *Rocky Marciano: Biography of a First Son*. Boston: Houghton-Mifflin, 1977.

—by SALVATORE D'ALESSANDRO

GUGLIELMO MARCONI (1874-1937)

Today's radio and television can be greatly attributed to this ingenious Italian American. His initial invention of the radio opened a whole new field of wireless communication. Marconi lived in the United States for over twenty years after his arrival in 1899, developing most of his ideas in the New York metropolitan area. Although he never became an American citizen, and he returned to Italy in the 1920s to accept a post as President of the Italian Academy, many consider him a *bona fide* Italian American. Disgruntled with Mussolini, Marconi helped and encouraged others to leave Italy, but he himself was never able to return to the U.S. having died in 1937.

Marconi was born in Bologna, Italy in 1874 to a fairly well-to-do family. His father was Italian and, interestingly, his mother was Irish. He had the advantage of private tutors, and he became particularly fascinated by physics and electricity. After years of private tutoring, he attended the University of Bologna. In 1894, at the age of twenty, Marconi became impressed by the writings of Heinrich Hertz, who had discovered radio waves. That stirred his imagination, and he dreamed of using Hertz's discovery to transmit telegraph messages without wires. He constructed these mechanisms for sending and receiving telegraph messages through the air, and he discovered that he was able to send messages up to a mile away with no wire connection. He presented his invention to the Italian government; and despite many accolades, it was rejected, being of no immediate significance to anyone.

Marconi continued his work, fired by the idea of this new method of sending messages. The possibilities seemed endless to him as he envisioned messages being sent to ships at sea,

or vice versa, ships in distress sending messages for help. Marconi had imagined the possibility of wireless communications to and from all parts of the globe. In 1896, he demonstrated his device in England, and he was issued his first patent for the invention in 1897. In the same month, Marconi formed a company and the first "Marconigrams" were sent. In the following year, he was able to send wireless messages across the English Channel.

His company was known as Marconi's Wireless Telegraph Company, Ltd., and it was the beginning of making him a wealthy man. One of the first practical uses of the wireless occurred in 1898. While following the Kingstown Regatta from a tugboat, Marconi immediately flashed the contest results in code to the offices of a Dublin newspaper. Then in 1899 when a lightship was rammed in a fog, they summoned help by using his wireless. Naval intelligence of many nations throughout the world suddenly became interested.

It was reported that Russian, French, and German scientists were trying to "catch up" with Marconi's developments. That's when he decided to come to the United States. On September 11, 1899, Marconi arrived in America. By November, Marconi became incorporated in New Jersey as the Marconi Wireless Company of America; and twenty years later, it would become the well-known Radio Corporation of America: RCA. He was also developing short wave transmission, and President Theodore Roosevelt would use this device to send a transatlantic message to Prince Edward VII in 1903. In 1909, the importance of the radio transmission became dramatically demonstrated when the S.S. Republic was damaged and was sinking at sea. Its radio messages brought help, and all but six persons were saved. It was becoming apparent that radio transmission had become one of the most significant inventions in history.

In the same year Marconi was recognized for his achievements, and he was awarded the Nobel Prize in Physics. The following year, he succeeded in sending a message from Ireland to Argentina, a distance of over 6,000 miles using the dot-and-dash system of the Morse code. It was also known that voice could be transmitted by radio, and after 1906 its application was slowly being introduced. However, radio broadcasting on a commercial basis (as we know it today) would begin in the early 1920s.

Marconi confounded his detractors, who had believed that radio waves would only travel in straight lines, thus being only able to transmit to the horizon and stopped by the curvature of the Earth. Contrary to their opinions, Marconi thought that the long waves he used would naturally follow the curvature of the Earth. In fact, he had already proven this when on December 12, 1901, he received signals in St. John's, Newfoundland, sent from a transmitter in Poldhu at the southwestern tip of England. Marconi persisted in improving his invention by sending messages farther away. In 1918, he sent a message from England around the globe to Australia. Other scientists would soon add their own inventions to the wireless. These included the vacuum tube amplifier and the audio tube.

By 1921, Marconi's wireless telegraphy would become wireless telephony, the "voice" of radio today. The imminence of the invention of the radio was of such magnitude that it had caused legal disputes over patent rights. These disputes died out in 1914 when the courts had recognized Marconi as having clear priority.

When long wave broadcasting became a practical reality, Marconi turned his attention to short waves. By 1922, he had perfected the transmission of short waves by focusing the waves with a parabolic reflector behind the antenna. This system is still used by most worldwide communication systems. Marconi also invented the radio "direction finder" by which ships and airplanes could fix their positions by using radio signals. In 1934, Marconi began demonstrating equipment that made instrument navigation of ships possible. He was also a pioneer in the use of ultrahigh frequency (UHF) waves for voice communications over short distances.

Marconi was both an inventor and the driving force behind many related technologies that would evolve from his basic wireless and navigational systems. His inventions involving the use of wireless transmission have had an immeasurable impact on the modern world. Untold numbers of lives have been saved through this medium alone. Aside factors of convenience and efficiency, communication has literally entered a new dimension and has approached new heights once unimaginable except by visionaries like Marconi.

General Sources:
1. Evans, Colin. *Guglielmo Marconi: The Power of Perseverance*. Las Cruces, NM: Sofwest Press, 1998.
2. Garratt, G.R.M. *The Early History of Radio: From Faraday to Marconi*. London, UK: Institution of Electrical Engineers & the Science Museum, 1994.
3. Hart, Michael H. *The 100: A Ranking of the Most Influential Persons in History*. Secaucus, NJ: Carol Pub. Group, 1992.
4. Morgan, Nina. *Guglielmo Marconi*. New York: Bookwright, 1991.
5. Null, Gary, and Stone, Carl. *The Italian-Americans*. Harrisburg, PA: Stackpole Books, 1976.
6. Parker, Steve. *Guglielmo Marconi and Radio*. New York: Chelsea House, 1995.
7. Tames, Richard. *Guglielmo Marconi*. New York: F. Watts, 1990.

—by JERRY F. TESTA

DAN MARINO (1961-   )

A legend in his own time, the Miami Dolphins quarterback Dan Marino has risen to National Football League (NFL) stardom status probably faster than any other football player in recent times. With a most extraordinary bullet-speed passing arm, he has defied traditional statistics, breaking scores of records, and holding seventeen NFL and twenty Dolphin team passing records. From the outset of his pro career, he distinguished himself as a frontrunner and as a record-breaking athlete.

In 1983, his very first year with the Dolphins, he led them to the American Football Conference (AFC) Eastern Division title and became the NFL's rookie of the year. Becoming the first quarterback to pass more than 5,000 yards in a single season (1984), Marino also broke the single-season record for touchdown passes. In 1985, he was mainly responsible for taking the Dolphins to the Super Bowl. More recently (1995), with a host of record-breaking feats, he was voted NFL player of the year, setting the NFL career records in passing completions, passing yardage, touchdown passes, and passing attempts. Because of his extraordinary and spectacular talents, his influence on pro football has already been compared to the effect that "Babe Ruth, Bill Russell, and Bobby Orr had on baseball, basketball, and hockey, respectively, during their careers."

Daniel Constantine Marino, Jr., better know as Dan Marino, was born on September 15, 1961 in Pittsburgh, Pennsylvania. The only son and oldest of three children, he was born to Dan Marino, Sr., and Veronica (nee Kolczynski) Marino. Raised in Pittsburgh's south Oakland area, mostly comprised of middle-class Italian, Irish, Polish, and African-American families, he attended St. Regis parochial grade school where he played quarterback for the school team which, coincidentally, his father coached. His dad, whose job schedule allowed him to be home in mid-afternoon, often played with young Marino, and they would practice tossing footballs to each other. Marino contends that his father was the best coach he ever had.

With a lackluster grade school academic record, he barely made it into the high school of his choice, Central Catholic, where he played both football and baseball exceptionally well and quickly established a statewide reputation in high school sports. He seemed destined for a great future in at least one of two sports since his most impressive pitching record of 25-1 and a batting average of .550 were yet eclipsed by his overall performance as a football player. Scouts from the University of Pittsburgh showed interest in Marino as early as his sophomore year, and by his senior year they were most eager for him to accept their football scholarship.

Before his high school year was concluded, he was bombarded by dozens of college football scholarships coming from all parts of the United States. He was also sought by the Kansas City Royals to play professional baseball. Deciding to remain local, he accepted the University of Pittsburgh's invitation whose campus was literally a few blocks away from his house. During his first three years in college football, he performed exceptionally well as a quarterback especially in the execution of touchdown passes.

It was during these three years that he was in great part responsible for the Pittsburgh "Pitt" Panthers winning the Fiesta, Gator, and Sugar Bowls, respectively, in three consecutive years. The year 1981 (his junior year) was the best of his collegiate years. His phenomenal playing—to include tossing three touchdowns (one touchdown with thirty-five seconds left to the game)—won the Sugar Bowl for the Pitt Panthers 11-1. Nominated fourth in the Heisman Trophy balloting for that year, he was expected to capture it in his senior year.

For a host of reasons, his fourth year's performance for the Pitt Panthers unfortunately failed to meet those high expectations. In all, despite the disappointment for some fans, by the time he completed his four years of college he had been very much involved in having led the Pitt Panthers to a 42-6 record (an 87% win percentage) and letting them finish four times in the Top Ten Associated Press selections. Marino was one of four Pitt Panthers whose jersey was retired.

Dan Marino, who was not a favorite in the NFL annual draft of college players because of alleged drug improprieties in his last year of college, was selected nonetheless by Don Shula of the Miami Dolphins who admired Marino's quarterback abilities. Marino went on to sign a four-year $2 million contract and was to serve as backup to David Woodley who previously had led the Dolphins to the Super Bowl. Yet Woodley's lackluster start in the first two games of the fall 1983 season found Marino replacing him in the third game and doing exceptionally well.

This season proved to be rewarding for Marino as he became the first rookie quarterback to start in the Pro Bowl. The 1984 season proved to be even better as he began breaking NFL records in completions, yards and touchdowns; he became the first quarterback to pass for more than 5,000 yards in a single season, and he broke the single-season record for touchdown passes. The year 1985 was a banner year for Marino who was voted NFL player of the year and led the Dolphins to the 1985 Super Bowl.

Since his first pro season in 1983, Marino has consistently been a major asset to the Miami Dolphins. Despite occasional injuries on the field, Marino has proven his stamina by having started in over 145 straight games which no other quarterback has been able to surpass. To date, he still holds 28 Dolphins team records and 25 NFL records. In the 1995 season, he became the All Time Leader in all NFL passing records surpassing many of Fran Tarkenton's records.

In the 1990s, Marino became heavily involved in charity work. After serving as a United Way representative in 1994, he also established the Dan Marino Foundation to help underprivileged children in south Florida. Marino, who in the past donated his time to the Leukemia Fund, now also sponsors its annual golf tournament. As an autobiographer (1997), he has shared his life experiences and has shown his more vulnerable side. Italian Americans can be very proud of his success in overcoming the challenges he faced. His attitude in tirelessly striving for perfection in a very competitive and demanding sport aptly serves as an example for people of all ages to admire and emulate.

General Sources:
1. *Current Biography Yearbook*. New York: Wilson, 1989.
2. Kennedy, Nick. *Dan Marino, Star Quarterback*. Springfield, NJ: Enslow Publishers, 1998.
3. Marino, Dan, and Greg Brown. *First & Goal*. Dallas, TX: Taylor, 1997.
4. Neft, David, et al. *The Football Encyclopedia: The Complete History of Professional Football from 1892 to the Present*. New York: St. Martin's Press, 1994.
5. "Player Profiles." 4 September 1998. <http://204.254.173.2/dolphins/player-profiles/dmarino.html>.
6. Wilner, Barry. *Dan Marino*. New York: Chelsea House, 1996.

—by LILLIAN MARCELLI

PENNY MARSHALL (1942-   )

Penny Marshall, most associated with her role as the street-smart and often cynical Laverne, the co-starring role in the hit TV situation comedy *Laverne and Shirley* (1976-1983), is also a very talented and successful director of Hollywood movies such as *Big* (1988), *Awakenings* (1990), and the unusually fascinating film *A League of Their Own* (1992) that deals with women's baseball from the 40s.

She was born in New York City on October 15, 1942. Penny was the third child of Tony and Marjorie Marshall. The family surname, Marshall, apparently represents an anglicized modification that was most likely based on one of three possible prior Italian variations: Masciarelli, Mascirelli or Mascarelli.

Penny's father who for many years had been a filmmaker would at a later point in time produce *Laverne and Shirley*, Penny's well-known TV series. Penny's mother, who operated a tap dancing school in the basement of a Bronx apartment complex, had Penny start practicing dance as early as three years of age. Despite the fact that a dance troupe, the Marshallettes, which had been organized and developed by her mother, was good enough to appear on *The Jackie Gleason Show* and on the *Ted Mack Amateur Hour*, Penny (who belonged to the group) had little or no interest in dance.

Depicting herself as a self-effacing tomboy whose interactive potential seemed for a while to lie more in friendship rather than romantic areas, Penny did not always feel she fit into the social scene during her teenage years. She often belied her loneliness by using humor as the antidote throughout that tough transitional period. After high school, she went to college, and at the behest of parental insistence, she attended the University of New Mexico in Albuquerque. Majoring in psychology and minoring in business and anthropology, she left college after her sophomore year to marry a football player, Michael Henry.

From that marriage, she had a daughter, Tracy; and soon after, the marriage ended in divorce. To support herself, she did some secretarial work and, ironically, ended up teaching dance and working as a choreographer at the Albuquerque Civic Light Opera Association. In 1967, she moved to Los Angeles where her brother Garry already a successful writer, producer and filmmaker, advised her to take acting and improvisation lessons. Having done so, she soon embarked upon doing commercials, becoming a stunt woman, and taking on small supporting roles as in the comedy *How Sweet It Is* (1968) and in the motorcycle melodrama *The Savage Seven* (1968). She also made her TV debut on *The Danny Thomas Hour* in 1968.

In 1970, Penny had auditioned and failed to obtain the part of Gloria in Norman Lear's pioneering sitcom, *All in the Family*. Yet, in 1971 as fate would have it, she met and married Rob Reiner who played the role of Mike Stivic, the "meathead," in that very sitcom she had missed. They met as members of a Los Angeles repertory theater group called The Committee. Penny was not at a loss for obtaining small parts on TV. On several occasions, she appeared on *The Odd Couple* playing the role of Myrna, Oscar Madison's lightheaded secretary.

Penny appeared in a number of other TV programs such as *The Bob Newhart Show*, *Friends and Lovers*, *The Super*, and in two made-for-TV films. Penny finally appeared in *Happy Days* that was her brother Garry's hit sitcom about a Milwaukee family and its teenage high school scene. Penny Marshall together with Cindy Williams emerged in one of the *Happy Days* episodes as a very interesting female duo. This successful event immediately suggested to Garry Marshall the idea for a spinoff. He proposed the idea to Fred Silverman, ABC's programming director, and the rest was history as a new sitcom was born: *Laverne and Shirley*.

It premiered on January 27, 1976, and by the time it had reached its second TV season (1977-78), it had become the highest rated TV series. The series chronicled the lives of two women, both assembly-line brewery workers who shared a basement apartment and whose attempts and misadventures in finding romance constituted most of the weekly storylines. Lasting nearly eight years, the final episode of the *Laverne and Shirley* series took place on May 10, 1983.

Prior to the conclusion of this notable sitcom series, she had co-starred with Bob Reiner in a 1978 made-for-TV movie romantic comedy, *More than Friends*, which Reiner had written. She also had a minor role in Spielberg's unsuccessful 1979 film named *1941* which dealt with Los Angeles life immediately after the attack on Pearl Harbor. After Penny's divorce in 1981, the *Laverne and Shirley* series was still two years away from its conclusion, and Penny was in the throes of struggling with her new situation as a divorced woman. She kept herself isolated and close to only a select group of friends such as Joe Pesci and James Belushi.

After *Laverne and Shirley*'s final episode, she appeared in some made-for-TV movies, and she made her stage debut in the 1985 Off-Broadway play, *Eden Court*. Though the play was short-lived, the critics liked her comic work with Ellen Barkin. Penny's trajectory was now turning upward once more. She was asked to direct her first movie, *Jumpin' Jack Flash* (1986), which starred Whoopi Goldberg. Though the movie did not prove to be a hit, she as director had surely shown her mettle by professionally completing this film under difficult production and personnel conditions.

Marshall's second movie, *Big* (1988), had immediate box-office success and was later nominated for Best Picture and Best Actor (Tom Hanks). She received many accolades for her direction and was now offered to direct at many Hollywood movie studios. Her third directorial effort, *Awakenings* (1990), represented a radical shift in theme. Based on Dr. Oliver Sacks' book regarding his study of post-encephalitic Parkinsonian patients warehoused in a psychiatric hospital, it starred two great actors Robert De Niro and Robin Williams. *Awakenings* received Oscar nominations for Best Picture, Best Actor and Best Screenplay.

Her fourth and most notable film, *A League of Their Own* (1992), in another radical shift in theme, dealt with the emergence of the first season of the All-American Girls Professional Baseball Leagues begun in 1943 during the wartime exodus of male players. A sensitive actress and a most versatile director, Penny Marshall has earned much respect and admiration as a very creative individual both by the film community and by her viewing public. Relatively young, Penny Marshall's future surely holds more challenges and rewards for her.

General Sources:
1. *Contemporary Theatre, Film and Television*. Detroit, MI: Gale Research, 1995.
2. *Current Biography Yearbook*. New York: Wilson, 1992.
3. Katz, Ephraim. *The Film Encyclopedia*. New York: HarperCollins, 1998.
4. Monaco, James. *The Encyclopedia of Film*. New York: Perigee Books, 1991.
5. Ragan, D. *Who's Who in Hollywood*. New York: Facts on File, 1992.
6. Siegel, Scott, and Barbara Siegel. *The Encyclopedia of Hollywood*. New York: Facts on File, 1990.

—by NANCY BENNETT

DEAN MARTIN (1917-1995)

Dino Crocetti, better known as Dean Martin, was born in Steubenville, Ohio on June 7, 1917. He would someday become the well-known baritone crooner, TV entertainer, actor, one-time partner of the famous Martin and Lewis comedy-singing act of stage and screen, and prominent member of Sinatra's rat pack. Often compared to Sinatra, one of his closest friends, Martin as an entertainer virtually left few stones unturned in his career in terms of showmanship versatility, crooning his way into the hearts of nationwide audiences, performing not only as a most popular singer in radio and in nightclubs but also as an adept movie actor, popular TV host-entertainer, and comedian.

His father Gaetano (Guy), an emigrant from the Abruzzi area of Italy came to live with his brothers in Steubenville. Barely speaking any English, he married Angela Barra, who coincidentally spoke no Italian. When they first met, she was still attending school in a convent, and their mutual attraction was apparently so great that they married only two weeks after their initial meeting. He went on to have his own successful barber shop business, and as a couple they raised a family.

Although their hometown of Steubenville was far from Chicago, it had been metaphorically dubbed "little Chicago" because of its rampant vice in such areas as its bootlegging and its gambling industries during the prohibition era. Dino, not being the best of students, quit high school in the tenth grade. He admitted, years later, that while he was in school he thought he was smarter than the teacher. Afterwards, quitting school did prove to be difficult as he had to work many odd jobs such as a shoeshine boy and a gas station attendant.

In 1931 in the heart of the Great Depression, under the name Kid Crochet he became a boxer at fourteen years of age in the welterweight division earning ten dollars per fight. During his short-lived boxing career, Dino managed to get his nose broken and a split lip, both requiring surgery. Ostensibly compelled to giving up boxing for awhile, he went from job to job, working a local steel mill, then delivering bootleg liquor across state lines, and finally being a clerk in a cigar store which covertly hosted a gambling casino in its back room.

Dino quickly learned to be a dealer and croupier, and he was soon earning as much as $20 a day plus tips, a handsome sum for that depressed era. Reportedly, it was his boss who, upon hearing him sing, kept urging him to pursue singing. One night in a club in August 1934, he was supposedly pushed on stage to sing, and that apparently started him crooning in Steubenville cafes under the name Dino Martini earning $50 a week.

After a few years experience locally, he started singing in Columbus and then finally in Cleveland in 1940. He was twenty-three years old and maturing as a singer; and as a featured vocalist, he had taken over the city of Cleveland by storm. He soon changed his name to an anglicized Dean Martin. By 1943 he signed a contract with MCA enabling him to sing at the Riobamba Room in New York, and by 1944 he had his own 15-minute radio program called *Songs by Dean Martin* from New York City.

Dean Martin and Jerry Lewis were introduced to each other in 1945, but they would not work together until a year later in the Havana-Madrid Club in March 1946. Later in July 1946, Dean appeared at the 500 Club, again on the same bill as Jerry. What started as a "horsing around with each other's acts" blossomed into performing as a team. They created their own unique routines, often improvising as they went along their scheduled performances. They had hit upon a fresh and effective entertainment combination that blended comedy and music that worked well on stage and that later would also work in their movies.

After appearing as a team at top-notch nightclubs such as the Copacabana and earning $5,000 per week, their manager Abby Greshler booked them on the west coast in Beverly Hills at Slapsie Maxie Rosenbloom's popular nightclub. There, a Paramount Pictures partner, Joseph Hazen, witnessing firsthand the Martin & Lewis performance, rushed to sign up this dynamic duo for a long-term movie contract.

Between 1949 and 1956, Martin & Lewis made sixteen successful films for Paramount. Beginning with *My Friend Irma* (1949) and concluding as a filmmaking duo with *Hollywood or Bust* (1956), they were earning, at times, as much as $2 million per year as a team. This rewarding amalgam of creative personalities came to an end in 1956 when each partner decided to go his own way.

Disappointing millions of devoted fans nationwide, their schism made immediate news headlines, and their split became the topic of everyday conversation for months on end even when it had become incredibly clear that they were no longer a team. This also became a rather dark period, however brief, in Dean's life when some critics contended that he would not be able to make it on his own especially after his first solo movie in 1957 (*Ten Thousand Bedrooms*) earned him only lackluster critiques.

In 1958, however, just a year later, Dean Martin appeared in what became a blockbuster of a movie based on Irwin Shaw's best-selling WWII novel, *The Young Lions*. Movie heavyweights such as Marlon Brando, Maximilian Schell, and Montgomery Clift headlined this film, and its overwhelming success had compelled viewing audiences across the nation to take note of Dean Martin's superb acting abilities that had gone well beyond his previous range of stereotypical comedic and singing roles.

From 1957 to 1984, Martin appeared in over thirty more films in a variety of acting settings and roles. Between 1965-1974 he also hosted his very own popular TV variety program, *The Dean Martin Show,* whose success won him a Golden Globe Award in 1967. In his fifty-years-plus music career, he had recorded over one hundred successful albums; and despite his failing health, he continued going on concert tours singing with fellow entertainers until he was well into his mid-70s. At age seventy-eight, Dean Martin died of respiratory failure in his Beverly Hills home on Christmas day in 1995.

He will always be remembered as a great Italian-American entertainer and a superb singer whose hit songs remain as popular today as ever before, especially on radio programs featuring old favorites and popular song classics. It remains a pleasant paradox that Dean Martin in addition to singing what might be characterized as, strictly speaking, American-style popular love songs, also performed many songs bearing an unmistakably Italian flavor, such as "That's Amore," that in fact have become part of Americana and its concomitant musical heritage.

General Sources:
1. Johnson, Karl B., comp. *Dean Martin: A Collecting Guide to His Recording, Sheet Music, Films, and Videos*. Tucson, AZ: J. Carlson Press, 1998.
2. Katz, Ephraim. *The Film Encyclopedia*. New York: HarperCollins, 1998.
3. Null, Gary, and Carl Stone. *The Italian-Americans*. Harrisburg, PA: Stackpole Books, 1976.
4. Tosches, Nick. *Dino: Living High in the Dirty Business of Dreams*. New York: Dell, 1993.

—by KATHLEEN ZAPPIA

GIAN CARLO MENOTTI (1911-   )

Best known for his *verismo* (realism) style of opera, Gian Carlo Menotti has been able to combine contemporary dramatic librettos (lyrics) with more traditional Italian opera. In many respects, he was a child prodigy, and he has had since his early years an impressively long list of musical accomplishments to his credit. Hailed as a modern-day Puccini, he still remains "the most often performed *living* composer of opera" in today's opera world.

Menotti was born on July 7, 1911 in Cadegliano on Lake Lugano near Milan, Italy. He was the sixth of ten children of a well-to-do, musically talented family. Under the influence of their talented mother, each Menotti child was trained to play a variety of instruments, and they practiced as a family at home. The Menotti family also had their own family box at La Scala, and Gian Carlo attended the opera regularly.

Menotti started composing music at the age of six, and by eleven he composed his first opera *The Death of Pierrot*. Since as a pastime he staged puppet shows, he had his first opera performed as a home puppet show. At seventeen he had already become an accomplished pianist; more interestingly, it was since the age of five he had been setting verse to piano music. At age thirteen, he wrote his "second childhood opera, *The Little Mermaid*, based on Hans Christian Andersen's fairy tale."

In 1924 when the Menotti family moved to Milan at the urging of his mother, Gian Carlo was enrolled in the Verdi Conservatory of Music. Living in Milan became a cultural catalyst causing him to develop an even greater interest not only in the world of opera and in fairy tales from around the world but also an interest in "the exotic, the theatrical, the occult, and the decadent."

In 1928, after his father's death and the collapse of the family coffee investment, he and his mother traveled to South America attempting to salvage the business, but it was to no avail. Before returning to Italy, they sailed to Philadelphia where she presented a letter from Toscanini to the Curtis Institute of Music recommending her son to study under Rosario Scalero, the institute's famous professor of music composition.

Scalero had characterized Gian Carlo as "undisciplined and raw," and he insisted that Menotti get down to serious business and work hard at learning his art. Scalero, no doubt a disciplinarian, was very influential in Menotti's development; under Scalero's rigid program, he mastered the art of musical composition. Although Menotti often felt he was undergoing a kind of "torture" in the study of music composition, he obviously acquired the necessary confidence and tools to succeed in such a challenging craft.

While at the Curtis Institute, Menotti also began a lifetime friendship with the American composer Samuel Barber. In 1933, after graduating together, they traveled to Austria, and Menotti relates that they were: "wasting a lot of time going to wild parties." When they settled down, Menotti says he began writing "his first mature opera," *Amelia al Ballo*. One of the few that he had written in Italian, the one-act opera dealt with a "frivolous woman determined not to let her husband's murderous rage at being cuckolded stand in the way of her going to a ball."

The opera translated into English as *Amelia Goes to the Ball* had its premiere in Philadelphia in 1937. The instant success of the American version led to the National

Broadcasting System (NBC) commissioning Menotti to write another opera for the radio. And so he wrote a humorous one-act opera, *The Old Maid and the Thief*, that dealt with the wiles of a "virtuous" spinster framing an unsuspecting drifter for her own needs. This opera, successfully broadcast in 1939, was later adapted for the stage.

In 1939 Gian Carlo wrote a ballet entitled *Sebastian*. This work was followed by Gian Carlo's first experiment with "grand" opera. Entitled *The Island God*, it premiered at the New York Metropolitan Opera in 1942. The work concerned religion and the conflict between faith and reality. The story dealt with two religious skeptics marooned on a Mediterranean island and their subsequent revelations summoned by their interaction with the discovery of an ancient Greek temple. Unfortunately, the opera proved to be a failure, one of the worst in Met history.

Nonetheless, the ensuing years proved to be exciting and rewarding for Menotti as his reputation soared. After composing his *Piano Concerto in A minor* in 1945, Menotti resumed his interest in opera with the composition of a two-act work called *The Medium*. Dealing with the world of séance, this play calls into question the relationship between the natural and supernatural worlds. With its companion piece, *The Telephone*, described as a *divertissement*, it ran on Broadway for 211 performances in 1947.

The Consul, a Broadway full-length opera, presents the tragic story of "political outcasts in a European totalitarian state seeking asylum through a foreign consulate" only to find unsuspectedly an equally frustrating bureaucracy of indifference. This opera earned Menotti a Drama Critics Circle Award and a Pulitzer Prize in 1950.

In 1951, *Amahl and the Night Visitors*, a one-act TV opera, depicted a pastoral scenario dealing with a crippled boy offering "his crutches to the Three Wise Men as a gift for the infant Jesus" and its ensuing miracle. Broadcast on TV for thirteen consecutive Christmas Eves, its stage production version broke all contemporary opera records running 587 performances. In the 1954-55 Broadway season, Menotti won his second Pulitzer Prize with a three-act opera entitled *The Saint of Bleeker Street*. In the milieu of very contemporary urban times, it dramatized the conflict between a cynical realism and the apparent anomaly of a pressing mysticism ever present in human existence.

Menotti has since composed many more musical works. He has written a total of twenty-one operas and remains as one of the very few successful contemporary opera composers. He is also a pioneer in having successfully introduced contemporary opera through the TV medium, doing in effect what Leonard Bernstein had done for symphonic music. Gifted and talented as a child and later in life prodigious and prolific as a composer, he aptly deserves the recognition of his being "the most performed living composer of opera."

General Sources:
1. *Current Biography/Yearbook*. New York: Wilson, 1947;1979.
2. Grieb, Lyndal. *The Operas of Gian Carlo Menotti 1937-1972: A Selective Bibliography*. Metuchen, NJ: Scarecrow Press, 1974.
3. Gruen, John. *Menotti: A Biography*. New York: Macmillan, 1978.
4. Guinn, John, and Les Stone, eds. *The St. James Opera Encyclopedia: A Guide to People and Works*. Detroit, MI: Visible Ink, 1997.
5. Menotti, Gian Carlo. *Amahl and the Night Visitors*. New York: Morrow, 1986.
6. Wlaschin, Ken. *Gian Carlo Menotti on Screen: Opera, Dance, and Choral Works on Film, Television, and Video*. Jefferson, NC: McFarland, 1999.

—by JERRY F. TESTA

EDUARDO MIGLIACCIO (1882-1946)

At the mere mention of theater impressionists and stage improvisators of the Italian-American vaudevillian era, the name of Eduardo Migliaccio invariably surfaces as its foremost figure. The acknowledged master of parody and comedy of his day, Eduardo Migliaccio's fame as entertainer swept the nation at all the key theaters frequented by Italian immigrants and second generation Italian Americans. In Italian communities during the radio days, his name had become a household word synonymous with comedy.

Eduardo Migliaccio was born on April 15, 1882 in a small town outside Naples called Cava dei Terreni. At a young age, he studied at the Istituto di Belle Arti where he learned about the arts and art design. As a young teenager he had also had the opportunity to learn about drama and comedy in the Neapolitan theater especially by watching Nicolò Maldacea, an impressionist at the Teatro Nuovo in Naples. These early influences would have a great creative impact on his life in the years to come.

Migliaccio's father was a fairly wealthy man. Unlike most immigrants who came to America precisely because they were poor, Migliaccio's father traveled to America for other reasons, mainly business. Typically, in those early days of Italian migration, the father traveled to America ahead of his family and later sent for them. Eduardo joined his father in Hazelton, Pennsylvania in 1897 at the age of 14. He immediately began work in his father's place of business, the Banca Sandolo. His father had indeed opened a bank: an anomaly for a recent immigrant. Eduardo's position in the bank involved customer service for the bank patrons, who were usually miners and laborers. Since many could neither read nor write, Eduardo usually wrote letters for them to be sent to relatives back in Italy or in the States. Eduardo took an instant aversion to his service position which often involved listening to the trials and tribulations of immigrants. Unwittingly, this position was preparing him, still a teenager, for his future career in entertainment (both in drama and in comedy) as it forced him to take a long hard look at the hardships, the likes and dislikes of immigrants, together with their problems with learning English and adapting to America.

Migliaccio had already experienced the exuberance of the New York City lifestyle during his early immigrant transition, and it did not take him long to decide to return there. He quickly found work through a family friend in a bank on Mulberry Street (lower Manhattan) where, ironically, he did the same thing he had done in his father's bank. However, on April 26, 1900, Eduardo firmly placed his feet on the Italian-American stage and would remain there for decades to come. He worked at his day job, and he performed at night, starting in drama then switching to song.

He signed his first contract to sing Neapolitan songs at the Caffè Concerto Pennacchio for four dollars a week on Mulberry St. Migliaccio's acquired the name "Farfariello" (little butterfly), the name of the character in his signature love song whose theme dealt with an unhappy affair. Along with his comedic song repertoire, he slowly introduced comic character sketches known as "macchiette," impersonations and parodies, which sometimes he put to music. Creatively employing song, comedy, and sketches, the daily fare of vaudeville, he soon became master of that art form. The growing ranks of New York audiences called him "Re dei macchiettisti" (king of the impersonators).

He often poked fun at specific individuals and stereotypes familiar to Italian immigrants. There wasn't an occupation left unscathed by Migliaccio parodies. In addition, he had a fondness for recasting English words into Italian-sounding structures around which he would then construct an entire sketch. For instance, one of his favorites was the undertaker, a popular comedic topic, spelled in its Italianized form "l'ondertecco."

Migliaccio was reputedly a master of disguises who in the blink of an eye through lightning-quick costume changes, replete with wigs and masks, could impersonate men and women, young and old alike. With time, both of Migliaccio's children, Almarinda and Teodorico, as well as his sister, Esterina Grimaldi, joined in his success and often worked together as a troupe. By 1914 he reportedly had a repertoire of 500 "macchiette" and soon after took his show on the road beyond the precincts of New York City.

He toured the United States for two years with his own company traveling under the name The Eduardo Migliaccio Vaudeville Company. He performed in cities with large concentrations of Italians such as Philadelphia, Chicago, St. Louis, and as far west as San Francisco in 1917-18. Everywhere he traveled, he brought along one of his favorite songs called "La sciabola" (the sabre) which contains an additional meaning of "shovel."

> This new world is upside down
> And the cafone here can smile
> For the coat of arms has no renown
> And the callouses are in style.
> There the *signore* raises his sabre
> When his sacred honor's hurt,
> But here the shovel's used in labor
> And mainly raises dirt.

When the new medium of radio broadcasting began its commercial phase in the early 20s, Migliaccio was also beginning to produce operettas (1924); and he wrote and performed for WAAT, the first radio program in the United States, spoken entirely in Italian. At the forefront of this fledgling media, radio only served to increase his fame and helped to bring laughter to more homes. In 1936 Migliaccio had the opportunity to tour Italy, and King Victor Emanuel III subsequently honored him as Cavaliere dell'Ordine della Corona D'Italia. Migliaccio, a legend in comedy, died on March 27, 1946. As he was an RCA Victor recording artist, his voice can still be heard on records and tapes.

In 1996, a unique presentation was organized by the Immigration History Research Center (IHRC) and the Great American History Theatre in Minneapolis, Minnesota to celebrate the IHRC's 30th anniversary. One of the five planned activities involved the performing arts of various immigrant groups. One portion was dedicated to the craft of Migliaccio. For a brief moment in time, Farfariello, his persona, came to life once more through the superb acting and singing of Christopher Bloch who had donned a dress, twirled a parasol, and sang in the Italian-American vaudevillian style of Migliaccio.

General Sources:

1. Aleandri, Emelise. "A History of Italian-American Theater: 1900-1905." Diss. City University of New York, 1983.

2. D'Acierno, Pellegrino, ed. *The Italian American Heritage: A Companion to Literature and Arts*. New York: Garland Publ., 1999.

3. Estavan, Lawrence, and Mary A. Burgess, eds. *The Italian Theater in San Francisco*. San Bernardino, CA: Bongo Press, 1991.

4. Mangione, Jerre, and Ben Morreale. *La Storia: Five Centuries of the Italian American Experience*. New York: HarperCollins, 1992.

—by LINDA D'ANDREA-MARINO

APRILE MILLO (1958-   )

An Italian-American soprano, accomplished in having already earned a worldwide reputation in opera, Aprile Millo is viewed today as being only at the beginning of an even greater operatic career.

Aprile was born on April 14, 1958 in New York City. She is one of three children of Giovanni Millo and Margherita Ghirosi, both successful opera singers in their own right. Her father, a tenor, was the first American singer to be hired by the famed opera company at La Scala di Milano after WWII. Her mother, a soprano, has also performed in many films and theatrical productions.

Much of Aprile's early childhood was spent with her brother Richard and sister Grace traveling around Europe with their parents. As obedient and attentive children of professional performers, all three attended with regularity their parents' performances, voice classes, rehearsals, and even coaching lessons. While seeming very much routine on the surface to an observer, Aprile contends that living as a child for periods of time in Europe's finest cities offered her and her siblings the opportunity to become "museum goers and voracious readers."

When the Millo family returned to the United States and settled in Hollywood, California around 1969, Aprile attended the local public schools. It was at this point, at age eleven, that she began her formal voice training under the tutelage of her own parents. To supplement her lessons, she regularly listened to the recordings of female opera notables such as Renata Tebaldi, Rosa Ponselle, Claudia Muzio, Maria Callas, and Zinka Milanov.

A good student in school and a good student in her home-based operatic training provided by her parents, Aprile was chosen to be one of eight "apprentices" at the San Diego Opera Center in 1977 after her high school graduation. The course of study (1977-80) involved training, competition, and the close scrutiny of professionals. In 1977 Licia Albanese, one of opera's most gifted and influential personalities, selected Millo to become the recipient of the annual Geraldine Farrar Award.

In the following year, Millo went on to win the first prize in the Concorso Internazionale di Voci Verdiane in Bussetto, Italy (1978). Only months later, she also won the Montserrat Caballé Award in the Francisco Vinas competition in Barcelona, Spain (1979). Subsequent to her return to the United States, she joined the Utah Opera Company in Salt Lake City. In 1980, she made her professional debut starring in the title role of Giuseppe Verdi's *Aida* (1871). A most difficult role to perform even for an established opera singer, she excelled; and later in the season she went on to sing the role of the female lead, Santuzza, in Mascagni's *Cavalleria Rusticana* (1890).

With many recent victories behind her, she decided to compete in the open-call auditions at the Metropolitan Opera in New York City. While rendering a Verdi aria, her powerful soprano voice impressed the Met's artistic and administrative directors. After a second audition, she was offered an invitation to join the Young Artists Development Program. She then spent the next few years (1980-84) learning new operatic roles and perfecting her style and vocal techniques.

In 1984, Millo signed a three-year contract with the Metropolitan Opera in which she would serve mainly as an understudy. On December 3, 1984, when Anna Tomowa-Sintow became ill at the last minute and was not able to sing the role of Amelia in Verdi's *Simon Boccanegra*, Millo stepped in to take her place. In fact, that very night, Millo effectively made her Metropolitan Opera debut, and she had done so without benefit of formal rehearsal time. In recognition of her excellent performance in this challenging situation, she received tremendous ovations from the audience and, subsequently, glowing reviews from the critics.

Three months later, in her capacity as understudy, she had the opportunity to substitute for Montserrat Caballé in the operatic role of Elvira in Verdi's *Ernani*. The newspaper critics, particularly Henahan from the *New York Times*, lauded the young soprano's talent and, especially her robust voice, a *sine qua non* for Verdi roles such as Elvira. In all, Millo had shown herself as quite capable of performing even under the pressure of being an understudy and singing difficult roles.

In 1985, while still under contract with the Met, she did some limited freelance appearances. First singing in the title role in *Aida* at the San Antonio Festival, she then went to Chile (South America) to sing the role of Maddalena in *Andrea Chénier* at the Santiago Opera. That year, she also earned for herself first prize in the Richard Tucker competition.

Perhaps one of her biggest personal challenges took place in the following year in January 1986. Since she believed strongly that in opera the acting component is indirectly involved in helping to inspire the quality of singing, she felt deeply challenged when, making her Carnegie Hall debut, she was limited to a "concert" version of Verdi's *I Lombardi alla Prima Crociata*. Despite her initial misgivings about singing "opera in concert form," she received at the conclusion of the performance incredibly enthusiastic applause and "a near-wild ovation."

Still as understudy, she received an equally resounding ovation when she completed her debut as Elisabetta in an unusually long five-hour production of *Don Carlo* at the Met on March 31, 1986. Her substitute performance went so well that the management of the Met decided to let her keep that role for the remaining performances of that opera season. Similarly, a month later, in an open-air performance also sponsored by the Met, she sang the role of *Aida* in New York City's Central Park much to the delight of the audience attending the free concert.

After her many successful experiences at the Metropolitan in the 80s, Aprile has continued to thrive with increasing success, enjoying an undeniable popularity and greater operatic professionalism as a reputedly seasoned Verdian soprano. In her career she has sung at the major operatic halls and centers in the United States and at those in Europe's more prestigious city opera centers such as Milan, Rome, Bologna, Verona, Turin, Vienna, Bonn, Munich, and Barcelona—not to mention her tours in the Far East, such as in Korea and in Japan. She has often come to describe herself as a "work in progress," and indeed, more like a high-quality reserve wine, she is improving with age.

General Sources:
1. *Current Biography Yearbook*. New York: Wilson, 1988.
2. Guinn, John, and Les Stone, eds. *The St. James Opera Encyclopedia: A Guide to People and Works*. Detroit, MI: Visible Ink, 1997.
3. "LaScala-Aprile Millo." 9 July 1998. <http://lascala.milano.it/ita/character/millo.html>.
4. *The New Grove Dictionary of Opera*. New York: Grove's Dictionaries of Music, 1992.
5. *New York* 21 April 1986: 91+.
6. *New York Times* 19 Jan. 1986, sec. II: 19.
7. *Opera News* 30 Jan. 1988: 8+.

—by DENNIS PIASIO

LIZA MINNELLI (1946-   )

Liza, the dynamic and multi-talented star of stage, screen, and television was born in Hollywood, California on March 12, 1946. The child of famous singer Judy Garland and well-known film director Vincente Minnelli, her life has been marked by many exciting and equally painful moments. Many critics have described her life experiences like that of a roller-coaster experiencing both the most titillating of triumphs and the very depths of despair.

Her survival of a host of personal challenges and ordeals that have punctuated various epochs of her life, however, only serves to recognize and accentuate her gifts and talents as a performer. Winning her first Tony Award at the mere age of nineteen, making her the youngest actress to receive such an award (*Flora, the Red Menace*, 1965), she went on to earn two more Tonys (*Liza at the Winter Garden,* in 1973 and *The Act* in 1978). Topped by an Oscar and an Emmy, she has been acknowledged by critics as one of the very few performers to have won the so-called "triple crown" of show business excellence in theater, film, and television.

She is the oldest of Judy Garland's three children and the only child from the Garland/Minnelli marriage. Her half-sister Lorna and half-brother Joseph came by way of Garland's third marriage to movie producer Sid Luft. Liza's early years were characterized by her fascination with being on the set watching her father's or her mother's creativity in action. Since Liza was interested particularly in dancing, she was enthralled by personally watching superstars like Fred Astaire, Gene Kelly, and Cyd Charisse rehearse their numbers. When she went home, she would "practice for hours in front of the mirror."

On the dark end of the spectrum, her parents' divorce in 1951 (when Liza was only five) would represent a sign of many future difficulties for young Liza. Her mother, whose frequent illnesses had made Liza a parentified child, surely imposed early adulthood status on her. Reportedly by age eleven, Liza was literally running the household to the point of paying bills and even hiring staff for her mother. In a *Time* magazine interview, she said "I don't really remember having any childhood. I always had responsibilities."

Perhaps the starting point for Liza's career might aptly begin with her witnessing a performance of *Bye Bye Birdie*. Animated by the Broadway production, she immediately joined her high school drama club in Scarsdale, a town in Westchester County, just north of New York City. After auditioning for *The Diary of Anne Frank* and then winning the lead role, the Scarsdale High School play was so successful that a sponsor paid for a 1961 summer tour of the play in Europe. A year later, Liza took on bit parts in musical comedies in Hyannisport, Massachusetts.

A few months after returning to high school in 1962, Liza quit traditional education deciding in favor of focusing on an acting career. In April 1963 at age seventeen, she appeared in *Best Foot Forward* at Stage 73, an Off-Broadway theater, whose audience was stacked with celebrities and critics who had come to see, no doubt, Judy Garland's daughter perform. The critics proved to be both kind and genuine in acknowledging her talents, and *Theater World* magazine selected her as one of the year's "promising personalities."

The critics were indeed right as her career would soon begin to skyrocket in the following year with bursts of activity both at home and abroad. At age eighteen, she cut her first album called *Liza! Liza!* (Capital, 1964), and she toured throughout the United States in "road company productions of *Carnival*, *The Fantasticks*, *Time Out for Ginger*, and *The Pajama Game*." In November of that year, she appeared with her mother at the London Palladium in a joint concert, taped for TV and recorded to be later released by Capital Records.

In May 1965, she starred in *Flora, the Red Menace*, a spoof of depression era communism in the United States. Though the critics remained disenchanted with the production as a whole, they loved Liza's dynamic performance, and this earned her a Tony Award for Best Actress in a musical. In the same year, Liza developed a cabaret act which took her to the best quality nightspots including the Shoreham Hotel Blue Room in Washington, D.C., the Persian Room in the New York City Plaza Hotel, and a host of other nightspots both at home and abroad.

Established as an international stage performer and having a Broadway Tony to her credit, Liza then began a film career. She made her film debut in the movie *Charlie Bubbles* (1968) where she received favorable reviews. This film was followed by *The Sterile Cuckoo* (1969) where she had a greater opportunity to portray her wide acting range and abilities. She did so well that she earned an Oscar nomination for Best Actress, and she won Italy's David di Donatello Prize as Best Foreign Actress.

In 1969, while Liza was working in her third movie (*Tell Me That You Love Me, Junie Moon*), her mother died from an overdose of sleeping pills. After handling all funeral arrangements and settling estate matters, Liza would later reveal that in having immersed herself in her work, at that time, she had not really allowed herself to mourn her mother's death and had no closure in that regard. Proceeding headlong with her work, she made her first TV special *Liza Minnelli* (NBC, 1970), and when she took her act overseas, it also became a success internationally.

With little time for rest, she started filming in 1971 *Cabaret* (1972), which for many, represents her most prominent work. Based on Isherwood's *Berlin Stories* and under Bob Fosse's film direction, Liza played the role of an American-born cabaret singer, adrift in Berlin's bohemianism of the 1930's. With her performance decidedly electric, she went on to win several awards that year including the Golden Globe award for Best Actress in a Musical, the American Guild of Variety Artists Entertainer of the Year, and finally an Oscar at the Academy Awards as the year's Best Actress. Before the year ended, she also won an Emmy for her TV special *Liza With a Z* (NBC, 1972).

Truly a gifted person, she has since gone on to do more notable TV specials, Hollywood films, and many more concert tours. She remains in the hearts of many who appreciate her stage presence and showmanship as an undeniably superb performer. She has met and has overcome many personal challenges to become a superstar not limited to movies, or to stage, or to TV but effectively encompassing all three media in one person in one lifetime.

General Sources:
1. *Contemporary Theatre, Film and Television*. Detroit, MI: Gale Research, 1988.
2. *Current Biography Yearbook*. New York: Wilson, 1988.
3. Katz, Ephraim. *The Film Encyclopedia*. New York: HarperCollins, 1998.
4. Leigh, Wendy. *Liza: Born A Star*. New York: Dutton, 1993.
5. Mair, George. *Under the Rainbow: The Real Liza Minnelli*. Secaucus, NJ: Carol Publ. Group, 1996.
6. *Who's Who in Entertainment*. 1998-1999 ed.

—by ANGELA HARRINGTON

VINCENTE MINNELLI (1903-1986)

Successful director of spectacular Broadway shows and lavish Hollywood film productions, exceptionally skilled in directing both drama and musicals, Vincente Minnelli's reputation among the general public has generally been associated with his great talents in creating memorable musicals. His movies won many Oscars, and perhaps his most memorable achievement still remains his eight-category Oscar-winning film *Gigi* (1958), which starred Leslie Caron and Maurice Chevalier. At that time, he was most likely the only Hollywood director to have two simultaneous Oscar nominations for Best Movie where one was a musical (*Gigi*) and the other a drama (*Some Came Running*).

Minnelli, whose first name ends with an "e," was born on February 28, 1903 in Chicago, Illinois. His birth graced him with a very talented family where his father was a musical conductor from Palermo (Sicily) and his French mother, May Le Beau, was an actress whose stage name was Mina Gennell. Vincente performed at an early age, making his debut at three-and-a-half, appearing on stage in the tent theater circuit in the Midwest during the summer months with his parents and uncle in a show called the Minnelli Brothers Tent Theater. During the school calendar months, he would live with his grandparents, and for a period of time he also attended a Catholic boarding school, St. Joseph, located outside of Cleveland.

When his parents ceased performing in the tent theater circuit due to the overwhelming competition from the movies, they settled in Delaware, Ohio. A determined and multi-talented youngster, he earned money—while still in grade school—by making illustrated signs for the local movie house. After attending St. Mary's High School for three years, he graduated at age 16 from Willis High School. He held various kinds of jobs which usually involved utilizing artistic talent and imagination such as doing display work, photography, drawing, and sketching. Apparently unable to attend college, he attended the Chicago Art Institute for a relatively short period of time.

He received his first significant break in show business when he found a job with a Chicago firm, Balaban and Katz, a motion picture theater and vaudeville chain whose program included an on-stage performance prior to showing the feature film. There he worked as an assistant stage manager and costume designer for its prefeature program. When the firm was absorbed by a merger with Broadway's Paramount Theater in 1931, Minnelli creatively made a quick lateral move for himself by switching to the New York City area where he became a set and costume designer for the Paramount Theater. Soon thereafter, with the recognition of his talents, he moved at a fast pace. He quickly became involved in doing the designing for the weekly shows and outside work.

Despite his growing reputation both at Paramount and in Broadway establishments, he remained without work for several months in late 1933 and early 1934 due to big bands supplanting the once daily fare of vaudeville shows at the Paramount Theater. In late February 1934, he began working for Radio City Music Hall as chief costume designer, and within little time he was entrusted with producing some of its stage show extravaganzas. Powerful Broadway producers quickly admired his work, and the Shubert brothers, in particular, offered him to direct a series of three shows. Minnelli left the music hall and directed these shows that all became hits: *At Home Abroad* (1935-36), *Ziegfeld Follies* (1936), and *The Show Is On* (1936-37).

After being disappointed at an uneventful schedule despite an enticing contract with Paramount Pictures in Hollywood, he returned to New York and supervised some Broadway productions. In 1940 Arthur Freed invited Minnelli to Hollywood to join their company to study film techniques and to experiment with all the phases of filmmaking—at MGM's expense. After directing special musical film sequences in *Strike Up the Band* (1940), *Babes on Broadway* (1941), and *Panama Hattie* (1942), he directed his first full-length film, *Cabin in the Sky* (1943). His "apprenticeship" paid off since *Cabin in the Sky*, which involved an all-black musical cast starring Ethel Waters, became a big hit; and Minnelli's many surprisingly technical innovations in the film introduced new dimensions for future filmmakers.

Especially after directing the musical *Meet Me in St. Louis* (1944) and the drama, *The Clock* (1945), both of which starred Judy Garland, and after directing Fred Astaire and Gene Kelly in *Ziegfeld Follies* (1944), Minnelli's fame began to skyrocket. *Meet Me in St Louis* had become MGM's second highest box-office success only after its number one movie, *Gone With the Wind* (1939). In 1945, Minnelli married Judy Garland, and in the following year their daughter Liza Minnelli was born. The remainder of the 40s and the two following decades were among Minnelli's most successful years professionally.

In many respects, Minnelli's craft as director was ahead of its time. This was evident in his creation of a surrealist ballet in *Yolanda and the Thief* (1945); in his creative integration of forms and colors with thematic structure in *The Pirate* (1948), which starred Gene Kelly and Judy Garland; in the integration of musical numbers with narrative sequence and thematic structure in *An American in Paris* (1951), which

won six Oscars, including Best Picture; and, the same may be said for *Gigi* (1958), winner of eight Oscars, including Best Picture and Best Director.

Minnelli's genius was not limited to creating a standard of excellence for the Hollywood movie musical. His dramatic talents were also evident in his filming of *Madame Bovary* (1949) based on Flaubert's classic novel. Probably even more exquisite in style was his film direction of *Lust for Life* (1956), based on Irving Stone's biography of Vincent Van Gogh. Throughout his career Minnelli had clearly established himself as an excellent director who had set a standard especially for the Hollywood musical. With many Oscar nominations and awards to his name, his direction became associated with the exquisite portrayal of dance, song, and dramatic sequencing that took into account the vivid use of color and designs.

In addition to many Hollywood awards, he won the French Legion of Honor award in 1986. When he passed away on July 25 of the same year, he left a Hollywood legacy that included a model for the film musical whose expression necessitated an artistic fit between the music and the thematic structure of the narrative. He directed over 40 films many of which are as enjoyable today as they were when they were originally released. His memorable works remain as a tribute to American culture.

General Sources:
1. *Current Biography Yearbook*. New York: Wilson, 1975; 1986.
2. Katz, Ephraim. *The Film Encyclopedia*. New York: HarperCollins, 1998.
3. Minnelli, Vincente, and Hector Arce. *I Remember It Well*. Garden City, NY: Doubleday, 1974.
4. Naremore, James. *The Films of Vincente Minnelli*. New York: Cambridge University Press, 1993.

—by SAM PITTARO

TINA MODOTTI (1896-1942)

Tina Modotti remained for many decades an unrecognized yet revolutionary photographer of the 20s and 30s. She was born on August 17, 1896 with an unusually long name, Assunta Adelaide Luigia Modotti Mondini, the child of Giuseppe and Assunta Modotti from Udine, Italy. As a child, her name became Assuntina and then was abbreviated to Tina. Her father's work as a machinist took him and his family further north into Austria for a time, and later back to their native town of Udine.

With job prospects sketchy for machinists, Giuseppe, like many others around the turn of the century, took off for America. He went alone with plans to earn enough money to eventually send for his entire family. His brother, Pietro, had a successful photography studio in Udine where Tina and her siblings visited and were often photographed. It seems that young Tina's future interests and growth in the field of photography had probably started in some way there in her uncle's studio.

In 1908, at age twelve, Tina worked in an Italian silk factory to assist with the family's financial needs. Tina's father was beginning the process of sending for family members, one at a time; and her older sister, Mercedes, was the first to leave Italy. In 1913, when it was her turn, she journeyed alone, coming through Ellis Island on her way to San Francisco where her sister and father resided and awaited her arrival. Eventually, the three of them working hard earned enough money to send for the rest of the family. Tina was first employed as a seamstress, but, because of her striking beauty, she was soon modeling the clothes designed by the company for which she had sewn.

By 1914 at age eighteen, she realized a great interest in the theater, and she attended performances regularly. Soon afterwards, she began acting in the local Italian theater productions in San Francisco's Little Italy where she performed in *Tosca* and *Scampolo*. Her performances were so well received that she later joined an acting company, Città di Firenze, where she performed and went on to receive favorable reviews for her roles in *La Morte Civile* and *La Nemica*.

In 1915 her growing thirst for beauty and culture led her to the Panama-Pacific Exhibition which took place in San Francisco's Palace of Fine Arts. It included an exhibit on photography, a topic for which she had always nurtured interest. There she met Robaix "Robo" de l'Abrie Richey, a poet and illustrator whose works were part of the exhibition. A serious friendship emerged from their meeting, and later she (at age twenty-two) married Robo in 1918, and moved to Los Angeles.

Tina and Robo were both creatively driven individuals with many artistic interests. Robo became known for designing fabrics using Javanese batik methods to create eye-catching designs, and Tina would sew the garments and model them. She also created whimsical and fanciful dolls. They worked together as a team and encouraged each other.

She continued her acting interests and appeared on the silver screen in the silent movie era in the early 20s. A strikingly beautiful woman, she was quick to capture attention and received the starring role in *The Tiger's Coat* (1920) where, coincidentally, she wore a batik dress designed by her husband. She also acted in *Riding with Death* (1921) and *I Can Explain* (1922), but disenchanted with her limited roles due in part to her ethnic flavor, she dropped movie acting. She met Edward Weston, a well-known photographer in whose work she had taken an avid interest.

Simultaneous to her meeting Weston, Tina and Robo decided to move to Mexico to pursue the artistic community life. Robo left first, but before she was able to follow him, she was notified that her husband had been taken ill with smallpox and that he was critical at a Mexico City hospital. He in fact died before she arrived, and she remained in Mexico for a period of time to insure that her husband's art exhibition opened as scheduled.

Tina then returned to Mexico in 1923 with Edward Weston. He photographed her quite extensively, and, as of this time, they had already become intimate, but they would not ever marry each other despite maintaining a lifelong friendship. Not content with merely posing for photographs, she decided to learn in depth the art and skills needed for fine-art photography in an effort to record, through that medium, her views and reactions to the world she knew and had experienced. They worked on a project together and their photos were incorporated in a 1929—now classic—book entitled *Idols Behind Altars*.

Tina's career as a photographer involved her interests in Mexican folk-art, flesh-and-blood men and women workers and farmers: the working classes. She also had interest in nature and, particularly, in flowers. Her photographs appeared in many publications of the day such as *Mexican Folkways* and *El Machete*. Two memorable classics were entitled "Roses" and "Flor de Manita." The latter consists of a flower which gives the appearance of a human hand, its palm and fingers, reaching upward, as if in prayer or in invocation. By the end of the 20s, she became indeed part of an avant-garde of artists and writers.

Tina's strong beliefs in radical socialist reform were just as intense as her passion for photography, often abandoning one in favor of the other. Unfortunately, her radical views caused her great pain and many upheavals in her public as well as her personal life. Despite some male relationships in her life, she never married after the death of her husband with whom she had formed an apparently definitive bond.

Compelled to travel for a variety of political reasons, she moved to Berlin (1930), Moscow (1931-34), France (1934), Spain (1935-38), and finally under an alias she returned illegally to Mexico. Pursuing her photography and her political work, she suddenly took ill on January 6, 1942, and a few hours later she reportedly died of congenital heart failure.

Despite a flurry of interest in her work at an exhibition in April 1942 right after her death in her American hometown of San Francisco, Modotti's art work was only recently redeemed. After many years of critical neglect, recognition began with a 1975 art exhibition. More recently in the latter part of the 1990s, Modotti also became the focus of two critical texts, one by Margaret Hooks and another by Patricia Albers. Both authors have conclusively presented Tina Modotti as a pioneer in the photography of her time. Modotti possessed the foresight in having appreciated and then creatively applied the available camera technology to the area of highly focused portraits, still lifes and even abstract compositions. As a dynamic early twentieth-century Italian-American woman, Modotti has finally acquired a fuller and more deserving recognition in the art of photography.

General Sources:
1.   Albers, Patricia. *Shadows, Fire, Snow: The Life of Tina Modotti*. New York: Clarkson Potter, 1999.
2.   Estavan, Lawrence, and Mary A. Burgess. *The Italian Theater in San Francisco*. San Bernardino: Bongo Press, 1991.
3.   Hooks, Margaret. *Tina Modotti: Photographer and Revolutionary*. San Francisco: Harper, 1995.

—by LINDA D'ANDREA-MARINO

ANNA MOFFO (1932-   )

Anna Moffo, a world-celebrated Italian-American coloratura soprano, daughter of Nicholas and Regina (nee Cinti) Moffo, was born on June 27, 1932 in Wayne, Pennsylvania. Naturally gifted with a beautiful voice, she amazed listeners with her musical abilities when she began her singing career as a child. She made her stage debut at the age of seven before a school assembly in a rendition of "Mighty Lak' a Rose." Without any formal training, she sang as a youngster at various recitals, at social and religious events such as weddings, funerals, and in choirs.

Anna attended Radnor High School where she was excellent in academics as well as in sports. A physically attractive and talented teenager, she was dedicated to her studies and graduated as valedictorian. Shortly after graduation she received an offer to appear in Hollywood films which she declined thinking that she might dedicate her life as a religious becoming a nun. After finally deciding to pursue a career in music, she applied at the renowned Curtis Institute of Music in Philadelphia where she won a four-year scholarship. Based in part on prior academic performance, she ultimately won the scholarship in great part by the qualifying performance of Puccini's "Un bel dì," from *Madama Butterfly*, the only operatic piece she knew at the time.

Dedicated as she was to her studies at the Curtis Institute, she studied diligently both voice and piano, and not surprisingly she concluded her years of study at Curtis by graduating with honors. She went on to receive two awards in 1955. One award was from the Young Artists Auditions offered by the Philadelphia Orchestra, and a second award was in the form of a Fulbright grant for vocal study abroad that made it possible for her to study in Rome, Italy under such distinguished teachers as Luigi Ricci and Mercedes Llopart.

Her abilities coupled with her studies shaped her into becoming a coloratura soprano, a singer who vocally is able to reach operatic trills and other difficult florid variations at unusually high ranges. Her training, operatic talents, and dynamic personality quickly propelled her into what became the beginning of an extensively rich operatic career. She made her debut in the same year (1955) in Spoleto (Italy) singing as Norina in Donizetti's *Don Pasquale*.

After her operatic theater debut in Italy, Anna Moffo began making several Italian radio engagements that were soon followed by 1956 appearances on the Italian state broadcasting system TV network, RAI, where she competed and won the title role in Puccini's *Madama Butterfly*. This performance was staged by Mario Lanfranchi, an Italian producer, whom she married on December 7, 1957, and who became her manager. With this performance, she achieved immediate nationwide success in Italy and subsequently received invitations to sing elsewhere throughout Europe. Within little time, the Europeans recognized her as possessing great operatic talent.

Numerous stage engagements soon followed her TV appearance. She later sang at Italy's most acclaimed opera house, La Scala di Milano, and at other major Italian opera houses; then, in London at its Covent Garden, in Aix-en-Provence (France), and in Austria at the Salzburg Festival. After rendering these notable European performances in such a relatively short period of time, Anna Moffo, a year later, in autumn of 1957 made her first operatic engagement in the United States. She appeared in Puccini's *La Bohème* with the Lyric Opera of Chicago where she would return a year later to sing. She sang on U.S. radio and appeared on the then well-known TV program *The Voice of Firestone* through which she reached a nationwide audience and became in a sense re-introduced to her native American public.

Two years later, she made he debut on the stage of the Metropolitan Opera House, appearing as Violetta in Verdi's *La Traviata*, a role that Moffo has sung to date more than 900 times, unofficially estimated. She was praised for her voice, dramatic qualities, and personal beauty, but some overly severe American critics felt she needed more time to fine tune some of her great talents. She continued with the Met, taking part in its 1960 spring tour throughout the United States. That year, she also sang with the San Francisco Opera Company both on its stage and on tour. One of her performances included a difficult title role favorite of coloratura sopranos, Bellini's *La Sonnambula*.

Later in 1960, she opened the Philadelphia Grand Opera Company's season with her rendition of *La Traviata*. Anna Moffo then returned to the Metropolitan for its 1960-61 season in new roles including Gilda in Verdi's *Rigoletto*, and Adina in Donizetti's *L'Elisir d'Amore*. It was during this season that New York City opera critics not only richly praised Anna Moffo's performance but also lauded her for a flawless presentation. This signified that she had made it to the top. In 1961 she also appeared there in Puccini's *Turandot*, an opera that had not been performed on the Met stage in more than 30 years. She sang with a brilliant cast including Birgit Nilsson and Franco Corelli. Anna Moffo sang the role of Liù, a tragic slave, whose role included many poignant moments.

In Italy, during the 1960s she had her own TV program called the *Anna Moffo Show* whose content dealt with opera and lasted three consecutive years on the air. For many reasons, Anna Moffo suffered a vocal breakdown in 1974-75, and it was roughly at the time she was divorcing Lanfranchi (1974). After her recovery, she went on to sing successfully the lead role in *Thais* in Seattle in 1976 and in *Adriana Lecouvreur* in Parma, Italy in 1978 and has since resumed her career.

With her appearances oscillating between Italy and the United States on the operatic stage, she has appeared not only in many American-made and Italian-made film versions of entire operas such as Verdi's *La Traviata* (1968), Donizetti's *Lucia di Lammermoor* (1973), and *Great Moments in Opera* (1997) but also in innumerable highlighted portions of feature movies or simply appearing in operatic voice backgrounds. As an Italian American whose operatic career has been second to none, Anna Moffo holds the Order of Merit Award from the Italian government. In the 60s the Italian public voted her as one of the ten most beautiful women in Italy.

General Sources:
1.   *Current Biography Yearbook*. New York: Wilson, 1961.
2.   *The Encyclopedia of Opera*. Ed. Leslie Orrey. New York: Scribner, 1976.
3.   Ewen, David. *The New Encyclopedia of the Opera*. New York: Hill and Wang, 1971.
4.   Hines, Jerome. "Anna Moffo." *Great Singers on Great Singing*. Garden City, NY: Doubleday, 1982.
5.   *History of Opera*. Ed. Stanley Sadie. New York: Norton, 1990.
6.   *International Who's Who*. 1995-96.
7.   *The Metropolitan Opera Encyclopedia: A Comprehensive Guide to the World of Opera*. Ed. David Hamilton. New York: Simon & Schuster, 1987.
8.   *The New Grove Dictionary of Opera*. Ed. Stanley Sadie. New York: Grove's Dictionaries of Music, 1992.

—by GABRIEL DE SABATINO

JOE MONTANA (1956-   )

Joseph C. Montana, Jr., better known as Joe Montana, enjoys being a professional football superstar. With a persistent drive for success, he has endured many challenges due to injuries and has always come back, rightly earning his superstar status. As a college quarterback for Notre Dame , he led the Fighting Irish to a national championship in 1977 and to Cotton Bowl victories in 1978 and 1979. Later, as a San Francisco 49er, he established several NFL records, but he is mostly admired for having taken the 49ers to four Super Bowl victories in the 1980s and has been selected Super Bowl MVP twice.

He was born on June 11, 1956, to Joseph, Sr., and Theresa Montana, who, like her husband, is Italian but also part Sioux Indian. Joe Montana was their only child, and under the special guidance of his father, a sports enthusiast, Joe learned to play sports at an early age. Joe grew up in Monongahela, a little town due south of Pittsburgh, Pennsylvania where both his parents worked for a firm called Civic Finance Company.

In addition to baseball and football, Joe was a top performer on the Ringgold High School basketball team. He did so well in sports in his senior year that he was awarded a scholarship grant to North Carolina State University in basketball which he declined after he received a scholarship offer in football from the University of Notre Dame.

In 1974 Montana played under the tutelage of Notre Dame Coach Dan Divine who "was not impressed by how Joe performed in practice." Yet during 1975-76, his second season, Joe's legendary football activities began, and they began to call him "the comeback kid." In one particular game, in his appearance during the 4th quarter, trailing 14-6, he suddenly became responsible for bringing his team in an heroic effort to a 21-14 victory over North Carolina. Again that year, the Air Force Academy was leading 30-10; and, after Joe had entered the game during the second half, within eight minutes he threw three touchdown passes winning the game 31-30.

Montana sat out in the 1976 season because of his first shoulder separation. When he returned in the 1977 season, he was the third-string quarterback. Once again, when he entered in the fourth quarter, trailing Purdue 24-10, Joe Montana brought the Fighting Irish back to winning another come-from-behind victory 31-24. This significant success encouraged Coach Divine to let Joe appear as the starting quarterback to finish the season.

As the starter, he led Notre Dame to first place in the National Collegiate standings, bringing his team in 1977 to a highly coveted national championship and to back-to-back Cotton Bowl victories in 1978 and 1979. In the 1978 Cotton Bowl, the Fighting Irish, under Montana's lead upset the unbeaten, first-rated, Texas 38-10. Notre Dame was "voted number-one team by the Associated Press and the United Press International polls."

Another amazing game came in 1978 against Pittsburgh. While trailing 17-7 with eight minutes remaining, Joe completed fifteen of twenty-five passes and won the game 26-17. This was the kind of miracle finish to which even his schoolmates became accustomed. In the same season, with forty-two seconds left against University of Southern California, he turned the score around from 24-6 to 27-25, to lose by a last second goal.

Once again, Notre Dame went to the

Cotton Bowl in Joe's last year, 1979. During that game, Montana, although terribly ill, came into the game late in the third quarter with Houston leading 34-12. He brought his team to a 35-34 victory in the final seconds. Upon his graduation from University of Notre Dame as a business major, Joe Montana, though confident, was not drafted until after the second round in the 1979 pro draft. Finally, after a third round decision, he was called in by Bill Walsh, the newly signed general manager and coach of the San Francisco football team. Coach Walsh also shared the same confidence in Joe Montana and wanted him on the team.

In 1979 the 49ers experienced a lackluster season of 2-14 with Montana making only brief appearances on the field. Bill Walsh and quarterback Coach Wyche then expertly worked Joe Montana into their offensive system to create a winning team. The team leaders, in addition to grooming Joe Montana, also worked closely with another rookie receiver, Dwight Clark. The remaining 1979 season was the last season where Joe was a back-up quarterback. Soon Coach Walsh started edging Montana into the number one starter position with Dwight Clark as his main receiver.

On December 7, 1980, Joe Montana established himself as the new field leader in a game against the New Orleans Saints. With the Saints leading in the second half, he led San Francisco in four touchdown drives, two by his pinpoint passing and two on the ground. The game went into overtime and Joe engineered a fifty-five yard drive that ended with the winning goal. For most football spectators, this game probably remains the greatest second-half in NFL history. The 1980 season ended with a 6-10 record for the 49ers and with great expectations for Joe.

During the 1981 season, Steve DeBerg was traded to the Denver Broncos leaving Montana as the lead man. By mid-season, Montana was to have "his first great season and also helped lead San Francisco to the National Football Conference (NFC) West Division title." The 49ers won the NFC West with thirteen wins, their most ever. Joe Montana's ability to throw on the run was his forte. This was again brought to light during the 1982 playoffs against the Dallas Cowboys. Joe brought his team eighty-nine yards with a last second on-the-run pass to Dwight Clark.

He was indeed responsible for bringing the 49ers to Super Bowl XVI. They eventually played the Super Bowl on January 24, 1982 against the Cincinnati Bengals and won 26-21. That year Joe was named Most Valuable Player of the game, and historically it was a most memorable game. During the first half, the 49ers put together the longest drive in Super Bowl history with ninety-two yards and a one-yard rush by Montana going into the second half with the Bengals 20-0. The Bengals rallied to a close score 26-21. It still remains one of the most exciting Super Bowl games ever.

In addition to bringing the 49ers to a total of four Super Bowl victories in the 1980s and being selected Super Bowl MVP twice, Joe Montana has set at least five NFL records and has earned over twenty awards and honors bestowed by both the football establishment and the nationwide media polls and surveys. He is surely a sports hero and a great tribute to his Italian heritage.

General Sources:
1. *Current Biography Yearbook*. New York: Wilson, 1983.
2. Montana, Joe, and Dick Schaap. *Montana*. Atlanta: Turner Pub., 1995.
3. Montana, Joe, and Richard Weiner. *Joe Montana's Art and Magic of Quarterbacking*. New York: Henry Holt, 1997.
4. Spence, Jim. *Joe Montana, the Comeback Kid*. Vero Beach, FL: Rourke Press, 1995.

—by DENNIS PIASIO

WILLIE MOSCONI (1913-1993)

William Joseph Mosconi, the billiards superstar, was born in Philadelphia, Pennsylvania on June 27, 1913. He was the oldest child of Helen (nee Reilly) and Joseph Mosconi, a tavern and billiard parlor owner and former prize fighter. Willie had four brothers, Charles, John, Joseph, and Louis, and a sister Marie. Surprisingly, his father would never allow young Willie to play billiards, and he made certain that the billiard balls and cue sticks were locked up at night. Willie had two uncles who were successful dancers in vaudeville, and Willie's father wanted him someday to go into show business with his uncles—not end up with billiards. At age six, Willie reluctantly became his uncles' pupil in dance.

One day, his uncle Charley challenged Willie to a game of pool. In an amazing feat, young Willie ran off 15 balls into the pockets. This inevitably led his father to discover that Willie used to practice at night at a very late hour creatively using a broomstick as a cue and potatoes as billiard balls. Suddenly aware of his son's talents, Joseph Mosconi aggressively arranged a series of exhibition matches for his six-year-old son.

The most memorable of these matches involved a game where young Willie was competing with a ten-year-old, Ruth McGinnis, in Philadelphia's National Billiard Academy where he ran 40 balls in the first round. After playing in a few more exhibitions, Willie "retired" at the age of seven as he had gotten "sick of the game," and he was ever mindful of the fact that his father had gone from one extreme to the other.

Young Mosconi graduated from Barrett Junior High School in 1931 and enrolled in Banks Business College. When both of his parents became seriously ill, he left school altogether and took a job as an upholsterer's apprentice. He did piecework and earned $40 per week, a relatively large sum for Depression days. After a disagreement with his foreman, he lost his job. On his way home that day, he saw a sign advertising a billiard tournament. He entered it and won the $75 first prize. Willie was suddenly on his way to becoming the greatest pocket billiard champion of his time.

In 1932 Mosconi played under the sponsorship of Izzie Goodman, the owner of the Fox Billiard Academy. In 1933 he represented them in a divisional tournament in Philadelphia. He won it and then went on to win the sectional tournament in New York City. Later, he went to Minneapolis for the National Championship and finished fourth. Willie soon signed on with Clyde Storer of the Brunswick Corporation. At twenty years of age in the height of the depression years, he was earning $600 per month becoming the youngest member of a 21-man billiard staff. This is when he realized how much money could be made in billiards.

His first job for Brunswick entailed going on a 112-day tour within Ralph Greenleaf who was then the world's billiard champion. Mosconi later revealed that he had learned a lot from Greenleaf, including from his mistakes. On tour, Greenleaf won 57 matches to Mosconi's 50. By the end of the tour Mosconi proved that he had learned his lessons well. In the following years Mosconi was almost always on tour, and it had become a tiring yet prosperous way of life. Willie played in world tournaments between 1933 and 1938. He always played well but never enough to win at the highest level. During 1939 it appeared that general interest in billiards was dropping and, more so, within Willie. He ended his contract with Brunswick and went on Hollywood where he spent a rather restless year.

In 1940 Bob McGirr, one of New York's biggest billiard operators agreed to sponsor Mosconi in the six-month tournament for the 1941 world championship. After winning the 1941 title in a memorable performance, Mosconi made the sport headlines. He had won the crown by an unheard of 32 games and by having 59 runs of 100 or more balls in his total of 224 games. Willie then lost the title for awhile and quickly regained it in November of 1942. World War II had already been a harsh and demanding reality, and Willie like so many others went into military service, and for the duration of the war he served in the special services of the Army.

When he was discharged in 1945 with a T-5 classification, he had seen himself as broke, and he stated that he was "sick of life in general and the billiard game in particular." He wanted a title match soon but only because he needed to make some money. When C.P. Binner, Brunswick's promotional manager, picked up on what Mosconi had said, he offered Mosconi an enticing long-range contract. In 1949 Mosconi lost the world championship title he had won to Jimmy Caras; finally, six years later in 1955 when Irving Crane held the world's champion crown, Mosconi in a challenge match regained the precious title he had once lost.

Perhaps Mosconi's greatest contribution to the game was his ability to have popularized it especially during the second half of the twentieth century through exhibitions and promotional interviews. In addition, partly on Mosconi's suggestions, Brunswick began to design billiard table surfaces with cloth covers in decorator colors like white, gold, blue, and tangerine rather than traditional green. The move was aimed at eradicating from the public's mind the unfortunate reputation the pool halls suggested. Mosconi also favored making table pockets the largest allowable sizes so as to minimize the frustration of the pool player's desire to pocket the ball.

In the early 1950s, Mosconi, who was earning about $50,000 a year, continued to give exhibitions where he generously demonstrated his "trick shots" which to this day his video-taped recordings of those shots still fascinate viewing audiences. In 1957 he suffered a stroke which influenced his decision to slow down his pace. Mosconi later became technical advisor on the set in the production of the now classic film, *The Hustler* (1961), which starred Paul Newman, Jackie Gleason, and George C. Scott.

Among his other credits, Willie Mosconi wrote three books one of which is entitled *Willie Mosconi on Pocket Billiards* where he traces the game of billiards back to fifteenth-century Europe to its royal—game of kings—origins in a concise style and in great detail. Mosconi also owned and operated an establishment called the Superior Billiard Academy in north Philadelphia, and he was proud that his clientele consisted mainly of college students.

Willie Mosconi died in 1993 at 80 years of age, and he will be remembered as he was, usually pictured in a business suit playing the game. Mosconi brought to the sport not only his expertise but also his inimitable style. He returned class and elegance to a game that had once begun as a sport of kings.

General Sources:
1. *Current Biography Yearbook*. New York: Wilson, 1963; 1993.
2. Mosconi, Willie. *Willie Mosconi on Pocket Billiards*. New York: Crown Trade Paperbacks, 1995.
3. Mosconi, Willie. *Willie's Game: An Autobiography*. New York: Macmillan, 1993.
4. Mosconi, Willie. *Winning Pocket Billiards*. New York: Crown Publ., 1965.
5. "Obituary." *New York Times* 18 Sept. 1993: 9.

—by DENNIS PIASIO

261

JOHN J. MUCCIO (1900-1989)

A career diplomat who had spanned most of the globe in his many years of service for the United States, John Muccio served at many ambassadorial posts in the Far East, including assignments in Hong Kong, South Korea; in many South and Central American countries, and in several European countries. After World War II, he served as delegate to the United Nations trusteeship council and to posts in Europe.

A highly respected representative of the United States government, he had spent forty consecutive years working in the U.S. Foreign Service. He served with the service both before and through World War II, during the Korean War, and throughout the 1950s when cold war tensions began to escalate. When he retired in 1961, he acquired the rank of career minister, the highest rank achievable in the American Foreign Service.

John Joseph Muccio was born in Italy in Valle Agricola on March 19, 1900. While John was still an infant, his parents decided to immigrate to the United States. They made their new home in Providence, Rhode Island. When John became of age, he eventually attended a local grammar school, and after completing high school, he entered Brown University. In 1918 before finishing the requirements for his degree, he served in the United States Army. He later graduated from Brown in 1921 with a degree in philosophy.

After graduation in June he applied for his naturalization papers so that he could enter the Foreign Service. With his papers in order, he entered the Foreign Service consular assistant program, which involved taking a two-year course of study at George Washington University. After receiving his M.A. degree in 1923, he was finally assigned the rank of Foreign Service Officer. His first assignment took him to Hamburg, Germany where he was titled vice-consul.

After serving two years in Germany, he was transferred in 1926 to the Far East for nine years. During that time his assignments took him to many places, but he spent most of his time in Hong Kong (2 years) and in Shanghai (four years). As a sequel to his nine-year assignment in the Far East, Muccio was sent in 1935 for another series of nine years to South and Central America, including posts in Bolivia, Panama, Nicaragua, and Cuba (Havana).

At the conclusion of WWII, he returned to Germany as assistant to Robert Murphy who was then political adviser on German affairs. After returning to Washington in 1946, he was sent once more to the Far East and assigned to the Inspector Corps of the Foreign Service whose responsibilities included increased travel and supervisory roles.

By the late 1940s, John Muccio had experienced over twenty-five years in the Foreign Service. By now a seasoned diplomat, John Muccio's Asian itinerary was re-routed by President Truman to the troubled area of Korea. Muccio was appointed the first United States Ambassador to South Korea on August 12, 1948. With the conclusion of World War II and the defeat and expulsion of the Japanese occupational forces from China, Communism took hold in most of southeast Asia. Intervention by the United Nations had created a Korea that was divided politically into North and South. North Korea was Communist, and South Korea was in the process of developing a government that was basically modeled on Western democracies.

In essence, John Muccio, an American civilian, replaced Lieutenant General John R. Hodges who had been the commander of the military government in South Korea from 1945-1948 when there was no Korean civilian government in place. Now with South Korea's newly elected government coming of age in a return to civilian control in 1948, it was John Muccio's mission as American ambassador to guarantee—from a United States perspective—the implementation of the United Nations resolutions insuring South Korea's right to self-determination and independence.

As America's highest ranking representative in South Korea, John Muccio handled the introduction and supervision of the United States economic assistance through the Economic Cooperation Administration program to South Korea. The economic accords were signed in late 1948 with Syngman Rhee as South Korea's first president. By early 1949, South Korea seemed to be well on the way to establishing "internal stability," and so Muccio was at the beginning of discussing the implementation of American military personnel withdrawal.

Yet by the end of the same year in the eyes of the American government, some major unacceptable reversals had taken place in South Korea's political and economic behavior. Syngman Rhee had postponed the democratic elections scheduled for May 1950, and its seems that the South Korean government's excessive expenditure of funds was causing unnecessarily high inflation on its fledgling democratic society. America threatened to cut off future aid because of South Korea's indiscretions. Muccio negotiated with the Korean government and by June of 1950 these problems were laid to rest.

In the same year, Muccio signed an agreement with South Korea amounting to $10 million in military aid. Yet with recent military tensions mounting in the territory that divided North from South Korea, Muccio who all along had feared an all-out invasion from the north urged Congress to increase military aid to South Korea.

On June 25, 1950, Muccio's worst fears were confirmed as North Korea attacked South Korea. This constituted the beginning of the Korean War that was euphemistically called the "Korean Conflict." Overnight, Muccio directed the evacuation of embassy personnel from Seoul. He remained among the last in the embassy while awaiting orders for his relocation to safer quarters in South Korea.

On July 13, 1950, Dean Acheson, Secretary of State, offered Muccio a commendation for his "courageous and effective performance of duty" during the crisis in Korea. On October 15 of the same year, on Wake Island (Pacific) President Truman, who had personally appointed Muccio to Korea's ambassadorship, conferred upon Muccio the Medal for Merit "for valor and courageous devotion to duty and superlative diplomatic skill."

Later in October, he returned to the United States to confer with various United Nations committees regarding Korea. His future assignments took him once more to Europe as ambassador to Iceland and then to Central America as ambassador to Guatemala. He retired in 1961 with the rank of career minister and resided in Washington, D.C. At eighty-nine years of age, John Muccio died at his home on May 19, 1989, survived by his wife and four children. Both to his family and to his country, he left a legacy of dedication, loyalty, and courage.

General Sources:
1.   *Current Biography/Yearbook*. New York: Wilson, 1951; 1989.
2.   *Newsweek* 13 Nov. 1950: 34.
3.   "Obituary." *New York Times* 22 May 1989: D11.
4.   *Who's Who in America*. 1950-51 ed.
5.   *Who's Who in New England*. 1949 ed.

—by PEGGY M. BOMPADRE

MICHAEL ANGELO MUSMANNO
(1897-1968)

Michael Angelo Musmanno was a person of many talents. A decorated hero of WWII, he was a judge at the well-known Nuremberg Trials of the post-WWII era where he presided over the largest trial consisting of twenty Nazi defendants. He authored sixteen books dealing with labor justice, constitutional issues, the Sacco and Vanzetti case, and the Holocaust. He also had two of them made into movies, *Black Fury* in 1935 and *The Last Ten Days* (1956).

He was born in 1897 in Stowe Township, Pennsylvania on the Ohio River outside of Pittsburgh. His father Antonio and his mother, Maddelena (nee Castellucci) Musmanno, were both Italian emigrants. Initially his father was a coal miner, then a railroad section hand, and, later in life, a policeman. As a young man, Michael aspired to become a lawyer as he demonstrated aptitude for logical argument, debate, and analysis.

Despite hard work as a coal loader, Michael managed to take law courses in the evening school at Georgetown University in Washington, D.C. His studies were interrupted by World War I where he served as an infantryman. After the war, he continued his course work at Georgetown, completing all the requirements for a Bachelor of Law degree; later, he went on to earn several other degrees totaling seven, which were obtained from five different universities.

Musmanno was admitted to the Pennsylvania bar in 1923, and despite his rich and varied preparation, he found it difficult to obtain a position as a new, young lawyer in an established firm. After writing an article, which to his elation the *New York Times* had published,

he secured a job at the firm of John R. K. Scott, a highly respected establishment in the Philadelphia area. While working for Scott's firm, Musmanno won the first forty-two cases that he had tried. Yet, after losing a mere five out of sixty-five cases that he had defended, he had doubts about himself, and so he decided to resign from Scott's firm. Feeling uncertain about his future in law, he left the United States and sailed for Italy in 1924.

On his visit to Italy, Musmanno became a frequent observer of the Italian court system operations, and within a few weeks he soon realized his irrepressible love for law. Deciding to stay in Rome, she studied Roman law at the University of Rome. He worked part-time as an English tutor, a news correspondent, and even as an extra in the MGM motion picture of *Ben Hur*, released in 1926. After he had fulfilled the degree requirements, he was awarded a *Dottore di Giurisprudenza* (Doctor of Jurisprudence) degree in 1925, having received the "highest possible score." Before returning to the U.S., Musmanno traveled to Paris and to London.

He began his private practice in Pittsburgh that same year. After a difficult start, he did establish a clientele and became known as the "champion of the underprivileged." In the celebrated 1927 court case, he became one of the members of the defense team for Nicola Sacco and Bartolomeo Vanzetti, who were convicted of murder. Though the legal defense proved unsuccessful for their clients, Musmanno would eventually write a "defense" of Sacco and Vanzetti in his 1939 book, *After Twelve Years.*

Musmanno's initial attempt at gaining public office in 1926 proved unsuccessful, but in

1928, once elected, he became the youngest state assemblyman in Pennsylvania after having to combat much prejudice against his Italian name. Reelected in 1930, he worked hard during his tenure to repeal the Coal and Iron Police Laws. After Musmanno had dramatized (in the form of a short story) the fatal beating of a miner by a policeman siding with a coal mining establishment, Musmanno's literary work became the subject of a 1935 Hollywood movie entitled *Black Fury.*

In 1932, he was elected judge of the Allegheny County Court. Two years later, after receiving the largest number of votes ever obtained by a local candidate, he was elected judge of the Court of Common Pleas. He served on the bench until the attack on Pearl Harbor. Musmanno was then commissioned in the United States Navy as lieutenant commander, and eventually he would rise to the rank of rear admiral. Because of his knowledge of the Italian language and Italy, he served in the Mediterranean in the invasion of Italy in 1943. While there, he served under General Mark Clark, and for six months, was military governor of Italy's Sorrentine peninsula. Twice wounded, he received many military decorations, including the Purple Heart, the Bronze Star for Valor, Legion of Merit, and many others.

Immediately following the war in Europe, he was assigned to a commission to investigate the veracity of Hitler's death. He interviewed over 200 Nazis many of whom were among Hitler's top brass. These interviews constituted the basis of another book that he wrote in 1950 which was entitled *Ten Days to Die.* As in the case of his short story, Hollywood would make a movie of this book in 1956, renaming it *The Last Ten Days.* In 1946, President Truman appointed Musmanno as one of the judges in the famous Nuremberg trials. Of that series of trials, Musmanno presided over the largest one, which was comprised of over twenty Nazi defendants. It was the *Einsatzgruppen* case, the members of which were charged with the murder of over one million Jews.

When Musmanno returned to the United States, he resumed his bench at the Court of Common Pleas until 1951. Then, elected judge to the Pennsylvania Supreme Court for a twenty-one year term, he became its first member of Italian descent. In 1961, the attorney general of Israel invited Musmanno to testify as a witness for the prosecution against Adolf Eichmann. He testified using information he had obtained from his WWII interviews with Herrmann Goering, Josef Goebbels, Martin Bormann, and Joachim von Ribbentrop. His testimony proved to be critical in incriminating Eichmann.

Musmanno spent his later years with persistent energy. When he died in 1968, he was still working avidly on his writings, and he had to his credit no less than sixteen books. He was highly immersed in history especially with the intricate issues of American constitutional law, and he enjoyed nonfictional narratives. A recipient of numerous awards, he was elected right before his death a fellow of the International Academy of Law and Sciences. Michael Angelo Musmanno who accomplished so much in one lifetime stands as a colossus of human dignity, justice, and humanitarianism.

General Sources:

1. *Current Biography Yearbook.* New York: Wilson, 1967; 1968.
2. Musmanno, Michael Angelo. *The Story of the Italians in America.* Garden City, NY: Doubleday, 1965.
3. Musmanno, Michael Angelo. *Ten Days to Live.* Garden City, NY: Doubleday, 1950.
4. Musmanno, Michael Angelo. *Verdict.* Garden City, NY: Doubleday, 1958.
5. "Obituary." *New York Times* 13 Oct. 1968.
6. *Who's Who in America.* 1966-67.

—by PETER PAUL FRANCO, M.D.

AMEDEO OBICI (1877-1947)

Amedeo Obici, the genius behind the Planters peanut empire in the United States, was born to Pietro and Carlotta (nee Sartor) Obici on July 15, 1877 in Odezo, Treviso, Italy. When his father died in 1884, Amedeo was only seven years of age. He was the oldest of four children, and despite his young age, he helped to support his family. Four years later in 1888, at age 11, he traveled alone to America to live with his mother's brother Victor in Scranton, PA. He lived with his uncle and worked hard in his ensuing teenage years. He would not get married until 1916 at age 39 to Louise Musante.

Amedeo attended school as a youngster, but it was short-lived. It seems that traditional education was apparently not to his liking at the time. He simply preferred working. In the Wilkes-Barre area of Pennsylvania, his first jobs included working in a cigar factory and later in a produce market. Young Amedeo then took to working as a barkeeper for Billy McLaughlin. While employed there he came to learn a great deal, and for a few years McLaughlin became his mentor helping him to improve his English and even introducing him to Shakespeare's writings.

Unfortunately, McLaughlin died by the time Obici reached seventeen years of age. Obici thereby lost one of the best relationships he had made in America and by now had experienced his second major loss in his personal life after his father's death. By the time Obici was nineteen, he had been so frugal and responsible that he saved enough money to bring his mother and two sisters to America in 1896. Obici had also made the decision to go into business for himself. While working for others he had made it a point to gather business insight. From his experience and observations, he had logically deduced that people were more apt to

make nickel purchases than dollar purchases since they viewed paper currency as hard-earned money but coins, especially small coins, more expendable. It was upon this premise that he would build his empire. He began by spending $4.50 for a simple peanut roasting machine. He built a stand and put up a sign that read "The Peanut Specialist." He began by selling small bags of roasted peanuts for a nickel.

Since this became his business, part of the procedure involved spending long periods of time insuring that the peanuts would not burn in the roasting process. One day, he got the novel idea to use a small fan motor and a series of pulleys to turn the peanuts over to prevent their getting overcooked or burnt on any one side. Throughout his lifetime it was his firm belief that it was he who had independently invented the first electrically operated peanut roaster.

Obici's next idea was promotional in nature. He had randomly placed coupons with the letters of his name in his roasted peanuts bags. When a person returned and could spell out his name Amedeo Obici, he would give away a watch that was valued at one dollar. It was reported that he had given away 10,000-20,000 watches before his lengthy promotional campaign would come to an end. To boost his sales, he subsequently introduced salted peanuts and then candied peanuts in his product line.

By 1907 his business was doing so well that together with Mario Peruzzi they founded the Planters Nut and Chocolate Company in Wilkes-Barre. They established delivery routes with draught animals, and during that same year, the company added a peanut candy bar to its product line as Obici always attempted to expand his business. In the ensuing years, he discovered that people preferred Virginia peanuts over Spanish peanuts. By 1910 he added chocolate covered nuts to his line hoping to secure more company stability and growth by offering a greater variety of products.

By 1912, the company showed its first net profit, and it paid out its first dividend to its stockholders. Experimentation and learning were Obici's catalysts for expansion. He learned the real estate business in order to buy buildings for his growing enterprise. He also invented a method for blanching the red skins of the peanuts. He had a sales force that did house-to-house free-sample promotions. A major move forward occurred in 1913 when Obici and Peruzzi purchased a peanut cleaning plant in Suffolk, Virginia. Within two years, leaving behind only the executive offices in Wilkes-Barre, they consolidated their assets by establishing in Virginia the entire manufacturing process of the business from cleaning, roasting, and can-packaging to distribution.

To make absolutely sure that his work as "The Peanut Specialist" would not be forgotten, he ingeniously utilized groups of school children as a resource for new ideas in the promotion of his peanut products on a commercial level. One child drew a peanut shell with a head and legs. Obici embellished the drawing with top hat, spats, and cane to create the emblem of Mr. Peanut, still seen today on Planters products.

By 1917 Planters first commercial ads were visible in the *Saturday Evening Post* and in similar magazines. Peanut products as we know them today had already become a common household word. Obici's business continued to flourish as San Francisco saw the opening of its first factory in 1921; and Toronto, Canada its first factory opening in 1924. Obici and Peruzzi expanded their operations by buying out other peanut companies.

New products were added to their product line that by now included peanut oil and an American favorite: peanut butter. Obici, always concerned with the well-being of his employees, had built in 1925 for his workers a club for R&R after work hours. Despite the depression of the 30s, the Planters Nut and Chocolate Company continued to expand in grand fashion with the addition of the Planters Edible Oil Company and the National Peanut Corp. which had thirty-five stores in operation. Despite the expansion in the development of new products, Obici concentrated on the sale of salted peanuts. His hunch was confirmed when he compared his 1937 sales of twenty-five million pounds of salted nuts with his 1940 sales of 100 million pounds.

Amedeo Obici was a member of many organizations including the Christopher Columbus Society, the Masons, and the Italo-American Society of Wilkes-Barre, PA. He also became director of the Farmers Bank of Nansemond, the town in which he had his estate. When Obici died on May 21, 1947, his company employed 2,000 people and grossed $40 million that year. Obici, an extraordinary entrepreneur, who, from his initial purchase of a $4.50 peanut roaster, made his dream a reality by treating each situation as an opportunity for growth, one nickel at a time. In Italy, it is no surprise that peanuts whose Italian equivalent is "arachidi," are referred to by the less technical and more endearing term "noccioline americane," or little American nuts.

General Sources:
1. DiStasi, Lawrence, ed. *The Big Book of Italian Culture*. New York: HarperCollins, 1990.
2. Mangione, Jerre, and Ben Morreale. *La Storia: Five Centuries of the Italian American Experience*. New York: HarperCollins, 1992.
3. *The National Cyclopedia of American Biography*. Vol. XXXVI. New York: James T. White, 1950.
4. "Obituary." *New York Times* 22 May 1947: 27.

—by LINDA D'ANDREA-MARINO

267

AL PACINO (1940-   )

Winner of an Obie Award for the Off-Broadway production of *The Indian Wants the Bronx* (1967-68), Al Pacino also went on to receive two Tony Awards, one for *Does a Tiger Wear a Necktie?* (1969) and another for *The Basic Training of Pavlo Hummel* (1977). Nominated several times for Best Actor at the Oscar presentations for his role in such films as *The Godfather Part II* (1974), *Serpico* (1973), *And Justice for All* (1979), he would eventually capture an Oscar for his performance in *Scent of a Woman* in 1992. Both in the theater and on the screen, he has rightfully earned respect and admiration for his superb acting in those especially difficult antiheroic leading roles where understatement often becomes a critical acting component.

Alfred James "Sonny" Pacino, of Sicilian descent, was born on April 25, 1940 in East Harlem, New York. He was the only child born of Salvatore and Rose Pacino. His father, a mason, left his family when Al was only two years old, leaving his mother Rose to cope with the upbringing of their child. Since she had to go to work to support him, they moved from their furnished apartment in Harlem to her parents, James and Kate Gerard, in a poor area in the Bronx not far from the Bronx Zoo.

Pacino spent his growing years in the Bronx. He was not studious in grammar school, but he showed talent, and it involved his enjoyment in acting out scenes from the movies that he had usually seen the night before with his mother. After seeing Pacino act in an eighth grade drama, a teacher of his voiced her opinion that he had "the fire of the great Sicilian actors." His mother was also instrumental in encouraging him to follow his acting abilities.

Despite poor grades, Al was voted "most likely to succeed" in junior high school because of his apparently good acting abilities. His scholastic levels were surely low, but on the strong and insistent recommendation of his drama teacher, he was accepted in Manhattan's High School of Performing Arts. Spending two years at this school did little for Pacino because he was failing in his scholastic areas. Eventually, after his mother became ill, Pacino dropped out of school. At the age of sixteen, he began to work to help support the household as a messenger, supermarket checker, office boy, and a variety of small jobs. With time he became restless and left home, moving in with a girl in another part of the Bronx. He sent money home to his mother assuring her that he'd succeed.

At age nineteen, Pacino moved to Greenwich Village where he had the good fortune to meet Charlie Laughton, an acting coach at the Herbert Berghof Studio, who would sponsor Al's apprenticeship at the studio. Ten years Al's senior, Laughton introduced him to writers, directors, and many others involved in the theater. Laughton foresaw a great future for Pacino as Al picked up bit acting parts over the next few years. The retention of the surname Pacino seemed apparently unsuitable at that time for many reasons, and so Al Pacino decided to use the stage name of "Sonny Scott."

At 22, Pacino suffered a major blow when his mother Rose, then 43, passed away. Al went to pieces only to suffer more when a year later his grandfather also passed away. After periods of excessive drinking, he resumed acting, picking up bit parts over the next few years. At age 26, the Actors Studio accepted Pacino for training where he began to receive more opportunities, and that December he'd appeared in a play with James Earl Jones.

Finally, in 1968, at the age of 28, Pacino played a role in an Off-Broadway play *The Indian Wants the Bronx*. It was a one-act play about two hoodlums who terrorize an old Indian man. After a run of 204 performances in New York City, Pacino won an Obie as Best Actor for that play in its Off-Broadway production for the 1967-68 season. Success had suddenly come to Pacino, and it would steadily grow, eventually leading him to Hollywood studios.

In February 1969, Pacino made his Broadway debut playing the role of a psychotic junkie in *Does a Tiger Wear a Necktie?* Despite the play's brief run of thirty-nine performances and the theater critics' less-than-enthusiastic appraisals of the play, they nonetheless extolled Pacino's brilliant portrayal of the suicidal and sadistic psychotic in a drug rehabilitation center. For this role he earned himself the coveted Antoinette Perry (Tony) Award in 1969 as the Best Dramatic Actor in a supporting role. Shortly thereafter, a *Variety* poll of drama critics proclaimed him the "most promising new Broadway actor."

In the same year, Pacino made his film debut in *Me, Natalie,* a rather unsuccessful film where Pacino played the role of a junkie once more. In 1971, two years later, he starred in *The Panic in Needle Park,* the story of a drug-addicted couple during a supposedly temporary shortage of drugs in New York City. Again, despite the critics' mixed reviews of the movie, Pacino came out with flying colors for his remarkable interpretation of the role. It was reported that, after viewing only a twelve-minute segment of that movie, Paramount Pictures executives concurred in considering Pacino for the role of Michael Corleone in Coppola's movie version of *The Godfather* (1972).

To many critics and moviegoers, he seemed born for the part of Michael Corleone, completing the movie trilogy in *The Godfather II* (1974) and *The Godfather III* (1990). He went on to be nominated for Best Supporting Actor for that role in *The Godfather* and later was nominated for Best Actor for his role in *Serpico* (1973), the story of an incorruptible New York City cop. After his role in *The Godfather*, his outstanding performance in his next movie in the starring role of *Scarecrow* (1973), the touching story of a luckless drifter, was instrumental in making that movie tie for first place in the May 1973 Cannes Film Festival. Taking a short respite from his screen successes, he appeared once more on Broadway in 1977 in *The Basic Training of Pavlo Hummel*, winning his second Tony Award.

While completing *The Godfather* trilogy, Pacino also appeared in several critically-acclaimed successes. They consisted of films such as *Dog Day Afternoon* (1975), *Scarface* (1983), *Sea of Love* (1989), *Frankie and Johnny* (1991), and *Scent of a Woman* (1992). In his career he had been nominated many times for an Academy Award, and finally in 1993 he won an Oscar for Best Actor in *Scent of a Woman.*

He remains today one of the most sought after actors in the film industry. His incredibly dynamic and electrifying style of acting is often immersed in difficult and realistic settings. Typically, he deals with one of the two ends of the societal spectrum in relation to power: the vulnerable and the commanding. From humble beginnings, Al Pacino has skyrocketed to the top of the film industry and the theater as a highly respected professional actor.

General Sources:

1. *Contemporary Theatre, Film and Television*. Detroit, MI: Gale Research, 1995.
2. *Current Biography Yearbook*. New York: Wilson, 1974.
3. Schoell, William. *The Films of Al Pacino*. Secaucus, NJ: Carol Pub., 1995.
4. Yule, Andrew. *Life on the Wire: The Life and Art of Al Pacino*. New York: D.I. Fine, 1991.

—by EDWARD MOTTOLA, Jr.

CAMILLE PAGLIA (1947-   )

After teaching college English in relative obscurity for twenty years, she quickly became a controversial personality when Yale Press decided to print her book *Sexual Personae: Art and Decadence from Nefertiti to Emily Dickinson*. Once just a manuscript that had been rejected for nine years by the publishing industry, it became a bestseller in 1990. Utilizing patterns of thought that availed themselves of the paradoxical elements in human existence, her prose typically invades practically everyone's comfort zone. Many hail her as a charismatic scholar and author. Her style might describe her at one moment reactionary, yet moments later liberal; and a feminist and, then, an anti-feminist. In all, she is complicated and always thought-provoking as she has a strong and exacting grasp of human history's vagaries and intricacies. She is generally characterized as a very controversial feminist, yet she is also feminism's severest critic.

Camille Paglia, born in Endicott, New York on April 2, 1947, had been an only child for fourteen years until one day her parents presented her with a sister Lenora, who is today an art conservator. Her father, Pasquale Paglia was a professor of Romance languages at the Jesuit Le Moyne College in Syracuse, New York. Her mother, Lydia, born in Ceccano, Italy, immigrated to the U. S. at the age of six.

Camille attended public schools in Syracuse. She received her undergraduate degree, *summa cum laude,* in English in 1968 from Harper College of SUNY at Binghamton. She obtained her Ph.D. in English in 1974 from Yale University where she was a Woodrow Wilson Fellowship Designate. She taught at Bennington College 1972-80; and subsequently, at Wesleyan University, at Yale University, and also at the University of New Haven before joining the Philadelphia College of Performing Arts (now the University of Arts) in 1984.

While at Yale, Paglia had as her mentor the renowned literary critic, Harold Bloom. He supervised her doctoral dissertation, *Sexual Personae*, and despite his continual support of her book, she met rejection time and time again. Dr. Paglia contends that her difficulties in finding a publisher were due to her criticism of the so-called politically correct liberal academic establishment. Yet she welcomed challenges to her ideas, particularly to one of her main themes, such as her conviction that "Judeo-Christianity never did defeat paganism, which still flourishes in art, eroticism, astrology and pop culture." It was this kind of statement that had touched a sensitive nerve in the intellectual "body" of Western thought; and, it proved to be too difficult to handle for many intellectuals. Finally in 1985, the first of two volumes was accepted by Yale University Press but would not be published until 1990.

It became a bestseller and was nominated for a National Book Critics Circle Award. Among her many controversial ideas, she championed a major educational reform by advocating a return to the classics and by endorsing an abolition of all feminist studies. The descriptive reactions to her book varied widely with adjectives such as brilliant, provocative, pagan, politically incorrect, and downright nasty.

For instance, her tantalizing statement: "I reaffirm and celebrate women's ancient mystery and glamour. I see the mother as an overwhelming force who condemns men to lifelong sexual anxiety from which they escape through rationalism and physical achievements," had feminist critics raging in that she had obviously written such ideas as a backlash to the women's movement. In contrast to the recent feminist perspectives, Paglia emphatically insisted that women should openly acknowledge the existence of male strength and men's achievements throughout history.

Camille's father encouraged her to pursue her ideas which ironically led her to reject many of his own ideas. She professes that her strong and determined character specifically resulted from her grandmothers who cared for her while her mother worked in banking. She also states that in another vein her mother's energy, optimism, and practicality also contributed to her personality. She attributes her intellectuality, studiousness, and severity to her father's personality. She credits her Italian heritage for her capacity for hard work; and her organizational abilities are attributed to the "ancient Roman genius" for administration.

Paglia believes that the experiences in her maturation process have made her a "better role model for women today than all these sex phobic feminists." With confidence, she assaults the modern feminist tendency toward beliefs that have summarily blamed men for the historical situation in which women find themselves today. Her thoughts provoke much controversy, and it is no surprise that counterattacks to her thoughts come especially from women. Yet she claims to desire only "to restore women to their unique power and vibrant potency," says her literary agent Lynn Nesbit. Dr. Paglia has managed to pierce through the armor of lifestyles and genres, and undauntedly she has fathomed the depths of thought from the most sacred of ideological abodes such as theological to the most corporeal of ideological abodes such as sexology.

At the core of Paglia's thought lies the essential psychic dualism that views the male and his drives as typically geared towards what Freud had best described as sublimation, i.e., the drive towards creativity and overcoming nature; the female counterpart, instead, gets more typically reflected towards the achievement of homeostasis or dynamic equilibrium, i.e., staying closer to the acceptable societal norms. "There is no female Mozart because there is no female Jack the Ripper. Great art and great crime are similar deviations from the norm that require a megalomania, an utter obsession.... Most women have too much empathy to want to be involved in anything like that."

Paglia declares that hard-core feminism has painted itself into the proverbial corner, stuck in its own closed-ended ideology, having wasted too much time trying to create sameness between men and women rather than discussing constructively their differences. According to Paglia, the women's movement has naively missed the dialectic between the sexes and has taken the erroneous route in futilely trying to homogenize everything and everybody.

Paglia's controversial thinking has enriched and expanded the ongoing debate between the various intellectual camps. She stands as a proud example of free thought based on serious scholarship and a healthy respect for challenging any kind of establishment whenever it has gone too far in its purported influence.

General Sources:
1. *Contemporary Literary Criticism.* "Camille Paglia." Detroit, MI: Gale Research, 1992.
2. *Current Biography Yearbook.* New York: Wilson, 1992.
3. Paglia, Camille. *The Birds.* London: BFI Pub., 1998.
4. Paglia, Camille. *Sex, Art, and American Culture: Essays.* New York: Vintage Books, 1992.
5. Paglia, Camille. *Sexual Personae. Art and Decadence from Nefertiti to Emily Dickinson.* New Haven: Yale University Press, 1990.
6. Paglia, Camille. *Vamps & Tramps: New Essays.* New York: Vintage, 1994.

—by NORINA ABRUZZESE SIGONA

LEON PANETTA (1938-   )

After having duly served eight full terms as a U.S. Representative from California's 16th District between 1977 and 1993, Leon Panetta went on to become director of the White House Office of Management and Budget (OMB) in the Clinton administration where after serving for barely a year, he was promoted to the onerous job of White House Chief of Staff in 1994 and served until 1997 when he resigned and returned to private life. He presently teaches at the newly formed California State University at Monterey Bay and writes about political topics on state and national issues.

On June 28, 1938 in Monterey, California, Leon Edward Panetta, the second of two sons, was born to Carmelo Frank Panetta and Carmelina Maria (Prochilo) Panetta. These Calabrian parents had emigrated from Italy to Wyoming to join relatives already living there. Working first as a copper miner, Carmelo Panetta then moved to California with his family and finally settled in Monterey where he opened Carmelo's Cafe, his wife working by his side, and Leon washing dishes. A popular spot with Italian-American servicemen from Fort Ord, Carmelo's ill health forced its sale in 1947. Profits from the sale went towards his next venture, a walnut ranch in Carmel Valley, the locale where Leon and his brother would spend most of their growing years.

Leon Panetta's schooling began at San Carlos Elementary. He went on to graduate Monterey High School (1956), the University of Santa Clara (1960) with a B.A. *magna cum laude*, and then the University of Santa Clara Law School (1963) with a J.D. While in law school, he married Sylvia Maria Varni. They now have three grown sons, Christopher, Carmelo, and James, and one grandchild.

Panetta practiced law in Monterey for one year. From 1964 to 1966, he served in the U.S. Army where he rose from second lieutenant to captain. In addition to his work in Army intelligence, Panetta acted as legal counsel in court martial cases on a volunteer basis. It was at this point in his life that he first experienced outright segregation in housing and public facilities, stationed in Fort Benning, Georgia.

Following his discharge from the Army, his involvement with civil rights issues continued during his work as legislative assistant to U.S. Senator Thomas H. Kuchel of California with his involvement in drafting the open housing bill of 1968. From 1969 to 1970, under the Nixon administration, Panetta served as director of the U.S. Office of Civil Rights where he was responsible for implementing the Civil Rights Act of 1964 barring segregation. His timetable in carrying out desegregation in the south was much shorter than that which President Nixon had envisioned.

This, coupled with John Ehrlichman's statement that "Blacks aren't where the votes are," influenced Leon Panetta to resign the office on February 17, 1970 and to switch from the Republican to the Democratic Party in 1971. In support of Panetta's stand, 125 of the Health, Education, and Welfare civil rights employees signed a protest petition. Panetta was awarded the National Education Association (NEA) Lincoln Award. His service as director of the Office of Civil Rights is recounted in his book *Bring Us Together* written in 1971.

From 1970-1971, Leon Panetta served as executive assistant to Mayor John Lindsay of New York City; and from 1971-1976, he was a partner in Panetta, Thompson & Panetta law firm. In 1976, Panetta was voted into office as a U.S. Representative in what was then California's 16th Congressional District. He continued to win this office by a 71 percent vote or better for a total of sixteen years in the House. Panetta became an expert in budgets and became known as a budgeter. He even purchased some of his office furniture at his own expense and used frequent-flyer bonuses rather than charge the taxpayers for his travel.

During the 1980s, Panetta criticized President Reagan for his policies on defense and foreign policy enterprises; he criticized aid to the Contras in Nicaragua and charged publicly that Colonel Oliver North's operations on behalf of the Contras was illegal. The son of a farmer and a member of the Agriculture Committee, Panetta helped pass the 1986 immigration reform bill that permitted farmers to use illegals to enter California for seasonal agricultural work. This, he insisted, was to protect the illegals from being exploited by farmers.

A recipient of the Bread for the World Award in 1978, 1980, and 1982, Panetta's concern with high unemployment and the fact that many Americans were starving drove the passage of the Hunger Relief Act of 1984 which primarily provided surplus dairy products and emergency shelter to the needy. His work to help hospice patients get Medicare and Medicaid reimbursement won him the National Hospice Organization Award in 1984.

A member of the House Budget Committee from 1979-1985, he was chair from 1989-1992 and was one of the chief players in the 1990 budget summit negotiations. On December 10, 1992, two days after the Democratic Caucus reelected Panetta as chair of the Budget Committee, President Clinton nominated him for director of Office of Management and Budget. Panetta initially enraged officials when he boldly stated that Clinton needed to prioritize elements of his economic plan, but they quietly concurred. Always looking to the long term, Panetta believes that passing a bill to balance the budget won't balance it. Raising taxes and cutting spending in all areas, even those most politically hypersensitive such as medicare, social security, and veterans' benefits, are a necessity.

On July 17, 1994, President Bill Clinton appointed Leon Panetta Chief of Staff. A zealous Roman Catholic, Leon Panetta took his work seriously, rising early in the morning for staff meetings, and staying up into the night to work on his justifiable drive and quasi-obsession in tackling the federal budget deficit. In addition to all his other involvements, Leon Panetta has served on the Parish Council at his church, Our Lady of Mount Carmel, is a founder of the Monterey College of Law, was vice president of Carmel Valley Little League, and it's no surprise that Panetta is probably one of the most knowledgeable individuals when it comes to federal budget issues.

On a less serious note, to contrast the $4 trillion debt that the feds had amassed, it seems that Panetta's parents had taught him all along as a youngster about budgets—you can buy whatever you want—cash!

General Sources:

1. Cooper, Matthew. "Panetta's Moment." *The New Republic* 6 Nov. 1995: 13-14.

2. *Current Biography Yearbook.* New York: Wilson, 1993.

3. Magnusson, Paul. "Man in the Middle of the Budget Battle." *Business Week* 8 March 1993: 32.

4. Panetta, Leon. "Hunger in America." *USA Today* May 1984: 38-41.

5. Panetta, Leon. *Restoring America's Future: Preparing the Nation for the 21st Century: A Report.* Washington, DC: G.P.O., 1991.

6. Panetta, Leon, and Peter Gall. *Bring Us Together: The Nixon Team and the Civil Rights Retreat.* Philadelphia: Lippincott, 1971.

—by DIANE M. EVANAC, Ed.D.

EMIL F. PASCARELLI (1930-   )

Medical doctor, researcher, consultant, university teacher, editor, and writer of over forty articles most of which have focused on repetitive strain injury (RSI), often called the computer users' epidemic of the 90s, includes medical conditions such as carpal tunnel syndrome and tendinitis. Dr. Pascarelli has been one of the pioneers in the field of RSI. In a relatively new area of concern in hi-tech societies, he has become an internationally recognized specialist having identified more than two dozen kinds of RSI, ranging from cervical radiculopathy to fibromyalgia. He has taught and lectured throughout the United States and is recognized as a specialist on the subject of RSI in industrialized countries.

He has also identified the causes of RSI and has advocated approaches to minimize their influence. He teaches a series of corrective behaviors, and he favors in most cases non-surgical treatments including acupuncture, nutritional and vitamin/mineral therapy, deep tissue massage such as Rolfing, and the use of Eastern (Buddhist) visualization techniques, recently adapted by Western psychology and used in psychotherapy, and more recently in medicine itself, called guided visualization.

Emil Pascarelli was born in New York City on July 19, 1930, the only child of Anna and Carlo Pascarelli. His immigrant parents traveled to Italy frequently, and young Emil grew up knowing both Italian and American cultures firsthand, remaining fluent in Italian and English. Young Emil was also blessed with the good fortune of having had parents who were well educated. His mother was an elementary school teacher and his father a physician. His parents had always expressed their desire to see him become a doctor, but while attending Columbia College, Emil had other ideas. Majoring in fine arts, he received his bachelors degree in 1952 and did some postgraduate work in fine arts for another year.

Then he took a trip to Italy where he pondered the possibility of entering medicine. Fluent in Italian and degreed from the United States, he was able to enroll at the University of Pavia, and by the year 1958 he earned his medical degree. Upon returning to the U.S., he did his medical internship in 1958 in New York City's Roosevelt Hospital where he also did a series of residencies from 1959 to 1962. His subsequent hospital appointments have been at St. Vincent's Hospital/Medical Center, St. Luke/Roosevelt Hospital Center, New York Hospital-Cornell Medical Center, Beekman Downtown Hospital, and Columbia Presbyterian Hospital, all located in NYC.

Having already written about twenty-four articles since 1964 on a varied number of medical topics (including arm and leg blood pressure in aortic insufficiency, drug addiction and dependency, methadone maintenance, mobile intensive care systems, dispatching medical procedures and response time in urban settings), in 1982 he completed his first book where he was the editor. Based on his hospital experiences and based on many articles that he himself had written, the book was entitled *Hospital-Based Ambulatory Care* which consisted of a number of topics all dealing with the improvement and the delivery of better health care in ambulatory, urban settings.

In September 1984, Dr. Pascarelli was appointed corporate medical director of Ambulatory Care at St. Luke/Roosevelt Hospital. A year later in 1985 in the same hospital, he struck upon a novel idea. Soliciting over one million dollars in grants from various foundations, he became the founder and medical director of the Kathryn and Gilbert Miller Health Care Institute for Performing Artists that was at that time the country's largest multi-specialty occupational health care facility dedicated to the care and treatment of problems unique to performing artists and allied professionals.

Based on his experiences especially in the treatment of musicians' problems, he became unusually attentive to their high frequency of repeated complaints regarding chronic pain, rigidity, numbness, and muscular spasms in upper body areas, particularly, the hands, forearms, neck, and shoulders. He took time to make a study of how they played their instruments, and he paid special attention to the neuromuscular relationships that were involved. Dr. Pascarelli came to realize that their troubles—aside from the repetitive aspect of their work—stemmed from many other causal factors including improper techniques, ill-fitting instruments, and poor physical conditioning. To treat this multi-causal problem, he prescribed a rehabilitation program to arrest, reverse, and minimize the effects of these job-related medical conditions called repetitive strain injury, RSI.

Soon many computer users also joined the ranks of musicians and began frequenting the institute, and they reported the same symptoms. After examining their situation, Dr. Pascarelli came to the conclusion that their problems were indeed similar to those of musicians, and he prescribed them virtually the same treatment. What became of his ten-year study was a book entitled *Repetitive Strain Injury: A Computer User's Guide* published in 1994. Dr. Pascarelli has had many concerns regarding RSI because—when untreated—it is more apt to cause an increase in chronicity and pain, and it may also lead to many professionals giving up their jobs and vocations needlessly. Equally pressing, there remains today the immediate problem of so many youngsters using the computer or other hi-tech equipment unabated without availing themselves of the benefits of knowing the preventative measures that have been recently acquired through studies on RSI.

Presently a professor of clinical medicine at Columbia University College of Physicians and Surgeons and also an adjunct associate professor of public health at Cornell Medical Center in NYC, Dr. Pascarelli maintains a private practice at Columbia Presbyterian's eastside facility where he has also established a cumulative trauma disorder center for patient treatment. He continues to lecture for industry professionals and artistic performers and writes journal articles. He has submitted a chapter to the third edition publication of the book entitled *Vascular Disorders of the Upper Extremity*, edited by H. Machleder, M.D.

Dr. Pascarelli, a recognized expert on cumulative trauma disorders, is also about to have published his third book concerned with upper body injuries. He has carved himself a niche in modern medicine by having addressed in depth repetitive strain injury, a disorder effecting so many people in today's society.

General Sources:

1. Arksey, Hilary. *RSI and the Experts: The Construction of Medical Knowledge*. London, UK: UCL Press, 1998.
2. Pascarelli, Emil F. Personal interview. 29 Nov. 1998.
3. Pascarelli, Emil F. "Understanding Occupational Repetitive Strain Injury." *1997 Yearbook of Science and Technology*. New York: McGraw-Hill, 1997.
4. Pascarelli, Emil F., ed. *Hospital-Based Ambulatory Care*. Norwalk, CT: Appleton-Century-Crofts, 1982.
5. Pascarelli, Emil F., and Deborah Quilter. *Repetitive Strain Injury: A Computer User's Guide*. New York: Wiley, 1994.

—by ANNA GATTUSO

JOHN PASTORE (1907-)

First elected as a Democrat to the Rhode Island House of Representatives in 1934 at twenty-seven years of age, John Pastore began a career in public service that would come to a conclusion in his retirement after forty-two years in government. After becoming Rhode Island's governor in 1945, he joined the U.S. Congress as a junior senator in 1950 to fill the vacated seat of J. Howard McGrath (who became U.S. Attorney General in the Truman administration). John Pastore was to be reelected in November 1952 and three other times, serving four full terms for an aggregate total of 26 years in Congress.

John Orlando Pastore was born on March 17, 1907, the second of five children to Michele and Erminia (nee Asprinio) Pastore in the Federal Hill District of Providence, Rhode Island. Both his father and mother were immigrants who had come to the United States in 1899 at the turn-of-the-century immigration wave. A tailor by trade, his father died in 1916 when John was barely nine years of age. For the next three years, both his older brother and his mother worked hard to maintain the family.

When his mother remarried her late husband's brother Pasquale, also a tailor by profession, her financial pressures diminished. All the family helped out in the home-based family tailor business with John doing the garment deliveries. John continued his education and worked during his summer vacations. In 1925, he graduated with honors from Classical High School in Providence. While he worked as a claims adjuster for the Narragansett Electric Company, he eventually enrolled in 1927 in an evening law program given by Northeastern University at the Providence YMCA. Four years later, he went on to receive his law degree (LL.B.) in 1931 and was admitted to the bar in 1932.

Becoming involved in Democratic politics, Pastore won both the Democratic nomination and the election for the State House of Representatives at the age of 27 in what was an essentially Republican district in 1934. Here is where he began his career of public service. Reelected in 1936 to the state House, he accepted an appointment to become an assistant to the state attorney general in 1937. Temporarily losing this appointed position because of a Republican victory in 1938, he was appointed once more assistant attorney general in 1940. In 1941, John and Elena Elizabeth (nee Caito) Pastore married and had three children: John, Jr., Frances Elizabeth and Luisa Marie.

In 1945, when Rhode Island's Governor McGrath resigned his position to work in the Truman administration, Pastore who had been elected McGrath's lieutenant governor in 1944, automatically became the new governor on October 6. John Pastore's achievements as governor were many, including the creation of a "State antipollution authority, a direct primary, and a fair employment practice law."

Because the postwar budgets of many states had to expand to catch up with deferred state projects and salary increases that necessarily had been put aside during the war years, it was indeed a difficult era for most governors in having to impose new taxes. With a divided state legislature (Democrats recommending more corporate taxes and the Republicans advocating a sales tax), Pastore was able to work out a compromise solution. This fair and just settlement spread the taxation responsibility equitably in order to raise those much needed dollars for the state.

What remains most notable about Pastore's leadership qualities in those years involved his decision not to featherbed his administration with Italian Americans. He chose, instead, the more difficult path selecting the best people for the job. It is no wonder that he kept a high popularity both with the citizenry and the state leadership of both parties, which was predominantly Irish American. In fact, in this very regard, Pastore was quoted as saying that in his administration he always sought to create "a record not an organization."

As a person who disliked bureaucracy, remonstrations, and investigations, Pastore liked to keep his "official house in order" by emphasizing a vigilant ad hoc approach to dealing with problems. So whenever new problems arose, he attempted to deal with them immediately and effectively. After his popular reelection in 1948, he canceled the inaugural ball claiming he had already had one in 1946 in his first elected term as governor, and another one now seemed unnecessary. Noted for his policy-making equanimity, Pastore soon after his election became chairman of the six-man New England Governors Conference.

After McGrath relinquished his senatorial seat to became Attorney General in 1949, Pastore had no trouble becoming the newly elected U.S. senator from Rhode Island in 1950. Acclaimed the "biggest vote-getter" in Rhode Island's election history, he also was one of the youngest senators at age 43. Being assigned to committees on Labor, Public Works, Post Office and Civil Service, he established the reputation of being a friend to the American worker and particularly to the federal worker.

As a U.S. senator, Pastore remained a champion for the rights of working people especially while serving on specific committees such as Labor, Public Welfare, Post Office and the Civil Service and the Committee for the District of Columbia. He served for nearly 27 years (1950-1977) under six presidential administrations spanning the Truman, Eisenhower, Kennedy, Johnson, and Nixon years up to the Ford years.

In particular, during the Kennedy, Johnson, and Nixon administrations, he was liberal on most domestic issues such as fighting poverty and anti-discrimination. Initially backing the logic of U.S. efforts in the Vietnam War, by 1970 he staunchly opposed U.S. activities there. Pastore's record in the Senate reflects the passage of legislation of many bills too numerous to mention that include: grants for public health, gun control, tax reform, and establishment of the consumer protection agency. In many respects, he was years ahead of his time in his repeated concerns to Congress about the federal budget deficits and the negative influence of excessive sex and violence in the media.

His Italian name, Pastore, implies shepherd or pastor. It stands very much in harmony with his endless caring and devotion in preserving quality of life and in respecting the worth of the worker and the everyday citizen. A perusal of his life indicates the history of a dedicated public servant who earned his reputation as a most trustworthy representative of the people. In a way, shepherd might be the very icon to reflect his moral stature and virtuous example for others to follow.

General Sources:

1.   *Current Biography*. New York: Wilson, 1953.

2.   Morgenthau, Ruth S. *Pride Without Prejudice: The Life of John O. Pastore*. Providence, RI: Rhode Island Historical Society, 1989.

3.   United States, 94th Congress, 2nd session, 1976, Senate. *Tributes to the Honorable John O. Pastore of Rhode Island: in the United States Senate, Upon the Occasion of His Retirement from the Senate*. Washington, DC: U.S. Government Printing Office, 1977.

—by JOHN BONIELLO

JOE PATERNO (1928-   )

Joe Paterno has been a part of the Penn State football coaching staff since 1950, first as an assistant coach for 16 years and then as an outstanding head coach, who has been named four times Coach of the Year by the American Football Coaches Association. Despite the fact that his name is synonymous with college football, he considers himself first an educator, holding his students, athletes, and his staff to the same rigorously high standards as he had set for himself many years ago.

He was born on December 21, 1928, the first of four children of Angelo "Pat" Paterno and Florence (nee Cafiero) Paterno. Both sides of Joe's Italian heritage seemed influential in his motivational development. On the Paterno side, Sicilian in origin, they were hard-working people, many of whom held professional jobs in the arts such as in music and in painting. On his maternal side (the Cafieros), Calabrian in origin, they were fiercely disciplined and driven to goal-directed activities.

Joe, his brother George, and his sister Florence attended Catholic grammar school in Brooklyn, New York. Later, Joe and George attended the prestigious Jesuit high school, Brooklyn Prep. Their parents recognized the importance of a good education and were willing to work hard and sacrifice for it. In fact, while the two boys were attending this prep school, their father attended law school in the evening, eventually completing his law degree while holding down a full-time job during the day.

The Paterno brothers always loved sports and both played football in high school. Joe did not make the team in his freshman year, played some football in his second year, but finally became a quarterback in his junior and senior years. His involvement helped to take what was a second-rate football team to an almost perfect record in his last year. They lost only one game—to St. Cecilia of New Jersey—a team coached at that time by Vince Lombardi. During his high school years, Paterno had become an outstanding scholar, student leader, and athlete. After serving in the military service, he accepted a full scholarship at Brown University where he played defensive back, quarterback and was team captain.

Joe graduated with a degree in English, and after scoring in the top ten percent on the law boards at Princeton, he had to decide whether or not to fulfill what had become a family dream that included following his father's example by going to law school and eventually setting up a father and son legal practice. Other factors would come into play and prevail. Rip Engle, who at that time was the Brown football coach, had been offered the top coaching job at Penn State, and he asked Paterno to come along as an assistant coach. A deal was struck. Joe would coach for one year, and then if it didn't work out, he would go to law school.

When Engle and Paterno arrived at Penn State in 1950, Paterno was only twenty-two years old. Together with Engle's leading role, they began to build a football program that became legendary. Joe, a shy guy off the field, worked hard at football, enjoying the game and the company of the players and coaches. He rented a room from one of the other assistant coaches and lived that way for many years.

Presumably he felt comfortable with that arrangement until he reached 36 years of age when he felt it was time to get married and start a family. He had met a pretty co-ed, Susan Pohland, 13 years his junior, and they married in

1964 with the blessing of both sides of the family. They would then have three children: Diana, Mary Kay, and Joe, Jr. In 1966 Paterno became the head coach of Penn State, and he went on to make football history.

Although Joe had been regularly offered head coaching jobs from many other teams, including professional teams, he never seriously considered leaving his beloved Nittany Lions. His record remains powerfully unique in the annals of college football. His teams have won the most bowl games in history. He is the only coach to have won four New Years Day games: the Rose, Sugar, Cotton and Orange Bowls. He has posted eleven or more victories in twelve of his seasons, has seven undefeated regular games, and has finished in the Top Ten twenty times.

One honor that makes Paterno especially proud was the Distinguished American Award granted by the National Football Foundation and the College Football Hall of Fame. He was the first active coach to receive this award, and it truly reflects both the kind of coach he exemplifies and the moral temperament he exhibits in his activities. He places emphasis on honesty with his players on and off the football field. He makes sure his players attend class, devote proper time to studies and graduate with degrees that will help them enter meaningful careers upon graduation. The term student-athlete is not an oxymoron at Penn State because Paterno expects his players to be both athletes and students who live up to what is expected of college students.

In order to offer a sense of fairness to the title National Championship, Paterno has often expressed the need for a National Championship game that would decide which college team wins for the year as opposed to the less reputable way it is presently decided. Although several of his teams have finished undefeated, they have lost the title, sometimes to lesser teams with easier schedules. He perceives his newly proposed system for crowning the National Champion would serve best since it eliminates the biases and political pressures from the process and makes it a fair contest for the players.

The Penn State football team under Coach Paterno has graduated 20 first team academic All-Americans, 14 Hall of Fame Scholar-Athletes, and 16 NCAA postgraduate scholarship winners. In all, they have a graduation rate of 71 percent. Paterno has coached players who have won all the major football awards including the Heisman, Maxwell, Lombardi, O'Brien, and Biletnikoff Awards.

On twenty-nine occasions he has seen at least one of his players selected as a first team All-American. More than 200 of his players have entered the National Football League, 22 as first-round draft picks. He was named *Sports Illustrated* 1986 Sportsman of the Year and his teams have won 2 National Championships. Paterno's long record of successes speaks for itself. An author of several books on football and coaching, his education has served him well. While a role model in the academic world for students to emulate, he remains a tribute to his Italian-American heritage for upholding and practicing his guiding principles that have earned him success and respect.

General Sources:
1. *Current Biography Yearbook*. New York: Wilson, 1984.
2. Neft, David S., et al. *The Football Encyclopedia: The Complete History of Professional Football from 1892 to the Present*. New York: St. Martin's Press, 1994.
3. O'Brien, Michael. *No Ordinary Joe: The Biography of Joe Paterno*. Nashville, TN: Rutledge Hill Press, 1998.
4. Paterno, George. *Joe Paterno, The Coach from Byzantium*. Champaign, IL: Sagamore, 1997.
5. Paterno, Joe. *Paterno: By the Book*. New York: Random House, 1989.

—by JANET B. TUCCI

ADELINA PATTI (1843-1919)

A world-renowned opera singer, "the Queen of Song," "the last of the great divas," business woman, woman of the world—such were the phrases associated with Adelina Patti, who in many ways would have been right at home in the latter part of 20th century. She gave her first public performance at the age of eight in 1851 in New York City, and she offered her last public performance in 1914 at the age of seventy-one in London's Albert Hall. In the time between those two dates, Patti was among the highest paid opera singers in the world and probably the most well known in Europe and in North and South America.

Born on February 10, 1843 in Madrid, Spain to Italian parents, Salvatore Patti and Caterina Barili-Patti, both opera singers, Adelina developed early in her youth an exceptionally talented singing voice. Her childhood years were spent in New York City where her parents and their eight children had settled in 1847. Signor Patti had been invited to help manage the eight-hundred-seat Palmo's Opera House on Chambers Street in lower Manhattan. Opera in New York, still a relatively new phenomenon, had begun its first season there only twenty-one years before. Music was an integral part of the Barili-Patti household, and Adelina's first music teachers were her stepbrothers Ettore and Antonio Barili and her sister Carlotta: all professional musicians.

Adelina was a highly spirited child whose passion and vindictive temper caused fear in the hearts of her childhood neighbors. This high spirit appears to have translated itself into the intense focus needed to dedicate herself to her voice and her art. At the age of eight, Adelina made her debut at New York's Tipler Hall, singing "Echo Song" and "I am a Bayadere."

The *New York Tribune* lauded the event; and shortly thereafter, Adelina gave seven more concerts in New York astounding audiences with her command of operatic arias at such a young age.

Her success inspired her father, who seemed always financially pressed, to plan a tour for her with Maurice Strakosch who would be both soloist and accompanyist. The tour, lasting from the fall of 1852 to the spring of 1854 earned Adelina—or rather Salvatore—$20,000! Not bad for an eleven year-old in those days.

At sixteen, Adelina made her opera debut in *Lucia*. The *Tribune* declared her "brilliant execution" as a marvel for her age, and they ranked her among the best singers of the time. Awareness of her success reached across the Atlantic whereby an English music agent offered her $1,000 per monthly engagement. Unfortunately, soon after her arrival there, Patti found that the opera season had been canceled. This minor setback led her to doing a free concert which, in turn, led her throughout England doing concerts and obtaining financial rewards and the admiration of the British public.

One of her admirers was the noted novelist, Charles Dickens, who wrote a glowing tribute. "Born in Madrid, Italian by parentage, trained exclusively in America, Mlle. Adelina Patti, on the first evening's appearance at our Italian Opera—nay, in her first song—possessed herself of her audience with a sudden victory which has scarcely a parallel." The reign of Patti had indeed begun. Her first full London season was in 1861 at the age of eighteen, and in June of that year, she sang in a command performance at Buckingham Palace for the members of Queen Victoria's family. Throughout her career she would come to know most of the crowned heads of Europe. She enjoyed a glittering social life in Europe, befriending the likes of Rossini and Verdi. In 1868 she married, much to her father's displeasure, an impoverished marquis, seventeen years her senior. The Marquis de Caux was known as a ladies' man who had an inflated ego and a cynical attitude. It was said of Patti that she loved the title more than the man. It came as no surprise that it was not a happy union. De Caux, dissatisfied with the marriage, took a mistress. In 1876, a love affair had begun between Patti and the French tenor Ernest Nicolini who was married and the father of five children.

The Victorian world shuddered. Morally outraged, women would turn their backs at Patti at social events. The press also reviled her. The Marquis sued her, and in August of 1877, he was awarded a separation. Patti paid all the expenses for the suit, and she had to turn over half her wealth to him. Patti's career was not damaged by the scandal in any major way. The Prince of Wales was an outspoken supporter; and audiences in London and in Vienna received her enthusiastically.

In October of 1878, Patti and Nicolini moved into the newly acquired estate in Wales which was to become her lifelong residence and refuge. Patti named it Craig-y-Nos. The estate ultimately included hot houses where exotic fruits and vegetables were grown, an icemaking plant, eighteen cottages, a farmyard with livestock, stables, a clock tower, a private theater, and much more. It required over forty domestics to run it.

Although Patti's stage appearance was much in demand all over the world, her engagements were not without controversy. Her scandalous private life caused her some unwelcome press and cold shoulders, especially in conservative New York. In 1885, the Marquis de Caux obtained a divorce from Patti; and the following year, Patti and Nicolini were married in a church near their home, Craig-y-Nos, greeted by a band and one thousand singing children.

By 1887, Nicolini's health had declined, and he often could not accompany Patti on her tours or social engagements. He died in January 1898, leaving Patti in deep mourning for several months. She wore widow's weeds for her first concert the May after his death. In November of that year, however, Patti surprised her friends by announcing that she intended to remarry. Thus, scarcely a year after Nicolini's death and shortly before her fifty-sixth birthday, Adelina Patti married Baron Rolf Cederstrom, Swedish-born and nearly twenty-eight years her junior.

In 1905, at age sixty-two, Patti was finally persuaded to make her first recording. It was so wildly received that she made another one the next year with her nephew, Alfredo Barili, accompanying her on the piano. Her singing career culminated with an operatic farewell tour in the provinces ending in November 1907. She and the Baron lived a full and happy life at Craig-y-Nos until her death in late 1919. Her body was interred at the famous Père Lachiase Cemetery in Paris where a tomb boldly dominates the area. The Queen of Song will long be remembered.

General Sources:
1. Cone, John F. *Adelina Patti: Queen of Hearts*. Portland, OR: Amadeus Press, 1993.
2. Gatti-Gasazza, Giulio. *Memories of the Opera*. New York: Vienna House, 1973.
3. Klein, Herman. *The Reign of Patti*. New York: Arno Press, 1977.
4. Lauw, Louisa. *Fourteen Years with Adelina Patti: Reminiscences of Louisa Lauw*. s.l.: La Sala Autographs, 1977.
5. Sadie, Stanley, ed. *History of Opera*. New York: Norton, 1990.
6. Sadie, Stanley, ed. *The New Grove Dictionary of Opera*. New York: Grove's Dictionaries of Music, 1992.

—by CONI GESUALDI

LUCIANO PAVAROTTI (1935-   )

Not since the legendary Enrico Caruso has an opera personality captured the world's imagination as the tenor Luciano Pavarotti, who has become the most recognized and the most recognizable opera singer around the globe today. According to a recent *Forbes* magazine article for the time frame 1995-1996, Pavarotti was ranked as the 28th highest paid entertainer in the world. With the advent of the worldwide satellite broadcasting of his outdoor concert performances, his fame seems to be growing more and more, and who knows just how high his fame will take him.

Born a baker's son, in the north-central Italian city of Modena, he lived as a child in a secluded 16-family apartment building in the city's outskirts. Despite the isolation from the city, he remembers being engulfed with love and attention: "When I was born on October 12, 1935, I was the first boy born in that building in ten years. That alone made me a superstar."

His father's name was Fernando, a baker with a fine tenor voice. Vocal music was very important to him, and he would bring home records of all the great tenors of the day. Luciano was about the age of five when he discovered that he, too, had a "voice." His father would play the records over and over again. Hearing those great voices all the time, it just seemed inevitable that Luciano would try to sing like that too.

Yet the dominant event of his childhood was World War II. At first, he was only dimly aware of it, but when the American and British forces starting bombing Modena, it became overwhelming. Suddenly, Modena became an important military target because of its industry. Everyone learned that an hour before the bombings when planes would fly overhead and drop smoke bombs to signal that the real bombs were on their way. At one point, when the bombings became very regular and intense, many families fled the city. The Pavarotti family left Modena and took refuge on a farm near the town of Carpi outside the village of Gargallo in 1943. Luciano was then only eight years old.

Despite the fact that the ground war was far away to the south, farm areas up north were full of partisans and underground military activity. Every night, partisans would conduct their private raids on local Fascists and Nazis. Luciano said that he often would fall asleep to the sound of gunfire. Humorously, he attributes his good sense of rhythm to the beat of automatic weapons that he had heard so often. Aside the dangers of civilians possibly being killed in the crossfire, food also had became scarce and expensive.

Although his family did survive the war in tact, many family members had close calls with death. His father was once arrested by accident, but luckily, he was spared execution through the influence of a family friend. Civilians also feared for their lives because whenever Italian partisans killed members of the Nazi occupational forces, reprisals inevitably would took place and local Italians often would be executed. With the acceleration of the ground and air war, the partisans increased their activities, creating then greater pressure on local inhabitants and raising the possibility of their being murdered in a Nazi reprisal.

By August 1944, the Allied Armies had fought their way as far north as Florence. Those remaining months right before the Nazis total collapse in Italy could be best described as the terrible months for northern Italians still living under German occupation. The worst reprisals of the war in Italy occurred only twenty-five miles from Modena in the town of Marzabotto, where, one day, 1,830 Italian civilians were rounded up and summarily executed.

Before reaching his tenth birthday in 1945, young Luciano fully comprehended the ugly meaning of war and death. Of that period, he says: "For me it was a terrible sight and it made me sick inside. I became an adult right away. Seeing that impressed on me how easy life can be destroyed, how quickly it can end. It has given me, I think, my terrific enthusiasm for life. That was an important effect the war had on me." After the liberation, he wasted no time getting down to the regular activities of a young boy, like playing soccer on the neighborhood lots.

Along with his father, he also began singing in the choir at the local church dedicated to the patron saint of Modena, San Gemignano. Often they would go there for the evening vespers, singing to the music of different composers. A most memorable event took place in Luciano's inner world when Luciano was about twelve years of age. Beniamino Gigli, at that time the world's most famous tenor, came to sing in Modena. Luciano was particularly thrilled about that as he had been listening to Gigli on his father's records for years. Luciano, who had made his way into Gigli's rehearsal, became ecstatic listening to Gigli sing in person.

Gigli, who was then in his late fifties, had his voice in excellent form. His singing apparently had enraptured young Luciano. And so, when Gigli finished his rehearsal, Luciano was so overwhelmed by Gigli's presence and performance that he went running up to him and burst out the news, declaring that when he would grow up, he wanted to be a tenor. Of course, the rest is history. Luciano would continue to sing and develop his talents, and, like Gigli, he would indubitably become a superstar.

Yet before traveling on the road to opera stardom, he had taken a small detour that is worthy of interest. Despite his great voice and his continuous involvement with singing, there was the matter of earning a living. After graduating from the Istituto Magistrale in Modena in 1955, he taught elementary school for two years. It was during this crucial period of deliberation that he finally decided to become a professional opera singer and take the necessary risks concomitant with entertainment.

As a reward for winning the Concorso Internazionale in 1961, he sang professionally in the city of Reggio Emilia, in the role of Rodolfo in *La Bohème*. He then made his American debut in Miami (Florida) in 1965. His career began to move very rapidly as he would make his Metropolitan Opera debut in New York City in 1968; and after delighting opera lovers, especially with his ability to hit the high "C" notes, he would achieve the status of superstardom in 1972, merely four years later. Today it comes as no surprise that he has achieved the status as the most well-known opera singer in the world.

General Sources:

1. Bonvicini, Candido. *The Tenor's Son: My Days with Pavarotti.* New York: St. Martin's Press, 1993.
2. Guinn, John, and Les Stone, eds. *The St. James Opera Encyclopedia: A Guide to People and Works.* Detroit, MI: Visible Ink, 1997.
3. Kesting, Jurgen. *Pavarotti: The Myth of the Tenor.* Boston: Northeastern University Press, 1996.
4. Pavarotti, Luciano, and William Wright. *Pavarotti, My Own Story.* Garden City, NY: Doubleday, 1981.
5. Pavarotti, Luciano, and William Wright. *Pavarotti, My World.* New York: Random House, 1995.
6. Sadie, Stanley, ed. *The New Grove Dictionary of Opera.* New York: Grove's Dictionaries of Music, 1992.

—by ROCKY PESIRI

MARIO PEI (1901-1978)

Italian-born Pei, world famous linguist and philologist, grew up in New York City and published close to thirty books in his lifetime. Having taught romance philology at Columbia University for over thirty years, he was a formidable force in influencing the study and growth of linguistics, philology, and foreign languages in the United States. He accomplished this in a time frame where he stood in direct confrontation with an era typified by American ethnocentricity and linguistic isolation. He consistently championed the study of languages as a means of closing the gap between nations and as a way of minimizing the potential for war and, correspondingly, as a means of insuring peace and greater understanding between the peoples of the world.

He acknowledged and endorsed an idea contained in Frederick Bodmer's 1944 book entitled *The Loom of Language* that the world adopt one common *second* language as a medium for international communication. The underlying idea was based on the notion that world citizens could communicate better with a common language that was supra-national in nature and not embedded in the politics of a national ideology. This theory has been slowly becoming a reality. It has not been by a collective conscious choice that it became reified in an agreement among nations. However, with the advent of the Internet, English has been assuming that role more and more in the 90s.

Mario (Andrew) Pei was born in Rome, Italy on February 16, 1901. He was one of two children (sister Mathilde) born to Francesco and Luisa (nee Ferri) Pei. His father operated a drugstore, and when it failed, the family moved to the United States. Mario was seven at the time, and he had already had two years of schooling in Italy. He never stopped speaking Italian in America as it was the common language spoken among family members at home. He grew up biculturally as he also continued to read books, magazines, and newspapers in Italian.

After attending St. John the Evangelist Parochial School, he won a scholarship to St. Francis Xavier High School. Both schools were in Manhattan. At Xavier he received an excellent Jesuit high school education where academics and the basic disciplines came before all else. His education included four years of Latin, three and a half years of Greek, and three years of French. After graduating high school in 1918, he attended the City College of New York (CCNY) in the evenings intending to enter its engineering school. After a year's study in math and science, he decided to switch to liberal arts.

During his first two years of study at CCNY, he also taught the sixth grade at St. Francis Xavier Grammar School. In 1920 he went to Cuba for a short time to teach President Menocal's three nephews several subjects including French and English. After his return to the U.S., he taught at Fordham Prep in 1921 and then at Regis High School in 1921-22. He took several years to complete his B.A. degree, but when he did in 1925, he graduated *magna cum laude* and as a Phi Beta Kappa member. From 1922 to 1936 he taught languages at CCNY and at its prep school called Townsend Harris High School.

His outstanding graduation record empowered him to immerse himself still more into languages, and he enrolled at Columbia University where he earned his doctorate in 1932 doing his dissertation on *The Language of the Eighth-Century Texts in Northern France*, a topic from which he would generate two more related books in 1948 and in 1952. He was hired by Columbia University in 1937 and would teach there until 1970 as professor of romance philology (1952-1970). The first book he published as a faculty member at Columbia was in 1941, *The Italian Language*, which has since remained a standard linguistic text in Italian.

During World War II he was a consultant to the Office of Strategic Services and to the Office of War Information. His contributions to the war effort included the creation of English radio lessons for the Latin American countries. Those lessons were later adapted for use in Europe, Asia, and Africa. During the war he also developed a thirty-seven-language course for servicemen which was titled "War Linguistics."

Two of his most popular books, *The Story of Language* (1949, revised 1965) and *The Story of the English Language* (1952), did much to disseminate the idea that linguistics did not have to remain limited to specialists in the field but could be appreciated and understood by many non-specialists as well. The sales of his 1949 book did so well that it became a Book-of-the-Month Club selection in 1950. The book was well received by the critics as well as by the great playwright George Bernard Shaw, who admired Pei's display of knowledge and memory. As a writer, Pei had apparently found and nurtured that highly coveted middle ground of the written spectrum where he could examine exacting thoughts and patterns and yet render them decipherable to the reader.

Pei's linguistic interests overflowed into the fascinating area of American politics and of the media's manipulations of words. As a staunch conservative living in the 60s and 70s, he strongly disliked the "soft-sell" embedded in the linguistic ploys of easy liberalism that benignly omitted the whole area of individual responsibility from the equation asserting rights and freedoms. At an international level, he supported Bodmer's view that a common language among nations would serve the purpose of fostering better understanding and peaceful initiatives among the peoples of the world. A common worldwide language would also act as an force to minimize the possible nationalistic machinations and their leaders' manipulations of their national language when no common language is available.

Pei, who died on March 2, 1978, won many commendations and awards including the title of Cavaliere Ufficiale of the Order of Merit from the Italian Republic (1958), Unico's Award for Literature (1959), the David McKay Humanities Award from Brigham Young University (1970), and numerous other awards from many language associations. He left a legacy that included a love of languages and a desire that the world be united by a common *second* language as a tool towards promoting lasting peace. A jovial, generous and self-described man as "warmhearted by nature," his fund of knowledge in languages that was encyclopedic in quality was only outweighed by his deep desire to visualize a world with justice, free of the ravages of wars.

General Sources:

1. *Current Biography Yearbook*. New York: Wilson, 1968; 1978.

2. Pei, Mario. *The America We Lost: The Concerns of a Conservative*. New York: World Publishing, 1968.

3. Pei, Mario. *The Italian Language*. New York: Columbia University Press, 1941.

4. Pei, Mario. *One Language for the World*. New York: Biblo and Tannen, 1968.

5. Pei, Mario. *The Story of Language*. Philadelphia: Lippincott, 1965.

6. Pei, Mario. *The Story of the English Language*. Philadelphia: Lippincott, 1952.

7. *Who's Who in America.* 1979-80 ed.

—by GEORGE CARPETTO, Ph.D.

EDMUND DANIEL PELLEGRINO (1920-)

As president of the Catholic University of America between 1978-1982, one of the most prestigious universities in the U.S. and founded in 1887, he has since continued as a leader in administration, philosophical writing, and teaching. Educated as a medical doctor with a distinguished background in the rapidly growing field of bioethics, Pellegrino has held a long series of positions in either administrative or teaching capacities at SUNY at Stony Brook, Georgetown and Yale Universities, the Universities of Kentucky and Tennessee, and the Kennedy Institute of Ethics.

Ethics has always been an integral part of medicine, and medical ethics had their historical precedent or model in the person of Hippocrates (c.460-c.377 B.C.) the "father of medicine" whose oath formed the foundation for the more recent Hippocratic oath (1740 A.D., England) usually taken by those who are about to enter the field. The oath serves to embody the duties and obligations of physicians to their patients.

When Dr. Pellegrino published his critical book, *Humanism and the Physician* in 1979, he opened the dialogue on many of today's ethically related medical problems especially those concerned with geriatric scenarios and the issues dealing with physician-assisted suicide (PAS). Outspoken on medical issues, he has taken a conservative view of PAS and stands in sharp contrast with the more liberal viewpoints.

Born in Newark, New Jersey on June 22, 1920, the son of Michael and Marie (nee Cartone) Pellegrino, Edmund attended Xavier High School, a New York City Catholic secondary school with high academic standards. Graduating *magna cum laude* with a B.S. in 1941 from St. John's University, he went on to earn an M.D. three years later at New York University. In 1944, the same year, he married Clementine Coakley, and they went on to have a family of six children: Thomas, Virginia, Michael, Andrea, Alice, and Leah.

He served several residencies including an internship at New York City Bellevue Hospital (1944-45), residency at Goldwater Memorial Hospital (1945-46), residency at Bellevue Hospital (1948-49), and research fellowship at New York University (1949-50). He worked in a tireless manner also serving as supervising physician at the Homer Folks Tuberculosis Hospital in Oneonta, NY (1950-53), director of internal medicine at the Hunterdon Medical Center in Flemington, NJ (1953-59) and also its medical director (1955-59), and chairman of the Department of Medicine at the University of Kentucky Medical Center (1959-66).

Dr. Pellegrino's university administrative trajectory then began to move more rapidly. When he assumed the position of professor of medicine at SUNY at Stony Brook in 1966, he quickly became the director of the Health Sciences Center and dean of its medical school. In 1973 in the state of Tennessee, he also served as chancellor of the University of Tennessee's medical units. In 1975 he became president of Yale University's Medical Center.

In 1978 he began his longest association with a university when he joined the Catholic University of America. There he became its president between 1978-1982; and, thereafter he held a series of concurrent positions teaching philosophy, biology, bioethics for Catholic University of America, Georgetown University, and the Kennedy Institute for Ethics. Aside exercising leadership roles in the span of time ranging from 1978 to the mid-90s, he was prolific in doing research, writing, and editing texts. It was during this time frame that the specific issues dealing with physician-assisted suicide and those dealing with managed health care became major problems especially in ethical matters.

In addition to his own seminal book, *Humanism and the Physician* (1979), he coauthored with Dr. Davis Thomasma three other books: *Philosophical Basis of Medical Practice* (1981), *For the Patient's Good* (1988), and *The Virtues in Medical Practice* (1993). He also coedited four other books whose thematic structures all dealt with medical ethics: *Ethics, Trust, and the Professions* (1991), *African-American Perspectives on Biomedical Ethics* (1992), *Transcultural Dimensions in Medical Ethics* (1992), and *Dignity and Dying* (1996).

In his 1975 interview with *U.S. News & World Report*, Dr. Pellegrino stated his essential viewpoint on euthanasia. He emphatically does *not* believe in "direct medical intervention to terminate the life of a patient." He clarified this position still further by saying that employing a "direct medical intervention to terminate the life of a patient" is *different* "from withdrawing medical intervention and allowing the natural disease process to take its course." Dr. Pellegrino would invariably reply "yes" to the following question: "Does a patient with an incurable illness and no possibility of a positive outcome have the right to participate in a decision to let nature take its course?"

Being concerned about doctors possible abuse of power in life and death situations, he views doctors' roles as twofold in these matters. First, doctors should provide the layman (patient and family members) with "information and technical knowhow which provide the basis for a rational decision." Second, doctors should "involve those who have most at stake—the patient or family—in arriving at the decision."

In a more recent interview in the magazine, *Christianity Today* (June 1997), Dr. Pellegrino, who is staunchly against physician-assisted suicide, pointed to his earlier fears as having become unfortunately realized, for instance, in Holland where PAS became legal. He cites a Dutch medical report, Remmelink, that "the Dutch government documented that 1,000 persons were *killed* without their giving consent in what was supposed to be a 'voluntary' program." Dr. Pellegrino foresees these kinds of situations worsening as more nations move towards PAS and as greater economic pressures and managed health care problems, particularly financial, enter the bioethical equation.

Dr. Pellegrino is the recipient of 41 honorary degrees and numerous awards from civic, medical, and scientific organizations, including the National Italian American Lifetime Achievement Award in 1980. He was the founding editor of the *Journal of Medicine and Philosophy* in 1983. With his long list of publications of books and articles, he is a model of an Italian American dedicated to the medical profession, its highest possible ethical ideals, and someone who has served his fellow citizens as an administrator, teacher, and motivator in the humane struggle to bring respect and dignity to the patient and particularly to the dying.

General Sources:

1. *American Men & Women of Science.* New Providence, NJ: Bowker, 1998.
2. Pellegrino, Edmund D. *Humanism and the Physician.* Knoxville: University of Tennessee Press, 1979.
3. Pellegrino, Edmund D. "The Right to Die—Should a Doctor Decide?" *U.S. News & World Report* 3 Nov. 1975: 53-54.
4. Pellegrino, Edmund D., et al. *Transcultural Dimensions in Medical Ethics.* Frederick, MD: University Pub. Group, 1922.
5. Thomas, Gary L. "Deadly Compassion." *Christianity Today* 16 June 1997: 14-21.

—by GEORGE CARPETTO, Ph.D.

MICHAEL PESCE (1943-   )

Upon achieving in the early 1970s the distinction of being the youngest assemblyman ever elected in the history of New York State government, Michael Pesce became an instant celebrity in the New York metropolitan area. Magazines and newspaper articles and TV coverage were quick to celebrate this event.

Before World War II, Francesco Pesce, Michael's father, had traveled to Brooklyn, NY from the small Adriatic seaside town of Mola di Bari in Italy. After working for a while on the Brooklyn docks, he returned to his native Italy to his wife Vincenza, and his two children, Isabella and Vito. Within a few years, Michael, who became their youngest child, was born into the Pesce family on March 1, 1943.

In early 1955, the entire Pesce family immigrated to the United States. They settled in Carroll Gardens—as it is called today—an established Italian area for almost fifty years. Michael recalls vividly the hard-working image he had of his parents, particularly his father who went to work as a longshoreman the day after their arrival. Unable to speak a word of English, young Michael started school in Brooklyn at age 12. With neither bilingual nor transitional programs available at the time, he was immersed in a totally American education—an experience not all immigrant youngsters successfully survived. Despite initial linguistic and cultural roadblocks, this newly-arrived young immigrant distinguished himself at his elementary school graduation by receiving an academic achievement medal.

Michael's high performance at Boys High School in Brooklyn qualified him for admission to City College of New York (CCNY) of the City University of New York (CUNY) system. Known for its high admissions standards, entrance to the then tuition-free CCNY was very competitive. It possessed an excellent academic reputation nationwide that included notable alumni such as former associate justice of the U.S. Supreme Court Felix Frankfurter, and polio-vaccine pioneer Dr. Jonas Salk.

In 1964, Michael Pesce received his bachelors degree in economics at CCNY. Two years later, he was awarded a masters degree at the New School for Social Research. Switching academic tracks from his enrollment in its doctoral program, Michael Pesce then entered the Detroit Law School and again distinguished himself by being on the dean's list. Within a year of graduation in 1969, he returned to New York and passed its bar examination. From 1969 to 1972, Pesce took an $8,600-a-year job as a legal aid attorney working in a Puerto Rican neighborhood in the Bronx with its underprivileged, poor, unemployed, and its newly-arrived immigrants who often spoke no English. It was this experience together with his own experiences as an immigrant that inspired him to enter the world of politics where he felt he could better serve the public by representing a larger number of people.

In 1971, Michael Pesce and other concerned citizens formed a group called the Independent Neighborhood Democrats and decided to make their office in a storefront in downtown Brooklyn. One week before its designated opening, the office was bombed. Despite the continuance of bomb threats, they resumed their agenda undaunted by the heavily entrenched Brooklyn Democratic machinery. Pesce was greatly assisted by vigorous campaign efforts of the Van Westerhout Mola Social Club, a civic association of Italian Americans with roots to Mola di Bari. In 1972, with a constituency of Italian Americans and many non-Italians, Pesce became the candidate for the Independent Neighborhood Democrats. He won an upset victory at the Democratic primary and then went on to win the election by a margin of 300 decisive votes.

In 1973, at age thirty, Michael Pesce became the youngest state assemblyman ever elected to Albany. Celebrated as he was by the media as a community-minded person, his hard work and his commitment allowed him to become reelected with little resistance until 1981. Representing the 52nd District, his track record both in Albany and in his downtown Brooklyn storefront office consistently reflected a deep respect for people from all walks of life.

In 1981, Pesce began his service in the court system as a civil court judge. From 1984-1989, he became acting supreme court judge, and in 1990, Judge Pesce became a supreme court judge for the state of New York. In April 1996, he moved even higher in rank when he was appointed administrative judge of the Second Judicial District having jurisdiction over Brooklyn and Staten Island. It is the largest single judicial district in New York State and the second largest in the nation. He was lauded not only by his former political constituents but also by the New York metropolitan area press for his new position.

In a 1995 article, Jack Newfield of the *New York Post* had already cited Michael Pesce as being among the top 13 judges in the New York State judicial system. His recent promotion came as no surprise to his admirers. Belonging to over a dozen professional and community associations, Judge Pesce, true to his engaging and dedicated personality, remains highly visible and active in his Brooklyn community of Carroll Gardens where he resides. Judge Pesce has been the recipient of numerous honors and distinctions including the National Hydrocephalus Research Foundation Humanitarian Award and the Italian Heritage and Cultural Committee of New York Man of the Year Award. He was also made Knight of the Republic of Italy: Cavaliere di Merito del Governo della Repubblica D'Italia.

As a frequent traveler to Italy, he has consistently encouraged and participated in exchange protocols involving cultural programs and government leaders in a world that is getting smaller each year by the increasing use of worldwide news satellite transmission and the Internet. A lover of active sports and also an active participant himself, particularly in soccer and sailing, Judge Pesce exemplifies the Greco-Roman ideal of a sound mind in a sound body.

General Sources:
1. Gelman, Mitch. "The Ball's in Judge's Court." *New York Newsday* 15 May 1994.
2. Jacoby, Susan. "A Dream Grows in Brooklyn." *The New York Times Magazine* 23 Feb. 1975.
3. Newfield, Jack. *New York Post* 1 March 1995.
4. New York State Legislature. Assembly. *Report on the Hearings of March 30, 1978, of the New York State Assembly Task Force on the Port of New York and the Waterfront*. Co-chairs Charles E. Schumer & Michael L. Pesce. Albany, NY: NYS Assembly, 1978.
5. Pesce, Michael. "Lindsay Years: Broken Streets, Broken Dreams." *Village Voice* 14 Jan. 1974.
6. Pesce, Michael. "Notes on a Blue Collar Reform Movement." *Pieces of Dream*. New York: Center for Migration Studies, 1973.
7. Ruggiero, Pino. "Da Mola a New York in Viaggio nel Sogno Americano." *La Gazzetta del Mezzogiorno* 28 Settembre 1994.
8. *Who's Who in American Politics*. 1997-1998 ed.

—by GEORGE CARPETTO, Ph.D.

JAMES CAESAR PETRILLO (1892-1984)

Beginning as a small-time union leader and then shaping the American Federation of Musicians into one of the most powerful and well-organized negotiating vehicles for American musicians, he clashed with everyone who stood in the way of respectful wages for working musicians. He clashed with President Roosevelt in 1942, and Petrillo even compelled recording companies to pay royalties to musicians and unions alike after an historic twenty-seven-month strike. True to his sense of labor justice, even after retirement, he fought segregation and racial prejudice in unions well before the 60s legislation insuring civil rights. A fiercely caring negotiator for those he represented in the evolution of American unionism, he was a brave and truly colorful figure, reputedly possessing a pistol close-by and traveling in a bulletproof car.

James Petrillo was born on March 16, 1892 in Chicago's notorious West Side. His father was an emigrant from Italy who labored digging ditches for the city's waste management system. Far from an ideal student, young James struggled through the elementary school system from which he would never graduate, quitting after nine years of uneventful attendance. He had started playing the trumpet at eight, and in his teens he was a member of a band called the *Daily News*. He held many odd jobs including working for the band. Being his own worst critic and possessing a unique and precipitately street-smart sense of humor, he openly avowed noticing little "audible improvement" in his playing even after many years of performing.

At one point in his teens, he had even organized his own band that played at Jewish and Italian weddings and at local beer gardens. In addition to being the band organizer, he presented himself as a trumpeter; but, reportedly, to appease his listeners, he soon switched to playing the drums "by popular request." A bit of an entrepreneur, he was also involved in many other small businesses from time to time. Not professing to having a perfect command of the "King's English," he was often colorfully metaphoric and eloquent when he spoke. For instance, when asked why he chose unionism as his lifetime work, he would answer, "I liked punching holes in the other guy's argument."

His union career began when he joined a Chicago independent union, the American Musicians Union (AMU). Later in 1914 at age twenty-two, he became its president and remained in that capacity for three years until 1917 when he lost his bid at reelection. Apparently no longer wanted by the AMU, he switched and joined the American Federation of Musicians (AFM). Despite experiencing some unpopular reactions in his earlier soundings of the AMU members, he was elected AFM vice president in 1919 and later in 1922 became its president earning a $100-a-week salary.

Once empowered as president, he began his ongoing fight for Chicagoan musicians and immediately achieved greater security and some remarkable benefits for his fellow musicians. At that time in history, broadcasting in commercial radio had become the new and exciting medium of expression just as TV would become the new medium phenomenon in the late 40s. When musicians were let go indiscriminately from radio programs—in this new fledgling industry—Petrillo fought to reinstate them; and, to boot, he engineered contracts so that musicians were no longer necessitated to work a seven-day work-week and were able to keep their seven-day salary. Petrillo was also responsible for negotiating union-rate salaries for radio broadcast-studio technicians who turned the records during airing times.

The year 1927 took him away from radio to another arena, the theater. This was the era of the so-called "roaring twenties," a time of relative prosperity in the United States. It appeared that many Chicago theater owners who were doing well had called into question Petrillo's rights as union leader and his powers over his members. He quickly retaliated by making his two-thousand-musician group go on strike, and within four days, the theater owners conceded to Petrillo. When the strike was ended, the remaining non-unionized musicians joined Petrillo's musicians union.

After the stock market crash struck American society in 1929, the effort to keep union leadership strong and its membership united became more difficult. Despite the hard times and the complexities of the 30s, in 1931 Petrillo still negotiated with Chicago hotels; he demanded that they had to sign contracts for their New Year's Eve musicians or they would go on strike. In a similar vein, in 1936 in an effort to cut short the all-too-easy road to making money by musicians bypassing union rules, Petrillo prohibited Chicago musicians from making recordings for use in broadcasting without union involvement.

A few years earlier in 1933, Petrillo, whose concern was for musicians being able to find work at union wages, had ingeniously gotten himself appointed to Chicago's Park Board. By the year 1935, he had managed to get the board's approval to let some of his union members give a series of free open-air concerts in Grant Park while payment to the musicians for their work would come directly out of union coffers. It proved to be a huge success, and for the next year and the ensuing years he managed to get the board to assume the responsibility for subsidizing the open-air concerts, which since the 1930s have become a Chicago tradition featuring blues, gospel, jazz, country, and symphonic music at Grant Park.

Petrillo's reputation for financial integrity, which withstood the acid test of audits throughout the tough and corruptible years of the 1930s earned him a $25,000 summer home in Wisconsin gifted to him by his union members. By the year 1940, his steadfastness as head of his Chicago AFM local caused him to earn a salary of $26,000 per annum. On June 24, 1940 with the help of his Chicago local, he reached the pinnacle of his career when he was elected president of the American Federation of Musicians (AMF) at the national level where he had the opportunity to wield his union principles nationwide, and he would soon become involved in a new area for musicians: TV in the late 40s. Petrillo would also begin a new fight against the prevailing racial segregation in unions.

An unsung hero of American unionism, James Petrillo probably did more for the financial stability, security, and respect for American musicians that any other person to date. Starting from humble beginnings and lacking the talent to be a great musician himself, he excelled in his ability to organize musicians, negotiate with management over working conditions, salaries and benefits, and royalty contracts. He died at age 92 on October 23, 1984 in his native city of Chicago where he is remembered by the Petrillo Music Shell in Grant Park, home of the Grant Park Symphony Orchestra whose summer music festivals are enjoyed yearly by millions of people.

General Sources:
1. *Current Biography/Yearbook*. New York: Wilson, 1940; 1985.
2. Leiter, Robert. *The Musicians and Petrillo*. New York: Octagon Books, 1974.
3. "Obituary." *New York Times* 25 Oct. 1984: B 22.

—by DENNIS PIASIO

ROCCO PETRONE (1926-   )

Along with Neil Armstrong and Christopher Kraft, Rocco Petrone was acclaimed in 1970 as three of the men most responsible for the success of the *Apollo 11* moon flight which included the world's first lunar landing, Armstrong's first step on the moon's surface on July 20, 1969, and the safe return of the Apollo astronaut team to Earth. The development of a winning strategy and the eventual victory of a lunar landing with all its historical significance was not without its frantic moments. This outstanding achievement, that involved a safe liftoff and a capable delivery system to the moon and back, clearly established the United States as the new leader in space technology and exploration.

Rocco Petrone was born on March 31, 1926 in Amsterdam, New York, a town not far from Schenectady. The son of Italian-American parents, Anthony and Theresa (nee DeLuca) Petrone, he obtained his B.S. at the United States Military Academy in 1946. He later earned a masters degree in mechanical engineering from the Massachusetts Institute of Technology in 1952 after which he worked as a research and development officer at the Redstone Missile Development Base in Huntsville, Alabama. Four years later, he moved to Washington, D.C. where he became a member of the Army general staff and served in that position until 1960. On October 29, 1955, he married Ruth Holley, and they would have a family of four children: Teresa, Nancy, Kathryn, and Michael.

In 1960 Petrone began his work with the Apollo program. He was selected by both Pentagon personnel and other government leaders for very specific reasons. He possessed first-rate credentials in the field of engineering, specifically in the field of rocketry science, which had begun with his work at the Redstone Missile Development Base in Alabama. He was also heavily involved with the development of the Saturn V booster rocket (under Dr. Wernher von Braun's direction), that had replaced the Saturn IB rocket and became the workhorse of the Apollo program, used to launch the *Apollo 11* spacecraft to the moon in the late 1960s and other crafts in the early 1970s. An impressive full-scale Saturn V booster rocket has been recently placed on permanent exhibition at the Apollo/Saturn V Center on Merritt Island, Florida.

Petrone was also selected for this project because he had demonstrated excellent leadership qualities. His administrative duties would necessarily involve dealing with a highly diverse blend of people consisting of concerned military personnel, a highly educated class of civilian scientists, an emerging specialized group of aerospace manufacturers, and a highly skilled technical and computer-driven work force. He was manager of the Apollo program at the Kennedy Space Center (KSC) for six years beginning in 1960. In 1966 Petrone moved from program manager to director of launch operations until 1969. After the success of the *Apollo 11* mission, he was promoted to director of the Apollo program at NASA.

Petrone was interviewed in his Washington, D.C. office in July 1970 on the occasion of the first anniversary of the eventful moon landing. When confronted with the issues of the exceedingly high costs of space exploration coupled with the reality of the federal government's budgetary limitations and its responsibilities to the people on welfare needing housing and education, he answered,

"You've got to have houses and cities. But you also must have something that will let men look up out of the muck and the mire." Within the context of the power of his position and the enormous responsibilities during the highly intricate pre-flight chronology whose game plan involved the fully functioning interplay of over one million parts and the ultimate safety of the astronaut team, he humbly and paradoxically stated that the success of *Apollo 11* signified "a sheer demonstration of power without arrogance."

This space adventure all began in the early 1960s when the United States was sorely lagging behind the Soviet Union in space exploration, and President Kennedy in May 1961 urged Congress to appropriate the necessary monies for the then young National Aeronautics and Space Administration (NASA) to do its work. He reiterated the importance of NASA's goals for landing a man on the moon and for creating a manned space station around the Earth. Kennedy's insistence on these goals captured new impetus when they became a media-driven nationwide mandate in the 60s.

NASA's Gemini series of flights lasting five years between 1961-1966 demonstrated clearly that spacecrafts could be piloted outside of the Earth's atmosphere and that orbital rendezvous, docking, and living for extended periods of time in outer space were all feasible. The Apollo series whose planning stages also dated back to the early 1960s were put into action in the winter of 1967. On January 27, 1967, during a "routine test" for the scheduled *Apollo 1*, a fire inside the command module tragically killed three astronauts at KSC. The tragedy caused Petrone to rally all the forces of the Kennedy Space Center to move forward despite the tragic loss.

Working harder than before, they were able—through the determined efforts of Petrone's leadership—21 months later on October 11, 1968 to successfully launch *Apollo 7* that became the first manned Apollo flight lasting eleven days in Earth orbit. This proved so successful that just two months later on December 21, 1968 they launched *Apollo 8* that became the first manned flight *around* the moon. All these missions were preparatory for the eventual *Apollo 11* moon landing mission.

Eight months later, they launched the history-making *Apollo 11*, and on a very memorable July 20, 1969 Armstrong became the first man to step on the surface of the moon where he and later Edwin Aldrin collected 48.5 pounds of soil and rock samples to bring to Earth for scientific research. Together with Michael Collins, the lunar team had remained on the moon for 23.5 hours. The moon landing and the moon walks became one of the most televised events in worldwide TV history. Then, everyone merely waited for the astronauts' safe return home to Earth.

Along with many honors, awards, and commendations, Rocco Petrone received an honorary doctorate from Rollins College in 1969 for his accomplishments. He retired from NASA in 1975 leaving behind a legacy of hard work, dedication, and the clear fulfillment of President Kennedy's mandate to put a man on the moon by the end of the 1960s. He took on the position of CEO at the National Center for Resource Recovery until 1981, and then after joining Rockwell International, he subsequently retired.

General Sources:

1. *American Men & Women of Science.* New Providence, NJ: Bowker, 1998.
2. Murray, Charles A. *Apollo: The Race to the Moon.* New York: Simon & Schuster, 1989.
3. *Newsweek* 27 July 1970: 76.
4. *U.S. News and World Report* 2 Aug. 1971: 21-2.
5. *U.S. News and World Report* 18 Dec. 1972: 17-19.
6. *Who's Who in America.* 1972-73 ed.

—by GEORGE CARPETTO Ph.D.

GIUSEPPE PETROSINO (1860-1909)

Giuseppe Michele Pasquale Petrosino, who would someday become one of New York City's most celebrated policemen and detectives, was the inventor of the "bomb squad," the first unit of its kind in the United States to fight the Black Hand. As head of a highly-select corps of Italian-American undercover cops, he was responsible for having deported to Italy no less than 500-1,000 criminals, mostly extortionists.

He was born on August 30, 1860 to Prospero and Maria (nee Arato) Petrosino in Salerno, Italy. His mother died at a young age, and after his father remarried, he moved the entire family to New York in 1873. At thirteen, Giuseppe helped out with the family finances by selling newspapers and shining shoes. Prophetically, his shoeshine stand stood just outside of the police headquarters on Mulberry Street (Little Italy) in lower Manhattan.

When Petrosino decided to join the police, his timing was right. He spoke English and many Italian dialects as well, and it was at a time in the 1880s when emigration from southern Italy to America was beginning to accelerate. The NYPD, primarily Irish, needed young Italian-American policemen like Petrosino to be able to communicate more effectively with Italian immigrants. Petrosino became in effect the first Italian-American cop recruited by the NYPD.

Petrosino spent almost ten years as a patrolman dealing with some unsavory immigrants who had crossed the ocean right along with their law-abiding counterparts. In 1890 he was promoted to the investigative area. The police commissioner at the time was Theodore Roosevelt who had appointed him sergeant in charge of detectives in undercover operations. After the underworld members became aware of this tactic, they used the word "petrosino" as a code word along with other words in sentences to indicate that Petrosino or his men were snooping around. In the southern Italian dialects, "petrosino" means parsley.

Petrosino dealt with many different facets of the underworld, which at that time was also loosely called the Black Hand. While the origin of this term historically had dealt more with anarchists, i.e., political subversives wanting to overthrow the government and killing government officials, for Petrosino it usually meant extortionists who exacted money from their own fellow Italians. Ironically, Petrosino in addition to dealing with extortionists did in fact uncover a plot to kill President William McKinley. He immediately went to Washington to warn the president of a threat against his life, but McKinley gave it little credence, and ignoring Petrosino's warning, he was assassinated shortly thereafter on December 6, 1901 as Petrosino had warned would happen.

However, most of the so-called Black Hand in Petrosino's purview were extortionists, and, characteristically, they would send "knife letters." Those letters bearing different emblems such as a clenched fists, daggers, swords, or skulls were designed to intimidate the recipient into paying "protection money." It was in this area that Giuseppe Petrosino had duly acquired a reputation for getting convictions for his captured criminals.

The year 1906 proved to be a very good year for Petrosino. Theodore A. Bingham, the new police commissioner, assigned Petrosino a newly created leadership post within the NYPD called the Italian Legion. In the same year, Giuseppe Petrosino, at age 46, also found love. He met, courted, and married Adelina Vinti a year later in April 1907. In the fall of 1908, Joe Petrosino experienced two wonderful events in his life. In October, he was presented with a gold watch by the Italian government for rounding up criminals who had run from Italian justice. More joy followed shortly thereafter when, on November 30, he became a father with the birth of his daughter, Adelina. Delighted with fatherhood, he'd rush home every night to be with his family.

A newly enacted U.S. immigration law had made the deportation of unwanted criminals possible. Joe Petrosino and his undercover policemen worked hard. They arrested well over 1,000 members of the Black Hand and managed to deport anywhere between 500 to 1,000 of them. Petrosino was also responsible for being the founder of the "bomb squad" to counter the Black Hand and its use of explosives in their extortion threats.

Petrosino's good fortune, however, would run out in February 1909 when he was compelled to travel to Sicily on a police assignment to gather intelligence information on the Black Hand. Bingham had become careless and leaked the story to the newspapers undermining Petrosino's cover. Joe Petrosino already in Italy remained unaware of this leak to the press. When he arrived in Palermo, he spoke with the local police commissioner, Baldassare Ceola on March 6th. Their meeting did not go well as they ended up arguing. After that disappointment, Petrosino spent his time taking notes, making observations, and making a list of criminals to be investigated in America for deportation. One of those names listed was that of Vito Cascio Ferro.

However, Petrosino would never have the chance to investigate the members on that list. It seems that on Friday, March 12, 1909 in the city of Palermo, Petrosino, the man who had once turned the criminal world upside down in the United States and in Italy, was murdered on the way back to his hotel room while his murderers disappeared into the night. The news of his death shocked the United States and American police authorities. After his body was returned to New York City, his funeral was reportedly attended by well over 200,000 people, and the procession itself was five-and-one-half hours in length. Commissioner Bingham was later removed from office. Detective Petrosino, in effect, had became the only NYPD officer killed in the line of duty outside of the United States.

An anonymous letter to the NYPD mentioned names of those responsible for the murder. The list included the name of Vito Cascio Ferro, who reportedly had always carried Petrosino's picture in his pocket and had said that one day he would kill him. Ferro was eventually imprisoned on other charges; and in a confession years later, he admitted to having been responsible. Ferro died in 1941, after having been "accidentally" left in his prison cell without food or water for an extended period.

Petrosino's life story was later made into a popular movie starring Ernest Borgnine, and it was entitled *Pay or Die* in 1960. There is a park in New York City named after him and a book written by Arrigo Petacco, entitled *Joe Petrosino*. Even today, the mention of the name Joe Petrosino to NYPD members or in the police museum in New York City brings instant recognition.

General Sources:
1. "Lieutenant Petrosino." *NYPD- Spring 3100*. 3 Apr. 1998. <http://www.ci.nyc.ny.us/nypd/html/3100/retro-22.html>.
2. Mangione, Jerre, and Ben Morreale. *La Storia: Five Centuries of the Italian American Experience*. New York: HarperCollins, 1992.
3. Petacco, Arrigo. *Joe Petrosino*. Trans. Charles Lam Markmann. New York: Macmillan, 1974.

—by LINDA D'ANDREA-MARINO

BRIAN PICCOLO (1943-1970)

Excelling in football, baseball, and basketball as a youngster, Brian Piccolo became a local superstar during his high school days at Central Catholic in Fort Lauderdale, Florida. After receiving a sports scholarship to attend Wake Forest College in North Carolina, he went on to become a great college football player happily fulfilling people's expectations. In his senior year of college, Brian held both the Atlantic Coast Conference (ACC) and the National titles in rushing yards, and was also named the ACC's Most Valuable Player. In 1970, at the young age of 26, in a cruel twist of fate during his professional football career with the Chicago Bears, he succumbed after a seven-month-long battle with one of the deadliest forms of cancer. To commemorate his life, Hollywood would make an inspiring film called *Brian's Song*.

Brian Piccolo was born on October 31, 1943 in Pittsfield, Massachusetts. At the time of his birth, he had two older brothers. Joe was eight years of age, and Dan was two. When Brian reached three years of age, the family moved to Fort Lauderdale where the three brothers grew up closely knit and playing lots of sports together. Brian's father, Joseph Piccolo, Sr., born in Naples, Italy was proud of his Italian heritage; and together with his wife Irene, who was of German-Hungarian extraction, they offered their boys a strong sense of family.

Brian began his sports career starring in Little League Baseball and in Boy's League Football. Later, as a 185-pound high school senior, he could block, tackle, and catch football like no one else in his area, and he made every local all-star team. He became noted both for his speed in carrying the football and for his good judgement in making the right moves for a touchdown. Football scouts had observed his excellent playing all along, and before graduation he was offered several scholarships. He finally chose to go to Wake Forest College in North Carolina.

As a freshman football player, Brian scored five touchdowns, four points after touchdown, and averaged 4.2 yards per carry. As a sophomore, Brian gained 400 yards and still averaged 4.2 yards. Despite his efforts, Wake Forest lost all ten games. In his junior year, Wake Forest lost eight straight games until Pic (Brian's nickname) squeaked a 20-19 win by kicking the extra point, and that was their only win of that season. Brian's reputation as a hard-running and quick-thinking player was growing.

His senior year (1964) proved to be his best college season. Pic scored three touchdowns in the very first game of the season when Wake Forest beat Virginia 31-21. Brian then went on to score all 20 points in Wake Forest's 20-7 victory against highly favored Duke. Impressed with Piccolo's playing, United Press International and *Sports Illustrated* named Brian Piccolo the Back of the Week. After Brian accumulated the ACC and the national titles in rushing yards (1,044) and scoring 111 points, he was named ACC's Most Valuable Player. Based on its prior history, Wake Forest had been expected to finish last, but through Brian's efforts and those of a new coach, Wake Forest concluded the season with a commendable 5-5 record. Piccolo also played baseball as a centerfielder for Wake Forest, and that year he hit a .375 average.

Despite reasonable expectations that Brian would be swooped up into the professional National Football League (NFL) on the first draft, all 440 college football players were drafted but not Piccolo. Later, after the drafting period and after turning down several offers such as those from the Cleveland Browns and the Baltimore Colts, he accepted an offer from the Chicago Bears where he joined as a free agent. At his wedding reception where 250 guests attended, he wanted to incorporate into his reception decorum his successful acceptance on the Bears football club. He cleverly had an ice-carved bear made and had it placed on display for his family and friends at his wedding.

Brian Piccolo's development on the Bears team started to take shape in a consistent and determined manner. After pulling a hamstring muscle in his early months, he was placed on the so-called "taxi squad" for most of the '65 season, practicing but not actively playing on Sunday games. By the '66 season, Brian Piccolo made the active roster and played football relegated to the "bomb" squad (kick-offs and punt returns). In the '67 and '68 seasons, both Brian Piccolo and Gale Sayers played so well that they had become outstanding players in the eyes of the media. Both seemed to be heading for fame and fortune in the coming years.

On November 24, 1969, after experiencing a persistently painful cough, Brian entered the New York City Sloan-Kettering Cancer Center for a biopsy and a battery of related tests. A terrible war with cancer had now begun. He had a tumor in his chest cavity, and the cancer was diagnosed as embryonal cell carcinoma. The next day, Brian underwent an operation during which the doctors removed a large tumor the size of a grapefruit that was adhering to his lung. The doctors also removed a significantly smaller tumor near one of his lymph nodes. At this stage, the prognosis seemed good, and since the early healing process also seemed to be progressing well, he was eventually discharged from the hospital.

In February 1970, he returned to the Sloan-Kettering Center with suspicions of additional cancer growth. On March 24, he underwent surgery to remove a tumor on his pectoral muscle, and this was followed by more surgery on April 9. On May 28, Brian returned with his wife Joy to Fort Lauderdale to be reunited with their three daughters. Joy, who was by his side throughout Brian's ordeal with cancer, spent her last day with Brian on June 15 as he passed on the next day at 2 a.m.

In 1971, one year after Brian's death, Hollywood decided to make a TV movie commemorating the football player's life story, and it was titled *Brian's Song*. It was a most uplifting movie for all ages but especially popular with teenagers and young adults. It starred James Caan whose stunning true-to-life performance of Brian Piccolo earned him an Emmy nomination. Billy Dee Williams, who played the role of Gale Sayers, together with Caan performed as the Chicago Bears' first interracial on-the-road roommates in the team's history. The story dealt poignantly with a host of football-related struggles and, of course, with Brian Piccolo's travails during his fatal illness and untimely death from cancer.

Today the film, *Brian's Song* (winner of five Emmy Awards) and the book, *Brian Piccolo: A Short Season*, stand as worthy commemorations of a loving and sensitive husband, a dedicated father of three children, a strong determined personality, and a great football player cut down by a fatal illness in his prime.

General Sources:
1. *Brian's Song*. Dir. Buzz Kulik. Perf. James Caan, Billy Dee Williams, and Jack Warden. Columbia TriStar, 1971.
2. Morris, Jeannie. *Brian Piccolo: A Short Season*. Chicago: Bonus Books, 1995.
3. Morris, Jeannie. *Brian Piccolo: A Short Season*. Chicago: Rand McNally, 1971.
4. *The Official Encyclopedia of Football*. South Brunswick, NJ: Barnes, 1976.

—by JOSEPH PIGNATIELLO

EZIO PINZA (1892-1957)

Gifted with an unusually rich and varied basso voice which easily carried over into baritone ranges, he was a concert singer, a member of the New York Metropolitan Opera House for twenty-two seasons (1926-1948), star of radio, film, stage, and early TV. Mostly acclaimed as an opera singer who for years had earned fame and recognition in such roles as Don Giovanni and Boris Godunoff, and as Mephistopheles in *Faust* at the Metropolitan Opera, he swept away audiences with his memorable role of Emile de Becque in the Broadway musical play, *South Pacific* (1949-1950), with his highly textured voice and charismatic Mediterranean charm. He also scored great success a few years later in another well-known and popular Broadway musical play, *Fanny* (1954-1956).

Ezio Pinza was born in Rome, Italy on May 18, 1892. He was the seventh of nine children of Cesare and Clelia (nee Bulgarelli), and he was one of only three children to have survived infancy. Years later, after Ezio's birth, his father moved the family, returning to his native city of Ravenna where Ezio spent his growing years. While in his teens Ezio became a helper in his father's carpentry shop and was also a delivery boy for a local baker. He desired to become a civil engineer, and after attending a technical school in the city of Ravenna for a short-lived duration of one year, he changed course deciding to become a professional bicycle racer. When he won no racing events, his father urged him to return to engineering.

Though until that time he had never seriously thought of a music career, his bicycle rider friends who had heard him sing were the ones responsible for first suggesting that he consider a singing career over his racing. Later, in negotiating vocational options with his father, Ezio finally worked out an agreement whereby he would drop racing and his father would support his decision to study music instead of going back to engineering. He attended the Bologna Conservatory of Music for two years.

In 1914, he made his opera debut in the role of a Druid priest in Bellini's *Norma*. The performance took place in Soncini, a small town outside of Milan where he later performed other roles as well. This series of performances had occurred right before Italy declared war on the Austro-Hungarian Alliance in May 1915, Italy's formal entrance into World War I. Pinza enlisted in the Italian Army; and after training, he was stationed in artillery in the Italian Alps where he remained until the end of the war. After doing riot-prevention duty in Naples, he was discharged in 1919 with the rank of captain, physically unscathed by war.

After a brief job with the railroads, he found work in opera by the end of 1919 in Rome at the Teatro Reale dell'Opera. For his first role, he appeared as King Mark in Wagner's *Tristan und Isolde*. Subsequent to this auspicious start in Rome, he remained there for two years after which he enjoyed having engagements in several cities including Turin, Naples, and Ravenna. In his hometown of Ravenna alone, he proudly sang in twenty consecutive performances as Mephistopheles in *Faust*. Ezio Pinza's experience and fame had grown, and for the next three years he would have the good fortune to appear at La Scala di Milano which at that time was under the direction of Arturo Toscanini.

During his stay at La Scala, Pinza was later assigned an important role in Arrigo Boito's world premiere performance of *Nerone* in 1924. The general manager of the New York

Metropolitan Opera, Giulio Gatti-Casazza, who had heard Pinza sing in that opera offered him an opportunity to sing at the Metropolitan Opera at some future time. Ezio Pinza finally made his debut at the Met on November 1, 1926 where he appeared as Pontifex Maximus in Spontini's *La Vestale*. Pinza's basso voice scored immediate success with New York critics and audiences.

As he became more appreciated, his roles at the Met increased. In 1929 Pinza was eventually given his first title role in Mozart's *Don Giovanni*, a role with which he would be associated throughout his career. His reputation for singing a variety of quality basso roles and for performing with a versatility of style (i.e., singing enhanced by good acting) grew consistently throughout the 1930s. Bruno Walter asked Pinza to sing at the prestigious Salzburg Festival in 1935 where he performed the role of Don Giovanni and was invited again in 1937 to sing in Mozart's *Marriage of Figaro*.

Before returning to the Metropolitan, he made a tour of Europe, Australia, and the United States. Towards the end of the 1930s, he had become so popular as a concert singer that in the United States alone he averaged as many as sixty concerts a year, often visiting as many as fifty different cities. Soon in 1939 Ezio Pinza inevitably became the new lead basso at the Metropolitan succeeding the one-time star basso, Chaliapin, who had died. Prior to World War II, Pinza had achieved some significant milestones in his life. He officially became an American citizen, was promoted to lead basso at the Met, and had acquired experience in over fifty distinct operatic roles.

In the 40s and 50s, Ezio Pinza reached the acme of his career, known worldwide for his basso voice and the basso roles he sang. In 1944, he was pronounced one of the ten most "glamorous men" by a *Harper's Bazaar* poll. He became known as a perfectionist in the roles he sang as he had acquired a reputation for having researched the historical backgrounds of the operatic characters portrayed. In all, as Met's new star basso, he remained there until 1948, completing twenty-two seasons with them.

Ezio Pinza had left few stones unturned throughout his long career. He appeared in about four films beginning with *Rehearsal* (1947), *Mr. Imperium* (1951), *Strictly Dishonorable* (1951), and *Tonight We Sing* (1953). He also appeared on many TV shows and eventually had his own program called *The Ezio Pinza Show*, appearing on alternate Friday evenings on NBC-TV in November 1951. In March 1953, he also had his own Saturday morning radio program called the *Ezio Pinza Radio Show*, a program designed as a "music appreciation course" appealing to all ages.

Despite his long and brilliant career at the New York Metropolitan Opera, Ezio Pinza will be best remembered for his most captivating and *enchanting* singing role that took place on Broadway. It was the role as the star of *South Pacific* (1949-1950) which he played for over a year, singing every night to capacity audiences. In particular, it included a song that would soon become his signature piece "Some Enchanted Evening." After a two-year appearance in another hit musical, *Fanny* (1954-1956), he died at 65 on May 9, 1957 leaving a legacy of superb showmanship, singing, and acting, always conveying a deep love and respect for music.

General Sources:
1. *Current Biography*. New York: Wilson, 1953; 1957.
2. Ewen, David. *The New Encyclopedia of the Opera*. New York: Hill and Wang, 1971.
3. Pinza, Ezio. *Ezio Pinza: An Autobiography*. New York: Arno Press, 1977.
4. Sadie, Stanley, ed. *The New Grove Dictionary of Opera*. New York: Grove's Dictionaries of Music, 1992.
5. *Who's Who in America*. 1952-1953 ed.

—by DENNIS PIASIO

WALTER PISTON (1894-1976)

A prolific music composer, author of four books on music composition, educator, and winner of two Pulitzer Prizes, once in 1948 for his *Third Symphony* and, again, in 1961 for his *Seventh Symphony*, Walter Piston became known internationally early in his career as an articulate American artist. In addition to his many compositions in symphonic, chamber and orchestral music, he enjoyed a rich and rewarding teaching career at Harvard University having instructed many students such as Leonard Bernstein who went on to compose and direct. A reputedly excellent teacher, Piston was also a creative theoretician whose books on harmonics, counterpoint, and orchestration are still in use today as standard music texts and have been translated into scores of languages including Chinese, Japanese, and Korean.

Walter Piston was born on January 20, 1894 in Rockland, Maine. He was one of four sons of Walter and Leona (nee Stover) Piston. His Italian ancestry goes back to his paternal grandfather, Antonio *Pistone* whose last name was abbreviated to the English-sounding Piston. In 1905 the Piston family moved from Rockland to Boston, Massachusetts where young Walter received most of his education. He did not come from a musical family, but his parents supported his interest in music when he decided to join his school orchestra where he played violin. After graduation from Mechanic Arts High School, he worked for a while as a draftsman for the Boston Elevated Railway Company.

From 1912 to 1916 he attended the Massachusetts Normal Art School. In the past, a normal school typically prepared students to become teachers. While going to school, Walter Piston supported himself by playing piano and violin music at restaurants, cafes, and at social functions. When World War I began, he applied to become a member of the United States Navy Band. He was accepted and was placed in its aeronautics division stationed at the Massachusetts Institute of Technology. By the end of WWI, he made a decision to devote his energies entirely to music. At age 26 in 1920, he entered Harvard University as a freshman.

He worked hard as a student, and he graduated in 1924 with a B.A. degree in music *summa cum laude* and earned membership in Phi Beta Kappa. More importantly, he was awarded a John Knowles Paine Fellowship, a two-year grant which afforded Piston a study program in Paris, France at the École Normale de Musique. While in France he had the opportunity to study music with mentors Nadia Boulanger and Paul Dukas. He had acquired a strong liking for French neoclassical music, and he also had the opportunity to enjoy a revival in the works of Bach which was taking place at the time.

During that two-year period, Piston was also actively composing music, and two of his works, a *Piano Sonata* and *Three Pieces for Flute, Clarinet, and Bassoon*, had their premiere performance in Paris. In addition to employing many traditional neoclassical techniques, Piston also experimented in the use of non-traditional blending of instruments such as in his *Three Pieces for Flute, Clarinet and Bassoon*. One of his early distinguishing traits as a composer involved creating new sounds through the innovative use of instrument combinations. This would become one of his signature techniques.

When he returned to the United States, he assumed faculty status at Harvard University's music department where he went on to earn a full professorship in 1944 and would remain at Harvard until retirement in 1959. In 1951, eight years before his retirement, he was awarded the Naumberg Professorship in Music, a prestigious chair from Harvard University's endowment organization. An author of no less than four books dealing with the quintessential topics of harmonics, counterpoint, and orchestration, his works have since become standard texts for many music students and have been translated into numerous languages for students abroad.

Piston prescribed that students aspiring to write music, in addition to studying theory, needed to study concrete examples of composers' works prior to the 1900s. The understanding of music begins with the study of harmonics, the simultaneous sounding of two or more tones (which produce chords) and their relationship to each other. These components in turn become the foundation for melody. Until the 1900s, harmonics was considered *tonal*, i.e. the traditionally established way of writing music. With the advent of the twentieth century, *atonality* (defined as both the absence of a functional center and tonic qualities) breaks most rules—if not all the rules—of harmonics.

Piston's great strength as a teacher, author of books, and as a composer himself allowed him to integrate the elements of this rather complex scenario of tonal and atonal music into a broad-based design, geared to an understanding which avoided narrowly focused interests of some teachers who promoted one composing style over another. Piston's methods of teaching proved successful as he was influential in offering a firm and rich background for his students, many of whom went on to be become well-known musicians and composers in their own right.

Walter Piston's fruitful career of honors and awards include grants, commissions, fellowships, and two Pulitzer Prizes. After earning his 1924 two-year scholarship allowing him to study in Paris, he also received a Guggenheim Fellowship in 1935. In the same year, he was also commissioned by the Elizabeth Sprague Coolidge Foundation to write a composition which resulted in his *Trio for Violin, Cello, and Piano* (1935). A grant from the Alice Ditson Fund allowed Piston to write his *Second Symphony,* first performed in 1944 in Washington, D.C., which earned him the New York Music Critics Circle Award.

Four years later, commissioned by the Koussevitzky Foundation, Piston went on to compose his *Third Symphony* that earned him both his first Pulitzer Prize in music in 1948 and the Boston Symphony's Horblit Award. In 1961 his *Seventh Symphony,* sponsored by the Philadelphia Orchestra Association, earned Piston his second Pulitzer Prize. The recipient of two more New York Music Critics Circle Awards for his *Viola Concerto* and *String Quartet No. 5*, Piston also was the recipient of eight honorary doctorates, including one from Harvard University. Walter Piston, who died November 12, 1976, left an enormous legacy in music. From his many notable works, he will probably be best remembered for his musical suites, *The Incredible Flutist* and *Three New England Sketches*.

General Sources:
1. *Current Biography Yearbook*. New York: Wilson, 1961; 1977.
2. *The New Grove Dictionary of American Music*. Ed. H. Wiley Hitchcock and Stanley Sadie. New York: New Grove's Dictionaries, 1986.
3. Piston, Walter. *Counterpoint*. New York: Norton, 1947.
4. Piston, Walter. *Harmony*. New York: Norton, 1978.
5. Piston, Walter. *Orchestration*. New York: Norton, 1955.
6. Pollack, Howard. *Harvard Composers: Walter Piston and His Students*. Metuchen, NJ: Scarecrow Press, 1992.
7. Pollack, Howard. *Walter Piston*. Ann Arbor, MI: UMI Research Press, 1982.

—by GEORGE CARPETTO, Ph.D.

RICK PITINO (1952-   )

A determined leader who early in his coaching career had established a reputation for turning around several losing teams into winners, Rick Pitino became especially sought after as a head coach when he took over the reins of the University of Kentucky's Wildcats. After reversing their downward spiral, Pitino brought the Wildcats to the NCAA championship in 1996, their first title in 18 years. Subsequent to that event, the New Jersey Nets reportedly made him an offer worth more than $30 million over a five-season time frame. Deciding to turn down the Nets' offer, he remained with Kentucky for another year, sticking with his $3 million per annum income. After compiling an overall record with Kentucky of 218 wins and 50 losses, he finally accepted a very lucrative offer from the Boston Celtics in May 1997.

Rick Pitino was born in Manhattan on September 18, 1952 to Rosario (Sal) and Charlotte (nee Newman) Pitino. Rick's father was a building superintendent whose parents had emigrated from Sicily and operated a fruit stand in New York City. When Rick was six, he, his two older brothers, and parents left Manhattan and went to reside in Cambria Heights, a predominantly residential community in the adjacent borough of Queens. Rick's mother was an administrator at Bellevue Hospital in Manhattan; and she and her husband commuted regularly into the city to work. By the time Rick was 14, the family moved to Bayville, a town on Long Island's north shore.

By this time in his life, Rick had become extremely involved in basketball. In his senior year at St. Dominic's High School, he was averaging 28 points and 10 assists a game. He became known as Rifle Rick, and he became a member of the Long Island Catholic High School All-Star team. He pursued his interests in basketball by attending Howard Garfinkel's well-known Five Star Basketball Camp in the Catskills during the summers, first, as a trainee and, later, as a counselor. The latter position served him well as he experienced his first exposure to playing a coaching role. This serendipitous event allowed him to discover his apparent great ability to inspire and motivate others on the basketball court.

Yet it must have been somewhat disappointing to Rick when he went on to the University of Massachusetts where after receiving an athletic scholarship, he experienced as a player a relatively lackluster record despite his playing good defense and offense in his junior and senior years. Determined to stay in basketball, he accepted his first job as assistant coach of the Rainbows at the University of Hawaii. After a two-year stint, he returned to New York City where he met Jim Boeheim, who had been recently appointed head basketball coach at the University of Syracuse. Boeheim offered Pitino a job as assistant coach, and Pitino remained with the Orangemen team until 1978 when he became head coach of the Terriers at Boston University.

Pitino now found himself faced with tremendous challenges since the Terriers "had little talent, no tradition, scant support from student fans, and had won a total of only 17 games in its last two seasons." Rick Pitino, determined to create a turnaround, worked his newly acquired team into shape, at times, working them even on holidays and doing some unorthodox drilling. After spending five seasons with the Terriers, Pitino had raised them to the level of being able to compete in the NCAA post-season tournament. This was a first in the

Terriers' history, and they had also amassed in that five-season period a record of 91 wins and only 51 losses. It was no surprise that Pitino had impressed the basketball world and was named New England's Coach of the Year in 1978 and 1979.

In 1983 Pitino made a big move going from collegiate to professional basketball coaching. Stepping down from head coach status at the collegiate level, he became assistant coach to Hubie Brown with the New York Knicks, a professional team. Pitino spent two years with the Knicks but then returned to the collegiate circuit. He again took on the challenge of working with another weak, non-competitive team, the Friars of Providence College in Rhode Island.

Beginning in 1985, following his own fine example of what he had done with the Terriers, Pitino worked the Friars hard into becoming achievers and contenders. Into his second season as their head coach, Pitino witnessed the Friars soar to a 25-9 record that allowed them to compete in the 1987 NCAA tournament. While the Friars who reached the Final Four lost the championship, they had made for themselves a solid track record. Pitino, who had repeated his achievement of the classic turnaround of a once weak team into a highly skilled, motivated, and articulate team, had conclusively proven his coaching regimen as one endowed with high leadership.

In 1987 Pitino returned once more to professional basketball and again to the New York Knicks—this time, however, as their head coach. Disappointing some of his detractors who had thought that Pitino's magic in motivating college would not work for those playing professional, Pitino went on to turn around the Knicks' dismal record just as he done for the college teams. In the '84-'85 season, the Knicks had finished last in the Atlantic Division, but with hard work and training in just one season, Pitino moved them out of the bottom up to the playoffs. In their second season, the Knicks took their first Atlantic Division title in 18 seasons.

In 1989 after two seasons with the Knicks, Pitino again returned to the collegiate circuit accepting the position of head coach for the University of Kentucky Wildcats. Again, Pitino ended their downward spiral, and the Wildcats went to the NCAA championship in 1996, beating the Syracuse Orangemen, coached by Jim Boeheim, Pitino's one-time boss. Pitino, who remained with Kentucky for another year, in effect turned down the Nets' attempt to recruit him with a handsome $30 million package. However, he did leave to become head coach for the Boston Celtics in May 1997 for an incredible 10-year contract valued at more than $50 million, making Pitino the highest paid coach in the league. The contract also made him the president of the Celtics team. Along the way, Pitino has also found the time to write some books about what he knows best: basketball.

General Sources:
1. *Current Biography Yearbook*. New York: Wilson, 1998.
2. *Inside Sports* Nov. 1987: 40+.
3. *New York Times* 3 Apr. 1996: B14.
4. Pitino, Rick. Foreword. *Refuse to Lose*. By John Calipari & Dick Weiss. New York: Ballantine Books, 1996.
5. Pitino, Rick, and Bill Reynolds. *Born to Coach: A Season with the New York Knicks*. New York: New American Library, 1988.
6. Pitino, Rick, and Dick Weiss. *Full-Court Pressure: A Year in Kentucky Basketball*. New York: Hyperion, 1992.
7. Pitino, Rick, and Bill Reynolds. *Success is a Choice: Ten Steps to Overachieving in Business and Life*. New York: Broadway Books, 1997.
8. *Sports Illustrated* 11 Dec. 1989: 54+.
9. *Sports Illustrated* 26 Feb. 1996: 81-87+.

—by DENNIS PIASIO

LEO POLITI (1908-1996)

Leo Politi, prolific author and famous illustrator of children's books, spent his entire lifetime in the cause of bringing joy to America's youngest and perhaps most precious readership. He was born on November 21, 1908 in the town of Fresno, California to Italian parents. His father was a horse dealer, and the family lived on a ranch. When Leo was seven, the family decided to move back to Italy to his mother's hometown of Brani near Milan. It was a change in venue that proved to be instrumental in shaping much of young Leo's mind towards his future career as illustrator and writer of children's books.

Leo's favorite childhood storybook was Carlo Collodi's classic *Pinnochio* as illustrated by Attilo Mussino, Leo's favorite illustrator. In 1923, at the age of fifteen, Leo received a scholarship to the National Art Institute at the Royal Palace of Monza, which had been at one time the residence of King Umberto I of Italy. Later Leo also had the good fortune to study in London for a year. Leo studied many forms of art, including sculpture, architecture and design. His training was preparing him to be a school teacher, but Leo had other plans.

Leo, who at an early age had a sharp eye, was a critical observer, truly treasuring Italy's churches and museums, as well as its gardens and zoos where he'd often stop to make sketches. He also appreciated the lakes, the hillsides and terrain of central Italy. Other unique inspirations for his future craft emanated from his experiences observing artists sketching on the sidewalks in London. Leo, in fact, actually began his career in Italy by helping to illustrate a textbook for teaching deaf mutes.

In 1931, at age 23, Politi moved back to California. He traveled by way of the Panama Canal and was enthralled by the scenic beauty of Central America. At a later date, he expanded his knowledge of that part of the world by traveling through Mexico. In time, he married Helen Fontes, and they moved to Olvera Street in the Spanish district of Los Angeles where he felt comfortable studying and developing his craft. His children, Paul and Susanne, were born in that area.

Leo was very inspired by the Mexican atmosphere of Olvera Street. He painted and sold paintings, illustrated for magazines, and painted murals for theaters. Politi had become a regular contributor of illustrations to a magazine published in Los Angeles called *Script*. He used some of those illustrations in *Little Pancho* (1938), his first illustrated book. His art also brought him to do illustrations not only in his books but also in those of others such as Ruth Sawyer's *The Least One* (1941) and Helen Garrett's *Angelo and the Naughty One* (1944). He himself wrote and illustrated *Pedro, the Angel of Olvera Street* (1946), which became a well-known Christmas story favorite.

In 1947, a unique book entitled *Illustrators of Children's Books* was published. In addition to displaying a sampling of the illustrators' works, illustrators were invited to write a brief autobiographical summary. Naturally, Leo was invited to contribute to this book where he revealed that he had already been drawing quite well by the age of seven. He also recounted that his mother once bought him an Indian chief outfit before they left the United States. In Italy, when Leo wore his costume to school, his classmates were so distracted from school work that he was no longer able to wear it. His family's move to Italy and the Indian chief costume episode in class would later become the material for his children's book, *Little Leo,* in 1951.

A crowning achievement in Leo Politi's career came in 1950 when he was awarded the Caldecott Medal of the American Library Association for *Song of the Swallows* (1949). This delightful book tells the story of the swallows predictable return to and departure from Capistrano each year. The Caldecott Medal has been awarded annually since 1938 by the Association for Library Service to Children and by the American Library Association. Because Leo received the prestigious Caldecott Award along with so many other awards, May Hill Arbuthnot, a noted writer and editor for ScottForesman in her 1955 book, *Children and Books,* included a Politi illustration from *Little Leo* (1951) with his illustrations in Alice Dagliesh's book, *The Columbus Story* (1955).

For his book, *Looking for Something* (1951), Leo was the recipient of the 1952 *New York Herald Tribune* Spring Book Festival Award for picture books. In 1961 for his book, *Moy Moy* (1960), Leo also received the Southern California Council on Literature for Children and Young People Award for his significant contribution to children's literature in illustrations. In 1966 and again in 1980, Leo also received the Regina Medal from the Catholic Library Association for his "continued distinguished contribution to children's literature."

Regarding Politi's *Song of the Swallows,* Arbuthnot alludes to his Olvera Street influence with particular regard to the Mexican-American ceremony involving the blessing of the animals whose origins are to be found in St. Francis of Assisi. She describes Leo Politi as having "gentleness and decorative grace" that are feelings so important in satisfying children's need for beauty. The theme of gentleness towards animals will be also developed in Politi's *Saint Francis and the Animals* in 1959.

Arbuthnot notes that in observing Politi's work, one can see that his greatest strengths lie in his illustrations more than in his words. In particular, his illustrations of children seemed to contain a certain "unforgettable" character about them. It comes as no surprise, then, that Politi once wrote that he loved to draw pictures of small children more than anything else.

Leo Politi continued to write and illustrate children's books almost yearly with titles such as *All Things Bright and Beautiful, Piccolo's Prank,* and *The Poinsettia.* His last work, *Mr. Fong's Toyshop,* was published in 1978. After a long and illustrious career of writing and illustrating his own books and illustrating the works of others, Leo Politi died in 1996. A lover of "people, animals, birds, and flowers" and of "simple, warm and earthy things," Politi's stories and illustrations have left a most precious yet invisible legacy that is in the hearts and minds of our young people. Because he encouraged love and sensitivity, one can only guess how much he affected our children.

General Sources:

1. Arbuthnot, May Hill, ed. *Children and Books.* Glenview, IL: ScottForesman, 1957.

2. *Contemporary Authors.* Detroit, MI: Gale Research, 1995.

3. Folmsbee, Beulah, et al. *Illustrators of Children's Books 1744-1945.* Boston: The Horn Book, 1947.

4. Huber, Miriam B. *Story and Verse for Children.* New York: Macmillan, 1965.

5. Politi, Leo. *Saint Francis and the Animals.* New York: Scribner, 1959.

6. Politi, Leo. *Song of the Swallows.* New York: Scribner's Sons, 1949.

7. Politi, Leo. *Three Stalks of Corn.* New York: Macmillan, 1994.

8. Weber, Francis. *Leo the Great: A Bio-Bibliographical Study of Leo Politi.* Mission Hills, CA: Archival Center, 1989.

—by LINDA D'ANDREA-MARINO

ROSA PONSELLE (1897-1981)

Rosa Ponselle, a superstar of twentieth-century opera, lived a life that in many ways reads like a Hollywood story. Born in Meriden, Connecticut to poor immigrant parents whose last name was Ponzillo, she was one of three children. Despite the family's lack of wealth, the children managed to take music lessons from a local music teacher, Anna Ryan. Both Rosa and her sister Carmela would show unusual musical abilities in their teenage years. At a certain point, they decided to put their talents to work, and so they sought to join the vaudeville circuit, working for B.F. Keith who owned the Palace Theatre in New York.

The girls performed on the "subway circuit," i.e., theaters near subway stations. They traveled from the Bronx to Brooklyn and to Off-Broadway theaters in Manhattan, doing two shows, sometimes four shows a day. Their travels sometimes took them as far away as Montreal and Ontario. The young performers often shared the stage with such notables as Jackie Coogan and Fred Astaire.

Noticing that their act was very popular with all the audiences, Rosa began to demand better billing, and she was not satisfied with earning seven hundred dollars a week, a sizable sum in those days. She asked for one thousand dollars per week; and when she was offered nine hundred, she refused the offer and resigned. It must be noted that her father's annual income for the year 1905 had been $1,500.

Upon the urging of a friend and admirer, Sylvester Z. Poli, she was introduced to a well-known teacher, William Thorner, a friend of Enrico Caruso, who was then singing at the Metropolitan Opera House. Upon hearing Rosa's voice, the teacher immediately began preparing her for an audition with Caruso. Rosa had known little about opera. The aria for her audition was "Casta Diva," a rather demanding aria from Bellini's opera, *Norma*. Upon singing the end of this demanding aria, Rosa promptly fainted in front of her listeners. Once revived, she was surprisingly offered a contract with the Metropolitan Opera House. She would make her world debut with the legendary Caruso in the lead role of Leonora in Verdi's *La Forza del Destino* on November 5, 1918 at the Met.

It may be said that Rosa Ponselle started at the top. She began her operatic lessons under the tutelage of Romano Romani, thus beginning her study of twenty-three operatic roles which would make her world renowned and wealthy. Romano would become Rosa's coach and friend for the remainder of her life. And it was for Rosa that he wrote the opera, *Fedra*. This opera was aimed at allowing her to show off all her brilliance, warmth, and range of voice.

After her successful debut with Caruso, there followed a role in *Cavalleria Rusticana*, and one success seemed to follow another. For the next two decades her name became synonymous with the Metropolitan Opera. Countless recitals, radio shows, recordings, and personal appearances would make Rosa internationally famous. As the years went by, her signature role became Norma. This extremely demanding role began to wear her out. She asked for new roles, new productions to keep her motivated and interested, but her audiences wanted to hear Norma.

She had always experienced some degree of nervousness prior to a performance, but now at the top of her career, she began to have doubts, fretting that she would not be able to live up to her own high standards. Rosa had always heard of the English and Italian audiences as being the most difficult to please in opera, and for this reason she had refused to sing abroad.

It wasn't until 1929, eleven years after her debut, that she decided to test the European audiences. Indeed, her Covent Garden performance of Norma was a smashing success. The English audience, usually not demonstrative, after completion of her "Casta Diva," burst into six minutes of uninterrupted applause. Similarly, the Italian audience in Florence would not allow the conductor to continue the opera, *La Vestale,* until an encore of the principal aria had been performed. These tributes were never forgotten by Rosa, and they would become her most memorable and cherished experiences.

Having become such a prominent figure, she met the most powerful and influential people in upper social circles. In 1936, she married Carle Jackson, the son of the mayor of Baltimore. Carle, who headed a private insurance firm, was about ten years Rosa's junior. They appeared happy as a couple, and they built a large and lavish home called Villa Pace on a 150-acre estate in an exclusive area, Green Spring Valley in the Baltimore suburbs that would become Rosa's home until her death in 1981.

In a twist of fate, she experienced not only ill-fated attempts at becoming a Hollywood screen diva but also rejection by the Met when she seemed to have found artistic differences with them. Yet, still in great demand, she did countless personal appearances, concerts, and recordings; and she became the recipient of many honorary degrees and awards, including the prestigious Peabody Award, her most cherished achievement.

In time, professional and personal demands upon her life began to take their toll. Soon after the death of her mother, Rosa began exhibiting bouts of depression, requiring hospitalization. Even Rosa's marriage to Carle would not endure the difficult times and her husband's repeated infidelities. She sued for divorce in 1949. Grief stricken by the slow disintegration of her life, Rosa turned to religion. She drew closer to the church, often singing at Sunday Mass to the delight of the congregation.

Rosa, who had always been an active, athletic woman, began feeling frequently ill, especially with respiratory ailments. Rosa spent most of her retirement years at Villa Pace, and during World War II, she opened parts of her large estate to war-weary servicemen for rest and relaxation. In 1952, President Eisenhower presented Rosa with an honorary plaque for her contribution to the war effort. Rosa also became involved with the Baltimore Opera Company. As operatic advisor and fund-raiser, she shaped it as one of the best opera houses in the U.S. In 1981, after a series of illnesses and weakened by a fall, Rosa Ponselle died at Villa Pace.

Upon the centennial of her birth, James A. Drake wrote her biography, *Rosa Ponselle: A Centenary Biography.* This book along with many releases of her recordings have initiated a renewed interest in her great talents and her charitable works as an outstanding opera singer who indeed attained the American Dream.

General Sources:
1. Aloi, Enrico. *My Remembrances of Rosa Ponselle.* New York: Vantage Press, 1994.
2. Drake. James A. *Rosa Ponselle: A Centenary Biography.* Portland, OR: Amadeus Press, 1997.
3. Ewen, David. *The New Encyclopedia of the Opera.* New York: Hill and Wang, 1971.
4. Phillips-Matz, Mary Jane. *Rosa Ponselle: American Diva.* Boston: Northeastern University Press, 1997.
5. Ponselle, Rosa, and James Drake. *Ponselle, A Singer's Life.* Garden City, NY: Doubleday, 1982.
6. Sadie, Stanley, ed. *History of Opera.* New York: Norton, 1990.

—by NORMA TRIVELLI

GREGORIO PRESTOPINO (1907-1984)

A prolific contemporary New York City artist depicting themes of social concern in the context of urban realities, employing art work in oil, watercolors and drawings, Gregorio Prestopino today has much of his work ensconced in the permanent collections of many well-known art museums and institutes throughout the United States. From a broad perspective, he is viewed essentially as an expressionist artist. Expressionism is generally defined as a style of art where forms derived from nature or from any environment are deliberately distorted, often two-dimensionally where the artists intensify the colors employed for expressive ends.

Despite the fact that Prestopino was initially attracted to the French impressionists whose late 19th-century style was characterized by short brush strokes of bright colors to reflect the effects of light on the subject, his initial style was different. After acknowledging the value of impressionism's style, he chose instead one of the more available paths of *expressionism* that decades had been referred to as "Ashcan" art. It is a contemporary style that is characterized by a richness of color and by a simplicity of lines, usually portrayed in a two-dimensionality approach. It is focused particularly on city life, its poverty, its humbler aspects, and often its oppressive aspects.

"Ashcan" art, a rather specific category under the broad heading of expressionism, was influenced by many conceptualistic traditions of modern abstract art where both mood and *idea* were the desired central affects of the artist's work on the observer. Hence, attempts at artistically representing reality, as if it were a copy such as in a "photographic" portrayal of a subject, were abandoned in favor of simplicity and abstract images. Prestopino's expressionism, whose works rely heavily on abstract art, emphasizes in particular his compassion and concern for the common person, especially for poor ethnic urbanites in their struggle to survive in an city environment, often unforgiving, brash, and painfully alienating.

A second-generation Italian, he was born in New York City's Little Italy on June 21, 1907. He was one of two sons of Anthony and Lillian (nee Rando) Prestopino. After attending his local elementary school, he went on to Murray Hill Vocational High School. In 1923, some years after graduating secondary school, he received a scholarship that allowed him to enroll in the National Academy of Design in New York City where he attended for the next six years. In 1929 he completed his studies, and he took to traveling in Mexico, in the American Southwest, and later in 1936 in Europe in the hope of experiencing new and different cultures firsthand.

During the 1930s he initiated his most basic social realism phase. His art works that generally contained depictions of the struggles of laborers and the listlessness of the unemployed were among his most common themes in this period and no doubt reflected the terrible psychological effects wielded by the depression of the time. The other rather familiar theme of poverty and its frequent cohort, inertia, are perhaps best illustrated in one particular work, *Portsmouth Street* (1936), an oil painting that depicts clusters of unemployed, hopeless men idling like meaningless forms occupying the inanimate space of city streets.

While the subject matter of his art remains essentially the same as he moves through the 40s decade (i.e., the travails of the workers), art critics have pointed out that his style underwent certain refinements that were characterized by a greater simplicity in the use of images and a greater expressiveness in the use of portraiture so that his paintings acquired more of the architectonics of art while losing its journalese appeal. In all, his style acquired more and more the stature of quality art that reflected an integrated consciousness. An example of his art that apparently reflected this flattering artistic critique is evidenced by an oil painting entitled *Winter* (1945) where Prestopino depicted working men boarding a streetcar: where form and content become one.

Perhaps Prestopino's most widely known series of art works remains that of his Harlem phase. It was an extensive series of drawings and works in oil and in watercolors done in the 1950s where the themes of suffering among the poor—in this case the Harlem poor—are evidenced and focused in their portraitures (their faces) amid the surroundings of oppressive streets, decaying structures, ominous skies, and hellish subway entrances. Here Prestopino reaches one of the high points of his style, and it is at this time he receives many commissions to do a commercial series of art works for magazines such as *Life* (September 1957).

After undergoing a phase where he worked almost exclusively on cloth with black dyes in the 1960s, he did an expansive series in the expressionistic style combining fantasy and urban detail depicting a macabre world—one decimated by a nuclear Armageddon—that is now inhabited by eerie human skeletons. By contrast, the remaining years before his passing showed a surprisingly definite return to the world of French impressionism. Leaving behind the world of "Ashcan" art, the very last phase of his artistic creativity involved not only a return to impressionism but also depictions of rural landscapes replete with nude figures.

A recipient of many honors, awards, and commissions from such sources as the National Institute of Arts and Letters, Prestopino has earned the status of an artist whose many works are found in the permanent collections of art centers including the Addison Gallery of Art, the Art Institute of Chicago, the Museum of Modern Art, and the Whitney Museum of American Art. An accomplished illustrator of books, he enjoyed an excellent reputation as a teacher of seminars at art institutes and at the School for Social Research; and also as a fine lecturer at the Museum of Modern Art in Manhattan and at the Brooklyn Museum.

Gregorio Prestopino died on December 16, 1984, leaving a legacy of art that illustrates—through his artistic persona that encapsulates a view of the less privileged—many new and different perspectives of an America as it moved through the throes of its great depression, its social ailments, its ethical challenges, its Cold War with Russia, and its fear of nuclear holocaust potentially terminating a humanity that he so loved.

General Sources:
1. Bertol, Roland. *Sundiata: The Epic of the Lion King, Retold*. New York: T.Y. Crowell, 1970.
2. *Current Biography Yearbook*. New York: Wilson, 1964; 1985.
3. Graham, Lorenz. *A Road Down in the Sea*. New York: T.Y. Crowell, 1970.
4. Grahame, Kenneth. *The Reluctant Dragon*. New York: Grosset & Dunlap, 1968.
5. *Harlem Wednesday: A Storyboard Production*. Dir. John Hubley and Faith Elliot. Audio-Brandon Films, 1957.
6. Joyce, Carolyn. *The Magic Donkey*. Lexington, MA: Ginn, 1972.
7. New Jersey State Museum. *Three Artists View the Human Condition*. Trenton, NJ: New Jersey State Museum, 1968.
8. "Obituary." *New York Times* 19 Dec. 1984: 22.

—by SAM PITTARO

MARIO PUZO (1920-1999)

Of Mario Puzo, a *Time* magazine author had aptly said, "If Mario Puzo never writes another word, he will already have earned the title of Godfather of the Paperbacks. Puzo's *The Godfather* and 'an offer you can't refuse,' have already become part of the language. This may find him a niche in American letters. He is already assured a place in American numbers." The enormous popularity of *The Godfather,* having sold more than 13 million copies, made Mario Puzo one of the most sought after novelists and screenwriters of our time.

Critics have generally suggested that Puzo's works remain useful to literary scholars due to the sociological and historical content of their themes—the themes of Italian immigrant struggles within the context of American urban environments, densely populated and stratified, within an industrial and technological society. Yet some organizations have pointed to the negative influence of his writings, and their tarnishing effects on the image of Italian Americans.

For example, statistics have shown that 85% of all "mob" movies have been produced *since* the 1972 advent of *The Godfather* movie. They maintain that equating Italian Americans with mobsterism has become the downside of Puzo's literary success. In other words, the Italian-American image has greatly suffered, in a sense, by Puzo's writing success. Thus this issue still remains controversial and emotions may understandably run high.

Mario Puzo was born to immigrant parents, Antonio and Maria Puzo, in New York City's Hell's Kitchen in 1920. He and his four brothers and two sisters were raised by their mother in what was then a predominantly Italian neighborhood. Recognizing the social intricacies and "organizational" nature of this community, Puzo was quick to learn of certain unique relationships existing among an especially small segment of Italians which mainstream America referred to as "the Mafia."

All his books are based on research and depict composites of characters he had met, observed, or studied in some manner. His tales are based on experience *and* on fact, a modern realism if you will. When viewed in that respect, it becomes clear that his works do *not* represent a writer's meanderings through a world of pure fiction as a deliberately vengeful ploy or convenient expedient whose hidden agenda would involve disparaging a people whose majority is otherwise hard working and dedicated to family life.

His own life experiences spanned quickly from inner city neighborhood activities to civilian public relations administration for the United States Air Force in Europe. While in Europe he met his wife (Erika Lina Broske) with whom he had five children. It was while in Germany that friends and fellow employees encouraged him to write after they would listen to his many characterizations and stories from his New York experiences of his younger years.

Many of his adolescent years had been spent at the Hudson Guild Settlement House where he was captain of its football team. Perhaps more importantly, to better understand his background and how it relates to his writing success, it is noteworthy that he was a frequent visitor to the Hudson Guild Library where he read a great deal of fiction and even completed the works of the famous Russian writer Dostoevsky. Then WWII came along, and though his youthful years were not quite finished, Puzo like so many others was drafted into military service and eventually was stationed in Germany.

He returned to the U.S. to work as a civil service administrator. During the late 1940s and 1950s, he studied literature and writing at Columbia University and at the New School for Social Research. He then began writing short stories and completed his first novel *The Dark Arena* in 1955. Considered a minor classic today, it depicted a post-war European cosmos and war's dehumanizing effects for both the conquerors and conquered.

In 1965 Puzo wrote his second novel, *The Fortunate Pilgrim*. Semi-autobiographical, this novel depicted the struggles of an Italian immigrant matriarch who had dedicated her entire life to her six children. It was considered a talented merging of social history and creative sensitivity to understanding interpersonal relationships. Gay Talese, another Italian-American author, congratulated Mario Puzo for having created "perhaps the best novel ever written about Italian Immigrants in America."

In the 1960s, Puzo deliberately took to writing novels with greater selling appeal. *The Godfather* and the trilogy, as depicted in the motion pictures, detail the rise and fall of Mafia Don Vito Corleone and his sons, Sonny and Michael. Sociologists have recognized in the trilogy's depiction a certain frustration in the characters' twisted realization of the American Dream, and how, when the avenues toward success get blocked, alternative means come into play—even illegal means.

In his self-defense (especially when accused of "glorifying the Mafia" and when presenting the illicit actions of the "Corleone family in a morally sympathetic light"), Puzo correctly and aptly pointed out that, "it is a novelist's job not to be a moralist but to make you care about the people in the book." Correspondingly, it becomes precisely the reader's job and the critic's responsibility to make moral calls.

The success of *The Godfather* as a book naturally led to selling the film rights to the movie industry for *The Godfather* (1972) and *The Godfather Part II* (1974). *Earthquake* (1974), one in a series of extremely successful disaster movies, was Puzo's third screenplay. These successes in turn led to more screenplays such as *Superman* and *Superman II*.

Subsequent novels include *Fools Die* based on the gambling scene in Las Vegas; *The Sicilian*, semi-fictional historical and revolutionary tale set in northern Sicily; *The Fourth K*, a political thriller roughly based on a distant Kennedy cousin; and *The Last Don* (made into two TV movies) depicting a crime family's struggles and its disintegration amidst a modern backdrop.

A best-selling novelist and screenwriter artistically adept at dealing successfully both in fantasy such as in *Superman* scenarios and in modern realism such as in immigrant struggles and in crime scenarios, Mario Puzo achieved much success. He died of heart failure on July 2, 1999 at his Bayshore, Long Island home.

General Sources:
1. Ciongoli, Kenneth A., and Jay Parini, eds. *Beyond the Godfather: Italian American Writers on the Real Italian American Experience*. Hanover, NH: University Press of New England, 1998.
2. *Contemporary Authors*. Detroit, MI: Gale Research, 1981.
3. *Dictionary of American Biography*. New York: Scribner's Sons, 1980.
4. Katz, Ephraim. The Film Encyclopedia New York: HarperCollins, 1998.
5. *Life* 10 July 1970: 41-44.
6. *Publisher's Weekly* 12 June 1978: 10-12.
7. Puzo, Mario. *The Fortunate Pilgrim*. New York: Atheneum, 1964.
8. Puzo, Mario. *The Godfather Papers and Other Confessions*. New York: Putnam, 1972.

—by MICHAEL BAGLINO, Ed.D.

LEONARD RIGGIO (1941-   )

Leonard Riggio, Chairman and CEO of Barnes & Noble, the largest retail chain of bookstores in the United States, oversees the operation of approximately 1,000 bookstores. Either under the name Barnes & Noble or under the title of other trade names such as B. Dalton Bookseller, Doubleday Book Shops, or Scribner's Bookstores, he professes to operate this growing network of retail stores with consumer needs in mind.

He is nowadays reputed to having created a model for retail bookstore ambiance that accommodates browsers and potential buyers by providing a slow-paced tempo in visually appealing, uncluttered surroundings that encourage browser friendliness. He contends that success is no accident; it is achieved in great part by actively gleaning consumer input and understanding consumer needs.

Leonard Riggio, the son of Stephen Riggio, a boxer and cab driver, was born in the Little Italy section of lower Manhattan, New York City in 1941. At age four, Leonard along with his family moved to Bensonhurst, Brooklyn, which has become since the 1940s another Little Italy. After finishing grammar school, he attended a somewhat well-known and highly reputable public high school called Brooklyn Tech whose programs prepare students for the sciences, engineering, and the more recent technologies developed.

Riggio's bookselling career began in the 1960s at the Campus Bookstore of New York University (NYU) at its main campus in the Greenwich Village area (Manhattan). As a sales clerk he sold textbooks during the day, and after work in the evening he studied metallurgical engineering at NYU's uptown campus in the Bronx. During this time his interests shifted to retailing, and he began taking course at NYU's School of Commerce.

In 1965 he started his own business, and he initiated his enterprise with a plan and a clear desire to improve upon the disappointing experiences he had in retailing. He opened up a rival bookstore just around the corner from where he had once worked. It was named the Waverly Student Book Exchange. By 1971, within six short years, he had expanded his operations to six other bookstores, including stores at Columbia University and at the Fashion Institute of Technology, both located in Manhattan.

More importantly, in 1971, Riggio acquired what was his prize possession, a well-known yet apparently struggling Barnes & Noble bookstore, which coincidentally was the only Barnes & Noble bookstore in existence at the time. It specialized in textbooks, a field with which Riggio was quite familiar, and so Riggio decided to make an offer to buy their firm. The owners of Barnes & Noble gladly accepted his $750,000 offer which would be amortized over a seven-and-a-half-year period.

When commenting on the propitious timing of purchasing not just the bookstore itself but acquiring the fine reputation of the Barnes & Noble enterprise, Riggio said, "When a business is floundering, people don't see what's right about it, just what's wrong. They thought we were textbook people since we ran college bookstores, but we saw that Barnes & Noble was much, much more than a textbook store."

With an ear pitched to customer needs, he first began to experiment with making the store more customer friendly. He accomplished this by adding seating areas, restrooms, small shopping carts, and also by developing a large children's department to meet the needs of a burgeoning sector of the book market. At first, these seemed perhaps uneventfully simple ideas, but Riggio's intuition proved to be correct since at a foundational level it served to accommodate customer needs and growing customer expectations. As the so-called information explosion, which had begun a few decades ago, was moving rapidly and headlong into the future, Riggio discovered a merchandising technique whereby his bookstores radiated a coffee-table-book effect.

During the 1980s Riggio moved to the next level by opening up superstores—huge stores with large book inventories, racks with an unusually large number of magazines, open areas for book presentations and authors' book signings. His policies also included an on-the-spot ordering of books presently unavailable to shorten the waiting time for a book needed by a customer. In some of his Barnes & Noble bookstores, he experimented with offering a cafe setting with a cosmopolitan nuance within the precincts of the bookstore environment so that customers could effectively enjoy reading and having coffee at the same time. Riggio had made an important correlation between what he probably experienced many times in his old Italian neighborhood where coffeehouse patrons would often read their newspapers *and* what people now wanted from their bookstores.

The experiment worked, and by 1993 Riggio signed an agreement with the Starbucks chain to offer their coffee in Barnes & Noble bookstores. His innovations had become an unbeatable combination whereby the bookstore and coffeehouse amalgamation became an inviting literary sanctuary away from the pressures of the outside world.

Reminiscent of the European tradition of coffeehouses, Riggio's model of the American modern bookstore suddenly acquired new warmth, meaning, and more—an irresistible homeliness. Surely for many, his new approach filled a void often sensed in most modern retail establishments with no service personnel available, too much glitz and glamour, and a lack of warmth.

Thanks to the success of these tried and tested policies to accommodate the modern book-buying customer, Riggio has been able to expand his company opening branches outside of New York City. His expansion program has involved closing down some of his smaller stores for the sake of cost effectiveness while opening as many as 90 new superstores a year throughout the United States.

He has indeed established himself as a trendsetter, and entrepreneurs everywhere are now emulating his business style. Between 1992 and 1996, Barnes & Noble more than doubled its yearly business going from a $1.08 billion to a $2.4 billion operation. Aware of the challenges that lie ahead, the talented and innovative Riggio has also entered the Internet book market population and is offering very challenging competition to Amazon Books which, not long ago, had established itself as the pioneer and front-runner in selling books on the Internet.

Riggio, who started with one bookstore just thirty years ago, has become a distinguished, self-made, Italian-American entrepreneur. In a new hi-tech business generation, he rightly deserves recognition for his business acumen and innovation in such a highly competitive era. In many respects, he has set modern standards in servicing, accommodating, and respecting the consumer and consumer needs in an age dominated by the computer and the information explosion.

General Sources:
1. *Current Biography Yearbook.* New York: Wilson, 1998.
2. Dugan, I. Jeanne. "The Baron of Books." *Business Week* 29 June 1998: 108-112+.
3. *New York Times* 3 Sept. 1993:1.

—by DENNIS PIASIO

FRANK RIZZO (1920-1991)

Frank Lazarro Rizzo, who became Philadelphia's most well-known mayor (1972-1980), exemplified the phenomenon of "blue-power," an urban "grass roots" backlash against civil disorder that had run rampant in the 60s and continued into the 70s. Emulating his father's spirit and drive to improve his status, Rizzo worked his way up from the rank of foot patrolman, became the police commissioner (1967-1971), and then the mayor of a very challenging urban city.

He was born on October 23, 1920 to his parents, Ralph and Teresa (nee Erminio) Rizzo. Frank's father, who was an emigrant from Calabria, Italy, became a policeman and worked his way up to the rank of sergeant on the Philadelphia force. When he retired, he had spent forty-one years on the force.

The Rizzo family consisted of four boys who were born and raised on South Rosewood Street, a predominantly Italian area, then a reputed tough neighborhood. In 1938 when his mother died during gall bladder surgery, Frank left his high school senior year unfinished and decided to join the Navy. Discharged early from the service for medical reasons (diabetes), Frank then worked as a laborer and a machine operator for a nearby steel corporation for several years. Frank and his wife, Carmela Silvestri, were married in 1942. Carmela's parents were from Monte Corvino Rovella, province of Salerno, Italy.

A year later on October 6, 1943, Frank joined the Philadelphia police force, and just like his father, became a policeman and confronted the challenges of Philadelphia's tough streets. His reputation as a brave and audacious policeman spread almost immediately. Dubbed "the Cisco Kid," he became known for taking risks and saving lives in perilous situations. Early in his career, he had predicted to his wife that he would someday become the commissioner of the Philadelphia Police Department. Indeed, all along the way he consistently presented himself as a man of determination, courage, and conviction who believed in law and order.

He rose through the ranks: first, sergeant (1951), acting captain (1952), captain (1954), inspector (1959), deputy commissioner (1964), and finally commissioner (1967). At this point in time in the second half of the 1960s, he and most other urban police commissioners had to face the growing unrest and crime rate sweeping the nation's urban areas. In the ensuing years as commissioner, Frank Rizzo had to face the toughest time in his career including urban drug proliferation, riots, and civil rights demonstrations gone awry.

As a conservative championing law and order, he eventually emerged the victor supported by many ethnic groups and by the majority of Philadelphia's citizenry. Yet many years of his police work involving a two-fisted, hands-on policy raised the issue of excessive force being exercised in the line of duty. On one occasion, he was even arraigned in court on legal charges, but they were dismissed. Often he would personally lead his men and regularly raid known drug hangouts operating in the guise of coffeehouses, and he had no misgivings about jailing civil rights activists who broke the law.

In fact, Rizzo and his Philadelphia police force made worldwide headlines when one of its task forces, in a predawn raid, stormed and rounded up local Black Panthers at their headquarters. The newspaper photographs of the militants, lined up and stripped of clothing, seemed to smack of racial exploitation. In his defense, Rizzo explained it was he who ordered the press to be present precisely to avoid those kinds of predictable false accusations. He further explained that the militants were scantily dressed because they were sleeping when the raid began and that they obviously had to be checked for weapons.

Despite the efforts of several civic organizations to effect charges against Rizzo's alleged violation of citizen rights at the federal level, Rizzo pointed out in rebuttal his demonstrably determined efforts at having recruited integrated two-man patrol cars, more black police officers, and special drug squads to apprehend peddlers in the poor neighborhoods. He had in fact increased the police force by nearly 1,200, and during his tenure, the crime rate in Philadelphia remained among the lowest of the highly-populated urban cities in the U.S.

In 1971, after twenty-eight years on the police force, Frank Rizzo resigned as police commissioner in order to begin his campaign to win the mayoral election in Philadelphia. While viewed as a popular candidate locally, he did not receive support from Democrats at the national level who viewed him as reactionary, nor did he receive any support from liberal and civil rights organizations. Yet with his slogan "Rizzo means business" and a host of good campaign strategies, such as visiting ethnic neighborhoods almost on a daily basis, he did much to improve his reactionary image.

His mayoral campaign included tax exemptions for businesses, tougher stands on illicit drug sales and court leniency, a crackdown on pornography, more efficient city budgeting, and a stronger police force. In May 1971, Rizzo went on to win the Democratic primary and in November won the election receiving 49% of the vote, despite his opponent's backing from two of Philadelphia's largest newspapers.

He took office in January 1972, and just after two weeks as mayor, Rizzo (a Democrat) was paid tribute when Nixon invited him to the White House. When he returned to business with his noteworthy take-charge attitude, he created programs, giving teachers more discretionary (disciplinary) power, appointed many Blacks to senior posts, fought off pornographic establishments, and brought membership in the police forces up to 9,500.

Despite his many successes as a two-term Democratic mayor, his future political career presented many difficulties. As a notable leader against civil disorder and social unrest, he had dedicated himself to the ideal of reversing the moral and social decay of urban areas. On the overall, he kept Philadelphia's rate of street crime and racial violence the lowest in the ten most populated cities in the U.S. Unable to run for a third consecutive term in 1979 because of city charter legislation, he lost the Democratic primary later in 1983.

While attempting one more time at running for the mayor's office at age 71, Mayor Frank Rizzo died on July 16, 1991. Despite a disappointing last attempt at re-entering mayoral politics, he had already become a legend in the hearts of many citizens in the city of Philadelphia and in America. In his death, Philadelphia lost a controversial yet great public servant, but more importantly, it lost a hero who was not afraid to show his values and have a ready willingness to fight for them.

General Sources:
1. *Amateur Night at City Hall: The Story of Frank L. Rizzo*. Dir. Robert Mugge. Direct Cinema Limited, 1978.
2. *Current Biography Yearbook*. New York: Wilson, 1973; 1991.
3. Daughen, Joseph, and Peter Binzen. *The Cop Who Would be King: Mayor Frank Rizzo*. Boston: Little Brown, 1977.
4. Paolantonio, S.A. *Frank Rizzo: The Last Big Man in Big City America*. Philadelphia: Camino Books, 1993.

—by ANTHONY SOLDANO

PHIL RIZZUTO (1918-   )

Phil Rizzuto, who would someday give new meaning to the word *shortstop* while playing for the New York Yankees, was born on September 25, 1918. He was one of five children of Philip, Sr., and Mary Rizzuto. His parents who had separately come from the same town in Italy did not know each other until they met in the United States. Philip, Sr., at first a dock worker on the New York waterfront, became a trolley car driver. He made a home for his family in the Ridgewood area of Brooklyn, which at that time was also called Little Italy.

When Phil junior was twelve, the family moved to Glendale, Queens. He started attending Richmond Hill High School where he not only played as quarterback on the football team but also served as captain of the baseball team. Reportedly, it was Al Kuntz, the baseball coach at Richmond Hill, who had seen the potential in Phil when he first tried out for the high school team. By the end of his graduation year (1937), he was offered two athletic scholarships: one for Columbia University and the other for Fordham University. He declined both scholarships because he was apparently more interested in trying out for baseball teams. After a dismal tryout with the Dodgers where he was hit by a wild pitch, he tried out for the New York Giants baseball team and was rejected by them also.

Much to his surprise, his tryout with the New York Yankees proved to be fruitful as the management sent him to Virginia to play shortstop for $75 a month on the Bassetts, a Yankee farm team. After sixty-seven games where he hit .310 and fielded .933, he was moved up to the Norfolk team in 1938. Rizzuto's batting average of .336 and fielding .938 now permitted him to move up one step higher into the Kansas City team which was part of the American Association, considered a top minor league. In 1939 after Rizzuto had hit .316 and fielded .944, *The Sporting News* named him Number One Minor League Player of the Year in 1940. He went on to conclude that year by stealing the most bases in the American Association League.

In 1941 he finally moved up to the New York Yankees where as a rookie Yankee he was earning $5,000 a year. Despite the fact that during that year he batted .307 and fielded .957, he was apparently benched for poor playing in the last portion of the season. In all, the rookie right-hander led the American League that year by participating in the most double plays. Rizzuto also got to play in his first World Series that year making two hits, twelve put-outs, and one error in five games.

In 1942 in his second World Series appearance, he really created a sensation. He made one home run and eight hits in five games with an average of .381; he fielded .967, and he made fifteen put-outs and one error. He created major league record history by participating in five double plays in just one game, by tying the major league record with five put-outs in one game, and by leading the league in double plays and in put-outs.

With a war going on in the world, he served for three years in the United States Navy. While stationed on duty in New Guinea, he caught malaria, and during his recuperation from the illness, he managed a Navy league baseball team. Later in 1944 he joined the Navy All-Stars, and playing third base he helped the Navy defeat the Army. After engaging in wartime activities in the Philippines, he was discharged in late 1945.

Returning to the New York Yankees in 1946, he consistently maintained his high averages. Participating in his third World Series in 1947, he fielded 1.000 and batted an average of .308. The year 1949 was considered by many as his most exemplary year fielding .971, thus leading the American League shortstops. Phil Rizzuto, often referred to as "the Scooter," was named Top Major League Shortstop each year from 1949 to 1952. For the year 1949 Rizzuto was also named runner-up for the Most Valuable Player in the American League (MVP) bestowed by the Association of Baseball Writers of America.

Because many sports people felt Rizzuto should have been named MVP in 1949 and not merely its runner-up position, the Association of Baseball Writers apparently reflected that sentiment in October 1950 by then bestowing the MVP title on Rizzuto. Receiving 16 of the 23 first-place votes, he was clearly a heavy favorite. His popularity with the fans kept increasing, and in November, he was named the "overwhelming favorite" in the Associated Press poll for the 1950 All-Star Baseball Team. Of the 360 ballots used in the voting, the Yankee shortstop's name appeared most frequently.

Phil Rizzuto played for the Yankees for a total of 13 years between 1941-42 and 1946-56. He led the American League in double plays three times, and twice in fielding percentage and in put-outs. He holds the record for playing 21 consecutive World Series games without an error, and the American League Most Valuable Player in 1950. Despite the fact that he hit over .300 only twice in his thirteen-year career, Rizzuto was an excellent bunter, and he led the American League in sacrifice hits for five consecutive years.

New York Times sports editor, Arthur Daley, correctly pointed out the fact that while Casey Stengel might have been rightfully called the "magician" because of his uncanny ability to pull a winning game out of the fire, it was also in part due to Phil Rizzuto's miracle performances always surprising the baseball fans with different and often impossible plays that saved the day.

In regard to his very early years after high school, Rizzuto on many occasions was told that he was too short for sports and that he'd be better off getting a "shoeshine box." Despite that kind of unwarranted criticism, he went on to become not only a success in the hearts and minds of millions of fans but also very popular among his fellow players. After leaving baseball as a player, he found a second career in baseball sportscasting, and so while he may have left the diamond in one way, he then saw it from another angle.

As a tribute to Rizzuto, in August 1984 the baseball authorities created Phil Rizzuto Day. Finally, in 1994 he was elected into the Hall of Fame in Cooperstown, New York. He will always be admired for his personality, professionalism, unique style, and his love of the game.

General Sources:

1. *Current Biography*. New York: Wilson, 1950.

2. *Great Athletes: The Twentieth Century*. Pasadena: Salem Press, 1992.

3. Hirshberg, Dan. *Phil Rizzuto: A Yankee Tradition*. Champaign, IL: Sagamore Pub., 1993.

4. Rizzuto, Phil. *The "Miracle" New York Yankees*. New York: Coward-McCann, 1962.

5. Rizzuto, Phil, and Tom Horton. *The October Twelve: Five Years of Yankee Glory—1949-1953*. New York: Forge, 1994.

6. Schoor, Gene. *The Scooter: The Phil Rizzuto Story*. New York: Scribner, 1982.

7. Trimble, Joe. *Phil Rizzuto, a Biography of the Scooter*. New York: A.S. Barnes, 1951.

—by THOMAS CASALINO

SABATO (SAM) RODIA (1875-1965)

Sabato (Sam) Rodia, born in Avellino, Italy in 1875, would make American folk art history years after he had created the now famous Los Angeles Watts Towers with their dreamlike structures composed of mosaic spires, still today a much discussed and controversial art work attracting high volume visitor attention.

When Sam came to the U.S. at age fourteen, he spent his early days working for the railroads as a laborer in Wyoming, Illinois and Colorado. Apparently, he bore just the ordinary skills of an Italian tilesetter, yet in retrospect his life and his unique creative energies still remain today an enigma filled with interesting contradictions and many unanswered questions. His very name and birth date were listed erroneously in the *Columbia Encyclopedia* as "Simon Rodilla" and as born in "1879."

The main reason for this major interest in his undeniably complex personality surrounds Rodia's life after he settled in the Watts area of Los Angeles. In 1921, he began a project which would take him about thirty-three years to complete. He started building 17 towers. Three would ultimately reach 55, 97, and 99 feet in height. To the world at large they would become known as the Watts Towers. These towers were systematically built around his place of residence, and eventually his house became encapsulated by the overwhelming structures.

The towers were constructed of steel rods, metal scraps, and cement. The components also included seashells that he would bring back from walks on the beach, and from broken bottles, pottery, wire mesh, hoops and assorted materials he chanced to find anywhere. Everything he designed was decorated with multicolored mosaics which in a sense incorporated the skills he had brought

from Italy. During the day, he worked for the railroads, and at night he worked approximately five hours for himself building the towers.

When he worked above ground level, he held on to his towers by a window washer's belt, and he typically would sing Italian operatic arias as he worked. Going about his work peaceably, he had neighbors who thought he was crazy, and there were also children who pelted rocks at him as he went about making his creation. Naturally, the city fathers were in a perpetual uproar over safety issues since he had no building permit. Yet as far safety was concerned, just over ten years after its initial date of construction, the towers failed to be moved or effected in any way by the 1933 Long Beach earthquake.

Rodia's towers bear his initials with the dates showing when certain sections were completed inscribed with the words "Nuestro Pueblo" (loosely translated "our town") to honor his Spanish neighbors. The larger towers were buttressed by smaller towers and embellished by fountains, gazebos, arches, love seats, and a ship called the "the Ship of Marco Polo." Rodia's art work, however, also extended beyond his home as well. He gave his sister and brother-in-law Sam Calicura large outdoor flower vases made of mosaic and cement, which he constructed in their yard.

One day, as unexpectedly as Rodia's mysterious lifestyle had commenced in the construction of this unorthodox and magical-looking structure, it ended. In 1954, Rodia deeded his property to a neighbor, and he simply and inexplicably walked away from his towers forever, never to return. Unfortunately, many other neighbors who did not appreciate the structure's beauty began dumping trash on the property, slowly creating a fire hazard. A few years had gone by, and eventually his house located within the towers was set afire and burned beyond repair in 1957.

By the end of the 1950s, Rodia was considered to be deceased by many given his rather strange and sudden disappearance coupled with his projected age. Yet he was very much alive, living as a recluse, remaining totally opposed to returning to see the towers he had built. In his later years, when asked what inspired him to build the towers, he would answer: books and museums. He also added that Buffalo Bill, Amerigo Vespucci, and Julius Caesar were among his favorite historical figures. Despite his reclusive style of living, his sister and her family continued to stay in close contact with him. He died in 1965 at the age of ninety in Martinez, California, but the controversy over his creation was far from over as safety became the apparent overriding issue.

The city of Los Angeles declared the structure hazardous and ordered the destruction of the towers. However, concerned citizens countered by acquiring the property and paying to have a stress test done. This involved the towers being able to withstand the equivalent of a 70 m.p.h. gale force wind. When the Watts Towers passed the test with flying colors, the city became compelled to allow the towers to stand.

In 1983, the Los Angeles Cultural Commission declared the towers to be a "monument which must be protected." That same year, in *Smithsonian Magazine*, Rodia's work was mentioned in an article entitled "The Transformed Trash of Untrained Artists." Although saved from destruction by a group of private citizens, the property was soon deeded to the City of Los Angeles because of the magnitude of the restoration project. The matter was soon in litigation because an agreeable solution could not be found, and it would take seven more years to resolve that issue.

With the exception of the visibility of their highest spires, the Watts Towers were covered with scaffolding for nearly ten years. The general public was not allowed inside, and only an occasional school group could enter briefly for educational purposes. Eventually the state of California offered its help in restoration, funding it with $1.2 million. Located on 107th Street in Watts, L.A., the Watts Towers Art Center now receives visitors on weekends. It hosts exhibitions, classes, special events, and a film production entitled "Daniel and the Towers" to commemorate Rodia's work whose esthetic qualities also raise many questions.

Sam has been designated many titles such as architect, sculptor, and folk artist to help define his complex work. The reasons for its creation have become perplexing. Yet whatever the explanations, this Italian American has assured himself a place in posterity as his Watts Towers have become recognized as a major achievement of 20th-century American art.

General Sources:
1.   DiStasi, Lawrence. *The Big Book of Italian American Culture*. New York: HarperCollins, 1990.
2.   Goldstone, Bud, and Arloa Paquin Goldstone. *The Los Angeles Watts Towers*. Los Angeles: Getty Conservation Institute, J. Paul Getty Museum, 1997.
3.   Placzek, Adolf K. *Macmillan Encyclopedia of Architects*. London, UK: Free Press, 1982.
4.   Rolle, Andrew. *The Italian Americans; Troubled Roots*. New York: Free Press, 1980.
5.   Tomasi, Lydio. *Italian Americans: New Perspectives in Italian Immigration and Ethnicity*. Staten Island, NY: Center for Migration Studies, 1985.
6.   Ward, Daniel Franklin. *Simon Rodia and His Towers in Watts*. Monticello, IL: Vance Bibliographies, 1986.

—by LINDA D'ANDREA-MARINO

PETER WALLACE RODINO, JR. (1909-   )

Noted for his leadership as chairman of the House Judiciary hearings during the 1974 Watergate proceedings, Peter Rodino has had a long and interesting career. Beginning with his wartime activities in north Africa and Italy which made him a highly decorated Army veteran in 1946, he later went on to grant the American public an incredibly long span of over forty years of dedicated public service in the legislative branch of the federal government.

Peter Rodino, Jr., was born in Newark, New Jersey to Peter and Margaret (nee Gerard) Rodino on June 7, 1909. His father, an emigrant from southern Italy, worked most of his life as a bricklayer, and raised a family in a tough—sometimes violent—neighborhood. Peter, Jr., through hard work and perseverance, received acceptance into college and earned his LL.B. degree in 1937 at the University at Newark (Rutgers Law School). In the same year, he was also admitted to the New Jersey bar.

Despite the fact that he was in the process of setting up a private legal practice in Newark, Rodino decided to volunteer for military service. He did so before the Pearl Harbor attack; yet, only a few weeks after that early December morning surprise raid, he and his bride, Marianna Stango, made a daring decision to get married, not knowing what the future would bring. That marriage would indeed go on to produce two children, Margaret Ann (Mrs. Charles Stanziale, Jr.) and Peter, III.

After Rodino volunteered in 1941, the Army commissioned him to work overseas, and he served in combat in the north African and European theaters of operation with the First Armored Division. He was also assigned to work with the military mission delegated to the Italian Army. By the end of the war, Rodino had became a highly decorated U.S. Army veteran, receiving many honors and awards, including the Bronze Star and the War Cross. He also received many decorations from the Republic of Italy, including the Knights of the Order of the Crown. When he was discharged in 1946, he had earned the rank of captain.

In 1948, just two years after the conclusion of his military service, Rodino was elected to Congress to the House of Representatives from the 10th Congressional District of New Jersey. Representing Newark and its adjacent areas, Rodino took office on January 3, 1949 in the 81st Congress, and he would become successfully reelected to each succeeding Congress until his retirement in 1988.

As an active Democratic congressman, Rodino was heavily involved as a member on several House committees, including Select House Committee on Narcotics Abuse and Control, Inter-Governmental Committee for European Migration, President's Select Commission on Immigration Refugee Policy, National Commission for Revised Antitrust Laws and Procedures, and North Atlantic Assembly—to mention but a few.

In the 1960s, he was particularly involved with immigration issues and the passage of a House bill that at once proposed to eliminate nationality quotas and offered just and more equitable procedures for all applicant ethnic groups. This culminated in the passage of the Immigration Reform and Control Act of 1966 which in effect halted an immigration system that had been inherently discriminatory.

Additionally, in the 1960s Rodino was actively involved in backing civil rights legislation such as in the enactment of the broad-based Civil Rights Act of 1966 and in another bill in 1969 (The Philadelphia Plan) which effectively compelled the hiring of minority workers for projects that were federally-financed. In the egalitarian spirit of 1960s statesmanship, his sustaining efforts and support of civil rights legislation was best recognized when he became the recipient of the Hubert H. Humphrey Civil Rights Award in 1978.

Of course, what made Rodino well known—at least in the eyes of the media in the 1970s—was his role as head of the Judiciary Committee whose task dealt with exploring the very serious matter of President Nixon's possible impeachment. Yet today what will be best remembered is his quiet and dispassionate leadership on the Judiciary Committee in what clearly remains such a difficult and painful event in modern American history.

With such a strenuous and perplexing dilemma before the committee and before Congress as a whole, both tempers and emotions often ran high. Partisan politics surely emerged with many Republicans defending Nixon and many Democrats advocating swift impeachment of Nixon. It thus became Rodino's responsibility to insure that the objectives of the committee inquiry remained clear and that justice was being served procedurally so that the very process of deciding the validity of evidence towards a potential impeachment remained unobstructed and valid in the eyes of history.

In keeping with his level-headedness and equanimity, Rodino did not support many House members' punitive craving to have impeachment hearings resume after Nixon resigned from office and President Gerald Ford subsequently pardoned him. It had been Rodino's contention during the impeachment hearings that this kind of inquiry should always remain above partisan thinking and that pursuance of those hearings after removal of a President from office was tantamount to harassment and would not serve the ends of justice.

In all, Rodino has received many awards and commendations, and he serves as an elegant example of a man of principles who has reified the intended and originating spirit of the law. He accomplished this through calm and forthright statesmanship in a most difficult time in American history. Exemplifying devoted service to his country for over forty years on the Hill together with a prior military service record that is second to none, Italian Americans can be proud of him in the certain knowledge that there are many government officials in high places who do belong there.

General Sources:
1. Fields, Howard. *High Crimes and Misdemeanors*. New York: Norton, 1978.
2. Marchione, Margherita. *Americans of Italian Heritage*. Lanham, MD: University Press of America, 1995.
3. Rodino, Peter. Introduction. *The Consular Dimension of Diplomacy: A Symposium*. Ed. Martin F. Herz. Lanham, MD: University Press of America, 1985.
4. Rodino, Peter. Preface. *Fourteen Years or Life: The Bankruptcy Court Dilemma*. By Robert E. DeMascio, et al. Washington, DC: National Legal Center for Public Interest, 1983.
5. Rodino, Peter. *Progress Report on the Control of Narcotics*. Brussels: North Atlantic Assembly, International Secretariat, 1972.
6. Rodino, Peter, et al. (United States Congress. House. Committee on the Judiciary). *Impeachment of Richard M. Nixon, President of the United States: Report of the Committee on the Judiciary, House of Representatives*. New York: Viking Press, 1974.
7. *Who's Who in America*. 1975 ed.

—by GRACE D. ROTONDO

MARIE ROSSI (1959-1991)

When a country is engaged in war, the announcement of cessation of hostilities is usually a happy event, a time for celebration, especially for those who have loved ones in the military. Families look forward to their return and their return to normalcy, peace, and tranquillity. And so it was with Gertrude and Paul Rossi, who were looking forward to the return of their 32-year old daughter, Major Marie Rossi, together with her husband of nine months, Chief Warrant Officer John Anderson (Andy) Cayton. Like his wife, Paul was also serving in the Persian Gulf War as a special-operations pilot but in another theater of operations. During Operation Desert Storm, Marie Rossi and her husband who were essentially newlyweds would be able to meet for only brief periods of time during their marriage that became unfortunately limited to a nine-month duration by fate.

The cease-fire in the Persian Gulf was to take effect at 8 a.m., February 28, 1991. Tragically, the next day on March 1, at 7:30 p.m. Major Marie Rossi was killed in a non-combat accident crashing into an unlit 375 foot microwave tower while flying her CH-47D Chinook cargo helicopter in bad weather in northern Saudi Arabia. Four of the five members of her crew died, and one survived with serious injuries. Her parents were soon notified of the untimely and tragic news. Marie Rossi, a career Army officer, paid with her life along with three other crew members on that ill-fated flight in the service of her country.

Marie was the third of four children (three girls and one boy) of Gertrude (nee Nolan) Rossi and Paul Rossi, a World War II decorated U.S. Marine. They lived in a modest two-story home in Oradell, New Jersey, a small town just a half-hour drive from New York City. Marie's father was employed as treasurer at a bookbindery, and her mother was employed as a secretary in a Wall Street firm in Manhattan.

Marie Rossi had always been an active and engaging child. She was a lover of animals, and she and her sister Beth used to work countless hours at a stable in an effort to help defray the cost of boarding a horse they both owned. In addition to loving animals, she also demonstrated her beliefs for animal rights. There was one incident that reflects this when she and some friends were shopping in a mall, and she noticed a woman wearing a fur coat. She promptly excused herself and walked over to the woman to remind her that many little animals had to be killed in order to make her fur coat.

Soon after entering high school, Marie was active in sports activities. After joining the swimming team , she became a lifeguard. When she graduated from River Dell High School in 1976, she went on to Dickenson College in Carlisle, Pennsylvania majoring in psychology. There she joined the Army ROTC, and upon graduation in 1980 she was commissioned second lieutenant. Her Army career eventually took her to Fort Bliss, Texas where she initially served as an artillery officer, and after completing a rotary wing flight program, she became a helicopter pilot in 1986.

She met her husband-to-be, John Cayton, in South Korea, and they became married in 1990 while she was stationed at Hunter Army Field in Georgia. Her peers and those who served under her command had a high regard and respect for her as she exercised her position and rank as an Army professional caring for her troops.

Her responsibilities were enormous, and

as company commander she was responsible for no less than 200 military, including officers and their support troops. Her company consisted mostly of men and 12 women who made up the personnel for a squadron of Chinook transport helicopters which usually number about 15 for which she was entirely responsible.

When her division, the 101st Airborne, became operational in the Persian Gulf War on February 24, 1991 and the ground attack began, she was among the first women officers to cross enemy lines piloting her helicopter. Traveling well beyond 50 miles inside the Iraqi border, she led her squadron of helicopters ferrying ammunition, fuel, supplies, and troops to the front lines.

In all, there were over 40,000 military women serving in key combat and non-combat positions in the Persian Gulf region during Operation Desert Storm. Military statistics released to the press via the Defense Department on July 17, 1991 indicated that casualty totals included 269 deaths of U.S. military personnel from August 1990 up to July 1991. Of this total there were 16 female military personnel deaths.

Women in the past have served in the United States military though the numbers were smaller compared to those of today's wars. Some women served in military roles as early as the American Civil War where it was recorded that over 60 women were either killed or wounded. Then, in the Spanish-American War of 1898, 22 Army female nurses died mostly from typhoid fever. Many military women, numbering in the hundreds, lost their lives in World War I; and, similarly it was estimated more than 400 women lost their lives in World War II. Additionally, the WASPs (Women Auxiliary Service Pilots) from World War II whose deaths numbered 38 were not given full military status until years later.

While in the Korean Conflict 19 military women lost their lives, there were five military women in Vietnam who died. Yet the Vietnam arena presented a more complicated scenario for female deaths during the war since there were women who were non-military who either worked in American governmental agencies or were non-government civilians such as journalists, missionaries, and American Red Cross help whose deaths numbered close to 50.

Like those women who preceded her in death in military service to their country, Major Marie Rossi was one of 16 female U.S. military personnel in the Persian Gulf War who gave of their lives. She met the challenges for which she had been trained, and in so serving her country she lost her life. She was given full military honors including burial in America's most respected place of honor where over 200,000 others share their final resting place.

The process of affirming women's rights in all areas of life has produced in the last forty years many substantial advances, yet those rights for their inclusion in the military still remain a painful situation for their loved ones, especially when tragedy occurs. Marie Rossi was buried on March 11, 1991 in Arlington National Cemetery, a 408-acre locale in north Virginia on the Potomac River opposite Washington D.C., where are found the burial sites of many military personnel who died in war, such as the Tomb of the Unknowns, and the late President Kennedy. Marie Rossi, an Italian-American woman who died in the line of military duty was also respected with an induction into the Army Aviation Hall of Fame, becoming the first woman to be so honored.

General Sources:
1.   *Facts on File* 28 Feb. 1991: 127.
2.   Francke, Linda Bird. "Requiem for a Soldier." *The New York Times Magazine* 21 April 1991: 24+.
3.   Kane, Joseph N. *Famous First Facts*. New York: Wilson, 1997.
4.   "Marie Rossi." *People Weekly* (Special Issue) Spring/Summer 1991: 12-15.

—by MARIO GUECIA

ALVIN RAY "PETE" ROZELLE
(1926-1996)

A U.S. sports executive and National Football League Commissioner and elected to the Pro Football Hall of Fame, Alvin Ray Rozelle made his mark on football. Aside from having engineered the precedent of lucrative contracts for just about everyone related to football, including owners, players, and management, he will probably be best remembered by football enthusiasts for having introduced *Monday Night Football* and the Super Bowl.

He was born on March 1, 1926, the only child of Ray and Hazel Viola (nee Healey) Rozelle, in the town of South Gate, California. "Pete," as he was known as of age five, had been quickly nicknamed by an uncle. Having been named at birth Alvin Ray, Rozelle has since said, "considering my real name, I am forever grateful to him." He was brought up in Lynwood, another suburb of Los Angeles. After he served two years in the U.S. Navy, he attended Compton Junior College after which he attended the University of San Francisco as an undergraduate where he acquired much media experience as its athletic news director.

Upon graduation in 1950 he remained there for two years as the University's assistant athletic director. Yet it would not be long before the Los Angeles Rams would offer him a position as their publicity director in 1952. And it was with this particular job that he began his long association with the National Football League except, of course, for a small hiatus between 1955-57. During that interval he was away from the National Football League to work for the P.K. Macker public relations firm in San Francisco doing promotional work for Australian athletes in the 1956 Melbourne Olympic games.

In order to quell internal discord among the L.A. Rams' owners, Commissioner Bert Bell suggested Rozelle as their new general manager, and so they did just that in 1957. Two years later, the National Football League Commissioner (NFL) Bert Bell died, and Rozelle replaced him. At the young age of 33, Rozelle was elected the NFL's sixth commissioner on January 26, 1960. He was a compromise choice winning on the 23rd ballot. Despite protestations of his inexperience, he set himself to work, and as one of his first projects, he expanded the NFL from twelve to fourteen teams adding the Dallas Cowboys in 1960 and the Minnesota Vikings in 1961.

Meanwhile, the American Football League that was itself founded in 1960, charged the National Football League's expansion into those two cities as an attempt to suppress new competition; they sued the older more established league (NFL) for $10 million. Legal research on antitrust laws which was carried out to a large extent by Commissioner Rozelle and his staff helped the National Football League's legal defense win the suit in 1963 at the U.S. Fourth Circuit Court of Appeals.

Making all the right moves, Rozelle negotiated in 1966 a merger of the two leagues, and for the first time in football history, a game between the champions of the American Football League and the National Football League was played in January 1967. This game went on to be known as the Super Bowl, which has become America's most watched sporting event. As its commissioner, Rozelle realized an unprecedented package from the television industry that in two years doubled the value of football team franchises. He set up a unified television policy whereby one network booked all league games in a single contract; yet, all teams would equally share in the profits, thus allowing teams in smaller market areas to share television revenues equally with the big market teams.

Rozelle found ways to increase revenue from other sources such as television ads and football picture cards. He also set up a more effective benefit plan for National Football League players, providing for life and medical insurance plus a pension for five-year players. Rozelle also engineered *Monday Night Football,* now the nation's longest running series. Since the National Football League had already made an agreement not to televise on Friday or Saturday which would have effectively undermined public viewing of high school and college football competition, he chose Monday as football night.

One of the most controversial decisions he had ever made in football was for the games to proceed as scheduled on the Sunday following the assassination of President John F. Kennedy. In his entire career, Rozelle's record shows that he consistently had to deal with the complicated negotiations that arose between television and player and owner rights. A tough negotiator with high standards of behavior, for nearly three decades he survived bidding wars with three rival leagues and three player strikes. He confronted players' drug and steroid use and gambling scandals. Pete's handling of the gambling scandal made everyone accept him as commissioner and made his position stronger than ever. Once and for all, he gained everyone's complete respect.

During his tenure, Pete truly made professional football big business, and it has become today the number one spectator sport in the United States. While the price of a franchise was approximately $1million in 1960 when he first became commissioner, the last club to change hands while he was still commissioner sold for $140 million. His undeniable impact on professional football has been such that he was elected to the Pro Football Hall of Fame in 1985, an honor usually bestowed to the candidate after retirement. Two seasons before allowing his contract to expire, he retired in 1989, claiming that the stress of ongoing legalities had taken the fun out of his job.

Rozelle, who had changed the way people spent Sunday afternoon in the fall, had served as commissioner of the National Football League from 1960 to 1989. He was chiefly responsible for the merger of the AFL into the NFL with its ultimate expansion from 12 to 28 teams. He obtained unprecedented TV sports contracts amounting to $240 million annually. No doubt, among his many legacies, his greatest creations remain the introduction of *Monday Night Football* and the heavily attended and TV-viewed Super Bowl series. He died on December 8, 1996 at the age of 70 at his home in Rancho Santa Fe, California, survived by his wife Caffie; a daughter, Anne Marie; and two grandchildren.

General Sources:

1. *Current Biography Yearbook*. New York: Wilson, 1964; 1997.
2. Null, Gary, and Carl Stone. *The Italian-Americans*. Harrisburg, PA: Stackpole Books, 1976.
3. Rozelle, Pete. Foreword. *The Super Bowl: Celebrating a Quarter-Century of America's Greatest Game*. By Ray Didinger. New York: Simon & Schuster, 1990.
4. Rozelle, Pete. Introduction. Ed. Wes Janz and Vickie Abrahamson. *25 Years of Super Bowl*. Minneapolis, MN: Bobbleheads Press, 1991.
5. *Who's Who in America*. 1964-65 ed.

—by LEW MAZZARELLA

PETER SAMMARTINO (1904-1992)

Peter Sammartino was born on August 15, 1904 in New York City. He was one of two children of Guy and Eva (Amendola) Sammartino. His father, born in Salerno, Italy immigrated to America in 1901; at first a pastry chef, he later became a wholesaler in pastry products. Peter attended Stuyvesant High School in New York City where he became highly active in leadership roles in many student clubs and associations and also edited the French Club's newsletter and the school's newspaper.

He attended the City College of New York (CCNY) where he again assumed many leadership roles, which included heading the Circolo Dante Alighieri and organizing a college band. He also played piano in the college orchestra. After a bachelor's degree in 1924 from CCNY, he pursued graduate work at New York University earning a masters in 1928 and a Ph.D. in 1931.

In 1933, he would marry his lifetime companion, Sylvia (Sally) Scaramelli. She hailed from Rutherford, New Jersey, a daughter of a prominent businessman. They worked together for their entire married life, achieving unimaginable heights including the creation of a junior college in 1942 that would someday be one of the largest privately run universities in the U.S.

Before embarking on this dream in which his wife would remain a full-time participant, he began his teaching career in 1924 in an elementary school. By 1928, he became a faculty member at CCNY, and by 1933, he became the language chairman for eight years at the New School at Columbia University. While in this capacity, he had the opportunity to participate in dialoguing with educators from the Rutherford area of New Jersey as to the paucity of schools of higher learning in that area. Dr. Sammartino became concerned since many high school graduates could not afford to go to a distant college nor were they able to get locally the needed technical training for their careers.

It wasn't long before Peter and Sally began dreaming of establishing, as a start, a junior college. With the moral insistence and persuasion of sixteen high school principals, they interested Colonel Fairleigh Dickinson (president of a surgical supply house) to purchase a decaying twenty-five room brownstone mansion in Rutherford which sat on a ten-acre site. Together with $15,000 from Sally's father, $15,000 of their own, and $30,000 from Colonel Dickinson, this became a reality. After its purchase, Colonel Dickinson turned it over to Sammartino for development.

With additional contributions, they managed to get this coeducational junior college operational by the fall of 1942 with 153 day and evening students. Within three years, its enrollment grew to 650. In 1948, it became a four-year college. By 1956, it would achieve university status having six "schools" of learning, including Arts & Sciences, Graduate School, Engineering, Business Administration, Education, and Dentistry.

Based on concepts from the New School, Sammartino kept his board of trustees small and highly selective. He worked closely with the surrounding communities. He especially worked in tandem with the high school principals and community business leaders to hammer out educational programs to assist students. The establishment of work-study programs would make it possible for students to work and still attend college, meeting their financial responsibilities. The career-training programs would also make it easier for students to secure future advancement once in the field. However, despite this heavy emphasis on work and career orientation, Sammartino did not sacrifice the importance of a good liberal arts background for students before graduating.

Since its inception in 1942, Fairleigh Dickinson University was becoming one of the fastest growing institutions of higher learning in recent United States educational history. Through Peter and Sally's vision and untiring efforts, Fairleigh Dickinson would acquire a lofty status among private schools of higher learning. By the time Peter and Sally retired in 1967, more than thirty years ago, Fairleigh Dickinson had officially become the eighth largest privately run university in the United States. It has grown even more since then; yet, at that time, it proudly claimed an enrollment of 20,000 students, 52 buildings, 7 campuses (two of which were overseas), an endowment of $62 million and a net value of $250 million.

Sammartino was the author of some 14 books; at least four of them textbooks in the area of languages (in French and Italian). As an expert in the area of higher education, he also wrote a number of books (e.g., *The President of a Small College*, 1954) depicting the challenges and the unique conditions that faced education especially in the post-war WWII economy, the growth of technology, and the education explosion of the 1950s.

A prolific writer for many professional journals, he was also associate editor for many journals including the *Literary Review*. In 1964, Peter founded the International Association of University Presidents (IAUP) which in 1992 boasted a membership of over 600 college presidents. In 1975, Peter became a founding member of the National Italian-American Foundation (NIAF) for the dissemination of Italian culture in the United States. In 1978, both he and Sally initiated the Ellis Island Restoration project by obtaining a congressional grant of $1 million, which was followed by another grant of $5 million.

Peter Sammartino received many awards, medals, titles, and commendations to honor his educational and administrative accomplishments together with his limitless generosity. These included recognition from French and Italian educational institutions, from American private and business associations, and from civic and ethnic groups in the United States. Sadly, Peter and Sally, after 52 years of marriage, died together on March 29, 1992, apparently taking their own lives, reportedly experiencing failing health. Bequeathing their entire estate to Fairleigh Dickinson University, they will be remembered as a devoted couple, exemplifying so well in one lifetime their high ideals of culture, education, and Christian charity.

General Sources:

1. *American Portrait. Peter Sammartino*. CBS-TV, 1986.

2. *Current Biography/Yearbook*. New York: Wilson, 1958; 1992.

3. Marchione, Margherita. *Americans of Italian Heritage*. Lanham, MD: University Press of America, 1995.

4. Marchione, Margherita. *Peter and Sally Sammartino*. New York: Cornwall Books, 1994.

5. Sammartino, Peter. *A History of Higher Education in New Jersey*. South Brunswick, NJ: A.S. Barnes, 1978.

6. Sammartino, Peter. *I Dreamed a College*. South Brunswick, NJ: A.S. Barnes, 1977.

7. Sammartino, Peter. *Of Colleges and Kings: The Autobiography of Peter Sammartino*. New York: Cornwall Books, 1985.

8. Sammartino, Peter. *Sicily: An Informal History*. New York: Cornwall Books, 1992.

9. *Who's Who in America*. 1958-59 ed.

—by MARGARET SCARFIA

SUSAN SARANDON (1946-   )

Nominated on several occasions for an Oscar, Susan Sarandon finally went on to receive one for Best Actress in 1996 for her poignant performance in *Dead Man Walking* (1995). She was born Susan Abigail Tomalin on October 4, 1946 in New York City. From a Welsh-Italian family of nine children (five girls and four boys), she was the eldest, and like her siblings, she spent her childhood years mostly in Edison, New Jersey. She first attended a Catholic elementary school and then switched to a public junior high school.

Reportedly it appears that "the discontentment of her conventional but unhappy youth" was in part attributed to her parents' uneasy marriage and, respectively, in turn each parent's difficult childhood. Her mother, Lenora, nee Criscione, who was the child of a teenage mother, had spent many years in a girl's boarding school. Philip Leslie Tomalin, her father, in addition to his own challenges as a growing boy, was first a nightclub singer, then a television producer, and later an advertising executive.

After high school, Susan attended Catholic University in Washington, D.C., where she initially lived with her grandparents off-campus. She worked as secretary for the university's drama department, and she did a variety of jobs, including modeling for an agency that produced a brochure endorsing the now infamous Watergate Hotel. She readily admits that she had never really wanted to become an actress. Though she majored in drama, it was not for professional reasons. This all began to change when she met Chris Sarandon, a graduate student and actor whom she later married before her senior year.

While her husband kept pursuing work in the regional theaters in and around Washington, D.C., she pursued a career in modeling after graduation. With regard to her acting career, things began to change only after she had accompanied her husband to read for a New York talent agent. Surprisingly, they were both invited to return in the fall to act. After they had moved to New York City, she did her first audition, and she landed not only her first professional role but also the female lead as well in the very same film. Her film debut took place in the film *Joe* (1970).

A story about troubled teenagers of the "hippie culture" of the 60s and early 70s, Sarandon had the role of Melissa, the daughter of an advertising executive. Her involvements took her to New York City's East Village, its drug culture, and its erotic allurements of a "free love" society. Her father together with a blue-collar worker, Joe, a role played by Peter Boyle, hunt down the hippie group where Melissa is believed to be located.

After their exposure to the hippie lifestyle and their interaction with the youths, the men become involved in a wild adventure that explodes in a tragic conclusion with Melissa getting shot accidentally. While the film won no awards, it made a terrifying statement about the drug culture generation of the early 70s. Sarandon was personally fortunate in the sense that this movie led to roles on TV soaps and in film.

In 1970 and 1971, in her portrayal of a neurotic woman, Patrice Kalham, on ABC's *World Apart*, Susan would earn as much as $1,000 a week. Later, she appeared in still another TV soap, *Search for Tomorrow*. Sarandon has since referred to both soap opera experiences as her "B-movies" where she learned acting techniques. In fact, the 70s were full of many acting challenges and experiences. On April 30, 1972, Sarandon made her Broadway debut in the role of Tricia Nixon in *An Evening with Richard Nixon,* a play by Gore Vidal. The play's brief run of sixteen weeks brought her back to TV where she appeared in *Calucci's Department* (1973) on CBS and went on to do three TV movies.

Sarandon appeared in many movie roles during that decade. She appeared in *Lady Liberty* (1972) which starred Sophia Loren; the wife of a journalist in *The Front Page* (1974) which starred Jack Lemmon; she worked opposite Robert Redford in *The Great Waldo Pepper*; held the starring female role in *The Rocky Horror Picture Show* (1975) which has since become for many a cult-classic spoofing the horror and musical movies of that era; she appeared in *The Other Side of Midnight* (1977) based on Sidney Sheldon's best-selling novel; *The Last of the Cowboys* which featured Henry Fonda; and she appeared as Hattie, Brook Shield's mother, in the controversial *Pretty Baby* (1978) directed by Louis Malle which dealt with the sensitive issue of child prostitution.

The 80s were better years in that her talents gained much recognition. Opposite Burt Lancaster in the film *Atlantic City* (1981), for her role as Sally, a clam-bar waitress who is also a croupier-in-training, she earned the Canadian Cinema Genie Award for Best Foreign Actress and an Academy Award nomination in the United States. In Mazursky's film version of Shakespeare's *Tempest* (1982), her performance in the role of Aretha also earned her the award for Best Actress at the Venice Film Festival in 1982. She also appeared in *Bull Durham* (1988) for which Sarandon received many accolades for her versatility in acting in the role of the worldly Annie Savoy.

Having appeared in forty-seven films in her career thus far, Sarandon found the 90s treating her quite well. She was nominated for four academy awards for her performances in *Thelma and Louise* (1991); *Lorenzo's Oil* (1992); *The Client* (1994); and *Dead Man Walking* (1995). She went on to win the Oscar for Best Actress in *Dead Man Walking*. Professionally at her best, she offered one of her finest film performances. She played the role of a Catholic nun and her spiritual relationship with a death-row inmate. The film, while overtly dealing with the present-day issue of capital punishment, treated with great sensitivity the eternally poignant yet dramatically difficult theme of spiritual redemption.

Although divorcing Chris Sarandon in 1979, she continues to bear his last name. After she and Louis Malle had a three-year relationship, it came to an end when Malle went on to marry Candice Bergen. She has three children: a daughter with Italian director Franco Amurri; and two sons with actor/director Tim Robbins with whom she resides. Taking advantage of her celebrity status, she has on many occasions communicated her views to the public about the need for social change. This includes the problems of the homeless, AIDS research, and the struggles of women and children in Central America.

General Sources:

1. *Celebrity Register*. New York: Simon & Schuster, 1990.
2. *Contemporary Theatre, Film and Television*. Detroit, MI: Gale Research, 1997.
3. *Current Biography Yearbook*. New York: Wilson, 1989.
4. Gerosa, Melina. "A Woman of Substance." *Ladies' Home Journal* Nov. 1997: 210-213+.
5. *International Directory of Film and Film Makers*. Detroit, MI: St. James Press, 1992.
6. Katz, Ephraim. *The Film Encyclopedia*. New York: HarperCollins, 1998.

—by IRENE LAMANO

JOHN ALFRED SCALI (1918-1995)

Entering the diplomatic arena as successor to George Bush as Permanent Representative of the United States to the United Nations in 1972, John A. Scali was a journalist of note who had worked with political personalities at the highest levels of government. A well-known leader among newspaper correspondents, he worked for the Associated Press (AP) and was nicknamed the AP's Premier Traveling Reporter. Covering the last two years of WWII in Europe and the subsequent Eisenhower years of the 50s, he was present at the celebrated "kitchen debate" in Moscow between Vice President Nixon and the Soviet Union Premier Nikita S. Khrushchev.

Scali, as correspondent, had worked behind the scenes as a patriotic citizen assisting in the resolution of one of the most delicate and potentially dangerous matters in recent history—the Cuban Missile Crisis during the Kennedy administration. Today as more information becomes available to the general public regarding that October 1962 crisis, its unfolding has revealed the depth of the previously *underestimated* near-disaster political proportions of a situation that could have ushered a full-scale nuclear war between the Soviet Union and the United States. As a correspondent and not in an official government position, John Scali played a significant role in abating and defusing a potentially destructive scenario that many political analysts believe was the closest humanity had come to using atomic weapons since WWII.

John Alfred Scali, born April 27, 1918 in Canton, Ohio was the son of Paul and Lucy (nee Leone) Scali who, several years after John's birth, moved to Boston. During high school, John was a reputed basketball star, and when he later attended Boston University, he proved himself to be gifted as a writer. By his senior year in college he became editor in chief of the campus newspaper. After graduating in 1942 with a B.S. degree in journalism, he became a reporter for the Boston *Herald* and soon afterwards joined the Boston bureau of United Press (UP) and was assigned to general reporting.

Dissatisfied with United Press for not allowing him to go on overseas assignments, in 1944 he joined the Associated Press, UP's major rival, and he would remain a loyal member of its staff for almost two decades until the beginning of the Kennedy administration. After his war correspondence years in 1944-45 in Europe, the Associated Press reassigned him to its Washington bureau, staying particularly close to the State Department where he often had the opportunity to do news correspondence accompanying diplomats and dignitaries in their travels at home and abroad.

In the 50s, during the Cold War when the word Communism evoked strong emotions, one of Scali's more important assignments took him to Moscow where at an American Expo of American goods he covered Vice President Nixon's participation in an unscheduled debate with Premier Khrushchev on the contrasting merits of their ideologies. Since the discussion took place in the exhibition's kitchen appliance showroom, it was nicknamed the "kitchen debate." An omen of things to come, Khrushchev's hard-nosed attitudes would later become realized in a dangerous scenario of nuclear brinkmanship during the Cuban Missile Crisis.

In the 50s, Scali as correspondent covered President Eisenhower's many state visits to different parts of Asia, Europe, and the Middle East. Energetic and resourceful, Scali seemed to be in the right place at the right time offering maximal high quality coverage of events. By the end of the 50s, Scali had acquired an excellent reputation for his knowledge of top-level political protocol. His unquestionable experience in dealing directly with diverse governments around the globe together with his personal acquaintance of political leaders constituted major factors that allowed him to make the transition from traditional press correspondence to TV media coverage for the American Broadcasting Company on February 27, 1961.

Scali's transition took place a month after Kennedy's inauguration. It was a period of time that was historically dangerous for the world, a time when America's direct involvement in Vietnam was beginning and would later escalate into a seemingly endless war that tore at the very fabric of America. It was also a perilous time when Khrushchev's nuclear militancy against the U.S. was approaching its apogee where, with Cuba's complicity, Khrushchev was having built a series of missile sites in Cuba replete with missiles capable of delivering nuclear strikes against the U.S. just miles away from Florida.

President Kennedy, who was completing his 20th month in office, announced to the nation in a televised address on October 22, 1962 that what the Soviets were doing constituted a direct threat to United States security and that within two days he would put in place a maritime quarantine, a naval blockade around Cuba. On October 26, two days after the blockade was put into effect, Scali was approached by an unannounced Russian to consider acting as an intermediary with President Kennedy. This mysterious offer came about in the Occidental Restaurant on Pennsylvania Avenue in Washington, D.C., by Aleksandr Fomin, ostensibly a top Russian Embassy Washington-based official who was a Soviet high level operative for Russian intelligence (KGB).

Trusted as a highly reliable person by so many around the world, ABC News correspondent Scali was targeted by the Russians to initiate a behind-the-scenes negotiation between them and the United States. Suddenly finding himself as an intermediary without any previous government directive or mandate, he handled the exchange of critically relevant information on both sides so that in effect he assisted in negotiating a deal *sub rosa* that saved face for the Russians but more importantly averted a potentially catastrophic nuclear war.

Scali's important role in this crisis did not become known until two years later. By 1967 he narrated many ABC-TV news specials such as those on the war in Vietnam, and he became anchorman for a weekly TV program *ABC Scope*. In 1971 he left ABC-TV News to become a foreign affairs adviser to President Nixon. In 1973, he was assigned by Nixon as ambassador to the United Nations. After two years of service, he returned to ABC News working until his retirement in 1993. When he died on October 9, 1995 in the nation's capital, he left an unusual legacy of a style of journalism that had always been enriched by his firsthand experience at the White House and his worldwide knowledge of diplomacy.

General Sources:
1. *Current Biography Yearbook*. New York: Wilson, 1973; 1996.
2. "Obituary." *New York Times* 10 Oct. 1995: A 20.
3. Scott, L.V. *Macmillan, Kennedy, and the Cuban Missile Crisis: Political, Military, and Intelligence Aspects.* New York: St. Martin's Press, 1999.
4. Valois, Karl E., ed. *The Cuban Missile Crisis: A World in Peril.* Carlisle, MA: Discovery Enterprises, 1998.
5. *Who's Who in America.* 1993 ed.

—by ELEANOR FEE

ANTONIN SCALIA (1936-   )

A specialist in constitutional law, a professor of law, and federal appellate judge, Antonin Scalia in 1986 became the first Italian American ever to be appointed to the highest court in the land, the Supreme Court. This event took place during President Ronald Reagan's administration. For many political critics, his approval to that post seemed to mark a clear movement to the right in America. For most Italian Americans, that appointment meant not only the just selection of a highly qualified man but also a refreshing look at the status of professional Italian Americans in recent history.

Antonin was born March 11, 1936 in Trenton, New Jersey, the only child of Eugene and Catherine Scalia, Sicilian emigrants. Both his parents were educated; Eugene, a literary scholar, and Catherine, a school teacher. While he was a child, the family moved to Elmhurst, Queens (New York) where he would spend most of his childhood years. He attended Xavier High School, a Catholic military academy in Manhattan where he graduated first in his class. He was known by his peers as a conservative Catholic and a brilliant student. He continued his formal education as a history major at Georgetown University in Washington, D.C., again graduating first in his class in 1957.

He enrolled at Harvard Law School and became editor of their publication, *The Law Review*, while also acquiring the reputation as an accomplished debater. Receiving his law degree in 1960, he joined the corporate law firm of Jones, Day, Cockley & Reavis in Cleveland, Ohio. During his seven-year tenure, Antonin was known as a most outspoken conservative on constitutional issues.

Despite the attractiveness of being offered a lucrative partnership, Scalia resigned in 1961, and he accepted a teaching position at the University of Virginia Law School where he cultivated an extensive knowledge of administrative law. In 1971, President Nixon appointed him to the part-time position of general counsel in the executive office of telecommunications policy. Two years later in 1974, in fact, he was promoted to assistant attorney general in charge of legal counsel, acting as an advisor to the President of the United States and to the attorney general, a position confirmed by Congress under the succeeding Ford administration.

During the Watergate scandal and the ensuing investigation, Scalia fought hard to state that the controversial Watergate tapes recorded during President Nixon's term were Nixon's personal property and not that of the United States. His legal opinion was later rejected by the Supreme Court. He worked full-time at the Justice Department until the Ford Administration left office in 1977.

With the incoming Carter administration, Scalia left government and became a visiting professor at Georgetown Law Center and a scholar-in-residence at the American Enterprise Institute, a conservative "think tank" located in Washington, D.C. Later, in 1977 he left Washington and became a professor at the University of Chicago Law School. He was coediting two scholarly journals that promoted free market policies: University of Chicago's *Regulation* and the American Enterprise Institute's *Journal on Government and Society*.

These publications gained him a national reputation as a strong advocate of federal and state deregulation. He maintained dissenting views with regard to Supreme Court rulings upholding affirmative action programs for schools and businesses that set numerical goals and timetables. He accused the Supreme Court of making decisions that led to preferential status to less qualified minority applicants and the effect of reverse discrimination.

Scalia opposed the 1974 Amendments to the Freedom of Information Act. He questioned the security risks, and he urged the amendments be modified to further restrict the flow of information dealing with law enforcement and national security. His request to modify and restrict those amendments and his opinions regarding the Gramm-Rudman budget balancing law as unconstitutional earned him the admiration of the Reagan administration. In 1982, he was appointed to the bench of the United State Supreme Court of Appeals for the District of Columbia, a position considered to be the most powerful federal tribunal in the country second only to the Supreme Court.

In his new position, Judge Scalia wasted no time in applying his doctrine of judicial restraint to render conservative opinions on some key social issues. Lethal drugs injected into condemned prisoners were required to meet Food and Drug Administration consumer standards. He rejected a ruling upholding a U.S. Navy regulation forbidding homosexuality in the service. He became a strong advocate for increasing the accountability of the news media in libel lawsuits filed by public figures. His staunch position earned him the label as the judge who is the worst enemy of free speech by *New York Times'* political columnist William Safire.

On many different occasions, he challenged the interference of the judicial system in areas of which they knew very little. Scalia was masterful in rejecting the Gramm-Rudman budget balancing law with his defense of the separation of powers within the legislative branch. The Supreme Court upheld the Scalia panel in a July 1986 decision.

The Justice Department, under the Reagan administration, was so impressed with his press libel rulings and his powers of persuasion that Scalia became frontrunner as a Supreme Court nominee. He was put to the test by his future colleagues for two days of questions in which he was admired by all, despite testimony against his nomination by civil rights leaders and feminist organizations.

Scalia skillfully avoided giving his personal opinions on controversial social issues on grounds that he might prejudice his impartiality in future court cases. He did, however, pledge to enforce affirmative action laws that had already existed. Soon after Scalia received the American Bar Association's highest rating for Supreme Court nominee, the Senate Committee approved him unanimously, and it was ratified with a 90-0 vote.

His colleagues describe him as a gifted storyteller, good humored and also a person who demands excellence from his workers. Feared by many in the opposition, he is a disciplined worker, typical of a self-made-man ethic, maintaining a strong competitive instinct, respect for authority, and a drive towards excellence. Nino, as Judge Scalia is known to his close friends, has been married to the former Maureen McCarthy since September 10, 1960. They have nine children and reside in the Washington suburb of McClean, Virginia.

General Sources:
1. Brisbin, Richard. *Justice Antonin Scalia and the Conservative Revival.* Baltimore, MD: Johns Hopkins University Press, 1997.
2. *Current Biography Yearbook.* New York: Wilson, 1986.
3. Italia, Bob. *Antonin Scalia.* Edina, MN: Abdo, 1992.
4. Scalia, Antonin. *A Matter of Interpretation: Federal Courts and the Law: An Essay.* Princeton, NJ: Princeton University Press, 1997.

—by SAM PITTARO

FRANCESCO SCAVULLO (1929-   )

A photographer of socialites and show business celebrities, high fashion models, photogenic beauties, author of several books, and an occasional director of film, Scavullo has carved out a niche for himself in the world of contemporary American life. Recognized by weekly news and fact-gathering kinds of magazines such as *Time* and *Newsweek*, and acknowledged by fashion plate magazines such as *Harper's Bazaar* and *Vogue,* Scavullo—for those in the media where the *image* depicted is crucial and central to meaning and influence—has become a legend in his time to such a point that the *Washington Post* has described him as "the court painter of our time" whose strategy to idealize his subjects before the eye of the camera has rendered him famous for his creation of photographic portraitures of the "beautiful people."

Francesco Scavullo was born on January 16, 1929 in Staten Island, New York. He was one of five children of Angelo and Margaret (nee Pavis) Scavullo. Francesco's father, who had been in the cooking utensil-business, moved up to Manhattan acquiring and operating a highly fashionable restaurant, the Central Park Casino in 1937. Living in a stylish and centrally located townhouse not far from the restaurant, young Scavullo, barely eight years of age at the time, would have the opportunity to take notice and experience in his growing years the most elegant of people who frequented his parents' posh restaurant.

Apparently sparked by intuition and much imagination, he enjoyed his mother's stories about the celebrities who dined there and his mother's shopping excursions at the expensive and lavishly furnished 5th Avenue boutique with their showcase window displays.

From a young age, he was visually sensitive, often remaining mesmerized as he thumbed through his mother's women's magazines, especially fashion magazines, their full-page display ads, their photo layouts depicting show business celebrities, their activities, whereabouts, and performances. The first movie he had ever seen was *Queen Christina* starring Greta Garbo whose statuesque beauty would make a lasting impression on him and his style of photography.

Unusually determined as a child in his fascination with visual representation through the camera, he regularly took snapshots with his father's camera, and in 1938 at the age of nine he had gone as far as swaying his mother into buying him a Univex motion picture camera. Using his new camera he would then re-create and then film "excerpts" mimicking the movies having his two older sisters and friends dress the part of the movie characters. One of his favorites was filming and photographing his re-creation of the leading female characters from *Gone With the Wind*. Eventually becoming expert at retouching photos, he developed a following consisting of his sisters' girlfriends who wanted to be photographed, and, of course, have their photos retouched for maximal effect.

It was in high school that he determined he would become a fashion photographer. During that period of time, he had several part-time jobs one of which allowed him the opportunity to take a photo of the famous Latin American singer Carmen Miranda as she boarded a cruise ship. Following his high school graduation in 1945, he worked his way up from a job in Becker's Studios, noted for its fashion catalogs, to *Vogue* magazine where he worked for three years on its staff as an assistant and apprentice. Then moving on to *Harper's Bazaar* magazine, Scavullo seized the opportunity to redesign a studio set from scratch. In doing a layout for a blouse advertisement, he did his first photograph on that set, and the style that emerged from that set would soon come to be known as the "Look."

The photograph attracted much attention in the industry, and it afforded him an opportunity to do free-lance photography for the front cover of the next issue of an entirely different magazine, *Seventeen*. The cover photograph depicting "two teenaged models dressed in yellow slickers and huddled under an umbrella" became an instant success photo in the industry, and Scavullo at age nineteen in 1948 was taken on immediately by *Seventeen* magazine. The new and more prestigious position allowed him to travel around the globe shooting fashion layouts in unlikely and wondrous locations such as in the Australian Outback and in the Andes of Peru at Machu Picchu.

It was at this time that Scavullo moved to a converted carriage house in Manhattan's Upper East Side which would become his permanent residence and studio. Not limited to his regular job at *Seventeen* magazine, he did covers and fashion layouts for other magazines such as *Ladies' Home Journal*, *Good Housekeeping*, *Woman's Home Companion*, *Today's Woman*, and *Town and Country*. It was in the last of this aforementioned list of magazines that he began a new era in his career photographing socialites and debutantes; and he recalls, as one of the most interesting in his entire career, once photographing Countess Anna Camerana Bozza who wore "nothing but jewelry" on her body.

As Scavullo worked in the 1950s, he slowly developed new techniques, including one that insisted on a "soft, natural daylight effect" in lighting his subjects. By the mid-1960s he felt certain about having achieved his own distinct innovative style of photographing which he deemed applicable to most areas, and he began doing extensive work for *Cosmopolitan* magazine. His innovations dealt mostly with lighting, makeup, correctly styling the hair of his subjects, and suggesting appropriate apparel. This series of procedures both in the preparation of the subject's appearance and the use of lighting on the subject was coined as the "Scavullo-ization" process. This was codified as a business strategy, and Scavullo offered his services as "image-maker" to performers and celebrities. It has been reported that in the 1970s this process which entailed an afternoon's work cost his clients as much $10,000 per sitting.

Despite protestations by critics as to Scavullo's elitist and supercilious attitudes towards the masses, Scavullo defended himself in his book, *Scavullo on Beauty* (1976). He rebutted the accusations by stating that the "average woman" can do much to bring out the best in herself with the proper knowledge in aesthetic care and with a concomitant belief in herself. The author of several books, Scavullo has had a selection of his photographs preserved for posterity at the permanent photography collection at the Metropolitan Museum of Art in New York City.

General Sources:
1. *Current Biography Yearbook*. New York: Wilson, 1985.
2. Scavullo, Francesco. *Scavullo: Francesco Scavullo Photographs 1948-1984*. New York: Harper & Row, 1984.
3. Scavullo, Francesco. *Scavullo on Beauty*. New York: Random House, 1976.
4. Scavullo, Francesco. *Scavullo: Photographs 50 years*. New York: Abrams, 1997.
5. Scavullo, Francesco, and Sean Byrnes. *Scavullo Women*. New York: Harper & Row, 1982.
6. *Who's Who in America*. 1995 ed.

—by DENNIS PIASIO

WALTER M. SCHIRRA, JR. (1923-   )

Walter Schirra, better known as Wally Schirra, used to watch a man in a white coverall being fired out of a cannon at the Barnum & Bailey Circus. A human cannonball: flying through the air and landing in a net on the other side of the arena. He thought: "what a nutty stunt," never thinking that, years later, he'd be strapped inside a capsule atop a mighty rocket fired into space in a much more "nutty stunt." Schirra would be one of the seven original astronauts selected for the American space program in April 1959.

He is of Swiss-Italian background, born on March 12, 1923 in Hackensack, New Jersey. The child of Florence Shillito Leach, from Brooklyn, and Walter M. Schirra, Sr., an engineer from Philadelphia, Wally was also the grandson of a world famous cornetist who played with the Philadelphia Symphony.

Wally's father, who had been an army pilot, flew bombing and reconnaissance missions over Germany in WWI. After the war, as an avocation, he became a barnstorming flier, doing stunts with his wife at county fairs in New Jersey. His wife would often do wing-walking in flight. When their son would later become part of the astronaut team and the subject of flying experience came up, Wally, Jr., would always claim to those at NASA his distinction of actually having flown before he was born since his mother did wing-walking and barnstorming during her pregnancy with him.

Wally grew up in Oradell, New Jersey. As a youngster, he would often spend days riding his bicycle around the Teterboro Airport (New Jersey) watching planes land and take off. As he grew older, his heros would become the daring pilots of the early days of flying like Charles Lindbergh and Clarence Chamberlin.

He would graduate from Dwight Morrow High School in 1940 in Englewood, New Jersey.

Entering Newark College of Engineering to study aeronautical engineering, he later applied and was accepted into the United States Naval Academy in 1942. Its usual program was five years, but because of the wartime effort to provide needed naval officers, the program was suddenly abbreviated to three years. Upon graduating with a B.S. degree and an ensign's commission, he joined the Pacific fleet aboard the cruiser *Alaska* in 1945. By the time he arrived in Japan, the war would be over. After the war in 1946 he met and married Josephine Cook Fraser who would be his wife for the next 50 plus years.

For the years immediately following the war, he devoted his time in the Seventh Fleet on Pacific assignments. In 1948, he entered flight training school at Pensacola Naval Air Station in Florida and earned his wings. His training, naturally, included doing carrier landings. When he become a naval aviator, he was assigned to Fighter Squadron 71. Much of his training had been with jets like the F-80 Shooting Star. When the Korean Conflict began on June 25, 1950, he was assigned as an exchange pilot with the 154th Fighter Bomber Squadron, flying F84E jets involving low-level bombing and strafing missions. This experience as a flyer in Korea would begin a new chapter in his life.

He flew 90 combat missions in 8 months, and had to his credit shooting down two MIGs. Awarded the Distinguished Flying Cross and two Air Medals after his Korean assignment, he become a test pilot at the Naval Ordinance Training Station in China Lake, California. Testing numerous types of aircraft, including prototype rocket planes, he was also involved in testing Sidewinder air-to-air missiles.

On December 17, 1958, on the fifty-fifth anniversary of the Wright brothers' first flight, the United States announced the birth of the manned satellite program. It would be called Mercury. A total of 508 service records were screened. In February of 1959, a short list of candidates consisting of no less than 30 fellow officers included Wally Schirra. Finally, on April 9, 1959, Schirra along with six other officers became selected to become the original seven NASA astronauts.

The seven veteran test pilots, who had flown experimental and sometimes dangerous aircraft, were not at all prepared for the sudden fame and publicity that the American public and the press would give their first astronauts. Yet they had total faith in each other's competence. They traveled throughout the U.S. investigating where the Mercury equipment and components were being manufactured. It was now 1960, and it was time to select America's first man in space. Alan B. Shepard drew the first assignment scheduled for May 5, 1961.

Schirra's turn came with the launching of *Sigma-7*, the fifth American manned space mission and third American orbital flight. The space mission took place on October 3, 1962 in the Mercury capsule *Sigma-7* whose goal consisted of a six-orbit flight around the Earth which lasted 9 hours and 13 minutes. Schirra's flight proved to be important because it reinstated the value of manned spacecraft as opposed to using robots as some planners would have wanted.

Schirra was able to demonstrate his control of the spacecraft, doing such things as saving fuel and performing maneuvers that would not have worked with a robot at that point in time. He also was able to show that by the use of hand controls he could change the spaceship attitude and make it possible to dock with other vehicles in space. Performing a near-perfect splashdown, he landed about four-and-one-half miles from the aircraft carrier Kearsarge. Being an engineer he was able to solve one of the problems with his space suit; he corrected its overheating by ingeniously hooking it up with a cooling water system.

Schirra was the only astronaut to fly in all three of the manned space programs: Mercury, Gemini, and Apollo. Perhaps his most important achievement, attributable to his flying skills, remains his having performed the world's first rendezvous of two manned crafts in outer space when he commanded *Gemini 6* and successfully docked with *Gemini 7* on December 15, 1965.

Schirra was promoted to captain after his Gemini flight and would retire at that rank after going on an Apollo mission. He entered several fields of endeavor including a leasing business, a vice president at Johns-Manville and an independent director of several companies and a consultant. Schirra was inducted into the National Aviation Hall of Fame in Dayton, Ohio in 1986. It was just one of the many honors bestowed on him for his accomplishments in aviation and space exploration.

General Sources:
1. Carpenter, M. Scott, et al. *We Seven*. New York: Simon & Schuster, 1962.
2. *Current Biography Yearbook*. New York: Wilson, 1966.
3. Knight, David, ed. *American Astronauts and Spacecraft: A Pictorial History from Project Mercury Through Project Apollo*. New York: F. Watts, 1972.
4. Manned Spacecraft Center (U.S.). *The Six Orbits of Sigma 7: Walter M. Schirra's Space Flight, October 3, 1962*. Washington, DC: NASA, 1963.
5. Schirra, Walter, Jr., and Richard N. Billings. *Schirra's Space*. Annapolis, MD: Naval Institute Press, 1995.
6. United States. NASA. *NASA Astronauts*. Washington, DC: U.S. G.P.O., 1967.

—by JEAN TESTA

MARTIN SCORSESE (1942-   )

Martin Scorsese, considered by many one of the world's most provocative filmmakers, was born on November 17, 1942 in Flushing, New York. His parents, Charles and Catherine (nee Cappa) Scorsese, had recently moved there from Little Italy in Manhattan. They both had jobs in the garment district, but because of apparent financial straits, they returned to their former home in New York City's Little Italy when Martin was eight. Living there until twenty-four years of age, he came to understand thoroughly the flavor and rhythm of its life.

Poor health, specifically asthma, prevented Martin Scorsese from fully joining his older brother Fred and his peers in their sports activities, urban street ventures, and job experiences. In this micro-world of Little Italy located within the macro-world of New York City, his health limitations made him at times an outsider: more an observer of his world rather than an active participant. It was a perspective and a role he would examine repeatedly in his films. In his younger years, to relieve his pain of loneliness and idleness, he would often go to the movies with his father. Afterwards, at home he would sketch motion picture scenes on his drawing pads.

Raised a Roman Catholic, Scorsese attended a Catholic grade school, and at fourteen with the intention of becoming a priest he enrolled in a junior seminary, New York City Cathedral College. Expelled at the end of the year reportedly for "roughhousing during prayers," he transferred to Cardinal Hayes High School in the Bronx and graduated with honors in 1960. After not meeting the requirements for Fordham University's divinity program, he planned on majoring in English in order to teach after he entered New York University.

He did not abandon the idea of the priesthood altogether until he found in filmmaking what he has come to call his true vocation. After discovering the university's film department, he devoted himself to the fundamentals of filmmaking. While studying for his B.S. degree in film communication (1964) and his masters degree (1966), he taught as an assistant instructor.

He soon started making films that won awards from the Edward L. Kingsley Foundation, the Screen Producers Guild, and the Brown University Film Festival. Scorsese's award-winning student films included *What's a Girl Like You Doing in a Place Like This?* (l963) and *Its Not Just You, Murray* (1964). There also emerged in him a fascination with violence surely obvious in the blood-drenched, six-minute color film *The Big Shave* (1967).

When Scorsese returned to the NYU faculty in 1968 to teach film until 1970, he wrote and directed his first feature film: *Who's That Knocking At My Door?* (1968), a story about the struggles of a young Catholic, Italian American growing up in New York City's Little Italy and his attempts at reconciling Catholic sexual codes with the contrasting realities around him. A very explicit sex scene caused considerable critical attention.

A subsequent movie, *Street Scenes* (1970), which Scorsese had generated while at NYU, documented a New York City anti-Vietnam demonstration. In the same year, working with director Michael Wadleigh, Scorsese became supervising editor and assistant director with another documentary, *Woodstock* (1970), a vivid description of the 1969 concentration of some half-million rock music fans in the New York Catskills area. In 1971 after moving to Hollywood and more filming activity, Scorsese was invited by producer Roger Corman to direct a low-budget film, *Boxcar Berta* (1972), based on the life story of a Depression-era young woman vagrant in the genre of *Bonnie and Clyde* movies.

Scorsese then filmed *Mean Streets* (1973), based on a script he had written with Mardik Martin seven years earlier. It dealt with the relationship between a small-time hood Charlie and his reckless friend Johnny Boy, both of whom were caught up in the criminal world of Little Italy. Torn between loyalty to a friend and the desire to move up the ranks in the crime organization, Charlie sacrifices his epileptic girlfriend and Johnny Boy. Using some of Cassavetes' improvisational skills, Scorsese directed Harvey Keitel and the then unknown Robert De Niro. Yet far from being a box-office smash, Scorsese received much critical acclaim at the New York Film Festival.

Hollywood's recognition of Scorsese's talents brought funding for his next movie, *Alice Doesn't Live here Anymore* (1975). A radical divergence from his previous work, it dealt with feminist themes and was based on Robert Getchell's TV screenplay about a mediocre singer seeking a career in music after she suddenly became widowed. Considered a sleeper at the box office, the film brought a Best Actress Oscar to Ellen Burstyn and in the eyes of Hollywood producers had finally made Scorsese a success.

Just a year later, the film *Taxi Driver* (1976) returned to the thematic violence of *Mean Streets* and received three Oscar nominations for Best Picture, Best Supporting Actress, and Best Actor. Depicting an ex-marine taxi driver gone psycho in his efforts to rid New York City of undesirables, the film dramatizes a very extreme condition of personal alienation and its terrible externalizations into bloody violence. Considered a masterpiece of its genre, Scorsese's film won the International Grand Prize at the Cannes Film Festival (1976).

Scorsese received his first Oscar nomination as Best Director for the black-and-white film *Raging Bull* (1980), a riveting biography of boxer Jake La Motta. Amazingly, the film also received six other nominations including Best Picture. De Niro in the title role won an Oscar, and Scorsese won the National Society of Film Critics Award for Best Director. Again, Scorsese received Best Director Award at Cannes Film Festival for a subsequent film *After Hours* (1985).

In 1988 he received an Oscar nomination as Best Director for *The Last Temptation of Christ*. Closely following Kazantzakis' novel, the film evoked enormous controversy among many religious groups because of its depiction of Christ's human, sensual, and vulnerable qualities. In 1990 he directed *Goodfellas*, a stunning return to mob violence that received an Oscar nomination for Best Picture. For that film he was voted Best Director by both the National Society of Film Critics (1990) and the Venice Film Festival (1991). Though not typically belonging to the Hollywood establishment, Scorsese's name has become synonymous with daring, unique, and provocative cinematography.

General Sources:
1.   Bliss, Michael. *Martin Scorsese and Michael Cimino*. Metuchen, NJ: Scarecrow Press, 1985.
2.   *Current Biography Yearbook*. New York: Wilson, 1979.
3.   Friedman, Lawrence. *The Cinema of Martin Scorsese*. New York: Continuum, 1998.
4.   Katz, Ephraim. *The Film Encyclopedia*. New York: HarperCollins, 1998.
5.   Scorsese, Martin. *A Personal Journey with Martin Scorsese Through American Movies*. New York: Hyperion, 1997.
6.   *Who's Who in Entertainment*. 1998-1999 ed.

—by ANTHONY TRIVELLI

JOHN H. SECONDARI (1919-1975)

Television producer, narrator, novelist, news commentator, and journalist, John Secondari remains one of the unsung heros of early television. He was best noted for his many award-winning documentaries which paved the way for the more modern kinds of TV documentaries viewed today. As a genre, the documentary and its spinoff, investigative reporting programs, have steadily earned a respectable share of TV viewing time and have also captured a greater part of the TV viewing audiences. While Secondari did not invent the TV documentary as a genre, he surely helped to develop it in its early years when the genre was in its infancy in the process of adapting itself to the TV screen. It was a transition that involved defining what a TV documentary was and what stylistic elements could be utilized from the precedents found in the old-time movie "news" documentaries and in the old radio-style documentaries heard where the commentator's personality was an integral part of the style.

Starting out as a news correspondent for CBS in Rome, Italy, he took leave from journalism in order to write novels such as *Coins in the Fountain*, eventually becoming a hit Hollywood movie renamed *Three Coins in the Fountain*. After his lengthy writing break, he joined ABC in the late 1950s as its Washington bureau chief. In the early 1960s, he spearheaded the organization of ABC's first TV documentary unit and became the executive producer of the historically important and notable series, *Saga of Western Man*, an Emmy award-winning TV program. He had also organized—together with Drew Associates—the initiation of a weekly TV documentary series called *Close-up!*, which represented one of the earliest TV investigative-type programs. As an innovator and developer of TV programming and a manager of information who would have gone much farther in the late 70s and 80s when TV was in its younger years, he died at the early age of 56 in 1975.

He was born on November 1, 1919 in Rome, Italy to Dr. Epaminonda and Linda (nee Agostini) Secondari. They lived in a small town called Bevagna just outside Rome. His father, apparently the product of a long line of Italian physicians, broke the family tradition when in 1924 he decided to move his family to America. Living in New York City, young Secondari received a top-quality education attending first Xavier High School, a Jesuit institution; then, Fordham University, another Jesuit institution where he received his B.A. in 1939; then, finally, Columbia University where he received his M.S. degree in journalism. His first job involved working for the United Press, a news gathering agency, in its radio section.

In 1941 after joining the U.S. Army, he was commissioned a second lieutenant. He fought in France, Germany, and Austria and was finally assigned to General Mark Clark's staff in Vienna. In 1946 he completed his military service with the rank of captain, and unlike most American soldiers, he remained in Europe to work. He became a reporter first for the *Daily American* back in his native city of Rome and then a news correspondent for CBS. Later, he left CBS radio network and joined the Economic Cooperation Administration (ECA) in its special mission to Italy, which in effect was the Italian-based component of America's Marshall Plan for Europe's economic recovery. In his three years at ECA, Secondari with a staff of 50 people produced 37 films and almost 10 weekly radio shows.

After partaking in Italy's economic recovery from the war in the revitalizing of its communications networks, Secondari left the ECA to write novels. He indeed wrote three novels, one which eventually became a Hollywood film, *Three Coins in the Fountain* (1954) starring superstars Clifton Webb and Dorothy McGuire. Later, when both NBC and CBS rebuffed airing a dramatic script of his that dealt with the highly sensitive theme of advertisers' influences on TV programming (a script he had written expressly for a TV drama presentation), he joined ABC in 1956 as its Washington bureau chief for three years. During that time he became moderator of an ABC program called *Open Hearing*, a public-service weekly TV program dealing with national and international current events.

In 1960 he became executive producer for ABC's special projects area—in those days that term meant documentaries. On March 29, 1960, Secondari demonstrated his innovation and talent in his production of *Korea—No Parallel*. It was a documentary that Secondari had also written and narrated, and it dealt with Korea's status seven years after the 1953 armistice. Many observers had recognized its value and hailed that program as a decidedly different and incisive kind of presentation that departed from TV's standard programming. Its investigative format had a definite journalistic style that would indeed effect changes in the style of future TV documentaries and TV reporting.

Perhaps his best remembered weekly documentary series was his *Close-Up!* This program (varying from one-half hour to one hour), which began in the fall of 1960 and lasted three TV seasons, investigated subject matter that most TV stations would avoid. For instance, Secondari's topics included programs on civil rights struggles, the spread of Communism in South America, and recent conservationist efforts at fighting wildlife extinction in Africa. His most remembered documentary in this series was called *Meet Comrade Student* presented in September 1962. Filmed in Russia at the height of the Cold War during the Kennedy years, it focused on contemporary Russians, their schools, their home life— in short, emphasizing their similarities more than their differences with Americans. It won the Overseas Press Club Award for Best Photographic Reporting for that year.

In a life span that was all too brief, Secondari's crowning achievement was his award-winning series, *The Saga of Western Man*. The series consisted of three TV seasons. The first, 1963-1964, focused on four major years in history: 1492, 1776, 1898, and 1964 all viewed as pivotal years in Western history. The second season, 1964-1965, dealt with specific men and events such as Leonardo da Vinci. The third and final season, 1965-1966, dealt with a variety of topics such as Beethoven's genius. In all, Secondari had created a new interest in programming better presentations in the area of documentaries. Well known and famous in his day, he—along with his wife who directed and did production work—won many awards, including an Emmy in 1965 for outstanding achievement in entertainment. A year prior, in 1964 he had received Italy's Gugliemo Marconi World Television Award. Secondari, in his mid-fifties, died on February 8, 1975 in New York City.

General Sources:

1.   Brown, Les. *Encyclopedia of Television*. Detroit, MI: Gale Research, 1992.
2.   *Current Biography Yearbook*. New York: Wilson, 1967; 1975.
3.   Secondari, John. *Coins in the Fountain*. Philadelphia: Lippincott, 1952.
4.   Secondari, John. *Spinner of the Dream*. Boston: Little, 1955.
5.   Secondari, John. *Temptation for a King*. Philadelphia: Lippincott, 1954.
6.   *Who's Who in America*. 1966-67 ed.

—by ROCKY PESIRI

SISTER BLANDINA SEGALE (1850-1941)

Sister Blandina Segale, whose given name was Rosa Maria Segale, was born on May 23, 1850 in Cicagna, Italy to Francesco and Giovanna (nee Malatesta) Segale. Francesco owned orchards, but the revolutionary atmosphere in Italy made him feel that emigration from Italy had become a necessity. Although his family landed in Louisiana, the city of Cincinnati, Ohio would be their destination. They had heard that Cincinnati was built on seven hills, and the Segales felt that it would remind them of home.

As a child, Rosa's first written words reportedly were Gesù Madre, surely an interesting way for a child to view Christ: as a mother. After grammar school, Rosa attended Mt. St. Vincent Academy in Cedar Grove which was run by the Sisters of Charity in Cincinnati. In time, her desire for a religious vocation grew, and she finally revealed to her family that she wished to become a nun in the Sisters of Charity.

Despite her mother's opposition, Rosa at sixteen in 1866, entered the mother convent house where she would take on the religious name Sister Blandina. Her biological sister, Maria Maddelena, would soon follow her and take on the habit becoming Sister Justina. In 1872, having obtained training as a teacher, Sister Blandina received orders to go to Trinidad, Colorado to teach in its public school system, and she was also told that she would be traveling alone to her new destination. This time it was her father who forbade her to go there. She was not afraid, and all along she had secretly wished to be sent further west to California.

As she traveled west, Sister Blandina had no idea that her experiences would take her far beyond the realm prescribed by teaching. She often took on the role of nurse, construction worker, and negotiator where everyday life offered her new challenges and meaning to her existence as a nun. A journal arose from the scraps of paper Sister Blandina had penned over the years. The journal encompassed twenty years (1872-1892) that she had spent out west, which included not only Trinidad, Colorado but also Santa Fe and Albuquerque, New Mexico. Sister Blandina had originally written her journal to share her experiences exclusively with her sister.

She writes in her journal of having met Billy the Kid on two occasions. The first time they met, Billy offered her safety and protection from the rowdiness of his gang after she had tended to one of them when he was injured. She crossed paths with him again when he was imprisoned for his attempt on the life of Governor Lew Wallace of New Mexico (author of *Ben Hur*). She saw Billy with his hands and feet cuffed while his body lay fastened to the floor. Sister Blandina commented in her journal that even though Billy was immobile, his thoughts considered the fate and condition of others. She remembered hearing Billy say that he wished he could have provided a chair for her, and he also asked her to try to do something to release the other prisoner in his cell.

One of the most touching references in Sister Blandina's journal tells of a man who had come to her hungry and his body frozen. She took care of him and treated him kindly. After he left her, he sent notes to her signed "The Outcast," suggesting that he had done some terrible wrongs in his past. Subsequent notes clearly revealed that he had changed his ways and had not done anything wrong since he met her. He told her that she had planted "a seed of kindness," and that the "gleamings of Faith" were slowly returning to him. In gratitude for how his life had changed, he told her he was returning to his home. She never heard from him again.

Sister Blandina, who had been expressly sent to the town of Trinidad in 1872, formed a caring community through social work and faith renewal to those who had gone astray. Upon being sent to Santa Fe, New Mexico in 1877, she was responsible for having a school built miraculously with no money of her own—just with the generosity of people's labor and materials. Charitable and most enterprising, she also helped in getting established St. Vincent's Hospital. At one point, the local county where she lived had decided to cut back on funding the burial of bodies without known families. Upon hearing the news, Sister Blandina rose to the occasion by offering to place those bodies without funding upon the coroner's doorstep.

She moved once again to Albuquerque, New Mexico where she worked to get a school built and negotiated back pay for some teachers. In 1881, she helped in the building of a sisters residence, that today is better known as Sister Blandina Convent. In 1889, when the laws changed, it seemed that nuns could no longer wear their habits in public schools, and so Sister Blandina who refused to give up her habit eventually moved to Pueblo, Colorado where in 1892 she became principal of a Catholic school.

In 1897, Sister Blandina returned to Cincinnati where she and her sister were reunited. Together they opened the Santa Maria Institute, offering a multitude of social services for immigrants and others in need. The services included a day and night school, clothing distribution for the needy, and a safe residence for working girls. She also traveled to New York City in 1910 to study how to educate the deaf in order that she might teach others back in Cincinnati.

In time, an editor for the *Santa Maria Magazine* learned of Sister Blandina's journal, and he requested her permission to print its contents in serial form in his magazine. Her consent to have historical data based on her personal experiences met with overwhelming interest. In 1932, Sister Blandina's journal became a book titled *At The End of the Santa Fe Trail*. Since then, it has gone through several editions and continues to draw interest. As if the book's tales and descriptions of the old west were not enough, its Forewords were equally fascinating to read. In the 1932 edition, she mentions her influence in abolishing the Lynch Law, and in the 1948 edition, she mentions her dubious distinction as a nun being appointed a probation officer in Cincinnati upon her return to that city.

The death of her biological sister, Sister Justina, in 1929 had devastated her world, but this did not slow her down. She traveled to the Vatican in 1932 requesting more clergy to assist the Italian immigrants. She continued her work until 1938 when she fell and broke her hip. In 1940, she fell again rendering her unable to leave her room. On February 23, 1941, at the age of 91, she whispered "Gesù Madre" and departed this life.

General Sources:
1. Johnson, Byron A. *Old Town, Albuquerque, New Mexico, A Guide to Its History and Architecture.* Albuquerque, NM: publisher unknown, 1980.
2. Pesko, S.J., Father Michael. *Catholic and American: A Popular History.* Huntington, IN: Our Sunday Visitor Press, 1989.
3. Segale, Sister Blandina. *At The End of the Santa Fe Trail.* Columbus, OH: Columbian Press, 1932.
4. Segale, Sister Blandina. *At The End of the Santa Fe Trail.* Ed. Sister Therese Martin McCarthy. Columbus, OH: Columbian Press, 1948.

—by LINDA D'ANDREA-MARINO

EMILIO SEGRÈ (1905-1989)

Emilio Gino Segrè, who together with the physicist Owen Chamberlain, discovered the antiproton for which the two would share the Nobel Prize in 1959, discovered new elements such as technetium, astatine, and plutonium-239, and did extensive research in the use of neutrons for splitting the atom.

The youngest of three sons, Emilio was born on January 30, 1905 in Tivoli, Italy. His father Giuseppe Abramo Segrè born in 1859 hailed from the town of Bozzolo. The Segrè lineage, which had been in Bozzolo for centuries, was probably from Spain at the time of the expulsion of the Jews in 1492.

Giuseppe, after working for various paper and ceramics manufacturers, became an assistant manager of a corporation which utilized a river near Tivoli for both hydroelectric power and irrigation. Eventually becoming manager, Giuseppe focused his attention on papermaking, his area of expertise, and hydroelectric power. Emilio's mother, Amelia Susanna Treves, of Italian-Jewish heritage, was born in Florence in 1860. The Treves had lived in Vercelli in Piedmont. Amelia's father Marco later moved to Florence to find a more enlightened attitude toward Jewish people.

As a child, young Emilio spent many hours at his father's hydroelectric plant. In 1922, he began his college studies at the University of Rome opting at first to prepare for engineering for predominately practical reasons. Then he struck up a friendship with a student friend Franco Rasetti, recently hired in physics at Enrico Fermi's suggestion. Enrico Fermi, who had just obtained his doctorate in physics in Pisa, gave a seminar which Segrè attended. Segrè remained impressed, and it wasn't long before Segrè thought of opting out of engineering and moving into physics.

In 1927, Segrè went to Lake Como to attend an International Physics Conference commemorating the hundredth anniversary of the death of Alessandro Volta. Though still not officially a physics student, he was intent on attending all the lectures presented by many of the notable physicists of the time: Max Planck, Ernest Rutherford, Niels Bohr, Robert Millikan, Wolfgang Pauli, and Werner Heisenberg.

This conference represented a major turning point in Segrè's career. Fermi and Rasetti began treating him as a future colleague, convincing him of the emerging opportunities in physics. Returning to Rome, he began attending physics classes. Segrè obtained his doctorate in physics on July 14, 1928.

After serving two years of compulsory military service, Segrè began doing research on "forbidden lines" in atomic spectra. This was the area of quadropole radiation, which involved the complexities of radiation when viewed as a patterned set of four accelerating charges. The results of this study were published as his first independent paper in 1930 earning him the nickname: "Lord Quadropole." Because his equipment was inadequate for what he had hoped to accomplish, he traveled to Holland to study under the famous Dutch physicist, Pieter Zeeman.

He met his future wife, Elfriede Spiro, the daughter of German-Jewish parents from the small town of Otrowo in East Prussia. Elfriede, like many other Jews, had fled the growing tide of Nazism. She ended up in Italy in 1933 where she met Segrè. In the next few years, he increasingly turned his scientific interest to nuclear physics. Like many of his colleagues, Segrè had heard that Frederic Curie and Jolet

Curie, pioneers in neutron physics, had bombarded elements ranging from atomic number 29 (flourine) to 92 (uranium) with neutrons. Their aim was to create new isotopes, i.e., atoms containing an increased number of neutrons. After bombarding uranium, an odd mixture surprisingly resulted that helped usher in both the marvels and dangers of the atomic age.

In 1936, Segrè won the chair in physics at the University of Palermo, and he would also marry Elfriede Spiro. He made his first visit to the United States visiting the University of California at Berkeley where he saw their cyclotron. This was of particular interest to him because for some time he had been searching for an element, the thus-far-undiscovered element of atomic number 43, to fill the gap between molybdenum, atomic number 42, and ruthenium, atomic number 44.

Ernest Lawrence, one of the scientists at Berkeley, gave him a sample of molybdenum which had been bombarded with deuterons, isotopes of hydrogen. Segrè took the sample back to Palermo and analyzed it with a colleague. They had, indeed, identified trace amounts of an element with the atomic number 43. Segrè named it technetium, from the Greek word, *technetos*, meaning artificial.

In 1938, on his second visit to Berkeley, he collaborated with Dale R. Corson and K.R. MacKenzie, synthesizing another artificial element dubbed astatine (atomic number 85). During that period, the Italian government passed anti-Semitic civil service laws. After his return to Italy, he decided to immigrate to the U.S., working as a research associate in physics at Berkeley. Segrè delved further into artificial radioactivity and nuclear isomerism.

Meanwhile, Fermi's neutron bombardment experiment with uranium determined that the uranium atom could be split into smaller atoms. This caused a great stir in the scientific community. It meant that splitting the uranium atom, a process known as fission, produced neutrons, which could also cause a self-sustaining chain reaction that could produce staggering amounts of explosive energy unlike anything humanity had ever seen before.

After Fermi was funded for further research, his work pointed toward the use of plutonium 239, an isotope, in a chain reaction device. Segrè, who would become an American citizen in 1944, assisted Fermi in this major enterprise that led to the development and implementation of the atomic bomb.

Later, in the early 1950s, Emilio Segrè and Owen Chamberlain joined forces to generate and detect the antiproton, the negatively charged twin of the proton whose existence had been predicted but not found because the accelerators (e.g., cyclotrons, syncrotrons) were not fast enough to produce one. However, that changed with the construction of the bevatron at Berkeley. The contribution of Segrè and Chamberlain consisted of the ingenious methods used in conclusively identifying antiprotons. They were both awarded the Nobel Prize in physics in 1959.

His wife Elfriede died in 1970. In 1972, Segrè married the former Rosa Minnes and also retired as professor emeritus. A prolific writer of books (including a biography of Enrico Fermi) and many articles, he died on April 22, 1989 leaving a legacy of critical research in discovering new atomic elements and their sub-atomic structures and energy.

General Sources:
1. Segrè, Emilio. *Enrico Fermi Physicist*. Chicago: University of Chicago, 1970.
2. Segrè, Emilio. *From Falling Bodies to Radio Waves: Classical Physicists and their Discoveries*. New York: Freeman, 1984.
3. Segrè, Emilio. *From X-Rays to Quarks: Modern Physicists and Their Discoveries*. San Francisco: W.H. Freeman, 1980.

—by MARK BATTISTE

LISA SERGIO (1905-1989)

Writer, editor, university teacher, lecturer, translator, radio news commentator, feminist predating the American Women's Liberation Movement, and polyglot, Lisa Sergio led a full and active life both in Italy and later in the United States. Known throughout Europe as the Golden Voice of Rome, she began her career in the era of Fascist Italy and became Europe's first woman radio commentator. Unhappy as she had become with political developments in Fascist Italy in the second half of the 30s, she fled to the United States in 1937 bringing with her a rich and thorough knowledge of the Fascist Party and the machinations of its leadership.

By 1939, one of New York City's best radio stations, WQXR, known at that time as "the radio station with a soul," achieved even greater popularity after having adopted Lisa Sergio to do its foreign affairs commentary where she editorialized about the war with incredible acumen as she had known the Fascists personally for years. Besides having been a radio news commentator in Italy, she had been a literary critic and brilliant translator, quite capable of simultaneous translations from Italian into English. In one well-known instance, in November 1936, in her translation of one of Mussolini's speeches into English, she became the first person to use the word axis that then became the standardized word to describe the coalition between Hitler and Mussolini such as in the phrase "Rome-Berlin axis."

She was born Elisa Sergio in Florence, Italy on March 17, 1905. Her father Baron Agostino Sergio, who was an active supporter of Italian unification in the 19th century, came from a Neapolitan family that traced its origins back 2,000 years to Pola, a seaside town on the Adriatic where an arch bearing the last name still remained. Lisa, whose name became modified from the original Elisa, was also half American as her mother Marguerite Fitzgerald came from a well-to-do Baltimore, Maryland family.

Lisa was a precocious child, who having had little exposure to formal education, did not have any diplomas to her name as she spent her younger years being privately tutored. She had also learned by traveling throughout Europe and by disciplining herself to speak English, French and German—not to mention her knowledge of Spanish and her native Italian. In her mid-teens, she was absorbed by the *Bible* and the plastic arts. She had even translated a French play which was later produced in Italian.

Being unusually well read for her age and self-disciplined in being able to integrate what she was constantly learning and absorbing, she rejected the usual roles accepted by most female teenagers. She had worked hard, and because of her excellent English, at age seventeen in 1922, she managed to become the associate editor of *Italian Mail*, a literary weekly serving British and American writers living in Italy. She eventually became its editor, but in 1928 she quit when Mussolini sought to make it a propaganda vehicle. She then pursued her interests in archaeology where she served as general secretary, bibliographer, and coordinator for the Association of Mediterranean Studies.

After several years of full-time involvement in archeology, including the writing of handbooks on Pompeii in three different languages, Sergio decided to live in Rome. In 1932, when the Italian government launched Europe's first shortwave broadcast in foreign languages, Sergio was asked to join the government program as a news commentator at the rather innocent urging of a family friend

Guglielmo Marconi. She became active broadcasting in English and in French. She established programs that were able to air in twenty-one different languages. Her success caused her to be called the Golden Voice of Rome, but that came to end when she began to disagree with the Italian government's policies and its attack on Ethiopia. In time, Mussolini ordered her dismissal. With the help of Marconi, she made arrangements to leave Italy, and she successfully slipped out before she could be interrogated or possibly arrested.

When she arrived in the United States in July 1937, she immediately filed for American citizenship and became an adamant critic of Mussolini and Fascism. She was soon hired in radio by David Sarnoff president of the Radio Corporation of America for many of his NBC programs. She also worked for other radio stations whose programs included WEAF's *Tales of Great Rivers* and WJZ's *Let's Talk It Over* where she interviewed international celebrities and stars from radio and film. Finally, in March 1939 she began broadcasting at WQXR where she enjoyed having her own news commentary program, *The Column of the Air*, which aired several times a week and focused on politics, government, and foreign affairs. She became a naturalized U.S. citizen in 1944, and she remained with WQXR until 1946.

After World War II from 1947 to 1950, she taught at Columbia University as a specialist in international affairs, specifically in the area of propaganda analysis. From 1960 to 1971, she received a Danforth visiting lectureship in international affairs where she traveled in the United States and Canada. In the 1960s, Sergio also took on the cause of human rights and rights for women worldwide. In addition to having written an abundance of articles for magazines, she also wrote several books most of which focused on history, politics, biography, and religion. While she hosted programs for NBC-TV and for ABC-TV, she never fully left the world of radio as she frequently hosted in Washington on WMAL radio a program entitled *Prayer Through the Ages* until just a few years before her death.

Lisa Sergio, a pioneer in the area of radio broadcasting in Italy in the early Mussolini days and then a determined antifascist news commentator in the U.S., died at 84 at her home in the nation's capital on June 22, 1989. She will be remembered for her innovative radio work in Italy and her role in the U.S. where she informed and alerted Americans of the meaning of European current events. She was also a friend and admirer of the arts as she frequently was a commentator or host for broadcasts of many music programs such as the Berkshire Music Festivals and those of the Metropolitan Opera. A recipient of many awards for her distinguished radio work, she also received many honorary college degrees in the 60s and 70s, an award of the Order of the Star of Italian Solidarity in 1975, and the award of the French Legion of Honor in 1947.

General Sources:
1. *Current Biography/Yearbook*. New York: Wilson, 1944; 1989.
2. "Obituary." *New York Times* 1 June 1989: B8.
3. Sergio, Lisa. *I Am My Beloved: The Life of Anita Garibaldi*. New York: Weybright and Talley, 1969.
4. Sergio, Lisa. *Jesus and Woman: An Exciting Discovery of What He Offered Her*. McLean, VA: EPM Publications, 1975.
5. Sergio, Lisa. *Lisa Sergio Papers*. Washington, DC: Georgetown University Special Collections Division.
6. Sergio, Lisa. *A Measure Filled: The Life of Lena Madesin Phillips*. New York: R.B. Luce, 1972.
7. *Who's Who of American Women*. 1958-1959 ed.

—by MARYANN PASSANISI

FRANK SINATRA (1915-1998)

Francis Albert Sinatra, born in Hoboken, NJ on December 12, 1915, spent many of his early childhood years in the care of his grandmother and his aunts Mary and Rosalie. From an early age he was an active performer, doing at first movie star and comic imitations. He was popular as a youngster, and he began his singing in 1930 at A.J. Demarest High School. Unable to graduate, he completed his formal education at Drake Business School. At age 17, Frank's first girlfriend and future wife was Nancy Barbato. At that time, his singing idol was Bing Crosby, and while attending one of Crosby's live performances, he told Nancy: "One day, that's gonna be me up there."

Frank had formed a musical group, the Hoboken Four that sang locally. He received his first break when he won first prize on *Major Bowes Amateur Hour.* This was followed by appearances on radio and small night clubs. In 1939, bandleader Harry James would discover him at the Rustic Cabin in New Jersey. Sinatra teamed up with Harry James on the Brunswick label, performing such songs as "From the Bottom of my Heart" and "All or Nothing at All." When Harry James died in 1983, Sinatra attributed the beginning of his success to the great bandleader.

During 1940-42, while singing swing music with trombonist Tommy Dorsey and his band, he began to emerge as a singer having a unique voice and personal style. Bobby-soxers, a term first used in 1943 to identify screaming and swooning teenagers, idolized "Frankie Boy" the skinny, vulnerable, blue-eyed baritone —often cited as the original teen idol. The superstar's twinkling eyes, soft voice, apparent shyness and quivering lower lip gave his fans a reason with which to be enthralled. He would create and maintain a superstar status for more than five decades.

The year 1940 had brought the Sinatras their first child, Nancy. At the same time, however, gossip columnists were busily reporting on his extra-curricular activities that included Marilyn Monroe and Lana Turner. In 1941, Sinatra appeared as a vocalist in Tommy Dorsey's band in *Las Vegas Nights*, Frank's first feature-length movie appearance. *Billboard* magazine named him Number One Male Vocalist of the Year. He had become dubbed: The Voice. The Army had classified him 4-F due to a punctured eardrum acquired at birth. Unable to enlist in the military service, he toured the country with Bob Hope, Bing Crosby, Ginger Rogers, and many other stars, entertaining the WWII servicemen.

In 1944, Frank Sinatra, Jr., was born while his father was 3,000 miles away in Hollywood singing his way into the hearts of his fans. In 1947, the press played havoc with photos depicting Sinatra with syndicated crime figures and dope-smoking musicians. Denial didn't seem to help reverse the newspaper stories, and this part of his life would remain like a cloud over his career for many years.

In 1948, Father's Day became a memorable event with the arrival of his second daughter, Christina. "Goodnight Irene" had risen to #5 on the charts, and Frank and his band played Atlantic City along with guest appearances on *Bob Hope's Holiday Special* and Milton Berle's popular *Texaco Star Theater*. Despite the magnitude of his apparent success, these would be Sinatra's darkest days, especially in those years from 1947 to 1952.

Reluctantly, he divorced Nancy. Then, he later married Ava Gardner in 1951, divorcing in 1957. In this very low point in his life, he attempted suicide with an overdose in 1951 and again in 1952. His career seemed finished especially when his vocal cords hemorrhaged in 1952. After much soul-searching, Frank fought back and made a dramatic comeback, wooing his fans again. During this new period of Sinatra's life, Sammy Cahn and Jimmy Van Heusen would write some of his most memorable recordings. The new Sinatra would emerge exemplifying confidence and maturity.

Over his lifetime, Sinatra would star or appear in more than 50 films. He had already won his first Oscar Award in 1945 for a patriotic film-short entitled *The House I Live In*. In 1953, he would receive the highly coveted Oscar Award for Best Supporting Actor for his role as Maggio in *From Here to Eternity*. In 1955, he would be nominated for Best Actor for his role as a drug addict in the film, *The Man With the Golden Arm*.

Ole' Blue Eyes also became known as King of the Strip on Las Vegas Blvd., and Marlena Dietrich would dub him The Mercedes Benz of Men. Friends like Sammy Davis, Jr. and Jerry Lewis would gladly fill in for him at engagements. Sinatra's image had soared and his wealth had jumped into the many millions, making him one of the wealthiest people in Hollywood. Mia Farrow would become his third wife for two years from 1966 to 1968.

In 1969, at the age of 54, Sinatra would record Paul Anka's hit, "My Way." It was at this time that he raised the funds and dedicated the Martin Anthony Sinatra Medical Education Center in Palm Springs to the memory of his father. The Academy of Motion Picture Arts and Sciences honored him with the Jean Hersholt Humanitarian Award because of his charity work. As he got older, it seemed that helping people came natural to The Chairman of the Board. Pope Paul VI was reported as saying to Sinatra's mother Dolly, "Your son is very close to God because he does God's work, and does not talk about it."

Lauren Bacall and Juliet Prowse might have been included on Sinatra's list of potential brides, but finally, Barbara Marx would win his heart for keeps. The Summit, or better known to the public as the Rat Pack, had included Humphrey Bogart, Lauren Bacall, Judy Garland, Peter Lawford, Sammy Davis, Jr., Dean Martin, Joey Bishop, Shirley McLaine, and Mike Romanoff.

Frank Sinatra's career included 58 films, over 100 albums, nearly 2,000 individual songs and many recording awards. On June 13, 1971, after 35 years of entertaining the world, he made a farewell appearance at the Los Angeles Music Center, but he would return occasionally to the concert stage to perform many special singing engagements. After several years of failing health, he died at eighty-three years of age on May 14, 1998. He will be remembered for his unique voice, a simple yet superb legendary style of twentieth-century popular song. The overpowering influence of his rich and velvety soft singing of romantic songs, now part of Americana, will be difficult to measure.

General Sources:
1. Ackelson, Richard W. *Frank Sinatra: A Complete Recording History of Techniques, Songs, Composers, Lyricists, Arrangers, Sessions, and First-Issue Albums, 1939-1984.* Jefferson, NC: McFarland, 1992.
2. Freedland, Michael. *All the Way: A Biography of Frank Sinatra.* New York: St. Martin's Press, 1997.
3. Friedwald, Will. *Sinatra! The Song is You: A Singer's Art.* New York: Scribner, 1995.
4. Katz, Ephraim. *The Film Encyclopedia.* New York: HarperCollins, 1998.
5. Sinatra, Nancy. *Frank Sinatra: An American Legend.* Santa Monica, CA: General Publishers Group, 1995.

—by IRENE LAMANO

JOHN J. SIRICA (1904-1992)

Nicknamed the Watergate Judge by the American press and the TV media, he was named Man of the Year by *Time* magazine in 1974 and remembered as the federal judge presiding with determination and equanimity over the Watergate trial of 1973. Judge John Sirica indeed faced many challenges in the investigation of the 1972 break-in and bugging by seven Republican Party secret operatives of the Democratic National Committee headquarters in Washington's Watergate Hotel. In an investigation whose conclusions would prove to be directly responsible for President Nixon's ultimate resignation from the land's highest office, Sirica, who had been a lifelong Republican, took the case himself rather than assign it to one of his fifteen federal judges in order to have the judicial system avoid any charges of partisan politics. Judge Sirica who had begun in private practice as a lawyer in the late 1920s, was eventually appointed to the Unites States District Court for the District of Columbia in 1957, and he would became its chief judge in 1971.

Born on March 19, 1904 in Waterbury, Connecticut, John Joseph Sirica was one of two sons of Federico and Rose (nee Zinno) Sirica. Federico, better known as Fred, had emigrated in 1887 from a small village called San Valentino located outside of Naples, Italy. Rose, also of Italian descent, was born in New Haven. A barber by trade, Fred had always been involved in one small business after another with no major successes. Young John's early years were in a sense most unusual as his parents moved frequently, and they usually moved great distances in the hope of securing better business opportunities. As a youngster, John had already experienced living in New Orleans, Richmond, Daytona, and Jacksonville.

By 1918, when he was fourteen, the family had settled for a while in Washington, D.C., where John was able to complete his high school education at Columbia Preparatory School. In 1921, at age seventeen, he began attending George Washington University Law School, but after only one month of school John inexplicably decided to drop out. He held a series of odd jobs, took up boxing at the YMCA, and considered going into a trade. His parents, resuming their trek in seeking business opportunities, left town. After considering this troublesome scenario, John enrolled once more—this time at Georgetown University—to again pursue legal studies. To support himself, he coached in boxing and sometimes did some boxing himself, doing three-rounders in smokers.

In 1926, he earned his LL.B. degree and visited his parents in Miami. At that time Miami was a fledgling resort for the wealthy where John focused on boxing once more and did some sparring with prominent and well-to-do personalities vacationing there. He returned to the D.C. area, passed the bar exam, and set up private practice by year's end. For the next four years, he worked hard establishing a clientele while doing much *pro bono* work for the indigent. In his desire to master legal tactics in trial procedures, he often spent much personal time in the courtroom observing the best trial lawyers in action.

On August 1, 1930, Sirica was appointed an assistant United States attorney for the District of Columbia, a federal job he held for four years after which he returned to private practice. In the years that followed, he had steadily established a wide reputation as a thorough and forthright lawyer, and despite many invitations to return to government (such as Senator Joseph McCarthy's efforts to recruit him in 1952), Sirica stayed clear of federal posts from 1934 onward. Yet while Sirica refrained from returning to federal service, he was politically active as a Republican. Beginning in 1936, he became involved in five presidential campaigns, and he often conducted liaison work between nationwide party affiliates.

Then in 1957, Sirica reversed his long-standing posture about accepting federal positions when President Eisenhower appointed him to the United States District Court for the District of Columbia. In that capacity he continued his hard long hours for nearly a decade-and-a-half in what is reputed to be one of the busiest court systems in the United States. During that time, where he presided over the large gamut of federal court cases ranging from homicides to costly antitrust suits, his reputation as a law-and-order judge earned him the nickname Maximum John for his penchant of assigning the longest allowable sentences. On April 2, 1971, at age sixty-seven, he became chief judge for the U.S. District Court where his duties included necessarily more supervisory and administrative demands.

In June of the same year, astounding developments took place during the election campaign. Seven undercover operatives were caught bugging the Democratic National Committee headquarters in the Watergate Hotel. As the preliminary investigations went on, more and more information seemed to corroborate the fact that many people close to the President and the President himself as being quite aware of the illegal activity. Nixon was elected in November of that year, but by the time the case came to Judge Sirica's district court in January 1973, the month of the presidential inauguration, Judge Sirica had already decided to try the case himself.

The so-called Watergate trial attracted media attention worldwide, and John Sirica became instantly recognized as the Watergate judge. Not without his critics from both sides of the spectrum regarding the eternal battle between personal rights versus authority, Judge Sirica made some difficult choices, and based on much research he ultimately ruled (with a host of constitutional implications) that Nixon had to deliver his personal White House tapes and that in this situation Nixon could not invoke executive privilege to avoid yielding the tapes. Sirica's ruling, which was later upheld by the U.S. Court of Appeals, marked the beginning of the end of Nixon's second term in office when on August 9, 1974, nearly a year later, Nixon in a televised address announced his resignation.

Judge John Sirica was applauded for his determination in affirming the constitutional imperatives of the judicial branch over the executive branch's breach of the public trust. Judge Sirica, who went into semi-retirement in 1977, retired fully in 1986 at age eighty-two. He passed away on August 14, 1992. The recipient of countless awards and honorary degrees, he has left a legacy of dedication to the public good, hoping to fulfill the realization of the moral edict that no one should be above the law, especially those in high political office.

General Sources:
1. *Current Biography Yearbook*. New York: Wilson, 1974; 1992.
2. Marchione, Margherita. *Americans of Italian Heritage*. Lanham, MD: University Press of America, 1995.
3. "Obituary." *New York Times* 15 Aug. 1992: 1.
4. Sirica, John J. *To Set the Record Straight: The Break-In, The Tapes, The Conspirators, The Pardon*. New York: Norton, 1979.
5. *Time* 7 Jan. 1974: 8-15+.
6. *Who's Who in America*. 1992-93 ed.
7. *Who's Who in Government*. 1992-1993 ed.

—by ROSE MARIE BONIELLO

CHARLES ANGELO SIRINGO (1855-1928)

A cowboy involved in the initial capture of Billy the Kid (1859-1881) in 1880, then a detective in apprehending anarchists in the aftermath of Chicago's Haymarket Riots (1886), together with a twenty-two year record as a detective for the Pinkerton National Detective Agency, and a deft writer of his many dangerous and colorful experiences, Charles Angelo Siringo—in his lifetime—became a popular legend of incredible insight, resourcefulness, and shrewdness. He became popularized by his own books which went on to become invaluable resources of facts and information in helping historians reconstruct a more accurate and expert assessment of America's southwest in the latter part of the 19th century.

Charles Siringo was born on February 7, 1855 in Matagorda County, Texas to an Irish mother and an Italian father. His father, who had immigrated to the United States, died when Charles was only one year old. His mother, Bridget, left alone to raise Charles and his older sister, was not able to offer her son a continuous formal education. Instead he received a combination of formal education and many life experiences. Aware of his mother's struggles, Charlie—as he was most often called—became a cowhand at age twelve. By the time his teenage years were over, he became a cowboy in the most grandiose sense of the word. From that time on, although almost always separated from his mother and sister, he would visit them whenever he could and would send home money to assist with the family finances.

His first employer was a well-known, memorable character of the old West called "Shanghai" Pierce. After Pierce had offered Charlie an education in cowboy matters and cattle rustling, he sent Siringo to help out in the development of the LX, a huge new ranch located in the Texas Panhandle in 1877. His employment initially consisted of branding and recovering missing or stolen cattle. Later in 1880, when he was twenty-five years of age, he was deemed so competent that he was sent out as a member of the tracking party to assist in capturing the legendary outlaw Billy the Kid. The adventuresome history in pursuing Billy proved to be successful for Charlie's experience when they had finally captured Billy, but Billy would not remain captured for long.

Siringo moved around a great deal during the next few years, traveling wherever the LX Ranch would send him to work. He would be given pocket money for these excursions, but he was self-reliant, always managing to find odd jobs along the way to earn extra income. By 1882, he found himself working in Chicago where he met and married Mamie Lloyd. The marriage was not a lengthy one as his wife would die only six years later, leaving Charlie with the responsibility of raising their daughter.

Charlie Siringo, an extremely resourceful man when it came to earning money, managed to publish his first of many books in 1885. Autobiographical in nature, it initially bore a long title: *A Texas Cowboy or Fifteen Years on the Hurricane Deck of a Spanish Pony*. In this book Siringo depicted his early adventures recovering stolen cattle. He also devoted three chapters to the capture of Billy the Kid where he described how Billy was not all bad and seemed to possess some good qualities.

Siringo's book has been often alluded to as the first autobiographical account ever written by a genuine cowboy. Will Rogers (1879-1935), the famous American humorist, often referred to as the "cowboy philosopher," was a great fan of

Siringo and called Siringo's first book the "cowboy's bible." Due to its great popularity, *A Texas Cowboy* was published by five different publishers over the course of its first forty years.

A year later, his life changed significantly as he went from Texas cowboy to Chicago detective. Due to the Haymarket Square Riot in Chicago on May 4, 1886, Siringo decided to join the Pinkerton's National Detective Agency to assist in the fight to apprehend the anarchists who were apparently responsible for the riot. It all began when a labor protest group numbering 1,500 demonstrated for an eight-hour work day. It turned into a riot after a bomb exploded in the midst of the demonstrators whereupon eleven persons were killed and over one hundred were wounded. Siringo, who managed to become part of the ongoing investigation, became highly involved in the apprehension of the anarchists responsible for causing the violence. Siringo proved to be of immediate help, and his efforts assisted in convicting seven of them; four were executed and three were given prison sentences.

In 1887 Siringo was sent to Pogosa Springs, Colorado where as an undercover agent for Pinkerton, he feigned being an outlaw. Gaining the confidence of a criminal group whose leader was named Taylor, he uncovered their plot to kill three town officers. After averting the killing of these three town commissioners, he then managed to have his investigation lead to a grand jury indictment of sixteen people who were trying to disrupt the town government. This assignment was followed by his work in Nebraska where he single-handedly apprehended a murderer, Ernest Bush, who was later tried and convicted for having killed a Civil War veteran. In 1890, again as an undercover agent for Pinkerton, he almost got killed infiltrating a union that was bent on creating labor riots in the mining town of Coeur d'Alene, Idaho after the town experienced its boom in the lead and silver mining industry.

In 1907, after having completed close to twenty-two years detective work for Pinkerton,

Siringo retired to his ranch near Santa Fe, New Mexico where he returned to his writing. He went on to write a book critical of the Pinkerton Agency's operations, and after many court battles with them, it was finally published in 1912 as *A Cowboy Detective*. Not satisfied with retirement, Siringo joined the Burns Detective Agency in Chicago for six years and later joined the New Mexico Rangers after which he published *A Lone Star Cowboy* (1919) and *Riata and Spurs* (1920).

A relatively recent Hollywood movie *Siringo* (1994) depicted his many exploits as an undercover operative for Pinkerton where he attempted to tame part of the wild Southwest. In all of his gun-toting years, he is remembered as an excellent shot who was never seen without his Colt .45 that had never been used to take a life away. He leaves a legacy of firsthand authoritative information chronicling a colorful and specific area of America's history written in a forthright and interesting manner.

General Sources:
1. DiStasi, Lawrence, ed. *The Big Book of Italian American Culture.* New York: HarperPerennial, 1990.
2. Haley, J. Evetts, ed. *Dictionary of American Biography.* New York: Scribner, 1936.
3. Pingenot, Ben E. *Siringo: The True Story.* College Station: Texas A&M University Press, 1989.
4. Sawey, Orlan. *Charles A. Siringo.* Boston: Twayne, 1981.
5. *Siringo.* WarnerVision Entertainment, 1994.
6. Siringo, Charles. *A Cowboy Detective.* Lincoln: University of Nebraska Press, 1988.
7. Siringo, Charles. *A Texas Cowboy.* Lincoln: University of Nebraska Press, 1979.

—by LINDA D'ANDREA-MARINO

ELEANOR MARIE CUTRI SMEAL
(1939-   )

Ellie Smeal was born Eleanor Marie Cutri on July 30, 1939. She would become an important social activist in the 1970s in the National Organization for Women (NOW) and the Feminist Majority organization. Succeeding Karen DeCrow as national NOW president in 1977, she would go on to show how she had doubled NOW's membership within two years of her presidency. Today its membership has grown steadily making it the world's largest feminist organization.

She was a homemaker from Pittsburgh, PA where she participated as a local NOW president in the town of South Hills before she took on the national leadership of NOW. Ellie was born in Ashtabula, Ohio, and she was the fourth child and first daughter of Peter Anthony Cutri from Calabria, Italy and Josephine Agresti, the daughter of Italian emigrants. She was raised Catholic and attended public schools.

When interviewed by a reporter and asked how she learned to debate and argue her point she replied "I started at 4 or 5, like in any good Italian family." When she attended Duke University in Durham, NC, she was a good student having many friends. But her stand against racism and for integration and affirmative action put her at odds with many of her peers.

In 1961, she graduated Phi Beta Kappa from Duke with a B.A. degree. Intending to pursue law, she changed her mind when she heard that "women lawyers seldom practice in courtrooms." She pursued, instead, studies in political science and public administration at the University of Florida where she earned her M.A. degree in 1963. In the same year, she would marry Charles R. Smeal, a student in metallurgical engineering.

She continued her graduate studies, but illness prevented her from completing the requirements for her doctorate, namely, her doctoral dissertation on the attitude of women toward women candidates for office. This general topic is something she would resume and bring to fruition with the publication of her book in 1984 entitled *Why and How Women Will Elect the Next President*.

However, in 1969, they moved to Pittsburgh where her husband became a researcher in his field of metallurgy. And again, Eleanor's doctoral dissertation would be put on hold because of illness. Both she and her husband joined NOW in 1970.

When asked later by the *Christian Science Monitor* in September 1979 about her initial involvement in women's activism she replied, "I made up my mind that the fight for the equality of women was the most important historical thing I could participate in and it would always be important to me."

She began as the organizer and the first president of a NOW chapter in her area from 1971 to 1973. Also with the help of her husband, she organized the first day care nursery in her community of South Hills, a Pittsburgh suburb. In 1972, she would also go on to become elected the first president of Pennsylvania NOW and remain in that position until 1975.

In 1975, she became the board president and director of NOW's Legal Defense and Education Fund. She emphasized the use of Title IX to fight for equality in educational issues and sports programs for girls. She decentralized

NOW, expanding it into the small communities thereby doubling NOW's membership. She organized the boycott of Nevada costing their capital city over $19 million in convention business. This was in response to the fight for acceptance of the Equal Rights Amendment.

Smeal, now considered a leading advocate for the fight for women's rights, has appeared frequently on TV and radio, and has testified before Congressional committees on women's issues. She has played a leading role in both national and state campaigns to win women's rights legislation, including some landmark state and local court cases. She has been referred to by many as the modern architect of the drive for women's rights.

Known both as a strategist and a grass-roots organizer, she was the first to identify the different ways women and men vote and she helped popularize their usage in political polling data. To intensify women's voting clout, Smeal called for the women's movement to return to the streets in the mid-1980's to demonstrate support for abortion rights. She led the first national abortion rights march in Washington, D.C. and in many other cities across the nation with over 100,000 supporters.

Smeal co-founded and became president of the Feminist Majority (FM). She headed the Feminist Majority Foundation One campaign. It has been called the Feminization of Power Campaign, a national movement focusing on recruitment of feminists to run for public office. It has also pressed for passage of gender-balance laws requiring governors and mayors to appoint equal numbers of women and men to cabinet posts.

The Foundation has specialized in education and research projects to empower women. It has encouraged empowering women to run for public office, to fight in issues over reproductive rights, to advance medicine and philanthropy, and to break through the glass ceiling in all sectors of society that delimit women's advancement. Moreover, the Foundation sponsors public education on the need for RU486 (the French Abortion Pill) and new forms of contraception.

Smeal as co-founder and president of FM has co-authored and co-produced two 30-minute award-winning videos. Both deal with abortion issues. On a national level, one video addresses the devastating effects on young women's lives with the issues of parental consent and notification laws on abortion. The other documentary deals with the mother's survival in regard to abortion issues at the global level. She also became a pioneer in introducing rights for gays and lesbians into NOW's agenda.

President Carter appointed her to the National Advisory Committee for Women in 1978. She was listed as one of the 25 most influential women in 1978 in *Time* magazine, appearing on its cover with that group. She is quoted as saying in a magazine interview: "I have begun to believe that what I'm doing is in the greatest tradition of our society, of one generation fighting for an improved life for the next generation."

General Sources:
1. *Current Biography Yearbook.* New York: Wilson, 1980.
2. Evans, Sara. *Born for Liberty: A History of Women in America.* New York: Free Press, 1989.
3. Kondratas, S. Anna. *Comparable Worth: Pay Equity or Social Engineering: A Debate Between S. Anna Kondratas and Eleanor Smeal.* Washington, DC: Heritage Foundation, 1986.
4. Smeal, Eleanor. *Eleanor Smeal, NOW President.* Washington, DC: National Public Radio, 1985.
5. Smeal, Eleanor. *Why and How Women Will Elect the Next President.* New York: Harper & Row, 1984.

—by KATHY FREEPERSON

ALFRED EMANUEL SMITH (1873-1944)

Alfred Emanuel Smith, the first Roman Catholic who ran for President of the United States, had been dubbed the "happy warrior" by Franklin Delano Roosevelt. A most popular four-term governor of New York State, Smith was born on December 30, 1873 in Manhattan, New York to Alfred Smith, an American Civil War veteran, and the elder Smith's second wife Catherine Mulverhill who was the daughter of English and Irish families. The governor's father, though curiously bearing the surname Smith, was the son of a German mother and an Italian father (Alfredo Emanuelo Smith). Two years after the birth of this younger fair-haired, blue-eyed Alfred Emanuel Smith (1873), a sister Mary was born bearing dark hair and olive complexion suggesting her father's Italian forebearers. Strangely enough, Governor Alfred E. Smith, long regarded as the most famous Irish American around, owed his heritage instead to a multicultural background of Italian, German, English, and Irish ancestry.

The Smith family lived in a five-room flat in Manhattan's Lower East Side. At that time, it was a pleasant residential neighborhood where a strong sense of community prevailed, and children were raised in a caring environment. Apparently their father who operated a small delivery business was a good provider. The young Smith was an altar boy at St. James Roman Catholic Church, and he attended the local parochial school.

He was reportedly just an average student, but he seemed to excel as a debater. At age eleven, he went on to win a silver medal in a citywide oration contest that was perhaps a good omen of his gift for making powerful and incisive speeches when he would enter politics at a later date. He would be credited as having said in a 1936 speech in attacking an opposing speaker's remarks: "No matter how thin you slice it, it's still baloney."

The ancestry of Governor Alfred E. Smith had been an enigma until Frances Perkins, a social worker and family friend did an interview of the governor's sister, Mary Glynn (nee Smith). The results of this conversation together with some in-depth research showed clearly that the governor's father was indeed Italian. First, Mary recalled that her father often boasted to his friends about having an uncle who was the bishop of Naples. Secondly, the New York State Census of 1855 showed that the governor's paternal grandfather, Alfredo Emanuelo Smith, was born in Genoa, Italy and that the governor's paternal grandmother was born in Germany. The same census also indicated that Smith (grandfather of the governor) was forty-two years of age at the time and his wife Magdalen was thirty-nine. Their children were Teresa, thirteen, and Alfred Emanuel Smith, fifteen (the father of the future governor).

While the above records did not indicate a surname for the governor's paternal grandfather, it clearly bore an Italian first name Alfredo and middle name, Emanuelo, a variation of the Italian Emanuele. It stated that he arrived in New York City in 1825 and his probable age was twelve or thirteen. As was so often the case at that time, the immigration officer probably could not speak Italian and the youngster did not speak English. Amid the confusion, the immigration officer most likely granted the boy an entrance card and as an expedient merely assigned him a last name (Smith) which was tacked onto Alfredo Emanuelo.

Al Smith (the governor), was only twelve

years old when his father, a Civil War veteran, died in 1885. In all, poverty soon ensued, and young Al dropped out of school when he was fourteen. At first he worked odd jobs, then at eighteen he became a general clerk for the Feeney Company, a wholesale commission house in the Fulton Fish Market. He was active in community theater and often appeared in the lead role in the St. James Dramatic Society. On May 6, 1900, after a five-year courtship, Al Smith married Catherine Dunn, an Irish woman from the Bronx and together raised a family of five children.

After work it was Al Smith's routine to visit the local saloon, have a beer and talk. There he befriended the owner, Tom Foley, a Tammany Hall precinct leader. Smith became involved in politics, and his activities reached such a point that he was considered a viable candidate for winning an assemblyman position. With self-determination and support from Tom Foley and Robert Wagner, Al Smith did win a seat as a state assemblyman. It appeared that all those positive qualities he had nurtured through the years helped him to quickly acquire a reputation for honesty, for fairness, and for being approachable by the public.

The famous 1911 Triangle Shirtwaist Company fire, a disaster that claimed the lives of 146 factory workers, mostly women and young girls, suddenly thrust Al Smith into the limelight. Being a man of the people and understanding poverty and poor urban working conditions, he rose to the occasion sponsoring legislation that established ongoing factory investigative commissions. By 1913 when he became the speaker of the assembly, he helped sponsor more social legislation concerning sanitation, health and fire hazards, wage and hour regulations, and workmen's compensation.

For many in positions of power, Al Smith's popularity in the Democratic Party and among the people clearly pointed to his being the logical candidate for the next governor of New York in 1918, and despite strong opposition from the Republican Party, he managed to win with a plurality of 15,000 votes.

During his four terms in office, he became the driving force in compiling an astounding record of administrative reforms and social legislation. He reorganized state government by streamlining operations yet making services more available, effective, and fair to all state residents. His social reforms included state support for low-cost housing, bond issues to develop an extensive state park recreational system, more funds for education, and the expansion of laws enforcing work-safety requirements and related labor laws.

Governor Smith's nationally recognized record of social and political reform placed him as one of the favorites of the presidential candidates at the 1924 Democratic Convention (Houston). Nominated on the first Democratic ballot, he did not win the election against Herbert Hoover, the Republican candidate. Ahead of his time on so many issues, Smith withdrew from politics disillusioned by so much religious bigotry that had tempered the presidential election.

He became head of the Empire State Building Corporation, active in church charities, and was later knighted by the Pope. His wife, Catherine, died in May 1944, and he died six months later on October 4, 1944 at the age of seventy. At that time, his death marked the second time that a non-cleric lay in state at New York City's St. Patrick's Cathedral.

General Sources:
1. *Dictionary of American Biography.* New York: Scribner, 1941-1945.
2. Josephson, Matthew and Hannah Josephson. *Al Smith, Hero of the Cities.* Boston: Houghton-Mifflin, 1969.
3. Smith, Alfred E. *Up to Now: An Autobiography.* New York: Viking Press, 1929.

—by PETER PAUL FRANCO, M.D.

SABATINO SOFIA (1939-   )

A distinguished Italian-American astronomer specializing in gathering data on solar activity, Sabatino Sofia is presently chairman at Yale University's well-known astronomy program. Experienced by his many prior roles with NASA, such as director of its Solar Radiation Office at NASA's Goddard Space Flight Center in Maryland in 1979, Sofia has gone on to writing and editing many books and articles in astronomy and astrophysics. Sofia along with two colleagues recently achieved greater prominence in the field of astrophysics with their invention of a device called a solar disk sextant, an instrument that serves to enhance scientists' abilities to measure solar activity, particularly its fluctuations in luminosity. This can and will serve as a tool in forecasting long-range periodic models for the Earth's climate.

Sabatino Sofia was born on May 14, 1939 in Episcopia, Italy. He immigrated to the United States in 1961, and two years later he married Tara Sibilia. His educational trajectory moved very rapidly from the time he set foot in America. He graduated from Yale University with a B.S. in 1963, a masters in astronomy in 1965, and in just one year a Ph.D. in astrophysics in 1966. His fine work as a graduate student made possible his being awarded a postdoctoral research fellowship in astrophysics at the Goddard Institute for Space Studies at NASA for one year (1966-67). In 1967, he became an associate professor at the University of South Florida (Tampa) and by 1973 earned his full-professorship status.

In the 70s, the pace of his activities and involvements increased, and during 1973-74 he was a visiting fellow at the Joint Institute Laboratory for Astrophysics in Boulder, Colorado; then, during 1974-75 he became a senior research associate at the University of Rochester in Rochester, New York. In 1975, he was an adjunct professor (and still continues to be so) at the University of Florida (Gainesville). At the same time, in 1975 he held a two-year post at NASA headquarters.

In the same year, he switched and went to work at NASA's Goddard Space Flight Center in Greenbelt, Maryland as a National Council Associate where in 1979 he was appointed the director of its Solar Radiation Office, a position he held until 1985. That year, he became a professor of astronomy at Yale University and concurrently a member of NASA's Space and Earth Science Advisory Committee until 1988. In 1993 Sabatino became chairman of the astronomy department and the associate director of the Center for Solar and Space Research at Yale.

In recent years, Sabatino and two colleagues invented the solar disk sextant with which they experimented in conjunction with high-altitude balloons (in 1992, 1994, 1995, and 1996) that have carried the solar disk sextant aloft for gathering solar data. The next mission which is slated for late 1999 or 2000 will employ rocketry and will gather data from the upper reaches of the Earth's atmosphere. The solar disk sextant is capable of measuring the size and shape of the solar disk to within a few mille-arc-seconds as viewed from the regions of the Earth's atmosphere.

These precise measurements can in turn be used to determine the relationship between changes in solar size (radius or diameter) and changes in the sun's total energy output called luminosity. Together with past data derived from the sun's radial fluctuations (such as those obtained from prior solar eclipses), present and future data will create an ongoing database to establish the construction of computer generated models of solar behaviors, a history of solar changes, and their forecasting potentials in regard to climate patterns on Earth.

Solar activity has always had implications for long-term climate change. For instance, from historically available information, scientists have been able to assert with much certainty that when solar activity was very high in the 11th and 12th centuries, global warming occurred, and it brought about climatic conditions that allowed the Vikings to inhabit Greenland. The Vikings historical developments changed radically when, afterwards, solar activity subsequently lessened.

In addition to dealing with solar patterns and changes in luminosity, Sabatino had also worked on his ability to predict the intensity of other specific solar activities such as sun spots and flares. He has achieved this ability by studying the huge magnetic field enveloping the sun. At the American Astronomical Society Meeting in Toronto in January 1997, Sabatino and his colleague, Kenneth Schatten of the Goddard Space Flight Center, presented some predictions—based on their studies—that raised many eyebrows. They happily forecast that the upcoming solar-activity peak will be lower than previous estimates and that the projected maximum will be the lowest in decades.

This was great news for the users or operators of hi-tech equipment whose components can easily become affected by solar flares. It was also great news for governmental and private industries that maintain satellites around the Earth. First, high levels of solar radiation due to solar flares can easily damage sensitive parts of electronic circuitry. These kinds of high level radiation might consist of a proton, an alpha particle (helium nucleus), or a photon. Secondly, satellites that orbit in the Earth's upper atmosphere are naturally subjected to friction, referred to as drag, a condition that erodes the satellite's orbit. Sun flares, it seems,

only hasten the eroding effect on a satellite's orbit. High levels of solar radiation whose scientific name is particulates (distinct outer space particles) despite their tiny size have the capacity to thicken the drag factors causing a satellite to fall from orbit and disintegrate prematurely.

Astronauts on a mission in outer space will also benefit from this predicted lull in solar flares since particulates of radiation may be very harmful and in some instances fatal, especially during space walks. Sabatino Sofia, whose career in astronomy and astrophysics exemplifies blending research and practice, has set a model of academic research excellence and potential applicability. Perhaps in the not too distant future, the solar disk sextant will assist even more in the practical aspects of planning globally in developing nations or in those countries whose agrarian economies are top priority.

General Sources:
1. *American Men & Women of Science.* 1998-99 ed.
2. "Astrophysics." 7 Mar. 1999. <http://www.yale.edu/physics/research/astrophysics.html>.
3. Devinney, Edward J., Haywood Smith, Jr., Sabatino Sofia. *Contemporary Astronomy.* Columbus, OH: Merrill, 1975.
4. Durney, Bernard R., and Sabatino Sofia, eds. *The Internal Solar Angular Velocity.* Proc. of the 8th National Solar Observatory Summer Symposium. Sunspot, New Mexico, 1986. Boston: Reidel Publishers, 1987.
5. Sofia, Sabatino, ed. *Variations of the Solar Constant.* Proc. held at the Goddard Space Flight Center. Greenbelt, MD: 1980. Washington, DC: National Aeronautics and Space Adm., 1981.
6. *Who's Who in America.* 1999 ed.

—by MARK BATTISTE

PAOLO SOLERI (1919-   )

Twentieth-century architect and urban planner, writer of seven books, Paolo Soleri, who holds a doctorate in architecture and is a former student of the great Frank Lloyd Wright dating back to 1947, is considered a visionary, an architectural strategist who is many decades before his time. After his fellowship with Wright in the late 40s, he returned to Italy, did research, designed and built two ceramics factories there, after which he returned to Arizona making Scottsdale his home and permanent laboratory for his architectural prototypes.

He has since designed and started building innovative homes in a planned community, in essence, creating a small town called Arcosanti. Though still considered a work-in-progress, the town's growth has generated many thought-provoking dialogues not only among architects but also among ecologists around the globe since the architecture of his structures in this desert climate works hand-in-hand with temperature control systems that are entirely based on ecological principles. Soleri has been hailed by many as a pioneer in a new architecture that is tantamount to that of a visionary, incorporating science, ecology, and aesthetics. His bold, forward-looking principles have also had the effect of raising some grave concerns over the lack of ecological prudence in contemporary industrialized nations.

Paolo was born on June 21, 1919 in Turin, Italy. In 1933 his family moved to Grenoble, France initially to escape the grips of the Fascist regime only to return to Turin in 1935. Showing great artistic sensibilities as a teenager, he attended the Torino Accademia Albertina where he chose a path leading to architecture. In 1941 when he entered the Torino Politecnico, his education was interrupted by the war. After serving in the corps of army engineers until Mussolini's government fell, he continued his studies at the Politecnico, and in 1946 he earned his doctorate in architecture graduating with highest honors.

He then applied for and won a fellowship in the United States. It was an 18-month apprenticeship with Frank Lloyd Wright at Taliesin West, located in Phoenix, Arizona. With time, it appears he experienced a falling out with Wright and went his own way after the apprenticeship ended. One of Soleri's first clients in Arizona was Mrs. Leonora Woods. With the assistance of a friend Mark Mills, also an ex-apprentice with Wright, Soleri designed and built what is called the Domed Desert House (or Woods House) in 1949-1950.

Still standing today, it is located in the desert at Cave Creek just outside of Phoenix. Its unusual roof was designed to rotate, open, and close according to weather conditions. Its design included the incorporation of passive principles for heating and cooling. During its construction in 1950, Soleri met and married his client's daughter, Carolyn Woods, with whom he would have two children. In the same year, Soleri and his wife took off for Italy with the overt purpose of doing research.

He ended up in fact designing and building two ceramics factories. One of them was the Solimene ceramics factory in a small town called Vietri-sul-Mare along the beautiful Amalfi coast, an area prized for ceramics. There, Soleri was able to incorporate many of Wright's ideas along with his own so that the ceramics factory blended perfectly with the ruggedly beautiful cliffs of the Amalfi coast in an ecologically sound design.

In regard to cooling and heating systems of the structure, Soleri took full advantage of the principles of the sunlight's energy properties and those from hydrology, i.e., the study of the circulation, distribution, and properties of the waters of the Earth and its atmosphere. Soleri also designed and built another ceramics factory located in Sicily in a town close to the city of Palermo. Again, using the same ecological principles for heating and cooling, and incorporating the utilization of local materials, Soleri created a structure not aesthetically in conflict with its environment but part of it.

In 1956, along with their two daughters, Soleri and his wife returned to Scottsdale, Arizona where they purchased land and established in 1962 the Cosanti Foundation, its headquarters, and the experimental "earth houses" whose major project has involved the design and creation of a 7,000-person prototype town called Arcosanti. Under construction since 1970, Arcosanti has had the benefits of Soleri's guiding principles (ecology and esthetics) on materials and temperature control.

The course work and workshops at the Cosanti Foundation are accredited by the College of Architecture of Arizona State University at Tempe. The work at Arcosanti is done mainly by summer apprentices and year-round volunteers. This program offers future architects and builders new ways to create and visualize future housing in light of their experience at this thirteen-acre, twenty-five story town growing vertically amid a beautiful 860 acre site.

To promote this remarkable project and do fundraising, Dr. Soleri travels and lectures around the world, but he also stages annual art shows and music festivals at Arcosanti itself. In addition, he also relies heavily upon the sale of his Soleri windbells which have now become world famous and are produced at Arcosanti. The larger version of an exhibition of his work titled "The Architectural Vision of Paolo Soleri" has traveled throughout the U.S. and continues to do so successfully. The smaller counterpart of his "earth houses" has also ventured into many parts of Europe. In all, his shows have as their inspirational model the celebrated exhibit which took place in 1970 at the Corcoran Gallery of Art in Washington, D.C.

Buckminster Fuller (1895-1983), inventor, philosopher and architectural genius of the twentieth century, who studied and admired Soleri's work, viewed him as a "strategist" with a dream to the future. Dr. Soleri holds three honorary doctorates and is titled as distinguished lecturer at the College of Architecture at Arizona State University. In addition to his Wright Foundation Fellowship from 1947, Dr. Soleri also was the recipient of a Graham Foundation Fellowship and two Guggenheim Fellowships. Dr. Soleri, who has sketched plans for a future city to accommodate as many as two million people in a process he has called the "humanization of the earth," has been aptly described as a cross between Leonardo da Vinci and H.G. Wells.

General Sources:

1. *Current Biography Yearbook*. New York: Wilson, 1972.

2. Pizarro, Rafael. *Paolo Soleri: An Introduction to Arcology*. Phoenix, AZ: 1997.

3. Soleri, Paolo. *Arcosanti: An Urban Laboratory*. Arcosanti, AZ: Cosanti Press, 1993.

4. Soleri, Paolo. *The Omega Seed: An Eschatological Hypothesis*. Garden City, NY: Anchor Press, 1981.

5. Soleri, Paolo. *Technology and Cosmogenesis*. New York: Paragon House, 1985.

6. Wall, Donald. *Visionary Cities: The Arcology of Paolo Soleri*. New York: Praeger, 1970.

7. *Who's Who in America*. 1999 ed.

—by JANET B. TUCCI

SYLVESTER STALLONE (1946-   )

Sylvester Stallone, actor, screenwriter, and filmmaker, whose life had been filled with many obstacles, finally had a winning script with *Rocky*. While he deservedly reaped the benefits of the film's success and that of its sequels, the fervor engendered in the Rocky icon filled a great spiritual void in America of the late 1970s.

Stallone was born on July 6, 1946 in the Hell's Kitchen area on the west side of Manhattan in NYC. He was the older of two sons of Frank Stallone, a hair dresser, and Jacqueline (nee Labofish) Stallone, a chorine at Billy Rose's Diamond Horseshoe who later became a practicing astrologer and a women's wrestling promoter. Stallone's difficulties had begun with a forceps-assisted birth during which time a facial nerve was severed, paralyzing the left side of his face and causing his left eyelid to droop. He developed a speech impediment that resulted in children taunting him. His father used to hit him on the head and told him his brain was "dormant" and that he would never amount to anything.

In his early childhood, he boarded with a woman in Queens, NY, and only saw his parents on weekends. Finding release from his loneliness in books, he fantasized about heroic deeds. At the age of five, he moved to Silver Springs, MD, with his brother Frank where their father had been operating a successful chain of hairstyling salons for six years. At fifteen, he left his father's home and went to live with his mother in northeast Philadelphia.

Having been expelled from most of the twelve schools he attended, he was sent to Devereux Manor, a private high school for troublesome teenagers where he found in sports a suitable outlet for his pent-up aggression. He had already started lifting weights at eleven years of age after he had seen Steve Reeves in the action adventure film *Hercules*. He had both the physical strength and the determination needed to excel in athletics, particularly in boxing after a boy kicked him in the groin. Because of his poor performance in school, he found it difficult to get into college. Too young to join the Navy, he applied to beauty school, but that didn't last long.

Eventually, in 1965, he obtained a working scholarship to attend the American College at Switzerland in Leysin where while he taught girls physical education, he studied drama. When he received a standing ovation for his performance as Biff in a student performance of Arthur Miller's *Death of a Salesman*, he knew he had found his calling.

Returning to the United States, he continued his training at the University of Miami in Florida. Three years later, when he was just three credits short of graduation, he dropped out of college and moved to New York City to pursue an acting career. During the next seven difficult years, he supported himself by taking a variety of jobs as a salesman, a pizza demonstrator, a deli-worker, a truckdriver, a bouncer, a security attendant, a short-order cook, and an usher.

On December 28, 1974, he married Sasha Czak whom he met while ushering at the Baronet Theater in Manhattan. While Sasha waitressed, he doggedly peddled scripts that he had written. In his spare time, he worked to eliminate speech defects by listening to his tape-recorded voice as he read aloud the works of Edgar Allen Poe, Walt Whitman, and Shakespeare. He diligently learned a new word every day to improve his vocabulary and to enable him to read the stories of his favorite authors.

The character of Rocky Balboa grew out of several sources, beginning with one of Stallone's earlier scripts called *Hell's Kitchen*. While writing another similar script on commission, he saw a boxing match in March 1975 between Muhammad Ali and a man named Chuck Wepner. Inspired by the fight, he made one of the persons in his story a boxer in honor of Wepner whose pride and dignity had greatly impressed him. For the Chuck Wepner character he derived the name Rocky Balboa from the boxer, Rocky Marciano, and the explorer, Asco Nunez de Balboa.

Film backers agreed to produce the movie provided Stallone allow Ryan O'Neal to play Rocky. Although he had only $106 to his name and his wife was pregnant with their first child, Stallone held out until the producers let him take the leading role for a reported $600 a week and 10% of the net profits.

Rocky earned $225 million in box office receipts. *Rocky* earned ten Oscar nominations, winning Best Picture, Best Editing, and Best Directing. He became the third person in film history to be nominated twice the same year for both acting and writing honors. *Rocky* also received a Golden Globe Award for Best Picture of 1976. He also received the Donatello Award given to him in Europe, a Bell Ringer Award from *Scholastic Magazine,* and a National Theater Owner's Award.

In the late 1980s, Stallone endured a relentless pummeling by the media. In addition to the tabloid haunts he received because of his two divorces, he was ridiculed for his Rambo movies. Stallone's popularity in Europe and Asia endures as his movies make more at the box office there than they do in the United States.

He was reportedly paid from $12 million to $15 million to play Lincoln Hawk, a trucker who enters an arm wrestling contest in order to gain self-respect and his son's affection in *Over the Top*. In 1991, he received an Artistic Achievement Award from the National Italian-American Foundation. On Feb. 22, 1992, he was presented with an Honorary Cesar, the French equivalent of the Oscar for career achievement. He also was admitted into France's Ordre des Arts et Lettres. Other honors included Show West Actor of the Year in 1979.

He is a member of the School Writers Guild, the Writers Guild, Stuntman Association (honorary), and the Directors Guild. An avid art collector, he himself is a painter, and his works have sold for as much as $40,000 each. Barely six feet in height, Stallone eats low fat meals and works out daily with weights for at least two hours.

He had two sons with his first wife. He plays golf regularly, and he drives a vintage Harley-Davidson. His business enterprises include a partnership in Planet Hollywood restaurants. Somewhat disillusioned by his wealth and fame, he has said: "Big money really does corrupt. It puts a beard on innocence, takes away the edge, the fun, the excitement of suddenly being able to afford certain luxuries. When you can buy anything, the thrill is gone. At least, it is for me."

General Sources:
1.   *Current Biography Yearbook*. New York: Wilson, 1977.
2.   Daly, Marsha. *Sylvester Stallone: An Illustrated Life*. New York: St. Martin's Press, 1984.
3.   Katz, Ephraim. *The Film Encyclopedia*. New York: HarperCollins, 1998.
4.   Simpson, Janice Claire. *Sylvester Stallone: Going the Distance*. St. Paul: EMC Corp., 1978.
5.   Stallone, Sylvester. *The Official Rocky Scrapbook*. New York: Grosset & Dunlap, 1977.
6.   *Washington Post Magazine* 26 Dec. 1976: 8+.

—by ANNE RESTIVO

FRANK STELLA (1936-   )

For many art aficionados, a Stella painting has become synonymous with great contemporary modern art. Frank Stella, one of the most successful painters of our time, enjoyed success relatively early in his career as early as twenty-three years of age, but not resting on his laurels, he has continued to produce art works which are eagerly sought after at art exhibitions and purchased for both private and corporate business art collections. As one of the most celebrated abstract artists of our time, Stella has undergone shifts in his development, going from early two-dimensional prototypical abstract representations to using abstract components in three-dimensional space.

Frank (Philip) Stella was born May 12, 1936, in Malden, Massachusetts, a working class town just north of Boston. He is the oldest of three children born to second-generation Italian-American parents: his father, Dr. Frank Stella, a gynecologist whose parents came from Sicily, and his mother, Constance who is of Calabrian descent.

As a youngster attending public school in Malden, Frank proved to be an unruly adolescent, engaged in juvenile mischief, cutting classes and the like. As a teenager, he painted houses to earn spending money, and he also became a wrestler finishing runner-up in a regional championship tournament sponsored by the New England Amateur Athletic Union. In 1950, his parents, concerned that young Frank needed to experience a more disciplined and more academic education, enrolled him in the well-known private school, Phillips Academy in Andover, Massachusetts.

There Frank was introduced to abstract painting by Patrick Morgan, an artist himself and an instructor at the academy. Reportedly, it seemed that as early as high school Frank was destined for success in modern art since he understood its concepts almost instinctively. Frank entered Princeton University in 1954, and before graduating in 1958 with a B.A. in history, he had had the opportunity to study painting with Stephen Greene, an abstract painter from New York City. Stella had also studied there with art historian William Seitz, an expert on abstract expressionism and a friend to many practicing abstract painters (like Willem de Kooning) in New York City which as an art center had come to replace Paris as the world capital for contemporary art.

Not acceding to his father's desire for Frank to attend law school and to desist from pursuing a precarious career in art, Stella took his father's $300 graduation gift and rented a one-room studio apartment in Manhattan's Lower East Side on Eldridge Street for fifty dollars a month. In order to support himself, he painted houses in Queens and in Brooklyn three days a week utilizing the rest of his time to paint on canvas. He painted in an artistic style which he later characterized with the heading "non-relational painting." Abandoning gestural brushwork, he focused on doing "striped paintings" such as his "Coney Island" and "Astoria," which became part of a group exhibition at Oberlin College in May 1959.

Influenced by the theories of critic Clement Greenberg, Stella did an entire series of large black paintings that were comprised of black bands arranged in vertical, horizontal or diagonal patterns whose uniqueness expressed an eye-catching immediacy. As critic Calvin Tomkins pointed out, "there was something compelling about them, a remote and majestic austerity. It seemed incredible that they had

364

been painted by someone who was only twenty-three years old."

During this very early period in Stella's development, his works had captured the attention of two important New York City individuals: Leo Castelli, an art gallery entrepreneur, and Dorothy Miller, the curator of the Museum of Modern Art (MOMA). In the fall of 1959, Castelli, who was looking for young artists for his gallery exhibitions, took Miller to view Stella's so-called black paintings at Stella's new location in Soho, a former warehouse district adjacent to Greenwich Village frequented by artists, writers, and performers.

While Miller selected four of Stella's paintings to be displayed at an exhibition of works by new artists that opened at MOMA that very December, Castelli took the remainder of Stella's works and put them on exhibition in both his gallery and in that of Tibor de Nagy. In 1960, Stella went on further to enjoy his first solo exhibition in Castelli's renowned gallery. Suddenly, with the advent of such an immediate high-profile exposure to public viewing, Stella's works came under the close scrutiny of New York City art critics. Like many young, innovative artists, Stella who was twenty-four, invariably received mixed criticism. Some of his unflattering critics, like Harold Rosenberg, described Stella's works as examples of "chessboard aesthetics."

The majority of critics, however, offered favorable reviews. In fact, the director of collections for MOMA, Alfred H. Barr, Jr., arranged for the museum to purchase one of Stella's art works entitled "The Marriage of Reason and Squalor." William Rubin, who became the director of MOMA's department of painting and sculpture in 1973, also became a steadfast Stella supporter in the coming years. From this rather successful beginning in the early 1970s, Stella's subsequent creative growth involved many innovations and changes which were reflected in a multiplicity of artistic phases. Throughout the process, he was earning a growing reputation, and he has become today one of the wealthiest artists in recent times. His earliest paintings are now worth in the millions of dollars.

Both his larger works that bedeck the lobbies of many corporate office buildings and his smaller works that adorn the homes of private collectors have yielded handsome sums of money. His fame has reached such a point that no museum dedicated to modern art is considered complete without a Stella. Having had exhibitions of his art in scores of major cities in the U.S. and also many exhibitions worldwide in such cities as London, Munich, Rome, Sakura (Japan), and Nagoya (Japan), he has also achieved an international reputation. As a recipient of many awards, fellowships, and honorary degrees, he brings honor to all Italian Americans who have always had a tradition of high investiture in the plastic arts and culture.

General Sources:
1. *Current Biography Yearbook*. New York: Wilson, 1988.
2. Fried, Michael. *Three American Painters: Kenneth Noland, Jules Olitski, Frank Stella*. Cambridge, MA: Fogg Art Museum, 1965.
3. Guberman, Sidney. *Frank Stella: An Illustrated Biography*. New York: Rizzoli International, 1995.
4. Rosenblum, Robert. *Frank Stella*. Harmondsworth, UK: Penguin Books, 1971.
5. Ruben, William Stanley. *Frank Stella, 1970-1987*. New York: Museum of Modern Art, 1987.
6. Stella, Frank. *Frank Stella: The Circuits Prints*. Minneapolis, MN: Walker Art Center, 1988.
7. Stella, Frank. *Working Space*. Cambridge, MA: Harvard University Press, 1986.

—by CHARLES HARRINGTON

PAUL TAGLIABUE (1940-   )

Lawyer and consultant to Pete Rozelle, then eventually his successor as commissioner of the National Football League in 1989, Paul John Tagliabue faced and overcame a very challenging set of circumstances. By the end of the 1980s, professional football had become big business. The growth of the Super Bowl from a simple championship game to a major media event driven by shrewd hi-tech marketing made the stakes far higher than they had ever been. Both team owners and football players had haplessly entered into a quarrelsome and litigious period. Tagliabue, who had served as Rozelle's outside legal counsel for nearly twenty years, was the best choice the team owners could have made to replace Pete Rozelle.

Paul Tagliabue was born in Jersey City, New Jersey on November 24, 1940. He is the third of four boys born to Charles and Mary Tagliabue. Paul's father Charles owned a small business where he did repair work at factories and loading docks on the New Jersey waterfront. Charles, a former basketball player himself in the early 1920s, set very high standards for his sons where athletics were important, but academics had higher priority. Paul's older brothers, Charles and Robert, became business executives and his younger brother John became a journalist. Paul's first love as a youngster was baseball, and he especially admired the Brooklyn Dodgers—until they moved to Los Angeles in 1958, and then he suddenly lost interest in them.

As an adolescent, he played football with the neighborhood boys, but his favorite sport was still basketball which he would practice for hours at a time in all kinds of weather. Often when the temperature was below freezing, he would tape his fingers to keep his skin from cracking. Attending St. Michael's High School

in Union City, New Jersey, he had the distinction of becoming its second best basketball player; the first was Tom Heinsohn, who later played for the Boston Celtics and became an NBA Hall of Famer.

An athletically talented adolescent, Paul won the state high-jump championship one year. Pursued by over twenty colleges with sports scholarship monies, Paul ultimately chose Georgetown University because of its high academic standards and its long Jesuit tradition in education. At Georgetown he played well, and he began to attract the attention of several scouts from professional basketball, but because of continued knee injuries during his college years, he was rendered unable to become a pro-basketball player.

Paul majored in government and was regularly on the dean's list. He was president of his senior class and a Rhodes scholar finalist. Reputed as quite disciplined in his study habits, it was no surprise that he graduated with honors in 1962 and was awarded the coveted Root-Tilden scholarship from New York University School of Law where he became editor of its law review. Receiving his law degree in 1965, he worked for a year as a law clerk in federal court in Washington, D.C.

In the same year on August 28, Paul married the former Elizabeth Chandler Minter, an English scholar, and they would have two children. In September of 1966 he switched to the Defense Department as a policy analyst on European and North Atlantic affairs. After three years of dedicated work for the government, he received the department's highest civilian award, the Meritorious Civilian Service Medal.

In June 1969, he joined the prestigious law firm of Covington and Burling where he remained for 20 years, eventually becoming a senior partner of the firm and serving on its five-member committee supervising the operations of 275 company lawyers. One of his assignments dealt with the National Football League account, and one of its first legal matters was advising Pete Rozelle regarding the highly publicized Joe Namath-Bachelors III affair. After jointly considering the legalities, Rozelle ordered Joe Namath to sell his half-interest in Bachelors III, a posh Manhattan bar and restaurant where gambling had allegedly been taking place regularly.

In the 1970s, after engineering highly lucrative and unprecedented contracts for TV football, Rozelle became the most admired and respected commissioner in recent sports history, and Paul Tagliabue became Rozelle's most valued legal counsel. However, as the 1980s approached with unparalleled sums of money contracted, there also came the phenomenon of disgruntled "underpaid" players, litigation, strikes, and labor disputes involving abbreviating the regular season. In addition, Paul and Pete had to contend with the legalities of Al Davis' actions which involved moving the Raiders from Oakland to Los Angeles.

Five years later in 1987, many players went on strike, and the owners finished the regular season with substitute players, trimming their regular sixteen-game season by nine games. Tagliabue and Rozelle had to struggle with antitrust lawsuits summoned by the NFL Players Association and the U.S. Football League (USFL). The USFL, a recently defunct league, sued for $1.69 billion in damages. Tagliabue achieved a major victory for his client when he advised Rozelle not to settle out of court. His advice proved correct when a federal jury awarded the USFL a nominal settlement of one dollar.

On March 22, 1989 after 29 years as football commissioner, Pete Rozelle announced his retirement at the annual meeting of the NFL. After much infighting over a period of seven long months with five contenders for Rozelle's position, on October 29, 1989 Paul Taliabue was finally elected commissioner of the NFL. The matter of negotiating new contracts with the television networks was among the major items on the agenda. In March 1990, Tagliabue and network executives hammered out a four-year $3.6 billion contract, amounting to the most lucrative TV sports agreement in history, which included a guaranteed $32 million for each club per season.

In order to increase the viewing range of American football overseas, Tagliabue negotiated agreements involving a preseason game in Berlin as well as one in Tokyo and London. Paul also declared college juniors eligible for the spring draft in 1990. The negotiations included two more wildcard teams to the season-ending play-off structure; and an expanded sixteen regular-season games to seventeen weeks in 1990 and 1991, and eighteen weeks in 1992 and 1993. He also negotiated new drug testing policies to include checking for performance enhancing drugs, creating a drug rehabilitation program, and enacting tougher guidelines for steroid testing. Paul Tagliabue, an educated, disciplined, hard-working man dedicated to his profession and family life, is a tough negotiator and a forthright football commissioner.

General Sources:
1. *Current Biography Yearbook*. New York: Wilson, 1992.
2. George, Thomas. "Tagliabue is Elected NFL Commissioner." *New York Times* 27 Oct. 1989.
3. Marchione, Margherita. *Americans of Italian Heritage*. Lanham, MD: University Press of America, 1995.
4. Thomas, Robert. "Family Man, Sports Fan, NFL Chief." *New York Times* 27 Oct. 1989.

—by RONALD BENNETT

GAY TALESE (1932-   )

Gay Talese was born on February 7, 1932 in Ocean City, New Jersey. His given name was Gaetano. The son of an Italian immigrant father Joseph Francis and his mother Catherine (Di Paola) Talese, he grew up as an Italian Catholic in an Irish parish, and lived in a predominately Protestant community. As a child living in Ocean City, a seaside resort town, he found it festive and bright in the summertime but dispirited the rest of the year. It was reported that as a child in grammar school, he was shy and a loner, doing poorly in most classes at the parochial school he attended. Later, in Ocean City High School, he started out as neither interested in playing sports nor in studying for his school subjects.

As Talese once explained in a magazine interview, characterizing himself as a very quiet and curious person, he focused much of his energies on studying people. His curiosity would soon grow into a desire to do newspaper reporting on events at his high school, its sports, and other related activities for the local weekly paper, the Ocean City *Sentinel-Ledger*. At age 13, it seems, he had made a major discovery that changed the course of his entire life. Whenever he was involved in newspaper reporting, he realized that his shyness did not interfere with his approaching total strangers and asking them questions. And so, throughout his high school years he would continue reporting the news.

He entered the University of Alabama in 1949, majoring in journalism. He wrote for the college newspaper and became a correspondent for the *Birmingham Post Herald*. Talese modeled much of his writing style on that of Red Smith's newspaper style. He hoped someday to become like Red Smith, a renowned sportswriter, who wrote for the *New York Herald Tribune*. Talese received his bachelor's degree from the University of Alabama in 1953.

In the same year, he began his writing career as a copy boy at the *New York Times* in New York City but not without first having some personal misgivings and disappointments. He had applied at the *New York Herald Tribune* and then at several other New York newspapers (some are now defunct), and they all rejected him. Ironically, the *New York Times*, which he thought would be the most difficult place to find a position, hired him without hesitation.

In just two years, he proved himself worthy to become a staff reporter. During that prior period (1953-1955) as copy boy, he had also done a two-year assignment in the military as an ROTC lieutenant in the Army. He would keep his full-time reporter job for the *New York Times* until 1965. In June 1959, Talese married Nan Ahearn, a publishing editor, and from their marriage they had two daughters: Pamela and Catherine.

In addition to doing job-related reporting in the 50s, he also continued his own writing. He would eventually receive acclaim and many awards in the coming decades. He began by writing essays and vignettes of his impressions of life in New York City, an exciting but sometimes impersonal domain, depicting its "odd, little noticed aspects." His persistence in adhering to his unique style and to the specific content of his work eventually bore fruit as *Times Magazine* decided to publish these essays and vignettes.

The most interesting of his initiatives appeared in the October 16, 1955 issue whose topic dealt with Nita Naldi, a once famous entertainer who had become a virtual unknown, living in Manhattan's frenzied pace, all but forgotten by her one-time admirers. The notion of the "impermanence of fame" would become a major thematic component in the style of Talese's works, and Naldi became his initial icon depicting the cruel metamorphosis from fame into relative obscurity.

Talese's first book, *New York: A Serendipiter's Journey*, was published in 1961, and it was composed largely of material from articles that had been already printed in the *New York Times*. While it had a small sales volume, critics were quick to admire Talese's style as having "a sense of pace, a crispness, a precision." This effort was followed by another collection of articles in 1965 called the *Over-reachers*, and it was preceded in 1964 by *The Bridge*. The latter is an account of the building of the Verrazzano-Narrows Bridge, blending drama and romance as integral elements of this bridge-building story. Though not a bestseller, it was critically well received.

As one of the pioneers of the new journalism of the time, Gay Talese was one of the first writers to apply modern fiction writing techniques to non-fictional narratives, making newspaper reporting or magazine writing read more like a short story or a novel. Considered to be classics of that genre, Talese's *Esquire* articles, written in this style, probed the private lives of celebrities such as Joshua Logan, Frank Sinatra, and Joe DiMaggio. Prompted by the popular success of these stories, Talese worked on bigger subjects.

In 1969, after two-and-a-half years of research, he produced his first bestseller, *The Kingdom and the Power*, a non-fiction work about the dramatic inner workings of the *New York Times* written in this new novelistic style, and as result of this book, he went on to receive the Christopher Book Award in 1970. Since then, Talese has thematically explored three major topics, all difficult and controversial: the Mafia in *Honor Thy Father* (1971); American sexuality vis-a-vis the First Amendment in *Thy Neighbor's Wife* (1980); and in his third area of concern, the issue of self-identity from the perspective of a post-immigration author in *Unto the Sons* (1992). So far, it is Talese's most challenging writing experience. Looking back in time, Talese's persona alters the initial first-person narrative, shifting subtly into a third-person point-of-view narration, integrating the historical profiles of past figures such as Garibaldi, Mussolini, and others in a non-fictional narrative.

Widely respected as a master of his craft, Talese has expressed his preference for non-fictional narratives: "I don't want to resort to changing names to fictionalizing. The reality is more fascinating. My mission is to get deep into the heart and soul of the people in this country." *Honor Thy Father*, a heavily researched, inside-look at the life of Joe ("Bananas") Bonanno, took six years in the making. It had a popular journalistic appeal, selling 300,000 copies in just four months of its publication. His other works include *Fame and Obscurity* (1970), and *The Literature of Reality* (1995) with co-author Barbara Lounsberry.

As an innovative writer bringing narrative verve and dramatic impact to non-fiction story-telling, he has earned the respect of many critics who have admired his pioneering work and who have compared him to Norman Mailer, Truman Capote, and Tom Wolfe.

General Sources:

1. *Contemporary Authors*. Detroit, MI: Gale Research, 1983.
2. *Current Biography Yearbook*. New York: Wilson, 1972.
3. D'Acierno, Pellegrino, ed. *The Italian American Heritage: A Companion to Literature and Arts*. New York: Garland, 1999.
4. Talese, Gay, and Barbara Lounsberry. *Writing Creative Nonfiction: The Literature of Reality*. New York: HarperCollins, 1996.

—by MARIE BULZACCHELLI

CHRISTINE M. TARTAGLIONE (1960-   )

Reelected on November 3, 1998 to serve a second term as state senator for the 2nd District of Philadelphia and also unanimously elected in the same year as chairperson of the Pennsylvania Democratic State Committee, Senator Christine Tartaglione shows incredible promise on her political horizon. As a relatively young state legislator, she possesses all the necessary ingredients for a bright future. Known for her passionate commitment to public service, she has a proven track record both before and during her years as senator. She exudes a generosity of spirit along with great vitality and drive.

Christine M. Tartaglione was born on September 21, 1960 to Eugene and Margaret (nee Warnecki) Tartaglione in Philadelphia, Pennsylvania where her grandfather Antonio Tartaglione had settled after he arrived from the city of Campobasso, the regional capital of Molise, one of the southern regions of Italy. One of five children, Senator Tartaglione claims to have been politically active "since birth" largely due to her family's intense passion for and involvement in politics and government.

Her mother established herself in 1975 as a political figure upon her election as chair of the Philadelphia County Commission. Her strong past alliance with the well-known and popular Italian-American mayor of Philadelphia, Frank Rizzo, had proven to be invaluable. Margaret Tartaglione, better known as "Marge," was elected to the chair of that commission in 1975 and has since remained in that office for well over twenty-five years. Now, recently reelected in 1999, she will continue for another four years. Marge has also been a member of the Philadelphia Democratic Committee for more than forty-three years, State Democratic Committee for thirty-two years, and National Democratic Committee for at least sixteen years.

Most of Senator Tartaglione's family members have expressed interest either in public service or in the civil service sector. Her sister, Renee Tartaglione, was and still is the chief deputy commissioner of Philadelphia; her brother, Eugene Tartaglione, Jr., was a zoning board commissioner in San Diego, California; and her younger sister, Mary Tartaglione Rossi, is presently a deputy sheriff in Philadelphia. Tartaglione cites both her mother and her aunt for the majority of early influences in her political upbringing. She states that as far as her family was concerned, "there were always people in our house" that had something to do with political activity. "It was constantly a revolving door since Mom and Dad were always helping people."

As a young adult, Tartaglione graduated from Peirce Junior College in 1980. She subsequently worked for the admiralty law firm of Palmer, Biezup & Henderson where she assisted in handling international claims including one historic case that involved recovering $35 million for the firm's client. When the 6th Council District of Philadelphia sought help in the year 1985, Tartaglione became the head of its Constituent Services and also handled budgetary and legislative issues.

This experience led her to a subsequent position where she became senior executive assistant to Pennsylvania Treasurer Catherine Baker Knoll. In that two-year capacity, lasting from December 1989 to December 1991, Tartaglione saved taxpayers millions of dollars by initially discovering that $75 million in state leasing proposals had not been placed in competitive bidding. This led her to begin a program that led to savings of $1.5 million per year. She was also instrumental with many other programs, including Home Start which allowed a qualifying family with an annual income less than $25,000 to purchase a home at a one percent discount below the original price. In 1994, Tartaglione became business manager for Local 1776 of the United Food & Commercial Workers composed of more than 1,200 people, one of the most vocal unions in Pennsylvania's history. She also assisted in unionizing the employees at the Pennsylvania Employees Benefit Trust Fund.

In 1994 she decided to challenge a controversial incumbent state senator who had succeeded long-time State Senator Frank Lynch, a Democrat. She ran a vigorous campaign through the neighborhoods using door-to-door voter contact and speaking passionately about politics and the new leadership that was needed in that district. With the help of an aggressive staff and hundreds of dedicated volunteers, she won an impressive victory on Election Day defeating Republican incumbent Bruce Marks. After she was sworn in as state senator in early 1995, her first appointment involved becoming Democratic Minority Chair of the Aging and Youth Committee. This was followed by obtaining membership in a long line of other committees, including Labor & Industry, Law & Justice, and Communications & High Technology, as well as the Intra-Governmental Council on Long-Term Care. These state Senate committees handle some of the most important and persistent issues of our day especially those involving the needs of the elderly, defining the growth and limits of information systems versus the rights of individual privacy, and defining what constitutes a criminal violation in hi-tech applications as employed in societal, business, governmental, and medical contexts.

As a state senator, Tartaglione has been a champion for the "little guy" speaking out against an increase in gasoline taxes in 1997 while voting for an increase in funds for the Children's Health Insurance Program (CHIP) to provide for low-cost health insurance for families unable to afford health insurance who cannot qualify for other assistance programs. She served for a number of years as a member of the Children's Trust Fund, which awarded grants to various organizations to fight child abuse.

In many ways, she has been inspired by her mother who has been her political role model. Following in mom's footsteps, Senator Tartaglione had been so active in her community, supporting firefighters, police and correctional officers, and retirees from other professions that she was named Woman of the Year in November 1998 by the Philadelphia Retired Police, Fire and Prison Employees. Again in 1998, in recognition of her tireless efforts in advocating programs for mental health and programs for those afflicted with mental retardation, Senator Tartaglione was one of only fifteen individuals in the United States to receive the John F. Kennedy Memorial Award, conferred annually by the Kennedy Foundation.

As a recently reelected state senator and as a newly elected chair of the Pennsylvania Democratic State Committee, Tartaglione will prosper and achieve many more contributions for America. Her broadened power base will mean not only an upward mobility in her personal status in an obviously burgeoning career but also a greater opportunity for her to serve in the public sector, which she has already done for many years.

General Sources:
1.   "Pennsylvania Senate - Tartaglione." <http://sengate.pasen.gov/members/sd02.html>.
2.   Tartaglione, Christine M. Personal interview. 4 Dec. 1998.
3.   *Who's Who in American Politics*. 1997-1998 ed.

—by MARIANNE MICCOLI

GIULIANA CAVAGLIERI TESORO
(1921-   )

An internationally recognized expert on both the scientific theory and applied technology of polymers (compounds of high molecular weight such as polyester fabrics, plastics, and resins), Dr. Giuliana Cavaglieri Tesoro, who in her career as administrator, researcher, inventor, university professor, writer, worldwide lecturer, and product developer, has been responsible for about 120 patents. She has been honored by industry, academia, and government alike for her contributions in quality assurance in the manufacture and use of consumer goods, and in the use of textile fibers in public conveyances.

She has made a long series of important contributions in industry not only in the synthesis of pharmaceutical products but also, more extensively, in the field of textiles in the development of textile chemicals, chemical modification of fibers, flame-retardants and antistatic chemicals for fabrics, and in developing improvements in the permanent press properties of textile fabrics and products. An active and engaging person, she has also had from time to time the challenging situation of having concurrent positions in industry with a university or with national councils for public safety.

Giuliana Cavaglieri was born in Venice, Italy on June 1, 1921. Of Jewish ancestry, she was one of three children born to Gino and Margherita (nee Maroni) Cavaglieri. Her father, who was a civil engineer by education but managed an insurance firm, died when Giuliana was only twelve. By 1938, when Giuliana was ready to continue her education beyond the secondary school level, Mussolini's government was entering a disgraceful phase of its development where it started employing overt discriminatory and repressive measures against its own native Italian Jews.

Like so many other Italian Jews, Giuliana knew that she would be denied access to Italy's university system, and so to escape the tyranny of Fascism's unrelenting pace, she moved to Switzerland where she studied X-ray technology for a short period of time. With a miraculous sense of timing, Giuliana immigrated to the United States in 1939. She arrived safely after having traveled in the perilous U-boat infested waters of the Atlantic just before Mussolini announced Italy's entrance into World War II.

Giuliana, who was only eighteen years of age, wanted to pursue one of her main goals of earning an advanced degree. Despite a difference in language, but bearing the benefits of a good high school education from Italy, she was allowed to enter Yale University's graduate program conditionally. Gifted intellectually and a hard worker, Giuliana Cavaglieri went on to finish her prerequisite courses and completed all of her doctoral courses and dissertation in record time. By 1943 at the age of twenty-one, she received a Ph.D. in organic chemistry, one of the most difficult areas in the field of chemistry. In the same year, she also married Victor Tesoro with whom she would have two children, Claudia Margaret and Andrew James.

In a long and fulfilling career in chemistry, she worked and generally maintained a home in and around the New York City Metropolitan area (working for chemical firms usually in New Jersey). From time to time, she also worked elsewhere such as at the Burlington Industries in Greensboro, North Carolina and at MIT in Cambridge, Massachusetts for varying periods of time. In 1943, Dr. Giuliana Tesoro's first job was in Boundbrook, New Jersey where she worked briefly for American Cyanamid as a research chemist; then for another short while, she worked in the same capacity at Calco Chemical in 1943-1944.

Finally, in 1944 in Jersey City, NJ she became employed by Onyx Oil and Chemical Company where she remained in its research department for over a decade until 1958 holding different administrative titles essentially in organic synthesis research. In 1958 she moved to J.P. Stevens in Garfield, New Jersey where she was appointed assistant director of organic research and remained there for almost a decade doing work in similar capacities as in her prior job. After doing work at the Textile Research Institute, Dr. Tesoro was appointed director of chemical research at Burlington Industries in Greensboro, North Carolina where she remained for three years. This time frame constituted one of the most prolific phases of her career where she created new products and developed new industrial processes. In the year 1970 alone, she received approval on more than two dozen patents.

After working almost three full decades in industry, Dr. Tesoro accepted a post as visiting professor at the prestigious Massachusetts Institute of Technology in 1972 until 1976; then remaining there on the faculty until 1982, she became adjunct professor and senior research scientist. In the latter half of 1982, Dr. Tesoro continued her newly found enjoyment in academia by becoming a research professor at the Polytechnic University in Brooklyn, New York. After having worked for many years in dealing with the demands of hi-tech industry in its quest for patents and business applications, Dr. Tesoro has been savoring the simple pleasure of teaching the general concepts and principles of science.

Dr. Tesoro has been a member of many national associations such as the American Association for the Advancement of Science, the American Institute of Chemists, and the American Chemical Society. She has also been a member of three National Research Council committees (1979-1985) and a contributing author of their publications dealing with fire safety and material toxicity. She has also served a term as president of the Fiber Society in 1974, and has been a columnist for the *Polymer News*.

As an international lecturer, Dr. Tesoro has given talks and presentations in Europe, the Middle East, and China, expounding on the topic of polymers, their latest developments and applications, especially in the area of flame-retardation. In 1963 the American Association of Textile Chemists and Colorists awarded her the Olney Medal. Similarly, in 1978, because of the enormity of her research contributions throughout her lengthy career, Dr. Giuliana Tesoro also received the Society of Women Engineers Achievement Award.

General Sources:

1. *American Men and Women of Science.* 1992-1993 ed.
2. Backer, Stanley, et al. *Textile Fabric Flammability.* Cambridge: MIT Press, 1976.
3. Bailey. Martha J. *American Women in Science: A Biographical Dictionary.* Santa Barbara, CA: ABC-CLIO, 1994.
4. Herzenberg, Caroline. *Women Scientists from Antiquity to the Present.* West Cornwall, CT: Locust Hill Press, 1986.
5. National Research Council (U.S.). Committee on Fire Safety Aspects of Polymeric Materials. *Fire Safety Aspects of Polymeric Materials.* Washington, DC: National Academy of Sciences, 1978.
6. *Notable Twentieth-Century Scientists.* Detroit, MI: Gale Research, 1995.
7. *Who's Who of American Women.* 1966-1967 ed.

—by GEORGE CARPETTO, Ph.D.

JOE TORRE (1940-   )

In his first season as manager of the New York Yankees, Joe Torre at age 56 made history in the fall of 1996 when he led the Bronx Bombers to their first World Series title since 1978. Joe Torre, whose career in baseball had been colorful and varied, spent 17 seasons as a ballplayer, 15 as a manager, and 5 as a sportscaster, but he had never participated as a player or manager in a World Series. During the Series, the Yankees had thrilled their audiences when, after losing the first two games, they went on to win 4 straight games to clinch the series.

Joe Torre, last of five children, was born on July 18, 1940 in the Marine Park section of Brooklyn, New York. His father, Joseph Torre, Sr., was a police detective, and his mother Margaret Torre was a homemaker. His parents separated in the early 50s; and Joe, the youngest child of the family, was reportedly spoiled to no end by his two brothers and two sisters. His two brothers acted as father figures to Joe who was only in his early teens when the parents separated.

His brothers also played as members of the Cadets, belonging to the oldest New York amateur baseball organization. All three brothers, in fact, shared a common passion for baseball, and Joe Torre too joined the Cadets after his graduation from St. Francis, a Roman Catholic prep high school. Frank, eight years older than Joe, was already in professional baseball and played first base for the Milwaukee Braves when Joe started with the Cadets. Rocco, the oldest of the three brothers, had already become a police officer.

At first rejected by the Milwaukee Braves, Joe tried again after he had lost some weight and was accepted into the farm system in August 1959. He began his first year playing for Eau Claire, located in Wisconsin, where he acquired "the highest batting average in the Northern League and was named the league's All-Star catcher." Based on the strength of his brief and strong record, Joe Torre made his major league debut at the end of the 1960 season, and in 1961 he joined his brother Frank as a regular on the Milwaukee Braves team. During his years with Milwaukee, Torre played side by side with such great hitters as Joe Adcock, Eddie Matthews, and Hank Aaron.

The 60s decade was a good one for Joe Torre. For the 1961 Rookie of the Year Award, he earned second place, and by the end of the 1963 season, he became Milwaukee's number-one catcher. In 1964 he broke a record by becoming the first catcher since 1955 to bat over .300 with 20 home runs and 100 runs batted in. In 1964 he also played in the National and American Leagues' Annual All-Star game, something he would do eight more times in his career.

In all, Joe was establishing himself on the field not only as a solid catcher but also as a consistently good hitter. He hit .321 in 1964 and displayed power by belting 20 home runs and driving in 109 runs. The 1964 season was the start of an eight-year stretch where Joe became viewed as one of the steadiest hitters in the National League. In 1965 he earned for himself a Gold Glove Award as the Best Fielding Catcher in his league.

Already a five-time All-Star participant while with the Milwaukee Braves, Torre was traded to the St. Louis Cardinals in 1969 where he would remain for the next five years. During that time he played third base in 1970 and then three years later, first base. In 1971 he was named the league's Most Valuable Player having earned a batting average of .363, 24 home runs, 230 hits, and 137 RBIs.

In 1974 he was traded to the New York Mets where after three seasons on June 18, 1977, he called it quits as a player, and at 37 years of age he took on the new responsibility as the Mets manager. In all, from his 2,209 games in the majors as a player, Torre had earned some commendable lifetime statistics including a "batting average of .297. He scored 996 runs and had 2,342 hits, 1,185 RBIs, 344 doubles, and 59 triples."

The next six years of Torre's life as manager would prove to be painful and frustrating as he inherited a host of problems that were beyond his control. Many of the Mets best talents had already been traded, and, to make matters worse, the Mets also traded away Tom Seaver, reputedly one the league's best players. In short, Torre had to work with a team that had been diminished in talent, and for the next three years (1977-1979), the Mets found themselves in last place in the National League East. When the Mets decided to overhaul the team, they fired Torre in October 1981 erroneously considering him to have been part of the problem.

Within a matter of days, however, Torre was quickly picked up by the Braves who had by now moved to Atlanta. The Braves, who had ended up in last place in 1981, now with Torre went on to open up the 1982 season winning 13 consecutive games—plus capturing the National League West championship. Despite such continued good work for another year, Torre was summarily fired by the Braves management who seemed to be more acutely concerned with popularity ratings than Torre's excellent work. For the next five years, Joe Torre made a career switch, turning to sportscasting for the California Angels. He felt comfortable in his new line of work until the Cardinals offered him a managerial job in 1990.

History, unfortunately, would repeat itself. After the Cardinals had reached the World Series three times in the 1980s, it became a team that, according to many baseball analysts, had now passed its prime, and there wasn't much Torre could do with them. And so, again, Joe Torre was fired in 1995, but the Yankees owner George Steinbrenner quickly swooped up Joe as the new manager—and the rest is history. In 1996, Joe Torre guided the Yankees to their first World Series in 18 years. Torre must have felt vindicated as a manager who had finally found the right conditions for victory, and he achieved his lifetime dream to win a World Series for a team from his native New York City.

In late 1998, baseball writers gave Torre 105 votes for inclusion into the Baseball Hall of Fame. Though it proved to be insufficient for induction at that time, it surely suggested the great respect that had been generated for the three-and-a-half decades of his life dedicated to baseball. He is a man who has won many awards, but, more importantly, he has been consistently described by his players and his colleagues as an unselfish man who is more concerned about the team's performance than his personal image.

General Sources:
1. *Current Biography Yearbook*. New York: Wilson, 1997.
2. *The Joe Torre Story—Curveballs Along the Way*. Video. Hallmark Entertainment, 1998.
3. Light, Jonathan Fraser. *The Cultural Encyclopedia of Baseball*. Jefferson, NC: McFarland, 1997.
4. Ryan, Nolan, Joe Torre, and Joel H. Cohen. *Pitching and Hitting*. Englewood Cliffs, NJ: Prentice Hall, 1977.
5. Torre, Joe, and Tom Verducci. *Chasing the Dream: My Lifelong Journey to the World Series: An Autobiography*. New York: Bantam, 1997.

—by LEW MAZZARELLA

ARTURO TOSCANINI (1867-1957)

Arturo Toscanini born on March 25, 1867 in Parma, Italy was to become the most internationally celebrated music conductor of his time. Known for his fiery temper and strict discipline in rehearsals, he had an iron memory learning musical scores by heart as a result of his failing eyesight. Today, as in the time in which he lived, the name Toscanini still remains synonymous with perfect orchestration and exacting precise interpretations of composers' desired directions from the musical scores.

Reportedly, he spent of good deal of his younger years working in his father's tailor shop. His father Claudio had been a member of Garibaldi's Red Shirts, the military that fought for Italy's independence and unification in the 1860s. Young Arturo apparently took pride in his father's prowess and political affiliations, and most certainly he received much of his courage and daring from his father. Despite his many brilliant achievements, Toscanini would profess later on in his life, still apparently loyal to his humble beginnings, that at heart he remained a *contadino*, or peasant, as he had always been.

Arturo's father, who loved to sing and made music prevail throughout the household, may have greatly contributed to his son's high regard for music. His parents had him enrolled in the Parma Conservatory of Music from which he graduated in 1885 at eighteen years of age. He was first employed for a period of time as cellist by the Buenos Aires Orchestra in South America. A year later, during a performance of Verdi's *Aida* in Rio de Janeiro, Brazil the orchestra conductor took ill, and Toscanini, who played cello, was unexpectedly asked to substitute. Arturo seized the opportunity and gladly served as conductor. After the initial pressure of the opening score, Arturo was able to direct the music of the entire opera without turning a page of the written score, directing the orchestra entirely from memory. He became an immediate success, and that performance was pivotal in helping him realize that becoming a renowned conductor was well within his reach.

Toscanini also had the good fortune to have experienced working under the aegis of Giuseppe Verdi and Giacomo Puccini, two of the greatest composers and *maestri* of their time. Their influence and their passion for music were qualities that Toscanini would never forget. As time passed, his fame grew in great measure throughout Italy, Germany, Austria, France, England, and Russia. His musical expertise and intuition allowed him to conduct each symphony in each of the countries as if he had been a native of that country's unique tastes. He was applauded and praised throughout the music world; his drive and authenticity as conductor could not be challenged by many others.

In 1898, at the age of 31, Arturo Toscanini became the principal conductor at the prestigious opera house, La Scala di Milano. During that time, another well-known opera house, The Vienna Opera House, was the home of another brilliant conductor, Gustav Mahler. Both Toscanini and Mahler became cultural rivals throughout most of their careers. Though each had radically different personalities, they were compatible in their ruthless idealism for achievement and perfection, which often caused turmoil and intrigue. With their highly excitable personalities, they both scorned their detractors. They had become celebrities who symbolized for many a new order in the world of music.

Arturo Toscanini was one of the handsomest men to wield a baton. While conducting, he gave an impression of excitement and spiritual light to his music. Known to be an irresistible philanderer and adored by the ladies, this only enhanced the aura of mystique that surrounded him. Gustav Mahler, on the other hand, whose career would include composing nine symphonies, had been described as manic and morbid. As conductors, their paths would soon cross in the land of opportunity, America.

In May 1907, the Metropolitan Opera House summoned Mahler. Several months later, in February 1908, Arturo Toscanini also arrived. Quite suddenly, these two individuals who had been competitors and who were held in high esteem in two different European countries, soon become rival conductors at the same opera house. In time, Toscanini's great talent and genius as an interpreter of music scores would eclipse Mahler's efforts in conducting.

Arturo remained at the Metropolitan Opera House until 1915. Returning to Italy during World War I, he volunteered his services by leading a military band into battle at the Italian front. His bravery was widely reported when on one evening in August of 1917 under the siege of bullets and cannon shells from the Austrian batteries, Toscanini performed his music to motivate the soldiers to charge. A Silver Medal for valor was later awarded to him.

Five years after World War I, Toscanini returned to America with his hand-picked La Scala Orchestra touring America. In sixteen weeks, the orchestra gave sixty-eight concerts in dozens of North American cities. Two concerts in New York's Hippodrome alone attracted sixteen thousand fans. Everywhere the orchestra toured, it was tumultuously received.

It was in New Jersey that the orchestra made a number of "talking machine recordings" for the RCA Victor Company. Since that company had established a policy of "presenting recordings of only the greatest artists," this had a reciprocal effect. The fact that Toscanini was now recording for RCA served only to enhance the company's image and vice versa.

While performing at the New York Philharmonic during the years 1926 through 1936, Toscanini was regularly proclaimed the world's greatest conductor. Following this success, he subsequently conducted the NBC Symphony (1937-1954) that had been created for him by David Sarnoff, President of RCA. Working with Sarnoff, Toscanini's fame increased even more. According to an article in *Life* magazine, Toscanini was as well known as Joe DiMaggio. He would adorn the cover of *Time* magazine on two separate occasions.

Toscanini, known for his fiery temper, excitable disposition, high standards, and unusually good memory in recalling entire musical scores, made a lasting impression on the music world. Though an equally brilliant conductor of philharmonic music, Toscanini was primarily praised by the public for conducting the operas of Verdi and Puccini. He had to his credit many opera premieres, including Leoncavallo's *Pagliacci* (1892), Puccini's *La Bohème* (1896), and Musorski's *Boris Godunov* (1913). Married to Carla dei Martini, the daughter of a Milan banker in 1897, they had three children: Walter, Wally, and Wanda, who would marry the concert pianist Vladimir Horowitz. Toscanini died in New York City on January 16, 1957, and was buried in Milan, Italy.

General Sources:
1. Ewen, David. *The Story of Arturo Toscanini.* New York: Holt, 1951.
2. Haggin, B.H. *Conversations with Toscanini: Contemporary Recollections of the Maestro.* New York: Da Capo Press, 1989.
3. Horowitz, Joseph. *Understanding Toscanini: A Social History of American Concert Life.* Berkeley: University of California Press, 1994.
4. Taubman, Hyman Howard. *The Maestro: The Life of Arturo Toscanini.* Westport, CT: Greenwood Press, 1977.

—by TINA PIASIO

JOHN TRAVOLTA (1954-   )

A highly popular TV and movie star since the '70s, John Travolta first began as a hit actor in one of TV's most popular TV sitcoms, *Welcome Back, Kotter* (1975-79). He then dazzled audiences with a powerfully stylized disco dancing that was matched by an equally fitting portrayal of Tony Manero, a Brooklyn disco king in the film *Saturday Night Fever* (1977), so far his signature film.

Coupled with another great performance in the popular film version of *Grease* (1978), a musical that focused on song and dance in a 50s high school setting, Travolta went on to appear in *Urban Cowboy* (1980), a film to which has been attributed much of the popularization of Western apparel and country dance whose trends reached their peak in the 80s and still endure in today's marketplace. A handsome and appealing blue-eyed, robust male with an attractive cleft chin, he is at once both masculine and vulnerable. If he had made no other films or TV appearances, Travolta would still be remembered for his role in the *Kotter* TV sitcom series and in these three most popular films.

John Travolta was born on February 18, 1954, in Englewood, New Jersey, a town adjacent to New York City. He is the youngest of six children of an Italian father, Salvatore "Dut" Travolta, and an Irish mother, Helen (nee Burke) Travolta. His father was a businessman in the tire industry; and, his mother, a former actress and champion swimmer, taught in high school and was its drama teacher and director. Because of their mother's influence, Travolta and his siblings all playacted as youngsters in their basement world putting on shows for themselves and for their parents. Travolta was reported as saying that he enjoyed a happy childhood along with all of his siblings, and he attributed much of

their happiness to their parent's selflessness and to their motivational attitudes that empowered their children to do creative activities.

He started acting before audiences at age 12 performing in community drama and musicals, and he joined the Actors Studio Workshop in Englewood whose members performed for local dinner-theater productions. At the same time, he pursued dance lessons, including tap-dancing lessons from Gene Kelly's brother Fred. With parental consent, at age 16 he withdrew from high school and was soon doing summer stock in New Jersey. He moved on to making TV commercials, and within a year he was residing with one of his sisters in New York City. By age 18 he made his Off-Broadway theater debut in *Rain* and two years later did his Broadway debut in a WWII Andrew Sisters musical called *Over There!*

In December 1972 he managed to obtain a minor role in *Grease*'s first touring company which enabled him to travel nationwide for ten months. After auditioning with no success for a part in Jack Nicholson's film, *The Last Detail*, its casting director positioned Travolta for the role of Vinnie Barbarino in *Welcome Back, Kotter* (1975-79) series. There he played the role of a likeable underachiever who heads an innocuous street gang that is bent on challenging the patience and benevolence of their high school teacher (Kotter) played by Gabe Kaplan. Intended to be a supporting role, it turned out that Travolta's portrayal of Barbarino often usurped the energy from Kaplan's teacher role.

The five-year TV series was no doubt the pivotal point in Travolta's career; and the eight-year time frame that begins at the inception of the sitcom series in 1975 proved to be full of activity for Travolta, constituting what most critics thus far believe to be the high point of his career. This was also a tragic period in his personal life as the ravages of cancer snuffed out the lives of two people whom he loved, his mother, and his girlfriend, actress Diana Hyland.

After playing a bit part in a horror movie, *The Devil's Rain* (1975), he acquired his first substantial role in director Brian De Palma's *Carrie* (1976). Based on Stephen King's bestseller of the same name, it was a popular horror movie dealing with a young naive girl with telekinetic powers who is taunted by classmates. Travolta, who plays the role of one of those twisted teenage classmates, is killed by her. In the same year in an almost complete reversal in roles in a made-for-TV film, *The Boy in the Plastic Bubble* (1976), Travolta plays the poignant and tender role of a teenager who has no natural immune system and is compelled to live a life confined to a germ-free plastic room.

It was during this period that Travolta cut three successful music albums: *Can't Let You Go* (1976), *John Travolta* (1976), and *Travolta Fever* (1978). It was also at about this time that the film *Saturday Night Fever* (1977) swept the nation. It featured John Travolta as Tony Manero dancing to disco music in his white three-piece suit to the rhythms of an outstanding series of Bee-Gees hit songs. Released months ahead of schedule, the film went on to gross $350 million and made a bold statement about young America's lifestyle in the disco era of the '70s that would influence the dance scene in urban areas around the world.

Riding on his success, Travolta appeared a year later in the lead role as Danny Zucco, again dancing—this time to the rhythms of *Grease* (1978)—epitomizing the consummate "coolness" of the juke-box 50s era where souped-up cars, swooning high school sweethearts, and leather jackets all symbolized teenage nostalgia at its best. Despite the passage of over twenty years, the movie *Grease* has withstood its initial test of time and still remains a favorite among video store patrons.

Travolta concluded this fruitful phase with *Urban Cowboy* (1980), a film that effected a sudden craze for country dancing and an appeal for Western apparel. A sequel to *Saturday Night Fever*, *Staying Alive* (1983), though not as popular as the original, focused on Tony Manero, who now older, is faced with a different set of challenges in his life.

Travolta has been in more than 34 films, and his most recent films include: *Pulp Fiction* (1994), *Get Shorty* (1995), *Broken Arrow* (1996), *Michael* (1996), *Phenomenon* (1996), *Face-Off* (1997), *Mad City* (1997), *She's so Lovely* (1997), *The Thin Red Line* (1998), *A Civil Action* (1998), *Primary Colors* (1998), and *The General's Daughter* (1999). Travolta has been the recipient of many awards and honors. In 1976 he earned *Billboard*'s Best Male Vocalist Award. In 1977 he earned an Oscar nomination, a Golden Globe Award nomination, and a National Board of Review Award for Best Actor for *Saturday Night Fever*. He garnered several awards from many worldwide film organizations and an Oscar nomination and a Golden Globe nomination for Best Actor for his role in *Pulp Fiction*. An ardent follower of Scientology, a flyer and owner of no less than three jets, John Travolta has also written a book of fiction and a body-training manual.

General Sources:
1. *Contemporary Theatre, Film and Television.* Detroit, MI: Gale Research, 1995.
2. *Current Biography Yearbook.* New York: Wilson, 1996.
3. Katz, Ephraim. *The Film Encyclopedia.* New York: HarperCollins, 1998.
4. Simpson, Rachel. *John Travolta.* Philadelphia: Chelsea House, 1997.
5. Travolta, John. *Propeller One-way Coach: A Fable for All Ages.* New York: Warner Books, 1997.

—by IRENE LAMANO

JOHN TURTURRO (1957-   )

Winner of the Obie Award in 1984 for his performance in *Danny and the Deep Blue Sea* (1983) and winner of two Cannes Film Festival Awards, one for Best Actor in 1991 for his role as the tormented playwright in *Barton Fink* (1991) and the Camera d'Or Award for directing *Mac* (1992) his first directorial debut, John Turturro is well on his way to realizing greater success. Even before he won these awards, he had become unforgettable in the minds of many moviegoers for his role as an antagonistic racist as Pino the pizza man in Spike Lee's film classic *Do the Right Thing* (1989). Turturro, true to his personal value system, has often professed that he maintains a greater interest and concern about obtaining interesting roles in good movies than simply becoming star status material.

John Turturro was born on February 28, 1957 in New York City's borough of Brooklyn to Nicholas and Katherine Turturro. His father had emigrated from Italy as a child, and he earned his livelihood as a home builder. John was the middle child, having an older brother Ralph and a younger brother Nicholas, Jr. Their mother, a homemaker who had once worked as a jazz singer, encouraged her children to study and find expression in the arts. At one point in time, the Turturro family decided to move to the borough of Queens, where the boys did most of their growing up particularly in the areas of Hollis and Rosedale, which typically consisted of ethnically diversified middle-class populations.

Like many young boys John loved sports, particularly basketball and boxing, and he dreamed of becoming a star athlete one day. This notion became shattered when he broke his leg. It was during the recuperation process at home that he gratified himself with watching movies, making scrapbooks of movie actors, and not only writing biographies of his Hollywood favorites but also sketching plays and short stories. In his high school years, he reportedly became curiously obsessed with Broadway-style musicals and staged abbreviated versions of them with his family members. Both he and his younger brother Nicholas (also an actor) have attributed their acting talents and creative drives to their mother.

Enthusiastic about plays and films, John attended SUNY at New Paltz where he majored in drama. Appearing in his first play at college, he had the role of the Chief in *One Flew Over the Cuckoo's Nest*. This role proved to be pivotal in his determined decision to become, once and for all, a professional actor. He graduated in 1978 and avidly sought acting jobs in New York City. To support himself, he worked in a variety of areas including teaching history in a Harlem high school and helping out his father in the building industry.

One night, Turturro received what was to be only an apparent lucky break when Robert De Niro, attending a performance of *The Tooth of Crime*, liked Turturro's acting and suggested he contact Martin Scorsese. Turturro concluded this episode of his life by happily obtaining a bit part in Scorsese's Oscar-winning film, *Raging Bull* (1980), a dramatic and often violent film of Jake LaMotta's biography. Despite Turturro's appearance in this notable film and being around people of influence, it still remained difficult for him to get better acting parts. He questioned what he might do to better his situation as he distinctly hated the whole idea of knocking on doors and doing self-promotion. He applied at Yale's drama school and became one of fifteen applicants accepted from a pool of approximately nine hundred people.

In 1983, after he received his Masters in Fine Arts (M.F.A.) from Yale, he landed the lead role in a play entitled *Danny and the Deep Blue Sea* (1983) whose story line dealt with a misfit who finds love with a lonely woman. Lauded by many New York City critics for his excellent and incredibly realistic acting performance, it was no surprise when John Turturro went on to win an Obie Award in 1984. After receiving the Obie, he focused his time in attempting to enter the film industry. He indeed went on to appear in five or so movies which he deemed mediocre until he finally played a more satisfying role in *Five Corners* (1987) that would at last establish his name in film. Having been typecast in his earlier movies as a socially unappealing person (often of Italian descent), he played to the hilt a very credible portrayal of the role of Heinz Sabatino, a crazed "sociopath ex-convict" who in one shocking scene throws his mother out of a window.

Spike Lee, who admired Turturro's acting work in *Five Corners*, invited him to appear in what turned out to be a highly acclaimed film, *Do the Right Thing* (1989). Turturro appeared as Pino, the bigoted son of a pizza store owner (performed by Danny Aiello), whose pizzeria is located in what was once an all-Italian neighborhood that has now become predominantly black. In Lee's poignant and in-depth exploration of the dangers and difficulties of racial bigotry, Turturro's superb acting proved to be engagingly realistic and touched many a fine nerve in the movie viewer.

Turturro then moved on to different areas. Joining the Coen brothers, Joel and Ethan, Turturro did an excellent portrayal in *Miller's Crossing* (1990) in the role of a homosexual bookie; and rejoining Spike Lee to appear in *Mo' Better Blues* (1990), John Turturro and his brother Nicholas played the roles of two Jewish jazz club owners who regularly cheated and abused their black musicians. Once more, returning to the Coen brothers, John gained the title role in *Barton Fink* (1991), a subtle and difficult parody of a neurotic playwright and his frustrating bouts with creativity. Turturro's incredibly superb acting went very deep in the difficult portrayal of a character's recursively introspective absorption in totally self-centered doubt, despair, and ineptitude. At an intuitive level, Turturro's acting, its sense of timing, and particularly, its emotional understatement made the character seem all too human, and understandable, and in a sense forgivable. The film captured three awards at the 1991 Cannes Film Festival. The film itself won the Palme d'Or; Joel Coen won Best Director; and, of course, Turturro earned the Best Actor Award. A year later, Turturro won once more an award winner at the Cannes Film Festival—this time for Best New Director for his film *Mac* (1992).

Winner of an Obie Award (1984) together with two Cannes Film Festival Awards, his reputation has grown as a highly engaging and versatile quality actor of many memorable portrayals. John Turturro has indeed established himself in the eyes of many critics as someone who will excel still further. With a list of film credits numbering close to thirty where appearances have ranged from lead roles to bit parts, John Turturro is only at the beginning of his career. His future will presumably present him with a greater array of challenges both as actor and director where he will illuminate daring scripts into first-class drama.

General Sources:

1. *Contemporary Theatre, Film and Television.* Detroit, MI: Gale Research, 1997.
2. *Current Biography Yearbook.* New York: Wilson, 1996.
3. Katz, Ephraim. *The Film Encyclopedia.* New York: HarperCollins, 1998.
4. *Who's Who in America.* 1999 ed.

—by GEORGE CARPETTO, Ph.D.

JACK VALENTI (1921-   )

A highly decorated WWII B-25 pilot, a Harvard University M.B.A. graduate, an advertising executive, the radio and TV Texas campaign manager for the Kennedy-Johnson ticket, special assistant to President Lyndon Johnson at the White House, and an enterprising film industry executive, Jack Valenti has realized many goals in one actively intense and fulfilling lifetime. He has managed to blend creatively his administrative and organizational savvy with his critical writing talents as is so evident from his numerous books and articles.

Jack Joseph Valenti was born on September 5, 1921 in Houston, Texas, the son of a county tax office clerk in Houston and the grandson of Sicilian emigrants. He and his sister Lorraine were raised according to old world family traditions of hard work and responsibility. As a boy, he sold newspapers and worked in grocery stores; later, he also served as an usher in a Houston movie theater, his first working contact with films.

Valenti attended Sam Houston High School where he was an honor student, a debating champion, and at 15 years of age he became the youngest graduate in the city's history. A year later, he went to work as an office boy with the Humble Oil and Refining Company, and wanting to continue his education, he enrolled in night classes at the University of Houston in 1938.

During World War II, Valenti served as a B-25 attack bomber pilot in Italy with the rank of first lieutenant. He flew more than 51 missions with the Twelfth Air Force and was decorated with the Distinguished Flying Cross, the Air Medal with four clusters, the Distinguished Unit Citation with one cluster, and the European Theater Ribbon with four battle stars. After the war he returned to the United States where he worked during the day and studied at night attending the University of Houston. He majored in business and graduated with honors in 1946. He then went on to Harvard University Graduate School of Business Administration where he received a master's degree. In 1948 he returned to Humble Oil as head of its advertising and promotion area.

In 1952 Valenti started an advertising agency called Weekley & Valenti with Weldon Weekley, a colleague from Humble Oil. While Weekley ran the office, Valenti went out to recruit commercial clients including Continental Oil Company. The agency later expanded into political campaign advertising and handled TV and radio ads for the presidential campaign of John F. Kennedy and Lyndon B. Johnson in Texas in 1960.

Valenti had met Johnson, then a U.S. senator from Texas in 1955. It was the start of a long and fruitful collaboration that would continue into the White House when Johnson would succeed Kennedy as President upon Kennedy's assassination in Dallas on November 22, 1963. Valenti was present in Dallas on that fateful day. He had accompanied Johnson from Fort Worth to Dallas where Kennedy was to have delivered a major address. Valenti was also present in the presidential motorcade when Kennedy, riding in an open car, was shot in Dealey Plaza. Summoned by Johnson, Valenti helped to arrange for Vice President Johnson's swearing-in ceremony, which was held aboard Air Force One at the Dallas Airport, and he accompanied the new President on the flight to Washington, D.C.

At the White House Valenti was named

special assistant to President Johnson. Valenti occupied an office next to the Oval office. He served as expediter, troubleshooter, and right-hand man to Johnson, who delegated a variety of duties to him. They included the handling of Congressional relations, foreign appointments, and the study of papers and documents before they reached the Presidential desk. Valenti also edited speeches for Johnson and undertook several foreign missions on his behalf, including traveling to South Vietnam. He became in effect the "indispensable man" of the White House staff.

On June 1, 1966, Valenti left the White House to become president and CEO of the Motion Picture Association of America (MPAA). It was a reluctant move, dictated by family and economic considerations; however, Valenti remained in close contact with Johnson, serving the President on various occasions and accompanying him on several foreign trips.

The MPAA had been founded in 1922 in response to public reaction against purported immoral content of Hollywood films. A film production code, known as the Hayes Code, was established severely restricting the depiction of sexuality in film and going so far as to require even married couples to be shown sleeping in separate beds. By the 1960s the code had clearly become anachronistic.

Under Valenti the MPAA began revising it to reflect the more liberal times. The aim was to provide guidance to moviemakers in avoiding the problems of the past while ensuring the artistic quality of their films. Valenti himself devised the current voluntary movie ratings system which became effective on November 1, 1968. The new ratings system established for the first time a grading system so as to enable parents to decide for themselves whether they or their children should see a certain film. The system was subsequently revised in order to render it more practicable and acceptable to parents and movie audiences.

Valenti also initiated action to promote and protect the interests of the American film industry, both commercially and artistically, at home and abroad. Through its foreign subsidiaries, Valenti as chairman and CEO of the MPAA sought to expand the distribution of U.S. films abroad (such as to China and South Korea) while safeguarding film rights from unfair competition and piracy.

On June 1, 1962, Valenti and Mary Margaret Wiley, former aide to the then Vice President Johnson, were married. Today, they have three children, Courtenay, John, and Alexandra, and they live in the Washington, D.C. Georgetown area from which Valenti divides his time between MPAA headquarters in the capital and Los Angeles. Valenti travels extensively and continues to write articles for newspapers and magazines and other publications. He has also written articles on Voltaire, Macauly, and other literary figures. He has authored four books of which three are nonfiction.

The recipient of many awards and commendations both from government and the film industry, Valenti was decorated Knight of the Grand Cross by the Italian government in 1967, and he also received France's highest award, the Legion of Honor. He has his own star on the Walk of Fame in Hollywood honoring the film industry's greats. A seemingly untiring personality, he sets a superb example of dedication, innovation, and creative activity in his multi-faceted career.

General Sources:

1. *Contemporary Theatre, Film and Television*. Detroit, MI: Gale Research, 1987.
2. *Current Biography Yearbook*. New York: Wilson, 1968.
3. Katz, Ephraim. *The Film Encyclopedia*. New York: HarperCollins, 1998.
4. Valenti, Jack. Personal interview. 6 September 1998.

—by GABRIEL DE SABATINO

JIM VALVANO (1946-1993)

An active sportsman winning honors in high school and named Senior Athlete of the Year while attending New Jersey's Rutgers University, he went on to coach several college teams and brought North Carolina's basketball team to glory when they won the NCAA championship in 1983. After winning many awards that recognized his coaching and managerial qualities, he became a highly sought and respected sports commentator/analyst who worked for the ESPN-TV network. Struck with bone cancer, he fought back bravely, and during the ten-month battle with that fatal disease he established—with the assistance of ESPN—a foundation for cancer research.

Jim (James Thomas) Valvano was born in Queens, New York on March 10, 1946 to Rocco and Marie (nee Vitale) Valvano. He attended Seaford High School where he demonstrated great athletic prowess becoming the school's only athlete to receive all-league honors in three sports in the same year. He went on to college studies at Rutgers University (1964-1967) where after three years of sports activity, he was named Senior Athlete of the Year (1967) after he had led the Scarlet Knights to a third place finish in the NIT. After earning a B.A. in English, he remained at Rutgers as assistant to Bill Foster for two seasons (1967-69) as freshman coach, and for a time did postgraduate work.

After a one-year stint as head coach at Johns Hopkins University for the 1969-70 season, he decided to work for Dee Rowe at the University of Connecticut at Storrs as assistant coach; and after two seasons, he left becoming head coach once more at Bucknell University from 1972 to 1975 with a record of 33-42. Things began to change significantly between

1975-1980 when he coached at Iona College where he finished with a 99-47 record and achieved two National Collegiate Athletic Association (NCAA) appearances. The momentum continued when he was hired by North Carolina State University (NCSU), also called NC State. Valvano's nine seasons there from 1980 to 1989 earned him a record of 209-114. Valvano was, at first, its head coach and then in 1986 became its athletic director.

In 1983 NC State's basketball team, the Wolfpack, whose record was 29-10, went on to win the NCAA championship, becoming the first team to ever win the NCAA Tournament after losing ten or more games during the regular season. Upsetting the top-ranked Houston Cougars in one of the most memorable performances in basketball history, Valvano's Wolfpack won the game on a slam dunk with only seconds left to effect a score of 54-52. Valvano concluded his coaching career at NC State in 1989. In addition to being 346-212 in his 19 seasons as an NCAA head coach, he appeared in eight NCAA Tournaments and captured a National Championship with NC State in 1983 leading its Wolfpack to a record of 209-114, and this included two ACC titles and three NCAA final eight finishes.

Before Valvano began his new career as a sportscaster, a book appeared on the market that made some strong accusations against his integrity. The book entitled *Personal Fouls* was written by Peter Golenbock, and it appeared in early January of 1989. In no uncertain terms, the writer accused Valvano and his staff of many disreputable acts including fixing grades, hiding drug test results, and diverting millions of dollars from the alumni club and paying off the players with cars. The NCAA investigation lasted eight long months and found Valvano guilty of nothing. However, NC State did incur a minor penalty, losing eligibility for the 1990 NCAA tournament and a two-year probation because some players had sold complimentary tickets and sneakers.

Valvano became a commentator/analyst for ESPN in 1991 for NCAA basketball, and not surprisingly that year he went on to win an ACE for excellence in cable television sports analysis. A year later in June 1992, Valvano was diagnosed with bone cancer after which he took a respite from his work to fight the disease. Through the media the public was made aware of Valvano's fatally difficult confrontation with the dreaded disease, and he quickly became known for his determination and strong will not to "ever give up" in the fight. He returned to ESPN as its color commentator during the preseason National Invitational Tournament (NIT) in November '92.

While time was running out for Valvano in 1993, he attended in Raleigh on February 21, NC State's celebration of the 10th Anniversary of its 1983 NCAA Basketball Championship. Two weeks later on March 4, Valvano received the Arthur Ashe Award for Courage at ESPN's very first ESPY's Award Show. It was during this program that, among other things, Valvano announced in his speech to the audience that in cooperation with ESPN he was starting The V Foundation for Cancer Research.

In his relatively brief but poignant talk, he encouraged people to live each day with laughter, with thought, and with feeling. He saw those as the three major ingredients that balanced human beings need in order to face each day of their lives. He also reiterated his fondness for his idol Vince Lombardi and Lombardi's motivational and inspirational film, *Commitment to Excellence*, citing the importance of family and religion in one's life. In addition to quoting Lombardi, Valvano also took the opportunity to quote Ralph Waldo Emerson in reference to encouraging people to be excited about life and to follow one's goals with alacrity: "Nothing great could be accomplished without enthusiasm."

Jim Valvano, proud of his Italian heritage, had served as a member of Lee Iacocca's Statue of Liberty Commission in 1986 where funds were raised for the statue's partial restoration and for the development of a newly envisioned Museum for Immigrants by reconditioning the remains of the immigration processing centers left abandoned on Ellis Island located not far from Liberty Island (Statue of Liberty) in New York City harbor. Jim Valvano also authored several books including *Too Soon to Quit*, *Jim Valvano's Guide to Great Eating*, *My Side*, and *They Gave Me a Lifetime Contract and Then They Declared me Dead*.

Jim Valvano leaves a legacy of hard work and dedication to what was in many ways a uniquely multi-faceted lifelong commitment to sports, excelling as a player, as a commentator, and as a writer. At age 47, Jim Valvano died on April 28, 1993 after an intense battle with bone cancer. About a month after his death, he was inducted into Rutgers University Basketball Hall of Fame.

General Sources:
1. Douchant, Mike, ed. *Encyclopedia of College Basketball*. Detroit, MI: Gale Research, 1995.
2. Savage, Jim. *The Encyclopedia of the NCAA Basketball Tournament*. New York: Dell, 1990.
3. Smith, G. "As Time Runs Out." *Sports Illustrated* 11 Jan. 1993: 10-14+.
4. Smith, G. "Obituary." *Sports Illustrated* 10 May 1993: 72.
5. Valvano, Jim. *Valvano: They Gave Me a Lifetime Contract, and Then They Declared Me Dead*. New York: Pocket Books, 1991.
6. *Who's Who in America*. 1993 ed.

—by DIANA VERICELLA

ROBERT CHARLES VENTURI (1925-)

One of the most original architects produced by the United States in recent history, Robert Venturi has demonstrated great leadership in having broken away from what has been called modern functional design. He is an architect who not only studied and appreciated the architecture from the recent and remote past but has also heeded the warnings and suggestions of contemporary urban sociologists who were concerned with urban sprawl and the dehumanization of the social milieu. In this context, Venturi has been credited for having clearly created a post-modernist movement in architecture. Controversial to many wedded to modernism, Venturi has been labeled counterrevolutionary to the modernist cause of functional design. Functionalism has been related to the Bauhaus School (1919-1933) in Germany, established by Walter Gropius who had emphasized functional design in architecture.

To a considerable degree, Venturi's postmodernist shift emanated from his seminal book, *Complexity and Contradiction in Architecture* (1966) that advocated a re-definition of what is associated with the term "modern" when referring to architecture. As a necessary condition to achieve a proper re-definition of what is modern, Venturi insisted that one must deal with "issues such as history, language, form, symbolism and the dialects of high and popular art" whose meaning and interpretation must then be integrated into the so-called modern. In short, the cold, hard, purely functional operational world suggested by the ongoing American functional modern architecture was no longer acceptable to Venturi. With functionalism it seemed as if people and their roles, their societal needs, their history, and their cultural values had been abrogated. It was therefore Venturi's strong desire to retrieve those elements and rightly reintegrate them into what is modern.

Robert Charles Venturi was born on June 25, 1925, in Philadelphia, Pennsylvania. He was the only child of Robert Charles, Sr. and Vanna (nee Lanzetta) Venturi. After attending an Episcopal Academy in Philadelphia where he graduated in 1944, he attended Princeton University to study architecture. In 1947, he graduated as a Phi Beta Kappa student with his B.A. degree in architecture *summa cum laude*. He remained at Princeton to pursue graduate work where he later became a recipient of a Palmer scholarship. In 1950, he graduated as a Master of Fine Arts that offered him a backdrop and a broader perspective. It would eventually serve him as an integrating tool and as an historically-based means for dealing with what he perceived as unacceptable and dehumanizing in the areas of modern functional architecture.

After his education at Princeton University, Venturi acquired experience working as a designer in two architectural firms, and in 1954 and 1956 he won the Rome Prize Fellowship which allowed him to study in Italy's capital and resume the formal aspects of education whereby the ongoing cultural growth enjoyed a symbiotic effect on his architectural perspectives. When he returned home to Philadelphia, Venturi had the fortunate opportunity to work for Louis I. Kahn.

It seems that both architects upheld philosophies that in many respects reflected a kindred spirit where admiration for past architectural achievements blended with many present techniques and values. In some ways, Kahn served as Venturi's mentor for a while, but they differed in that Venturi placed a growing emphasis on social contexts and concerns, much more than Kahn would be willing to admit. While maintaining close ties with Kahn, Venturi left the firm in 1958, and in Philadelphia he attempted his first partnership, Venturi, Cope and Lippincott. Three year later, Venturi started his second partnership, Venturi and Short, and then his third, named Venturi and Rauch. Since his return from Italy in 1957, he taught at the University of Pennsylvania where by 1965 he became an associate professor.

The year 1966 proved to be a pivotal period in his life. Venturi began teaching at Yale University in its architectural program, and he also returned to Italy to lecture as an architect in residence at the American Academy in Rome and, later, as visiting lecturer at the University of California at Los Angeles. In all, 1966 was a busy year because during this time he also published his much quoted fundamental text *Complexity and Contradiction in Architecture*. Many architectural specialists and critical thinkers akin to Venturi's philosophies have since considered that publication crucial for understanding Venturi's outright rejection of an architectural mentality that in the forty years prior to his 1966 book had proclaimed itself the orthodoxy of modern architecture.

For the architectural purists of the modern orthodox school, always striving to preserve the objective of a "pure, clear ordered, functional design" of a utopian unity unimpeded by the so-called "corrupting influences of the traditional," Venturi responds with many paradoxical replies. For instance, he says that he prefers the *hybrid* over the *pure*, the *redundant* over the *simple*, and the *accommodating* over the *exclusionary*. In short, he righteously asserted that he preferred employing old decorative themes as opposed to fostering the new, distancing, cold, stripped-down thematics of massive business buildings.

When Venturi made the paradoxical statement, "I am for messy vitality over obvious unity," he heartily encouraged the "apparent irrationality of a part" of any architecture if eventually it can be "justified by the resultant rationality of the whole." That is why he viewed the purists as strangely myopic in their thought, refusing to acknowledge the obvious truth that elements that might have been viewed as disparate to those within a *prior* architectural period seem to us today surprisingly unified.

As author and coauthor of several books, and, of course, as the subject of hundreds of books and articles and, therefore, one of the most quoted architects in recent times, Robert Venturi has done much to raise the awareness levels of both architects and the public in focusing on the relationship between building design and people, their needs, activities, and sense of belonging. In attempting to understand and then illustrate this relationship, he has developed a philosophy linking past and present societies via the study of the undeniably reciprocal influence generated between people's needs (especially their sense of belonging) and their surrounding architectural environments.

General Sources:
1. *Contemporary Architects*. Detroit, MI: Gale Research, 1993.
2. *Current Biography Yearbook*. New York: Wilson, 1975.
3. *Encyclopedia of American Architecture*. 1995 ed.
4. Venturi, Robert. *Complexity and Contradiction in Architecture*. New York: Museum of Modern Art, 1966.
5. Venturi, Robert. *Iconography and Electronics Upon a Generic Architecture*. Cambridge, MA: MIT Press, 1996.
6. Venturi, Robert, et al. *Learning from Las Vegas: The Forgotten Symbolism of Architectural Form*. Cambridge, MA: MIT Press, 1972.

—by GEORGE CARPETTO, Ph.D.

GIANNI VERSACE (1946-1997)

Fashion designer of men's and women's clothing, innovatively blending disparate fabrics and styles, and technologically integrating woven metal and silk or leather and rubber, author of several books on fashion design, he rose from the relatively small industrial town of Reggio Calabria where he assisted his talented mother design and tailor clothing for local patrons to the heights of fashion-conscious clienteles and fashion-center cities like Milan, Paris, London, and New York.

Ever since his designer clothes came into being in 1978 bearing his own label, he became immediately associated as an equal to the superstars of the fashion industry. His designs were so inventive that a number of them have been included as part of various permanent collections gracing the galleries in many renowned museums throughout the world such as the Art Institute of Chicago, the Metropolitan Museum of Art in New York, and the Tokyo Fashion Institute.

He was born on December 2, 1946 in Reggio Calabria, a town situated at the very toe of the Italian peninsula that faces the straits of Messina and is across from the island of Sicily. Gianni was the second of three children; his sister Donatella and his brother Santo have since also become involved in fashion and remain today in respectfully high positions in the industry. Their father Antonio was an appliance salesman; and their mother Francesca was a boutique owner, dressmaker, and a rather gifted designer herself.

Gianni avowed that he learned all the basics he needed to know from his talented mother and that he knew from his early years that he wanted to be a fashion designer. His mother's shop had become for him like a playground where he exercised his mind designing projects and his hands cutting materials, sewing things together into something new and creative. Gianni often mentioned that he remembered so vividly the day when in his mother's shop he watched his mother drape a piece of black velvet around the body of a rather beautiful woman and the esthetic effect it would have on him. It was a mental image and a corresponding feeling from his childhood years that he would never forget. It remained crystallized in his memory, marking one of those inspirationally esthetic moments captured in time.

In addition to these deep ruminations for wanting to design clothing as early as seven years of age, he also desired in his teenage years to study music and art away from home in Rome. But out of respect for his mother's wishes to remain locally, he also acquiesced to his father's desire for him to study architectural draftsmanship, and he indeed earned the title of land surveyor by the age 18. Yet instead of pursuing work in the world of construction and architecture, he decided to focus on being a part-time buyer for his mother's dress business. As he attended more and more fashion shows in Rome, Milan, and Paris, he desired less and less the world of architecture and construction.

By the time he was 22 years old, Gianni was creating his own clothing designs. He so impressed a local clothing manufacturer that Gianni was commissioned to design a small collection of clothing which would be, of course, manufactured locally and then displayed and distributed in local businesses like Gianni's mother's boutique. They had arranged a small fashion show in Reggio Calabria displaying Gianni's recent works. It seems that his creations caught on not only in that part of the Italian peninsula but also in Milanese fashion circles by word of mouth. This crucially important episode took place in 1970, a pivotal year in his life, whereby a Milanese manufacturer subsequently invited Gianni to work in Milan to do more fashion designing.

After Gianni accepted the invitation and worked there for two years, he also began doing freelance work for well-known companies such as Complice, Callaghan and Genny, initiating his *prêt-à-porter* (ready-to-wear) designs. In 1978 working for himself, he designed his first collection of women's ready-to-wear clothing under his own label. That year in Milan, his work was successfully presented at a fashion show at Palazzo della Permanente, and he opened his own boutique. By September, he also presented his first menswear collection under his label. Four years later in 1982, Versace achieved what perhaps best defined his creative personality. In collaboration with German engineers, he created the woven metal mesh dress.

Taking this prototype one step further, he treated the lightweight metal mesh with an anodizing process, i.e., treating the mesh with an electrolytic coating (as is often done with jewelry) making it impervious to weather and other external conditions. The anodized mesh could then be matched and merged side by side with creative blends of cotton, silk, wool, leather, or suede. From his experimentations, Gianni achieved a new level of creativity by utilizing laser technology to attach leather to rubber materials in a permanent bond which entirely eliminated the necessity of stitching. Innovations like these constituted what allowed Versace's fame to flourish rather quickly in the fashion industry, earning his designs permanent status in art museums worldwide.

In his relatively brief lifetime, Versace earned numerous awards and honors both for men's and women's fashion designs. These included winning in 1982 his first of four of Italy's L'Occhio d'Oro awards for best fashion design, France's Grande Medaille de Vermeil de la Ville de Paris (1986) and the United States American Fashion Oscar Award (1993). His designs were used in theatrical productions, operatic programs, and fashion shows in cities such as Milan, Paris, Brussels, Frankfurt, Berlin, London, Leningrad, and New York.

Claiming distribution in 130 boutiques worldwide, Versace's worth was recently placed at being just under $1 billion. A family company, it is run essentially by Gianni's older brother Santo and younger sister Donatella, who are both designers. Because of Gianni's influence, he had licensed his name to many fashion-related manufacturers whose products include sunglasses, fragrances, lingerie, bathing merchandise, and footwear.

On July 15, 1997, at the entrance to his Miami Beach mansion, Gianni Versace, at the age of 50, lost his life, shot twice in the head allegedly at the hands of a one-time friend, Andrew Cunanan, who later in turn was also found dead. While Gianni's death still remains veiled in mystery, his passion for life, fashion esthetics, business, and writing came to an abrupt halt all too quickly. One can only imagine what else he could have invented or designed if his life had not ended so soon.

General Sources:
1. *Current Biography Yearbook.* New York: Wilson, 1993; 1997.
2. Martin, Richard. *Gianni Versace.* New York: Metropolitan Museum of Art, 1997.
3. "Obituary." *New York Times* 16 July 1997: 1.
4. Turner, Lowri. *Gianni Versace: Fashion's Last Emperor.* London: Bainbridge Books, 1997.
5. Versace, Gianni. *Rock and Royalty.* New York: Abbeville Press, 1996.

—by CARMELA NESCI

EDWARD VILLELLA (1939-   )

Edward Villella rose from a tough, blue-collar neighborhood in Queens, New York to become one of America's greatest ballet artists and directors. Once a scrappy, athletic kid who especially loved baseball, Edward reluctantly used to tag along to his older sister's ballet classes, but with time in an ironic twist he became engrossed by the movement and the motion of ballet, and he developed a passion for it. In his lifetime, he became a winner of many national and international awards for dance. He has also been a member of the National Endowment for the Arts, and in 1985 he became the founding artistic director of the well-known Miami City Ballet.

Born on October 1, 1939 in Bayside, Queens, Villella, like most boys his age, typically enjoyed sports and was not considered as having a penchant for any of the arts despite the fact that his father was a part-time jazz musician and his mother often spoke of her dreams of a career in dance. Edward's parents, Joseph and Mildred (nee di Giovanni) Villella, had both immigrated to the United States from Italy and had met for the first time years later at a dance hall where Joseph led a dance band and where Mildred and her friends went for dancing and entertainment. Mildred would sit with Joseph during the band breaks and their romance soon blossomed.

Joseph, a quiet, hard-working man, drove a truck to earn a living to support his family. Mildred, who was orphaned as an infant, had few opportunities, it seems, in her earlier years to have developed a professional dancing career. Her disappointment was known to her family members, and she encouraged her two children all the more to succeed, pushing them up the ladder of personal development.

Edward's sister Carolyn, whom Edward called Carol, used her talent at the piano and as a student at the Anne Garrison School of Dance. When Edward suffered a serious head injury while playing sandlot baseball, his mother took him along to his sister's dance lessons so that she could keep an eye on him. After enduring many hours of watching the young ballerinas, Edward was invited to take lessons. Reluctantly, at his mother's insistence, he agreed.

Edward used to wear his baseball outfit to ballet practice, but soon his friends discovered what he was up to, and he had to endure the taunting that went along with being a boy doing ballet. Although Edward did not feel he fit into the world of ballet at first, he enjoyed the physical thrill of twisting and turning, and before long he looked forward to each lesson. When Carol was accepted at George Balanchine's School of American Ballet (SAB) in Manhattan, Mildred suggested that her 10 year-old Edward go along. Thrilled to get any male who would be willing to do ballet and dance, the SAB quickly accepted Edward.

Edward quickly found a place at SAB and attended for five years of dance training on a full scholarship program while getting his academic education at the New York City High School of Performing Arts. At SAB, he marveled at performers like Jerome Robbins and Robert Joffrey who danced and taught there. In another peculiar twist of fate at age fifteen Edward was requested by his mother to quit ballet. He switched educational tracks and prepared for something different by first attending the Rhodes School in Manhattan and then later enrolling at the New York Maritime College, which was closer to his home in Queens. In college he pursued football, baseball, and boxing. He went on to win the campus welterweight boxing championship and was a member of the varsity baseball team.

On Christmas night in 1955, Villella was assaulted by a thief and suffered a serious brain concussion. In the long recuperative process, he secretly resumed taking dance lessons in New York as a form of therapy for his injury while still attending the Maritime College. To earn money for his dance lessons, he would sell beer to fellow students at the college, a serious violation of school rules. He further violated policy by having to sneak out for lessons three times a week, either walking along the seawall or being transported out of the school facility in the trunk of a friend's car.

Since the Maritime College offered travel to Europe, Villella seized the opportunity knowing he would be able to visit some of Europe's finest dance studios. When he returned to the United States, he made the decision to return to dance full-time much to the anger and disappointment of his parents who now refused to talk to him. The NYC Ballet welcomed him so quickly that he did not have time to complete the final semester at the Maritime College in 1957 and would not complete his degree for another two years until 1959. In the fall of 1957 on his 21st birthday, Villella officially joined the NYC Ballet Company and became part of its dance corps, and things began to move rapidly.

Within weeks Villella was chosen by Jerome Robbins as the lead male dancer in *Afternoon of the Faun*. Later, he discovered that Robbins had written the ballet with the younger 16-year-old Villella in mind after seeing him one afternoon standing at the window of the SAB years earlier. In the fall of 1958, Villella also danced in the principal role of *Symphony in C*. His parents who were present at this performance ended their estrangement with their son Edward with tearful embraces. Villella went on to dance some of the greatest roles in the NYC Ballet repertory. These included *Prodigal Son, Tarantella, A Midsummer Night's Dream,*

Jewels, Dances at a Gathering, and many others with powerful and passionate performances.

After many years of dance performance and stage experience, he eventually ventured into directing choreography. Villella first was artistic coordinator of the Eglevsky Ballet from 1979 to 1984 and then became the director of the Oklahoma Ballet from 1983 to 1985. He became a principal figure in enhancing and popularizing the role of the male performer in ballet. His efforts at augmenting the role of male dancers proved exciting, and they were well received. He himself moved from lead dancer to behind-the-scenes artistic director and planner. His power, grace, and passion made the male role, which had been traditionally that of protecting the female artist, more visible and significant throughout the ballet world.

Villella has continued to be a leading advocate for ballet in America. He was the winner of the 38th Annual Capezio Dance Award, and he has served on the National Endowment for the Arts Dance Advisory Panel. In 1985, he became the founding artistic director of the Miami City Ballet and remains active in that organization which has since won honors worldwide. Villella and his wife Linda have a son and two daughters. In the hearts and minds of ballet lovers, he is reputed as one of the world's most gifted artists and choreographers.

General Sources:

1.   Chujoy, Anatole. *The New York City Ballet: The First Twenty Years.* New York: Da Capo Press, 1982.
2.   *International Dictionary of Ballet.* Detroit; MI: St. James Press, 1993.
3.   *International Encyclopedia of Dance.* New York: Oxford Univ. Press, 1998.
4.   Villella, Edward, and Larry Kaplan. *Prodigal Son: Dancing for Balanchine in a World of Pain and Magic.* New York: Simon & Schuster, 1992.

—by JANET B. TUCCI

HENRY VISCARDI, JR. (1912-   )

Born with a physical disability, he exceeded expectations at school and at work, and he later created innovative programs both for the disabled soldiers returning home from WWII and for the disabled in general. Historically, he represented the post-WWII wake-up call to both the armed forces and industry that the disabled were citizens who were due their training, acceptance, respect, and jobs. Anticipating and indeed setting the stage for major reforms many of which would not materialize until decades later, he was a principal force in the advancement and respect for the rehabilitation of the disabled in America in this century. For this reason, he was a consultant to practically every President in the last 50 years.

Henry Viscardi, Jr., was born on May 10, 1912 in Manhattan, New York City. His immigrant parents, Henry and Anna (nee Esposito) Viscardi, had five children of whom Henry, Jr. was the second oldest child and the only boy. His sisters were Theresa, the oldest, followed by Lillian, Victoria, and Rose. Coming into this world with unusual circumstances, young Henry was born without feet or knees. As a child, he spent the first six years of his life in hospital charity wards and at the Hospital for Deformities and Joint Diseases in Manhattan's Upper East Side where through surgery doctors did all they could to make him mobile. For legs he had two stumps encased in padded boots.

Because Henry's arms almost touched the ground as he moved around on his short legs, many neighborhood children called him the "ape man." By the time he was ten years old and about to enter the fifth grade, the family decided to move to Elmhurst, Queens (New York). Gifted with many emotional strengths particularly a strong will, he learned to deal with that nickname, excelling in school work compressing twelve years of elementary and high school education into eight years, and graduating at eighteen.

When he attended Newtown High School in Queens, he had acquired a great interest in sports, and he became manager of the basketball team. His father Henry, Sr., a barber who owned his own shop, died while his son was still in high school. Young Henry helped the family finances by working as a basketball referee and as a school sports reporter for the *New York Times*. After high school he attended Fordham University in 1930.

In order to pay for part of his tuition, he worked at many jobs including that of busboy in the dining hall, a library assistant, switchboard operator, and administrative clerk. Yet because of insufficient funds, he dropped out of college in 1933. Working as a clerk in the law firm of Gellman and Gellman in Corona, Queens, he became acquainted with the local operations of the newly formed Home Owners Loan Corporation (HOLC). Soon he found himself accepting a position in HOLC's taxation division in New York City. The traveling and the job proved too intense for his legs. He subsequently withdrew from the evening courses he had been taking all along at St. John's University in another borough, and he was unable to complete his senior year of college.

In 1936 with the help of Dr. Robert R. Yanover, a Long Island surgeon, he made the acquaintance of a Manhattan prosthesis specialist, George Dorsch. Challenged by the fact that prior specialists had said it would be close to impossible to make a workable prosthetic appliance for Henry, Dorsch went on to disprove them. With experimentation and time, Dorsch not only designed and fitted Henry with a pair of artificial legs which increased Henry's height by two feet but also taught him to balance himself so well that he was now able to enjoy things he had never before experienced. While having to bear only a slightly "perceptible limp" to his gait, the success of this event took place in 1938, and Henry remembers this as the "springtime" of his life where "every hour was the exploration of a new world."

The rest of Henry's life goes on to reveal a dramatic reflection and enactment of his new strengths and powers which he devoted to aiding the disabled. With the advent of WWII, he wanted to join the armed forces to help amputees adjust to their physical situation. Rejected by the Army, the Navy, and the Marines, he finally found acceptance in the Red Cross. He became a special field service officer in training at Fort Dix, New Jersey. Later he was assigned to Walter Reed Hospital in Washington, D.C. where from 1943 to 1945 he became an adviser to disabled veterans in their search for meaningful employment.

Viscardi indeed worked with disabled war veterans, but he became frustrated by the inadequacies of rehabilitation programs both within the armed forces and within the public sector. He openly challenged the *status quo*, but while his petitions were dismissed by many, his prophetic voice made an impact on some people of influence such as Eleanor Roosevelt and Colonel Howard A. Rusk (M.D.), an Air Force Medical Officer. Viscardi challenged the armed services and industry at large to respect the disabled by training and hiring them. That became his lifetime mission statement.

In 1948 Dr. Rusk became director of physical medicine and rehabilitation at New York University's Bellevue Medical Center. Heeding the challenges established by Viscardi's pleas for helping the disabled, he founded in 1949 Just One Break (JOB), a corporation of which Orin Lehman, an amputee from the war, became its president. Later in 1949 Viscardi joined JOB as its executive director. This was the first program of its kind in that it mapped out the use of the media to disseminate information regarding the disabled and to place individuals at work. Essentially, it was an effort to change attitudes in industry and in labor in effecting fair and just treatment of the disabled.

In 1952 Viscardi founded Abilities, Inc. in West Hempstead, Long Island where people with disabilities earned competitive wages and benefits doing contract work, manufacturing for major corporations. In the late 1950s, Dr. Viscardi moved his program to Albertson, Long Island. In 1962, he also founded a school for children with severe physical disabilities and a vocational rehabilitation program to help disabled adults receive proper training and job placement. This facility, known as the National Center for Disability Services, serves over 2,000 people.

Dr. Viscardi retired in 1981, but he remains a member of the board of directors as its founder and director emeritus. He received the Horatio Alger Award for Distinguished Americans in 1983 and the Andrus Award in 1992. He has been an advisor to every U.S. President since WWII in matters of the nation's disabled citizens. In addition to many honors and citations, he holds 25 honorary degrees. He and his wife Lucille live in Kings Point. They have raised four daughters, and have nine grandchildren and two great-grandchildren.

General Sources:
1. *Current Biography/Yearbook*. New York: Wilson, 1954; 1966.
2. Viscardi, Henry. *Give Us the Tools*. New York: Eriksson, 1959.
3. Viscardi, Henry. *A Letter to Jimmy*. New York: Eriksson, 1962.
4. Viscardi, Henry. *The Phoenix Child: A Story of Love*. New York: Eriksson, 1975.

—by DENNIS PIASIO

JOHN ANTHONY VOLPE (1908-1994)

John Anthony Volpe, businessman, engineer, administrator in Eisenhower's federal highway program, governor of Massachusetts, Secretary of Transportation in the Nixon cabinet, Ambassador to Italy, and publisher of two Massachusetts newspapers (*Malden News*, *Medford Daily Mercury*), is recognized for many years of excellence in public service. A multitalented Italian American of immigrant parents, he has earned respect and admiration not only for having utilized his diversified energies but also for having graced the highest levels of government with integrity.

He was born on December 8, 1908 in Wakefield, Massachusetts, the son of Vito and Filomena (nee Benedetto) Volpe both of whom were emigrants from a village near Teramo in the Abruzzi area of Italy. John, the second of five children (four boys and one girl), attended Malden High School where his extracurricular activities included track and orchestra. Unable to attend the Massachusetts Institute of Technology to study engineering because his father's business had failed, he graduated high school in 1926 and subsequently entered the workforce as a journeyman plasterer.

In 1928, he enrolled in the Wentworth Institute in Boston for its evening study program where he majored in architectural construction. He graduated in 1930 and began working as a timekeeper for a Boston construction firm. In March 1933, in the midst of the depression era and many financial struggles, he boldly founded the John A. Volpe Construction Company. In 1934, he married Jennie Benedetto, a nurse by profession.

Despite the difficulties of the economic depression of the era, his company prospered steadily into the 1940s, and it was only because he decided to join the Navy in 1943 that he temporarily shut down his firm. He volunteered for the Navy Civil Engineer Corps, and after his training period he was commissioned a lieutenant. He in turn trained Seabees (construction and engineering) in Camp Peary, Virginia for part of the war; and for the remainder, he spent time in Washington working in the Bureau of Naval Personnel interviewing candidates for the Civil Engineer Corps. His three brothers followed in his footsteps and joined the Navy. Discharged in 1946 with the rank of lieutenant commander, Volpe went on to receive the Navy's Civilian Service Award for outstanding service.

Volpe then began the process of resuscitating his construction company from its inactivity. Taking full advantage of his talents and experiences in engineering, his company moved swiftly in the next fifteen years building structures of all kinds both in Massachusetts and in other parts of the country. This included construction of schools, hospitals, military installations, and the latest showpiece in construction, shopping centers. With offices in Massachusetts and in Miami, Florida during that decade-and-a-half, his company had grown into a multimillion-dollar organization.

While nurturing the growth of his construction firm, he also had become involved in Republican politics. In 1950 after he was elected deputy chairman of the Republican State Committee, he also became an alternate delegate to the Republican National Convention two years later. Appointed by the governor as commissioner of public works for Massachusetts in 1953, he reorganized the structure, policies, and practices of that department at the state level. Meanwhile Volpe had also captured President

Eisenhower's attention since the President soon appointed him interim Federal Highway Administrator in 1956.

In 1958, Volpe seemed to be the frontrunner in the Republican party's choice for governor. Then, after much internal party debate, he won the Republican nomination and went on to defeat his Democratic opponent, Joseph Ward. When he began his first two-year term office in January 1961, he found himself in a strange situation; he was both the new governor and the only elected Republican who now had to deal with an all-Democratic cabinet. Despite this seemingly disparate situation, he did well as governor and returned to that office in 1965-66 and 1967-68.

When President Nixon appointed Volpe Secretary of Transportation in 1969, this event made him the third Italian American to hold a cabinet post. His accomplishment was preceded by that of Charles Bonaparte who had been Attorney General in the early 1900s in the Theodore Roosevelt Administration and by Anthony Celebrezze who was the head of HEW beginning in 1962 in the Kennedy administration and in the subsequent Johnson administration. As transportation secretary, Volpe had a twofold plan for urban transportation infrastructures and for the national highway system.

His plan embodied improving the transit infrastructure of urban areas while setting up a highway network known as the Interstate Highway System. While these plans indicated the way of the future in facilitating modern national transportation, he did not always get financial support and backing from Congress. Among other things, he also was a leading supporter of the supersonic jet transport (SST) as well as an endorser of nationwide no-fault insurance programs.

When Nixon was reelected in 1972 and restructured his cabinet, Volpe was assigned the ambassadorship post in Italy where he served for the next four years (1973-77). It was an uneasy and often challenging job since it was during this period that Italy was plagued with strikes, threats of terrorism, and anti-American sentiment against U.S. activities in Vietnam.

After 1977, John Volpe returned to private life, gave lectures, and still headed conferences on governmental matters. He was reputed as having received 34 honorary degrees, and his lifetime record also indicates his active involvement in many charitable causes and his loyal participation in many civic and cultural organizations such as the Order Sons of Italy in America. When he died at age 86 on November 11, 1994 in Nahunt, Massachusetts, he left a legacy of an Italian American who had held many lofty and responsible positions in government and had been an entrepreneur in construction whose responsibilities he performed with incredible energy and integrity.

General Sources:
1. *Current Biography Yearbook*. New York: Wilson, 1962; 1995.
2. Geiger, Theodore, John Volpe, and Ernest H. Pregg. *North American Integration and Economic Blocs*. London, UK: Trade Policy Research Centre, 1975.
3. Kilgore, Kathleen. *John Volpe: The Life of an Immigrant's Son*. Dublin, NH: Yankee Books, 1987.
4. Volpe, John. *Assessing U.S. Competitiveness in World Markets*. Washington, DC: International Division, Chamber of Commerce, 1979.
5. Volpe, John. *Industrial Incentive Policies and Programs in the Canadian-American Context*. Montreal: Canadian-American Committee, 1976.
6. Volpe, John. *Relazioni fra Italia e Stati Uniti, Presente e Futuro*. Roma, IT: Banco di Roma, 1974.
7. *Who's Who in Government*. 1973 ed.

—by ROSE MARIE BONIELLO

HARRY WARREN (1893-1981)

Composer, songwriter, and winner of three Academy Awards, Harry Warren led a full and creative life, writing for stage and screen in a career that spanned almost sixty years. As a self-taught musician, he composed more than three hundred popular songs in collaboration with lyricists Al Dublin, Johnny Mercer, Mack Gordon, Ira Gershwin, and Billy Rose. In his early years of show business, he wrote mostly for Broadway shows and worked closely with Billy Rose, but in 1931 he officially moved to California to work for the Warner Brothers Film Studios. The "talkies" had already supplanted silent movies in the late 20s, and the Hollywood of the 30s had replaced New York City as the film capital of the United States. With composers like Harry Warren seasoned by Broadway hits, Hollywood was now ready for the era of motion picture musical extravaganzas, going well beyond what could be done on the Broadway stage. In 1935 Harry Warren went on to win his first Academy Award for *Lullaby of Broadway*, and his career would continue to flourish for decades to come.

Salvatore Guaragna, better known later as Harry Warren, was born on Christmas Eve 1893 to Anthony and Rachel (nee DeLuca) Guaragna in Brooklyn, New York. Salvatore, who would not change his name until 1926 when he decided to publish his more recent songs under his stage name, was the eleventh and last child of the family. His father was a bootmaker who barely managed to provide the basics for such a large family. With no discretionary monies available to enhance Salvatore's early inclinations towards a musical career, he took advantage of the opportunity to sing in the choir at the local Catholic church, Our Lady of Loretto. A nearby barber, who sold musical instruments as a sideline, was sympathetic to Salvatore's obvious interests in music and allowed him to try them out. Salvatore settled on the drums, and not before long, he was performing at local weddings and dances.

Later, Salvatore, who had been attending Commercial High School, dropped out at age sixteen (1909) to join his godfather's carnival band. With the money he had saved that season, he paid $70 for a used piano. Salvatore could not read music, and so he played by ear teaching himself to play the piano. He had also taught himself to play his father's old Italian accordion, and he again rejoined his godfather's carnival show. Aspiring for something more challenging, he switched to working as a stagehand for Loew's Liberty Theatre where he earned $9 a week, but when the stagehands decided they wanted union representation, Salvatore, who would not strike with them, left the job.

He became part of a quartet at Vitagraph Film Studios, and he also played piano music that served as background to the actors during the shooting of silent movies. His hard work paid off as he eventually became an assistant director at the Vitagraph studios. On December 19, 1917, he married Josephine Wensler, and in time they would have two children. He enlisted in the Navy in 1918, but when he returned home from the war, Vitagraph, inexplicably, would not take him back. To earn a living, Salvatore took to playing piano wherever he could at movie theaters, beer gardens, and dance halls.

By 1920 he began to have a series of jobs—all related to song writing—first with Stark and Cowan and then later with Shapiro and Bernstein. By 1923 he published his first collection of songs including "Back Home in Pasadena" and "I Love My Baby." These songs enjoyed such an immediate popularity that he now knew for sure that song writing would be a good profession for his future. In 1924 he wrote more songs such as "I Found a Million Dollar Baby in a Five and Ten Cent Store." They soared on the music charts to become instant hits and have since become popular classics.

With fame now certain on the horizon, Salvatore Guaragna in 1926 decided to take the stage name Harry Warren. His song writing abilities kept growing, and when his tune, "I Love My Baby, My Baby Loves Me," that year gained instant popularity, Harry Warren joined the Remick Music Company in New York and became a staff composer where he began actively writing songs for Broadway shows. When Warner Brothers film studios bought out Remick, Harry was invited to Hollywood to write for his first movie, *Spring is Here* (1930) whose songs ended up being more successful than the movie itself. He returned to New York, but a year later, he moved permanently to Hollywood where he would compose songs for more than seventy-five films.

In many respects, the early years of the 30s marked the beginning of Hollywood's legendary musicals. Warner Brothers, who just a few years before in 1927 had made motion picture history with the filming of *The Jazz Singer*, the first film with synchronized songs and lines of dialogue, was ready to launch the era of the Hollywood musical. In collaboration with Al Dublin, Harry Warren worked on his second movie, *42nd Street*. Starring Dick Powell and Ruby Keeler who sang and danced in what was their film debut, the film was a huge success and with it the memorable hit "You're Getting to Be a Habit with Me." The 30s and 40s, which constituted Warren's most prolific decades, included such classic songs as: "Jeepers Creepers," "You Must Have Been a Beautiful Baby," "I Only Have Eyes For You," "That's Amore," "The More I See You," and "There Will Never Be Another You."

In all, forty-two of his songs made the Top Ten lists from 1932 to 1957. He earned three Academy Awards for the hit songs "Lullaby of Broadway" from the *Gold Diggers of Broadway* (1935), "You'll Never Know" from *Hello Frisco Hello* (1940), and "On the Atchison, Topeka and the Santa Fe" from *The Harvey Girls* (1946). The movies for which he wrote songs included the superstars of the Hollywood musical era such as Dick Powell, Carmen Miranda, Gene Kelly, Bing Crosby, Fred Astaire, and Judy Garland.

After experiencing a rich and rewarding lifetime of successful song writing that gained the deep appreciation of the general public as well as that of his peers, Harry Warren died in Los Angeles, California on September 22, 1981 at age eighty-eight. While much of his music typified the era of the Hollywood musical at its best, it also contained those qualities that transcended that era. Warren's reputation as a composer of high-quality popular music has made him among the most influential and admired songwriters of the twentieth century in America and helped set the standard for good quality musicals in film.

General Sources:
1. *Current Biography/Yearbook*. New York: Wilson, 1943; 1981.
2. *The Guinness Encyclopedia of Popular Music*. Chester, CT: New England Publishing, 1992.
3. Katz, Ephraim. *The Film Encyclopedia*. New York: HarperCollins, 1998.
4. *The New Grove Dictionary of American Music*. New York: Grove's Dictionaries of Music, 1986.
5. *The New Grove Dictionary of Music and Musicians*. New York: Grove's Dictionaries of Music, 1980.
6. Thomas, Tony. *Harry Warren and the Hollywood Musical*. Secaucus, NJ: Citadel Press, 1975.

—by LINDA D'ANDREA-MARINO

LOUIS ZAMPERINI (1917-   )

A major winner in the 1936 Berlin Olympics, a famous WWII bombardier, a POW survivor, and later a religious educator, Louis Zamperini has a biography that reads like fiction; yet at the same time, his story exemplifies the paradox that truth is often stranger and more interesting than fiction. Legendary Lou had immortalized his life story some fifty years ago when he wrote his 1956 best-selling book *Devil at My Heel* whose Foreword was penned by the Reverend Billy Graham. Today, Zamperini's biography is slated to become a Hollywood motion picture.

Louis Zamperini was born on January 26, 1917, in Olean, New York to hard-working emigrant parents from Verona, Italy. His father had immigrated to the United States when he was thirteen years old, and beginning as a worker in the Pennsylvania coal mines, he studied and worked his way up to railroad electrician. In 1920 when the brutal northern winters proved too much for Louis' younger brother who had health problems, the family moved to Torrance, California where Louis began his lifelong adventures.

Louis admits to having been a rather mischievous and daring youngster who often took risks that endangered his life. In one such incident, he had once climbed an aging wooden oil derrick. Losing his grasp, he fell into a pool of petroleum and nearly drowned. When he started attending Torrance High School, he put his energies to good use, winning nearly every track event he entered. Locally, he had won everyone's attention when as a junior in 1934 he set a world interscholastic record (that lasted for 20 years) by running a 4:21:2 mile.

Earning a scholarship to the University of California (USC), he quickly became a champion runner who set an NCCA record for the mile. Qualifying for the 1936 U.S. Olympic team, he became its youngest member at age 17. He went on to Berlin, Germany and won the 5,000-meter competition beating the world recordholder Don Lash. His final lap time of 57 seconds apparently impressed Hitler who asked to meet young Zamperini and whom he had described as "the American boy with the fast finish."

After having met Hitler, and later, after having had a few beers, Lou Zamperini kept an eye on Hitler's chancellery. When he saw Hitler get out of a staff car and when the area seemed apparently clear of people, Lou scaled the chancellery fence and seized the staff car flag. While absconding with the memento, he was stopped in his tracks by a hail of bullets. When the incident was resolved, General Werner Von Frisch gifted Zamperini with the flag, which Lou still has in his possession.

In 1938 at USC, he set a national collegiate (NCAA) mile mark of 4:08:2 which would remain unbeaten for 15 years. Later in 1940 he also ran an indoor mile in 4:07:6 at New York City's Madison Square Garden. On September 28, 1941, just months before the Japanese attack on Pearl Harbor, Lou Zamperini enlisted in the military. By January 1942, he entered the Army Air Force training center in Texas to become a bombardier. Eight months later in August 1942, he was commissioned a second lieutenant, and by October 26, he was stationed at Kualoa Field in Oahu, Hawaii with the 307th Bombardment Group, 7th Air Force, ready to fight in the Pacific theater of WWII.

It is here that the most incredible part of his story begins as a bombardier on B-24s. He had flown many missions over enemy held territories in the Pacific, taking part in raids over such places as Wake, Nairu, Makin, and Tarawa Islands. On one such dangerous mission, his B-24 miraculously made it back to the airfield. His bomber was riddled with over 500 bullet holes, its right tail shot off, its landing wheel missing, and half its crew dead or wounded.

Another hair-raising incident occurred when the bomb bay doors remained stuck open and the radio operator inadvertently fell through. He remained hanging by his finger tips traveling 10,000 feet over the Pacific Ocean. Zamperini, true to his personality, risked his life and managed to bring him back on board. Yet these incidents are relatively small in comparison to what awaited him in the near future. It would involve a rescue mission to save the members of a downed B-25.

On May 27, 1943, flying the only craft available at the moment, a bulky Green Hornet, the search team began their mission in pursuit of a B-25 reportedly shot down near Palmyra Island. By two that afternoon, after both port engines had failed, the plane hit the water and exploded. Of the ten-man crew, there were only three who survived: Lou, pilot Russell Phillips, and tail gunner Francis MacNamara. Spending 47 days adrift on a life raft, fighting starvation, and swimming in shark-infested waters to avoid enemy strafing, only two of them survived the ordeal by eating raw fish and drinking rainwater.

This was the longest known period of time military men spent on a raft adrift in the ocean. After making landfall in the Marshall Islands still held by Japanese forces, Zamperini and Phillips were picked up by a harbor boat. Lou who had weighed 165 pounds dropped to 79 pounds. He was to spend the next two-and-a-half years in a series of brutal concentration camps where he experienced sadistic beatings by prison guards and endured the terrible rigors of the elements.

Because of his disappearance, he had been officially declared dead. When the war was over, a *New York Times* reporter picked up on Lou's incredible story, and it was featured a few days later in the newspapers, which now had generated nationwide momentum. When Lou finally arrived in the U.S. on October 5, 1945 at Long Beach, California, besides being given a promotion to captain, he was awarded many medals, including a Purple Heart. To honor his courage, his hometown of Torrance renamed its local airport Zamperini Field in 1946.

Despite a detour with alcoholic episodes that, no doubt, represented an escape from his nightmares and flashbacks recalling his prison torture and his ordeal adrift in the Pacific Ocean for 47 days, he became a convert joining Billy Graham's movement; and he has since devoted much of his life to Christian works and services. In 1956 he wrote his autobiography, *The Devil at My Heels*, achieving much popularity. After offering more than 40 years of religious and social assistance to fellow humans, he is surely an outstanding model of citizenship and spirituality. Typical of his seemingly endless drive, in January 1998 at age 81, he fittingly ran a kilometer leg of the Olympic Torch run at the Nagano Winter Olympics in Japan.

General Sources:
1. "Louis Zamperini—Our Olympic Hero." 13 Aug. 1998. <http://www.fpch.org/zamperini/zam web.html">.
2. Murray, Jim. *Los Angeles Times* 12 Dec. 1991.
3. "The Story of Louis S. Zamperini." 13 Aug. 1998. <http://home.earthlink.net/toaairfair/lza mp.html>.
4. Zamperini, Louis. *The Devil at My Heels*. New York: Dutton, 1956.
5. Zamperini, Louis. Personal interview. 7 June 1998.
6. *Zamperini: Still Carrying the Torch*. Dir. Michael Sajbel. World Wide, 1992.

—by JERRY F. TESTA

FRANK ZAPPA (1940-1993)

Frank Zappa, born in 1940, would die an early death at 53 from prostate cancer. Many major aspects of his personal life have remained rather "unimpeachable" as he was abstinent from drugs and alcohol. Yet his music represented an unusual and highly controversial phenomenon, a paradox. While his lyrics and his music titles riled the sensitivities of many individuals and civic groups who thought him radically scatological, countercultural, and too obscene, the music (understood as the melodic aspects and not the lyrics) reflected a highly developed and complicated artistry, often based on classical composers and classic models.

Born in Baltimore on December 21, 1940, he was the oldest of four children who came from an economically modest beginning. Italian was spoken in the house but was not imparted to the children by the parents who were from Sicily. His father was a meteorologist at nearby Edgewood Arsenal, and reportedly each member of the family possessed a gas mask in case of a mustard gas leak. When Frank was about ten, the family moved to Monterey, California.

As he grew into his teenage years, he didn't particularly like school or teachers. He taught himself how to compose music by going to the library to read difficult texts and by listening to records. In high school he favored playing the drums, and he was an avid listener of music composed by Edgar Varese, Igor Stravinsky, and Anton Webern—all fairly difficult and innovative composers. It was in high school that Frank met friend and collaborator Don Van Vliet. Frank also spent much of his time and money amassing used rhythm and blues and rock 'n' roll singles. He played in an R&B band called the Ramblers and in a country blues band

named the Black-Outs.

At first having no interest in higher education, he decided to attend junior college for its social opportunities. Frank was twenty when he married Kay Sherman and then dropped out of junior college. He played electric guitar in a four-piece lounge band but soon tired of the restrictive atmosphere and quit. Frank wrote the score for a low-budget film called *Run Home Slow*. With his income from the film, he was able to open his own somewhat primitive recording studio named Studio Z. The twelve-hour work days and little money took their toll on his marriage, and it ended in divorce.

In 1964 Frank joined a band that would eventually call themselves Mothers and started performing in Los Angeles and San Francisco. When everyone around him seemed to be "dropping" acid and doing other drugs, he stuck to his coffee and cigarettes. The years were lean. The group hired a manager, but it ended up working more gigs and making even less money. In 1965 the band recorded a double album called *Freak Out!* for MGM whose reps insisted that the band alter its name to the Mothers of Invention to be more marketable.

After much touring, Frank returned to Los Angeles, and he fell in love with and married Gail Sloatman, a secretary at the famous Whisky-a-Go-Go. They moved to New York in 1967, and at the Garrick Theater his musical group experimented with "rock theater" by calling up members of the audience to perform skits to their music. Frank and Gail returned to California in 1968. Along with manager Herb Cohen, he formed his own record label and recorded such artists as Alice Cooper, Captain Beefheart, and the GTO'S. In 1970 the Mothers of Invention broke up, and Frank Zappa recorded his first non-group album, *Hot Rats,* that included violinist Jean-Luc Ponty. That same year Frank performed his music with Zubin Mehta and the L.A. Philharmonic to a sell-out crowd.

The Zappas had four children who bear unusual names: Moon Unit, Dweezil, Ahmet, and Diva. Frank encouraged his children to think for themselves as he did not believe in the school system because it wanted everyone to conform. Frank felt that conformity stifles creativity. He also believed that failure also had its good side, and that it was a significant part of life. Yet, he insisted, it was a part of life that most people (who always play it safe) run away from and consequently do not take any chances.

Frank Zappa took risks in his music, both in the writing of provocative lyrics and in venturing beyond the standard musical formulas and chord changes. An intricately metered jazz-rock fusion became his hallmark. He was fond of saying that without deviation from the norm, "progress" wasn't possible. Frank Zappa had become a prolific composer with over sixty albums to his credit. His satirical lyrics were meant to expose the dangers of institutionalized control and indoctrination as in the song "Who are the Brain Police?" And sometimes his words are just plain fun as in "Valley Girl" or his 1980's hit, "Dancin' Fool," which lampoons the disco craze that swept the country. No group is exempt from Frank's humorous prodding with such songs as "Catholic Girls" or "Jewish Princess." When Mercury Records refused to release "I Don't Wanna Get Drafted," he started his own label, Barking Pumpkin.

In the mid-1980s Frank took on Tipper Gore's group, Parents Music Resource Center (PMRC), that wanted to rate music CDs as the Motion Picture Association of America does for films. He wrote protest letters, including one to the President, condemning the group's actions. On September 19, 1984, Frank Zappa shared his views about censorship with a Senate subcommittee. He considered himself a "practical conservative," desiring less intrusive government, lower taxes, and no censorship in the realm of music. Frank also decried the extremism and the unnecessary growing political influence of fundamentalist religious groups.

The 1980s were good for Zappa especially when Pierre Boulez, the well-known composer, had released in 1984 *Boulez Conducts Zappa*: *The Perfect Stranger,* an album that reached number seven on the classical charts. In 1988 Zappa went on to win a Grammy for *Jazz from Hell* as Best Rock Instrumental Performance. In 1989, he published his autobiography, *The Real Frank Zappa Book.* In 1990 Vaclav Havel, President of Czechoslovakia and an avid fan of Zappa, convinced him to serve as Czechoslovakia's Trade, Tourism, and Cultural liaison to the Western countries. As one might have expected, it was short-lived, and Zappa was soon back at his studio recording more CDs. Sadly, after being diagnosed with prostate cancer, he died on December 4, 1993 at his home, just weeks before his 53rd birthday. His musical innovations and unique style have left a special legacy to those who admired him and emulated his style.

General Sources:
1. Assante, Ernesto, and Enzo Capua, eds. *I Trasgressori: Jimi Hendrix, Frank Zappa, Velvet Underground, Fugs, Iggy Pop, MC5.* Roma, IT: Savelli, 1982.
2. Romanowski, Patricia, and Holly George Warrens, eds. *The New Rolling Stone Encyclopedia of Rock and Roll.* New York: Fireside Press, 1995.
3. Walley, David. *No Commercial Potential: The Saga of Frank Zappa and the Mothers of Invention.* New York: Outerbridge & Lazard, 1972.
4. Zappa, Frank, and Peter Occhiogrosso. *The Real Frank Zappa Book.* New York: Poseidon Press, 1989.

—by PAUL DE LUCIA

Index of Contributing Authors by Florida Lodge Location

Jackson, Ursula	Greater Gainesville #2660, Gainesville
Lamano, Irene	St. Cloud/Kissimmee #2731, St. Cloud
Lamano, Vincent, Sr.	St. Cloud/Kissimmee #2731, St. Cloud
Lanzelotti, Lorraine	Sons of Italy of Orlando #2463, Orlando
Liles, Marian	Unita #2015, Tampa
Marcelli, Lillian	Lake Worth/Boynton Beach #2304, Lake Worth
Maturo, Lee	Lake Worth/Boynton Beach #2304, Lake Worth
Mazzarella, Lew	Greater Gainesville #2660, Gainesville
Miccoli, Marianne	Sunrise Tamarac #2542, Tamarac
Minafra, Anthony	John Paul I #2427, St. Petersburg
Morse, James L.	Lake Worth/Boynton Beach #2304, Lake Worth
Mottola, Edward, Jr.	Sgt. F.M. Bonanno #2549, Boca Raton
Nesci, Carmela	John Paul I #2427, St Petersburg
Passanisi, Maryann	Township Sons of Italy #2624, Coconut Creek
Passarella, Victor	Lake Worth/Boynton Beach #2304, Lake Worth
Pesiri, Dolores	Lake Worth/Boynton Beach #2304, Lake Worth
Pesiri, Rocky	Lake Worth/Boynton Beach #2304, Lake Worth
Piasio, Dennis	Lake Worth/Boynton Beach #2304, Lake Worth
Piasio, Tina	Lake Worth/Boynton Beach #2304, Lake Worth
Pignatiello, Joseph	Friendship Lodge #2728, Hudson
Pittaro, Sam	Delray Lodge #2719, Delray Beach
Restivo, Anne	Lake Worth/Boynton Beach #2304, Lake Worth
Rizzo, Annette	Greater Gainesville #2660, Gainesville
Rotondo, Grace D.	Cuore D'Italia #2703, Jupiter
Scarfia, Margaret	John Paul I #2427, St. Petersburg
Sigona, Carmelo J.	Greater Gainesville #2660, Gainesville
Sigona, Norina Abruzzese	Greater Gainesville #2660, Gainesville
Smeraldi, Gomy	Lake Worth/Boynton Beach #2304, Lake Worth
Soldano, Anthony	Lake Worth/Boynton Beach #2304, Lake Worth
Spera, Paul	Lake Worth/Boynton Beach #2304, Lake Worth
Susca, Frank	La Nuova Sicilia #1251, Tampa
Terrana, Judy	Unita #2015, Tampa
Terrana, Vincent	Unita #2015, Tampa
Testa, Jean	Osceola County #2523, Kissimmee
Testa, Jerry F.	Osceola County #2523, Kissimmee
Trivelli, Anthony	Township Sons of Italy #2624, Coconut Creek
Trivelli, Norma	Township Sons of Italy #2624, Coconut Creek
Tucci, Janet B.	Greater Gainesville #2660, Gainesville
Vascellaro, Andrew	Stuart #2337, Stuart
Vericella, Diana	Central Gulf Coast #2708, Tarpon Springs
Walker, Gloria Scalzitti	Joseph B. Franzalia #2422, Ft. Walton Beach
Walker, William	Joseph B. Franzalia #2422, Ft. Walton Beach
Zanatta, Leo V.	Nature Coast Lodge #2502, Spring Hill
Zappia, Kathleen	St. Cloud/Kissimmee #2731, St. Cloud
Zappia, Anthony	St. Cloud/Kissimmee #2731, St. Cloud

Bibliography

REFERENCE SOURCES

American Men and Women of Science. New Providence, NJ: R.R. Bowker, 1998-99.

Amory, Cleveland. *The Celebrity Register*. New York: Harper & Row, 1963.

Baker's Biographical Dictionary of Twentieth-Century Classical Musicians. New York: Schirmer Books, 1997.

Cawkwell, Tim, and John Smith. *The World Encyclopedia of Film*. New York: Galahad, 1972.

The Celebrity Who's Who. New York: World Almanac, 1986.

Chambers Biographical Dictionary. New York: Larousse, 1997.

The Concise Columbia Encyclopedia. New York: Columbia University Press, 1989.

Concise Dictionary of American Biography. New York: Scribner, 1990.

Concise Encyclopedia of Music. New York: Norton, 1988.

Contemporary American Dramatists. Detroit: St. James Press, 1994.

Contemporary Dramatists. New York: St. Martin's Press, 1973.

Contemporary Women Dramatists. Detroit: St. James Press, 1994.

Current Biography/Yearbook. New York: Wilson, 1940-1999.

Dictionary of American Biography. New York: Scribner, 1977.

Dictionary of American Catholic Biography. Garden City, NY: Doubleday, 1984.

Dictionary of American Medical Biography. Westport, CT: Greenwood Press, 1984.

Directory of American Scholars. Lancaster, PA: Science Press, 1942-1982.

The Encyclopedia of Hollywood. New York: Facts on File, 1990.

Encyclopedia of Major League Baseball Team Histories. Westport, CT: Meckler, 1991.

The Encyclopedia of New York City. Ed. K.T. Jackson. New Haven: Yale University Press, 1995.

The Encyclopedia of Popular Music. Ed. Colin Larkin. London, UK: MUZE UK Ltd, 1998.

Hoover's Handbook of American Business. Austin, TX: Hoover's Business Press, 1998.

The International Who's Who. London: Europa Publications Ltd., 1935-1999.

The International Who's Who in Poetry and Poets' Encyclopedia. Cambridge, Eng.: International Biographical Centre, 1993.

The International Who's Who of Women. London: Europa Publications, 1992.

The Italian American Heritage: A Companion to Literature and Arts. Ed. Pellegrino D'Acierno. New York: Garland, 1999.

Katz, Ephraim. *The Film Encyclopedia*. Rev. ed., Fred Klein and Ronald Dean Nolen. New York: HarperCollins, 1998.

Kinkle, Roger. *The Complete Encyclopedia of Popular Music and Jazz 1900-1950*. New Rochelle, NY: Arlington House Publishers, 1974.

The McGraw-Hill Encyclopedia of World Biography. New York: McGraw-Hill, 1973.

Monaco, James. *The Encyclopedia of Film*. New York: Perigee Books, 1991.

The New Grove Dictionary of American Music. Ed. Wiley Hitchcock and Stanley Sadie. London: Macmillan, 1989.

The New Grove Dictionary of Opera. Ed. Stanley Sadie. New York: Grove's Dictionaries of Music, 1992.

Nobel Prize Winners: An H.W. Wilson Biographical Dictionary. New York: Wilson,1987.

Notable 20th-Century Scientists. Detroit, MI: Gale Research, 1995.

Null, Gary, and Carl Stone. *The Italian-Americans.* Harrisburg, PA: Stackpole Books, 1976.

Schiavo, Giovanni. *Four Centuries of Italian-American History.* Staten Island, NY: Center for Migration Studies, 1992.

Shaw, Arnold. *Dictionary of American Pop/Rock.* New York: Schirmer, 1982.

Siegel, Scott, and Barbara Siegel. *The Encyclopedia of Hollywood.* New York: Facts On File, 1990.

Tinling, Marion. *Women Remembered.* Westport, CT: Greenwood Press, 1986.

Twentieth-Century Culture: A Biographical Companion. Ed. Alan Bullock and R.B. Woodings. New York: Harper & Row, 1983.

Uglow, Jennifer S. *The Continuum Dictionary of Women's Biography.* New York: Continuum, 1989.

Who's Who in America. New Providence, NJ: Marquis Who's Who, 1899-present.

Who's Who in American Art. New Providence, NJ: Marquis Who's Who.

Who's Who in American Education. New Providence, NJ: Marquis Who's Who.

Who's Who in American Law. New Providence, NJ: Marquis Who's Who.

Who's Who in American Politics. New Providence, NJ: Marquis Who's Who.

Who's Who in Entertainment. New Providence, NJ: Marquis Who's Who.

Who's Who in Finance and Industry. New Providence, NJ: Marquis Who's Who.

Who's Who in Hollywood. New York: Facts on File, 1992.

Who's Who in Medicine and Health Care. New Providence, NJ: Marquis Who's Who.

Who's Who in Opera. New York: Arno Press, 1976.

Who's Who in Religion. New Providence, NJ: Marquis Who's Who.

Who's Who in Science and Engineering. New Providence, NJ: Marquis Who's Who.

Who's Who in the Media and Communications. New Providence, NJ: Marquis Who's Who.

Who's Who in the United Nations and Related Agencies. New York: Arno Press, 1975.

Who's Who of American Women. Chicago: Marquis Who's Who.

Who Was Who in America. New Providence, NJ: Marquis Who's Who.

BOOKS

Alba, Richard, ed. *Ethnicity and Race in the USA: Toward the Twenty-First Century.* Boston: Routledge & Keagan Paul, 1985.

Alba, Richard. *Italian Americans: Into the Twilight of Ethnicity.* Englewood Cliffs, NJ: Prentice Hall, 1985.

Alfonsi, Ferdinando. *Incontri italoamericani di successo.* Catanzaro: Antonio Carello Editore, 1983.

Alfonsi, Ferdinando, ed. *Poeti Italo-Americani.* Catanzaro: Antonio Carello Editore, 1985.

Amfitheatrof, Eric. *The Children of Columbus.* Boston: Little, Brown & Company, 1973.

Avrich, Paul. *Sacco and Vanzetti: The Anarchist Background.* Princeton, NJ: Princeton University Press, 1991.

Barnes, Charles B. *The Longshoremen.* New York: Survey Associates, 1915.

Barolini, Helen. *Umbertina.* New York: Seaview Books, 1979.

Barzini, Luigi. *The Italians.* New York: Atheneum, 1964.

Battistella, Graziano, ed. *Italian Americans in the `80s: A Socio-demographic Profile.* Staten Island, NY: Center for Migration Studies, 1989.

Bike, William S. *Streets of the Near West Side.* Chicago: ACTA Publications, 1996.

Bolton, Herbert E. *Rim of Christendom: A Biography of Eusebio Francisco Kino, Pacific Coast Pioneer*. New York: Macmillan, 1936.

Bona, Mary Jo. *The Voices We Carry: Recent Italian American Women's Fiction*. Montreal, Guernica, 1994.

Bona, Mary Jo, and Anthony Julian Tamburri, eds. *Through the Looking Glass: Italian/American Images in the Media*. Proc. of American Italian Association. Chicago, 1994. Staten Island, NY: American Italian Association, 1996

Boniello, Rose Marie, ed. *Preserving Our Italian Heritage*. Memphis: Wimmer Brothers, 1991.

Brockway, Wallace, and Herbert Weinstock. *The World of Opera*. New York: Pantheon Books, 1962.

Capozzola, Richard A. *Five Centuries of Italian-American History*. New Orleans, LA: American Italian Renaissance Foundation, 1992.

Carmack, Sharon DeBartolo. *Italian-American Family History: A Guide to Researching and Writing about Your Heritage*. Baltimore, MD: Genealogical Publishing, 1997.

Carpenter, Niles. *Immigrants and their Children*. New York: Arno Press, 1969.

Caso, Adolph. *They, Too, Made America Great: Lives of the Italian Americans*. Boston: Branden Press, 1978.

Ciongoli, Kenneth, and Jay Parini, eds. *Beyond the Godfather: Italian American Writers on the Real Italian American Experience*. Hanover, NH: University Press of New England, 1998.

Collburn, David R., and George E. Pozzetta, eds. *America and the New Ethnicity*. Port Washington, NY: Kennikat Press, 1979.

Corte, Robert. *They Made it in America: A Celebration of the Achievements of Great Italian Americans*. New York: William Morrow, 1993.

D'Acierno, Pellegrino, ed. *The Italian American Heritage: A Companion to Literature and Arts*. New York: Garland, 1999.

D'Alfonso, Antonio. *In Italics: In Defense of Ethnicity*. Toronto: Guernica, 1996.

D'Agostino, Guido. *Olives on the Apple Tree*. New York: Arno Press, 1975.

Dana, Julian. *A.P. Giannini, Giant in the West*. New York: Prentice Hall, 1947.

Dash, Joan. *The Triumph of Discovery: Women Scientists Who Won the Nobel Prize*. Englewood Cliffs, NJ: Julian Messner, 1991.

De Conde, Alexander. *Half Bitter, Half Sweet: An Excursion into Italian American History*. New York: Charles Scribner & Sons, 1971.

Di Donato, Pietro. *Christ in Concrete*. New York: Bobbs Merrill, 1939.

Di Donato, Pietro. *Immigrant Saint: The Life of Mother Cabrini*. New York: McGraw-Hill, 1960.

Di Franco, Philip. *The Italian Americans*. New York: Chelsea House, 1988.

DiStasi, Lawrence, ed. *The Big Book of Italian American Culture*. Berkeley, CA: Sanniti Publications, 1996.

Elliot, Lawrence. *Little Flower*. New York: Morrow, 1983.

Emanuel, Muriel, ed. *Contemporary Architects*. New York: St. Martin's Press, 1980.

Fenton, Edwin. *Immigrants and Unions, A Case Study: Italians and American Labor*. New York: Arno Press, 1975.

Gallo, Patrick. *Old Bread, New Wine: A Portrait of Italian-Americans*. Chicago: Nelson-Hall, 1981.

Gambino, Richard. *Blood of My Blood: The Dilemma of the Italian-Americans*. Berkeley: University of California Press, 1992.

Gambino, Richard. *Vendetta*. Garden City, NY: Doubleday, 1970.

Gardaphé, Fred. *Dagoes Read: Tradition and the Italian/American Writer*. Toronto: Guernica, 1996.

Gardaphé, Fred. *The Italian American Writer: An Essay and An Annotated Checklist*. Spencertown, NY: Forkroads, 1995.

Gardaphé, Fred. *Italian Signs, American Streets: Evolution of the Italian American Narrative.* Durham, NC: Duke University Press, 1996.

Giovanetti, Alberto. *The Italians of America.* New York: Manor Books, 1979.

Green, Rose Basile. *The Italian-American Novel: A Document of the Interactions of Two Cultures.* Rutherford, NJ: Fairleigh Dickinson University Press, 1974.

Grossman, Ronald P. *Italians in America.* Minneapolis: Lerner Publications, 1993.

Harney, Robert, and J. Vincenza Scarpaci, eds. *Little Italies in North America.* Toronto: The Multicultural History Society of Ontario, 1981.

Hoobler, Dorothy. *The Italian American Family Album.* New York: Oxford University Press, 1994.

Immerso, Michael. *Newark's Little Italy: The Vanished First Ward.* New Brunswick, NJ: Rutgers University Press, 1997.

Iorizzo, Luciano, and Salvatore Mondello. *The Italian Americans.* New York: Twayne Publishers, 1971.

Johnson, Colleen Leahy. *Growing Up and Growing Old in Italian-American Families.* New Brunswick: Rutgers University Press, 1985.

Juliani, Richard, and Philip Cannistraro, eds. *Italian Americans: The Search for a Usable Past.* Staten Island, NY: American Italian Historical Association, 1986.

Kessner, Thomas. *Fiorello H. LaGuardia and the Making of Modern New York.* New York: McGraw-Hill, 1989.

Kessner, Thomas. *The Golden Door: Italian and Jewish Immigrant Mobility in New York City, 1880-1915.* New York: Oxford University Press, 1977.

Krase, Jerome, and Charles LaCerra. *Ethnicity and Machine Politics.* Lanham, MD: University Press of America, 1991.

Krase, Jerome, and Judith N. DeSena, eds. *Italian Americans in a Multicultural Society.* Proc. of the Symposium of the American Italian Historical Association held at St John's University. 11-13 Nov. 1993. Stony Brook, NY: *Forum Italicum,* 1994.

Krase, Jerome, and William Egelman, eds. *The Melting Pot and Beyond: Italian Americans in the Year 2000.* Staten Island, NY: The American Italian Historical Association, 1987.

LaGuardia, Fiorello H. *An Autobiography.* New York: Capricorn Books, 1961.

LaGumina, Salvatore. *From Steerage to Suburb: Long Island Italians.* Staten Island, NY: Center for Migration Studies, 1988.

LaGumina, Salvatore. *The Immigrants Speak: Italians Tell Their Story.* Staten Island, NY: Center for Migration Studies, 1979.

LaGumina, Salvatore. The Italian American Experience: An Encyclopedia. New York: Garland Publishing, 1999.

LaGumina, Salvatore. *New York at Mid-Century: The Impellitteri Years.* Westport, CT: Greenwood Press, 1992.

LaGumina, Salvatore, ed. *Wop: A Documentary History of Anti-Italian Discrimination in the U.S.* San Francisco: Straight Arrow Books, 1973.

Lee, Kathleen. *American Origins: Tracing our Italian Roots.* Santa Fe: J. Muir Publications, 1993.

Lepis, Louis. *Italian Heroes in American History.* New York: Americans of Italian Descent, Inc., 1976.

Litoff, Judy Barrett. *European Immigrant Women in the United States: A Biographical Dictionary.* New York: Garland Press, 1994.

Lopreato, Joseph. *Italian Americans: Ethnic Groups in Comparative Perspective.* New York: Random House, 1970.

Magagnotti, Paolo. *The Word of Cardinal Bernardin.* Staten Island, NY: Center for Migration Studies, 1996.

Mangione, Jerre, and Ben Morreale. *La Storia: Five Centuries of the Italian American Experience.* New York: HarperCollins, 1992.

Marchione, Margherita. *Americans of Italian Heritage.* Lanham, MD: University Press of America, 1995.

Marinacci, Barbara. *They Came from Italy: The Stories of Famous Italian Americans.* New York: Dodd Mead, 1967.

Musmanno, Michael A. *The Story of the Italians in America.* New York: Doubleday, 1965.

Massaro, Dominic. *Cesare Beccaria—The Father of Criminal Justice: His Impact on Anglo-American Jurisprudence.* Pescia: International UP, 1991.

Napolitano, Louise. *An American Story: Pietro Di Donato's Christ in Concrete.* New York: P. Lang, 1994.

Nelli, Humbert. *From Immigrants to Ethnics: The Italian Americans.* Oxford: Oxford University Press, 1983.

Nye, F. Ivan, and Felix M. Berardo, eds. *Emerging Conceptual Frameworks in Family Analysis: With a New Introduction for the 1980s.* New York: Praeger, 1981.

Nye, F. Ivan, and Felix M. Berardo. *The Family: Its Structure and Interaction.* New York: Macmillan, 1973.

Parillo, Vincent. *Strangers to These Shores.* 2nd ed. New York: John Wiley, 1985.

Perspectives in Italian Immigration and Ethnicity. Proc. of the Symposium held at Casa Italiana, Columbia University. 21-23 May 1976. New York: Center for Migration Studies, 1977.

Pescosolido, Carl, and Pamela Gleason. *The Proud Italians: Our Great Civilizers.* Seabrook, NH: Latium,1991.

Petacco, Arrigo. *Joe Petrosino.* New York: Macmillan, 1924.

Picardo, Eddie S. *Tales of a Tail Gunner: A Memoir of Seattle and World War II.* Seattle: Hara Publishing, 1996.

Pisani, Lawrence F. *The Italians in America.* New York: Exposition Press, 1957.

Pozzetta, George E., ed. *Pane e Lavoro: The Italian American Working Class.* Staten Island, NY: The American Italian Historical Association, 1978.

Pozzetta, George E., and Gary Ross Mormino. *The Immigrant World of Ybor City: Italians and their Latin Neighbors in Tampa 1885-1985.* Urbana: Univ. of Ill. Press, 1987.

Puzo, Mario. *The Fortunate Pilgrim.* New York: Bantam Books, 1985.

Read, Phyllis. *The Book of Women's Firsts.* New York: Random House, 1992.

Rolle, Andrew. *The Italian Americans: Troubled Roots.* New York: Macmillan, 1980.

Salvato, Cynthia. *The Dowry Cookbook.* Nashville: FRP, 1996.

Scalia, Antonin. *A Matter of Interpretation: Federal Courts and the Law.* Princeton, NJ: Princeton University Press, 1997.

Scarpaci, Vincenza. *A Portrait of the Italians in America.* New York: Scribners, 1982.

Scelsa, Joseph, Salvatore LaGumina, and Lydio Tomasi, eds. *Italian Amercians in Transition.* New York: The American Italian Association, 1990.

Schoener, Allon. *The Italian Americans.* New York: Macmillan, 1987.

Segrè, Emilio. *A Mind Always in Motion: The Autobiography of Emilio Segrè.* Berkeley: University of California Press, 1993.

Smith, Payton. *Rosellini: Immigrants' Son and Progressive Governor.* Seattle: University of Seattle Press, 1997.

Smith, Thomas W. *A Profile of Italian-Americans 1972-1991.* Chicago: National Opinion Research Center, University of Chicago, 1992.

Starr, Dennis J. *The Italians of New Jersey: A Historical Introduction and Bibliography.* Newark, NJ: New Jersey Historical Society, 1985.

Suskin, Steven. *Opening Night on Broadway.* New York: Schirmer Books, 1990.

Tomasi, Lydio. *The Italian American Family.* Staten Island, NY: Center for Migration Studies, 1972.

Tomasi, Lydio, ed. *Italian Americans: New Perspectives in Italian Immigration and Ethnicity.* Staten Island, NY: Center for Migration Studies, 1985.

Tomasi, Lydio, ed. *The Italians in America: The Progressive View, 1891-1914.* Staten Island, NY: Center for Migration Studies, 1978.

Tomasi, Silvano. *Perspectives on Italian Immigration and Ethnicity.* Staten Island, NY: Center for Migration Studies, 1977.

Tomasi, Silvano, and Madeline Engel, eds. *The Italian Experience in the United States.* Staten Island, NY: Center for Migration Studies, 1970.

Tomkins, Calvin. *Merchants and Masterpieces: The Story of the Metropolitan Museum of Art.* New York: Dutton, 1970.

Vecoli, Rudolph, ed. *Italian Immigrants in Rural and Small Town America.* Staten Island, NY: American Italian Historical Association, 1981.

Vecoli, Rudolph, ed. *Old World Origins and New World Developments.* Staten Island, NY: The American Italian Historical Association, 1974.

Walter, Claire. *The Book of Winners.* New York: Facts On File, 1978.

Wiley, Mason, and Damien Bona. *Inside Oscar.* New York: Ballatine, 1987.

Yans-McLaughlin, Virginia. *Family and Community: Italian Immigrants in Buffalo 1880-1930.* Ithaca: Cornell University Press, 1977.

Zinn, Howard. *A People's History of the United States.* New York: HarperCollins, 1980.